DODGE

CARAVAN & VOYAGER
1984-91 REPAIR MANUAL

CHILTON'S

Sr. Vice President	Ronald A. Hoxter
Publisher and Editor-In-Chief	Kerry A. Freeman, S.A.E.
Managing Editors	Peter M. Conti, Jr. □ W. Calvin Settle, Jr., S.A.E.
Assistant Managing Editor	Nick D'Andrea
Senior Editors	Richard J. Rivele, S.A.E. □ Ron Webb
Director of Manufacturing	Mike D'Imperio
Manager of Manufacturing	John F. Butler
Editor	Peter M. Conti, Jr.

CHILTON BOOK COMPANY

ONE OF THE *DIVERSIFIED PUBLISHING COMPANIES*,
A PART OF *CAPITAL CITIES/ABC, INC.*

Manufactured in USA
© 1991 Chilton Book Company
Chilton Way Radnor, Pa. 19089
ISBN 0–8019–8155–7
Library of Congress Catalog Card No. 90–056089

2 3 4 5 6 7 8 9 0 1   1 0 9 8 7 6 5 4 3 2

Contents

Contents

SAFETY NOTICE

Proper service and repair procedures are vital to the safe, reliable operation of all motor vehicles, as well as the personal safety of those performing repairs. This manual outlines procedures for servicing and repairing vehicles using safe, effective methods. The procedures contain many NOTES, CAUTIONS and WARNINGS which should be followed along with standard safety procedures to eliminate the possibility of personal injury or improper service which could damage the vehicle or compromise its safety.

It is important to note that the repair procedures and techniques, tools and parts for servicing motor vehicles, as well as the skill and experience of the individual performing the work vary widely. It is not possible to anticipate all of the conceivable ways or conditions under which vehicles may be serviced, or to provide cautions as to all of the possible hazards that may result. Standard and accepted safety precautions and equipment should be used when handling toxic or flammable fluids, and safety goggles or other protection should be used during cutting, grinding, chiseling, prying, or any other process that can cause material removal or projectiles.

Some procedures require the use of tools specially designed for a specific purpose. Before substituting another tool or procedure, you must be completely satisfied that neither your personal safety, nor the performance of the vehicle will be endangered

Although information in this manual is based on industry sources and is complete as possible at the time of publication, the possibility exists that some car manufacturers made later changes which could not be included here. While striving for total accuracy, Chilton Book Company cannot assume responsibility for any errors, changes or omissions that may occur in the compilation of this data.

PART NUMBERS

Part numbers listed in this reference are not recommendations by Chilton for any product by brand name. They are references that can be used with interchange manuals and aftermarket supplier catalogs to locate each brand supplier's discrete part number.

SPECIAL TOOLS

Special tools are recommended by the vehicle manufacturer to perform their specific job. Use has been kept to a minimum, but where absolutely necessary, they are referred to in the text by the part number of the tool manufacturer. These tools can be purchased under the appropriate part number, from your Chrysler, Dodge or Plymouth dealer or regional distributor or an equivalent tool can be purchased locally from a tool supplier or parts outlet. Before substituting any tool for the recommended one, read the SAFETY NOTICE at the top of this page.

ACKNOWLEDGMENTS

The Chilton Book Company expresses its appreciation to Chrysler Motors Corporation, Detroit, Michigan for their generous assistance.

General Information and Maintenance

HOW TO USE THIS BOOK

Chilton's Total Car Care Manual for the Dodge Caravan/Plymouth Voyager is intended to teach you about the inner workings of your van and save you money on its upkeep.

The first two Sections will be the most used, since they contain maintenance, tune-up information and service procedures. Studies have shown that a properly tuned and maintained vehicle will get better gas mileage (which translates into lower operating costs) and periodic maintenance will catch minor problems before they turn into major repair bills. The other Sections deal with the more complex systems of your car. Operating systems from engine through brakes are covered. It will give you the detailed instructions to help you change your own brake pads and shoes, tune-up the engine, replace spark plugs and filters, and do many more jobs that will save you money, give you personal satisfaction and help you avoid expensive problems.

Before attempting any repairs or service on your vehicle, read through the entire procedure outlined in the appropriate section. This will give you the overall view of what tools and supplies will be required. Many times a description of the system function and operation is given, helping you to understand what repairs must be done.

Two basic mechanic's rules should be mentioned here. First, whenever the LEFT side of the car or engine is referred to, it is meant to specify the DRIVER'S side of the car. Conversely, the RIGHT side of the car means the PASSENGER'S side. Second, all screws and bolts are removed by turning counterclockwise, and tightened by turning clockwise (unless otherwise noted).

Safety is always the most important rule. Constantly be aware of the dangers involved in working on or around an automobile, and take proper precautions to avoid the risk of personal injury or damage to the vehicle. See the section, Servicing Your Vehicle Safely, and the SAFETY NOTICE on the acknowledgment page before attempting any service procedures. Pay special attention to the instructions provided.

There are 3 common mistakes in mechanical work:

1. Incorrect order of assembly, disassembly or adjustment. When taking something apart or putting it together, doing things in the wrong order usually just costs you extra time; however, it CAN break something. Read the entire procedure before beginning disassembly. Do everything in the order in which the instructions say you should do it, even if you can't immediately see a reason for it. When you're taking apart something that is very intricate (for example a carburetor), you might want to draw a picture of how it looks when assembled at one point in order to make sure you get everything back in its proper position. We will supply exploded views whenever possible, but sometimes the job requires more attention to detail than an illustration provides. When making adjustments (especially tune-up adjustments), do them in order. One adjustment often affects another, and you cannot expect satisfactory results unless each adjustment is made in accordance with its sequence.

2. Overtorquing (or undertorquing) nuts and bolts. While it is more common for overtorquing to cause damage, undertorquing can cause a fastener to vibrate loose and cause serious damage, especially when dealing with aluminum parts. Pay attention to torque specifications and utilize a torque wrench in assembly. If a torque figure is not available remember that, if you are using the right tool to do the job, you will probably not have to strain yourself to get a fastener tight enough. The pitch of most threads is so slight that the tension you put on the wrench will be multiplied many times in actual force on what you are tightening. A good example of how critical torque is can be seen in the case of spark plug installation, especially where you are putting the plug into an aluminum cylinder head. Too little torque can fail to crush the gasket, causing leakage of combustion gases, and consequent overheating of the plug and engine parts. Too much torque can damage the threads or distort the plug, which changes the spark gap. Since more and more manufacturers are using aluminum in their engine and chassis parts to save weight, a torque wrench should be in any serious do-it-yourselfer's tool box.

NOTE: There are many commercial chemical products available for ensuring that fasteners won't come loose, even if they are not torqued just right (a very common brand is Loctite®). If you're worried about getting something together tight enough to hold, but loose enough to avoid mechanical damage during assembly, one of these products might offer substantial insurance. Read the label on the package and make sure the product is compatible with the materials, fluids, etc. involved before choosing one.

3. Cross Threading. This occurs when a part such as a bolt is screwed into a nut or casting at the wrong angle and forced, causing the threads to become damaged. Crossthreading is more likely to occur if access is difficult. It helps to clean and lubricate fasteners, and to start threading with the part to be installed going straight in, using your fingers. If you encounter resistance, unscrew the part and start over again at a different angle until it can be inserted and turned several times without much effort. Keep in mind that many parts, especially spark plugs, use tapered threads so that gentle turning will automatically bring the part you're threading to the proper angle if you don't force it or resist a change in angle. Don't put a wrench on the part until it's been turned in a couple of times by hand. If you suddenly encounter resistance and the part has not seated fully, don't force it. Pull it back out and make sure it's clean and threading properly.

Always take your time and be patient; once you have some experience, working on your car will become an enjoyable hobby.

TOOLS AND EQUIPMENT

Naturally, without the proper tools and equipment it is impossible to properly service your vehicle. It would be impossible to catalog each tool that you would need to perform each or every operation in this book. It would also be unwise for the amateur to rush out and buy an expensive set of tools, on the theory that he may need one or more of them at sometime.

The best approach is to proceed slowly, gathering together a good quality set of those tools that are used most frequently. Don't be misled by the low cost of bargain tools. It is far better to spend a little more for better quality. Forged wrenches, 6- or 12-point sockets and fine tooth ratchets are by far preferable to their less expensive counterparts. As any good mechanic can tell you, there are few worse experiences than trying to work on a car with bad tools. Your monetary savings will be far outweighed by frustration and mangled knuckles.

Begin accumulating those tools that are used most frequently; those associated with routine maintenance and tune-up.

In addition to the normal assortment of screwdrivers and pliers you should have the following tools for routine maintenance jobs:

1. SAE/Metric wrenches, sockets and combination open end/box end wrenches in sizes from ⅛ in. (3mm) to ¾ in. (19mm), and a spark plug socket ($^{13}/_{16}$ in. or ⅝ in.). If possible, buy various length socket drive extensions. One break in this department is that the metric sockets available in the U.S. will all fit the ratchet handles and extensions you may already have (¼, ⅜, and ½ in. drive).
2. Jackstands for support.
3. Oil filter wrench.
4. Oil filler spout or funnel.
5. Grease gun for chassis lubrication.
6. Hydrometer for checking the battery.
7. A low flat pan for draining oil.
8. Lots of rags for wiping up the inevitable mess.

In addition to the above items there are several others that are not absolutely necessary, but handy to have around. These include oil-dry, a transmission fluid funnel and the usual supply of lubricants, antifreeze and fluids, although these can be purchased as needed. This is a basic list for routine maintenance, but only your personal needs and desires can accurately determine your list of necessary tools.

The second list of tools is for tune-ups. While the tools involved here are slightly more sophisticated, they need not be outrageously expensive. A basic list of tune-up equipment could include:

1. Tachometer
2. Spark plug wrench
3. Timing light
4. Wire spark plug gauge/adjusting tools

In addition to these basic tools, there are several other tools and gauges you may find useful. These include:

1. A compression gauge. The screw-in type is slower to use, but eliminates the possibility of a faulty reading due to escaping pressure
2. A manifold vacuum gauge
3. A test light
4. An induction meter. This is used for determining whether

The tools and equipment shown here will handle the majority of the maintenance on your vehicle

or not there is current in a wire. These are handy for use if a wire is broken somewhere in a wiring harness.

As a final note, you will probably find a torque wrench necessary for all but the most basic work. The beam type models are perfectly adequate, although the newer click (breakaway) type are more precise, and you don't have to crane your neck to see a torque reading in awkward situations. The breakaway torque wrenches are more expensive and should be recalibrated periodically.

Torque specification for each fastener will be given in the procedure in any case that a specific torque value is required. If no torque specifications are given, use the following values as a guide, based upon fastener size:

Bolts marked 6T
- 6mm bolt/nut: 5–7 ft. lbs.
- 8mm bolt/nut: 12–17 ft. lbs.
- 10mm bolt/nut: 23–34 ft. lbs.
- 12mm bolt/nut: 41–59 ft. lbs.
  14mm bolt/nut: 56–76 ft. lbs.

Bolts marked 8T
- 6mm bolt/nut: 6–9 ft. lbs.
- 8mm bolt/nut: 13–20 ft. lbs.
- 10mm bolt/nut: 27–40 ft. lbs.
- 12mm bolt/nut: 46–69 ft. lbs.
- 14mm bolt/nut: 75–101 ft. lbs.

Special Tools

Normally, the use of special factory tools is avoided for repair procedures, since these are not readily available for the do-it-yourselfer mechanic. When it is possible to perform the job with more commonly available tools, it will be pointed out, but occasionally, a special tool was designed to perform a specific function and should be used. Before substituting another tool, you should be convinced that neither your safety nor the performance of the vehicle will be compromised.

Some special tools are available commercially from major tool manufacturers. Others can be purchased from Miller Special Tools; Division of Utica Tool Company, 32615 Park Lane, Garden City, Michigan 48135.

SERVICING YOUR VEHICLE SAFELY

It is virtually impossible to anticipate all of the hazards involved with automotive maintenance and service but care and common sense will prevent most accidents.

The rules of safety for mechanics range from "don't smoke around gasoline", to "use the proper tool for the job." The trick to avoiding injuries is to develop safe work habits and take every possible precaution.

Do's

- Do keep a fire extinguisher and first aid kit within easy reach.
- Do wear safety glasses or goggles when cutting, drilling, grinding or prying. If you wear glasses for the sake of vision, then they should be made of hardened glass that can serve also as safety glasses, or wear safety goggles over your regular glasses.
- Do shield your eyes whenever you work around the battery. Batteries contain sulfuric acid. In case of contact with the eyes or skin, flush the area with water or a mixture of water and baking soda and get medical attention immediately.
- Do use safety stands for any under-car service. Jacks are for raising vehicles; safety stands are for making sure the vehicle stays raised until you want it to come down. Whenever the vehicle is raised, block the wheels remaining on the ground and set the parking brake.
- Do use adequate ventilation when working with any chemicals. Asbestos dust resulting from brake lining wear cause cancer.
- Do disconnect the negative battery cable when working on the electrical system.
- Do follow manufacturer's directions whenever working

with potentially hazardous materials. Both brake fluid and antifreeze are poisonous if taken internally.
- Do properly maintain your tools. Loose hammerheads, mushroomed punches and chisels, frayed or poorly grounded electrical cords, excessively worn screwdrivers, spread wrenches (open end), cracked sockets, slipping ratchets, or faulty droplight sockets can cause accidents.
- Do use the proper size and type of tool for the job being done.
- Do when possible, pull on a wrench handle rather than push on it, and adjust you stance to prevent a fall.
- Do be sure that adjustable wrenches are tightly adjusted on the nut or bolt and pulled so that the face is on the side of the fixed jaw.
- Do select a wrench or socket that fits the nut or bolt. The wrench or socket should sit straight, not cocked.

Always use jackstands when working under the vehicle

• Do strike squarely with a hammer. avoid glancing blows.
• Do set the parking brake and block the wheels if the work requires that the engine be running.

Don'ts

• Don't run an engine in a garage or anywhere else without proper ventilation—EVER! Carbon monoxide is poisonous. It is absorbed by the body 400 times faster than oxygen. It takes a long time to leave the human body and you can build up a deadly supply of it in your system by simply breathing in a little every day. You may not realize you are slowly poisoning yourself. Always use power vents, windows, fans or open the garage doors.
• Don't work around moving parts while wearing a necktie or other loose clothing. Short sleeves are much safer than long, loose sleeves. Hard-toed shoes with neoprene soles protect your toes and give a better grip on slippery surfaces. Jewelry such as watches, fancy belt buckles, beads, or body adornment of any kind is not safe while working around a car. Long hair should be hidden under a hat or cap.
• Don't use pockets for toolboxes. A fall or bump can drive a screwdriver deep into you body. Even a wiping cloth hanging from the back pocket can wrap around a spinning shaft or fan.
• Don't smoke when working around gasoline, cleaning solvent or other flammable material.
• Don't smoke when working around the battery. When the battery is being charged, it gives off explosive hydrogen gas.
• Don't use gasoline to wash your hands. There are excellent soaps available. Gasoline may contain lead, and lead can enter the body through a cut, accumulating in the body until you are very ill. Gasoline also removes all the natural oils from the skin so that bone dry hands will suck up oil and grease.
• Don't service the air conditioning system unless you are equipped with the necessary tools and training. The refrigerant, R-12, is extremely cold and when exposed to the air, will instantly freeze any surface it comes in contact with, including your eyes. Although the refrigerant is normally non-toxic, R-12 becomes a deadly poisonous gas in the presence of an open flame. One good whiff of the vapors from burning refrigerant can be fatal.

NOTE: **The Dodge and Plymouth vehicles described in this manual are metric-specified. While some inch-standard parts are used, body panels, fasteners, drivetrain components, and tires are all specified according to the Metric System. Dimensions and performance data are also expressed in metric units.**

Use the proper size wrench and place it properly on the flats of the nut or bolt

Power tools should always be properly grounded

MODEL IDENTIFICATION

The Caravan and Voyager models covered in this manual have remained much the same since their introduction. There are a few variations on the basic model, these include the Mini Ram Van, the 1991 Chrysler Town & Country and the Plymouth Grand Voyager. All of these models are still based on the Caravan and Voyager, and are only different in trim configurations.

For 1991 Chrysler is offering both anti-lock brakes and All Wheel Drive (AWD) as an option on the entire Caravan and Voyager line.

SERIAL NUMBER IDENTIFICATION

ENGINE APPLICATION CHART

Years	Engine Code	No. Cyl.	Actual Displacement			Type	Fuel System	Built By
			Cu. In.	cc	Liters			
1984	C	4	135	2,212	2.2	OHC	2BBL	Chrysler
	G	4	156	2,556	2.6	OHC	2BBL	Mitsubishi
1985	C	4	135	2,212	2.2	OHC	2BBL	Chrysler
	G	4	156	2,556	2.6	OHC	2BBL	Mitsubishi
1986	C	4	135	2,212	2.2	OHC	2BBL	Chrysler
	G	4	156	2,556	2.6	OHC	2BBL	Mitsubishi
1987	C	4	135	2,212	2.2	OHC	2BBL	Chrysler
	K	4	153	2,507	2.5	OHC	EFI	Chrysler
	G	4	156	2,556	2.6	OHC	2BBL	Mitsubishi
1988	K	4	153	2,507	2.5	OHC	EFI	Chrysler
	3	6	181	2,966	3.0	OHC	EFI	Mitsubishi
1989	K	4	153	2,507	2.5	OHC	EFI	Chrysler
	J	4	153	2,507	2.5	OHC	EFI ①	Chrysler
	3	6	181	2,966	3.0	OHC	EFI	Mitsubishi
1990	K	4	153	2,507	2.5	OHC	EFI	Chrysler
	J	4	153	2,507	2.5	OHC	EFI ①	Chrysler
	3	6	181	2,966	3.0	OHC	EFI	Mitsubishi
	R	6	201	3,294	3.3	OHV	EFI	Chrysler
1991	K	4	153	2,507	2.5	OHC	EFI	Chrysler
	3	6	181	2,966	3.0	OHC	EFI	Mitsubishi
	R	6	201	3,294	3.3	OHV	EFI	Chrysler

① Turbocharged Engine

Vehicle Identification Number (V.I.N.)

The vehicle identification number (VIN) consists of seventeen numbers and letters embossed on a plate, located on the upper left corner of the instrument panel, near the windshield.

Engine Identification Number (E.I.N.)

All engine assemblies carry an engine identification number (E.I.N.). On 2.2 liter and 2.5 liter engines, the E.I.N. is located on the face of the engine block, directly under the cylinder head (left side of vehicle).

On the 2.6 liter, 3.0 liter and 3.3 liter engines, the E.I.N. is located on the left side of the engine block between the core plug and the rear face of the block (radiator side of vehicle).

Engine Serial Number

In addition to the previously covered E.I.N., each engine assembly carries an engine serial number which must be referenced when ordering engine replacement parts.

On the 2.2 liter, and 2.5 liter engines, the engine serial number is located on the rear face of the engine block, directly below the cylinder head (below E.I.N.). On 2.6 liter, 3.0 and 3.3 liter

Location of VIN plate

EIN location on 2.2L and 2.5L engines

engines, the engine serial number is located on the exhaust manifold stud (dash panel side of vehicle).

Transaxle

The transaxle identification number (T.I.N.) is stamped on a boss that is located on the left upper transaxle housing.

In addition to the T.I.N., each transaxle carries an assembly part number. On manual transaxles, the assembly part number is located on a metal tag at the front of the transaxle. On automatic transaxles, the assembly part number is located just above the oil pan at the rear of the assembly.

EIN location on 2.6L and 3.0L engines

Location of Transaxle Identification Number (T.I.N.) on transaxle and assembly part number location (automatic)

ROUTINE MAINTENANCE

Air Cleaner

The air cleaner element on vehicles equipped with 2.2 liter engine should be replaced every 52,000 miles. Vehicles equipped with 2.5L, 2.6L, 3.0L and 3.3L engines should be replaced every 30,000 miles. However, if the vehicle is operated frequently through dusty areas; it will require periodic inspection at least every 15,000 miles.

REMOVAL AND INSTALLATION

2.2L Engine

1. Unfasten the three hold down clips and remove the three wing nuts that retain the top of the air cleaner housing.
2. Remove the top of the air cleaner housing and position out of the way with the breather hose attached.
3. Remove the air cleaner element from the housing.
4. Clean the inside of the housing but take care not to allow the dirt to enter the carburetor air intake.
5. Install a new air cleaner element with the screen side up into the plastic housing.
6. Position the steel top cover so that the hold down clips and support bracket studs are aligned.

NOTE: The procedures in the next steps should be followed as stated to prevent loosening and air leaks.

7. Install the wing nuts on both carburetor studs and tighten them to 14 inch lbs. Install the wing nut that attaches the air cleaner tab to the support bracket and tighten to 14 inch lbs.

2.2L engine air cleaner filter

8. Fasten the hold down clips.

2.5L, 2.6L, 3.0L and 3.3L Engines

1. Unfasten the hold down clips that retain the air cleaner cover.
2. Remove the air cleaner housing cover with intake hose attached and position out of the way.
3. Remove the air cleaner element from the housing.
4. Clean the inside of the air cleaner housing.
5. Install a new cleaner element and position the cover on the air cleaner housing. Secure the hold down clips.

Fuel Filter

─── CAUTION ───

Don't smoke when working around gasoline, cleaning solvent or other flammable material.

The fuel system on all vehicles incorporate two fuel filters. One is part of the fuel gauge unit; located inside the fuel tank at the fuel suction tube. Routine servicing of this filter is not necessary. However, if limited vehicle speed or hard starting is exhibited, it should be inspected.

The second filter is located in the fuel line between the fuel pump and the carburetor or fuel injector rail. Replacement of this filter is recommended every 52,000 miles.

2.6L engine air cleaner filter

2.5L air cleaner assembly

3.0L air cleaner assembly

Air cleaner assembly — 2.5L Turbo engine

Fuel filter vapor separator 2.2L engine

Typical inline filter

AIR CLEANER COVER

PAPER AIR FILTER ELEMENT

COVER HOLD DOWN BAILS (2)

FIBER CRANKCASE FILTER (CLEAN AND OIL LIGHTLY)

Air cleaner assembly — 3.3L engine

FUEL TUBES SHIELD

PRESSURE RELIEF/ ROLLOVER VALVE

FUEL PUMP ASSEMBLY

FUEL SUPPLY HOSE

FUEL RETURN HOSE

VIEW IN DIRECTION OF ARROW X

FUEL VAPOR TUBE

FUEL FILTER ASSEMBLY

DRAIN TUBE

FUEL RETURN HOSE

VIEW Y

CLAMPS

VIEW IN DIRECTION OF ARROW Z

FUEL TANK ASSEMBLY

Fuel tank, filter and hose routing

REMOVAL AND INSTALLATION

2.2L and 2.6L Engines

1. Clean the area at the filter and clamps with a suitable solvent
2. Loosen the clamps on both ends of filter.
3. Wrap a shop towel or clean rag around the hoses to absorb fuel.
4. Remove the hoses from the filter, and discard the clamps and filter.
5. Install the new filter between the fuel lines and clamp.
6. Tighten the clamps to 1 Nm (10 inch lbs.)

2.5L, 3.0L and 3.3L Engines

The fuel filter on these vehicles is located along the chassis, mounted just ahead of the fuel tank. To remove the filter, the vehicle will have to be raised slightly.

—————— CAUTION ——————

Before servicing any components within the fuel system, the system pressure must first be released.

1. Loosen the gas cap to release tank pressure.
2. On the 2.5L engine, disconnect the harness connector from the injector
3. On the 3.0L and 3.3L engines, disconnect the harness connector from any injector
4. Ground one terminal of the injector.
5. Connect a jumper to the other terminal and momentarily touch the positive terminal of the battery for no longer than 10 seconds. This releases the system pressure.
6. Raise the vehicle slightly and safely support it. Remove the retaining screw and filter assembly from the chassis rail.
7. Loosen the clamps on both ends of the fuel filter.
8. Wrap a shop towel or clean rag around the hoses to absorb fuel
9. Remove the hoses from the filter, and discard clamps and filter.
10. Install the new filter between the hoses and clamp.
11. Tighten the clamps to 1 Nm (10 inch lbs.).
12. Position the filter assembly on the chassis rail.
13. Tighten the mounting screw to 8 Nm (75 inch lbs.)

PCV Valve

2.2L, 2.5L, 3.0L and 3.3L Engines

Crankcase vapors and piston blow-by are removed from the engine by intake manifold vacuum. The emissions are drawn through the PCV valve (usually located in the top of the engine valve cover) into the intake manifold where they become part of the air/fuel mixture. Crankcase vapors are then burned and pass through the exhaust system. When there are not enough vapors or blow-by pressure in the engine, air is drawn from the air cleaner. With this system no outside air enters the crankcase.

The PCV valve is used to control the rate at which crankcase vapors are returned to the intake manifold. The action of the valve plunger is controlled by intake manifold vacuum and the spring. During deceleration and idle, when manifold vacuum is high, it overcomes the tension of the valve spring and the plunger bottoms in the manifold end of the valve housing. Because of the valve construction, it reduces, but does not stop, the passage of vapors to the intake manifold. When the engine is lightly accelerated or operated at constant speed, spring tension matches intake manifold vacuum pull and the plunger takes a mid-position in the valve body, allowing more vapors to flow into the manifold.

2.2L engine crankcase module and PCV valve

2.5L PCV system

3.0L PCV system

2.6L Engine

Intake manifold vacuum draws air from the air cleaner through the valve cover into the engine, the outside air is mixed with crankcase vapors and piston blow-by and drawn through the PCV valve (located in the top end of the engine cover) and into the intake manifold where it becomes part of the air/fuel mixture. The vapors are burned and expelled with exhaust gases.

TESTING

1. Place the vehicle in Park, or Neutral (if manual transaxle). Set the parking brake and block the wheels.

Checking for vacuum at PCV valve

PCV VALVE
(PCV SHUTTLE
VALVE MUST RATTLE)

PCV VALVE SEAT

To be considered serviceable, the PCV valve must rattle when shaken

CRANKCASE VENT
HOSE

PCV VALVE

INTAKE MANIFOLD
VACUUM HOSE

3.3 LITRE V6

PCV system — 3.3L engine

2. Start the engine and allow to idle until normal operating temperature is reached.

3. With the engine idling, remove the PCV valve, with hose attached, from its rubber molded connector.

4. When the PCV valve is free of its mounting, a hissing noise will be heard and a strong vacuum felt when a finger is placed over the valve inlet. When the engine is turned off, the valve should rattle when shaken. If the valve is not operating properly it must be replaced.

REMOVAL AND INSTALLATION

1. With the engine off, clean PCV valve area with a suitable solvent.

2. Remove the PCV valve from the mounting grommet on the top cover (2.6L, 2.5L, 3.0L and 3.3L) or from the vent module (2.2L) engines. Disconnect the hose from the valve.

3. Examine the vacuum hose and replace if the hose is cracked, broken or dried out. Always check the vent hose for clogging. If clogged, replace or clean as necessary.

4. Install a new PCV valve into the hose and install into mounting grommet.

Crankcase Vent Filter

All engines, except the 3.3L, are equipped with a crankcase vent filter which is used to filter the outside air before it enters the PCV system. The filter is located in the air cleaner housing on 2.6L and 2.5L, or in the vent module on 2.2L engines. The filter is located inside the filter element box on 3.0L engines. Replacement should be performed every 52,000 miles.

VENT FILTER SERVICE

1. On models equipped with the 2.2L engine, remove the PCV valve from the vent module and remove the vent module from the engine cover. Wash the module thoroughly in kerosene or safe solvent.

2. Lubricate or wet the filter with SAE 30 weight oil. Reinstall the module, PCV valve and hose.

3. On models equipped with the 2.5L and 2.6L engine, remove the vent filter from the air cleaner housing. Replace with a new element. Wet the new element slightly with SAE 30 weight oil before installation.

4. Models equipped with the 3.0L engine, remove the filter from the filter element box. Renew filter.

Evaporative Charcoal Canister

All vehicles are equipped with a sealed, maintenance free charcoal canister, located in the wheel well area of the engine compartment. Fuel vapors, from the carburetor float chamber and from the gas tank, are temporarily held in the canister until they can be drawn into the intake manifold and burned in the engine.

SERVICING

Periodic inspection of the vent hoses is required. Replace any hoses that are cracked, torn or become hard. Use only fuel resistant hose if replacement becomes necessary.

Battery

Loose, dirty, or corroded battery terminals are a major cause of "no-start." Every 3 months or so, remove the battery terminals and clean them, giving them a light coating of petroleum jelly when you are finished. This will help to retard corrosion.

Check the battery cables for signs of wear or chafing and replace any cable or terminal that looks marginal. Battery terminals can be easily cleaned and inexpensive terminal cleaning tools are an excellent investment that will pay for themselves many times over. They can usually be purchased from any well-equipped auto store or parts department. Side terminal batteries require a different tool to clean the threads in the battery case. The accumulated white powder and corrosion can be

The battery is equipped with a built in test indicator

cleaned from the top of the battery with an old toothbrush and a solution of baking soda and water.

Unless you have a maintenance-free battery, check the electrolyte level (see Battery under Fluid Level Checks) and check the specific gravity of each cell. Be sure that the vent holes in each cell cap are not blocked by grease or dirt. The vent holes allow hydrogen gas, formed by the chemical reaction in the battery, to escape safely.

MAINTENANCE FREE BATTERIES

All models are factory equipped with a maintenance free battery. Maintenance free batteries are as the name implies, totally free of maintenance as far as adding water is concerned. The battery is generally completely sealed except for some small vent holes that allow gases, produced in the battery, to escape. Battery terminal and cable end connector maintenance is required. Also, the cables should be disconnected, and the terminals and clamps cleaned at least once a year.

The factory installed battery contains a visual test indicator which signals when an adequate charge level exists. The test indicator is a built-in hydrometer that is equipped with a sight glass and is permanently installed in the battery cover. The sight glass indicator will show green when the battery has from a 75% to full charge. The glass will appear dark if the battery needs recharging and show yellow when replacement may be needed.

CAUTION

Batteries contain electrolyte, a mixture of sulphuric acid and distilled water. The use of adequate eye protection, and a suitable pair of rubber gloves is strongly recommended when working with batteries. In any event, if battery acid comes in contact with the skin or eyes, flush the affected area with plenty of clear water, and seek medical attention.

REPLACEMENT BATTERIES EXCEPT MAINTENANCE FREE

If a replacement battery of the non-maintenance free type has been installed in your vehicle, be sure to check the fluid level at least once a month. During warm weather or during periods of extended service, more frequent checking is necessary.

The fluid level can be checked through the case on translucent polypropylene batteries. The cell caps must be removed on other styles. The fluid (electrolyte) level should be kept filled to the split ring inside each cell filler opening, or to the line marked or molded on the outside of the battery case.

If the fluid level is low, add water (distilled water only) through the top openings until the correct level is reached. Each cell is separated and must be checked and filled individually.

If water is added in freezing weather, the vehicle should be driven several miles to allow the water to mix with the electrolyte.

SPECIFIC GRAVITY (EXCEPT MAINTENANCE FREE BATTERIES)

At least once a year, check the specific gravity of the battery. It should be between 1.20 in. Hg and 1.26 in. Hg at room temperature.

The specific gravity can be check with the use of a hydrometer, an inexpensive instrument available from many sources, including auto parts stores. The hydrometer has a squeeze bulb at one end and a nozzle at the other. Battery electrolyte is sucked into the hydrometer until the float is lifted from its seat. The specific gravity is then read by noting the position of the float. Generally, if after charging, the specific gravity between any two cells varies more than 50 points (0.50), the battery is bad and should be replaced.

It is not possible to check the specific gravity in this manner on sealed (maintenance free) batteries. Instead, the indicator built into the top of the case must be relied on to display any signs of battery deterioration. Refer to section marked "MAINTENANCE FREE BATTERIES".

A small puller will easily remove the cable from the terminals

An inexpensive tool easily cleans the battery terminals

Clean the inside of the terminal cap

CABLES AND CLAMPS

Once a year, the battery terminals and the cable clamps should be cleaned. Loosen the clamps and remove the cables, negative cable first. On batteries with posts on top, the use of a puller specially made for the purpose is recommended. These are inexpensive, and available in auto parts stores. Side terminal battery cables are secured with a bolt.

Clean the cable lamps and the battery terminal with a wire brush, until all corrosion, grease, etc., is removed and the metal is shiny. It is especially important to clean the inside of the clamp thoroughly, since a small deposit of foreign material or oxidation there will prevent a sound electrical connection and inhibit either starting or charging. Special tools are available for cleaning these parts, one type for conventional batteries and another type for side terminal batteries.

Before installing the cables, loosen the battery hold down clamp or strap, remove the battery and check the battery tray. Clear it of any debris, and check it for soundness. Rust should be wire brushed away, and the metal given a coat of anti-rust paint. Replace the battery and tighten the hold down clamp or strap securely, but be careful not to over tighten, which will crack the battery case.

After the clamps and terminals are clean, reinstall the cables, negative cable last; do not hammer on the clamps to install. Tighten the clamps securely, but do not distort them. Give the clamps and terminals a thin external coat of grease after installation, to retard corrosion.

Check the cables at the same time that the terminals are cleaned. If the cable insulation is cracked or broken, or if the ends are frayed, the cable should be replaced with a new cable of the same length and gauge.

─── CAUTION ───
Keep flame or sparks away from the battery; it gives off explosive hydrogen gas. Battery electrolyte contains sulphuric acid. If you should splash any on your skin or in your eyes, flush the affected area with plenty of clear water. If it lands in your eyes, get medical help immediately.

Drive Belts

INSPECTION

Check the condition and tension of all drive belts every 12,000 miles, or at least once a year. Loose drive belts can lead to poor engine cooling and diminished alternator, power steering pump, air conditioning compressor, or emission air pump output. A belt that is too tight places a strain on the bearings in the driven component.

Replace any drive belt that is glazed, worn, cracked, or stretched to the point where correct adjustment tension is impossible. If two belts are used to drive a component, always replace both belts when replacement is necessary. After installing a new belt, run the engine for ten minutes, shut off the engine and recheck the belt tension. Readjust if necessary.

CHECKING DRIVE BELT ADJUSTMENT

Two popular methods of checking drive belt adjustment are; the Belt Tension Gauge Method and the Belt Deflection Method. The former requires a special gauge and the latter requires a straight edge and scale or just a good eye for measurement. The deflection method will be used in the following belt replacement instructions. A rule of thumb for checking belt tension by the deflection method is to determine the midpoint between two pulleys of the drive belt and press down at that point with moderate thumb pressure. The belt should deflect to the measurement indicated in the following installation procedures. Adjustment is necessary if the belt is either too loose or too tight.

REMOVAL AND INSTALLATION

NOTE: Jack up the front of the vehicle, support on jack stands and remove the lower splash shield if access is hampered due to space limitations when changing drive belts.

2.2L Engine BELTS—TENSION CHART and REMOVE/INSTALL-ADJUST

Accessory Drive Belt		Gauge	Deflection	Torque
Air Conditioning Compressor	New	105 lb.	8mm (5/16 in.)	54 N·m (40 ft. lbs.)
	Used	80 lb.	9mm (7/16 in.)	41 N·m (30 ft. lbs.)
Air Pump	New	—	5mm (3/16 in.)	61 N·m (45 ft. lbs.)
	Used	—	6mm (1/4 in.)	47 N·m (35 ft. lbs.)
Alternator/Water Pump "V" Belt and Poly "V"	New	115 lb.	3mm (1/8 in.)	149 N·m (110 ft. lbs.)
	Used	80 lb.	6mm (1/4 in.)	108 N·m (80 ft. lbs.)
Power Steering Pump	New	105 lb.	6mm (1/4 in.)	102 N·m (75 ft. lbs.)
	Used	80 lb.	11mm (7/16 in.)	75 N·m (55 ft. lbs.)

2.2L engine belt tension chart

2.5L Engine BELTS—TENSION CHART and REMOVE/INSTALL-ADJUST

Accessory Drive Belt		Gauge	Deflection	Torque
Air Conditioning	New	105 lb.	8mm (5/16 in.)	54 N·m (40 ft. lbs.)
Compressor	Used	80 lb.	11mm (7/16 in.)	41 N·m (30 ft. lbs.)
Alternator/Water Pump	New	115 lb.	3mm (1/8 in.)	149 N·m (110 ft. lbs.)
Poly ''V''	Used	80 lb.	6mm (1/4 in.)	108 N·m (80 ft. lbs.)
Power Steering Pump	New	105 lb.	6mm (1/4 in.)	102 N·m (75 ft. lbs.)
	Used	80 lb.	11mm (7/16 in.)	75 N·m (55 ft. lbs.)

2.5L engine belt tension chart

2.6L Engine BELTS-TENSION CHART and REMOVE/INSTALL-ADJUST

Accessory Drive Belt		Gauge	Deflection	Torque
Power Steering Pump	New	95 lb.	6mm (¼ in.)	149 N·m (110 ft. lbs.)
	Used	80 lb.	9mm (⅜ in.)	102 N·m (75 ft. lbs.)
Alternator	New	115 lb.	4mm (³/₁₆ in.)	—
	Used	80 lb.	6mm (¼ in.)	—
Alternator/Air Conditioning Compressor	New	115 lb.	6mm (¼ in.)	—
	Used	80 lb.	8mm (⁵/₁₆ in.)	—
Water Pump	New	—	8mm (⁵/₁₆ in.)	—
	Used	—	9mm (⅜ in.)	—

2.6L engine belt tension chart

3.0L Engine BELTS—TENSION CHART and REMOVE/INSTALL-ADJUST

Accessory Drive Belt		Gauge	Deflection
Air Conditioning	New	125 lb.	8mm (5/16 in.)
Compressor	Used	80 lb.	8mm (5/16 in.)
Alternator/Water Pump/	New		
Power Steering Pump	Used	Dynamic Tensioner	

3.0L engine belt tension chart

2.2L drive belt adjusting points

2.2L alternator belt adjustment

3. Using a breaker bar and socket apply torque to welded nut provided on the mounted bracket to obtain proper tension.
4. Tighten the locking screw first, followed by pivot screw. Tighten to 40 ft. lbs.

A/C Compressor Drive Belt 2.2L Engine

1. Loosen the idler pulley bracket pivot screw and the locking screw.
2. Remove the belt and install replacement.

Alternator Drive Belt 2.2L Engines (Chrysler Type)

If removal of the alternator belt is required, the A/C belt must first be removed.

1. Loosen the pivot nut, locking screw, and the adjusting screw.

HOW TO SPOT WORN V-BELTS

V–Belts are vital to efficient engine operation—they drive the fan, water pump and other accessories. They require little maintenance (occasional tightening) but they will not last forever. Slipping or failure of the V–belt will lead to overheating. If your V–belt looks like any of these, it should be replaced.

Cracking or Weathering

This belt has deep cracks, which cause it to flex. Too much flexing leads to heat build–up and premature failure. These cracks can be caused by using the belt on a pulley that is too small. Notched belts are available for small diameter pulleys.

Softening (Grease and Oil)

Oil and grease on a belt can cause the belt's rubber compounds to soften and separate from the reinforcing cords that hold the belt together. The belt will first slip, then finally fail altogether.

Glazing

Glazing is caused by a belt that is slipping. A slipping belt can cause a run-down battery, erratic power steering, overheating or poor accessory performance. The more the belt slips, the more glazing will be built up on the surface of the belt. The more the belt is glazed, the more it will slip. If the glazing is light, tighten the belt.

Worn Cover

The cover of this belt is worn off and is peeling away. The reinforcing cords will begin to wear and the belt will shortly break. When the belt cover wears in spots or has a rough jagged appearance, check the pulley grooves for roughness.

Separation

This belt is on the verge of breaking and leaving you stranded. The layers of the belt are separating and the reinforcing cords are exposed. It's just a matter of time before it breaks completely.

2. Remove the belt and install replacement.
3. Adjust to specification by tightening the adjusting screw.
4. Tighten the locking screw to 25 ft. lbs.
5. Tighten the pivot nut to 30 ft. lbs.

Alternator Belt 2.2L Engines (Bosch Type)

If removal of the alternator belt is required, the A/C belt must first be removed.
1. Loosen the pivot nut, locking nut, and adjusting screw.
2. Remove the belt and install replacement.
3. Adjust to specification by tightening the adjusting screw.
4. Tighten the locking nut to 25 ft. lbs.
5. Tighten the pivot nut to 30 ft. lbs.

Power Steering Belt 2.2L Engine

If removal of the power steering belt is required, the A/C and alternator belts must first be removed.
1. Loosen the locking screw, and pivot screw.
2. Remove the belt and install replacement.
3. Install a ½ in. breaker bar into the pump bracket slot, apply pressure with the breaker bar and adjust the belt to specification.
4. Tighten the locking screw first, then the pivot screw. Tighten to 40 ft. lbs.

Air Pump — 2.2L Engine

NOTE: When servicing the air pump, use the square holes provided in the pulley to prevent camshaft rotation.

1. Remove the nuts and bolts retaining the drive pulley cover.
2. Remove the locking bolt and pivot bolt from the pump bracket, and remove the pump.
3. Remove the belt and install replacement.
4. Position the pump, and install the locking bolt and pivot bolt finger tight.
5. Install a ½ in. breaker bar into the bracket assembly (block the drive pulley to prevent camshaft rotation), and adjust the belt to specification.
6. Tighten locking bolt and pivot bolt to 25 ft. lbs.

2.2L air pump belt adjustment

Air Conditioning Compressor — 2.5L Engine

1. Loosen the idler bracket pivot screw and the locking screws to replace, or adjust belt.
2. Remove the belt and install replacement.
3. Adjust the belt to specification by applying torque to weld nut on the idler bracket.
4. Tighten locking screw first, followed by the pivot screw. Tighten to 40 ft. lbs.

Alternator Belt 2.5L Engine

If replacement of the alternator belt is required, the A/C drive belt must first be removed.
1. Loosen the pivot nut, locking nut, and adjusting screw.
2. Remove the belt and install replacement.
3. Adjust the belt to specification by tightening the adjusting screw.

2.5L drive belt adjustment points

2.6L drive belt adjustment points

4. Tighten the locking nut to 25 ft. lbs.
5. Tighten the pivot nut to 30 ft. lbs.

Power Steering Pump 2.5L Engines

If replacement of the power steering belt is required, the A/C and alternator belts must first be remove.
1. Loosen the locking screw and pivot screw to replace, or adjust the belt.
2. Remove the belt and install replacement.
3. Using a ½ in. breaker bar positioned in adjusting bracket slot, adjust the belt to specification.
4. Tighten the locking screw followed by the pivot screw. Tighten to 40 ft. lbs.

Alternator/Air Conditioning Compressor — 2.6L Engine

1. Loosen the locking screw, jam nut, and pivot nut.
2. Loosen the adjusting screw.
3. Remove the belt and install replacement.
4. Adjust the belt to specification by tightening the adjusting screw.

3.0L belt tensioner release

5. Tighten the locking screw followed by the pivot nut. Tighten to 195 inch lbs.
6. Tighten the jam nut to 250 inch lbs.

Power Steering Pump Belt 2.6L Engines

If replacement of the power steering belt is required, the alternator and A/C belt must first be remove.
1. Loosen the pivot screw, and the locking screw.
2. Remove the timing pickup.
3. Remove the belt and install replacement.
4. Install a ½ in. breaker bar in the adjusting bracket slot, torque to specification.
5. Tighten the locking screw, followed by the pivot screw. Tighten to 40 ft. lbs.
6. Install the timing pick-up, and tighten to 160 inch lbs.

Air Conditioning Compressor Belt — 3.0L Engine

1. Loosen the locknut on the idler pulley.
2. Loosen the adjusting screw on the idler pulley.
3. Remove the belt and install replacement.
4. Adjust to specification by tightening the adjusting screw.
5. Tighten the idler pulley locknut to 40 ft. lbs.

3.0L drive belt adjustment points

Accessory drive belt routing — 3.3L engine

HOW TO SPOT BAD HOSES

Both the upper and lower radiator hoses are called upon to perform difficult jobs in an inhospitable environment. They are subject to nearly 18 psi at under hood temperatures often over 280°F, and must circulate nearly 7500 gallons of coolant an hour—3 good reasons to have good hoses.

Swollen Hose

A good test for any hose is to feel it for soft or spongy spots. Frequently these will appear as swollen areas of the hose. The most likely cause is oil soaking. This hose could burst at any time, when hot or under pressure.

Cracked Hose

Cracked hoses can usually be seen but feel the hoses to be sure they have not hardened; a prime cause of cracking. This hose has cracked down to the reinforcing cords and could split at any of the cracks.

Frayed Hose End (Due to Weak Clamp)

Weakened clamps frequently are the cause of hose and cooling system failure. The connection between the pipe and hose has deteriorated enough to allow coolant to escape when the engine is hot.

Debris In Cooling System

Debris, rust and scale in the cooling system can cause the inside of a hose to weaken. This can usually be felt on the outside of the hose as soft or thinner areas.

Alternator/Power Steering Pump Belt — 3.0L Engine

If replacement of the alternator/power steering drive belt is required, the air conditioner drive belt must first be removed.
1. Install a ½ in. breaker bar into the tensioner slot, and rotate counterclockwise to release belt tension.
2. Remove the belt and install replacement.
3. Proper belt tension is maintain by the dynamic tensioner.

Accessory Drive Belt — 3.3L Engine

All of the belt driven accessories on the 3.3L engine are driven by a single serpentine belt. The belt tension is maintained by am automatic tensioner.
1. Raise the front of the vehicle and safely support it with jack stands.
2. Remove the right front splash shield.
3. Install a ½ in. breaker bar into the tensioner slot, and rotate counterclockwise to release belt tension.
4. ‹Remove the belt and install replacement.
5. Proper belt tension is maintain by the dynamic tensioner.
6. Install the right front splash shield. Lower the front of the vehicle.

Hoses

———————— CAUTION ————————

On models equipped with an electric cooling fan, disconnect the negative battery cable, or fan motor wiring harness connector before replacing any radiator/heater hose. The fan may come on, under certain circumstances, even though the ignition is Off.

REMOVAL AND INSTALLATION

Inspect the condition of the radiator and heater hoses periodically. Early spring and at the beginning of the fall or winter, when you are performing other maintenance, are good times. Make sure the engine and cooling system are cold. Visually inspect for cracking, rotting or collapsed hoses, replace as necessary. Run your hand along the length of the hose. If a weak or swollen spot is noted when squeezing the hose wall, replace the hose.
1. Drain the cooling system into a suitable container (if the coolant is to be reused).

———————— CAUTION ————————

When draining the coolant, keep in mind that cats and dogs are attracted by the ethylene glycol antifreeze, and are quite likely to drink any that is left in an uncovered container or in puddles on the ground. This will prove fatal in sufficient quantity. Always drain the coolant into a sealable container. Coolant should be reused unless it is contaminated or several years old.

2. Loosen the hose clamps at each end of the hose that requires replacement.
3. Twist, pull and slide the hose off the radiator, water pump, thermostat or heater connection.
4. Clean the hose mounting connections. Position the hose clamps on the new hose.
5. Coat the connection surfaces with a water resistant sealer and slide the hose into position. Make sure the hose clamps are located beyond the raised bead of the connector (if equipped) and centered in the clamping area of the connection.
6. Tighten the clamps to 20–30 inch lbs. Do not overtighten.
7. Fill the cooling system.
8. Start the engine and allow it to reach normal operating temperature. Check for leaks.

Air Conditioning System

SAFETY PRECAUTIONS

Because of the importance of the necessary safety precautions that must be exercised when working with air conditioning systems and R-12 refrigerant, a list of the safety precautions are outlined.
 • Avoid contact with a charged refrigeration system, even when working on another part of the air conditioning system or vehicle. If a heavy tool comes into contact with a section of copper tubing or a heat exchanger, it can easily cause the relatively soft material to rupture.
 • When it is necessary to apply force to a fitting which contains refrigerant, as when checking that all system couplings are securely tightened, use a wrench on both parts of the fitting involved, if possible. This will avoid putting torque on the refrigerant tubing. (It is advisable, when possible, to use tube or line wrenches when tightening these flare nut fittings.)
 • Do not attempt to discharge the system by merely loosening a fitting, or removing the service valve caps and cracking these valves. Precise control is possibly only when using the service gauges. Place a rag under the open end of the center charging hose while discharging the system to catch any drops of liquid that might escape. Wear protective gloves when connecting or disconnecting service gauge hoses.
 • Discharge the system only in a well ventilated area, as high concentrations of the gas can exclude oxygen and act as an anesthetic. When leak testing or soldering this is particularly important, as toxic gas is formed when R-12 contacts any flame.
 • Never start a system without first verifying that both service valves are back seated, if equipped, and that all fittings are throughout the system are snugly connected.
 • Avoid applying heat to any refrigerant line or storage vessel. Charging may be aided by using water heated to less than 125°F (52°C) to warm the refrigerant container. Never allow a refrigerant storage container to sit out in the sun, or near any other source of heat, such as a radiator.
 • Always wear goggles when working on a system to protect the eyes. If refrigerant contacts the eye, it is advisable in all cases to see a physician as soon as possible.
 • Frostbite from liquid refrigerant should be treated by first gradually warming the area with cool water, and then gently applying petroleum jelly. A physician should be consulted.
 • Always keep refrigerant can fittings capped when not in use. Avoid sudden shock to the can which might occur from dropping it, or from banging a heavy tool against it. Never carry a refrigerant can in the passenger compartment of a van.
 • Always completely discharge the system before painting the vehicle (if the paint is to be baked on), or before welding anywhere near the refrigerant lines.

GENERAL SERVICING PROCEDURES

The most important aspect of air conditioning service is the maintenance of pure and adequate charge of refrigerant in the system. A refrigeration system cannot function properly if a significant percentage of the charge is lost. Leaks are common because the severe vibration encountered in an automobile can easily cause a sufficient cracking or loosening of the air conditioning fittings. As a result, the extreme operating pressures of the system force refrigerant out.

The problem can be understood by considering what happens to the system as it is operated with a continuous leak. Because the expansion valve regulates the flow of refrigerant to the evaporator, the level of refrigerant there is fairly constant. The receiver/drier stores any excess of refrigerant, and so a loss will first appear there as a reduction in the level of liquid. As this level nears the bottom of the vessel, some refrigerant vapor bubbles will begin to appear in the stream of liquid supplied to the expansion valve. This vapor decreases the capacity of the expansion valve very little as the valve opens to compensate for its presence. As the quantity of liquid in the condenser decreases, the operating pressure will drop there and throughout the high side of the system. As the R-12 continues to be expelled, the pressure available to force the liquid through the expansion valve will continue to decrease, and, eventually, the valve's orifice will prove to be too much of a restriction for adequate flow even with the needle fully withdrawn.

At this point, low side pressure will start to drop, and severe reduction in cooling capacity, marked by freeze-up of the evaporator coil, will result. Eventually, the operating pressure of the evaporator will be lower than the pressure of the atmosphere surrounding it, and air will be drawn into the system wherever there are leaks in the low side.

Because all atmospheric air contains at least some moisture, water will enter the system and mix with the R-12 and the oil. Trace amounts of moisture will cause sludging of the oil, and corrosion of the system. Saturation and clogging of the filter/drier, and freezing of the expansion valve orifice will eventually result. As air fills the system to a greater and greater extend, it will interfere more and more with the normal flows of refrigerant and heat.

A list of general precautions that should be observed while doing this follows:

1. Keep all tools as clean and dry as possible.
2. Thoroughly purge the service gauges and hoses of air and moisture before connecting them to the system. Keep them capped when not in use.
3. Thoroughly clean any refrigerant fitting before disconnecting it, in order to minimize the entrance of dirt into the system.
4. Plan any operation that requires opening the system beforehand in order to minimize the length of time it will be exposed to open air. Cap or seal the open ends to minimize the entrance of foreign material.
5. When adding oil, pour it through an extremely clean and dry tube or funnel. Keep the oil capped whenever possible. Do not use oil that has not been kept tightly sealed.
6. Use only refrigerant 12. Purchase refrigerant intended for use in only automotive air conditioning system. Avoid the use of refrigerant 12 that may be packaged for another use, such as cleaning, or powering a horn, as it is impure.
7. Completely evacuate any system that has been opened to replace a component, other than when isolating the compressor, or that has leaked sufficiently to draw in moisture and air. This requires evacuating air and moisture with a good vacuum pump for at least one hour.

If a system has been open for a considerable length of time it may be advisable to evacuate the system for up to 12 hours (overnight).

8. Use a wrench on both halves of a fitting that is to be disconnected, so as to avoid placing torque on any of the refrigerant lines.

ADDITIONAL PREVENTIVE MAINTENANCE CHECKS

Antifreeze

In order to prevent heater core freeze-up during A/C operation, it is necessary to maintain permanent type antifreeze protection of $+15°F$ ($-9°C$) or lower. A reading of $-15°F$ ($-26°C$) is ideal since this protection also supplies sufficient corrosion inhibitors for the protection of the engine cooling system.

WARNING: Do not use antifreeze longer than specified by the manufacturer.

Radiator Cap

For efficient operation of an cooling system, the radiator cap should have a holding pressure which meets manufacturer's specifications. A cap which fails to hold these pressure should be replaced.

Condenser

Any obstruction of or damage to the condenser configuration will restrict the air flow which is essential to its efficient operation. It is therefore, a good rule to keep this unit clean and in proper physical shape.

NOTE: Bug screens are regarded as obstructions.

Condensation Drain Tube

This single molded drain tube expels the condensation, which accumulates on the bottom of the evaporator housing, into the engine compartment.

If this tube is obstructed, the air conditioning performance can be restricted and condensation buildup can spill over onto the vehicle's floor.

TEST GAUGES

Most of the service work performed in air conditioning requires the use of a set of two gauges, one for the high (head) pressure side of the system, the other for the low (suction) side.

Manifold gauge set connections

The low side gauge records both pressure and vacuum. Vacuum readings are calibrated from 0 to 30 inches Hg and the pressure graduations read from 0 to no less than 150 psi.

The high side gauge measures pressure from 0 to at least 300 psi.

With the gauge set you can perform the following procedures:
1. Test high and low side pressures.
2. Remove air, moisture, and contaminated refrigerant.
3. Purge the system of refrigerant.
4. Charge the system with refrigerant.

All gauge sets must have 3 hoses, with 1 being for center manifold outlet.

WARNING: When connecting the hoses to the compressor service ports, the manifold gauge valves must be closed!

The suction gauge valve is opened to provide a passage between the suction gauge and the center manifold outlet. The discharge gauge valve is opened to provide a passage between the discharge pressure gauge and the center manifold outlet.

SYSTEM INSPECTION

━━━ CAUTION ━━━
The compressed refrigerant used in the air conditioning system expands into the atmosphere at a temperature of −21.7°F (−30°C) or lower. This will freeze any surface, including your eyes, that it contacts. In addition, the refrigerant decomposes into a poisonous gas in the presence of a flame. Do not open or disconnect any part of the air conditioning system.

Sight Glass Check

You can safely make a few simple checks to determine if your air conditioning system needs service. The tests work best if the temperature is warm (about 70°F [21°C]).

NOTE: If your vehicle is equipped with an after market air conditioner, the following system check may not apply. You should contact the manufacturer of the unit for instructions on systems checks.

1. Place the automatic transmission in Park or the manual transmission in Neutral. Set the parking brake.

2. Run the engine at a fast idle (about 1,500 Rpm) either with the help of a friend or by temporarily readjusting the idle speed screw.

3. Set the controls for maximum cold with the blower on High.

4. Locate the sight glass in one of the system lines. Usually it is on the left alongside the top of the radiator.

5. If you see bubbles, the system must be recharged. Very likely there is a leak at some point.

6. If there are no bubbles, there is either no refrigerant at all or the system is fully charged. Feel the two hoses going to the belt driven compressor. If they are both at the same temperature, the system is empty and must be recharged.

7. If one hose (high pressure) is warm and the other (low pressure) is cold, the system may be all right. However, you are probably making these tests because you think there is something wrong, so proceed to the next step.

8. Have an assistant in the van turn the fan control on and off to operate the compressor clutch. Watch the sight glass.

9. If bubbles appear when the clutch is disengaged and disappear when it is engaged, the system is properly charged.

10. If the refrigerant takes more than 45 seconds to bubble when the clutch is disengaged, the system is overcharged. This usually causes poor cooling at low speeds.

WARNING: If it is determined that the system has a leak, it should be corrected as soon as possible. Leaks may allow moisture to enter and cause a very expensive rust problem.
   Exercise the air conditioner for a few minutes, every two weeks or so, during the cold months. This avoids the possibility of the compressor seals drying out from lack of lubrication.

TESTING THE SYSTEM

1. Connect a gauge set.
2. Close (clockwise) both gauge set valves.
3. Park the van in the shade, at least 5 feet from any walls. Start the engine, set the parking brake, place the transmission in N and establish an idle of 1100–1300 Rpm.
4. Run the air conditioning system for full cooling, in the

Troubleshooting Basic Air Conditioning Problems

Problem	Cause	Solution
There's little or no air coming from the vents (and you're sure it's on)	• The A/C fuse is blown • Broken or loose wires or connections • The on/off switch is defective	• Check and/or replace fuse • Check and/or repair connections • Replace switch
The air coming from the vents is not cool enough	• Windows and air vent wings open • The compressor belt is slipping • Heater is on • Condenser is clogged with debris • Refrigerant has escaped through a leak in the system • Receiver/drier is plugged	• Close windows and vent wings • Tighten or replace compressor belt • Shut heater off • Clean the condenser • Check system • Service system

Troubleshooting Basic Air Conditioning Problems (cont.)

Problem	Cause	Solution
The air has an odor	• Vacuum system is disrupted • Odor producing substances on the evaporator case • Condensation has collected in the bottom of the evaporator housing	• Have the system checked/repaired • Clean the evaporator case • Clean the evaporator housing drains
System is noisy or vibrating	• Compressor belt or mountings loose • Air in the system	• Tighten or replace belt; tighten mounting bolts • Have the system serviced

Sight glass condition
  Constant bubbles, foam or oil streaks
  Clear sight glass, but no cold air
  Clear sight glass, but air is cold
  Clouded with milky fluid
	• Undercharged system
	• No refrigerant at all
	• System is OK
	• Receiver drier is leaking dessicant
		• Charge the system
		• Check and charge the system
		• Have system checked

Large difference in temperature of lines	• System undercharged	• Charge and leak test the system
Compressor noise	• Broken valves • Overcharged • Incorrect oil level • Piston slap • Broken rings • Drive belt pulley bolts are loose	• Replace the valve plate • Discharge, evacuate and install the correct charge • Isolate the compressor and check the oil level. Correct as necessary. • Replace the compressor • Replace the compressor • Tighten with the correct torque specification
Excessive vibration	• Incorrect belt tension • Clutch loose • Overcharged • Pulley is misaligned	• Adjust the belt tension • Tighten the clutch • Discharge, evacuate and install the correct charge • Align the pulley
Condensation dripping in the passenger compartment	• Drain hose plugged or improperly positioned • Insulation removed or improperly installed	• Clean the drain hose and check for proper installation • Replace the insulation on the expansion valve and hoses
Frozen evaporator coil	• Faulty thermostat • Thermostat capillary tube improperly installed • Thermostat not adjusted properly	• Replace the thermostat • Install the capillary tube correctly • Adjust the thermostat
Low side low—high side low	• System refrigerant is low • Expansion valve is restricted	• Evacuate, leak test and charge the system • Replace the expansion valve
Low side high—high side low	• Internal leak in the compressor—worn	• Remove the compressor cylinder head and inspect the compressor. Replace the valve plate assembly if necessary. If the compressor pistons, rings or

Troubleshooting Basic Air Conditioning Problems (cont.)

Problem	Cause	Solution
Low side high—high side low (cont.)		cylinders are excessively worn or scored replace the compressor
	• Cylinder head gasket is leaking	• Install a replacement cylinder head gasket
	• Expansion valve is defective	• Replace the expansion valve
	• Drive belt slipping	• Adjust the belt tension
Low side high—high side high	• Condenser fins obstructed	• Clean the condenser fins
	• Air in the system	• Evacuate, leak test and charge the system
	• Expansion valve is defective	• Replace the expansion valve
	• Loose or worn fan belts	• Adjust or replace the belts as necessary
Low side low—high side high	• Expansion valve is defective	• Replace the expansion valve
	• Restriction in the refrigerant hose	• Check the hose for kinks—replace if necessary
Low side low—high side high	• Restriction in the receiver/drier	• Replace the receiver/drier
	• Restriction in the condenser	• Replace the condenser
Low side and high normal (inadequate cooling)	• Air in the system	• Evacuate, leak test and charge the system
	• Moisture in the system	• Evacuate, leak test and charge the system

MAX or COLD mode.

5. The low pressure gauge should read 5–20 psi; the high pressure gauge should indicate 120–180 psi.

WARNING: These pressures are the norm for an ambient temperature of 70–80°F (21–27°C). Higher air temperatures along with high humidity will cause higher system pressures. At idle speed and an ambient temperature of 110°F (43°C), the high pressure reading can exceed 300 psi.

Under these extreme conditions, you can keep the pressures down by directing a large electric floor fan through the condenser.

DISCHARGING THE SYSTEM

1. Remove the caps from the high and low pressure charging valves in the high and low pressure lines.
2. Turn both manifold gauge set hand valves to the fully closed (clockwise) position.
3. Connect the manifold gauge set.
4. If the van does not have a service access gauge port valve, connect the gauge set low pressure hose to the evaporator service access gauge port valve.
5. Place the end of the center hose away from you, preferably into a container such as an old coffee can to catch the refrigerant oil.
6. Open the low pressure gauge valve slightly and allow the system pressure to bleed off.
7. When the system is just about empty, open the high pressure valve very slowly to avoid losing an excessive amount of refrigerant oil. Allow any remaining refrigerant to escape.

EVACUATING THE SYSTEM

NOTE: This procedure requires the use of a vacuum pump.

1. Connect the manifold gauge set.
2. Discharge the system.
3. Make sure that the low pressure gauge set hose is connected to the low pressure service gauge port on the top center of the accumulator/drier assembly and the high pressure hose connected to the high pressure service gauge port on the compressor discharge line.
4. Connect the center service hose to the inlet fitting of the vacuum pump.
5. Turn both gauge set valves to the wide open position.
6. Start the pump and note the low side gauge reading.
7. Operate the pump until the low pressure gauge reads 25–30 in.Hg. Continue running the vacuum pump for 10 minutes more. If you've replaced some component in the system, run the pump for an additional 20–30 minutes.
8. Leak test the system. Close both gauge set valves. Turn off the pump. The needle should remain stationary at the point at which the pump was turned off. If the needle drops to zero rapidly, there is a leak in the system which must be repaired.

LEAK TESTING

Some leak tests can be performed with a soapy water solution. There must be at least a ½ lb. charge in the system for a leak to be detected. The most extensive leak tests are performed with either a Halide flame type leak tester or the more preferable electronic leak tester.

In either case, the equipment is expensive, and, the use of a Halide detector can be **extremely** hazardous!

CHARGING THE SYSTEM

CAUTION

Never open the high pressure side with a can of refrigerant connected to the system! Opening the high pressure side will over pressurize the can, causing it to explode!

1. Connect the gauge set.
2. Close (clockwise) both gauge set valves.
3. Connect the center hose to the refrigerant can opener valve.
4. Make sure the can opener valve is closed, that is, the needle is raised, and connect the valve to the can. Open the valve, puncturing the can with the needle.
5. Loosen the center hose fitting at the pressure gauge, allowing refrigerant to purge the hose of air. When the air is bled, tighten the fitting.

CAUTION

If the low pressure gauge set hose is not connected to the accumulator/drier, keep the can in an upright position!

6. Start the engine and move the air conditioning controls to the low blower position.
7. Open the low side gauge set valve and the can valve.
8. Allow refrigerant to be drawn into the system. Adjust the valve so that charging pressure does not exceed 50 psi.

NOTE: The low pressure (cycling) cut-out switch will prevent the compressor clutch from energizing until refrigerant is added to the system. If the clutch does not engage, replace the switch.

9. When no more refrigerant is drawn into the system, start the engine and run it at about 1,300 Rpm. Turn on the system and operate it at the full high position. The compressor will operate and pull refrigerant gas into the system.

NOTE: To help speed the process, the can may be placed, upright, in a pan of warm water, not exceeding 125°F (52°C).

10. If more than one can of refrigerant is needed, close the can valve and gauge set low side valve when the can is empty and connect a new can to the opener. Repeat the charging process until the sight glass indicates a full charge. The frost line on the outside of the can will indicate what portion of the can has been used.

CAUTION

Never allow the high pressure side reading to exceed 240 psi.

11. When the charging process has been completed, close the gauge set valve and can valve. Remove the jumper wire and reconnect the cycling clutch wire. Run the system for at least five minutes until it to normalize. Low pressure side reading should be 4–25 psi; high pressure reading should be 120–210 psi at an ambient temperature of 70–90°F (21–32°C).
12. Loosen both service hoses at the gauges to allow any refrigerant to escape. Remove the gauge set and install the dust caps on the service valves.

NOTE: Multi-can dispensers are available which allow a simultaneous hook-up of up to four 1 lb. cans of R-12.

Windshield Wipers

Wiper blades exposed to the weather over a period of time tend to lose their wiping effectiveness. Clean the wiping surface of the blade with a sponge and a mild solution of water and detergent. If the blades continue to smear, they should be replaced with either a new blade or refill.

BLADE REFILLS

1. Turn the wiper switch to the ON position. Turn the ignition switch ON. When the blades reach a convenient place on the windshield, turn the ignition switch to OFF, thus stopping the blades.
2. Lift the wiper arm to raise the blade from the windshield.
3. Insert a small blade type tool into the release slot of wiper blade and pry slightly upward.
4. Pinch lock on each end of blade and slide wiping element out of blade.
5. Install a new wiping element into blade. Make certain each release points are properly locked in position.
6. Install blade on wiper arm.

Most Anco® styles uses a release button that is pushed down to allow the refill to slide out of the yoke jaws. The new refill slides in and locks in place. Some Trico® refills are removed by locating where the metal backing strip of the refill is wider. Insert a small screwdriver blade between the frame and metal backing strip. Press down to release the refill from the retaining tab.

The Trico® style is unlocked at one end by squeezing 2 metal tabs, and the refill is slide out of the frame jaws. When the new refill is installed, the tabs will click into place, locking the refill.

The polycarbonate type is held in place by a locking lever that is pushed downward out of the groove in the arm to free the refill. When the new refill is installed, it will lock in place automatically.

The Tridon® refill has a plastic backing strip with a notch about 1 in. (25mm) from the end. Hold the blade (frame) on a hard surface so that the frame is tightly bowed. Grip the tip of the backing strip and pull up while twisting counter clockwise. The backing strip will snap out of the retaining tab. Do this for the remaining tabs until the refill is free of the arm. The length of these refills is molded into the end and they should be replaced with identical types.

No matter which type of refill you use, be sure that all of the frame claws engage the refill. Before operating the wiper, be sure that no part of the metal frame is contacting the windshield.

Tires and Wheels

TIRE ROTATION

Tires installed on the front or rear of any vehicle are subjected to different loads, breaking, or steering functions. Because of these conditions, tires develop uneven wear patterns. Rotating the tires every 6000 miles or so will result in increased thread life. Use the correct pattern for tire rotation. Refer to Tire Rotation Patterns chart.

Most automotive experts are in agreement that radial tires are better all around performers, giving prolonged wear and better handling. An added benefit which you should consider when purchasing tires is that radials have less rolling resistance and can give up to a 10% increase in fuel economy over a bias-ply tire.

TIRE INFLATION

Check the air pressure in your vehicle's tires every few weeks. Make sure that the tires are cool. Air pressure increases with higher temperature, and will indicate false reading. A decal located on the glove box door or side door frame will tell you the proper tire pressure for the standard equipment tires.

Tread depth can be roughly checked with a Lincoln penny. If the top of Lincoln's head is visible, replace the tires

NOTE: Never exceed the maximum inflation pressure on the side of the tire. Also never mixed tires of different size or construction (Belted vs Bias-ply, or Radial vs Belted etc.).

It pays to buy a tire pressure gauge to keep in your vehicle, since those of service stations are often inaccurate or broken. While you are checking the tire pressure, take a look at the tread. The tread should be wearing evenly across the tire. Excessive wear in the center of the tread indicates over inflation. Excessive wear on the outer edges indicates under inflation. An irregular wear pattern is usually a sign of incorrect front wheel alignment or wheel balance.

A front end that is out of alignment will usually pull to one side when the steering wheel is released. Conditions which relate to front end alignment are associated by tire wear patterns. Tire treads being worn on one side more than the other, or wear on the tread edges may be noticeable. Front wheels which are incorrectly balance, is usually accompanied by high speed vibration.

TIRE ROTATION

It is recommended that you have the tires rotated and the balance checked every 6,000 miles. There is no way to give a tire rotation diagram for every combination of tires and vehicles, but the accompanying diagrams are a general rule to follow. Radial tires should not be cross-switched; they last longer if their direction of rotation is not changed. Truck tires and some high-performance tires sometimes have directional tread, indicated by arrows on the sidewalls; the arrow shows the direction of rotation. They will wear very rapidly if reversed. Studded snow tires will lose their studs if their direction of rotation is reversed.

NOTE: Mark the wheel position or direction of rotation on radial tires or studded snow tires before removing them.

If your van is equipped with tires having different load ratings on the front and the rear, the tires should not be rotated front to rear. Rotating these tires could affect tire life (the tires with the lower rating will wear faster, and could become overloaded), and upset the handling of the van.

When installing the wheels on the vehicle, tighten the lug nuts in a criss-cross pattern. Lug nuts should be torqued to 85 ft. lbs.

TIRE USAGE

The tires on your van were selected to provide the best all around performance for normal operation when inflated as specified. Oversize tires will not increase the maximum carrying capacity of the vehicle, although they will provide an extra margin of tread life. Be sure to check overall height before using larger size tires which may cause interference with suspension components or wheel wells. When replacing conventional tire sizes with other tire size designations, be sure to check the manufacturer's recommendations. Interchangeability is not always possible because of differences in load ratings, tire dimensions, wheel well clearances, and rim size. Also due to differences in handling characteristics, 70 Series and 60 Series tires should be used only in pairs on the same axle; radial tires should be used only in sets of four.

NOTE: Many states have vehicle height restrictions; some states prohibit the lifting of vehicles beyond their design limits.

The wheels must be the correct width for the tire. Tire dealers have charts of tire and rim compatibility. A mismatch can cause sloppy handling and rapid tread wear. The old rule of thumb is that the tread width should match the rim width (inside bead to inside bead) within 1 in. (25mm). For radial tires, the rim width should be 80% or less of the tire (not tread) width.

The height (mounted diameter) of the new tires can greatly change speedometer accuracy, engine speed at a given road speed, fuel mileage, acceleration, and ground clearance. Tire manufacturers furnish full measurement specifications. Speedometer drive gears are available for correction.

NOTE: Dimensions of tires marked the same size may vary significantly, even among tires from the same manufacturer.

The spare tire should be of the same size, construction and design as the tires on the vehicle. It's not a good idea to carry a spare of a different construction.

TIRE DESIGN

For maximum satisfaction, tires should be used in sets of five. Mixing or different types (radial, bias-belted, fiberglass belted) should be avoided. Conventional bias tires are constructed so that the cords run bead-to-bead at an angle. Alternate plies run at an opposite angle. This type of construction gives rigidity to both tread and sidewall. Bias-belted tires are similar in construction to conventional bias ply tires. Belts run at an angle and also at a 90° angle to the bead, as in the radial tire. Tread life is improved considerably over the conventional bias tire. The radial tire differs in construction, but instead of the carcass plies running at an angle of 90° to each other, they run at an angle of 90° to the bead. This gives the tread a great deal of rigidity and the sidewall a great deal of flexibility and accounts for the characteristic bulge associated with radial tires.

When radial tires are used, tire sizes and wheel diameters should be selected to maintain ground clearance and tire load capacity equivalent to the minimum specified tire. Radial tires should always be used in sets of five, but in an emergency, radial tires can be used with caution on the rear axle only. If this is done, both tires on the rear should be of radial design.

WARNING: Radial tires should never be used on only the front axle!

Troubleshooting Basic Wheel Problems

Problem	Cause	Solution
The car's front end vibrates at high speed	• The wheels are out of balance • Wheels are out of alignment	• Have wheels balanced • Have wheel alignment checked/adjusted
Car pulls to either side	• Wheels are out of alignment • Unequal tire pressure • Different size tires or wheels	• Have wheel alignment checked/adjusted • Check/adjust tire pressure • Change tires or wheels to same size
The car's wheel(s) wobbles	• Loose wheel lug nuts • Wheels out of balance • Damaged wheel • Wheels are out of alignment • Worn or damaged ball joint • Excessive play in the steering linkage (usually due to worn parts) • Defective shock absorber	• Tighten wheel lug nuts • Have tires balanced • Raise car and spin the wheel. If the wheel is bent, it should be replaced • Have wheel alignment checked/adjusted • Check ball joints • Check steering linkage • Check shock absorbers
Tires wear unevenly or prematurely	• Incorrect wheel size • Wheels are out of balance • Wheels are out of alignment	• Check if wheel and tire size are compatible • Have wheels balanced • Have wheel alignment checked/adjusted

Troubleshooting Basic Tire Problems

Problem	Cause	Solution
The car's front end vibrates at high speeds and the steering wheel shakes	• Wheels out of balance • Front end needs aligning	• Have wheels balanced • Have front end alignment checked
The car pulls to one side while cruising	• Unequal tire pressure (car will usually pull to the low side) • Mismatched tires • Front end needs aligning	• Check/adjust tire pressure • Be sure tires are of the same type and size • Have front end alignment checked
Abnormal, excessive or uneven tire wear See "How to Read Tire Wear"	• Infrequent tire rotation • Improper tire pressure • Sudden stops/starts or high speed on curves	• Rotate tires more frequently to equalize wear • Check/adjust pressure • Correct driving habits
Tire squeals	• Improper tire pressure • Front end needs aligning	• Check/adjust tire pressure • Have front end alignment checked

Tire Size Comparison Chart

| "Letter" sizes | | | Inch Sizes | Metric-inch Sizes | | |
"60 Series"	"70 Series"	"78 Series"	1965–77	"60 Series"	"70 Series"	"80 Series"
			5.50-12, 5.60-12	165/60-12	165/70-12	155-12
		Y78-12	6.00-12			
		W78-13	5.20-13	165/60-13	145/70-13	135-13
		Y78-13	5.60-13	175/60-13	155/70-13	145-13
			6.15-13	185/60-13	165/70-13	155-13, P155/80-13
A60-13	A70-13	A78-13	6.40-13	195/60-13	175/70-13	165-13
B60-13	B70-13	B78-13	6.70-13	205/60-13	185/70-13	175-13
			6.90-13			
C60-13	C70-13	C78-13	7.00-13	215/60-13	195/70-13	185-13
D60-13	D70-13	D78-13	7.25-13			
E60-13	E70-13	E78-13	7.75-13			195-13
			5.20-14	165/60-14	145/70-14	135-14
			5.60-14	175/60-14	155/70-14	145-14
			5.90-14			
A60-14	A70-14	A78-14	6.15-14	185/60-14	165/70-14	155-14
	B70-14	B78-14	6.45-14	195/60-14	175/70-14	165-14
	C70-14	C78-14	6.95-14	205/60-14	185/70-14	175-14
D60-14	D70-14	D78-14				
E60-14	E70-14	E78-14	7.35-14	215/60-14	195/70-14	185-14
F60-14	F70-14	F78-14, F83-14	7.75-14	225/60-14	200/70-14	195-14
G60-14	G70-14	G77-14, G78-14	8.25-14	235/60-14	205/70-14	205-14
H60-14	H70-14	H78-14	8.55-14	245/60-14	215/70-14	215-14
J60-14	J70-14	J78-14	8.85-14	255/60-14	225/70-14	225-14
L60-14	L70-14		9.15-14	265/60-14	235/70-14	
	A70-15	A78-15	5.60-15	185/60-15	165/70-15	155-15
B60-15	B70-15	B78-15	6.35-15	195/60-15	175/70-15	165-15
C60-15	C70-15	C78-15	6.85-15	205/60-15	185/70-15	175-15
	D70-15	D78-15				
E60-15	E70-15	E78-15	7.35-15	215/60-15	195/70-15	185-15
F60-15	F70-15	F78-15	7.75-15	225/60-15	205/70-15	195-15
G60-15	G70-15	G78-15	8.15-15/8.25-15	235/60-15	215/70-15	205-15
H60-15	H70-15	H78-15	8.45-15/8.55-15	245/60-15	225/70-15	215-15
J60-15	J70-15	J78-15	8.85-15/8.90-15	255/60-15	235/70-15	225-15
	K70-15		9.00-15	265/60-15	245/70-15	230-15
L60-15	L70-15	L78-15, L84-15	9.15-15			235-15
	M70-15	M78-15				255-15
		N78-15				

NOTE: Every size tire is not listed and many size comaprisons are approximate, based on load ratings. Wider tires than those supplied new with the vehicle should always be checked for clearance

FLUIDS AND LUBRICANTS

Fuel Recommendations

Chrysler recommends that unleaded fuel only with a minimum octane rating of at least 87 be used in your vehicle, if equipped with a catalytic converter. The use of unleaded gasoline is required in order to meet all emission regulations, and provide excellent fuel economy.

Fuels of the same octane rating have varying anti-knock qualities. Thus, if your engine knocks or pings, try switching brands of gasoline before trying a more expansive higher octane fuel.

Your engine's fuel requirements can change with time, due to carbon buildup which changes the compression ratio. If switching brands or grades of gas doesn't work, check the ignition timing. If it is necessary to retard timing from specifications, don't change it more than about 4°. Retarded timing will reduce power output and fuel mileage and increase engine temperature.

Engine

OIL RECOMMENDATIONS

A high quality heavy-duty detergent oil having the proper viscosity for prevailing temperatures and an SG/CC service rating should be used in your vehicle. A high quality SG/CC rated oil should be used for heavy duty service or turbocharged equipped engines. The SG/CC and SG/CD rated oil contain sufficient chemical additives to provide maximum engine protection.

Pick an oil with the viscosity that matches the anticipated temperature of the region your vehicle will be operated in before the next oil change. A chart is provided to help you with your selection. Choose the oil viscosity for the lowest expected temperature and you will be assured of easy cold weather starting and sufficient engine protection.

OIL LEVEL CHECK

The engine oil level is checked with the dipstick which is located on the radiator side of the engine.

NOTE: The oil should be checked before the engine is started or five minutes after the engine has shut off. This gives the oil time to drain back to the oil pan and prevents an inaccurate oil level reading.

Remove the dipstick from the tube, wipe it clean, and insert it back into the tube. Remove it again and observe the oil level. It should be maintained within the full range on the dipstick.

NOTE: Do not overfill the crankcase. This will cause oil aeration and loss of oil pressure.

Oil dipstick

OIL AND FILTER CHANGE

The recommended mileage figures for oil and filter changes are 7,500 miles or 12 months whichever comes first, assuming normal driving conditions. If your vehicle is being used under dusty conditions, frequent trailer pulling, excessive idling, or stop and go driving, it is recommended to change the oil and filter at 3,000 miles.

NOTE: Improper disposing of all lubricants (engine, trans., and differential), can result in environmental problems. Contact your local dealerships of service stations for advice on proper disposal.

Always drain the oil after the engine has been running long enough to bring it to operating temperature. Hot oil will flow easier and more contaminants will be removed along with the oil than if it were drained cold.

Chrysler recommends changing both the oil and filter during the first oil change and the filter every other oil change thereafter. For the small price of an oil filter, it's cheap insurance to replace the filter at every oil change. One of the larger filter manufacturers points out in its advertisements that not changing the filter leaves one quart of dirty oil in the engine. This claim is true and should be kept in mind when changing your oil.

1. Run the engine until it reaches normal operating temperature.
2. Jack up the front of the vehicle and support on jack stands, remove the shield if it will cause interference.
3. Slide a drain pan of at least 6 quarts capacity under the oil pan.

—————— **CAUTION** ——————
The engine oil will be hot! Keep your arms, face and hands away from the oil as it drains out!

4. Loosen the drain plug. It is located in the lowest point of the oil pan. Turn the plug out by hand. By keeping an inward pressure on the plug as you unscrew it, oil won't escape past the threads and you can remove it without being burned by hot oil.
5. Allow the oil to drain completely and then install the drain plug. Don't over tighten the plug, it will result in stripped threads.
6. Using a strap wrench, remove the oil filter. Keep in mind that it's holding about one quart of dirty, hot oil.

—————— **CAUTION** ——————
The EPA warns that prolonged contact with used engine oil may cause a number of skin disorders, including cancer! You should make every effort to minimize your exposure to used engine oil. Protective gloves should be worn when changing the oil. Wash your hands and any other exposed skin areas as soon as possible after exposure to used engine oil. Soap and water, or waterless hand cleaner should be used.

Recommended SAE Viscosity Grades

		20W-40, 20W-50, 30
	10W-30, 10W-40, 10W-50	
	10W	
	5W-30, 5W-40	
*5W-20		

°F	−20	−10	10	32	60	80	100
°C	−29	−23	−12	0	16	27	38

Temperature range anticipated before next oil change

*SAE 5W-20 <u>Not</u> recommended for sustained high speed vehicle operation.

Oil viscosity chart

Lubricate the gasket on a new filter with clean engine oil

7. Empty the old filter into the drain pan and dispose of the filter.

8. Using a clean rag, wipe off the filter adapter on the engine block. Be sure that the rag doesn't leave any lint which could clog an oil passage.

9. Coat the rubber gasket on the filter with fresh oil. Spin it onto the engine by hand; when the gasket touches the adapter surface give it another ½–¾ turn. No more, or you'll squash the gasket and it will leak.

10. Refill the engine with the correct amount of fresh oil. See the Capacities Chart.

11. Run the engine at idle for approximately one minute. Shut the engine off. Wait a few minutes and recheck oil level. Add oil, as necessary to bring the level up to **Fill**.

12. Shut the engine off and lower the vehicle.

—————————— **CAUTION** ——————————

You now have 4 quarts of used engine oil. Please store this oil in a secure container, such as a 1 gallon windshield washer fluid bottle. Locate a service station or garage which accepts used oil for recycling and dispose of it there.

Transaxle

FLUID RECOMMENDATION

Both the manual (4- or 5-speed) and the automatic transaxles use Dexron®II type automatic transmission fluid. Under normal operating conditions, periodic fluid change is not required. If the vehicle is operating under severe operating conditions change the fluid, or fluid and filter every 15,000 miles.

FLUID LEVEL CHECK

Manual Transaxle

1. The fluid level is checked by removing the fill plug on the end cover side of the transaxle.

Manual transaxle filler plug location

Automatic transaxle dipstick location

Automatic transaxle dipstick markings

2. The fluid level should be between the top of the fill hole and a point not more than ⅛ in. (3mm) below the bottom of the fill hole.

3. Add Dexron®II type fluid as necessary. Secure the fill plug.

Automatic Transaxle

NOTE: When checking the fluid level, the condition of the fluid should be observed. If severe darkening of the fluid and a strong odor are present, the fluid, filter and pan gasket (RTV sealant) should be changed and the bands readjusted.

Automatic transaxle fill tube — A604 Ultradrive transaxle

Form a silicone gasket as shown

1. Make sure the vehicle is on level ground. The engine should be at normal operating temperatures, if possible.
2. Apply the parking brake, start the engine and move the gear selector through each position. Place the selector in the PARK position.
3. Remove the dipstick and determine if the fluid is warm or hot.
4. Wipe the dipstick clean and reinsert until fully seated. Remove and take note of the fluid level.
5. If the fluid is hot, the reading should be in the crosshatched area marked **HOT**.
6. If the fluid is warm, the fluid level should be in the area marked **WARM**.
7. If the fluid level checks low, add enough fluid (Dexron®II®) through the fill tube, to bring the level within the marks appropriate for average temperature of the fluid.
8. Insert the dipstick and recheck the level. Make sure the dipstick is fully seated to prevent dirt from entering. Do not overfill the transaxle.

DRAIN AND REFILL

Manual Transaxle

1. Raise and support the front of the vehicle on jack stands.
2. Remove the undercarriage splash shield if it will interfere with fluid change.
3. Position a drain pan underneath the end of the transaxle and remove the differential end cover where the fill plug is located. Loosen the bolt slightly and pry the lower edge away so that the fluid will drain.

Power Transfer Unit (PTU) — fill plug location

4. Remove the cover completely. Clean the gasket surfaces of the case and cover. Clean the magnet located on the cover.
5. Use an even ⅛ in. (3mm) bead of RTV sealant to form a gasket on the cover and reinstall on the transaxle case.
6. Refill the transaxle with Dexron®II.

Automatic Transaxle

NOTE: Band readjustment and filter replacement are recommended when the fluid is changed. Refer to "Drive Train" for required procedures.

Differential

The transmission and differential share a common housing. Fluid check and change procedures are covered in the "Drive" Train Section.

Power Transfer Unit (PTU)

On models with All Wheel Drive (AWD), a power transfer unit is used that is connected to the transaxle. This unit is separate from the other drive train components.

FLUID RECOMMENDATION

Chrysler recommends the use of Mopar® Gear Lube, SAE 85W–90 or equivalent. The correct quantity of oil is 1.22 qts.

DRAIN AND REFILL

The PTU cannot be serviced. If fluid leakage is detected, the unit must be disassembled and the seals replaced.

Drive Line Module

On models with All Wheel Drive (AWD), the rear wheels are driven by shafts from the Drive Line Module. This module serves as the rear drive axle.

As well as containing the rear differential, this module contains a set of overrunning clutches in their own case. This clutch assembly serves to control differences in drive line speed and traction.

Overrunning clutch fill plug — All Wheel Drive equipped models

Drive line module fill plug — All Wheel Drive equipped models

FLUID RECOMMENDATION

Drive Line Module

Chrysler recommends the use of Mopar® Gear Lube, SAE 85W–90 or equivalent. The module is full when the fluid level is ⅛ in. (3mm) below the fill plug.

Overrunning Clutch

Chrysler recommends the use of Mopar® ATF type 7176 or equivalent. The oil level should be at the bottom of the oil fill opening.

Cooling System

FLUID RECOMMENDATION

A 50/50 mixture of water and ethylene glycol type antifreeze (containing Alguard or silicate type inhibiter) that is safe for use in aluminum components is recommended. The 50/50 mixture offers protection to −34°F (−37°C). If addition cold weather protection is necessary a concentrate of 65% antifreeze may be used.

LEVEL CHECK

All vehicles are equipped with a transparent coolant reserve container. A minimum and maximum level mark are provided for a quick visual check of the coolant level.
1. Run the engine until normal operating temperature is reached.
2. Open the hood and observe the level of the coolant in the reserve.
3. Fluid level should be between the two lines. Add coolant, if necessary, through the fill cap of the reserve tank.

DRAIN AND REFILL

1. If the lower splash shield is in the way, remove it.
2. Place the heater control lever on the dash control to full on.
3. Place a drain pan under the radiator and open the drain cock. When the coolant reserve tank is drained completely, remove the radiator cap.

CAUTION

When draining the coolant, keep in mind that cats and dogs are attracted by the ethylene glycol antifreeze, and are quite likely to drink any that is left in an uncovered container or in puddles on the ground. This will prove fatal in sufficient quantity. Always drain the coolant into a sealable container. Coolant should be reused unless it is contaminated or several years old.

4. If your vehicle is equipped with the 2.2L engine, removal of the vacuum valve (located above the thermostat housing), is necessary to provide air displacement. If your vehicle is equipped with the 2.5L engine, removal of the drain/fill plug (located above the thermostat housing), is necessary to provide air displacement.
5. To remove the vacuum valve, disconnect the hose connector plug, and carefully unscrew the valve using the proper size wrench.
6. After draining the system, refill with water and run the engine until normal operating temperature is reached. (See the following refill procedures). Drain the system again, repeat procedure until the drained water runs clear.
7. Close the radiator drain cock.
8. Fill the system with a 50/50 mixture of ethylene glycol type antifreeze.
9. When the coolant reaches the hole in the water box at thermostat housing (2.2L and 2.5L engines), install the vacuum valve or drain/fill plug to 20 N.m (15 ft. lbs.)
10. Continue filling system until full.
11. Install the radiator cap, start the engine, and run until normal operating temperature is reached. Fill the coolant reserve tank to **Max** mark. Stop engine and allowed to cool.

NOTE: It may be necessary to warm up and cool down engine several times to remove trapped air. Recheck level in reserve tank, and adjust level if necessary.

CHECK THE RADIATOR CAP

While you are checking the coolant level, check the radiator cap for a worn or cracked gasket. If the cap doesn't seal properly, fluid will be lost in the form of steam and the engine will overheat. Replace the cap with a new one, if necessary.

CLEAN RADIATOR OF DEBRIS

Periodically clean any debris—leaves, paper, insects, etc.—from the radiator fins. Pick the large pieces off by hand. The smaller pieces can be washed away with water pressure from a hose.

Carefully straighten any bent radiator fins with a pair of needle nose pliers. Be careful—the fins are very soft! Don't wiggle the fins back and forth too much. Straighten them once and try not to move them again.

2.2L engine vacuum valve location

Check the radiator cap gasket

Remove debris from the cooling fins

Check the antifreeze protection

Master Cylinder

FLUID RECOMMENDATION

Use only a DOT 3 approved brake fluid in your vehicle. Always use fresh fluid when servicing or refilling the brake system.

LEVEL CHECK

The fluid level in both reservoirs of the master cylinder

Check the master cylinder fluid level

Anti-lock brake system fluid reservoir

should be maintained at the bottom of the fill split rings visible after removing the covers. Add the necessary fluid to maintain proper level. A drop in the fluid level should be expected as the brake pads and shoes wear. However, if an unusual amount of fluid is required, check for system leaks.

Power Steering Pump

FLUID RECOMMENDATIONS

Power steering fluid such as Mopar Power Steering Fluid

Check the power steering fluid level

Power steering reservoir dipstick — 3.3L engine

(Part Number 4318055) or equivalent should be used. Only petroleum fluids formulated for minimum effect on the rubber hoses should be added. Do not use automatic transmission fluid.

——————— CAUTION ———————
Check the power steering fluid level with engine off, to avoid injury from moving parts.

LEVEL CHECK

1. Wipe off the power steering pump reservoir cap with a cloth before removal.
2. A dipstick is built into the cover. Remove the reservoir cover cap and wipe the dipstick with a cloth.
3. Reinstall the dipstick and check the level indicated.
4. Add fluid as necessary, but do not overfill.

Steering Gear

NOTE: The steering gear is lubricated and sealed at the factory, periodic lubrication is not necessary.

Chassis Lubrication

All vehicles have two lower ball joints in the front suspension that are equipped with grease fittings as are the tie rod ends. Periodic lubrication (every 24,000 miles) using a hand grease gun and NLGI Grade 2, Multipurpose grease is required. Connect

Inspect U-joint seal for leakage

Check the tie rod end ball joint seals

Check the ball joints for damaged seals

the grease gun to the fitting and pump until the boot seal on the tie rod ends or ball joints start to swell. Do not overfill until grease flows from under the boot edges.

Body Lubrication

The following body parts and mechanisms should be lubricated periodically at all pivot and sliding points. Use the lubricant specified;
Engine Oil:
 • Door Hinges at pin and pivot contact area.
 • Hinges
 • Liftgate Hinges
 • Sliding Door at center hinge pivot.
White Spray Lube:
 • Hood Hinge cam and slide
 • Lock cylinders
 • Parking Brake Mechanisms
 • Window Regulator: remove trim panel
 • Liftgate Latches
 • Liftgate Prop Pivots
 • Ash Tray Slide
Multi-purpose Lubricant (Water Resistant):
 • Door Latch, Lock control Linkage and Remote Control Mechanism (trim panel must be removed)
 • Latch Plate and Bolt
Multi-purpose Grease, NLGI Grade 2:
 • Sliding Door: lower, center and upper tracks. Open position striker spring.
 • Fuel Tank Door

ROLLER CAGE CUP HUB SPINDLE SEAL CONE NUT LOCK GREASE HUB CAVITY

Rear wheel bearing assembly — component view

Rear Wheel Bearings
Front Wheel Drive Only

SERVICING

NOTE: Sodium-based grease is not compatible with lithium-based grease. Read the package labels and be careful not to mix the two types. If there is any doubt as to the type of grease used, completely clean the old grease from the bearing and hub before replacing.

Before handling the bearings, there are a few things that you should remember to do and not to do.

Remember to DO the following:
● Remove all outside dirt from the housing before exposing the bearing.
● Treat a used bearing as gently as you would a new one.
● Work with clean tools in clean surroundings.
● Use clean, dry canvas gloves, or at least clean, dry hands.
● Clean solvents and flushing fluids are a must.
● Use clean paper when laying out the bearings to dry.
● Protect disassembled bearings from rust and dirt. Cover them up.
● Use clean rags to wipe bearings.
● Keep the bearings in oil-proof paper when they are to be stored or are not in use.

● Clean the inside of the housing before replacing the bearing.

Do NOT do the following:
● Don't work in dirty surroundings.
● Don't use dirty, chipped or damaged tools.
● Try not to work on wooden work benches or use wooden mallets.
● Don't handle bearings with dirty or moist hands.
● Do not use gasoline for cleaning; use a safe solvent.
● Do not spin-dry bearings with compressed air. They will be damaged.
● Do not spin dirty bearings.
● Avoid using cotton waste or dirty cloths to wipe bearings.
● Try not to scratch or nick bearing surfaces.
● Do not allow the bearing to come in contact with dirt or rust at any time.

The rear wheel bearings should be inspected and relubricated whenever the rear brakes are serviced or at least every 30,000 miles. Repack the bearings with high temperature multi-purpose grease.

Check the lubricant to see if it is contaminated. If it contains dirt or has a milky appearance indicating the presence of water, the bearings should be cleaned and repacked.

Clean the bearings in kerosene, mineral spirits or other suitable cleaning fluid. Do not dry them by spinning the bearings. Allow them to air dry.

1. Raise and support the vehicle with the rear wheels off the floor.
2. Remove the wheel grease cap, cotter pin, nut-lock and bearing adjusting nut.
3. Remove the thrust washer and bearing.
4. Remove the drum from the spindle.
5. Thoroughly clean the old lubricant from the bearings and hub cavity. Inspect the bearing rollers for pitting or other signs of wear. Light discoloration is normal.
6. Repack the bearings with high temperature multi-purpose EP grease and add a small amount of new grease to the hub cavity. Be sure to force the lubricant between all rollers in the bearing.
7. Install the drum on the spindle after coating the polished spindle surfaces with wheel bearing lubricant.
8. Install the outer bearing cone, thrust washer and adjusting nut.
9. Tighten the adjusting nut to 20–25 ft. lbs. while rotating the wheel.
10. Back off the adjusting nut to completely release the preload from the bearing.
11. Tighten the adjusting nut finger-tight.
12. Position the nut-lock with one pair of slots in line with the cotter pin hole. Install the cotter pin.
13. Clean and install the grease cap and wheel.
14. Lower the vehicle.

TOWING

The vehicle can be towed from either the front or rear. If the vehicle is towed from the front for an extended distance make sure the parking brake is completely released.

Manual transmission vehicles may be towed on the front wheels at speeds up to 30 Mph, for a distance not to exceed 15 miles, provided the transmission is in neutral and the drive line has not been damaged. The steering wheel must be clamped in a straight ahead position.

WARNING: Do not use the steering column lock to secure front wheel position for towing.

Automatic transmission vehicles may be towed on the front wheels at speeds not to exceed 25 Mph for a period of 15 miles.

WARNING: If this requirement cannot be met the front wheels must be placed on a dolly.

JUMP STARTING A DEAD BATTERY

The chemical reaction in a battery produces explosive hydrogen gas. This is the safe way to jump start a dead battery, reducing the chances of an accidental spark that could cause an explosion.

Jump Starting Precautions

1. Be sure both batteries are of the same voltage.
2. Be sure both batteries are of the same polarity (have the same grounded terminal).
3. Be sure the vehicles are not touching.
4. Be sure the vent cap holes are not obstructed.
5. Do not smoke or allow sparks around the battery.
6. In cold weather, check for frozen electrolyte in the battery. Do not jump start a frozen battery.
7. Do not allow electrolyte on your skin or clothing.
8. Be sure the electrolyte is not frozen.

CAUTION: Make certin that the ignition key, in the vehicle with the dead battery, is in the OFF position. Connecting cables to vehicles with on-board computers will result in computer destruction if the key is not in the OFF position.

Jump Starting Procedure

1. Determine voltages of the two batteries; they must be the same.
2. Bring the starting vehicle close (they must not touch) so that the batteries can be reached easily.
3. Turn off all accessories and both engines. Put both vehicles in Neutral or Park and set the handbrake.
4. Cover the cell caps with a rag—do not cover terminals.
5. If the terminals on the run-down battery are heavily corroded, clean them.
6. Identify the positive and negative posts on both batteries and connect the cables in the order shown.
7. Start the engine of the starting vehicle and run it at fast idle. Try to start the car with the dead battery. Crank it for no more than 10 seconds at a time and let it cool for 20 seconds in between tries.
8. If it doesn't start in 3 tries, there is something else wrong.
9. Disconnect the cables in the reverse order.
10. Replace the cell covers and dispose of the rags.

MAKE CERTAIN VEHICLES DO NOT TOUCH

1 CONNECT JUMPER CABLE TO DEAD BATTERY (+ TERMINAL)

2 CONNECT OTHER + END OF JUMPER CABLE TO GOOD BATTERY (+ TERMINAL)

BATTERY IN VEHICLE THAT IS DISCHARGED/DEAD

BATTERY IN VEHICLE WITH CHARGED/GOOD BATTERY

ENGINE

JUMPER CABLE

JUMPER CABLE

ENGINE

4 MAKE LAST CONNECTION OF SECOND JUMPER CABLE (−) TO ENGINE IN CAR WITH DEAD BATTERY; MAKE CONNECTION AWAY FROM BATTERY.

3 CONNECT SECOND JUMPER CABLE TO GOOD BATTERY (− TERMINAL)

FOR NEGATIVE GROUND VEHICLES

Side terminal batteries occasionally pose a problem when connecting jumper cables. There frequently isn't enough room to clamp the cables without touching sheet metal. Side terminal adaptors are available to alleviate this problem and should be removed after use

JACKING

The standard jack utilizes special receptacles located at the body sills. They accept the scissors jack supplied with the vehicle, for emergency road service only. The jack supplied with the vehicle should never be used for any service operation other then tire changing. Never get under the vehicle while it is supported by only a jack. Always block the wheels when changing tires.

The service operations in this book often require that one end or the other, or both, of the vehicle be raised and safely supported. The ideal method, of course, would be a hydraulic hoist. Since this is beyond both the resource and requirement of the do-it-yourselfer, a small hydraulic floor jack is recommended for certain procedures in this guide. Two sturdy jack stands should be acquired if you intend to work under the vehicle at any time. An alternate method of raising the vehicle would be drive-on ramps, Which are available commercially. Be sure to block the wheels when using ramps.

—————————— CAUTION ——————————
Concrete blocks are not recommended for supporting the vehicle. They are likely to crumble if the load is not evenly distributed. Boxes and milk crates of any description must not be used to support the vehicle!

TRAILER TOWING

Factory trailer towing packages are available on most vans. However, if you are installing a trailer hitch and wiring on your van, there are a few thing that you ought to know.

Trailer Weight

Trailer weight is the first, and most important, factor in determining whether or not your vehicle is suitable for towing the trailer you have in mind. The horsepower-to-weight ratio should be calculated. The basic standard is a ratio of 35:1. That is, 35 pounds of GVW for every horsepower.

To calculate this ratio, multiply you engine's rated horsepower by 35, then subtract the weight of the vehicle, including passengers and luggage. The resulting figure is the ideal maximum trailer weight that you can tow. One point to consider: a numerically higher axle ratio can offset what appears to be a low trailer weight. If the weight of the trailer that you have in mind is somewhat higher than the weight you just calculated, you might consider changing your rear axle ratio to compensate.

Hitch Weight

There are three kinds of hitches: bumper mounted, frame mounted, and load equalizing.

Bumper mounted hitches are those which attach solely to the vehicle's bumper. Many states prohibit towing with this type of hitch, when it attaches to the vehicle's stock bumper, since it subjects the bumper to stresses for which it was not designed. Aftermarket rear step bumpers, designed for trailer towing, are acceptable for use with bumper mounted hitches.

Frame mounted hitches can be of the type which bolts to two or more points on the frame, plus the bumper, or just to several points on the frame. Frame mounted hitches can also be of the tongue type, for Class I towing, or, of the receiver type, for Classes II and III.

Load equalizing hitches are usually used for large trailers. Most equalizing hitches are welded in place and use equalizing bars and chains to level the vehicle after the trailer is hooked up.

The bolt-on hitches are the most common, since they are relatively easy to install.

Check the gross weight rating of your trailer. Tongue weight is usually figured as 10% of gross trailer weight. Therefore, a trailer with a maximum gross weight of 2,000 lb. will have a maximum tongue weight of 200 lb. Class I trailers fall into this category. Class II trailers are those with a gross weight rating of 2,000–3,500 lb., while Class III trailers fall into the 3,500–6,000 lb. category. Class IV trailers are those over 6,000 lb. and are for use with fifth wheel trucks, only.

When you've determined the hitch that you'll need, follow the manufacturer's installation instructions, exactly, especially when it comes to fastener torques. The hitch will subjected to a lot of stress and good hitches come with hardened bolts. Never substitute an inferior bolt for a hardened bolt.

Wiring

Wiring the van for towing is fairly easy. There are a number of good wiring kits available and these should be used, rather than trying to design your own. All trailers will need brake lights and turn signals as well as tail lights and side marker lights. Most states require extra marker lights for overly wide trailers. Also, most states have recently required back-up lights for trailers, and most trailer manufacturers have been building trailers with back-up lights for several years.

Additionally, some Class I, most Class II and just about all Class III trailers will have electric brakes.

Add to this number an accessories wire, to operate trailer internal equipment or to charge the trailer's battery, and you can have as many as seven wires in the harness.

Determine the equipment on your trailer and buy the wiring kit necessary. The kit will contain all the wires needed, plus a plug adapter set which included the female plug, mounted on the bumper or hitch, and the male plug, wired into, or plugged into the trailer harness.

When installing the kit, follow the manufacturer's instructions. The color coding of the wires is standard throughout the industry.

One point to note, some domestic vehicles, and most imported vehicles, have separate turn signals. On most domestic vehicles, the brake lights and rear turn signals operate with the same bulb. For those vehicles with separate turn signals, you can purchase an isolation unit so that the brake lights won't blink whenever the turn signals are operated, or, you can go to your local electronics supply house and buy four diodes to wire in series with the brake and turn signal bulbs. Diodes will isolate the brake and turn signals. The choice is yours. The isolation units are simple and quick to install, but far more expensive than the diodes. The diodes, however, require more work to install properly, since they require the cutting of each bulb's wire and soldering in place of the diode.

One final point, the best kits are those with a spring loaded cover on the vehicle mounted socket. This cover prevents dirt and moisture from corroding the terminals. Never let the vehicle socket hang loosely. Always mount it securely to the bumper or hitch.

Cooling

ENGINE

One of the most common, if not THE most common, problem associated with trailer towing is engine overheating.

With factory installed trailer towing packages, a heavy duty cooling system is usually included. Heavy duty cooling systems are available as optional equipment on most vans, with or without a trailer package. If you have one of these extra-capacity systems, you shouldn't have any overheating problems.

If you have a standard cooling system, without an expansion tank, you'll definitely need to get an aftermarket expansion tank kit, preferably one with at least a 2 quart capacity. These kits are easily installed on the radiator's overflow hose, and come with a pressure cap designed for expansion tanks.

Another helpful accessory is a Flex Fan. These fan are large diameter units are designed to provide more airflow at low speeds, with blades that have deeply cupped surfaces. The blades then flex, or flatten out, at high speed, when less cooling air is needed. These fans are far lighter in weight than stock fans, requiring less horsepower to drive them. Also, they are far quieter than stock fans.

If you do decide to replace your stock fan with a flex fan, note that if your van has a fan clutch, a spacer between the flex fan and water pump hub will be needed.

Aftermarket engine oil coolers are helpful for prolonging engine oil life and reducing overall engine temperatures. Both of these factors increase engine life.

While not absolutely necessary in towing Class I and some Class II trailers, they are recommended for heavier Class II and all Class III towing.

Engine oil cooler systems consist of an adapter, screwed on in place of the oil filter, a remote filter mounting and a multi-tube, finned heat exchanger, which is mounted in front of the radiator or air conditioning condenser.

TRANSMISSION

An automatic transmission is usually recommended for trailer towing. Modern automatics have proven reliable and, of course, easy to operate, in trailer towing.

The increased load of a trailer, however, causes an increase in the temperature of the automatic transmission fluid. Heat is the worst enemy of an automatic transmission. As the temperature of the fluid increases, the life of the fluid decreases.

It is essential, therefore, that you install an automatic transmission cooler.

The cooler, which consists of a multi-tube, finned heat exchanger, is usually installed in front of the radiator or air conditioning compressor, and hooked in line with the transmission cooler tank inlet line. Follow the cooler manufacturer's installation instructions.

Select a cooler of at least adequate capacity, based upon the combined gross weights of the van and trailer.

Cooler manufacturers recommend that you use an aftermarket cooler in addition to, and not instead of, the present cooling tank in your van's radiator. If you do want to use it in place of the radiator cooling tank, get a cooler at least two sizes larger than normally necessary.

NOTE: A transmission cooler can, sometimes, cause slow or harsh shifting in the transmission during cold weather, until the fluid has a chance to come up to normal operating temperature. Some coolers can be purchased with or retrofitted with a temperature bypass valve which will allow fluid flow through the cooler only when the fluid has reached operating temperature, or above.

Lubrication and Maintenance Schedules

SCHEDULED MAINTENANCE FOR EMISSION CONTROL AND PROPER VEHICLE PERFORMANCE
Inspection and Service should also be performed any time a malfunction is observed or suspected. O = Except California Vehicles

Component	Service Interval		7.5	15	22.5	30	37.5	45	52.5	60	67.5	75	82.5	90	97.5	105	112.5	120
	Mileage in thousands		7.5	15	22.5	30	37.5	45	52.5	60	67.5	75	82.5	90	97.5	105	112.5	120
	Kilometers in thousands		12	24	36	48	60	72	84	96	108	120	132	144	156	168	180	192
Change engine oil every 12 months		Or	X	X	X	X	X	X	O	O	O	O	O	O	O	O	O	O
Change engine oil filter every second oil change (1)		Or		X		X		X		O		O		O		O		O
Inspect & adjust drive belts tension; replace as necessary		At		O		X		O		O		O		O		O		O
Replace spark plugs		At				X				O				O				O
Replace engine air filter		At				X				O				O				O
Replace oxygen sensor		At							O						O			
Replace EGR valve & tube & clean passages at 60 months		Or							O						O			
Replace PCV filter		At				X				O				O				O
Replace PCV valve at 60 months		Or							O						O			
Replace vacuum operated emission components at 60 months		Or							O						O			
Inspect timing belt 3.0L only		At							O						O			
Adjust ignition timing if not to specifications		At							O									O
Replace ignition cables, distributor cap & rotor		At							O									O
Flush & replace engine coolant at 36 months & 24 months or 30,000 miles (48 000 Km) thereafter		Or						O										
Replace alternator brushes		At										O						
Check engine coolant condition, coolant hoses & clamps every 12 months																		

(1) Note: If mileage is less than 7,500 miles (12 000km) each 12 months, replace oil filter at each oil change.

GENERAL MAINTENANCE SERVICES FOR PROPER VEHICLE PERFORMANCE

General Maintenance	Service Intervals		7.5	15	22.5	30	37.5	45
	Mileage in Thousands		7.5	15	22.5	30	37.5	45
	Kilometers in Thousands		12	24	36	48	60	72
Cooling System	Check & Service As Required Every 12 Months							
	Drain Flush, and Refill At 36 Months Or 52,500 Miles (84 000 Kilometers) And Every 24 Months Or 30,000 Miles (48 000 Kilometers) Thereafter							
Brake Hoses	Inspect For Deterioration And Leaks Whenever Brake System is Serviced And Every 7,500 Miles (12 000 km) Or 12 Months, Whichever Occurs First, For Non-turbocharged Vehicles and 7,500 Miles (12 000 km) or 6 Months, Whichever Occurs First, For Turbocharged Vehicles, Replace if Necessary.							
Brake Linings—Front	Inspect	At				X		X
Brake Linings—Rear	Inspect	At				X		X
Rear Wheel Bearings	Inspect	At				X		X
Tie Rod Ends and Steering Linkage	Lubricate Every 3 Years	Or				X		
Drive Shaft Boots	Inspect For Deterioration And Leaks Every Oil Change. Replace if Necessary	Or	X	X	X	X	X	X

SEVERE SERVICE MAINTENANCE*

	Service Intervals	Mileage in Thousands	3	6	9	12	15	18	21	24	27	30	33	36	39	42	45	48
		Kilometers In Thousands	4.8	9.6	14	19	24	29	34	38	43	48	53	58	62	67	72	77
Brake Linings (Front & Rear) and Rear Wheel Bearings	Inspect					X		X			X			X			X	
Constant Velocity Universal Joints	Inspect at every oil change																	
Engine Oil	Change every 3 months or		X	X	X	X	X	X	X	X	X	X	X	X	X	X	X	X
Engine Oil Filter	Change at every second oil change																	
Front Suspension Ball Joints	Inspect at every oil change																	
Transmission Fluid and Filter—Automatic	Change at (adjust bands at time of fluid and filter change)							X				X				X		
Steering Linkage Tie Rod Ends	Lubricate every 18 months or							X				X				X		
Engine Air Filter	Inspect and replace if required							X				X				X		

*Driving under any of the following operating conditions: Stop and go driving in dusty conditions, extensive idling, frequent short trips, operating at sustained high speeds during hot weather (above +90°F, +30°C)

CAPACITIES CHART

Year	Vin	Engine No. Cyl. Liters	Crankcase Includes Filter (qts)	Transmission (pts)			Fuel Tank (Gal)	Cooling System (qts) ③
				4-sp	5-sp	Auto		
1984	C	4-2.2L	4	8	—	①	15②	8.5
	G	4-2.6L	5	—	9	①	15②	9.5
1985	C	4-2.2L	4	8	—	①	15②	8.5
	G	4-2.6L	5	—	9	①	15②	9.5
1986	C	4-2.2L	4	8	—	①	15②	8.5
	G	4-2.6L	5	—	9	①	15②	9.5
1987	C	4-2.2L	4	8	—	①	15②	8.5
	K	4-2.5L	4	—	9	①	15②	8.5
	G	4-2.6L	5	—	9	①	15②	9.5
1988	K	4-2.5L	4	—	9	①	15②	8.5
	3	6-3.0L	4	—	—	①	15②	10.5
1989	K	4-2.5L	4	—	9	①	15②	8.5
	J	4-2.5L	4	—	9	①	15②	8.5
	3	6-3.0L	4	—	—	①	15②	10.5
1990	K	4-2.5L	4	—	9	①	15②	8.5
	J	4-2.5L	4	—	9	①	15②	8.5
	3	6-3.0L	4	—	—	①	15②	10.5
	R	6-3.3L	4	—	—	①	15②	10.5
1991	K	4-2.5L	4	—	—	①	15②	8.5
	3	6-3.0L	4	—	—	①	15②	10.5
	R	6-3.3L	4	—	—	①	15②	10.5

① A413/A470 Transaxles (except Fleet):
   17.8 pts.
   A413/A470 Transaxles (Fleet): 18.4 pts.
   A413/A460 Transaxles with Lockup Converter:
   17.0 pts.
   A604 Transaxles: 18.2 pts
② Standard: 15 Gal.
   Optional: 20 Gal.
③ Add 1 qt. when equipped with rear heater

MANUAL TRANSMISSION APPLICATION CHART

Years	Transmission	Models
1984–87	A-460 4 speed	Caravan, Voyager
1984–85	A-465 5 speed	Caravan, Voyager
1984–86	A-525 5 speed	Caravan, Voyager
1987–89	A-520 5 speed	Caravan, Voyager
1989	A-555 5 speed	Caravan, Voyager
1990	A-523 5 speed	Caravan, Voyager
1990	A-568 5 speed	Caravan, Voyager

AUTOMATIC TRANSMISSION APPLICATION CHART

Years	Transmission	Models
1984–91	A-413 3 speed	Caravan, Voyager
1984–87	A-470 4 speed	Caravan, Voyager
1988–91	A-670 3 speed	Caravan, Voyager
1989–91	A-604 4 speed	Caravan, Voyager
1991	A-604 4 speed	Town & Country

CONVERSION CHARTS

LENGTH

To convert	to	multiply by
inches	millimeters	25.4
millimeters	inches	0.03937
feet	meters	0.304
meters	feet	3.28
miles	kilometers	1.609
kilometers	miles	0.625

VOLUME

To convert	to	multiply by
pints	liters	0.473
liters	pints	2.11
quarts	liters	0.946
liters	quarts	1.06
gallons	liters	3.785
liters	gallons	0.264
cubic inches	liters	0.016
liters	cubic inches	61.02
cubic inches	cubic centimeters	16.39
cubic centimeters	cubic inches	0.061
cubic feet	liters	28.3
liters	cubic feet	0.0353

CONVERSION CHARTS

MASS

To convert	to	multiply by
ounces	grams	28.35
grams	ounces	0.035
pounds	kilograms	0.4536
kilograms	ounces	2.20

AREA

To convert	to	multiply by
square inches	square centimeters	0.645
square centimeters	square inches	0.155
square yards	square meters	0.836
square meters	square yards	1.196

FORCE (TORQUE)

To convert	to	multiply by
pounds	Newtons (N)	4.448
Newtons (N)	pounds	0.225
ft. lbs.	kilogram-meters (Kg-m)	0.138
kilogram-meters (Kg-m)	ft. lbs.	7.23
ft. lbs.	Newton-meters (Nm)	1.36
Newton-meters (Nm)	ft. lbs.	0.7376
inch lbs.	Newton-meters (Nm)	0.112
Newton-meters (Nm)	inch lbs.	8.844

PRESSURE

To convert	to	multiply by
pounds per square inch (psi)	atmospheres	0.068
atmospheres	pounds per square inch (psi)	14.7
pounds per square inch (psi)	kilopascals (kpa)	6.89
kilopascals (kpa)	pounds per square inch (psi)	0.145

TEMPERATURE

To convert	to	multiply by
Degrees Fahrenheit (subtract 32)	Degrees Celsius	0.555
Degrees Celsius (add 17.8)	Degrees Fahrenheit	1.8

AUTOMOTIVE FACTORS

To convert	to	multiply by
SAE horsepower	DIN horsepower	0.9861
DIN horsepower	SAE horsepower	1.104
SAE horsepower	kilowatts (kw)	0.746
kilowatts (kw)	SAE horsepower	1.34
miles per hour (mph)	kilometers per hour (Km/h)	1.60
kilometers per hour (Km/h)	miles per hour (mph)	0.625
miles per gallon (mpg)	kilometers per liter (Km/L)	0.425
kilometers per liter (Km/L)	miles per gallon (mpg)	2.35

TORQUE SPECIFICATIONS

Component	English	Metric
Air cleaner wing nut:	14 inch lbs.	1.5 Nm
A/C Compressor		
Exc. 2.6L engine		
Locking and pivot screws:	40 ft. lbs.	54 Nm
2.6L engine		
Locking screw and pivot nut:	16 ft. lbs.	22 Nm
Jam nut:	21 ft. lbs.	29 Nm
A/C Compressor idler pulley locknut		
3.0L Engine:	40 ft. lbs.	54 Nm
Air Pump locking and pivot bolts:	25 ft. lbs.	34 Nm
Alternator		
Exc. 2.6L engine		
Locking screw:	25 ft. lbs.	34 Nm
Pivot nut:	30 ft. lbs.	41 Nm
2.6L engine		
Locking screw and pivot nut:	16 ft. lbs.	22 Nm
Jam nut:	21 ft. lbs.	29 Nm
Carburetor stud nuts:	14 inch lbs.	1.5Nm
Cooling system hose clamps:	20–30 inch lbs.	2–3 Nm
Cooling system vacuum valve or drain/fill plug:	15 ft. lbs.	20 Nm
Fuel filter line clamps:	10 inch lbs.	1 Nm
Fuel filter mounting screw:	75 inch lbs.	8 Nm
Power Steering Pump locking and pivot screws:	40 ft. lbs.	54 Nm
Wheel lug nuts:	85 ft. lbs.	116 Nm

Engine Performance and Tune-Up

2

TUNE-UP SPECIFICATIONS CHART

TUNE-UP SPECIFICATIONS CHART

Years	VIN	Engine No. Cyl. Liters	Spark Plugs Type	Gap (in.)	Ignition Timing (deg.) MT	AT	Compression Pressure (psi)	Fuel Pump (psi)	Idle Speed (rpm) MT	AT	Valve Clearance In.	Ex.
1984	C	4–2.2L	65PR	0.035	12B	12B	100②	4.5–6.0	850	900	Hyd.	Hyd.
	G	4–2.6L	65PR	0.041①	—	12B	100②	4.5–6.0	—	800	0.005	0.010
1985	C	4–2.2L	65PR	0.035	12B	12B	100②	4.5–6.0	850	900	Hyd.	Hyd.
	G	4–2.6L	65PR	0.041①	—	12B	100②	4.5–6.0	—	800	0.005	0.010
1986	C	4–2.2L	65PR	0.035	12B	12B	100②	4.5–6.0	850	900	Hyd.	Hyd.
	G	4–2.6L	65PR	0.041①	—	12B	100②	4.5–6.0	—	800	0.005	0.010
1987	C	4–2.2L	RN12YC	0.035	6B	6B	100②	4.5–6.0	850	900	Hyd.	Hyd.
	K	4–2.5L	RN12YC	0.035	12B	12B	100②	15	—	800	Hyd.	Hyd.
	G	4–2.6L	RN12YC	0.040	—	7B	100②	4.5–6.0	—	800	0.005	0.010
1988	K	4–2.5L	RN12YC	0.035	6B	—	100②	15	850	—	Hyd.	Hyd.
	3	6–3.0L	RN11YC4	0.040	—	12B	100②	48	—	700	Hyd.	Hyd.
1989	K	4–2.5L	RN12YC	0.035	12B	12B	100②	15	850	850	Hyd.	Hyd.
	J	4–2.5L	RN12YC	0.035	12B	12B	100②	55	900	900	Hyd.	Hyd.
	3	6–3.0L	RN11YC4	0.040	—	12B	100②	48	—	700	Hyd.	Hyd.
1990	K	4–2.5L	RN12YC	0.035	12B	12B	100②	15	850	850	Hyd.	Hyd.
	J	4–2.5L	RN12YC	0.035	12B	12B	100②	55	900	900	Hyd.	Hyd.
	3	6–3.0L	RN11YC4	0.040	—	12B	100②	48	—	700	Hyd.	Hyd.
	R	6–3.3L	RN16YC5	0.050	—	16B	100②	43–53	—	750	Hyd.	Hyd.
1991	K	4–2.5L	RN12YC	0.035	—	12B	100②	55	900	900	Hyd.	Hyd.
	3	6–3.0L	RN11YC4	0.040	—	12B	100②	48	—	700	Hyd.	Hyd.
	R	6–3.3L	RN16YC5	0.050	—	16B	100②	43–53	—	750	Hyd.	Hyd.

① Canada 0.030
② Minimum compression pressure

Diagnosis of Spark Plugs

Problem	Possible Cause	Correction
Brown to grayish-tan deposits and slight electrode wear.	• Normal wear.	• Clean, regap, reinstall.
Dry, fluffy black carbon deposits.	• Poor ignition output.	• Check distributor to coil connections.
Wet, oily deposits with very little electrode wear.	• "Break-in" of new or recently overhauled engine. • Excessive valve stem guide clearances. • Worn intake valve seals.	• Degrease, clean and reinstall the plugs. • Refer to Section 3. • Replace the seals.
Red, brown, yellow and white colored coatings on the insulator. Engine misses intermittently under severe operating conditions.	• By-products of combustion.	• Clean, regap, and reinstall. If heavily coated, replace.

Diagnosis of Spark Plugs

Problem	Possible Cause	Correction
Colored coatings heavily deposited on the portion of the plug projecting into the chamber and on the side facing the intake valve.	• Leaking seals if condition is found in only one or two cylinders.	• Check the seals. Replace if necessary. Clean, regap, and reinstall the plugs.
Shiny yellow glaze coating on the insulator.	• Melted by-products of combustion.	• Avoid sudden acceleration with wide-open throttle after long periods of low speed driving. Replace the plugs.
Burned or blistered insulator tips and badly eroded electrodes.	• Overheating.	• Check the cooling system. • Check for sticking heat riser valves. Refer to Section 1. • Lean air-fuel mixture. • Check the heat range of the plugs. May be too hot. • Check ignition timing. May be over-advanced. • Check the torque value of the plugs to ensure good plug-engine seat contact.
Broken or cracked insulator tips.	• Heat shock from sudden rise in tip temperature under severe operating conditions. Improper gapping of plugs.	• Replace the plugs. Gap correctly.

TUNE-UP PROCEDURES

Neither tune-up nor troubleshooting can be considered independently since each has a direct relationship with the other.

It is advisable to follow a definite and thorough tune-up procedure. Tune-up consists of three separate steps: Analysis, (the process of determining whether normal wear is responsible for performance loss, and whether parts require replacement or service); Parts Replacement or Service; and Adjustment, (where engine adjustments are performed).

The manufacturer's recommended interval for tune-ups on non-catalyst vehicles is 15,000 miles. Models with a converter, every 30,000 miles. Models equipped with a 2.6L engine require a valve lash adjustment every 15,000 miles. this interval should be shortened if the vehicle is subjected to severe operating conditions such as trailer pulling or stop and start driving, or if starting and running problems are noticed. It is assumed that

the routine maintenance has been kept up, as this will have an effect on the result of the tune-up. All the applicable tune-up steps should be followed, as each adjustment complements the effects of the other. If the tune-up (emission control) sticker in the engine compartment disagrees with the information presented in the Tune-up Specifications chart in this section, the sticker figures must be followed. The sticker information reflects running changes made by the manufacturer during production.

Troubleshooting is a logical sequence of procedures designed to locate a particular cause of trouble. While the apparent cause of trouble, in many cases, is worn or damaged parts, performance problems are less obvious. The first job is to locate the problem and cause. Once the problem has been isolated, repairs, removal or adjustment procedures can be performed.

It is advisable to read the entire section before beginning a tune-up, although those who are more familiar with tune-up procedures may wish to go directly to the instructions.

Spark Plugs

A typical spark plug consists of a metal shell surrounding a ceramic insulator. A metal electrode extends downward through the center of the insulator and protrudes a small distance. Located at the end of the plug and attached to the side of the outer metal shell is the side electrode. The side electrode bends in at a 90° angle so that its tip is even with, and parallel to, the tip of the center electrode. The distance between these two electrodes (measured in thousandths of an inch) is called the spark plug gap. The spark plug in no way produces a spark but merely provides a gap across which the current can arc. The coil produces anywhere from 20,000 to 40,000 volts which travels to the distributor where it is distributed through the spark plug wires to the spark plugs. The current passes along the center electrode and jumps the gap to the side electrode, and, in do doing, ignites the air/fuel mixture in the combustion chamber.

SPARK PLUG HEAT RANGE

Spark plug heat range is the ability of the plug to dissipate heat. The longer the insulator (or the farther it extends into the engine), the hotter the plug will operate; the shorter the insulator the cooler it will operate. A plug that absorbs little heat and remains too cool will quickly accumulate deposits of oil and carbon since it is not hot enough to burn them off. This leads to plug fouling and consequently to misfiring. A plug that absorbs too much heat will have no deposits, but, due to the excessive heat, the electrodes will burn away quickly and in some instances, preignition may result. Preignition takes place when plug tips get so hot that they glow sufficiently to ignite the fuel/air mixture before the actual spark occurs. This early ignition will usually cause a pinging during low speeds and heavy loads.

The general rule of thumb for choosing the correct heat range when picking a spark plug is: if most of your driving is long distance, high speed travel, use a colder plug; if most of your driving is stop and go, use a hotter plug. Original equipment plugs are compromise plugs, but most people never have occasion to change their plugs from the factory-recommended heat range.

REMOVAL AND INSTALLATION

1. Before removing the spark plugs, number the plug wires so that the correct wire goes on the plug when replaced. This can be done with pieces of adhesive tape.
2. Next, clean the area around the plugs by blowing with compressed air. You can also loosen the plugs a few turns and crank the engine to blow the dirt away.

——————— CAUTION ———————

Wear safety glasses to avoid possible eye injury due to flying dust particles.

3. Disconnect the plugs wires by twisting and pulling on the rubber cap, not on the wire.
4. Remove each plug with a rubber insert spark plug socket. make sure that the socket is all the way down on the plug to prevent it from slipping and cracking the porcelain insulator.
5. After removing each plug, evaluate its condition. A spark plug's useful life is approximately 30,000 miles. Thus, it would make sense to replace a plug if it has been in service that long.
6. If the plugs are to be reused, file the center and side electrodes flat with a fine, flat point file. Heavy or baked on deposits can be carefully scraped off with a small knife blade, or the scraper tool of a combination spark plug tool. However, it is suggested that plugs be test and cleaned on a service station sand-

Remove the spark plugs with a ratchet and long extension

Check the spark plug gap with a feeler gauge

blasting machine. Check the gap between the electrodes with a round wire spark plug gapping gauge. Do not use a flat feeler gauge; it will give an inaccurate reading. If the gap is not as specified, use the bending tool on the spark plug gap gauge to bend the outside electrode. Be careful not to bend the electrode tool far or too often, because excessive bending may cause the electrode to break off and fall into the combustion chamber. This would require removing the cylinder head to reach the broken piece, and could also result in cylinder wall, piston ring, or valve damage.

7. Clean the threads of old plugs with a wire brush. Lubricate the threads with a drop of oil.
8. Screw the plugs in finger tight, and then tighten them with the spark plug socket to 26 ft. lbs. Be very careful not to over tighten them.
9. Reinstall the wires. If, by chance, you have forgotten to number the plug wires, refer to the Firing Order illustrations.

Spark Plug Wires

Check the spark plug wire connections at the coil, distributor cap towers, and at the spark plugs. Be sure they are fully seated, and the boot covers are not cracked or split. Clean the cables with a cloth and a non-flammable solvent. Check for brittle or cracked insulation, replace wires as necessary. If a wire is suspected of failure, test it with an ohmmeter. Test as follows:

1. Remove the plug wire from the spark plug. Twist the boot and pull. Never apply pressure to the wire itself.

Removing the plug wires from the distributor cap

NOTE: The 3.3L engine is equipped with a distributorless electronic ignition system. The plug wires run directly from the coil pack to the spark plugs.

2. Remove the distributor cap from the distributor with all wires attached.

NOTE: Do not pull plugs wires from distributor cap, they must first be released from inside of cap.

3. Connect the ohmmeter between the spark plug terminal, and the corresponding electrode inside the distributor cap. Resistance should be within limits of the cable resistance chart. If resistance is not within specs, remove the wire from the distributor cap and retest. If still not within specs, replace the wire.

4. Install the new wire into cap tower, then squeeze the wire nipple to release any trapped air between the cap tower and nipple.

CABLE RESISTANCE CHART	
Minimum	Maximum
250 Ohms Per Inch	600 Ohms Per Inch
3000 Ohms Per Foot	7200 Ohms Per Foot

Spark plug cable resistance

5. Push firmly to properly seat wire electrode into cap.
6. Install plug end of wire onto plug until it snaps into place.

WARNING: Do not allowed plug wires to contact exhaust manifold or any moving parts.

FIRING ORDERS

NOTE: To avoid confusion, remove and tag the wires one at a time, for replacement.

Mitsubishi 3.0L engine
 Engine firing order: 1-2-3-4-5-6
 Distributor rotation: counterclockwise

Chrysler Corp. (Mitsubishi) 2.6L engine
 Engine firing order: 1-3-4-2
 Distributor rotation: clockwise

Chrysler Corp. 2.2L and 2.5L engines
 Engine firing order: 1-3-4-2
 Distributor rotation: clockwise

FIRING ORDERS

NOTE: To avoid confusion, remove and tag the wires one at a time, for replacement.

Chrysler Corp. 3.3L engine
Engine firing order: 1-2-3-4-5-6
Distributorless Ignition System

Distributor cap terminal routing (view from top of the cap) — 3.0L engine

CHRYSLER HALL EFFECT ELECTRONIC IGNITION

Spark Control Computer (SCC) System

The Hall Effect electronic ignition is used in conjunction with the Chrysler Spark Control Computer (SCC) controlling the entire ignition. It consists of a sealed Spark Control Computer, specially calibrated carburetor and various engine sensors, such as the vacuum transducer, coolant switch, Hall Effect pick-up assembly, oxygen sensor and carburetor switch.

SCC SYSTEM COMPONENTS

Spark Control Computer

During cranking, an electrical signal is sent from the distributor to the computer. This signal will cause the computer to fire the spark plugs at a fixed amount of advance. Once the engine starts, the timing will then be controlled by the computer based on the information received from the various sensors.

There are essentially 2 modes of operation of the Spark Control computer: the start mode and the run mode. The start mode is only used during engine cranking. During cranking, only the Hall Effect pick-up signals the computer. These signals are interpreted to provide a fixed number of degrees of spark advance.

After the engine starts and during normal engine operation, the computer functions in the run mode. In this mode, the Hall Effect pick-up serves as only one of the signals to the computer. It is a reference signal of maximum possible spark advance. The computer then determines, from information provided by the other engine sensors, how much of this advance is necessary and delays the coil saturation accordingly, firing the spark plug at the exact moment this advance (crankshaft position) is reached.

There is a third mode of operation which only becomes functional when the computer fails. This is the limp-in mode. This mode functions on signals from the pick-up only and results in very poor engine performance. However, it does allow the car to be driven to a repair shop. If a failure occurs in the pick-up assembly or the start mode of the computer, the engine will neither start nor run.

Hall Effect Pick-Up

The Hall Effect pick-up is located in the distributor assembly and supplies the engine Rpm and ignition timing data to the SCC to advance or retard the ignition spark as required by current operating conditions.

Coolant Sensor

The coolant temperature sensor is located on the thermostat

housing and provides the SCC with engine temperature data. The SCC uses this data to control various engine functions such as spark advance, fuel mixture, emission controls operation and radiator fan.

Vacuum Sensor

The vacuum transducer is located on the Spark Control Computer and informs the SCC as to the manifold vacuum during operation. The engine vacuum is one of the factors that will determine how the computer will advance/retard ignition timing and with the feedback carburetor, how the air/fuel ration will be changed.

Carburetor Switch

The carburetor switch is located on the left side of the carburetor; it provides the SCC with throttle open or throttle closed signal.

2.2L oxygen sensor

2.2L coolant temperature sensor location

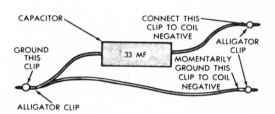

Special jumper wire construction for grounding the coil

2.2L spark control vacuum transducer

Oxygen Sensor

The oxygen sensor (used with feedback carburetors) is located in the exhaust manifold and signals the computer how much oxygen is present in the exhaust gases. Since this amount is proportional to rich and lean mixtures, the computer will adjust the air/fuel ration to a level which will maintain operating efficiency of the 3-way catalyst system and engine.

Single Module Engine Controller (SMEC)

The Hall Effect electronic ignition is used in conjunction with the Single Module Engine Controller (SMEC). The system features improved decision making capabilities and offers almost infinite control of fuel and spark advance.

SMEC SYSTEM COMPONENTS

Single Module Engine Controller (SMEC)

The SMEC controls the entire ignition system. It gives the capability of igniting the fuel mixture according the different engine conditions during a run/drive period by constantly altering the electronic spark advance curves. The SMEC has a built-in microprocessor which receives input from the engine monitoring sensors. The computer then advances or retards the ignition timing electronically to provide even driveability.

During periods of cranking and starting, the SMEC provides a fixed amount of advanced timing. During the running period, the timing is altered according to the sensor inputs. These operating modes may be referred to as the START (or CRANKING) mode and the RUN mode.

2.2L carburetor switch

HALL EFFECT ELECTRONIC SPARK ADVANCE SYSTEM DIAGNOSIS

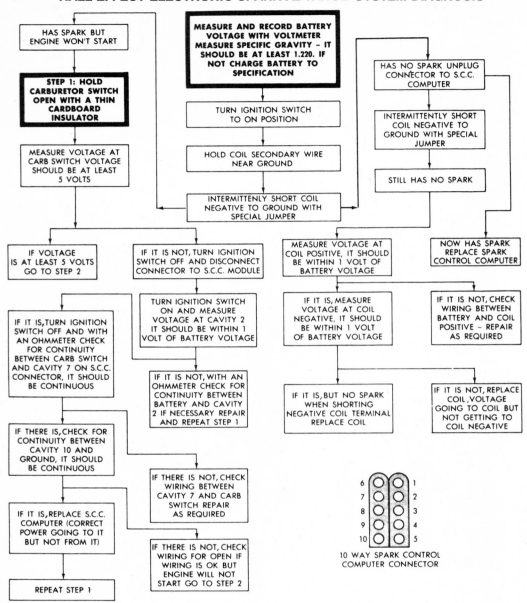

The amount of electronic spark advance provided is determined by 3 input factors: coolant temperature, engine Rpm and available manifold vacuum. The SMEC also receives input from the oxygen sensor and adjusts the air/fuel mixture to assure efficient combustion.

Hall Effect Pick-Up

The Hall Effect pick-up is located in the distributor assembly and supplies the engine Rpm, ignition timing, and on turbo engines, fuel synchronization data to the SMEC to advance or retard the ignition spark as required by current operating conditions.

Coolant Temperature Sensor

The coolant temperature sensor is mounted near the thermo-stat housing and provides data on engine operating temperature to the SMEC.

Incorporated into the digital microprocessor electronics are some unique spark advance schedules which will occur during cold and warm engine operation. They have been added to reduce engine emissions and improve driveability. (Because they will be changing at different engine operating temperatures during warm-up, all spark advance testing should be done with the engine fully warmed up and at normal operating temperature.) This data allows the SMEC to demand slightly richer air/fuel mixtures and higher idle speeds until normal operating temperatures are achieved.

The sensor is a variable resistor with a range of $-40°F$ ($-40°C$) to $265°F$ ($130°C$). The sensor is also used to control the radiator fan.

HALL EFFECT ELECTRONIC SPARK ADVANCE SYSTEM DIAGNOSIS

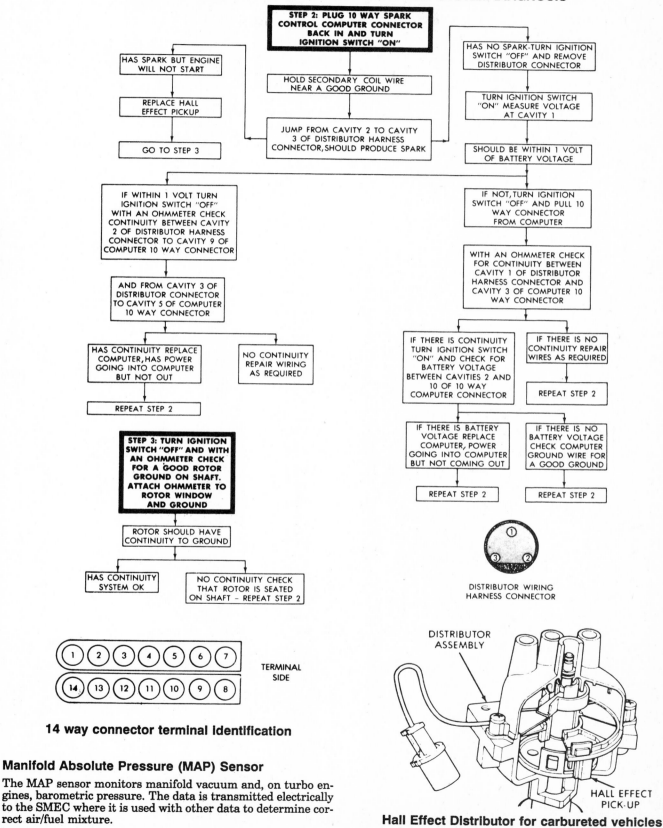

14 way connector terminal identification

DISTRIBUTOR WIRING HARNESS CONNECTOR

Hall Effect Distributor for carbureted vehicles

Manifold Absolute Pressure (MAP) Sensor

The MAP sensor monitors manifold vacuum and, on turbo engines, barometric pressure. The data is transmitted electrically to the SMEC where it is used with other data to determine correct air/fuel mixture.

Depending on engine and type of fuel injection, the MAP sensor may be located on the right front shock tower or fire wall (connected by a vacuum hose to a nipple on the throttle body or the intake manifold), the left side of the engine tunnel, the alternator bracket or directly mounted on the throttle body.

Automatic Shutdown (ASD) Relay

When there is no ignition signal present with the key in RUN position, there is no need for fuel delivery. When this condition occurs, the ASD relay interrupts power to the electric fuel pump, fuel injectors and ignition coil.

DIAGNOSIS AND TESTING

NOTE: Apply parking brake and block wheels before performing any engine running tests, including idle or timing checks and adjustments.

Testing for Spark at Coil

Remove coil secondary cable from distributor cap. Using a suitable tool, hold end of cable about ¼ in. from good engine ground. Crank engine and look for good, constant spark at coil secondary wire. If spark is constant, have a helper continue to crank engine while moving coil secondary cable away from ground. Look for arcing at the coil tower. If arcing occurs, replace the coil. If no arcing occurs, ignition system is producing the necessary high secondary voltage. Make certain this voltage is getting to spark plugs by checking distributor rotor, cap, spark plug wires and spark plugs. If all check in good condition, ignition system is NOT cause of problem.

If spark is weak, not constant or not present, continue with Failure To Start test.

Ignition System Starting Test

1. With a voltmeter measure voltage at battery and record it. Battery specific gravity must be 12.20. If if is not, charge batter to specification.
2. Turn ignition switch ON.
3. Remove coil wire from the distributor cap. Using a suitable tool, hold wire about a ¼ in. away from a good ground.
4. Intermittently jump coil negative to ground while looking for a good spark at coil wire.
5. If there is spark at coil wire it must be constant and bright blue in color. If spark is good, slowly move coil wire away from ground while looking for arcing at coil tower. If arcing occurs replace coil. If spark is weak or not constant, proceed to "Failure to Start Test".

Failure to Start Test

NOTE: Before proceeding with this test, make certain that "Testing for Spark at Coil" has been performed. Failure to do so may lead to unnecessary diagnostic time and incorrect test results.

SPARK CONTROL COMPUTER SYSTEM

NOTE: If a good spark was obtained during Ignition Starting Test, go to Step 8.

1. Turn ignition switch to OFF position and disconnect SCC 10-way connector. Turn ignition switch ON and remove coil wire from distributor cap. Using a suitable tool, hold end of wire ¼ in. away from a good ground.
2. Intermittently short coil negative wire to ground. If spark is obtained replace spark control computer.
3. If no spark is obtained, check for battery voltage at coil positive terminal with ignition switch ON. It should be within 1 volt of battery voltage. If voltage is correct go to Step 5.
4. If voltage is incorrect, check continuity of wiring between battery and coil positive terminal. Repair wiring and repeat Step 3.

5. Check for battery voltage at coil negative terminal, it should be within 1 volt of battery voltage. If it is correct go to Step 7.
6. If voltage is incorrect, replace coil.
7. If voltage is correct, but no spark is obtained when shorting negative terminal, replace coil.
8. Spark is obtained but engine will not start, turn ignition switch to RUN position and with positive lead of a voltmeter, measure voltage from cavity 1 of SCC 10-way connector, to ground of disconnected lead from computer. Voltage should be within 1 volt of battery voltage. If voltage is correct, proceed to Step 10. If not, continue to Step 9.
9. If voltage in Step 8 is not correct, check wire for an open between coil and SCC 10-way connector. Repair wire and repeat Step 8.
10. Place a thin insulator (piece of paper or cardboard) between curb idle adjusting screw and carb switch.
11. Connect negative lead of a voltmeter to a good engine ground.
12. Turn ignition switch to RUN position and measure voltage at carb switch.
   a. If voltage is approximately 5 volts, proceed to Step 14.
   b. If voltage is not at least 5 volts, turn ignition switch to OFF position. Turn ignition switch back to RUN position and measure voltage at terminal 2 of SCC 10-way connector. Voltage should be within 1 volt of battery voltage.
   c. If voltage is correct, repeat Step 10.
   d. If voltage is incorrect, check wiring between terminal 2 and ignition switch for open, shorts or poor connections.
13. Turn ignition switch OFF, check for continuity between terminal 7 of SCC 10-way connector and carb switch terminal. There should be continuity between these 2 points.
   a. If there is no continuity, check wire for opens, shorts or poor connections.
   b. If there is continuity, check for continuity between terminal 10 and engine ground.
   c. If there is continuity between terminal 10 and engine ground, replace Spark Control Computer (SCC).
   d. If there is no continuity, repeat Step 13; only proceed to Step 14 if engine still does not start.
14. Turn ignition switch to OFF position and, with an ohmmeter, measure resistance between terminals 5 and 9 of SCC 10-way connector for run pick-up coil and between terminals 3 and 9 for start pick-up coil. The resistance should be between 150-900 ohms.

Single Module Engine Controller (SMEC) mounting location

Hall Effect pick-up — SMEC system

Relay Identification

a. If resistance is correct, proceed to Step 15.

b. If resistance is not correct, disconnect pick-up coil leads from distributor. Measure resistance at lead going into distributor.

c. If resistance is now between 150-900 ohms, this means there is an open, shorted, or poor connection between the distributor connector and terminals 5 and 9 or 3 and 9 of the SCC 10-way connector.

d. Repair wire and repeat Step 14. If resistance is still out of specification, pick-up coil is bad. Replace pick-up coil and repeat Step 14.

15. Connect 1 lead of ohmmeter to an engine ground and, with other lead, check for continuity at each terminal lead going into distributor. There should be no continuity. Reconnect distributor lead and proceed to Step 16. If there is continuity, replace pick-up coil.

16. Remove distributor cap and check air gap of pick-up coil. If it is not within specification, adjust it. If it is within specification, proceed to Step 17.

17. Install distributor cap, reconnect all wiring and try to start engine. If engine still fails to start, replace Spark Control Computer.

SMEC SYSTEM

1. Check battery voltage and determine that a minimum of 12.4 volts is available for operation of cranking and ignition systems.

2. Crank engine for 5 seconds while monitoring voltage at coil positive terminal. If voltage remains near 0 during entire period of cranking, pleas refer to Section 5 in this book for on-board diagnostic checks of SMEC and ASD relay.

3. If measured voltage is near battery voltage but drops to 0 after 1-2 seconds of cranking, please refer to Section 5 in this book for on-board diagnostic checks of distributor reference pick-up circuit to SMEC.

4. If measured voltage remains near battery voltage for entire 5 second cranking period, turn key OFF and remove SMEC 14-way connector.
Check 14-way connector for any spread terminals.

5. Remove wire to coil positive terminal and connect regular jumper wire between coil positive terminal and battery positive terminal.

6. Using special jumper cable, momentarily ground terminal No. 12 of 14-way connector. A spark should be generated when ground is removed.

7. If spark is generated, replace SMEC.

8. If no spark is seen, use special jumper to ground coil negative terminal directly.

Testing carburetor switch

9. If spark is produced, trace and repair open condition within wiring harness.

10. If no spark is produced, replace ignition coil.

Testing for Poor Engine Performance

Before performing test, make sure "Testing for Spark at Coil" has been carried out. Failure to do so may lead to unnecessary diagnostic time and incorrect test results.

Correct basic engine timing is essential for optimum vehicle performance and must be checked before any of the following testing procedures are performed. Refer to the individual vehicle section for ignition timing procedures and/or refer to the Vehicle Information label, located in the engine compartment.

Spark Control Computer System

CARBURETOR SWITCH TEST

NOTE: Grounding carburetor switch lead wire will give a fixed air/fuel ratio.

1. With key OFF, disconnect 10-way dual connector from computer.

2. With throttle completely closed, check continuity between cavity 7 of 10-way connector and a good ground. If there is no continuity, check wire and carburetor switch.

3. With throttle open, check continuity between cavity 7 of connector and a good ground. There should be no continuity.

COOLANT TEMPERATURE SENSOR TEST

1. With key in OFF position, disconnect wire connector from coolant sensor.

2. Connect 1 lead of ohmmeter to terminal 1 (common) of coolant sensor.

3. Connect other lead of ohmmeter to terminal 3 (fan control circuit).
Resistance between terminals 1 and 3 should be:
Below 150°F (66°C): 20-200Ω
150–200°F (66–93°C): 100-1500Ω
Above 200°F (93°C): 400-6000Ω

4. Remove ohmmeter lead from terminal 3.

5. Connect ohmmeter lead to terminal 2 (SCC control circuit). Resistance between terminals 1 and 2 should be:
50–100°F (10–38°C): 3,300-36,000Ω
140–245°F (60–118°C): 176-3,900Ω

ELECTRONIC THROTTLE CONTROL SYSTEM

Incorporated within the spark control computer is the electronic throttle system. A solenoid, which regulates a vacuum dash-pot is energized when the air conditioner or electronic timers are activated. The 2 timers, incorporated within the ignition electronics, operate when the throttle is closed, plus a time delay of 2 seconds or after an engine start condition. To test the system:

1. Connect a tachometer to engine.

2. Start engine and run it until it reaches normal operating temperature.

3. Depress accelerator and release it. A higher than curb idle speed should be seen for a specified time.

4. On vehicles equipped with A/C, a slight decrease in idle speed will be noted when A/C is turned ON; turning OFF A/C will produce normal idle speed.

NOTE: The A/C clutch will cycle on and off as system is in operation. This should not be mistaken as part of electronic control system.

5. As A/C compressor clutch cycles on and off, sole kicker plunger should extend and retract.

6. If plunger does not move with A/C clutch cycling or after a start-up, check kicker system for vacuum leaks.

7. If speed increases do not occur, disconnect 6-way connector at carburetor.

8. Check solenoid with an ohmmeter by measuring resistance between terminal that contains black wire and ground. Resistance should be between 20-100 ohms. If not within specifications, replace solenoid.

9. Start vehicle and before time delay has timed out, measure voltage across vacuum solenoid terminals. The voltage should be within 2 volts of charging system voltage. If not within specifications, replace computer.

10. Turning A/C ON should also produce charging system voltage after time delay has timed out. If not, check wiring back to instrument panel for an open circuit.

SPARK ADVANCE OF SPARK CONTROL COMPUTER

Incorporated in the digital microprocessor electronics are some unique spark advance schedules, which will occur during cold and warm engine operation. These commands have been added to reduce engine emissions and improve driveability. Because they will be changing at different engine operating temperatures during the engine warm-up, all spark advance testing should be done with the engine at normal operating temperature.

1. Adjust the basic timing to specifications.

2. Have engine at normal operating temperature. The coolant temperature sensor must be connected and operating correctly.

3. Remove and plug vacuum hose at vacuum transducer.

4. Connect an auxiliary vacuum supply to vacuum transducer; draw and hold vacuum to 16 in Hg.

5. Start and raise engine speed to 2000 Rpm. Wait 1 minute and check specifications.

NOTE: The use of a metal exhaust tube is recommended for this test. Using rubber hose may result in a fire due to high temperatures and a long test period.

6. The advance specifications are in addition to basic advance. If correct advance is not obtained, replace spark plug control computer.

SMEC Systems

COOLANT TEMPERATURE SENSOR TEST

1. With key OFF, disconnect wire connector from coolant temperature sensor.

2. Connect one lead of an ohmmeter to one terminal of sensor.

3. Connect other ohmmeter lead to other sensor terminal; ohmmeter should read: Coolant at operating temperature (200°F [93°C]): Approximately 700-1000 ohms. Coolant at room temperature (70°F [21°C]): Approximately 7,000-13,000 ohms.

HALL EFFECT DISTRIBUTOR WIRING HARNESS CONNECTOR

JUMPER WIRE

Jumping cavities 2 and 3 of the distributor harness

Testing cavities 2 and 9, then cavities 3 and 5 for continuity

Checking voltage between cavities 2 and 10

Testing coolant temperature sensor

Coolant temperature sensor location

SPARK ADVANCE OF SMEC SYSTEM

1. Adjust basic timing to specifications.
2. Have engine at normal operating temperature. The coolant temperature sensor must be connected and operating correctly.
3. Start and raise engine speed to 2000 Rpm. Wait 1 minute and check specifications.

NOTE: The use of a metal exhaust tube is recommended for this test. Using rubber hose may result in a fire due to high temperatures and a long test period.

4. The advance specifications are in addition to basic advance. If correct advance is not obtained, SMEC must be replaced.

Spark Control Computer System— Component Replacement

REMOVAL AND INSTALLATION

Spark Control Computer

1. Disconnect 10-way and 14-way dual connectors and outside air duct from SCC. Remove vacuum line from transducer.
2. Remove 4 mounting screws that hold computer in place.
3. Install new computer and secure mounting screws.
4. Reconnect vacuum line to transducer, making sure vacuum line is not pinched. Reconnect dual connectors and outside air duct to SCC unit.

NOTE: Do not remove grease from 10-way or 14-way dual connector or connector cavities in spark control computer. The grease is used to prevent moisture from corroding terminals. If there isn't at least ⅛ in. grease on bottom of computer connector cavities, apply multi-purpose grease over entire end of connector plug before reinstalling.

Vacuum Transducer

If vacuum transducer fails, complete computer unit (SCC) must be replaced.

Coolant Temperature Sensor

1. Disconnect electrical connector from sensor. Remove sensor from engine. Some coolant may be lost from system.
2. Install new sensor and tighten to 20 ft lbs. Reconnect electrical connector.
3. Replace lost coolant.

Hall Effect Pick-Up

1. Remove splash shield from distributor and remove distributor cap.
2. Pull straight up on rotor and remove it from shaft.
3. Remove Hall Effect pick-up assembly.
4. Install new pick-up assembly onto distributor.

NOTE: Hall Effect assembly wiring leads may be damaged if not properly reinstalled.

5. Install distributor rotor.
6. Install distributor cap and splash shield.

Distributor

1. Disconnect the negative battery cable.
2. Disconnect the distributor pickup lead wires and vacuum hose(s), if equipped. Remove the splash shield, if equipped.
3. Unfasten the distributor cap retaining clips or screws and lift off the distributor cap with all ignition wires still connected. Remove the coil wire if necessary.

4. Matchmark the rotor to the distributor housing.

NOTE: Do not crank the engine during this procedure. If the engine is cranked, the matchmark must be disregarded.

5. Remove the hold-down bolt and clamp.
6. Remove the distributor from the engine.

To install:
7. Install a new distributor housing O-ring.
8. Install the distributor in the engine so the rotor is lined up with the matchmark on the housing. Make sure the distributor is fully seated and that the distributor shaft is fully engaged.
9. If the engine has been cranked, position the engine so that the No. 1 piston is at TDC of the compression stroke and the mark on the vibration damper is lined up with **0** on the timing indicator. Then install the distributor so the rotor is aligned with the position of the No. 1 ignition wire on the distributor cap.

NOTE: There are distributor cap runners inside the cap on 3.0L engines. Make sure the rotor is pointing to where the No. 1 runner originates inside the cap and not where the No. 1 ignition wire plugs into the cap.

10. Install the hold-down clamp and snug the hold-down bolt. Connect the vacuum hose(s), if equipped.
11. Connect the distributor pickup lead wires. Install the splash shield, if equipped.
12. Install the distributor cap and snap the retaining clips into place or tighten the screws.
13. Connect the negative battery cable.
14. Adjust the ignition timing and tighten the hold-down bolt.

Ignition Coil

The ignition coil is designed to operate without an external ignition resistor. Inspect coil for external leaks and arcing. Test primary and secondary circuit resistances, replacing any coil that dose not meet the manufacturers specifications.

Every time an ignition coil is replaced because of a burned tower or carbon tracking, always replace coil secondary wire.

Distributor Cap and Rotor

The distributor cap and rotor must be inspected for flash over, cracking, burning and/or worn terminals. Check carbon button in cap for cracking. Light scale may be removed with a sharp knife. Heavy deposits on the cap terminal or the rotor, require replacement of the component.

Single Module Engine Controller (SMEC) System—Component Replacement

REMOVAL AND INSTALLATION

Single Module Engine Control Unit

1. Disconnect the negative battery cable.
2. Disconnect the air cleaner duct from the SMEC unit.
3. Carefully disconnect the connectors from the unit.

NOTE: Make sure there is at least an 1/8 in. of grease in the connectors.

4. Install the connectors on the replacement unit.
5. Mount the unit in position and make sure the connectors are secure.
6. Install the air cleaner duct and connect the battery cable.

Hall Effect Pick-Up

1. Disconnect the negative battery cable.
2. Remove the distributor cap and remove the rotor.
3. Remove the screws that retain the pick-up assembly. Disconnect the electrical lead from the pick-up.
4. Carefully remove the assembly from the distributor.
5. Install the new pick-up assembly and connect the electrical lead.
6. Install the retaining screws. Install the cap and rotor.
7. Connect the negative battery cable.

Coolant Temperature Sensor

1. Disconnect electrical connector from sensor. Remove sensor from engine. Some coolant may be lost from system.
2. Install new sensor and tighten to 20 ft lbs. Reconnect electrical connector.
3. Replace lost coolant.

CHRYSLER OPTICAL DISTRIBUTOR SYSTEM

THis ignition system is used in vehicles with the 3.0L engine. The system is similar to the SMEC system in operation except that it uses a different type of distributor. The computer receives its input from an optical distributor. The signals are used to control fuel injection, ignition timing and engine idle speed.

The timing member in the distributor is a thin disk, driven at half the speed of the engine, from the left camshaft. The disk has 2 sets of slots in it. The outer, high data rate slots, occur at 2 degrees of engine rotation. They are used for ignition timing at engine speed of up to 1200 Rpm.

The inner, or low data rate set, contains 6 slots which are correlated to TDC of each cylinder. This is used to trigger the fuel injection system. At engine speed over 1200 Rpm, this set also controls the ignition timing.

3.0L distributor assembly

Light emitting diodes and photo sensors are mounted in facing positions on opposite sides of the disk in the distributor. Masks over the LED's and the diodes focus the light beams onto the photo diodes. As each slot passes between the diodes, the light beam is turned on and off. This creates an alternating voltage in each photo diode, which is converted into on/off pulses by an integrated circuit within the distributor.

The distributor also delivers firing pulses from the coil to each of the cylinders through the cap and rotor.

Component Replacement and Testing

The replacement of components and their testing in the optical distributor system are the same as the SMEC system.

DIRECT IGNITION SYSTEM

General Information

Vehicle equipped with the 3.3L engine use a distributorless ignition system. The system has 3 main components, the coil, the camshaft reference sensor and the crankshaft timing sensor.

The Single Board Engine Controller (SBEC) receives its engine speed and crankshaft position signal from a sensor located in the transaxle housing. This crankshaft position sensor senses slots located around an extension on the torque converter drive plate. A camshaft sensor located in the timing case cover, supplies cylinder identification to the SBEC, by sensing slots located on the camshaft sprocket.

Ignition coil removal and installation — 3.3L engine

Crankshaft position sensor location — 3.3L engine

Component Replacement

REMOVAL AND INSTALLATION

Ignition Coil

1. Disconnect the negative battery cable.
2. Remove the spark plug wires from the coil.
3. Disconnect the electrical connector.
4. Remove the coil fasteners.
5. Remove the coil from the ignition module.
6. The installation is the reverse of the removal procedure.

Crank Position Sensor

1. Disconnect the negative battery cable.
2. Disconnect the sensor lead at the harness connector.
3. Remove the sensor retainer bolt.
4. Pull the sensor straight up and out of the transaxle housing.
5. If the removed sensor is being reinstalled, clean off the old

Camshaft position sensor location — 3.3L engine

spacer completely and attach a new spacer to the sensor. If a new spacer is not used, the sensor will not function properly. New sensors are equipped with a new spacer.

To install:

6. Install the sensor in the transaxle housing and push the sensor down until contact is made with the drive plate.
7. Hold in this position and install the retaining bolt. Torque to 9 ft. lbs. (12 Nm).
8. Connect the sensor lead wire.

Cam Position Sensor

1. Disconnect the negative battery cable.
2. Disconnect the sensor lead at the harness connector.
3. Loosen the sensor retaining bolt enough to allow the slot to slide past the bolt.
4. Pull the sensor (not by the wire) straight up and out of the chain case cover. Resistance may be high due to the presence of the rubber O-ring.
5. If the removed sensor is being reinstalled, clean off the old spacer completely and attach a new spacer to the sensor. If a new spacer is not used, the sensor will not function properly. New sensors are equipped with a new spacer.

To install:

6. Inspect the O-ring for damage and replace if necessary.
7. Lubricate the O-ring lightly with oil. Install the sensor to the chain case cover and push the sensor into its bore in the chain case cover until contact is made with the cam timing gear.
8. Hold in this position and tighten the bolt to 9 ft. lbs. (12 Nm).
9. Connect the connector and rout it away from the belt.

Ignition Timing

Basic timing should be checked at each tune-up in order to gain maximum engine performance. While timing isn't likely to change very much with electronic ignition system, it become a critical factor necessary to reduce engine emission and improve driveability.

A stroboscopic (dynamic) timing light must be used, because static lights are too inaccurate for emission controlled engines.

Some timing light have other features built into them, such as dwell meters or tachometers. These are nice, in that they reduce the tangle of wires under the hood when you're working, but may duplicate the functions of tools your already have. One worthwhile feature, which is becoming more of a necessity with higher voltage ignition systems, is an inductive pickup. The inductive pickup clamps around the No. 1 spark plug wire, sensing the surges of high voltage electricity as they are sent to the plug.

The advantage is that no mechanical connection is inserted between the wire and the plug, which eliminates false signals to the timing light. A timing light with an inductive pickup should be used on electronic ignition systems

IGNITION TIMING ADJUSTMENT

CAUTION

Always apply parking brake and block wheels before performing any engine running tests.

2.2L and 2.6L Engines

1. With engine off, clean off the timing marks.
2. Mark the pulley or damper notch and the timing scale with white chalk or paint. If the timing notch on the damper or pulley is not visible, bump the engine around with the starter or turn the crankshaft with a wrench on the front pulley bolt to get it to an accessible position.
3. Connect a suitable inductive timing light to number one cylinder plug wire.
4. Connect a tachometer unit, Positive Lead to the negative terminal of the coil and the Negative Lead to a known good engine ground. Select the tachometer appropriate cylinder position.
5. Warm the engine to normal operating temperature. Open the throttle and release to make sure idle speed screw is against its stop, and not on fast idle.
6. On vehicles equipped with a carburetor switch, connect a jumper wire between the carburetor switch and ground to obtain specified Rpm. Disconnect and plug vacuum hose at the Spark Control Computer. (See specifications decal under the hood for specific instructions).
7. Read engine Rpm on the tachometer 1,000 Rpm scale, and adjust curb idle to specification noted on the under hood label.
8. Aim the timing light toward timing indicator, and read degree marks. If flash occurs when timing mark is before specification, timing is advanced. If flash occurs when timing mark is after specification, timing is retarded.

NOTE: Models equipped with the 2.2L engine have a notch on the torque converter or flywheel, with the numerical timing marks on the bell housing. Models equipped with the 2.6L engine have the timing marks on the front crankshaft pulley.

9. If adjustment is necessary, loosen the distributor hold down screw. Turn the distributor slowly to specified value, and tighten hold down screw. Recheck timing and curb idle. If curb idle have change, readjust to specified value and reset ignition timing. Repeat curb idle setting, and ignition timing until both are within specification.
10. Disconnect timing light, and reconnect all vacuum hoses necessary.
11. Turn engine off and remove jumper wire, and tachometer.

2.5L and 3.0L Engines

1. With the engine off, clean off the timing marks.
2. Mark the pulley or damper notch and the timing scale with white chalk or paint. If the timing notch on the damper or pulley is not visible, bump the engine around with the starter or turn the crankshaft with a wrench on the front pulley bolt to get it to an accessible position.
3. Connect a suitable inductive timing light to number one cylinder plug wire.
4. Connect a tachometer unit, positive lead to the negative terminal of the coil and the negative lead to a known good engine ground. Select the tachometer appropriate cylinder position.

2.2L timing mark location

2.6L timing marks

2.5L timing marks

3.0L timing marks

2.5L coolant temperature sensor

3.0L coolant temperature sensor

5. Warm the engine to normal operating temperature.

6. With engine at normal operating temperature, disconnect coolant temperature sensor. Radiator fan and instrument panel check engine lamp should come on. (See specifications decal under the hood for specific instructions).

7. Read engine Rpm on the tachometer 1,000 Rpm scale, and adjust curb idle to specification noted on the under hood label.

8. Aim the timing light toward timing indicator, and read degree marks. If flash occurs when timing mark is before specification, timing is advanced. If flash occurs when timing mark is after specification, timing is retarded.

NOTE: Models equipped with the 2.5L engine have the timing marks visible through a window on the transaxle housing. Models equipped with the 3.0L engine have the timing marks on the front crankshaft pulley.

9. If adjustment is necessary, loosen the distributor hold down screw. Turn the distributor slowly to specified value, and tighten hold down screw. Recheck ignition timing.

10. Turn the engine off and removed the tachometer and timing light.

11. Connect the coolant temperature sensor.

NOTE: Reconnecting the coolant temperature sensor will turn the check engine lamp off; however, a fault code will be stored in the SMEC. After 50 to 100 key on/off cycles the SMEC will cancel the fault code. The code can also be canceled by disconnecting the battery.

3.3L Engine

The 3.3L engine uses an electronic distributorless ignition system. The ignition timing cannot be changed or set in any way.

VALVE LASH

Valve adjustment determines how far the valves enter the cylinder and how long they stay open and closed.

If the valve clearance is too large, part of the lift of the camshaft will be used in removing the excess clearance. Consequently, the valve will not be opening as far as it should. This condition has two effects: the valve train components will emit a tapping sound as they take up the excessive clearance and the engine will perform poorly because the valves does not open fully and allow the proper amount of gases to flow in and out of the engine.

If the valve clearance is too small, the intake valve and the exhaust valves will open too far and they will not fully seat on the cylinder head when they close. As a result, the valves will also become overheated and will warp, since they cannot transfer heat unless they are touching the valve seat in the cylinder head.

NOTE: While all valve adjustments must be made as accurately as possible, it is better to have the valve ad-justment slightly loose then slightly tight as a burned valve may result from overly tight adjustments.**

Valve Adjustment

Valve adjustment must be performed after any engine overhaul or when the valve train components emit a tapping sound requiring valve adjustment service.

———————————— CAUTION ————————————
Always apply parking brake and block wheels before performing any engine running tests.

2.2L, 2.5L, 3.0L and 3.3L Engines

The 2.2L, 2.5L and 3.0L engines use hydraulic lash adjusters. No periodic adjustment or checking is necessary.

Adjusting the valve lash on the 2.6L engine

Exhaust Valve Closing	Adjust
No. 1 Cylinder	No. 4 Cylinder Valves
No. 2 Cylinder	No. 3 Cylinder Valves
No. 3 Cylinder	No. 2 Cylinder Valves
No. 4 Cylinder	No. 1 Cylinder Valves

Valve adjustment sequence

2.6L Engine (With Jet Valves)

A jet valve is added on some models. The jet valve adjuster is located on the intake valve rocker arm and must be adjusted before the intake valve.

1. Start the engine and allow it to reach normal operating temperature.
2. Stop the engine and remove the air cleaner and its hoses. Remove any other cables, hoses, wires, etc., which are attached to the valve cover, and remove the valve cover.

3. Disconnect the high tension coil-to-distributor wire at the distributor, and allow it to contact a known good engine ground.
4. Torque the cylinder head bolts.
5. Have a helper bump the ignition switch. Watch the rocker arms until piston No. 4 cylinder is at Top Dead Center (TDC) and adjust jet valves as follow.
6. Back out the intake valve adjusting screw two or three turns.
7. Loosen the locknut on the jet valve and back out jet valve adjusting screw.
8. Install a 0.15mm feeler gauge between the jet valve stem and the jet valve adjusting screw.
9. Turn in jet valve adjusting screw until it slightly makes contact with the jet valve stem. While holding jet valve adjusting screw in place tighten jet valve lock nut. Recheck clearance.
10. Complete the adjustment by adjusting intake and exhaust valve clearance on the same cylinder as jet valve you've finished. Refer to Valve Clearance Specification Chart.

2.6L Engine (Without Jet Valves)

1. Start the engine and allow it to reach normal operating temperature.
2. Stop the engine and remove the air cleaner and its hoses. Remove any other cables, hoses, wires, etc., which are attached to the valve cover, and remove the valve cover.
3. Disconnect the high tension coil-to-distributor wire at the distributor, and allow it to contact a known good engine ground.
4. Torque cylinder head bolts.
5. Have a helper bump the ignition switch. Watch the rocker arms until piston is at Top Dead Center (TDC) of the compression stroke (both valves closed).
6. Loosen valve adjuster lock nut. Back out valve adjusting screw and install a feeler gauge between adjusting screw and valve stem.
7. Turn in valve adjusting screw until it slightly touches the feeler gauge. While holding the adjusting screw in place tighten adjusting screw lock nut. Refer to Valve Clearance Specification Chart.
8. Perform Step 5 thru 7 on the remaining three cylinders.

IDLE SPEED AND MIXTURE ADJUSTMENTS

IDLE SPEED ADJUSTMENT

—————— **CAUTION** ——————
Always apply the parking brake and block wheels before performing idle adjustment, or any engine running tests.

Holley 5220/6520—2.2L Engine

1. Check and adjust the ignition timing.
2. Disconnect and plug the vacuum connector at the Coolant Vacuum Switch Cold Closed (CVSCC) located on the top of the thermostat housing.

3. Unplug the connector at the radiator fan and connect a jumper wire so that the cooling fan will run constantly. Remove the PCV valve from the engine and allow it to draw under hood air.
4. Connect a tachometer to the engine.
5. Ground the carburetor switch with a jumper wire.
6. On models equipped with a 6250 carburetor (6250 models are equipped with an oxygen sensor) disconnect the oxygen system test connector on the left fender shield.
7. Start the engine and run until normal operating temperature is reached.
8. Turn the idle adjustment screw until required Rpm is

Model 5220 carburetor

reached. (Refer to the Under hood Specification Label or Tune-Up Chart). Shut off engine.

9. Reconnect the PCV valve, oxygen connector, vacuum connector (CVSCC) and remove the carb switch jumper. Remove the radiator fan jumper and reconnect harness.

NOTE: After Step 9 is completed, the idle speed might change, this is normal and the engine speed should not be readjusted.

10. Refer to Fuel System Section for fast idle, air conditioning idle speed check and choke kick adjustment procedures.

Mikuni Carburetor — 2.6L Engine

1. Connect a tachometer to the engine.
2. Check and adjust the ignition timing.
3. Start and run the engine until normal operating temperature is reached.
4. Disconnect the cooling fan harness connector.
5. Run at 2500 Rpm for 10 seconds. Return the engine to idle.
6. Wait two minutes and check engine Rpm indicated on the tachometer. If the idle speed is not within specs indicated on the under hood sticker or Tune-Up Chart, adjust the idle speed screw as necessary.

7. Models equipped with air condition, set temperature control lever to coldest position and turn on air conditioning. With compressor running, set idle speed to 900 Rpm with idle up screw.

8. After adjustment is complete, shut off the engine, disconnect the tachometer and reconnect the cooling fan harness.

Electronic Fuel Injected Engines

The idle speed is controlled by the Automatic Idle Speed motor (AIS) which is controlled by the logic module. The logic module receives data from various sensors in the system and adjusts the engine idle to a predetermined speed. Idle speed specifications can be found on the Vehicle Emission Control Information (VECI) label, located in the engine compartment. If the idle speed is not within specification and there are no problems with the system, the vehicle should be taken to an authorized dealer for service.

IDLE MIXTURE ADJUSTMENT

The following procedure uses a propane enrichment method of adjusting the idle. Use extreme care when using the propane

Model 6520 carburetor

Carburetor switch location — 2.2L engine

tank. Make sure that it is in a secure location and that the fittings are not leaking.

Holley and Mikuni Carburetors

1. Disconnect and plug the EGR hose. Disconnect the oxygen sensor, if equipped.
2. Disconnect and plug the hose at the canister.
3. Remove the PCV hose from the valve cover and allow it to draw under hood air.
4. Ground the carburetor switch with a jumper wire, if equipped.
5. Disconnect the vacuum hose from the computer, if equipped and connect an auxiliary vacuum supply of 16 Hg in.
6. Remove the concealment plug. Disconnect the vacuum supply hose to the tee and install a propane supply hose in its place.
7. Make sure all accessories are off. Install a tachometer and start the engine. Allow the engine to run for 2 minutes to stabilize.
8. Open the main propane valve. Slowly open the propane metering valve until the maximum engine Rpm is reached. When too much propane is added, the engine will begin to stumble; at this point back off until the engine stabilizes.
9. Adjust the idle Rpm to obtain the specified propane Rpm. Fine tune the metering valve to obtain the highest Rpm again. If there has been a change to the maximum Rpm, readjust the idle screw to the specified propane Rpm.

Mikuni carburetor

Correct location for drilling the hole at the idle mixture screw

10. Turn the main propane valve off and allow the engine to run for 1 minute to stabilize.

11. Adjust the mixture screw to obtain the smoothest idle at the specified idle Rpm.

12. Open the main propane valve. Fine tune the metering valve to obtain the highest Rpm. If the maximum engine speed is more that 25 Rpm different than the specified propane Rpm, repeat the procedure.

13. Turn the propane valves off and remove the propane canister. Reinstall the vacuum supply hose to the tee.

14. Perform the idle speed adjustment procedure.

Adjusting the mixture using an Allen wrench

15. Connect all wires and hoses that were previously disconnected.

Engine and Engine Overhaul

3

UNDERSTANDING THE ENGINE ELECTRICAL SYSTEM

The engine electrical system can be broken down into 3 separate and distinct systems:
1. The starting system.
2. The charging system.
3. The ignition system.

BATTERY AND STARTING SYSTEM

Basic Operating Principles

The battery is the first link in the chain of mechanisms which work together to provide cranking of the automobile engine. In most modern cars, the battery is a lead/acid electro-chemical device consisting of six 2v subsections connected in series so the unit is capable of producing approximately 12v of electrical pressure. Each subsection, or cell, consists of a series of positive and negative plates held a short distance apart in a solution of sulfuric acid and water. The 2 types of plates are of dissimilar metals. This causes a chemical reaction to be set up, and it is this reaction which produces current flow from the battery when its positive and negative terminals are connected to an electrical appliance such as a lamp or motor. The continued transfer of electrons would eventually convert the sulfuric acid in the electrolyte to water, and make the 2 plates identical in chemical composition. As electrical energy is removed from the battery, its voltage output tends to drop. Thus, measuring battery voltage and battery electrolyte composition are 2 ways of checking the ability of the unit to supply power. During the starting of the engine, electrical energy is removed from the battery. However, if the charging circuit is in good condition and the operating conditions are normal, the power removed from the battery will be replaced by the generator (or alternator) which will force electrons back through the battery, reversing the normal flow, and restoring the battery to its original chemical state.

The battery and starting motor are linked by very heavy electrical cables designed to minimize resistance to the flow of current. Generally, the major power supply cable that leaves the battery goes directly to the starter, while other electrical system needs are supplied by a smaller cable. During starter operation, power flows from the battery to the starter and is grounded through the car's frame and the battery's negative ground strap.

The starting motor is a specially designed, direct current electric motor capable of producing a very great amount of power for its size. One thing that allows the motor to produce a great deal of power is its tremendous rotating speed. It drives the engine through a tiny pinion gear (attached to the starter's armature), which drives the very large flywheel ring gear at a greatly reduced speed. Another factor allowing it to produce so much power is that only intermittent operation is required of it. This, little allowance for air circulation is required, and the windings can be built into a very small space.

The starter solenoid is a magnetic device which employs the small current supplied by the starting switch circuit of the ignition switch. This magnetic action moves a plunger which mechanically engages the starter and electrically closes the heavy switch which connects it to the battery. The starting switch circuit consists of the starting switch contained within the ignition switch, a transmission neutral safety switch or clutch pedal switch, and the wiring necessary to connect these in series with the starter solenoid or relay.

A pinion, which is a small gear, is mounted to a one-way drive clutch. This clutch is splined to the starter armature shaft. When the ignition switch is moved to the **start** position, the solenoid plunger slides the pinion toward the flywheel ring gear via a collar and spring. If the teeth on the pinion and flywheel match properly, the pinion will engage the flywheel immediately. If the gear teeth butt one another, the spring will be compressed and will force the gears to mesh as soon as the starter turns far enough to allow them to do so. As the solenoid plunger reaches the end of its travel, it closes the contacts that connect the battery and starter and then the engine is cranked.

As soon as the engine starts, the flywheel ring gear begins turning fast enough to drive the pinion at an extremely high rate of speed. At this point, the one-way clutch begins allowing the pinion to spin faster than the starter shaft so that the starter will not operate at excessive speed. When the ignition switch is released from the starter position, the solenoid is de-energized, and a spring contained within the solenoid assembly pulls the gear out of mesh and interrupts the current flow to the starter.

Some starter employ a separate relay, mounted away from the starter, to switch the motor and solenoid current on and off. The relay thus replaces the solenoid electrical switch, buy does not eliminate the need for a solenoid mounted on the starter used to mechanically engage the starter drive gears. The relay is used to reduce the amount of current the starting switch must carry.

THE CHARGING SYSTEM

Basic Operating Principles

The automobile charging system provides electrical power for operation of the vehicle's ignition and starting systems and all the electrical accessories. The battery services as an electrical surge or storage tank, storing (in chemical form) the energy originally produced by the engine driven generator. The system also provides a means of regulating generator output to protect the battery from being overcharged and to avoid excessive voltage to the accessories.

The storage battery is a chemical device incorporating parallel lead plates in a tank containing a sulfuric acid/water solution. Adjacent plates are slightly dissimilar, and the chemical reaction of the 2 dissimilar plates produces electrical energy when the battery is connected to a load such as the starter motor. The chemical reaction is reversible, so that when the generator is producing a voltage (electrical pressure) greater than that produced by the battery, electricity is forced into the battery, and the battery is returned to its fully charged state.

The vehicle's generator is driven mechanically, through V-belts, by the engine crankshaft. It consists of 2 coils of fine wire, one stationary (the stator), and one movable (the rotor). The rotor may also be known as the armature, and consists of fine wire wrapped around an iron core which is mounted on a shaft. The electricity which flows through the 2 coils of wire (provided initially by the battery in some cases) creates an intense magnetic field around both rotor and stator, and the interaction between the 2 fields creates voltage, allowing the generator to power the accessories and charge the battery.

There are 2 types of generators: the earlier is the direct current (DC) type. The current produced by the DC generator is generated in the armature and carried off the spinning armature by stationary brushes contacting the commutator. The commutator is a series of smooth metal contact plates on the end of the armature. The commutator is a series of smooth metal contact plates on the end of the armature. The commutator plates, which are separated from one another by a very short gap, are connected to the armature circuits so that current will flow in one directions only in the wires carrying the generator output. The generator stator consists of 2 stationary coils of wire which draw some of the output current of the generator to form a powerful magnetic field and create the interaction of fields which generates the voltage. The generator field is wired in series with the regulator.

Newer automobiles use alternating current generators or alternators, because they are more efficient, can be rotated at higher speeds, and have fewer brush problems. In an alternator, the field rotates while all the current produced passes only through the stator winding. The brushes bear against continuous slip rings rather than a commutator. This causes the current produced to periodically reverse the direction of its flow. Diodes (electrical one-way switches) block the flow of current from traveling in the wrong direction. A series of diodes is wired together to permit the alternating flow of the stator to be converted to a pulsating, but unidirectional flow at the alternator output. The alternator's field is wired in series with the voltage regulator.

The regulator consists of several circuits. Each circuit has a core, or magnetic coil of wire, which operates a switch. Each switch is connected to ground through one or more resistors.

The coil of wire responds directly to system voltage. When the voltage reaches the required level, the magnetic field created by the winding of wire closes the switch and inserts a resistance into the generator field circuit, thus reducing the output. The contacts of the switch cycle open and close many times each second to precisely control voltage.

While alternators are self-limiting as far as maximum current is concerned, DC generators employ a current regulating circuit which responds directly to the total amount of current flowing through the generator circuit rather than to the output voltage. The current regulator is similar to the voltage regulator except that all system current must flow through the energizing coil on its way to the various accessories.

ENGINE ELECTRICAL

NOTE: Refer to Section 2 for further ignition system diagnosis and component replacement.

Ignition Coil

TESTING

All Models

NOTE: On models equipped with the 3.3L engine, the spark at the coil is tested in the same ways as models with a distributor. But each of the coils towers must be checked for spark.

1. Remove the coil wire from the distributor cap. Hold the end of the wire about ¼ in. away from a good engine ground point.
2. Have a helper crank the engine. Check for a spark between the coil wire end and the ground point.
3. If there is a spark, it must be constant and bright blue in color.
4. Continue to crank the engine. Slowly move the wire away

from the ground point. If arching at the coil tower occurs, replace the coil.
5. If the spark is good and no arching at the coil tower occurs, the ignition system is producing the necessary high secondary voltage.
6. Check to make sure that the voltage is getting to the spark plugs. Inspect the distributor cap, rotor, spark plug wires and spark plugs.
7. If all of the components check okay, the ignition system is probably not the reason why the engine does not start.
8. Check the fuel system and engine mechanical items such as the timing belt.

Ignition Coil

REMOVAL AND INSTALLATION

All Engines Except 3.3L

1. Disconnect the negative battery cable.
2. Remove the coil wire from the top of the coil.
3. Remove the wires from the top of the coil.
4. Remove the coil mounting bolt and remove the coil.
5. Mount the replacement coil in position and reconnect all of the wires.
6. Connect the battery cable.

3.3L Engine

1. Disconnect the negative battery cable.
2. Remove the electrical connector from the coil assembly. Tag and disconnect the spark plug wires from the coil assembly.
3. Remove the coil mounting bolts and remove the coil assembly from the engine.
4. Mount the coil in position and connect all of the wires. Tighten the coil assembly mounting bolts to 105 inch lbs. (12 Nm).
5. Connect the negative battery cable.

Checking for spark

ALTERNATOR TO INTAKE MANIFOLD BOLT — IGNITION COILS FASTENERS (4)

IGNITION COILS ELECTRICAL CONNECTOR

Ignition coil assembly removal — 3.3L engine

Distributor Cap

REMOVAL AND INSTALLATION

1. Remove the splash shield retaining screws and the splash shield.
2. Loosen the distributor cap retaining screws.
3. Remove the distributor cap
4. Inspect the inside, of the cap, for spark flash over (burnt tracks on cap or terminals), center carbon button wear or cracking, and worn terminals. Replace the cap if any of these problems are present or suspected.
Light deposits on the terminals can be cleaned with a knife, heavy deposits or scaling will require cap replacement.
Wash the cap with a solution of warm water and mild detergent, scrub with a soft brush and dry with a clean soft cloth to remove dirt and grease.
5. If cap replacement is necessary, take notice of cap installed position in relationship to distributor assembly.
6. Number each plug wire so that the correct wire goes on the proper cap terminal when replaced. This can be done with pieces of adhesive tape.

NOTE: Do not pull plugs wires from distributor cap, they must first be released from inside of cap.

7. Position the replacement cap on the distributor assembly, and tighten the distributor cap retaining screws.
8. Push the wire terminals firmly to properly seat the wires into the cap.
9. Reinstall the splash shield.

Distributor Rotor

With the distributor cap removed, remove the rotor. Inspect the rotor for cracks, excessive wear or burn marks and sufficient spring tension of the spring to cap carbon button terminal. Clean light deposits, replace the rotor if scaled or burnt heavily. Clean the ground strap on the inner side of the shaft mount. Take care not to bend any of the shutter blades, if blades are bent replace the rotor.

Distributor

REMOVAL AND INSTALLATION

NOTE: Although not absolutely necessary, it is probably easier (for reference reinstallation, especially if the engine is rotated after distributor removal) to bring the engine to No. 1 cylinder at TDC (top dead center) before removing the distributor.

1. Disconnect the distributor lead wires, and vacuum hose as necessary.
2. Remove the distributor cap.
3. Rotate the engine crankshaft (in the direction of normal rotation) until No. 1 cylinder is at TDC on compression stroke. make a mark on the block where the rotor points for installation reference.
4. Remove the distributor hold down bolt.
5. Carefully lift the distributor from the engine. The shaft will rotate slightly as the distributor is removed.
6. If the engine was not disturbed while the distributor was out, lower the distributor into the engine, engaging the gears and making sure that the gasket is properly seated in the block. The rotor should line up with the mark made before removal.
7. Install the distributor cap.
8. Tighten the hold down bolt. Connect the wires and vacuum hose as necessary.
9. Check and, if necessary, adjust the ignition timing.

NOTE: The following procedure is to be used if the engine was cranked with the distributor removed.

10. If the engine has been cranked/turned while the distributor was removed, rotate the crankshaft until the number one piston is at TDC on the compression stroke. This will be indicated by the O mark on the flywheel (2.2L and 2.5L engines) aligned with the pointer on the clutch housing, or crank pulley (2.6L and 3.0L engines) aligned with the pointer on engine front cover.
11. Position the rotor just ahead of the No. 1 terminal of the

HOLD DOWN SCREW

Distributor hold down — 2.2L engine

HIGH VOLTAGE LEAD

IGNITION COIL

COIL MOUNTING BOLT

HOLD DOWN NUT

DISTRIBUTOR

HIGH VOLTAGE LEAD

Distributor hold down — 2.6L engine

Distributor hold down nut location — 3.0L engine

cap and lower the distributor into the engine. With the distributor fully seated, the rotor should be directly under the No. 1 terminal.

12. Install the distributor cap.

13. Tighten the hold down bolt. Connect the wires and vacuum hose as necessary.

14. Check and, if necessary, adjust the ignition timing.

Alternator

The alternator charging system is a negative (−) ground system which consists of an alternator, a regulator, a charge indicator, a storage battery and wiring connecting the components, and fuse link wire.

The alternator is belt-driven from the engine. Energy is supplied from the alternator/regulator system to the rotating field through 2 brushes to 2 slip-rings. The slip-rings are mounted on the rotor shaft and are connected to the field coil. This energy supplied to the rotating field from the battery is called excitation current and is used to initially energize the field to begin the generation of electricity. Once the alternator starts to generate electricity, the excitation current comes from its own output rather than the battery.

The alternator produces power in the form of alternating current. The alternating current is rectified by 6 diodes into direct current. The direct current is used to charge the battery and power the rest of the electrical system.

When the ignition key is turned on, current flows from the battery, through the charging system indicator light on the instrument panel, to the voltage regulator, and to the alternator. Since the alternator is not producing any current, the alternator warning light comes on. When the engine is started, the alternator begins to produce current and turns the alternator light off. As the alternator turns and produces current, the current is divided in 2 ways: part to the battery to charge the battery and power the electrical components of the vehicle, and part is returned to the alternator to enable it to increase its output. In this situation, the alternator is receiving current from the battery and from itself. A voltage regulator is wired into the current supply to the alternator to prevent it from receiving too much current which would cause it to put out too much current. Conversely, if the voltage regulator does not allow the alternator to receive enough current, the battery will not be fully charged and will eventually go dead.

The battery is connected to the alternator at all times, whether the ignition key is turned on or not. If the battery were shorted to ground, the alternator would also be shorted. This would damage the alternator. To prevent this, a fuse link is installed in the wiring between the battery and the alternator. If the battery is shorted, the fuse link is melted, protecting the alternator.

ALTERNATOR PRECAUTIONS

Some precautions should be taken when working on this, or any other, AC charging system.

1. Never switch battery polarity.

2. When installing a battery, always connect the grounded terminal first.

3. Never disconnect the battery while the engine is running.

4. If the molded connector is disconnected from the alternator, never ground the hot wire.

5. Never run the alternator with the main output cable disconnected.

6. Never electric weld around the truck without disconnecting the alternator.

7. Never apply any voltage in excess of battery voltage while testing.

8. Never jump a battery for starting purposes with more than 12v.

CHARGING SYSTEM TROUBLESHOOTING

There are many possible ways in which the charging system can malfunction. Often the source of a problem is difficult to diagnose, requiring special equipment and a good deal of experience. This is usually not the case, however, where the charging system fails completely and causes the dash board warning light to come on or the battery to become dead. To troubleshoot a complete system failure only 2 pieces of equipment are needed: a test light, to determine that current is reaching a certain point; and a current indicator (ammeter), to determine the direction of the current flow and its measurement in amps.

This test works under 3 assumptions:

1. The battery is known to be good and fully charged.

2. The alternator belt is in good condition and adjusted to the proper tension.

3. All connections in the system are clean and tight.

NOTE: In order for the current indicator to give a valid reading, the car must be equipped with battery cables which are of the same gauge size and quality as original equipment battery cables.

1. Turn off all electrical components on the car. Make sure the doors of the car are closed. If the car is equipped with a clock, disconnect the clock by removing the lead wire from the rear of the clock. Disconnect the positive battery cable from the battery and connect the ground wire on a test light to the disconnected positive battery cable. Touch the probe end of the test light to the positive battery post. The test light should not light. If the test light does light, there is a short or open circuit on the car.

2. Disconnect the voltage regulator wiring harness connector at the voltage regulator. Turn on the ignition key. Connect the wire on a test light to a good ground (engine bolt). Touch the probe end of a test light to the ignition wire connector into the voltage regulator wiring connector. This wire corresponds to the I terminal on the regulator. If the test light goes on, the charging system warning light circuit is complete. If the test light does not come on and the warning light on the instrument panel is on, either the resistor wire, which is parallel with the warning light, or the wiring to the voltage regulator, is defective. If the test light does not come on and the warning light is not on, either the bulb is defective or the power supply wire form the battery through the ignition switch to the bulb has an open circuit. Connect the wiring harness to the regulator.

3. Examine the fuse link wire in the wiring harness from the starter relay to the alternator. If the insulation on the wire is cracked or split, the fuse link may be melted. Connect a test light to the fuse link by attaching the ground wire on the test light to an engine bolt and touching the probe end of the light to the bottom of the fuse link wire where it splices into the alternator output wire. If the bulb in the test light does not light, the fuse link is melted.

4. Start the engine and place a current indicator on the positive battery cable. Turn off all electrical accessories and make sure the doors are closed. If the charging system is working properly, the gauge will show a draw of less than 5 amps. If the system is not working properly, the gauge will show a draw of more than 5 amps. A charge moves the needle toward the battery, a draw moves the needle away from the battery. Turn the engine off.

5. Disconnect the wiring harness from the voltage regulator at the regulator at the regulator connector. Connect a male spade terminal (solderless connector) to each end of a jumper wire. Insert one end of the wire into the wiring harness connector which corresponds to the **A** terminal on the regulator. Insert the other end of the wire into the wiring harness connector which corresponds to the **F** terminal on the regulator. Position the connector with the jumper wire installed so that it cannot contact any metal surface under the hood. Position a current indicator gauge on the positive battery cable. Have an assistant start the engine. Observe the reading on the current indicator. Have your assistant slowly raise the speed of the engine to about 2,000 Rpm or until the current indicator needle stops moving, whichever comes first. Do not run the engine for more than a short period of time in this condition. If the wiring harness connector or jumper wire becomes excessively hot during this test, turn off the engine and check for a grounded wire in the regulator wiring harness. If the current indicator shows a charge of about 3 amps less than the output of the alternator, the alternator is working properly. If the previous tests showed a draw, the voltage regulator is defective. If the gauge does not show the proper charging rate, the alternator is defective.

REMOVAL AND INSTALLATION

Chrysler Alternator
2.2L Engine

1. Disconnect the negative battery cable.
2. Disconnect the wiring and label for easy installation.
3. Remove the air conditioning compressor drive belt if equipped.
4. Loosen the alternator adjusting bracket bolt and adjusting bolt. Remove the alternator belt.
5. Remove the bracket bolt and the mounting bolt.
6. Remove the pivot bolt and nut.
7. Remove the alternator.
8. Position the alternator against the engine.
9. Install the pivot bolt and nut.
10. Install the mounting bracket bolts, and adjusting bolt.
11. Install drive belts and adjust to specification.
12. Tighten all the mounting bolts and nuts.
13. Connect all alternator terminals.
14. Connect the negative battery cable.

Bosch Alternator
2.2L Engine

1. Disconnect the negative battery cable.
2. Disconnect the wiring and label for easy installation.
3. Remove the air conditioning compressor drive belt.
4. Loosen the alternator adjusting bracket lock nut and adjusting screw. Remove the alternator belt.
5. Remove the bracket locknut and mounting bolt.
6. Remove the pivot bolt and nut.
7. Remove the alternator.
8. Position the alternator against the engine.
9. Install pivot bolt and nut.
10. Set the mounting bracket in place and install the bracket mounting bolt and locknut.
11. Install the drive belts and adjust to specification.
12. Tighten all the mounting bolts and nuts.
13. Connect all alternator terminals.
14. Connect the negative battery cable.

Alternator mounting — 2.2/2.5L engine

Disconnecting alternator wiring — 2.2/2.5L engines

Bosch and Chrysler Alternators
2.5L Engine

1. Disconnect the negative battery cable.
2. Remove the drive belts.
3. Remove the adjusting bracket to engine mounting bolt.
4. Remove the adjusting locking bolt and nut, and remove the mounting bracket.
5. Position the alternator to gain access to the wiring.
6. Disconnect the wiring and label for easy installation.
7. Remove the pivot bolt, nut, and washers.
8. Remove the alternator assembly from the engine.
9. Position the alternator assembly against the engine.
10. Loosely install the pivot bolt, washers, and nut.
11. Install all wiring.
12. Position the mounting bracket and install engine mounting bolt.
13. Loosely install the adjusting locking bolt and nut.
14. Install the drive belts, and adjust to specification.
15. Tighten all mounting bolts and nuts.
16. Connect the negative battery cable.

Mitsubishi Alternator
2.6L Engine

1. Disconnect the negative battery cable.
2. Disconnect the wiring and label for easy installation.
3. Remove the adjusting strap mounting bolt.
4. Remove the drive belts.
5. Remove the support mounting bolt and nut.

Disconnecting alternator wiring — 3.0L engine

Alternator mounting — 3.0L engine

Alternator mounting — 3.3L engine

6. Remove the alternator assembly.
7. Position the alternator assembly against the engine and install the support bolt.
8. Install the adjusting strap mounting bolt.
9. Install the alternator belts and adjust to specification.
10. Tighten all the support bolts and nuts.
11. Connect all alternator terminals.
12. Connect the negative battery cable.

Bosch and Nippondenso Alternator
3.0L Engine

1. Disconnect the negative battery cable.
2. Install a ½ in. breaker bar in the tensioner slot. Rotate counterclockwise to release belt tension and remove poly-V belt.
3. Remove the alternator mounting bolts (2).
4. Remove the wiring and remove alternator.
5. To install, position the alternator and install wiring.
6. Set the alternator against the mounting bracket and install the mounting bolts.
7. Rotate the tensioner counterclockwise and install poly-V belt.
8. Connect the negative battery cable.

Nippondenso Alternator
3.3L Engine

1. Disconnect the negative battery cable.
2. Remove the alternator drive belt, by relieving the tension on the dynamic tensioner.
3. Loosen the nut on the support bracket at the exhaust manifold, do not remove it.
4. Remove the alternator tensioner/power steering bracket bolt.
5. Remove the tensioner stud nut and remove the tensioner.
6. Remove the alternator mounting bolts.
7. Remove the power steering reservoir from the mounting bracket, do not disconnect the hoses, and position it out of the way.
8. Remove the alternator support bracket bolts. Remove the intake plenum to alternator bracket bolt and remove the alternator support bracket from the engine.
9. Remove the alternator from the engine and disconnect the electrical leads.

To install:
10. Install the alternator in position on the engine and connect the electrical leads.
11. Install the alternator support bracket, tighten the retaining bolts to 40 ft. lbs. (54 Nm).
12. Install the power steering reservoir on the mounting bracket.
13. Install the alternator mounting bolts, tighten the bolts to 40 ft. lbs. (54 Nm).
14. Install the tensioner and tensioner mounting stud. Install the retaining nut on the exhaust manifold.
15. Install the alternator belt, insert a ½ in. extension into the

Troubleshooting Basic Charging System Problems

Problem	Cause	Solution
Noisy alternator	• Loose mountings • Loose drive pulley • Worn bearings • Brush noise • Internal circuits shorted (High pitched whine)	• Tighten mounting bolts • Tighten pulley • Replace alternator • Replace alternator • Replace alternator
Squeal when starting engine or accelerating	• Glazed or loose belt	• Replace or adjust belt
Indicator light remains on or ammeter indicates discharge (engine running)	• Broken fan belt • Broken or disconnected wires • Internal alternator problems • Defective voltage regulator	• Install belt • Repair or connect wiring • Replace alternator • Replace voltage regulator
Car light bulbs continually burn out—battery needs water continually	• Alternator/regulator overcharging	• Replace voltage regulator/alternator
Car lights flare on acceleration	• Battery low • Internal alternator/regulator problems	• Charge or replace battery • Replace alternator/regulator
Low voltage output (alternator light flickers continually or ammeter needle wanders)	• Loose or worn belt • Dirty or corroded connections • Internal alternator/regulator problems	• Replace or adjust belt • Clean or replace connections • Replace alternator or regulator

square hole in the tensioner and turn the tensioner. Tighten the tensioner bolt.

16. Connect the negative battery cable.

Regulator

REMOVAL AND INSTALLATION

Chrysler Alternator (Early Models)

1. Disconnect the negative battery cable.
2. Remove the electrical connection from voltage regulator assembly.
3. Remove the mounting bolts and remove the regulator.
4. This regulator is not adjustable and must be replaced as a unit if found to be defective.
5. Clean any dirt or corrosion from the regulator mounting surface, including mounting holes.
6. Install the replacement electronic voltage regulator.
7. Secured the mounting screws.
8. Connect the voltage regulator wiring connector. Connect the negative battery cable.

NOTE: All Bosch, Nippondenso, Mitsubishi, and Chrysler (Late Models) alternators have an integral electronic voltage regulator. Voltage regulator replacement on these models requires removal and disassembly of the alternator.

Starter

TEST PROCEDURES (ON VEHICLE)

NOTE: The battery is the heart of the electrical system. If the battery is not up to specification it will not deliver the necessary amperage for proper starter operation.

Starter Does Not Operate

——————— CAUTION ———————

Before performing this test, disconnect the coil wire from the distributor cap center tower and secure to a good engine ground. This will prevent the engine from starting.

1. Connect a voltmeter across the battery terminals and confirm that battery voltage (12.4 volts) is available for the ignition and cranking system.
2. Turn the headlights on.
3. If the headlights do not operate. Check the battery cables for loose or corroded connection.
4. If the headlights glow normally, have a helper operate the ignition switch. Headlights should remained reasonably bright when ignition switch is operated. If the headlights dim considerably or go out when the ignition switch is operated, the problem is battery related.
5. If headlights remain bright when the ignition switch is operated. The problem is at the starter relay, wiring, or starter motor.

Bosch direct drive starter motor

Nippondenso direct drive starter motor

6. Connect a test light to the battery feed terminal of the starter relay. The test light should go on. If the test light is off, check the battery feed wire to starter relay.

7. Connect the test light to the ignition switch terminal of starter relay and a known good engine ground. Have a helper operate the ignition switch. If the test light does not come on when the ignition switch is operated, check the wiring from the ignition switch to the relay. Test light should have came on.

8. Test light on.

9. Connect a heavy jumper wire, between the battery relay feed and the relay solenoid terminal. If the starter motor operates replace the starter relay. If the motor does not operate, remove the starter for repairs.

2.6L ENGINE
A-470 AUTOMATIC
TRANSAXLE STARTER

SOLENOID

Nippondenso reduction gear starter motor

REMOVAL AND INSTALLATION

1. Disconnect the negative battery cable.
2. Remove the heat shield and its clamps if so equipped.
3. On the 2.2L and 2.5L engine loosen the air pump tube at the exhaust manifold and move the tube bracket away from the starter.
4. Remove the electrical connections from the starter.
5. Remove the bolts attaching the starter to the flywheel housing and the rear bracket to the engine or transaxle.
6. Remove the starter.
7. Position the replacement starter against the mounting surface.
8. Install the mounting bolts.
9. Connect the starter wiring.
10. On 2.2L and 2.5L engines, position the air pump tube toward starter and connect tube bracket the to exhaust manifold.
11. Install the heat shield and clamp.
12. Connect the negative battery cable.

SOLENOID REPLACEMENT

1. Remove the starter as previously outlined.
2. Disconnect the field coil wire from the solenoid.
3. Remove the solenoid mounting screws.

Exploded view of Bosch starter

Exploded view of Nippondenso starter

**Removing pinion, clutch and drive gear —
Nippondenso starter**

4. Work the solenoid off of shift fork lever and remove the solenoid.
  5. Install plunger on replacement solenoid.
  6. Install plunger on shift fork lever.
  7. Secure solenoid with mounting screws.

STARTER GEAR AND CLUTCH REPLACEMENT

1. Disconnect the negative battery cable.
2. Remove the starter from the vehicle.
3. Remove the 2 gear housing attaching screws from the starter.
  4. Separate the gear housing from the solenoid housing. The pinion, pinion gear bearing and drive gear will all be loose between the 2 housings. The starter gear and clutch can also be removed at this time.
  5. To reinstall the pinion gear and bearing, wipe clean with a rag and coat with light weight wheel bearing grease.
  6. Place the bearing and gear over the shaft in the housing. Reinstall the starter gear and clutch if removed.
  7. Install the housings and reinstall the retaining screws.
  8. Install the starter in the vehicle and connect the negative battery cable.

Troubleshooting Basic Starting System Problems

Problem	Cause	Solution
Starter motor rotates engine slowly	• Battery charge low or battery defective	• Charge or replace battery
	• Defective circuit between battery and starter motor	• Clean and tighten, or replace cables
	• Low load current	• Bench-test starter motor. Inspect for worn brushes and weak brush springs.
	• High load current	• Bench-test starter motor. Check engine for friction, drag or coolant in cylinders. Check ring gear-to-pinion gear clearance.
Starter motor will not rotate engine	• Battery charge low or battery defective	• Charge or replace battery
	• Faulty solenoid	• Check solenoid ground. Repair or replace as necessary.
	• Damage drive pinion gear or ring gear	• Replace damaged gear(s)
	• Starter motor engagement weak	• Bench-test starter motor
	• Starter motor rotates slowly with high load current	• Inspect drive yoke pull-down and point gap, check for worn end bushings, check ring gear clearance
	• Engine seized	• Repair engine
Starter motor drive will not engage (solenoid known to be good)	• Defective contact point assembly	• Repair or replace contact point assembly
	• Inadequate contact point assembly ground	• Repair connection at ground screw
	• Defective hold-in coil	• Replace field winding assembly

Troubleshooting Basic Starting System Problems

Problem	Cause	Solution
Starter motor drive will not disengage	• Starter motor loose on flywheel housing • Worn drive end busing • Damaged ring gear teeth • Drive yoke return spring broken or missing	• Tighten mounting bolts • Replace bushing • Replace ring gear or driveplate • Replace spring
Starter motor drive disengages prematurely	• Weak drive assembly thrust spring • Hold-in coil defective	• Replace drive mechanism • Replace field winding assembly
Low load current	• Worn brushes • Weak brush springs	• Replace brushes • Replace springs

ENGINE MECHANICAL

Engine Overhaul Tips

Most engine overhaul procedures are fairly standard. In addition to specific parts replacement procedures and complete specifications for your individual engine, this section also is a guide to accept rebuilding procedures. Examples of standard rebuilding practice are shown and should be used along with specific details concerning your particular engine.

Competent and accurate machine shop services will ensure maximum performance, reliability and engine life.

In most instances it is more profitable for the do-it-yourself mechanic to remove, clean and inspect the component, buy the necessary parts and deliver these to a shop for actual machine work.

On the other hand, much of the rebuilding work (crankshaft, block, bearings, piston rods, and other components) is well within the scope of the do-it-yourself mechanic.

TOOLS

The tools required for an engine overhaul or parts replacement will depend on the depth of your involvement. With a few exceptions, they will be the tools found in a mechanic's tool kit (see "General Information and Maintenance"). More in-depth work will require any or all of the following:
- A dial indicator (reading in thousandths) mounted on a universal base
- Micrometers and telescope gauges
- Jaw and screw-type pullers
- Scraper
- Valve spring compressor
- Ring groove cleaner
- Piston ring expander and compressor

- Ridge reamer
- Cylinder hone or glaze breaker
- Plastigage®
- Engine stand

The use of most of these tools is illustrated in this section. Many can be rented for a one-time use from a local parts jobber or tool supply house specializing in automotive work.

Occasionally, the use of special tools is called for. See the information on Special Tools and Safety Notice in the front of this book before substituting another tool.

INSPECTION TECHNIQUES

Procedures and specifications are given in this section for inspecting, cleaning and assessing the wear limits of most major components. Other procedures such as Magnaflux® and Zyglo® can be used to locate material flaws and stress cracks. Magnaflux® is a magnetic process applicable only to ferrous materials. The Zyglo® process coats the material with a fluorescent dye penetrant and can be used on any material Check for suspected surface cracks can be more readily made using spot check dye. The dye is sprayed onto the suspected area, wiped off and the area sprayed with a developer. Cracks will show up brightly.

OVERHAUL TIPS

Aluminum has become extremely popular for use in engines, due to its low weight. Observe the following precautions when handling aluminum parts:
- Never hot tank aluminum parts (the caustic hot tank solution will eat the aluminum.
- Remove all aluminum parts (identification tag, etc.) from engine parts prior to the tanking.

- Always coat threads lightly with engine oil or anti-seize compounds before installation, to prevent seizure.
- Never over-torque bolts or spark plugs especially in aluminum threads.

Stripped threads in any component can be repaired using any of several commercial repair kits (Heli-Coil®, Microdot®, Keenserts®, etc.).

When assembling the engine, any parts that will be frictional contact must be prelubed to provide lubrication at initial start-up. Any product specifically formulated for this purpose can be used, but engine oil is not recommended as a prelube.

When semi-permanent (locked, but removable) installation of bolts or nuts is desired, threads should be cleaned and coated with Loctite® or other similar, commercial non-hardening sealant.

REPAIRING DAMAGED THREADS

Several methods of repairing damaged threads are available. Heli-Coil® (shown here), Keenserts® and Microdot® are among the most widely used. All involve basically the same principle—drilling out stripped threads, tapping the hole and installing a prewound insert—making welding, plugging and oversize fasteners unnecessary.

Two types of thread repair inserts are usually supplied: a standard type for most Inch Coarse, Inch Fine, Metric Course and Metric Fine thread sizes and a spark lug type to fit most spark plug port sizes. Consult the individual manufacturer's catalog to determine exact applications. Typical thread repair kits will contain a selection of prewound threaded inserts, a tap (corresponding to the outside diameter threads of the insert) and an installation tool. Spark plug inserts usually differ because they require a tap equipped with pilot threads and a combined reamer/tap section. Most manufacturers also supply blister-packed thread repair inserts separately in addition to a master kit containing a variety of taps and inserts plus installation tools.

Before effecting a repair to a threaded hole, remove any snapped, broken or damaged bolts or studs. Penetrating oil can be used to free frozen threads; the offending item can be removed with locking pliers or with a screw or.stud extractor. After the hole is clear, the thread can be repaired, as follows:

Checking Engine Compression

A noticeable lack of engine power, excessive oil consumption and/or poor fuel mileage measured over an extended period are all indicators of internal engine war. Worn piston rings, scored or worn cylinder bores, blown head gaskets, sticking or burnt valves and worn valve seats are all possible culprits here. A check of each cylinder's compression will help you locate the problems.

As mentioned in the Tools and Equipment section, a screw-in type compression gauge is more accurate that the type you simply hold against the spark plug hole, although it takes slightly longer to use. It's worth it to obtain a more accurate reading. Follow the procedures below.

1. Warm up the engine to normal operating temperature.
2. Remove all spark plugs.
3. Disconnect the high tension lead from the ignition coil.
4. On fully open the throttle either by operating the carburetor throttle linkage by hand or by having an assistant floor the accelerator pedal.
5. Screw the compression gauge into the no.1 spark plug hole until the fitting is snug.

NOTE: Be careful not to cross thread the plug hole. On aluminum cylinder heads use extra care, as the threads in these heads are easily ruined.

6. Ask an assistant to depress the accelerator pedal fully on both carbureted and fuel injected trucks. Then, while you read the compression gauge, ask the assistant to crank the engine 2 or 3 times in short bursts using the ignition switch.
7. Read the compression gauge at the end of each series of cranks, and record the highest of these readings. Repeat this procedure for each of the engine's cylinders. Compare the highest reading of each cylinder to the compression pressure specification in the Tune-Up Specifications chart. The specs in this chart are maximum values.

A cylinder's compression pressure is usually acceptable if it is not less than 80% of maximum. The difference between each cylinder should be no more than 12-14 pounds.

8. If a cylinder is unusually low, pour a tablespoon of clean engine oil into the cylinder through the spark plug hole and repeat the compression test. If the compression comes up after adding the oil, it appears that the cylinder's piston rings or bore are damaged or worn. If the pressure remains low, the valves may not be seating properly (a valve job is needed), or the head gasket may be blown near that cylinder. If compression in any 2 adjacent cylinders is low, and if the addition of oil doesn't help the compression, there is leakage past the head gasket. Oil and coolant water in the combustion chamber can result from this problem. There may be evidence of water droplets on the engine dipstick when a head gasket has blown.

Troubleshooting Engine Mechanical Problems

Problem	Cause	Solution
External oil leaks	• Fuel pump gasket broken or improperly seated	• Replace gasket
	• Cylinder head cover RTV sealant broken or improperly seated	• Replace sealant; inspect cylinder head cover sealant flange and cylinder head sealant surface for distortion and cracks
	• Oil filler cap leaking or missing	• Replace cap

Troubleshooting Engine Mechanical Problems (cont.)

Problem	Cause	Solution
External oil leaks	• Oil filter gasket broken or improperly seated	• Replace oil filter
	• Oil pan side gasket broken, improperly seated or opening in RTV sealant	• Replace gasket or repair opening in sealant; inspect oil pan gasket flange for distortion
	• Oil pan front oil seal broken or improperly seated	• Replace seal; inspect timing case cover and oil pan seal flange for distortion
	• Oil pan rear oil seal broken or improperly seated	• Replace seal; inspect oil pan rear oil seal flange; inspect rear main bearing cap for cracks, plugged oil return channels, or distortion in seal groove
	• Timing case cover oil seal broken or improperly seated	• Replace seal
	• Excess oil pressure because of restricted PCV valve	• Replace PCV valve
	• Oil pan drain plug loose or has stripped threads	• Repair as necessary and tighten
	• Rear oil gallery plug loose	• Use appropriate sealant on gallery plug and tighten
	• Rear camshaft plug loose or improperly seated	• Seat camshaft plug or replace and seal, as necessary
	• Distributor base gasket damaged	• Replace gasket
Excessive oil consumption	• Oil level too high	• Drain oil to specified level
	• Oil with wrong viscosity being used	• Replace with specified oil
	• PCV valve stuck closed	• Replace PCV valve
	• Valve stem oil deflectors (or seals) are damaged, missing, or incorrect type	• Replace valve stem oil deflectors
	• Valve stems or valve guides worn	• Measure stem-to-guide clearance and repair as necessary
	• Poorly fitted or missing valve cover baffles	• Replace valve cover
	• Piston rings broken or missing	• Replace broken or missing rings
	• Scuffed piston	• Replace piston
	• Incorrect piston ring gap	• Measure ring gap, repair as necessary
	• Piston rings sticking or excessively loose in grooves	• Measure ring side clearance, repair as necessary
	• Compression rings installed upside down	• Repair as necessary
	• Cylinder walls worn, scored, or glazed	• Repair as necessary
	• Piston ring gaps not properly staggered	• Repair as necessary
	• Excessive main or connecting rod bearing clearance	• Measure bearing clearance, repair as necessary

Troubleshooting Engine Mechanical Problems (cont.)

Problem	Cause	Solution
No oil pressure	• Low oil level	• Add oil to correct level
	• Oil pressure gauge, warning lamp or sending unit inaccurate	• Replace oil pressure gauge or warning lamp
	• Oil pump malfunction	• Replace oil pump
	• Oil pressure relief valve sticking	• Remove and inspect oil pressure relief valve assembly
	• Oil passages on pressure side of pump obstructed	• Inspect oil passages for obstruction
	• Oil pickup screen or tube obstructed	• Inspect oil pickup for obstruction
	• Loose oil inlet tube	• Tighten or seal inlet tube
Low oil pressure	• Low oil level	• Add oil to correct level
	• Inaccurate gauge, warning lamp or sending unit	• Replace oil pressure gauge or warning lamp
	• Oil excessively thin because of dilution, poor quality, or improper grade	• Drain and refill crankcase with recommended oil
	• Excessive oil temperature	• Correct cause of overheating engine
	• Oil pressure relief spring weak or sticking	• Remove and inspect oil pressure relief valve assembly
	• Oil inlet tube and screen assembly has restriction or air leak	• Remove and inspect oil inlet tube and screen assembly. (Fill inlet tube with lacquer thinner to locate leaks.)
	• Excessive oil pump clearance	• Measure clearances
	• Excessive main, rod, or camshaft bearing clearance	• Measure bearing clearances, repair as necessary
High oil pressure	• Improper oil viscosity	• Drain and refill crankcase with correct viscosity oil
	• Oil pressure gauge or sending unit inaccurate	• Replace oil pressure gauge
	• Oil pressure relief valve sticking closed	• Remove and inspect oil pressure relief valve assembly
Main bearing noise	• Insufficient oil supply	• Inspect for low oil level and low oil pressure
	• Main bearing clearance excessive	• Measure main bearing clearance, repair as necessary
	• Bearing insert missing	• Replace missing insert
	• Crankshaft end play excessive	• Measure end play, repair as necessary
	• Improperly tightened main bearing cap bolts	• Tighten bolts with specified torque
	• Loose flywheel or drive plate	• Tighten flywheel or drive plate attaching bolts
	• Loose or damaged vibration damper	• Repair as necessary

Troubleshooting Engine Mechanical Problems (cont.)

Problem	Cause	Solution
Connecting rod bearing noise	• Insufficient oil supply	• Inspect for low oil level and low oil pressure
	• Carbon build-up on piston	• Remove carbon from piston crown
	• Bearing clearance excessive or bearing missing	• Measure clearance, repair as necessary
	• Crankshaft connecting rod journal out-of-round	• Measure journal dimensions, repair or replace as necessary
	• Misaligned connecting rod or cap	• Repair as necessary
	• Connecting rod bolts tightened improperly	• Tighten bolts with specified torque
Piston noise	• Piston-to-cylinder wall clearance excessive (scuffed piston)	• Measure clearance and examine piston
	• Cylinder walls excessively tapered or out-of-round	• Measure cylinder wall dimensions, rebore cylinder
	• Piston ring broken	• Replace all rings on piston
	• Loose or seized piston pin	• Measure piston-to-pin clearance, repair as necessary
	• Connecting rods misaligned	• Measure rod alignment, straighten or replace
	• Piston ring side clearance excessively loose or tight	• Measure ring side clearance, repair as necessary
	• Carbon build-up on piston is excessive	• Remove carbon from piston
Valve actuating component noise	• Insufficient oil supply	• Check for: (a) Low oil level (b) Low oil pressure (c) Plugged push rods (d) Wrong hydraulic tappets (e) Restricted oil gallery (f) Excessive tappet to bore clearance
	• Push rods worn or bent	• Replace worn or bent push rods
	• Rocker arms or pivots worn	• Replace worn rocker arms or pivots
	• Foreign objects or chips in hydraulic tappets	• Clean tappets
	• Excessive tappet leak-down	• Replace valve tappet
	• Tappet face worn	• Replace tappet; inspect corresponding cam lobe for wear
	• Broken or cocked valve springs	• Properly seat cocked springs; replace broken springs
	• Stem-to-guide clearance excessive	• Measure stem-to-guide clearance, repair as required
	• Valve bent	• Replace valve
	• Loose rocker arms	• Tighten bolts with specified torque
	• Valve seat runout excessive	• Regrind valve seat/valves
	• Missing valve lock	• Install valve lock
	• Push rod rubbing or contacting cylinder head	• Remove cylinder head and remove obstruction in head
	• Excessive engine oil (four-cylinder engine)	• Correct oil level

Troubleshooting the Cooling System

Problem	Cause	Solution
High temperature gauge indication—overheating	• Coolant level low • Fan belt loose • Radiator hose(s) collapsed • Radiator airflow blocked • Faulty radiator cap • Ignition timing incorrect • Idle speed low • Air trapped in cooling system • Heavy traffic driving • Incorrect cooling system component(s) installed • Faulty thermostat • Water pump shaft broken or impeller loose • Radiator tubes clogged • Cooling system clogged • Casting flash in cooling passages • Brakes dragging • Excessive engine friction • Antifreeze concentration over 68% • Missing air seals • Faulty gauge or sending unit • Loss of coolant flow caused by leakage or foaming • Viscous fan drive failed	• Replenish coolant • Adjust fan belt tension • Replace hose(s) • Remove restriction (bug screen, fog lamps, etc.) • Replace radiator cap • Adjust ignition timing • Adjust idle speed • Purge air • Operate at fast idle in neutral intermittently to cool engine • Install proper component(s) • Replace thermostat • Replace water pump • Flush radiator • Flush system • Repair or replace as necessary. Flash may be visible by removing cooling system components or removing core plugs. • Repair brakes • Repair engine • Lower antifreeze concentration percentage • Replace air seals • Repair or replace faulty component • Repair or replace leaking component, replace coolant • Replace unit
Low temperature indication—undercooling	• Thermostat stuck open • Faulty gauge or sending unit	• Replace thermostat • Repair or replace faulty component
Coolant loss—boilover	• Overfilled cooling system • Quick shutdown after hard (hot) run • Air in system resulting in occasional "burping" of coolant • Insufficient antifreeze allowing coolant boiling point to be too low • Antifreeze deteriorated because of age or contamination • Leaks due to loose hose clamps, loose nuts, bolts, drain plugs, faulty hoses, or defective radiator	• Reduce coolant level to proper specification • Allow engine to run at fast idle prior to shutdown • Purge system • Add antifreeze to raise boiling point • Replace coolant • Pressure test system to locate source of leak(s) then repair as necessary

Troubleshooting the Cooling System (cont.)

Problem	Cause	Solution
Coolant loss—boilover	• Faulty head gasket • Cracked head, manifold, or block • Faulty radiator cap	• Replace head gasket • Replace as necessary • Replace cap
Coolant entry into crankcase or cylinder(s)	• Faulty head gasket • Crack in head, manifold or block	• Replace head gasket • Replace as necessary
Coolant recovery system inoperative	• Coolant level low • Leak in system • Pressure cap not tight or seal missing, or leaking • Pressure cap defective • Overflow tube clogged or leaking • Recovery bottle vent restricted	• Replenish coolant to FULL mark • Pressure test to isolate leak and repair as necessary • Repair as necessary • Replace cap • Repair as necessary • Remove restriction
Noise	• Fan contacting shroud • Loose water pump impeller • Glazed fan belt • Loose fan belt • Rough surface on drive pulley • Water pump bearing worn • Belt alignment	• Reposition shroud and inspect engine mounts • Replace pump • Apply silicone or replace belt • Adjust fan belt tension • Replace pulley • Remove belt to isolate. Replace pump. • Check pulley alignment. Repair as necessary.
No coolant flow through heater core	• Restricted return inlet in water pump • Heater hose collapsed or restricted • Restricted heater core • Restricted outlet in thermostat housing • Intake manifold bypass hole in cylinder head restricted • Faulty heater control valve • Intake manifold coolant passage restricted	• Remove restriction • Remove restriction or replace hose • Remove restriction or replace core • Remove flash or restriction • Remove restriction • Replace valve • Remove restriction or replace intake manifold

NOTE: *Immediately after shutdown, the engine enters a condition known as heat soak. This is caused by the cooling system being inoperative while engine temperature is still high. If coolant temperature rises above boiling point, expansion and pressure may push some coolant out of the radiator overflow tube. If this does not occur frequently it is considered normal.*

Troubleshooting the Serpentine Drive Belt

Problem	Cause	Solution
Tension sheeting fabric failure (woven fabric on outside circumference of belt has cracked or separated from body of belt)	• Grooved or backside idler pulley diameters are less than minimum recommended • Tension sheeting contacting (rubbing) stationary object • Excessive heat causing woven fabric to age • Tension sheeting splice has fractured	• Replace pulley(s) not conforming to specification • Correct rubbing condition • Replace belt • Replace belt
Noise (objectional squeal, squeak, or rumble is heard or felt while drive belt is in operation)	• Belt slippage • Bearing noise • Belt misalignment • Belt-to-pulley mismatch • Driven component inducing vibration • System resonant frequency inducing vibration	• Adjust belt • Locate and repair • Align belt/pulley(s) • Install correct belt • Locate defective driven component and repair • Vary belt tension within specifications. Replace belt.
Rib chunking (one or more ribs has separated from belt body)	• Foreign objects imbedded in pulley grooves • Installation damage • Drive loads in excess of design specifications • Insufficient internal belt adhesion	• Remove foreign objects from pulley grooves • Replace belt • Adjust belt tension • Replace belt
Rib or belt wear (belt ribs contact bottom of pulley grooves)	• Pulley(s) misaligned • Mismatch of belt and pulley groove widths • Abrasive environment • Rusted pulley(s) • Sharp or jagged pulley groove tips • Rubber deteriorated	• Align pulley(s) • Replace belt • Replace belt • Clean rust from pulley(s) • Replace pulley • Replace belt
Longitudinal belt cracking (cracks between two ribs)	• Belt has mistracked from pulley groove • Pulley groove tip has worn away rubber-to-tensile member	• Replace belt • Replace belt
Belt slips	• Belt slipping because of insufficient tension • Belt or pulley subjected to substance (belt dressing, oil, ethylene glycol) that has reduced friction • Driven component bearing failure • Belt glazed and hardened from heat and excessive slippage	• Adjust tension • Replace belt and clean pulleys • Replace faulty component bearing • Replace belt
"Groove jumping" (belt does not maintain correct position on pulley, or turns over and/or runs off pulleys)	• Insufficient belt tension • Pulley(s) not within design tolerance • Foreign object(s) in grooves	• Adjust belt tension • Replace pulley(s) • Remove foreign objects from grooves

Troubleshooting the Serpentine Drive Belt (cont.)

Problem	Cause	Solution
"Groove jumping" (belt does not maintain correct position on pulley, or turns over and/or runs off pulleys)	• Excessive belt speed • Pulley misalignment • Belt-to-pulley profile mismatched • Belt cordline is distorted	• Avoid excessive engine acceleration • Align pulley(s) • Install correct belt • Replace belt
Belt broken (Note: identify and correct problem before replacement belt is installed)	• Excessive tension • Tensile members damaged during belt installation • Belt turnover • Severe pulley misalignment • Bracket, pulley, or bearing failure	• Replace belt and adjust tension to specification • Replace belt • Replace belt • Align pulley(s) • Replace defective component and belt
Cord edge failure (tensile member exposed at edges of belt or separated from belt body)	• Excessive tension • Drive pulley misalignment • Belt contacting stationary object • Pulley irregularities • Improper pulley construction • Insufficient adhesion between tensile member and rubber matrix	• Adjust belt tension • Align pulley • Correct as necessary • Replace pulley • Replace pulley • Replace belt and adjust tension to specifications
Sporadic rib cracking (multiple cracks in belt ribs at random intervals)	• Ribbed pulley(s) diameter less than minimum specification • Backside bend flat pulley(s) diameter less than minimum • Excessive heat condition causing rubber to harden • Excessive belt thickness • Belt overcured • Excessive tension	• Replace pulley(s) • Replace pulley(s) • Correct heat condition as necessary • Replace belt • Replace belt • Adjust belt tension

GENERAL ENGINE SPECIFICATIONS

Years	VIN	Engine No. Cyl. Liters	Fuel System Type	SAE Net Horsepower @ rpm	SAE Net Torque @ rpm (ft. lbs.)	Bore × Stroke (in.)	Compression Ratio	Oil Pressure @ rpm
1984	C	4–2.2L	2BBL	84 @ 4800	111 @ 2400	3.44 × 3.62	8.5:1	60–90 @ 2000
	G	4–2.6L	2BBL	92 @ 4500	131 @ 2500	3.59 × 3.86	8.2:1	56 @ 2000
1985	C	4–2.2L	2BBL	84 @ 4800	111 @ 2400	3.44 × 3.62	8.5:1	60–90 @ 2000
	G	4–2.6L	2BBL	92 @ 4500	131 @ 2500	3.59 × 3.86	8.2:1	56 @ 2000
1986	C	4–2.2L	2BBL	96 @ 5200	119 @ 3200	3.44 × 3.62	9.5:1	50 @ 2000
	G	4–2.6L	2BBL	101 @ 5600	140 @ 2800	3.59 × 3.86	8.7:1	85 @ 2500
1987	C	4–2.2L	2BBL	96 @ 5200	119 @ 3200	3.44 × 3.62	9.5:1	50 @ 2000
	K	4–2.5L	EFI	100 @ 4800	135 @ 2800	3.44 × 4.09	8.9:1	30–80 @ 3000
	G	4–2.6L	2BBL	101 @ 5600	140 @ 2800	3.59 × 3.86	8.7:1	85 @ 2500
1988	K	4–2.5L	EFI	100 @ 4800	135 @ 2800	3.44 × 4.09	8.9:1	30–80 @ 3000
	3	6–3.0L	EFI	142 @ 5000	173 @ 2800	3.59 × 2.99	8.9:1	30–80 @ 3000
1989	K	4–2.5L	EFI	100 @ 4800	135 @ 2800	3.44 × 4.09	8.9:1	30–80 @ 3000
	J	4–2.5L	TURBO	150 @ 4800	180 @ 2000	3.44 × 4.09	7.8:1	30–80 @ 3000
	3	6–3.0L	EFI	142 @ 5000	173 @ 2800	3.59 × 2.99	8.9:1	30–80 @ 3000

GENERAL ENGINE SPECIFICATIONS

Years	VIN	Engine No. Cyl. Liters	Fuel System Type	SAE Net Horsepower @ rpm	SAE Net Torque @ rpm (ft. lbs.)	Bore × Stroke (in.)	Compression Ratio	Oil Pressure @ rpm
1990	K	4–2.5L	EFI	100 @ 4800	135 @ 2800	3.44 × 4.09	8.9:1	30–80 @ 3000
	J	4–2.5L	TURBO	150 @ 4800	180 @ 2000	3.44 × 4.09	7.8:1	30–80 @ 3000
	3	6–3.0L	EFI	142 @ 5000	173 @ 2800	3.59 × 2.99	8.9:1	30–80 @ 3000
	R	6–3.3L	EFI	150 @ 4000	185 @ 3600	3.66 × 3.19	8.9:1	30–80 @ 3000
1991	K	4–2.5L	EFI	100 @ 4800	135 @ 2800	3.44 × 4.09	8.9:1	30–80 @ 3000
	3	6–3.0L	EFI	142 @ 5000	173 @ 2800	3.59 × 2.99	8.9:1	30–80 @ 3000
	R	6–3.3L	EFI	150 @ 4000	185 @ 3600	3.66 × 3.19	8.9:1	30–80 @ 3000

VALVE SPECIFICATIONS CHART

Years	VIN	Engine No. Cyl. Liters	Seat Angle (Deg.)	Face Angle (Deg.)	Spring Test Pressure (lbs.)	Spring Installed Height (in.)	Stem-To-Guide Clearance In. Intake	Stem-To-Guide Clearance In. Exhaust	Stem Diameter (in.) Intake	Stem Diameter (in.) Exhaust
1984	C	4–2.2L	45	45	95	1.65	0.001–0.003	0.0030–0.0047	0.3124	0.3103
	G	4–2.6L	45	45	61	1.59	0.001–0.004	0.0020–0.0060	0.3150	0.3150
1985	C	4–2.2L	45	45	95	1.65	0.001–0.003	0.0030–0.0047	0.3124	0.3103
	G	4–2.6L	45	45	61	1.59	0.001–0.004	0.0020–0.0060	0.3150	0.3150
1986	C	4–2.2L	45	45	95	1.65	0.001–0.003	0.0030–0.0047	0.3124	0.3103
	G	4–2.6L	45	45	61	1.59	0.001–0.004	0.0020–0.0060	0.3150	0.3150
1987	C	4–2.2L	45	45	95	1.65	0.001–0.003	0.0030–0.0047	0.3124	0.3103
	K	4–2.5L	45	45	115	1.65	0.001–0.003	0.0030–0.0047	0.3124	0.3103
	G	4–2.6L	45	45	61	1.59	0.001–0.004	0.0020–0.0060	0.3150	0.3150
1988	K	4–2.5L	45	45	115	1.65	0.001–0.003	0.0030–0.0047	0.3124	0.3103
	3	6–3.0L	44.5	45.5	73	1.59	0.001–0.002	0.0020–0.0030	0.3130–0.3140	0.3120–0.3130
1989	K	4–2.5L	45	45	115	1.65	0.001–0.003	0.0030–0.0047	0.3124	0.3103
	J	4–2.5L	45	45	115	1.65	0.001–0.003	0.0030–0.0047	0.3124	0.3103
	3	6–3.0L	44.5	45.5	73	1.59	0.001–0.002	0.0020–0.0030	0.3130–0.3140	0.3120–0.3130
1990	K	4–2.5L	45	45	115	1.65	0.001–0.003	0.0030–0.0047	0.3124	0.3103
	J	4–2.5L	45	45	115	1.65	0.001–0.003	0.0030–0.0047	0.3124	0.3103
	3	6–3.0L	44.5	45.5	73	1.59	0.001–0.002	0.0020–0.0030	0.3130–0.3140	0.3120–0.3130
	R	6–3.3L	45	44.5	60	1.56				
1991	K	4–2.5L	45	45	115	1.65	0.001–0.003	0.0030–0.0047	0.3124	0.3103
	3	6–3.0L	44.5	45.5	73	1.59	0.001–0.002	0.0020–0.0030	0.3130–0.3140	0.3120–0.3130
	R	6–3.3L	45	44.5	60	1.56	0.002–0.016	0.0020–0.0160	0.3110–0.3120	0.3110–0.3120

CAMSHAFT SPECIFICATIONS

Years	Vin	Engine No. Cyl. Liters	Journal Diameter (in.) 1	2	3	4	5	Bearing Clearance (in.)	Camshaft Endplay (in.)
1984	C	4–2.2L	1.375–1.376	1.375–1.376	1.375–1.376	1.375–1.376	1.375–1.376	0.002–0.004	0.005–0.013
	G	4–2.6L	—	—	—	—	—	0.002–0.008	0.004–0.008
1985	C	4–2.2L	1.375–1.376	1.375–1.376	1.375–1.376	1.375–1.376	1.375–1.376	0.002–0.004	0.005–0.013
	G	4–2.6L	—	—	—	—	—	0.002–0.008	0.004–0.008
1986	C	4–2.2L	1.375–1.376	1.375–1.376	1.375–1.376	1.375–1.376	1.375–1.376	0.002–0.004	0.005–0.013
	G	4–2.6L	—	—	—	—	—	0.002–0.008	0.004–0.008
1987	C	4–2.2L	1.375–1.376	1.375–1.376	1.375–1.376	1.375–1.376	1.375–1.376	0.002–0.004	0.005–0.013
	K	4–2.5L	1.375–1.376	1.375–1.376	1.375–1.376	1.375–1.376	1.375–1.376	0.002–0.004	0.005–0.020
	G	4–2.6L	—	—	—	—	—	0.002–0.008	0.004–0.008
1988	K	4–2.5L	1.375–1.376	1.375–1.376	1.375–1.376	1.375–1.376	1.375–1.376	0.002–0.004	0.005–0.020
	3	6–3.0L	—	—	—	—	—		

CAMSHAFT SPECIFICATIONS

| Years | Vin | Engine No. Cyl. Liters | Journal Diameter (in.) | | | | | Bearing Clearance (in.) | Camshaft Endplay (in.) |
			1	2	3	4	5		
1989	K	4–2.5L	1.375–1.376	1.375–1.376	1.375–1.376	1.375–1.376	1.375–1.376	0.002–0.004	0.005–0.020
	J	4–2.5L	1.375–1.376	1.375–1.376	1.375–1.376	1.375–1.376	1.375–1.376	0.002–0.004	0.005–0.020
	3	6–3.0L	—	—	—	—	—	—	—
1990	K	4–2.5L	1.375–1.376	1.375–1.376	1.375–1.376	1.375–1.376	1.375–1.376	0.002–0.004	0.005–0.020
	J	4–2.5L	1.375–1.376	1.375–1.376	1.375–1.376	1.375–1.376	1.375–1.376	0.002–0.004	0.005–0.020
	3	6–3.0L	—	—	—	—	—	—	—
	R	6–3.3L	1.997–1.999	1.980–1.982	1.965–1.96	1.949–1.952	—	0.001–0.005	0.005–0.012
1991	K	4–2.5L	1.375–1.376	1.375–1.376	1.375–1.376	1.375–1.376	1.375–1.376	0.002–0.004	0.005–0.020
	3	6–3.0L	—	—	—	—	—	—	—
	R	6–3.3L	1.997–1.999	1.980–1.982	1.965–1.96	1.949–1.952	—	0.001–0.005	0.005–0.012

CRANKSHAFT AND CONNECTING ROD SPECIFICATIONS

| Years | VIN | Engine No. Cyl. Liters | Crankshaft | | | | Connecting Rod | | |
			Main Brg. Journal Dia.	Main Brg. Oil Clearance	Shaft End-Play	Thrust On No.	Journal Diameter	Oil Clearance	Side Clearance
1984	C	4–2.2L	2.3630–2.3630	0.0003–0.0031	0.002–0.007	3	1.9680–1.9690	0.0008–0.0034	0.005–0.013
	G	4–2.6L	2.3622	0.0008–0.0028	0.002–0.007	3	2.0866	0.0008–0.0028	0.004–0.010
1985	C	4–2.2L	2.3630–2.3630	0.0003–0.0031	0.002–0.007	3	1.9680–1.9690	0.0008–0.0034	0.005–0.013
	G	4–2.6L	2.3622	0.0008–0.0028	0.002–0.007	3	2.0866	0.0008–0.0028	0.004–0.010
1986	C	4–2.2L	2.3630–2.3630	0.0003–0.0031	0.002–0.007	3	1.9680–1.9690	0.0008–0.0034	0.005–0.013
	G	4–2.6L	2.3622	0.0008–0.0028	0.002–0.007	3	2.0866	0.0008–0.0028	0.004–0.010
1987	C	4–2.2L	2.3630–2.3630	0.0003–0.0031	0.002–0.007	3	1.9680–1.9690	0.0008–0.0034	0.005–0.013
	K	4–2.5L	2.3630–2.3630	0.0003–0.0031	0.002–0.007	3	1.9680–1.9690	0.0008–0.0034	0.005–0.013
	G	4–2.6L	2.3622	0.0008–0.0028	0.002–0.007	3	2.0866	0.0008–0.0028	0.004–0.010
1988	K	4–2.5L	2.3630–2.3630	0.0003–0.0031	0.002–0.007	3	1.9680–1.9690	0.0008–0.0034	0.005–0.013
	3	6–3.0L	2.3610–2.3630	0.0006–0.0020	0.002–0.010	3	1.9680–1.9690	0.0008–0.0028	0.004–0.010
1989	K	4–2.5L	2.3630–2.3630	0.0003–0.0031	0.002–0.007	3	1.9680–1.9690	0.0008–0.0034	0.005–0.013
	J	4–2.5L	2.3630–2.3630	0.0003–0.0031	0.002–0.007	3	1.9680–1.9690	0.0008–0.0034	0.005–0.013
	3	6–3.0L	2.3610–2.3630	0.0006–0.0020	0.002–0.010	3	1.9680–1.9690	0.0008–0.0028	0.004–0.010
1990	K	4–2.5L	2.3630–2.3630	0.0003–0.0031	0.002–0.007	3	1.9680–1.9690	0.0008–0.0034	0.005–0.013
	J	4–2.5L	2.3630–2.3630	0.0003–0.0031	0.002–0.007	3	1.9680–1.9690	0.0008–0.0034	0.005–0.013
	3	6–3.0L	2.3610–2.3630	0.0006–0.0020	0.002–0.010	3	1.9680–1.9690	0.0008–0.0028	0.004–0.010
	R	6–3.3L	2.5190	0.0007–0.0022	0.001–0.007	2	2.283	0.0008–0.0030	0.005–0.015
1991	K	4–2.5L	2.3630–2.3630	0.0003–0.0031	0.002–0.007	3	1.9680–1.9690	0.0008–0.0034	0.005–0.013
	3	6–3.0L	2.3610–2.3630	0.0006–0.0020	0.002–0.010	3	1.9680–1.9690	0.0008–0.0028	0.004–0.010
	R	6–3.3L	2.5190	0.0007–0.0022	0.001–0.007	2	2.283	0.0008–0.0030	0.005–0.015

PISTON AND RING SPECIFICATIONS

| Years | VIN | Engine No. Cyl. Liters | Piston Clearance | Ring Gap | | | Ring Side Clearance | | |
				Top Compression	Bottom Compression	Oil Control	Top Compression	Bottom Compression	Oil Control
1984	C	4–2.2L	0.0005–0.0015	0.0110–0.0120	0.0110–0.0120	0.0160–0.0550	0.0016–0.0028	0.0008–0.0020	0.0008–0.0020
	G	4–2.6L	0.0008–0.0016	0.0100–0.0180	0.0100–0.0180	0.0078–0.0350	0.0015–0.0031	0.0015–0.0037	—

PISTON AND RING SPECIFICATIONS

Years	VIN	Engine No. Cyl. Liters	Piston Clearance	Ring Gap			Ring Side Clearance		
				Top Compression	Bottom Compression	Oil Control	Top Compression	Bottom Compression	Oil Control
1985	C	4-2.2L	0.0005-0.0015	0.0110-0.0120	0.0110-0.0120	0.0160-0.0550	0.0016-0.0028	0.0008-0.0020	0.0008-0.0020
	G	4-2.6L	0.0008-0.0016	0.0100-0.0180	0.0100-0.0180	0.0078-0.0350	0.0015-0.0031	0.0015-0.0037	—
1986	C	4-2.2L	0.0005-0.0015	0.0110-0.0120	0.0110-0.0120	0.0160-0.0550	0.0016-0.0028	0.0008-0.0020	0.0008-0.0020
	G	4-2.6L	0.0008-0.0016	0.0100-0.0180	0.0100-0.0180	0.0078-0.0350	0.0015-0.0031	0.0015-0.0037	—
1987	C	4-2.2L	0.0005-0.0015	0.0110-0.0120	0.0110-0.0120	0.0160-0.0550	0.0016-0.0028	0.0008-0.0020	0.0008-0.0020
	K	4-2.5L	0.0005-0.0015	0.0110-0.0120	0.0100-0.0120	0.0160-0.0550	0.0016-0.0028	0.0008-0.0020	0.0008-0.0020
	G	4-2.5L	0.0005-0.0015	0.0110-0.0120	0.0100-0.0120	0.0160-0.0550	0.0016-0.0028	0.0008-0.0020	0.0008-0.0020
1988	K	4-2.5L	0.0005-0.0015	0.0110-0.0120	0.0110-0.0120	0.0160-0.0550	0.0016-0.0028	0.0008-0.0020	0.0008-0.0020
	3	6-3.0L	0.0008-0.0015	0.0120-0.0180	0.0100-0.0160	0.0120-0.0350	0.0020-0.0035	0.0008-0.0020	—
1989	K	4-2.5L	0.0005-0.0015	0.0110-0.0120	0.0110-0.0120	0.0160-0.0550	0.0016-0.0028	0.0008-0.0020	0.0008-0.0020
	J	4-2.5L	0.0006-0.0018	0.0100-0.0200	0.0080-0.0190	0.0150-0.0550	0.0016-0.0030	0.0016-0.0030	0.0002-0.0080
	3	6-3.0L	0.0008-0.0015	0.0120-0.0180	0.0100-0.0160	0.0120-0.0350	0.0020-0.0035	0.0008-0.0020	—
1990	K	4-2.5L	0.0005-0.0015	0.0110-0.0120	0.0110-0.0120	0.0160-0.0550	0.0016-0.0028	0.0008-0.0020	0.0008-0.0020
	J	4-2.5L	0.0006-0.0018	0.0100-0.0200	0.0080-0.0190	0.0150-0.0550	0.0016-0.0030	0.0016-0.0030	0.0002-0.0080
	3	6-3.0L	0.0008-0.0015	0.0120-0.0180	0.0100-0.0160	0.0120-0.0350	0.0020-0.0035	0.0008-0.0020	—
	R	6-3.3L	0.0009-0.0022	0.0120-0.0220	0.0120-0.0220	0.0100-0.0400	0.0012-0.0037	0.0012-0.0037	0.0005-0.0089
1991	K	4-2.5L	0.0005-0.0015	0.0110-0.0120	0.0110-0.0120	0.0160-0.0550	0.0016-0.0028	0.0008-0.0020	0.0008-0.0020
	3	6-3.0L	0.0008-0.0015	0.0120-0.0180	0.0100-0.0160	0.0120-0.0350	0.0020-0.0035	0.0008-0.0020	—
	R	6-3.3L	0.0009-0.0022	0.0120-0.0220	0.0120-0.0220	0.0100-0.0400	0.0012-0.0037	0.0012-0.0037	0.0005-0.0089

TORQUE SPECIFICATIONS

All readings in ft. lbs.

Years	VIN	Engine No. Cyl. Liters	Cylinder Head	Main Bearing	Rod Bearing	Crankshaft Damper	Flywheel	Manifold	
								Intake	Exhaust
1984	C	4-2.2L	①	30 ②	40 ②	50	70	17	17
	G	4-2.6L	70	58	34	87	70	13	13

TORQUE SPECIFICATIONS
All readings in ft. lbs.

Years	VIN	Engine No. Cyl. Liters	Cylinder Head	Main Bearing	Rod Bearing	Crankshaft Damper	Flywheel	Manifold Intake	Manifold Exhaust
1985	C	4-2.2L	①	30②	40②	50	70	17	17
	G	4-2.6L	70	58	34	87	70	13	13
1986	C	4-2.2L	①	30②	40②	50	70	17	17
	G	4-2.6L	70	58	34	87	70	13	13
1987	C	4-2.2L	①	30②	40②	50	70	17	17
	K	4-2.5L	①	30②	40②	50	70	17	17
	G	4-2.6L	70	58	34	87	70	13	13
1988	K	4-2.5L	①	30②	40②	50	70	17	17
	3	6-3.0L	70	60	38	110	70	17	17
1989	K	4-2.5L	①	30②	40②	50	70	17	17
	J	4-2.5L	①	30②	40②	50	70	17	17
	3	6-3.0L	70	60	38	110	70	17	17
1990	K	4-2.5L	①	30②	40②	50	70	17	17
	J	4-2.5L	①	30②	40②	50	70	17	17
	3	6-3.0L	70	60	38	110	70	17	17
	R	6-3.3L	③	30②	40②	40	70	17	17
1991	K	4-2.5L	①	30②	40②	50	70	17	17
	3	6-3.0L	70	60	38	110	70	17	17
	R	6-3.3L	③	30②	40②	40	70	17	17

① Tighten in 3 steps:
1st Step: 45 ft. lbs.
2nd Step: 65 ft. lbs.
3rd Step: 65 ft. lbs. plus additional 90 degree turn

② Plus an additional 90 degree turn
③ Tighten in 3 steps:
1st Step: 45 ft. lbs.
2nd Step: 65 ft. lbs.

3rd Step: 65 ft. lbs. plus additional 90 degree turn
Last, torque the small bolt in the rear of the head to 25 ft. lbs.

Engine

REMOVAL AND INSTALLATION

Engine Removal and Installation procedures are similar on all models.
1. Disconnect the negative battery cable.
2. Scribe the hood hinge outlines on the hood, and remove the hood.
3. Drain the cooling system. Remove the radiator hoses from the radiator and engine connections.

— CAUTION —

When draining the coolant, keep in mind that cats and dogs are attracted by the ethylene glycol antifreeze, and are quite likely to drink any that is left in an uncovered container or in puddles on the ground. This will prove fatal in sufficient quantity. Always drain the coolant into a sealable container. Coolant should be reused unless it is contaminated or several years old.

4. Remove the radiator and fan assembly.
5. Remove the air conditioner compressor from the engine and mounting brackets and hoses connected. Position the assembly to the side and secure out of the way.
6. Remove the power steering pump from the engine with mounting brackets and hoses connected. Position the assembly to the side and secure out of the way.
7. Disconnect all electrical connectors at the alternator, carburetor, injection unit and engine.

8. Disconnect the fuel line from the gas tank at the fuel pump. Disconnect the heat hoses from the engine. Disconnect the accelerator cable at the carburetor.
9. Remove the alternator. Disconnect the clutch cable from the clutch lever, if equipped with a manual transaxle.
10. Remove the transaxle case lower cover.
11. Automatic transaxle, mark the flex plate to torque converter location.
12. Remove the bolts that mount the converter to the flex plate. Attach a small C-clamp to the front bottom of the converter housing to prevent the converter from falling off of the transaxle.
13. Disconnect the starter motor wiring and remove the starter motor.
14. Disconnect the exhaust pipe from the exhaust manifold.
15. Remove the right inner engine splash shield. Drain the engine oil and remove the oil filter. Disconnect the engine ground strap.

— CAUTION —

The EPA warns that prolonged contact with used engine oil may cause a number of skin disorders, including cancer! You should make every effort to minimize your exposure to used engine oil. Protective gloves should be worn when changing the oil. Wash your hands and any other exposed skin areas as soon as possible after exposure to used engine oil. Soap and water, or waterless hand cleaner should be used.

16. Attach hoist to the engine.
17. Support the transaxle. Apply slight upward pressure with the chain hoist and remove the through bolt from the right (timing case cover) engine mount.

RIGHT ENGINE MOUNT ASSEMBLY
TIGHTEN YOKE **NUT** FIRST
TIGHTEN YOKE SCREW SECOND

Ⓑ YOKE SCREW

STRUT

Ⓒ YOKE NUT

RIGHT RAIL

LEFT RAIL

WEIGHT

INSULATOR

FRONT CROSSMEMBER

Ⓨ FRONT MOUNT ASSEMBLY

FRONT MOUNT ASSEMBLY
TIGHTEN FOUR BRACKET SCREWS
IN SEQUENCE - 1,2,3,4 TO TORQUE

W = 12 mm
X = 7 mm

PASS SIDE W — X DRIVER SIDE

FWD

VIEW IN DIRECTION OF ARROW Y

TORQUE	
A — 169 N•m (125 FT. LBS.)	
B — 133 N•m (100 FT. LBS.)	
C — 102 N•m (75 FT. LBS.)	
D — 68 N•m (50 FT. LBS.)	
E — 54 N•m (40 FT. LBS.)	
F — 21 N•m (16 FT. LBS.)	

Engine assembly mounting — 2.2/2.5L engines

RIGHT ENGINE MOUNT
ASSEMBLY
TIGHTEN YOKE NUT FIRST
TIGHTEN YOKE SCREW SECOND

DAMPENER WEIGHT

LEFT RAIL

RIGHT ENGINE SUPPORT ASSEMBLY

LEFT INSULATOR

YOKE NUT Ⓒ

RIGHT RAIL

YOKE SCREW Ⓑ

FWD

FRONT CROSSMEMBER

VIEW IN DIRECTION OF ARROW Y

W = 12 MM
X = 7 MM

PASS SIDE W — X DRIVER SIDE

FWD

FRONT ENGINE SUPPORT ASSEMBLY

VIEW IN DIRECTION OF ARROW X

TORQUE	
A — 169 N•m (125 FT. LBS.)	
B — 133 N•m (100 FT. LBS.)	
C — 102 N•m (75 FT. LBS.)	
D — 68 N•m (50 FT. LBS.)	
E — 54 N•m (40 FT. LBS.)	
F — 21 N•m (16 FT. LBS.)	
G — 23 N•m (200 IN. LBS.)	

Engine assembly mounting — 3.0L engine

	TORQUE	
A	68 N·m (50 FT. LBS.)	
B	136 N·m (100 FT. LBS.)	
C	102 N·m (75 FT. LBS.)	
D	23 N·m (200 IN. LBS.)	
E	54 N·m (40 FT. LBS.)	

Engine assembly mounting — 3.3L engine

NOTE: **If the complete engine mount is to be removed, mark the insulator position on the side rail to insure exact reinstallation location.**

18. Remove the transaxle to cylinder block mounting bolts.
19. Remove the front engine mount through bolt. Remove the manual transaxle anti-roll strut.
20. Remove the insulator through bolt from the inside wheel house mount, or remove the insulator bracket to transaxle mounting bolt.
21. Raise the engine slowly with the hoist (transaxle supported). Separate the engine and transaxle and remove the engine.
To install:
22. With the hoist attached to the engine. Lower the engine into engine compartment.
23. Align the converter to flex plate and the engine mounts. Install all mounting bolts loosely until all are in position, then tighten to 40 ft. lbs.
24. Install the engine to transaxle mounting bolts. Tighten to 70 ft. lbs.
25. Remove the engine hoist and transaxle support.
26. Secure the engine ground strap.
27. Install the inner splash shield.
28. Install the starter assembly.
29. Install the exhaust system.
30. Install the transaxle case lower cover. (Manual Transaxle)
31. Remove the C-clamp from the torque converter housing, (Automatic Transaxle)
32. Align flex plate and torque converter with mark previously made. (Automatic Transaxle).
33. Install the convertor to flex plate mounting screws. Tighten to (40 ft. lbs.).
34. Install the case lower cover. (Automatic Transaxle).
35. Connect the clutch cable. (Manual Transaxle)

36. Install the power steering pump.
37. Install the air conditioning compressor.
38. Install the alternator.
39. Connect all wiring.
40. Install the radiator, fan and shroud assembly.
41. Connect all cooling system hoses, accelerator cable and fuel lines.
42. Install the engine oil filter. Fill the crankcase to proper oil level.
43. Fill the cooling system.
44. Adjust linkages.
45. Install the air cleaner and hoses.
46. Install the hood.

Electric cooling fan and motor

A-28 N•m (250 IN. LB.)
B-95 N•m (70 FT. LBS.)

Right side engine mount — 4 cylinder engines

A-95 N•m (70 FT. LBS.)
B-54 N•m (40 FT. LBS.)

Front engine mount — 4 cylinder engines

68 N•m
(50 FT. LBS.)

54 N•m
(40 FT. LBS.)

Left side engine mount — 4 cylinder engines

47. Connect the battery cables, positive cable first.
48. Start the engine and run until normal operation temperature is indicated. Adjust the carburetor.

ENGINE/TRANSAXLE POSITIONING

The insulator on the frame rail (right side) and on the transmission bracket (left side) are adjustable to allow right/left drive

Left side engine mount movement

train adjustment in relation to the driveshaft distress, front end damage or insulator replacement.

Adjustment

1. Remove the load on the engine mounts by carefully supporting the weight of the engine/transaxle assembly on a floor jack.
2. Loosen the right engine mount insulator vertical mounting bolts and the front engine mount bracket to cross member mounting nuts and bolts. The left insulator is sleeved to provide lateral movement.
3. Pry the engine/transaxle assembly to the left or right as required.
4. Tighten the right engine mount to 20 ft. lbs. and front engine mount to 40 ft. lbs.

Rocker (Valve) Cover

REMOVAL AND INSTALLATION

2.2L Engine

1. Disconnect the negative battery cable.
2. Remove the air cleaner assembly. Remove or relocate any hoses or cables that will interfere with rocker cover removal.
3. Depress the retaining clip that holds the PCV module in the rocker cover and turn the module counterclockwise to remove the module.
4. Remove the cover mounting bolts and the rocker cover from the cylinder head.
5. Clean the cover and head mounting surfaces. Install the PCV module in rocker cover. Turn clockwise to install.

NOTE: With PCV module installed, snorkel must point upward, toward top of valve cover. Snorkel should be free to rotate.

6. Apply RTV sealant to the rocker cover mounting rail, or install a new cover gasket if provided.
7. Install the rocker cover and tighten to 105 inch lbs.
8. Install the vacuum hoses and spark plug wires.
9. Install the air cleaner assembly.
10. Connect the battery cable.

2.5L Engine

A curtain aiding air/oil separation is located beneath the rocker cover on the cylinder head. The curtain is retained by rubber bumpers.

1. Disconnect the negative battery cable.
2. Remove the air cleaner assembly.
3. Remove any vacuum hoses necessary and relocate spark plug wires.
4. Remove the cover screws and remove the cover.
5. Remove the air/oil separation curtain.

2.2L PCV module

6. Clean the cylinder head, curtain and cover mating surfaces before installation.

7. Install a gasket on the valve cover while pushing the tabs through slots in cover.

8. Install the curtain (manifold side first) with cutouts over cam towers and against cylinder head. Press opposite side into position below the cylinder head rail.

9. Install the cover and tighten to 105 inch lbs..

10. Install the vacuum hoses and spark plug wires.

11. Install the air cleaner assembly.

12. Connect the battery cable.

2.6L Engine

1. Disconnect the negative battery cable.

2. Remove the air cleaner assembly. Remove or relocate any hoses or cables that will interfere with rocker cover removal.

3. Disconnect the hoses to the PCV tube.

4. Remove the cover mounting bolts and remove the rocker cover from the cylinder head. The water pump pulley belt shield is attached at rear of rocker cover.

5. Clean the cover and head mounting surfaces.

6. Apply RTV sealant to the top of the rubber cam seal and install the rocker cover.

7. With rocker cover installed, apply RTV sealant to top of semi-circular packing.

8. Tighten screws to 55 inch lbs..

9. Install the vacuum hoses and spark plug wires.

10. Install the air cleaner assembly.

11. Connect the battery cable.

3.0L Engine

1. Disconnect the negative battery cable.

2. Remove the air cleaner assembly.

3. Remove any vacuum hoses necessary and relocate spark plug wires.

4. Remove the cover screws and remove cover.

5. Clean the cylinder head and cover mating surfaces before installation.

6. Install a new gasket. Apply RTV sealant to cover ends.

7. Install the cover and tighten to 68 inch lbs.

8. Install the vacuum hoses and spark plug wires.

9. Install the air cleaner assembly.

10. Connect the battery cable.

3.3L Engine

1. Disconnect the negative battery cable.

2. Remove the air intake tube and disconnect it from the intake manifold.

2.5L valve cover curtain

2.6L sealer application points

3. Remove the upper intake manifold, disconnecting any hoses or wires.

4. Remove the spark plug wires. Disconnect the closed ventilation system and evaporation control from the valve cover.

5. Remove the cover and gasket.

6. Install a new gasket and the cover. Tighten the cover retaining bolts to 102 inch lbs.

7. Reinstall all ventilation control components and the upper intake manifold.

3.0L sealer application points

8. Reconnect the air intake tube to the intake manifold.
9. Connect the negative battery cable.

Rocker Arms and Shafts

REMOVAL AND INSTALLATION

2.2L and 2.5L Engines

1. Disconnect the negative battery cable.
2. Remove the valve cover.
3. Rotate the camshaft until the lobe base is on the rocker arm that is to be removed.
4. Slightly depress the valve spring using Chrysler tool-4682 or the equivalent. Slide the rocker off the lash adjuster and valve tip and remove. Label the rocker arms for position identification. Proceed to next rocker arm and repeat Steps 3 and 4.
5. Remove the lash adjuster if servicing is necessary.
To install:
6. If the lash adjuster was previously removed, partially fill with oil and install.
7. Rotate the camshaft until lobe base is in position with rocker arm. Slightly depress the valve spring using Chrysler tool 4682 or equivalent. Slide rocker arm in position.

NOTE: When depressing the valve spring with Chrysler tool 4682, or the equivalent, the valve locks can become dislocated. Check and make sure both locks are fully seated in the valve grooves and retainer.

8. Install the valve cover.
9. Connect the battery cable.

2.6L Engine

1. Disconnect the negative battery cable.
2. Remove the valve cover.
3. Loosen the camshaft bearing cap bolts. Do not remove bolts from bearing cap.
4. Remove the rocker arm, rocker shafts and bearing caps as an assembly.
5. Remove the bolts from the camshaft bearing caps and remove the rocker shafts, waved washers, rocker arms and springs. Keep all parts in order. Note the way the rocker shaft, rocker arms, bearing caps and springs are mounted. The rocker arm shaft on the Left side has 12 oil holes at shaft bottom, and the Right side shaft has 4 oil holes at shaft bottom.
6. Inspect the rocker arms mounting area and rockers for damage. Replace if worn or heavily damaged.
To install:
7. Position the camshaft bearing caps with arrows pointing toward the timing chain and in numerical order.
8. Insert both shafts into the front bearing cap and install bolts to hold shafts in position.
9. Install the wave washers, rocker arms, bearing caps, and springs. Install bolts in the rear cap to retain assembly.
10. Place the assembly into position.
11. Tighten the camshaft bearing cap bolts in sequence to 10 Nm (85 inch lbs.) as followed:
    a. No. 3 Cap
    b. No. 2 Cap
    c. No. 4 Cap
    d. Front Cap
    e. Rear Cap
12. Repeat Step 12 and increase torque to 175 inch lbs.
13. Install the distributor drive gear, timing chain/camshaft sprocket, and sprocket bolt. Torque sprocket bolt to 40 ft. lbs.

NOTE: After servicing the rocker shaft assembly, Jet Valve Clearance (if used) and Intake/Exhaust Valve Clearance must be performed.

2.2L and 2.5L rocker arm and lash adjuster

2.2L and 2.5L — compressing a valve spring

14. Install the water pump (upper shield) and valve cover.
15. Connect the battery cable.

3.0L Engine

1. Disconnect the negative battery cable.
2. Remove the valve cover.
3. Loosen the camshaft bearing cap bolts. Do not remove bolts from bearing cap.
4. Remove the rocker arm, rocker shafts and bearing caps as an assembly.
5. Remove the bolts from the camshaft bearing caps and remove the rocker shafts and arms. Keep all parts in order. Note the way the rocker shaft, rocker arms, bearing caps and springs are mounted. The rocker arm shaft on the Intake side has a 3mm diameter oil passage hole from the cylinder head. The exhaust side does not have this oil passage.
6. Inspect the rocker arm mounting area and rocker for damage. Replace if worn or heavily damaged.
To install:
7. Identify No. 1 bearing cap, (No. 1 and No. 4 caps are similar). Install the rocker shafts into the bearing cap with notches in proper position. Insert the attaching bolts to retain assemble.
8. Install the rocker arms, springs and bearing caps on shafts in numerical sequence.
9. Align the camshaft bearing caps with arrows (depending on cylinder bank).

Rocker arm and shaft assemblies — 2.6L engines

3.0L number 1 camshaft bearing cap

3.0L rocker shaft identification

10. Install the bolts in number 4 cap to retain assembly.
11. Apply sealant at bearing cap ends.
12. Install the rocker arm shaft assembly.

NOTE: Make sure the arrow mark on the bearing caps and the arrow mark on the cylinder heads are in the same direction. The direction of arrow marks on the front and rear assemblies are opposite to each other.

3.0L rocker shaft assembly installation

13. Tighten the bearing caps bolts to 85 inch lbs. in the following manner:
    a. No. 3 Cap
    b. No. 2 Cap
    c. No. 1 Cap
    d. No. 4 Cap
14. Repeat Step 13 increasing torque to 180 inch lbs.
15. Install the valve cover.
16. Connect the battery cable.

3.3L Engine

1. Disconnect the negative battery cable.
2. Remove the upper intake manifold assembly.
3. Remove the rocker arm cover.
4. remove the 4 rocker shaft retaining bolts and retainers.
5. remove the rocker arms and shaft assembly.
6. If you are disassembling the rocker shaft, be sure to install the rocker arms in their original locations.

OIL INTAKE SHAFT
HAS EXTRA HOLE
IN BOTTOM

SHAFTS

CAP NO. 3

CAP NO. 4

CAP NO. 1

CAP NO. 2
WITH OIL
INLET (INTAKE)
FROM CYLINDER
HEAD

SPRING

ROCKER ARM

3.0L rocker arm and shaft assemblies

COMMON ROCKER ARMS

Rocker shaft assembly — 3.3L engine

To install:

7. Install the rocker arm and shaft assembly, using the 4 retainers. Tighten the retaining bolts to 250 inch lbs. (28 Nm).

NOTE: The rocker arm shaft should be torqued down slowly, starting with the center bolts. Allow 20 minutes for tappet bleed down after installation, before engine operation.

8. Install the rocker cover.
9. Install the crankcase ventilation components and connect the spark plug wires.
10. Install the upper intake manifold assembly. Connect the negative battery cable.

Thermostat

REMOVAL AND INSTALLATION

The thermostat is located in a water box at the side of the en-

gine (facing grille) 2.2L and 2.5L engines. The thermostat on 2.6L, 3.0L and 3.3L engines is located in a water box at the timing belt end of the intake manifold.

1. Drain the cooling system to a level below the thermostat.

—————— **CAUTION** ——————
When draining the coolant, keep in mind that cats and dogs are attracted by the ethylene glycol antifreeze, and are quite likely to drink any that is left in an uncovered container or in puddles on the ground. This will prove fatal in sufficient quantity. Always drain the coolant into a sealable container. Coolant should be reused unless it is contaminated or several years old.

2. Remove the hoses from the thermostat housing.
3. Remove the thermostat housing.
4. Remove the thermostat and discard the gasket. Clean the gasket surfaces thoroughly.
5. Install a new gasket on water box housing 2.2L and 2.5L engines. Center the thermostat in the water box on gasket surface. Install the thermostat housing on gasket. Make sure thermostat sits in its recess of the housing. Tighten bolts to 15 ft. lbs. On 2.6L engine position gasket on water box. Center thermostat in water box and attached housing. Tighten bolts to 15 ft. lbs. On 3.0L and 3.3L engines position thermostat in water box pocket. Make sure thermostat flange in seated properly in flange groove of the water box. Position the new gasket on water box and install housing. Tighten bolts to 15 ft. lbs.
6. Connect the radiator hose to the thermostat housing. Tighten the hose clamp to 35 inch lbs.
7. Fill the cooling system.

Intake Manifold

REMOVAL AND INSTALLATION

2.6L Engine

1. Disconnect the negative battery cable.
2. Drain the cooling system and disconnect the hoses from the water pump to the intake manifold.

2.6L intake manifold assembly

GASKET

SCREW
17 N•m
(150 IN. LBS.)

───── CAUTION ─────

When draining the coolant, keep in mind that cats and dogs are attracted by the ethylene glycol antifreeze, and are quite likely to drink any that is left in an uncovered container or in puddles on the ground. This will prove fatal in sufficient quantity. Always drain the coolant into a sealable container. Coolant should be reused unless it is contaminated or several years old.

3. Disconnect the carburetor air horn adapter and move to one side.
4. Disconnect the vacuum hoses and throttle link,age from the carburetor.
5. Disconnect the fuel inlet line at the fuel filter.
6. Remove the fuel filter and fuel pump and move to one side.
7. Remove the intake manifold retaining nuts and washers and remove the manifold.
8. Remove old gasket. Clean cylinder head and manifold gasket surface. Check for cracks or warpage. Install a new gasket on cylinder head.
9. Install manifold to cylinder head. Install washers and nuts. Refer to Torque Specification Chart.
10. Install the fuel pump and filter.
11. Install the carburetor air horn.
12. Install the throttle control cable.
13. Install the cooling system hose from water pump to manifold.
14. Install the vacuum hoses.
15. Connect the negative battery cable.

3.0L Engine

1. Release fuel system pressure.
2. Disconnect the negative battery cable.
3. Drain the cooling system.

───── CAUTION ─────

When draining the coolant, keep in mind that cats and dogs are attracted by the ethylene glycol antifreeze, and are quite likely to drink any that is left in an uncovered container or in puddles on the ground. This will prove fatal in sufficient quantity. Always drain the coolant into a sealable container. Coolant should be reused unless it is contaminated or several years old.

4. Remove the air cleaner.
5. Remove the throttle cable and transaxle kickdown cable.
6. Remove the electrical and vacuum connections from throttle body.
7. Remove the air intake hose from air cleaner to throttle body.

8. Remove the EGR tube to intake plenum.
9. Remove the electrical connection from charge temperature and coolant temperature sensor.
10. Remove the vacuum connection from the pressure regulator and remove the air intake connection from the manifold.
11. Remove fuel hoses to fuel rail connection.
12. Remove the air intake plenum to manifold bolts (8) and remove air intake plenum and gasket.

WARNING: Whenever the air intake plenum is removed, cover the intake manifold properly to avoid objects from entering cylinder head.

13. Disconnect the fuel injector wiring harness from the engine wiring harness.
14. Remove the pressure regulator attaching bolts and remove pressure regulator from rail.
15. Remove the fuel rail attaching bolts and remove fuel rail.
16. Remove the radiator hose from thermostat housing and heater hose from pipe.
17. Remove the intake manifold attaching nuts and washers and remove intake manifold.
18. Clean the gasket material from cylinder head and manifold gasket surface. Check for cracks or damaged mounting surfaces.
To install:
19. Install a new gasket on the intake surface of the cylinder head and install the intake manifold.
20. Install the intake manifold washers and nuts. Tighten in sequence shown. Refer to Torque Specification Chart.
21. Clean the injectors and lubricate the injector O-rings with a drop of clean engine oil.
22. Place the tip of each injector into their ports. Push assembly into place until the injectors are seated in their ports.
23. Install rail attaching bolts and tighten to 115 inch lbs.
24. Install pressure regulator to rail. Install pressure regulator mounting bolts and tighten to 95 inch lbs.
25. Install fuel supply and return tube holldown bolt and vacuum crossover tube holddown bolt. Torque to 95 inch lbs.
26. Torque fuel pressure regulator hose clamps to 10 inch lbs.
27. Connect injector wiring harness to engine wiring harness.
28. Connect vacuum harness to fuel rail and pressure regulator.
29. Remove covering from intake manifold.
30. Position the intake manifold gasket, beaded side up, on the intake manifold.
31. Put the air intake plenum in place. Install attaching bolts and tighten in sequence to 115 inch lbs.
32. Connect the fuel line to fuel rail. Tighten clamps to 10 inch lbs.
33. Connect the vacuum hoses to intake plenum.
34. Connect the electrical connection to coolant temperature sensor and charge temperature sensor.
35. Connect the EGR tube flange to intake plenum and torque to 15 ft. lbs.
36. Connect the throttle body vacuum hoses and electrical connections.

3.0L intake manifold torque sequence

Intake plenum tightening sequence — 3.0L engine

Intake manifold gasket retainers — 3.3L engine

37. Install the throttle cable and transaxle kickdown linkage.
38. Install the radiator and heater hose. Fill the cooling system.
39. Connect the negative battery cable.

3.3L Engine

1. Disconnect the negative battery cable. Relieve the fuel pressure. Drain the cooling system.
2. Remove the air cleaner to throttle body hose assembly.
3. Disconnect the throttle cable and remove the wiring harness from the bracket.
4. Remove AIS motor and TPS wiring connectors from the throttle body.
5. Remove the vacuum hose harness from the throttle body.
6. Remove the PCV and brake booster hoses from the air intake plenum.
7. Disconnect the charge temperature sensor electrical connector. Remove the vacuum harness connectors from the intake plenum.
8. Remove the cylinder head to the intake plenum strut.
9. Disconnect the MAP sensor and oxygen sensor connectors. Remove the engine mounted ground strap.
10. Remove the fuel hoses from the fuel rail and plug them.
11. Remove the DIS coils and the alternator bracket to intake manifold bolt.
12. Remove the upper intake manifold attaching bolts and remove the upper manifold.
13. Remove the vacuum harness connector from the fuel pressure regulator.
14. Remove the fuel tube retainer bracket screw and fuel rail attaching bolts. Spread the retainer bracket to allow for clearance when removing the fuel tube.
15. Remove the fuel rail injector wiring clip from the alternator bracket.

Intake manifold torque sequence — 3.3L engine

16. Disconnect the cam sensor, coolant temperature sensor and engine temperature sensor.
17. Remove the fuel rail.
18. Remove the upper radiator hose, bypass hose and rear intake manifold hose.
19. Remove the intake manifold bolts and remove the manifold from the engine.
20. Remove the intake manifold seal retaining screws and remove the manifold gasket.
21. Clean out clogged end water passages and fuel runners.
To install:
22. Clean and dry all gasket mating surfaces.
23. When the bolts are torqued, inspect the seals to ensure that they have not become dislodged.
26. Lubricate the injector O-rings with clean oil and position the fuel rail in place. Install the rail mounting bolts.
27. Connect the cam sensor, coolant temperature sensor and engine temperature sensor.
28. Install the fuel rail injector wiring clip to the alternator bracket.
29. Install the fuel rail attaching bolts and fuel tube retainer bracket screw.
30. Install the vacuum harness to the pressure regulator.
31. Install the upper intake manifold with a new gasket. Install the bolts only finger tight. Install the alternator bracket to

Intake manifold gasket sealing — 3.3L engine

2.6L exhaust manifold assembly

intake manifold bolt and the cylinder head to intake manifold strut and bolts. Torque the intake manifold mounting bolts to 21 ft. lbs. (28 Nm) starting from the middle and working outward. Torque the bracket and strut bolts to 40 ft. lbs. (54 Nm).

32. Install or connect all items that were removed or disconnected from the intake manifold and throttle body.

33. Connect the fuel hoses to the rail. Push the fittings in until they click in place.

34. Install the air cleaner assembly.

35. Connect the negative battery cable and check for leaks using the DRB I or II to activate the fuel pump.

Exhaust Manifold

REMOVAL AND INSTALLATION

2.6L Engine

1. Disconnect the negative battery cable.
2. Remove the air cleaner assembly.
3. Remove the belt from the power steering pump.
4. Raise the vehicle and make sure it is supported safely.
5. Remove the exhaust pipe from the manifold.
6. Disconnect the air injection tube assembly from the exhaust manifold and lower the vehicle.
7. Remove the power steering pump assembly and move to one side.
8. Remove the heat cowl from the exhaust manifold.
9. Remove the exhaust manifold retaining nuts and remove the assembly from the vehicle.
10. Remove the carburetor air heater from the manifold.
11. Separate the exhaust manifold from the catalytic converter by removing the retaining screws.
12. Clean gasket material from cylinder head and exhaust manifold gasket surfaces. Check mating surfaces for cracks or distortion.
13. Install a new gasket between the exhaust manifold an catalytic converter. Install mounting screws and tighten to 32 Nm (24 ft. lbs.).
14. Install the carburetor air heater on manifold and tighten to 80 inch lbs.
15. Lightly coat the new exhaust manifold gasket with sealant (P/N 3419115) or equivalent on cylinder head side.
16. Install the exhaust manifold and mounting nuts. Refer to Torque Specification Chart.
17. Install the heat cowl to manifold and tighten screws to 80 inch lbs.
18. Install the air cleaner support bracket.
19. Install the power steering pump assembly.
20. Install the air injection tube assembly to air pump.

21. Raise the vehicle and install air injection tube assembly to exhaust manifold.
22. Install the exhaust pipe to manifold.
23. Lower the vehicle and install power steering belt.
24. Fill the cooling system.
25. Install the air cleaner assembly.
26. Connect the negative battery cable.

3.0L Engine

1. Disconnect the negative battery cable.
2. Raise vehicle and support properly.
3. Disconnect the exhaust pipe from the rear (cowl side) exhaust manifold at articulated joint.
4. Remove the EGR tube from the rear manifold and disconnect oxygen sensor lead.
5. Remove the attaching bolts from crossover pipe to manifold.
6. Remove the attaching nuts which retained manifold to cylinder head and remove manifold.
7. Lower the vehicle and remove bolt securing front heat shield to front exhaust manifold.
8. Remove the bolts retaining crossover pipe to front exhaust manifold and nuts retaining manifold to cylinder head. Remove manifold assembly.
9. Clean all gasket material from cylinder the head and exhaust manifold gasket surfaces. Check mating surfaces for cracks or distortion.
10. Install the new gasket with the numbers 1-3-5 stamped on the top on the rear bank. The gasket with the numbers 2-4-6 must be installed on the front bank (radiator side).
11. Install rear exhaust manifold and tighten attaching nuts to 15 ft. lbs.
12. Install exhaust pipe to manifold and tighten shoulder bolts to 20 ft. lbs.
13. Install crossover pipe to manifold and tighten bolts to 69 Nm (51 ft. lbs.).
14. Install oxygen sensor lead and EGR tube.
15. Install front exhaust manifold and attach exhaust crossover.
16. Install front manifold heat shield and tighten bolts to 10 ft. lbs.
17. Connect the negative battery cable.

3.3L Engine

1. Disconnect the negative battery cable.
2. If removing the rear manifold, raise the vehicle and support safely. Disconnect the exhaust pipe at the articulated joint from the rear exhaust manifold.
3. Separate the EGR tube from the rear manifold and disconnect the oxygen sensor wire.
4. Remove the alternator/power steering support strut.

2.2L and 2.5L combination manifold bolt locations

**15 N•m
(130 IN. LBS.)**

**AIR INTAKE
PLENUM**

GASKET

**20 N•m
(174 IN. LBS.)**

**INTAKE (CROSS)
MANIFOLD**

**EXHAUST
CROSSOVER
PIPE**

**69 N•m
(51 FT. LBS.)**

GASKET

**GASKET
(CROSSOVER)**

**GASKET
(MANIFOLD)**

**22 N•m
(191 IN. LBS.)**

**GASKET
(CROSSOVER)**

**HEAT
SHIELD**

**15 N•m
(130 IN. LBS.)**

**20 N•m
(174 IN. LBS.)**

**REAR EXHAUST
MANIFOLD**

FRONT

Manifold assemblies — 3.0L engine

5. Remove the bolts attaching the crossover pipe to the manifold.

6. Remove the bolts attaching the manifold to the head and remove the manifold.

7. If removing the front manifold, remove the heat shield, bolts attaching the crossover pipe to the manifold and the nuts attaching the manifold to the head.

8. Remove the manifold from the engine.

9. The installation is the reverse of the removal procedure. Torque all exhaust manifold attaching bolts to 17 ft. lbs. (23 Nm).

10. Start the engine and check for exhaust leaks.

Combination Manifold

REMOVAL AND INSTALLATION
2.2L and 2.5L Engines

WITHOUT TURBOCHARGER

1. Disconnect the battery negative cable.
2. Drain the cooling system.

3. Remove the air cleaner, disconnect all vacuum lines, electrical wiring and fuel lines from carburetor and intake manifold.

4. Remove the throttle linkage.

5. Remove the water hoses from water crossover.

6. Raise the vehicle and remove exhaust pipe from manifold.

7. Remove power steering pump and set aside.

8. Remove intake manifold support bracket and EGR tube.

9. On Canadian cars remove (4) air injection tube bolts and injection tube assembly.

10. Remove the intake manifold retaining screws.

11. Lower vehicle and remove the intake manifold.

12. Remove exhaust manifold retaining nuts and remove exhaust manifold.

13. Clean gasket surface of both manifold and cylinder block surface.

14. Install a new gasket on exhaust and intake manifold. Coat manifold with Sealer (P/N 3419115) or equivalent on manifold side.

15. Position the exhaust manifold against cylinder block and install nuts. Tighten nuts from center while alternating outward in both direction. See Torque Specification Chart.

16. Position the intake manifold against cylinder head.

17. From beneath the vehicle tighten intake manifold screws. Start at the center while alternating outward in both direction. See Torque Specification Chart.

18. Install the exhaust pipe to exhaust manifold.

19. On Canadian cars install air injection tube assembly.

20. Install the intake manifold support bracket and EGR tube.

21. Install the power steering pump assembly and power steering belt.

22. Install the water hoses to water crossover.

23. Install the fuel lines, vacuum lines, and electrical wiring.

24. Fill the cooling system.

25. Connect the negative battery cable.

WITH TURBOCHARGER

NOTE: On some vehicles, some of the manifold attaching bolts are not accessible or too heavily sealed from the factory and cannot be removed on the vehicle. Head removal would be necessary in these situations.

1. Disconnect the negative battery cable. Drain the cooling system. Raise and safely support the vehicle.

2. Disconnect the accelerator linkage, throttle body electrical connector and vacuum hoses.

8. Relocate the fuel rail assembly. Remove the bracket to intake manifold screws and the bracket to heat shield clips. Lift and secure the fuel rail (with injectors, wiring harness and fuel lines intact) up and out of the way.

9. Disconnect the turbocharger oil feed line at the oil sending unit Tee fitting.

10. Disconnect the upper radiator hose from the thermostat housing.

11. Remove the cylinder head, manifolds and turbocharger as an assembly.

12. With the assembly on a workbench, loosen the upper turbocharger discharge hose end clamp.

NOTE: Do not disturb the center deswirler retaining clamp.

13. Remove the throttle body to intake manifold screws and throttle body assembly. Disconnect the turbocharger coolant re-turn tube from the water box. Disconnect the retaining bracket on the cylinder head.

14. Remove the heat shield to intake manifold screws and the heat shield.

15. Remove the turbocharger to exhaust manifold nuts and the turbocharger assembly.

16. Remove the intake manifold bolts and the intake manifold.

17. Remove the exhaust manifold nuts and the exhaust manifold.

To install:

18. Place a new 2-sided Grafoil type intake/exhaust manifold gasket; do not use sealant.

19. Position the exhaust manifold on the cylinder head. Apply anti-seize compound to threads, install and torque the retaining nuts, starting at center and progressing outward in both directions, to 17 ft. lbs. (23 Nm). Repeat this procedure until all nuts are at 17 ft. lbs. (23 Nm).

20. Position the intake manifold on the cylinder head. Install and torque the retaining screws, starting at center and progressing outward in both directions, to 19 ft. lbs. (26 Nm). Repeat this procedure until all screws are at 19 ft. lbs. (26 Nm).

21. Connect the turbocharger outlet to the intake manifold inlet tube. Position the turbocharger on the exhaust manifold. Apply anti-seize compound to threads and torque the nuts to 30 ft. lbs. (41 Nm). Torque the connector tube clamps to 30 inch lbs. (41 Nm).

22. Install the tube support bracket to the cylinder head.

23. Install the heat shield on the intake manifold. Torque the screws to 105 inch lbs. (12 Nm).

24. Install the throttle body air horn into the turbocharger inlet tube. Install and torque the throttle body to intake manifold screws to 21 ft. lbs. (28 Nm). Torque the tube clamp to 30 inch lbs.

25. Install the cylinder head/manifolds/turbocharger assembly on the engine.

26. Reconnect the turbocharger oil feed line to the oil sending unit Tee fitting and bearing housing, if disconnected. Torque the tube nuts to 10 ft. lbs. (14 Nm).

27. Install the air cleaner assembly. Connect the vacuum lines and accelerator cables.

28. Reposition the fuel rail. Install and torque the bracket screws to 21 ft. lbs. (28 Nm). Install the air shield to bracket clips.

29. Connect the turbocharger inlet coolant tube to the engine block. Torque the tube nut to 30 ft. lbs. (41 Nm). Install the tube support bracket.

30. Install the turbocharger housing to engine block support bracket and the screws hand tight. Torque the block screw 1st to 40 ft. lbs. (54 Nm). Torque the screw to the turbocharger housing to 20 ft. lbs. (27 Nm).

31. Reposition the drain back hose connector and tighten the hose clamps. Reconnect the exhaust pi at the EGR valve.

Turbocharger

REMOVAL AND INSTALLATION

2.5L Turbocharged Engine

1. Disconnect the negative battery cable. Drain the cooling system.

2. Disconnect the EGR valve tube at the EGR valve.

3. Disconnect the turbocharger oil feed at the oil sending unit hex and the coolant tube at the water box. Disconnect the oil/coolant support bracket from the cylinder head.

4. Remove the right intermediate shaft, bearing support bracket and outer drive shaft assemblies.

5. Remove the turbocharger to engine block support bracket.

6. Disconnect the exhaust pipe at the articulated joint. Disconnect the oxygen sensor at the electrical connection.

Manifolds, turbocharger and related components — 2.5L turbo charged engine.

7. Loosen the oil drain-back tube connector clamps and move the tube hose down on the nipple.

8. Disconnect the coolant tube nut at the block outlet (below steering pump bracket) and tube support bracket.

9. Remove the turbocharger to exhaust manifold nuts. Carefully routing the oil and coolant lines, move the assembly down and out of the vehicle.

To Install:

NOTE: Before installing the turbocharger assembly, be sure it is first charged with oil. Failure to do this may cause damage to the assembly.

10. Position the turbocharger on the exhaust manifold. Apply an anti-seize compound, Loctite® 771–64 or equivalent, to the threads and torque the retaining nuts to 40 ft. lbs. (54 Nm).

11. Connect the coolant tube to engine block fitting. Torque the tube nut to 30 ft. lbs. (41 Nm).

12. Position the oil drain-back hose and torque the clamps to 30 inch lbs.

13. Install and torque the:
- Turbocharger to engine support bracket block screw to 40 ft. lbs. (54 Nm).
- Turbocharger housing screw to 20 ft. lbs. (27 Nm).
- Articulated joint shoulder bolts to 21 ft. lbs. (28 Nm).

14. Install the right drive shaft assembly, the starter and the oil feed line at the sending unit hex. Torque the oil feed tube nut to 10 ft. lbs. (14 Nm) and the EGR tube to EGR valve nut to 60 ft. lbs. (81 Nm).

15. Refill the cooling system. Connect the negative battery cable and check the turbocharger for proper operation.

Air Conditioning Compressor

REMOVAL AND INSTALLATION

1. Disconnect the negative battery cable.

2. Properly discharge the air conditioning system. Refer to Section 1 for discharge, evacuate and recharge procedures.

Air conditioning compressor mounting — 2.2/2.5L engines

COMPRESSOR

COMPRESSOR
MOUNTING
BRACKET

Air conditioning compressor mounting — 3.0L engine

MOUNTING
BRACKET

A/C COMPRESSOR

Air conditioning compressor mounting — 3.3L engine

3. Remove the compressor drive belt(s). Disconnect the compressor lead.

4. Raise and safely support the vehicle, if necessary. Remove the refrigerant lines from the compressor and discard the gaskets. Cover the exposed ends of the lines to minimize contamination.

5. Remove the compressor mounting nuts and bolts.

6. Lift the compressor off of its mounting studs and remove from the engine compartment.

CLAMP TORQUE 4 N•m (35 INCH POUNDS)
DO NOT OVERTIGHTEN

HOSE
HOSE
O/B
FWD
U
V

HOSE
FWD
W

HOSE
O/B
O/B
X
Y
HOSE
O/B
Z

CLAMP POSITION AS VIEWED IN
DIRECTION OF LETTERED ARROWS

STRAP

INLET

OUTLET

2.6L ENGINE
RADIATOR HOSES

HOSE
CLAMP

TYPICAL SECTION

SCREW AND WASHER-2
NUT AND WASHER
2 N•m
(110 IN. LBS.)

U-NUT

INLET HOSE

OUTLET HOSE

CLIP

FWD

CLIP

FAN AND SUPPORT
2.2L AND 2.6L ENGINES

2.2L ENGINE
RADIATOR HOSES

OUTLET HOSE
ASSEMBLY

VIEW IN DIRECTION
OF ARROW T

ENGINE SUPPORT
(REFERENCE)

Radiator assembly mounting

To install:

7. Install the compressor and tighten all mounting nuts and bolts.

8. Coat the new gaskets with wax-free refrigerant oil and install. Connect the refrigerant lines to the compressor and tighten the bolts.

9. Install the drive belt(s) and adjust to specification. Connect the electrical lead.

10. Evacuate and recharge the air conditioning system.

11. Connect the negative battery cable and check the entire climate control system for proper operation and leaks.

Radiator

REMOVAL AND INSTALLATION

1. Disconnect the negative battery cable.
2. Drain the cooling system.

─────── **CAUTION** ───────

When draining the coolant, keep in mind that cats and dogs are attracted by the ethylene glycol antifreeze, and are quite likely to drink any that is left in an uncovered container or in puddles on the ground. This will prove fatal in sufficient quantity. Always drain the coolant into a sealable container. Coolant should be reused unless it is contaminated or several years old.

─────────────────────────

3. Remove the upper and lower hoses and coolant recovery tank tube to filler neck.
4. Disconnect the wiring harness from fan motor.
5. Remove the upper mounting bolts from fan assembly.
6. Lift fan assembly from bottom ring retaining clip.
7. Remove the radiator upper mounting bolts and carefully lift radiator from engine compartment.
8. Carefully slide the radiator into place while aligning radiator with holes in radiator support seat.
9. Install the upper radiator mounting bolts and tighten to 105 inch lbs.
10. Install the lower radiator hose and tighten to 35 inch lbs.
11. Carefully install the fan assembly while aligning lower fan support into retaining clip.
12. Attach washers and nuts to upper fan support.

REFRIGERANT LINE NUT

CONDENSER ASSEMBLY

REFRIGERANT LINE TO CONDENSER GASKET

Air conditioning condenser mounting

13. Connect the fan electrical connector.
14. Install the upper radiator hose and tighten clamp to 35 inch lbs.
15. Fill the cooling system.

Air Conditioning Condenser

REMOVAL AND INSTALLATION

1. Disconnect the negative battery cable.
2. Properly discharge the air conditioning system.
3. Remove the headlight bezels in order to gain access to the grille. Remove the grille assembly. A hidden screw fastens the grille to the center vertical support.
4. Remove the refrigerant lines attaching nut and separate the lines from the condenser sealing plate. Discard the gasket.
5. Cover the exposed ends of the lines to minimize contamination.
6. Remove the bolts that attach the condenser to the radiator support.
7. Remove the condenser from the vehicle.

To install:

8. Position the condenser and install the bolts.
9. Coat the new gasket with wax-free refrigerant oil and install. Connect the lines to the condenser sealing plate and tighten the nut.
10. Install the grille assembly.
11. Evacuate and recharge the air conditioning system. Add 1 oz. of refrigerant oil during the recharge.
12. Connect the negative battery cable and check the entire climate control system for proper operation and leaks.

Electric Cooling Fan

─────── **CAUTION** ───────

Make sure the key is in the OFF position when checking the electric cooling fan. If not, the fan could turn ON at any time, causing serious personal injury.

─────────────────────────

TESTING

1. Unplug the fan connector.
2. Using a jumper wire, connect the female terminal of the fan connector to the negative battery terminal.
3. The fan should turn on when the male terminal is connected to the positive battery terminal.
4. If not, the fan is defective and should be replaced.

REMOVAL AND INSTALLATION

1. Disconnect the negative battery cable.
2. Unplug the connector.
3. Remove the mounting screws.
4. Remove the fan assembly from the vehicle.
5. The installation is the reverse of the removal procedure.
6. Connect the negative battery cable and check the fan for proper operation.

Automatic Transmission Oil Cooler

REMOVAL AND INSTALLATION

The transmission oil cooler used on these models are externally mounted ahead of the radiator. This is considered an oil-to-air type system.

1. Remove the electrical cooling fan assembly and remove radiator. Refer to Radiator Removal procedures.

2. Loosen the clamps retaining the hoses from the transmission cooler lines.

3. Place an oil drain pan under the hoses and remove hoses from the cooler assembly.

4. Remove (2) screws retaining the cooler assembly to support and remove cooler assembly.

5. If reusing the cooler assembly, reverse flush the cooler.

6. Position the cooler assembly against its support.

7. Install the cooler mounting bolts and tighten to 35 inch lbs.

8. Install hoses from the cooler lines to cooler assembly and tighten clamps to 16 inch lbs.

9. Install the radiator and cooling fan assembly. Refer to Radiator procedures previously outlined.

Water Pump

REMOVAL AND INSTALLATION

2.2L and 2.5L Engine

1. Disconnect the negative battery cable.
2. Remove the drive belts.
3. Drain the cooling system.

------------------ CAUTION ------------------

When draining the coolant, keep in mind that cats and dogs are attracted by the ethylene glycol antifreeze, and are quite likely to drink any that is left in an uncovered container or in puddles on the ground. This will prove fatal in sufficient quantity. Always drain the coolant into a sealable container. Coolant should be reused unless it is contaminated or several years old.

4. Remove the upper radiator hose.
5. Without discharging the system, remove the air conditioning compressor from the engine brackets and set to one side.
6. Remove the alternator and move to one side.
7. Disconnect the lower radiator hose and heater hose.
8. Remove (3) upper screws and (1) lower screw retaining water pump to the engine and remove pump assembly.
9. Position the replacement pump against the engine and install mounting screws. Tighten the (3) upper screws to 20 ft. lbs. and lower screw to 50 ft. lbs.
10. Install heater hose and lower radiator hose. Tighten clamps to 16 inch lbs.
11. Install air conditioning compressor and alternator.
12. Install the drive belts and adjust to specification.
13. Fill the cooling system.
14. Connect the negative battery cable.

2.6L Engine

1. Drain the cooling system.

------------------ CAUTION ------------------

When draining the coolant, keep in mind that cats and dogs are attracted by the ethylene glycol antifreeze, and are quite likely to drink any that is left in an uncovered container or in puddles on the ground. This will prove fatal in sufficient quantity. Always drain the coolant into a sealable container. Coolant should be reused unless it is contaminated or several years old.

2. Remove the radiator hose, by-pass hose and heater hose from the water pump.
3. Remove the drive pulley shield.
4. Remove the locking screw and pivot screws.
5. Remove the drive belt and water pump from the engine.
6. Install a new O-ring gasket in O-ring groove of pump body assembly to cylinder block.
7. Position the water pump assembly against the engine and install pivot screws and locking screw finger tight.

SCREW
30 N•m
(250 IN. LBS.)

SCREW
68 N•m
(50 FT. LBS.)

Water pump assembly — 2.2L and 2.5L engines

PIVOT SCREWS
23 N•m
(204 IN. LBS.)

(W) LOCKING SCREW
23 N•m
(204 IN. LBS.)

Water pump assembly — 2.6L engine

O-RING   WATER PIPE

GASKET

WATER PUMP

Water pump mounting — 3.0L engine

8. Install the water pump drive belt and adjust to specification. New belt 8mm deflection, used belt 9mm deflection.
9. Install drive belt pulley cover.
10. Install the radiator hose, by-pass hose and heater hose.
11. Fill the cooling system.

3.0L Engine

1. Disconnect the negative battery cable.
2. Remove the drive belts.
3. Drain the cooling system.

— **CAUTION** —

When draining the coolant, keep in mind that cats and dogs are attracted by the ethylene glycol antifreeze, and are quite likely to drink any that is left in an uncovered container or in puddles on the ground. This will prove fatal in sufficient quantity. Always drain the coolant into a sealable container. Coolant should be reused unless it is contaminated or several years old.

4. Remove the timing case cover and timing belt. Refer to Timing Belt Covers and Timing Belt Removal procedures.
5. Remove the pump assembly mounting bolts.
6. Separate the pump assembly from water pipe and remove.
7. Clean gasket and O-ring mounting surfaces.
8. Install a new O-ring on water pipe and lubricate with water.
9. Install a new gasket on pump body.
10. Press the water pump assembly into water pipe.
11. Install pump mounting bolts and tighten to 27 Nm (20 ft. lbs.).
12. Install timing belt and cover. Refer to Timing Belt procedures.
13. Install drive belts.
14. Fill the cooling system.

3.3L Engine

1. Disconnect the negative battery cable.
2. Drain the cooling system.
3. Remove the serpentine belt.
4. Raise the vehicle and support safely. Remove the right front tire and wheel assembly and lower fender shield.
5. Remove the water pump pulley.
6. Remove the 5 mounting screws and remove the pump from the engine.
7. Discard the O-ring.

To install:

8. Using a new O-ring, install the pump to the engine. Torque the mounting bolts to 21 ft. lbs. (30 Nm).
9. Install the water pump pulley.
10. Install the fender shield and tire and wheel assembly. Lower the vehicle.
11. Install the serpentine belt.
12. Remove the engine temperature sending unit. Fill the radiator with coolant until the coolant comes out the sending unit hole. Install the sending unit and continue to fill the radiator.
13. Connect the negative battery cable, run the vehicle until the thermostat opens, fill the radiator completely and check for leaks.
14. Once the vehicle has cooled, recheck the coolant level.

Cylinder Head

REMOVAL AND INSTALLATION

2.2L and 2.5L Engines

1. Relieve the fuel pressure if equipped with fuel injection. Disconnect the negative battery cable and unbolt it from the head. Drain the cooling system. Remove the dipstick bracket nut from the thermostat housing.
2. Remove the air cleaner assembly. Remove the upper radiator hose and disconnect the heater hoses.
3. Disconnect and label the vacuum lines, hoses and wiring connectors from the manifold(s), carburetor or throttle body and from the cylinder head. Remove the air pump, if equipped.

4 STEP TORQUE PROCEDURE IN SEQUENCE SHOWN
1. 41 N•m (30 FT. LBS.)
2. 61 N•m (45 FT. LBS.)
3. 61 N•m (45 FT. LBS.)
4. + 1/4 TURN

Cylinder head torque sequence — 2.2L and 2.5L engines

4. Disconnect the all linkages and the fuel line from the carburetor or throttle body. Unbolt the cable bracket. Remove the ground strap attaching screw from the fire wall.
5. If equipped with air conditioning, remove the upper compressor mounting bolts. The cylinder head can be remove with the compressor and bracket still mounted. Remove the upper part of the timing belt cover.
6. Raise the vehicle and support safely. Disconnect the converter from the exhaust manifold. Disconnect the water hose and oil drain from the turbocharger, if equipped.
7. Rotate the engine by hand, until the timing marks align (No. 1 piston at TDC). Lower the vehicle.
8. With the timing marks aligned, remove the camshaft sprocket. The camshaft sprocket can be suspended to keep the timing intact. Remove the spark plug wires from the spark plugs.
9. Remove the valve cover and curtain, if equipped. Remove the cylinder head bolts and washers, starting from the middle and working outward.
10. Remove the cylinder head from the engine.

NOTE: Before disassembling or repairing any part of the cylinder head assembly, identify factory installed oversized components. To do so, look for the tops of the bearing caps pained green and O/SJ stamped rearward of the oil gallery plug on the rear of the head. In addition, the barrel of the camshaft is painted green and O/SJ is stamped onto the rear end of the camshaft. Installing standard sized parts in an head equipped with oversized parts—or visa versa—will cause severe engine damage.

11. Clean the cylinder head gasket mating surfaces.
12. Using new gaskets and seals, install the head to the engine. Using new head bolts assembled with the old washers, torque the cylinder head bolts in sequence, to 45 ft. lbs. Repeating the sequence, torque the bolts to 65 ft. lbs. With the bolts at 65 ft. lbs., turn each bolt an additional 1/4 turn.

NOTE: Head bolt diameter for 1986–91 vehicles is 11mm. These bolts are identified with the number 11 on the head of the bolt. The 10mm bolts used on previous vehicles will thread into an 11mm bolt hole, but will permanently damage the engine block. Make sure the correct bolts are being used.

13. Install the timing belt.
14. Install or connect all items that were removed or disconnected during the removal procedures.
15. Refill the cooling system. Connect the negative battery cable. Start the engine and check for leaks.

Cylinder head and related components — 2.2L engine

2.6L Engine

1. Disconnect the negative battery cable and unbolt if from the head.

2. Drain the cooling system. Remove the upper radiator hose and disconnect the heater hoses. Remove the air cleaner assembly.

3. Remove the dipstick bracket bolt from the thermostat housing.

4. Remove the carburetor to valve cover bracket. Remove the valve cover. Remove and plug the fuel lines to the carburetor.

5. Matchmark the distributor gear to its drive gear and remove the distributor. Remove the camshaft bolt and remove the distributor drive gear. Remove the camshaft gear with the chain installed from the camshaft and allow to rest on the holder just below it. This will not upset the valve timing. Do not crank the engine until the distributor has been reinstalled or the timing will be lost and timing components could be damaged.

6. Remove the water pump drive pulley retaining bolt and remove the pulley from the camshaft.

7. Disconnect and label the vacuum lines, hoses and wiring

94 N•m (69 FT. LBS.) COLD ENGINE
103 N•m (75 FT. LBS.) HOT ENGINE

18 N•m (156 IN. LBS.)

Cylinder head torque sequence — 2.6L engine

connectors from the manifold(s), carburetor and cylinder head. Since some of the vacuum lines from the carburetor connect to a solenoid pack on the right side inner fender, unbolt the solenoids from the fender with the vacuum lines attached and fold the assembly over the carburetor.

8. Disconnect all the linkages and the fuel line from the carburetor. Remove the ground strap attaching screw from the fire wall. Unbolt the power steering pump from the bracket and position to the side.

9. Raise the vehicle and support safely. Disconnect the vacuum hoses from the source below the carburetor and disconnect the air feeder tubes.

10. Remove the exhaust pipe from the exhaust manifold. Lower the vehicle.

6 N•m
(53 IN. LB.)

54 N•m
(40 FT. LBS.)

12 N•m
(105 IN. LBS.)

103 N•m (HOT)
(76 FT. LBS.)

54 N•m
(40 FT. LBS.)

18 N•m
(156 IN. LBS.)

SEMI-CIRCULAR
SEAL

Cylinder head and related components — 2.6L engine

11. Remove the small end bolts from the head first, then remove the remaining head bolts, starting from the outside and working inward.

12. Remove the cylinder head from the engine.

13. Clean the cylinder head gasket mating surfaces.

To install:

14. Install a new head gasket to the block and install all head bolts and washers. Torque the bolts in sequence to 34 ft. lbs. (40 Nm). Repeat the sequence increasing the torque to 69 ft. lbs. (94 Nm). Tighten the small end bolts to 13 ft. lbs. (18 Nm).

15. Install the camshaft gear with the timing chain. If the timing will not allow for gear installation, reach into the case with a long, thin tool and push the rubber foot into the oil pump to allow for more chain movement. Install the distributor drive gear, bolt and washer. Torque the bolt to 40 ft. lbs. (54 Nm). Install the distributor, aligning the match marks.

16. Install or connect all items that were removed or disconnected during the removal procedure.

17. Refill the cooling system. Connect the negative battery cable. Start the engine and check for leaks. Adjust the timing as required.

3.0L Engine

1. Relieve the fuel pressure. Disconnect the negative battery cable. Drain the cooling system.

Cylinder head bolt loosening sequence — 3.0L engine

Cylinder head bolt tightening sequence — 3.0L engine

2. Remove the drive belt and the air conditioning compressor from its mount and support it aside. Using a ½ in. drive breaker bar, insert it into the square hole of the serpentine drive belt tensioner, rotate it counterclockwise (to reduce the belt tension) and remove the belt. Remove the alternator and power steering pump from the brackets and move them aside.

3. Raise the vehicle and support safely. Remove the right front wheel assembly and the right inner splash shield.

4. Remove the crankshaft pulleys and the torsional damper.

5. Lower the vehicle. Using a floor jack and a block of wood positioned under the oil pan, raise the engine slightly. Remove the engine mount bracket from the timing cover end of the engine and the timing belt covers.

6. To remove the timing belt, perform the following procedures:

a. Rotate the crankshaft to position the No. 1 cylinder on the TDC of its compression stroke; the crankshaft sprocket timing mark should align with the oil pan timing indicator and the camshaft sprockets timing marks (triangles) should align with the rear timing belt covers timing marks.

b. Mark the timing belt in the direction of rotation for reinstallation purposes.

c. Loosen the timing belt tensioner and remove the timing belt.

NOTE: When removing the timing belt from the camshaft sprocket, make sure the belt does not slip off of the other camshaft sprocket. Support extension.

7. Remove the camshaft bearing assembly to cylinder head bolts (do not remove the bolts from the assembly). Remove the rocker arms, rocker shafts and bearing caps as an assembly, as required. Remove the camshafts from the cylinder head and inspect them for damage, if necessary.

8. Remove the intake manifold assembly.

9. Remove the exhaust manifold.

10. Remove the cylinder head bolts starting from the outside and working inward. Remove the cylinder head from the engine.

11. Clean the gasket mounting surfaces and check the heads for warpage; the maximum warpage allowed is 0.008 in. (0.20mm).

To install:

12. Install the new cylinder head gaskets over the dowels on the engine block.

13. Install the cylinder heads on the engine and torque the cylinder head bolts in sequence using 3 even steps, to 70 ft. lbs. (95 Nm).

14. Install or connect all items that were removed or disconnected during the removal procedure.

15. When installing the timing belt over the camshaft sprocket, use care not to allow the belt to slip off the opposite camshaft sprocket.

16. Make sure the timing belt is installed on the camshaft sprocket in the same position as when removed.

17. Refill the cooling system. Connect the negative battery cable. Start the engine and check for leaks using the DRB I or II to active the fuel pump. Adjust the timing as required.

3.3L Engine

1. Relieve the fuel pressure. Disconnect the negative battery cable. Drain the cooling system.

2. Remove the intake manifold with throttle body.

3. Disconnect the coil wires, sending unit wire, heater hoses and bypass hose.

4. Remove the closed ventilation system, evaporation control system and cylinder hear cover.

5. Remove the exhaust manifold.

6. Remove the rocker arm and shaft assemblies. Remove the pushrods and identify them in ensure installation in their original positions.

Cylinder head components — 3.0L engine

Cylinder head bolt tightening sequence — 3.3L engine

Cylinder head gasket installation — 3.3L engine

7. Remove the head bolts and remove the cylinder head from the block.
To install:
8. Clean the gasket mounting surfaces and install a new head gasket to the block.

9. Install the head to the block. Before installing the head bolts, inspect them for stretching. Hold a straight edge up to the threads. If the threads are not all on line, the bolt is stretched and should be replaced.
10. Torque the bolts in sequence to 45 ft. lbs. (61 Nm). Repeat

the sequence and torque the bolts to 65 ft. lbs. (88 Nm). With the bolts at 65 ft. lbs., turn each bolt an additional ¼ turn.

11. Torque the lone head bolt to 25 ft. lbs. (33 Nm) after the other 8 bolts have been properly torqued.

12. Install the pushrods, rocker arms and shafts and torque the bolts to 21 ft. lbs. (12 Nm).

13. Place a drop of silicone sealer onto each of the 4 manifold to cylinder head gasket corners.

—————————— CAUTION ——————————

The intake manifold gasket is composed of very thin and sharp metal. Handle this gasket with care or damage to the gasket or personal injury could result.

14. Install the intake manifold gasket and torque the end retainers to 105 inch lbs. (12 Nm).

15. Install the intake manifold and torque the bolts in sequence to 10 inch lbs. Repeat the sequence increasing the torque to 17 ft. lbs. (23 Nm) and recheck each bolt for 17 ft. lbs. of torque. After the bolts are torqued, inspect the seals to ensure that they have not become dislodged.

16. Lubricate the injector O-rings with clean oil and position the fuel rail in place. Install the rail retaining bolts.

17. Install the valve cover with a new gasket. Install the exhaust manifold.

18. Install or connect all remaining components that were removed or disconnected during the removal procedures.

19. Refill the cooling system. Connect the negative battery cable. Start the engine and check for leaks.

CYLINDER HEAD CLEANING AND INSPECTION

1. Turn the cylinder head over so that the mounting surface is facing up and support evenly on wooden blocks.

2. Use a scraper and remove all of the gasket material and carbon stuck to the head mounting surface and engine block. Mount a wire carbon removal brush in an electric drill and clean away the carbon on the valve heads and head combustion chambers.

NOTE: **When scraping or decarbonizing the cylinder head, take care not to damage or nick the gasket mounting surface or combustion chamber.**

3. Clean cylinder head oil passages.
4. After cleaning check cylinder head for cracks or damage.
5. Check cylinder head flatness. Flatness must be within 0.1mm.

CYLINDER HEAD RESURFACING

If the cylinder head is warped, resurfacing by a automotive machine shop will be required. After cleaning the gasket surface, place a straight-edge across the mounting surface of the head, diagonally from one end to the other. Using a feeler gauge , determine the clearance at the center and alone the length between the head and straight-edge.

Valves

REMOVAL

The following procedures to be performed with cylinder head removed from engine.

1. Compress valve springs using Tool C-3422A or equivalent. Do not mix removed parts. Place the parts from each valve in a separate container, numbered and identified for the valve and cylinder.

2. Remove valve retaining locks, valve spring retainers, valve stem seal, valve springs and valve spring seats.

Removing the valve springs

Measuring valve spring height — 2.2L engine shown

Checking the valve spring installed height — 2.2L engine shown

Valve seat width and centering

Valve stem oil seals — 2.2L engine shown

2.2L oil pan RTV sealer application

NOTE: Before removing valve assembly remove any burrs from valve stem lock grooves to prevent damage to valve guides.

3. Remove valve assembly.

INSPECTION

1. Clean valves thoroughly.
2. Check valve stem tip for pitting or depression.
3. Check for ridge wear on valve stem area.
4. Inspect valve (with Prussian blue) for even contact between valve face and cylinder head valve seat.
5. Gently remove valve stem seals with a pliers or screwdriver by prying side-to-side. Do not reused old seals.
6. Remove carbon and varnish deposits from inside of valve guides of cylinder head with a suitable guide cleaner.
7. Use an electric drill and soft rotary wire brush to clean the intake and exhaust valve ports, combustion chamber and valve seats. In some cases, the carbon build-up will have to be chipped away. Use a blunt pointed drift for carbon chipping, be careful around valve seat areas.

NOTE: When using a wire brush to clean carbon on the valve ports, valves, etc., be sure the deposits are actually removed, rather then burnished.

8. Wash and clean all valve spring, locks, retainers etc., in safe solvent. Remember to keep parts from each valve separate.

NOTE: If valve guide replacement is necessary, or valve or seat refacing is necessary, the job must be handled by a qualified machine shop.

If a valve seat is damaged, burnt or loose, the seat may be resurfaced or replaced as necessary. The automotive machine shop can handle the job for you.

CHECKING VALVE SPRINGS

Place the valve spring on a flat surface next to a carpenters square. Measure the height of the spring, and rotate the spring against the edge of the square to measure distortion. If the spring height varies (by comparison) by more than $\frac{1}{16}$ in. or if the distortion exceeds $\frac{1}{16}$ in., replace the spring.

Have the valve springs tested for spring pressure at the installed and compressed (installed height minus valve lift) height using a valve spring tester. Springs should be within one pound, plug or minus each other. Replace springs as necessary.

INSTALLATION

1. Coat valve stems with lubrication oil and install in cylinder head.
2. Install a new valve stem seal on the valve. The valve stem seal should be install firmly and squarely over the valve guide. The lower edge of the seal should rest on the valve guide boss.
3. Install the valve spring seat, valve spring, and retainer.
4. Using Tool C-3422A or equivalent compress valve spring only enough to install retainer locks. Install retainer locks and make certain locks are in their correct location before removing valve compressor.
5. Repeat step 1 thru 4 on remaining valves.

Oil Pan

REMOVAL AND INSTALLATION

2.2L Engine

1. Raise and safely support the vehicle on jackstands. Drain the oil pan.

— **CAUTION** —

The EPA warns that prolonged contact with used engine oil may cause a number of skin disorders, including cancer! You should make every effort to minimize your exposure to used engine oil. Protective gloves should be worn when changing the oil. Wash your hands and any other exposed skin areas as soon as possible after exposure to used engine oil. Soap and water, or waterless hand cleaner should be used.

2. Remove the oil pan attaching bolts and remove oil pan.
3. Clean the oil pan and engine block gasket surfaces thoroughly.

RTV application on the front and rear oil pan seals

23 N•m
(200 IN. LBS.)

ANTI-DRAIN BACK VALVE
(SEALING-SEE TEXT)
41 N•m (30 FT. LBS.)

1"-12

3/4"-16

"O" RING

12 N•m
(105 IN. LBS.)

END GASKET

OIL PAN
SIDE GASKETS

28 N•m
(250 IN. LBS.)

OIL PICKUP

M8-23 N•m
(200 IN. LBS.)

M6-12 N•m
(105 IN. LBS.)

27 N•m
(240 IN. LBS.)

2.5L engine lubrication components

4. Apply RTV sealant to oil pan side rails.

5. Install new oil pan seals and install oil pan. Torque the pan screws to 15 ft. lbs.

6. Refill the crankcase, start the engine and check for leaks.

2.5L Engine

1. Raise and safely support the vehicle on jackstands. Drain the oil pan.

— **CAUTION** —

The EPA warns that prolonged contact with used engine oil may cause a number of skin disorders, including cancer! You should make every effort to minimize your exposure to used engine oil. Protective gloves should be worn when changing the oil. Wash your hands and any other exposed skin areas as soon as possible after exposure to used engine oil. Soap and water, or waterless hand cleaner should be used.

2. Remove the oil pan attaching bolts and remove oil pan.

3. Clean oil pan and engine block gasket surfaces thoroughly.

4. Apply RTV sealant to oil pan rail at the front seal retainer parting line.

5. Attach the oil pan side gaskets using heavy grease or RTV to hold the gasket in place.

6. Install the new oil pan seals and apply RTV sealant to the ends of the seals at junction where seals and gasket meets.

7. Install oil pan and tighten M8 screws to 15 ft. lbs., and M6 screws to 105 inch lbs.

2.6L Engine

1. Raise and safely support the vehicle on jackstands. Drain the oil pan.

3.0L oil pan RTV sealer application

Oil pan gasket installation — 3.3L engine

— **CAUTION** —

The EPA warns that prolonged contact with used engine oil may cause a number of skin disorders, including cancer! You should make every effort to minimize your exposure to used engine oil. Protective gloves should be worn when changing the oil. Wash your hands and any other exposed skin areas as soon as possible after exposure to used engine oil. Soap and water, or waterless hand cleaner should be used.

2. Remove the oil pan attaching bolts and remove oil pan.

3. Clean oil pan and engine block gasket surfaces thoroughly.

4. Install a new pan gasket.

5. Install oil pan and tighten screws to 60 inch lbs.

3.0L Engine

1. Raise and safely support the vehicle on jackstands. Drain the oil pan.

— **CAUTION** —

The EPA warns that prolonged contact with used engine oil may cause a number of skin disorders, including cancer! You should make every effort to minimize your exposure to used engine oil. Protective gloves should be worn when changing the oil. Wash your hands and any other exposed skin areas as soon as possible after exposure to used engine oil. Soap and water, or waterless hand cleaner should be used.

2. Remove the oil pan attaching bolts and remove oil pan.

3. Clean oil pan and engine block gasket surfaces thoroughly.

4. Apply RTV sealant to oil pan.

5. Install oil pan to engine and tighten screws in sequence, working from the center toward the ends, to 50 inch lbs.

3.3L Engine

1. Disconnect the negative battery cable.

2. Raise the vehicle and support safely.

3. Remove the torque converter bolt access cover, if equipped.

4. Drain the engine oil.

5. Remove the oil pan retaining screws and remove the oil pan and gasket.

Oil pump application — 2.2L and 2.5L engine

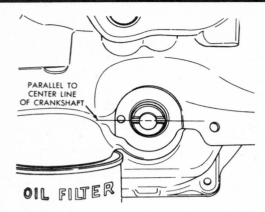

Oil pump shaft alignment — 2.2L engine

To install:

6. Thoroughly clean and dry all sealing surfaces, bolts and bolt holes.

7. Apply silicone sealer to the chain cover to block mating seam and the rear main seal retainer to block seam, if equipped.

8. Install a new pan gasket or apply silicone sealer to the sealing surface of the pan and install to the engine.

9. Install the retaining screws and torque to 200 inch lbs. (23 Nm).

10. Install the torque converter bolt access cover, if equipped. Lower the vehicle.

11. Install the dipstick. Fill the engine with the proper amount of oil.

12. Connect the negative battery cable and check for leaks.

Oil Pump

REMOVAL AND INSTALLATION

2.2L and 2.5L Engine

1. Raise and safely support the vehicle.
2. Drain the oil and remove engine oil pan. See Oil Pan Removal.

2.6L oil pump assembly

CAUTION

The EPA warns that prolonged contact with used engine oil may cause a number of skin disorders, including cancer! You should make every effort to minimize your exposure to used engine oil. Protective gloves should be worn when changing the oil. Wash your hands and any other exposed skin areas as soon as possible after exposure to used engine oil. Soap and water, or waterless hand cleaner should be used.

---

3. Remove the pump mounting bolts.
4. Pull the pump down and out of the engine.
5. Prime, by filling pump with fresh oil. Check crankshaft/intermediate shaft timing and oil pump drive alignment. Adjust if necessary.
6. Install pump and rotate back and forth slightly to ensure full surface contact of pump and block.
7. While holding pump in fully seated position, install pump mounting bolts. Torque to 15 ft. lbs.
8. Install engine oil pan. Refer to Oil Pan Installation procedures.
9. Refill crankcase, start engine.
10. Check engine oil pressure.

2.6L Engine

1. Remove accessory drive belts.
2. Remove the timing chain case cover. Refer to Timing Chain Case Cover Removal procedures.
3. Remove the silent shaft chain assembly and timing chain assembly. Refer to Timing Chain Removal procedures.
4. Remove the silent shaft bolt (bolt directly above the silent chain sprocket).
5. Remove the oil pump bolts and pull the pump housing straight forward. Remove the gaskets and the oil pump backing plate.
6. Clean gasket from mounting surfaces.
7. Install new gaskets/seals, align mating marks of the oil pump gears, refill the pump with oil, and install the pump assembly.
8. Install oil pump silent shaft sprocket and sprocket bolt. Tighten sprocket bolt to 34 Nm (25 ft. lbs.).
9. Install timing chain and silent shaft chain assembly. Refer to Timing Chain Installation procedures.
10. Install timing chain case cover. Refer to Timing Chain Case Cover Installation procedures.
11. Install accessory drive belts.
12. Reconnect battery negative cable.
13. Start engine and check engine oil pressure.

3.0L Engine

The oil pump assembly used on this engine is mounted at the front of the crankshaft. The oil pump also retains the crankshaft front oil seal.

3.0L oil pump components

1. Remove accessory drive belts.
2. Remove the timing belt cover and timing belt. Refer to Timing Belt Removal procedures.
3. Remove the crankshaft sprocket.
4. Remove the oil pump mounting bolts (5), and remove oil pump assembly. Mark mounting bolts for proper installation during reassembly.
5. Clean the oil pump and engine block gasket surfaces thoroughly.
6. Position a new gasket on pump assembly and install on cylinder block. Make sure correct length bolts are in proper locations and torque all bolts to 10 ft. lbs.
7. Install the crankshaft sprocket and timing belt. Recheck engine timing marks. Refer to Timing Belt Installation procedures.
8. Install the timing belt covers. Refer to Timing Belt Cover Installation procedures.
9. Install accessory drive belts.
10. Refill the crankcase and start the engine.
11. Check engine oil pressure.

3.3L Engine

1. Disconnect the negative battery cable. Remove the dipstick.
2. Raise the vehicle and support safely. Drain the oil and remove the oil pan.
3. Remove the oil pickup.
4. Remove the chain case cover.
5. Disassemble the oil pump as required.

To install:
6. Assemble the pump. Torque the cover screws to 10 ft. lbs. (12 Nm).
7. Prime the oil pump by filling the rotor cavity with fresh oil and turning the rotors until oil comes out the pressure port. Repeat a few times until no air bubbles are present.
8. Install the chain case cover.
9. Clean out the oil pickup or replace as required. Replace the oil pickup O-ring and install the pickup to the pump.
10. Install the oil pan.
11. Install the dipstick. Fill the engine with the proper amount of oil.
12. Connect the negative battery cable and check the oil pressure.

CHECKING

2.2L and 2.5L Engines

1. Remove the cover from the oil pump.
2. Check endplay of the inner rotor using a feeler gauge and a straight edge placed across the pump body. The specification is 0.001–0.004 in. (0.03–0.09mm).
3. Measure the clearance between the inner and outer rotors. The maximum clearance is 0.008 in. (0.20mm).
4. Measure the clearance between the outer rotor and the pump body. The maximum clearance is 0.014 in. (0.35mm).
5. The minimum thickness of the outer rotor is 0.944 in. (23.96mm). The minimum diameter of the outer rotor is 2.77 in. (62.70mm). The minimum thickness of the inner rotor is 0.943 in. (23.95mm).
6. Check the cover for warpage. The maximum allowable is 0.003 in. (0.076mm).
7. Check the pressure relief valve for damage. The spring's free length specification is 1.95 in. (49.50mm).
8. Assemble the outer rotor with the larger chamfered edge in the pump body. Torque the cover screws to 10 ft. lbs. (12 Nm).

2.6L Engine

1. Remove the cover from the oil pump.
2. Measure the clearance between the gears and their bearings. The specification for both is 0.0008–0.0020 in. (0.02–0.05mm).
3. Check the clearance between the gears and the housing. The specification for both gears is 0.004–0.006 in. (0.11–0.15mm).
4. Check endplay of the gears using a feeler gauge and a straight edge placed across the pump body. The specification for both is 0.002–0.004 in. (0.04–0.11mm).
5. Check the pressure relief valve for damage. The spring's free length specification is 1.85 in. (47.00mm).
6. If the gears were removed from the body, install them with the mating aligned. If they are not aligned properly, the silent shaft will be out of time.
7. Torque the cover screws to 13 ft. lbs. (18 Nm).

3.0L Engine

1. Remove the rear cover.
2. Remove the pump rotors and inspect the case for excessive wear.
3. Measure the diameter of the inner rotor hub that sits in the case. Measure the inside diameter of the inner rotor hub bore. Subtract the first measurement from the second; if the result is over 0.006 in. (0.15mm), replace the oil pump assembly.
4. Measure the clearance between the outer rotor and the case. The specification is 0.004–0.007 in. (0.10–0.18mm).
5. Check the side clearance of the rotors using a feeler gauge and a straight edge placed across the case. The specification is 0.0015–0.0035 in. (0.04–0.09mm).
6. Check the relief plunger and spring for damage and breakage.
7. Install the rear cover to the case.

3.3L Engine

1. Thoroughly clean and dry all parts. The mating surface of the chain case cover should be smooth. Replace the pump cover if it is scratched or grooved.
2. Lay a straight edge across the pump cover surface. If a 0.076mm feeler gauge can be inserted between the cover and the straight edge, the cover should be replaced.
3. The maximum thickness of the outer rotor is 0.301 in. (7.63mm). The minimum diameter of the outer rotor is 3.14 in. (79.78mm). The minimum thickness of the inner rotor is 0.301 in. (7.64m).
4. Install the outer rotor onto the chain case cover, press to one side and measure the clearance between the rotor and case. If the measurement exceeds 0.022 in. (56mm) and the rotor is good, replace the chain case cover.
5. Install the inner rotor to the chain case cover and measure the clearance between the rotors. If the clearance exceeds 0.008 in. (0.203mm), replace both rotors.
6. Place a straight edge over the chain case cover between bolt holes. If a 0.004 in. (0.102mm) thick feeler gauge can be inserted under the straight edge, replace the pump assembly.
7. Inspect the relief valve plunger for scoring and freedom of movement. Small marks may be removed with 400-grit wet or dry sandpaper.
8. The relief valve spring should have a free length of 1.95 in.
9. Assemble the pump using new parts where necessary.

Timing Gear/Belt/Chain Cover and Seal

REMOVAL AND INSTALLATION

2.2L and 2.5L Engine

1. Remove the accessory drive belts.
2. Remove the alternator.
3. Remove the air condition compressor belt idler bracket and

CAMSHAFT SPROCKET

88 N•m (65 FT. LBS.)

INTERMEDIATE SHAFT SPROCKET

FOAM STUFFER BLOCK

ENGINE BRACKET (REFERENCE)

TENSIONER

SNOW GUARD

88 N•m (65 FT. LBS.)

68 N•m (50 FT. LBS.)

CRANKSHAFT SPROCKET

12 N•m (105 IN. LBS.)

Timing belt and cover assembly — 2.2L and 2.5L engines

disconnect air conditioning compressor and locate out of the way.

4. Remove the power steering pump lock screw. Remove the pivot bolt and nut. Remove the power steering pump and mounting bracket. The hoses need not be disconnected, locate the pump out of the way.

5. Loosen and remove the water pump pulley mounting screws and remove the pulley.

6. Support the vehicle on jackstands and remove the right inner splash shield.

7. Remove the crankshaft pulley.

8. Remove the nuts at upper portion of timing cover and screws from lower portion and remove both halves of cover.

9. Install the cover. Secure the upper section to cylinder head with nuts and lower section to cylinder block with screws.

10. Install the crankshaft pulley and tighten the bolt to 20 ft. lbs., lower vehicle.

11. Install the water pump pulley and tighten screws to 105 inch lbs.

12. Install the power steering pump assembly.

13. Install the air conditioning compressor assembly.

14. Install the alternator assembly.

15. Install the accessory drive belts.

2.6L Engine

1. Disconnect the negative battery cable.

2. Remove the air cleaner assembly.

3. Remove the accessory drive belts.

4. Remove the alternator mounting bolts and remove alternator.

5. Remove the power steering mounting bolts and set power steering pump aside.

6. Remove the air condition compressor mounting bolts and set compressor aside.

7. Support the vehicle on jackstands and remove right inner splash shield.

8. Drain the engine oil.

CAUTION

The EPA warns that prolonged contact with used engine oil may cause a number of skin disorders, including cancer! You should make every effort to minimize your exposure to used engine oil. Protective gloves should be worn when changing the oil. Wash your hands and any other exposed skin areas as soon as possible after exposure to used engine oil. Soap and water, or waterless hand cleaner should be used.

9. Remove the crankshaft pulley.

Description	Flaw conditions
1. Hardened back surface rubber	Back surface glossy. Non-elastic and so hard that even if a finger nail is forced into it, no mark is produced.
2. Cracked back surface rubber	
3. Cracked or exfoliated canvas	
4. Badly worn teeth (initial stage)	Canvas on load side tooth flank worn (Fluffy canvas fibers, rubber gone and color changed to white, and unclear canvas texture)
5. Badly worn teeth (last stage)	Canvas on load side tooth flank worn down and rubber exposed (tooth width reduced)
6. Cracked tooth bottom	
7. Missing tooth	
8. Side of belt badly worn	
9. Side of belt cracked	

Note: Normal belt should have clear-cut sides as if cut by a sharp knife.

Checking the timing belt wear

10. Lower the vehicle and place a jack under the engine with a piece of wood between jack and lifting point.

11. Raise the jack until contact is made with the engine. Relieve pressure by jacking slightly and remove the center bolt from the right engine mount. Remove right engine mount.

12. Remove the engine oil dipstick.

13. Remove the engine valve cover. Refer to Rocker Cover Removal procedures.

14. Remove the front (2) cylinder head to timing chain cover bolts. DO NOT LOOSEN ANY OTHER CYLINDER HEAD BOLTS.

15. Remove the oil pan retaining bolts and lower the oil pan.

16. Remove the screws holding the timing indicator and engine mounting plate.

17. Remove the bolts holding the timing chain case cover and remove cover.

18. Clean and inspect chain case cover for crack or other damage.

19. Position a new timing chain case cover gasket on case cover. Trim as required to assure fit at top and bottom.

20. Coat the cover gasket with sealant (P/N 3419115) or equivalent. Install chain case cover and tighten mounting bolts to 13 ft. lbs.

21. Install the (2) front cylinder head to timing chain case cover mounting bolts and tighten to 13 ft. lbs.

22. Install the engine oil pan tighten screws to 53 inch lbs.

23. Install the engine mounting plate and timing indicator.

24. Install the crankshaft pulley.

25. Install the right engine mount, lower engine and install right engine mount center bolt.

26. Install the engine valve cover. Refer to Rocker Cover Installation procedures.

27. Install the engine oil dipstick.

28. Install the air conditioner compressor.

29. Install the power steering pump.

30. Install the alternator.

31. Install the accessory drive belts.

32. Fill the engine crankcase with recommended engine oil.

33. Install the air cleaner assembly.

34. Connect the negative battery cable.

3.0L Engine

1. Disconnect the negative battery cable.

2. Remove the accessory drive belts.

3. Remove the air conditioner compressor mounting bracket bolts and lay compressor aside.

4. Remove the air conditioner mounting bracket and adjustable drive belt tensioner from engine.

5. Remove the steering pump/alternator belt tensioner mounting bolt and remove belt tensioner.

6. Remove the power steering pump mounting bracket bolts, rear support lock nut and set power steering pump aside.

7. Raise the vehicle and support on jackstands.

8. Remove the right inner splash shield.

9. Remove the crankshaft drive pulley bolt, drive pulley and torsional damper.

10. Lower the vehicle and place a floor jack under the engine. Separate engine mount insulator from engine mount bracket.

11. Raise the engine slightly and remove engine mount bracket.

12. Remove the timing belt covers.

13. Install the timing belt covers and tighten all screws to 10 ft. lbs.

14. Raise the engine slightly and install engine mount bracket.

15. Install the engine mount insulator into engine mount bracket.

16. Install the torsional damper, drive pulley and drive pulley bolt. Torque bolt to 110 Nm (150 ft. lbs.). Install the right inner splash shield.

17. Install the power steering mounting bracket and install the power steering pump.

18. Install the steering pump/alternator belt tensioner.

19. Install the air conditioner adjustable drive belt tensioner and mounting bracket.

20. Install the air conditioner compressor.

21. Install the accessory drive belts.

22. Connect the negative battery cable.

3.3L Engine

1. Disconnect the negative battery cable. Drain the cooling system.

2. Support the engine with a suitable engine support device and remove the right side motor mount.

3. Raise the vehicle and support safely. Drain the engine oil and remove the oil pan.

4. Remove the right wheel and tire assembly and the splash shield.

5. Remove the drive belt.

6. Unbolt the air conditioning compressor and position it to the side. Remove the compressor mounting bracket.

7. Remove the crankshaft pulley bolt and remove the pulley using a suitable puller.

Timing case cover assembly — 2.6L engine

Front timing cover mounting — 3.0L engine

Timing chain case cover retaining bolts — 3.3L engine

Timing chain case cover gaskets and O-rings — 3.3L engine

8. Remove the idler pulley from the engine bracket and remove the bracket.

9. Remove the cam sensor from the timing chain cover.

10. Unbolt and remove the cover from the engine. Make sure the oil pump inner rotor does not fall out. Remove the 3 O-rings from the coolant passages and the oil pump outlet.

To install:

11. Thoroughly clean and dry the gasket mating surfaces. Install new O-rings to the block.

12. Remove the crankshaft oil seal from the cover. The seal must be removed from the cover when installing to ensure proper oil pump engagement.

13. Using a new gasket, install the chain case cover to the engine.

14. Make certain that the oil pump is engaged onto the crank-

shaft before proceeding, or severe engine damage will result. Install the attaching bolts and torque to 20 ft. lbs. (27 Nm).

15. Use tool C–4992 to install the crankshaft oil seal. Install the crankshaft pulley using a 5.9 in. suitable bolt and thrust bearing and washer plate L–4524. Make sure the pulley bottoms out on the crankshaft seal diameter. Install the bolt and torque to 40 ft. lbs. (54 Nm).

16. Install the engine bracket and torque the bolts to 40 ft. lbs. (54 Nm). Install the idler pulley to the engine bracket.

17. To install the cam sensor, first clean off the old spacer from the sensor face completely. Inspect the O-ring for damage and repalce if necessary. A new spacer must be attached to the cam sensor, prior to installation; if a new spacer is not used, engine performance will be affected. Oil the O-ring lightly and push the sensor in to its bore in the timing case cover until contact is made with the cam timing gear. Hold in this position and tighten it to 9 ft. lbs. (12 Nm).

18. Install the air conditioning compressor and bracket.

19. Install the drive belt.

20. Install the inner splash shield and the wheel and tire assembly.

21. Install the oil pan with a new gasket.

22. Install the motor mount.

23. Remove the engine temperature sensor and fill the cooling system until the level reaches the vacant sensor hole. Install the sensor and continue to fill the radiator. Fill the engine with the proper amount of oil.

24. Connect the negative battery cable and check for leaks.

Timing Belt and/or Chain

REMOVAL AND INSTALLATION

2.2L and 2.5L Engine

1. Remove the accessory drive belts.

2. Remove the timing belt cover. Refer to Timing Belt Cover Removal procedures.

3. Loosen the timing belt tensioner screw, rotate the hex nut, and remove timing belt.

4. Turn the crankshaft and intermediate shaft until markings on both sprockets are aligned.

5. Rotate the camshaft so that the arrows on the hub are in line with No. 1 camshaft cap to cylinder head line. Small hole must be in vertical center line.

6. Install the timing belt over the drive sprockets and adjust.

7. Tighten the tensioner by turning the tensioner hex to the right. Tension should be correct when the belt can be twisted 90 degrees with the thumb and forefinger, midway between the camshaft and intermediate sprocket.

8. Turn the engine clockwise from TDC 2 revolutions with crankshaft bolt. Check the timing marks for correct alignment.

WARNING: Do not used the camshaft or intermediate shaft to rotate the engine. Also, do not allow oil or solvent to contact timing belt as they will deteriorate the belt and cause slipping.

9. Tighten lock nut on tensioner while holding weighted wrench in position to 61 Nm (45 ft. lbs.).

10. Install the timing belt cover. Refer to Timing Belt Cover Installation procedures.

11. Install the accessory drive belts.

NOTE: With timing belt cover installed and number one cylinder at TDC, the small hole in the cam sprocket should be centered in timing belt cover hole.

2.6L Engine

1. Disconnect the negative battery cable.

Crankshaft and intermediate shaft timing mark alignment — 2.2L and 2.5L engines

Camshaft sprocket timing alignment

Mark the chain and sprockets and remove the bolt, washer, distributor drive gear and sprocket — 2.6L engine

2. Remove the accessory drive belts.

3. Remove the timing chain case cover. Refer to Timing Chain Case Cover Removal Procedures.

4. Remove the bolts securing the silent shaft chain guides. Mark all parts for proper location during assembly.

5. Remove the sprocket bolts, silent shaft drive chain, crankshaft/silent sprocket, silent shaft sprockets and spacer.

Timing chain components — 2.6L engine

Timing chain installation — 2.6L engine

6. Remove the camshaft sprocket bolt and washer.

7. Remove the distributor drive gear.

8. Remove the camshaft sprocket holder and timing chain guides.

9. Depress the tensioner and remove the timing chain and camshaft sprocket.

10. Remove the crankshaft sprocket.

11. Remove the tensioner shoe, washer and spring.

12. Clean and inspect all parts.

13. Check the tensioner shoe for wear or damage and tensioner spring for deterioration. Spring free length 65.7mm.

14. Check the chain cover for damage or cracks.

15. Check the silent shaft and camshaft chain guides for damage or excessive wear.

16. Check the silent shaft sprocket cushion ring for free and smooth rotation and ring guides for damage.

17. Check the silent chain and timing chain for excessive play, wear or damage links.

Timing/silent shaft chain and drive components — 2.6L engine

Dowel pin set at 12 o'clock — 2.6L engine

18. Check all sprockets for wear or damage teeth.
19. Rotate the camshaft until the dowel pin is at vertical center line with cylinder.
20. Install the timing chain sprocket holders.
21. Rotate the crankshaft until No. 1 piston is at Top Dead Center (TDC) of its compression stroke.
22. Install the timing chain tensioner spring, washer and shoe on oil pump body.
23. Assemble the timing chain on the camshaft and crankshaft sprockets.

NOTE: The mating mark on the camshaft and crankshaft sprocket teeth must line up with plated links on timing chain.

24. While holding the sprockets and chain as an assembly, install the crankshaft sprocket to key way of crankshaft and camshaft sprocket to dowel pin of camshaft.
25. Install the distributor drive gear, camshaft sprocket bolt and washer, and torque bolt to 54 Nm (40 ft. lbs.).
26. Install the silent shaft chain drive sprocket on crankshaft.

Oil pump and silent shaft installation — 2.6L engine

27. Assemble the silent shaft chain to oil pump sprocket and to silent shaft sprocket.

NOTE: The timing marks on the sprockets teeth must line up with plated links on of silent shaft chain.

28. While holding the parts as an assembly, align the crankshaft sprocket plated link with the punch mark on the sprocket. With the chain installed on crankshaft sprocket, install the oil pump sprocket and silent chain sprocket on their respective shafts.

Timing mark alignment for silent shaft timing chain installation — 2.6L engine

29. Install the oil pump and silent shaft sprocket bolts and tighten to 34 Nm (25 ft. lbs.).

30. Loosely install the 3 silent shaft chain guides and adjust silent shaft chain tension as follows.

    a. Tighten chain guide **A** mounting screws.

    b. Tighten chain guide **C** mounting screws.

    c. Slightly rotate the oil pump and silent shaft sprockets to remove any slack in the silent shaft chain.

    d. Adjust the position of chain guide **B** so that when the chain is pulled inward, the clearance between chain guide **B** and the chain links will be 1.0-3.5mm. Tighten chain guide **B** mounting screws.

31. Install a new timing case cover gasket and install timing case cover.

Silent shaft chain adjustment — 2.6L engine

Sprocket timing for belt installation — 3.0L engine

Secure the sprocket when removing or installing the nut

SILENT SHAFT CHAIN ADJUSTMENT

If necessary silent shaft chain adjustment may be performed without removing timing chain case cover. Proceed as followed:
1. Remove the access cover from the timing case cover.
2. Through the access hole loosen special bolt **B**
3. Using your finger only push on boss to apply tension.
4. While applying tension tighten special bolt **B** to 13 ft. lbs.
5. Install access cover to timing chain case cover.

3.0L Engine

NOTE: The timing belt can be inspected by removing the upper (front outer) timing cover.

1. Disconnect the negative battery cable.
2. Remove the accessory drive belts.
3. Remove the timing belt covers. Refer to Timing Belt Cover Removal Procedures.
4. Identify the timing belt running direction to avoid reversal during installation.
5. Loosen timing belt tensioner bolt and remove timing belt.
6. Remove the crankshaft sprocket flange.
7. Rotate the crankshaft sprocket until timing mark on crankshaft sprocket is lined up with the oil pump timing mark at 1 o'clock position.
8. Rotate the (inner) camshaft sprocket until mark on (inner) camshaft sprocket is lined up with the timing mark on alternator bracket.
9. Rotate the (outer) camshaft sprocket (radiator side) until mark on the sprocket is lined up with the timing mark on the timing belt inner cover. Refer to timing belt illustration.
10. Install the timing belt on the crankshaft sprocket while maintaining pressure on the tensioner side.
11. Position the timing belt over the camshaft sprocket (radiator side). Next, position the belt under the water pump pulley, then over the (inner) sprocket and finally over the tensioner.
12. Apply rotating force in the opposite direction to the camshaft sprocket (radiator side) to create tension on the timing belt tension side.
13. Rotate the crankshaft in a clockwise direction and recheck engine timing marks.
14. Install the crankshaft sprocket flange.
15. Loosen the tensioner bolt and allow tensioner spring to tension the belt.
16. Again rotate the crankshaft in a clockwise direction (2) full turns. Recheck the engine timing. Tighten the tensioner bolt to 31 Nm (23 ft. lbs.).
17. Install the timing covers.

Timing belt tensioner — 3.0L engine

Positioning the tensioner — 3.0L engine

Timing mark alignment — 3.3L engine

18. Install the accessory drive belts.
19. Connect battery negative cable.

3.3L Engine

1. If possible, position the engine so that the No. 1 piston is at

TDC on the compression stroke. Disconnect the negative battery cable. Drain the coolant.

2. Remove the timing chain case cover.

3. Remove the camshaft gear attaching cup washer and remove the timing chain with both gears attached. Remove the timing chain snubber.

To install:

4. Assemble the timing chain and gears.

5. Turn the crankshaft and camshaft to line up with the key way locations of the gears.

6. Slide both gears over their respective shafts and use a straight edge to confirm alignment.

7. Install the cup washer and camshaft bolt. Torque the bolt to 35 ft. lbs. (47 Nm).

8. Check camshaft endplay. The specification with a new plate is 0.002–0.006 in. (0.051–0.052mm) and 0.002–0.010 in. (0.51–0.254mm) with a used plate. Replace the thrust plate if not within specifications.

9. Install the timing chain snubber.

10. Thoroughly clean and dry the gasket mating surfaces.

11. Install new O-rings to the block.

12. Remove the crankshaft oil seal from the cover. The seal must be removed from the cover when installing to ensure proper oil pump engagement.

13. Using a new gasket, install the chain case cover to the engine.

14. Make certain that the oil pump is engaged onto the crankshaft before proceeding, or severe engine damage will result. Install the attaching bolts and torque to 20 ft. lbs. (27 Nm).

15. Use tool C–4992 to install the crankshaft oil seal. Install the crankshaft pulley using a 5.9 in. suitable bolt and thrust bearing and washer plate L–4524. Make sure the pulley bottoms out on the crankshaft seal diameter. Install the bolt and torque to 40 ft. lbs. (54 Nm).

16. Install all other parts removed during the chain case cover removal procedure and fill the engine with oil.

19. Connect the negative battery cable, road test the vehicle and check for leaks.

Timing Sprockets/Gears

REMOVAL AND INSTALLATION

2.2L and 2.5L Engines

1. Remove the drive belts, timing belt cover and timing belt. See Timing Belt Cover and Timing Belt Removal Procedures as previously outlined.

2. Remove the crankshaft sprocket bolt.

3. Remove the crankshaft sprocket using Tool C-4685 and Tool L-4524 or an equivalent puller. If crankshaft seal removal is necessary, remove with Tool C-4679 (2.2L) or Tool C-4991 (2.5L), or an equivalent tool.

4. Clean the crankshaft seal surface with 400 grit paper.

5. Lightly coat the seal (Steel case seal) outer surface with Loctite Stud N' Bearing Mount (P/N 4057987) or equivalent. A soap and water solution is recommended to lubricate (Rubber Coated Case Seal) outer surface.

6. Lightly lubricate the seal lip with engine oil.

7. Install seal with Tool No. C-4680 (2.2L) or Tool No. C-4992 (2.5L).

8. Install the sprocket and install sprocket bolt.

9. Remove and install the camshaft and intermediate shaft sprockets with Tool C-4687 and Tool C-4687-1 in similar fashion.

10. Install the timing belt and timing belt cover. See Timing Belt and Timing Belt Cover Installation Procedures as previously outlined.

11. Install the accessory drive belts.

Suspending the sprocket to retain the engine timing

2.6L Engine

Refer to Timing Chain Case Cover Removal procedures.

3.0L and 3.3L Engine

Refer to Timing Case Cover Removal procedures.

Camshaft and Bearings

REMOVAL AND INSTALLATION

2.2L and 2.5L Engines

The following procedure is preformed with the engine in the vehicle.

NOTE: Removal of the camshaft requires removal of the camshaft sprocket. To maintain proper engine timing, the timing belt can be left indexed on the sprockets and suspended under light pressure. This will prevent the belt from coming off and maintain timing.

1. Disconnect the negative battery cable. Relieve the fuel pressure, if equipped with fuel injection.

2. Turn the crankshaft so the No. 1 piston is at the TDC of the compression stroke. Remove the upper timing belt cover. Remove the air pump pulley, if equipped.

3. Remove the camshaft sprocket bolt and the sprocket and suspend tightly so the belt does not lose tension. If it does, the belt timing will have to be reset.

4. Remove the valve cover.

5. If the rocker arms are being reused, mark them for installation identification and loosen the camshaft bearing bolts, evenly and gradually.

6. Using a soft mallet, rap the rear of the camshaft a few times to break the bearing caps loose.

7. Remove the bolts, bearing caps and the camshaft with seals.

NOTE: Before replacing the camshaft, identify factory installed oversized components. To do so, look for the tops of the bearing caps pained green and O/SJ stamped rearward of the oil gallery plug on the rear of the head. In addition, the barrel of the camshaft is painted green and O/SJ is stamped onto the rear end of the camshaft. Installing standard sized parts in an head equipped with oversized parts-or vice versa-will cause severe engine damage.

Checking camshaft lobe wear

Camshaft bearing caps — 2.2L and 2.5L engines

Measuring camshaft end play

8. Check the oil passages for blockage and the parts for damage. Clean all mating surfaces.

To Install:

9. Transfer the sprocket key to the new camshaft. New rocker arms and a new camshaft sprocket bolt are normally included with the camshaft package. Install the rocker arms, lubricate the camshaft and install with end seals installed.

10. Place the bearing caps with No. 1 at the timing belt end and No. 5 at the transaxle end. The camshaft bearing caps are numbered and have arrows facing forward. Torque the camshaft bearing bolts evenly and gradually to 18 ft. lbs. (24 Nm).

NOTE: Apply RTV silicone gasket material to the No. 1 and 5 bearing caps. Install the bearing caps before the seals are installed.

11. Mount a dial indicator to the front of the engine and check the camshaft endplay. Play should not exceed 0.006 in.

12. Install the camshaft sprocket and the new bolt. Install the air pump pulley, if equipped.

13. Install the valve cover with a new gasket.

14. Connect the negative battery cable and check for leaks.

2.6L Engine

1. Disconnect the negative battery cable.

2. Remove the valve cover.

3. Remove the camshaft gear retaining bolt and match mark the distributor gear to its drive gear. Remove the distributor. Pry the distributor drive gear off of the cam gear.

4. Remove the cam gear from the camshaft and allow it to rest on the holder below it.

5. Remove the water pump pulley.

6. Remove the camshaft cap bolts evenly and gradually.

7. Remove the caps, shafts, rocker arms and bolts together as an assembly.

8. Remove the camshaft with the rear seal from the engine.

To install:

9. Install a new roll pin to the camshaft. Lubricate the camshaft and install with the rear seal in place. Install the camshaft in position so the hole in the gear will line up with the roll pin.

10. Install the rocker caps, shafts and arms assembly. Tighten the camshaft bearing cap bolts in the following order to 85 inch lbs. (10 Nm): No. 3, No. 2, No. 4, front cap, rear cap. Repeat the sequence increasing the torque to 175 inch lbs. (19 Nm).

11. Install the gear to the camshaft engaging the roll pin. Install the distributor drive gear and install the bolt and washer. Torque the bolt to 40 ft. lbs. (54 Nm). Install the distributor.

12. Install the valve cover and all related parts.

3.0L Engine

1. Disconnect the negative battery cable. Remove the air cleaner assembly and valve covers.

2. Install auto lash adjuster retainers MD998443 or equivalent on the rocker arms.

3. If removing the right side (front) camshaft, remove the distributor extension.

4. Remove the camshaft bearing caps but do not remove the bolts from the caps.

5. Remove the rocker arms, rocker shafts and bearing caps, as an assembly.

6. Remove the camshaft from the cylinder head.

7. Inspect the bearing journals on the camshaft, cylinder head and bearing caps.

Camshaft thrust plate — 3.3L engine

To Install:

8. Lubricate the camshaft journals and camshaft with clean engine oil and install the camshaft in the cylinder head.

9. Align the camshaft bearing caps with the arrow mark (depending on cylinder numbers) and in numerical order.

10. Apply sealer at the ends of the bearing caps and install the assembly.

11. Torque the bearing cap bolts, in the following sequence: No. 3, No. 2, No. 1 and No. 4 to 85 inch lbs. (10 Nm).

12. Repeat the sequence, increasing torque to 175 inch lbs. (18 Nm).

13. Install the distributor extension, if it was removed.

14. Install the valve cover and all related components.

3.3L Engine

1. Relieve the fuel system pressure. Disconnect the negative battery cable.

2. Remove the engine from the vehicle. Remove the intake manifold, cylinder heads, timing chain cover and timing chain from the engine.

3. Remove the rocker arm and shaft assemblies.

4. Label and remove the pushrod and lifters.

5. Remove the camshaft thrust plate.

6. Install a long bolt into the front of the camshaft to facilitate its removal. Remove the camshaft being careful not to damage the cam bearings with the cam lobes.

To install:

7. Install the camshaft to within 2 in. of its final installation position.

8. Install the camshaft thrust plate and 2 bolts and torque to 10 ft. lbs. (12 Nm).

9. Place both camshaft and crankshaft gears on the bench with the timing marks on the exact imaginary center line through both gear bores as they are installed on the engine. Place the timing chain around both sprockets.

10. Turn the crankshaft and camshaft so the keys line up with the key ways in the gears when the timing marks are in proper position.

11. Slide both gears over their respective shafts and use a straight edge to check timing mark alignment.

12. Measure camshaft endplay. If not within specifications, replace the thrust plate.

13. If the camshaft was not replaced, lubricate and install the lifters in their original locations. If the camshaft was replaced, new lifters must be used.

14. Install the pushrods and rocker shaft assemblies.

15. Install the timing chain cover, cylinder heads and intake manifold.

16. Install the engine in the vehicle.

17. When everything is bolted in place, change the engine oil and replace the oil filter.

NOTE: If the camshaft or lifters have been replaced, add 1 pint of Mopar crankcase conditioner, or equivalent when replenishing the oil to aid in break in. This mixture should be left in the engine for a minimum of 500 miles and drained at the next normal oil change.

18. Fill the radiator with coolant.

19. Connect the negative battery cable, set all adjustments to specifications and check for leaks.

CAMSHAFT INSPECTION

1. Inspect the camshaft bearing journals for wear or damage.

2. Inspect the cylinder head and check oil return holes.

3. Check the tooth surface of the distributor drive gear teeth of the right camshaft for wear or damage.

4. Check both camshaft surfaces for wear or damage.

5. Remove the distributor drive adaptor seal.

6. Check camshaft lobe height and replace if out of limit. Standard value is 41.00mm.

Auxiliary (Idler) Shaft
REMOVAL AND INSTALLATION

2.2L and 2.5L Engines

The following procedures to be performed with engine removed from vehicle.

1. Remove the distributor assembly.

2. Remove the fuel pump.

3. Remove timing case cover, and timing belt.

4. Remove the intermediate shaft sprocket. See Sprocket Removal Procedures.

5. Remove the intermediate shaft retainer screws and remove retainer.

6. Remove the intermediate shaft and inspect journals and bushing.

7. When installing the shaft, lubricate the fuel pump eccentric and distributor drive gear. Install the intermediate shaft.

8. Inspect the shaft seal in retainer. Replace if necessary.

9. Lightly lubricate the seal lip with engine oil.

10. Install the intermediate shaft retainer assembly and retainer screws. Tighten screws to 105 inch lbs. On 2.5L engine apply anaerobic (Form-in-Place) gasket material to retainer sealing surface before installing.

11. Install the intermediate shaft sprocket.

12. Check engine timing. See Engine Timing Check Procedures.

13. Install the timing belt and adjust.

14. Install the timing belt cover.

15. Install the fuel pump.

16. Install the distributor. See Distributor Installation Procedures.

Balance Shafts

The 2.5L engine is equipped with 2 balance shafts located in a housing attached to the lower crankcase. These shafts are driven by a chain and 2 gears from the crankshaft at 2 times crankshaft speed. This counterbalance certain engine reciprocating masses.

Balance shaft timing — 2.5L engine

FASTNER TORQUE			
LETTER	N·m	IN. LBS.	FT. LBS.
A	12	105	—
B	28	250	—
C	54	—	40
★D	★41	—	★30
E	95	—	70
F	(PLUG - LOCTITE 277)		
G	15	130	—

★SPECIFIED TORQUE
<u>PLUS</u> 1/4 TURN

Balance shaft assembly — 2.5L engine

Balance shaft chain tensioner adjustment — 2.5L engine

Removing the intermediate shaft sprocket

REMOVAL AND INSTALLATION

1. Remove the engine from vehicle.
2. Remove the timing case cover, timing belt and sprockets.
3. Remove the engine oil pan.

Balance shaft removal and installation — 2.5L engine

Balance shaft gear timing — 2.5L engine

4. Remove the front crankshaft seal retainer.
5. Remove the balance shafts chain cover.
6. Remove the chain guide and tensioner.
7. Remove the balance shafts sprocket retaining screws and crankshaft chain sprocket torx screws. Remove the chain and sprocket assembly.
8. Remove the balance shafts carrier front gear cover retaining double ended stud. Remove the cover and balance shafts gears.
9. Remove the carrier rear cover and balance shafts.
10. To separate the carrier, remove (6) crankcase to carrier attaching bolts and remove carrier.
11. Take notice of all parts to avoid interchanging.
To install:
12. Install both shafts into carrier the assembly from rear of carrier.
13. Install the rear cover.
14. Install the balance shafts drive and driven gears to shafts.
15. Position the carrier assembly on crankcase and tighten (6) bolts to 54 Nm (40 ft. lbs.).
16. Crankshaft to Balance Shaft Timing must be established. Rotate both balance shafts until the key ways are in the Up position.
17. Install the short hub drive gear on balance shaft driving shaft.
18. Install the long hub gear on the driven shaft.
19. With both gears on the balance shafts and key ways Up, the timing marks should be meshed.

20. Align the balance shaft carrier cover with the carrier housing dowel pin and install double ended stud. Tighten to 105 inch lbs.
21. Install the crankshaft sprocket and tighten sprocket torx screw to 11 ft. lbs.
22. Turn the crankshaft until number one cylinder is at TDC. The timing marks on the chain sprocket should line up with the parting line on the left side of number one main bearing cap.
23. Install the chain over the crankshaft sprocket so the nickel plated link of the chain is over the timing mark on the crankshaft sprocket.
24. Install the balance shaft sprocket into the timing chain so that the timing mark on the sprocket (yellow dot) mates with the yellow painted link on the chain.
25. With the balance shaft key way in 12 o'clock position slide the balance shaft sprocket on the nose of the balance shaft. The balance shaft may have to be pushed in slightly to allow for clearance.

NOTE: The timing mark on the sprocket, the painted link, and the arrow on the side of the gear cover should line up if the balance shafts are timed correctly.

26. Install the balance shaft bolt and tighten to 21 ft. lbs. Placed a wooden block between the crankcase and crankshaft counterbalance to prevent crankshaft from turning.
27. Proper balance shaft Timing Chain Tension must be established.
28. Place a shim 1.0mm thick by 70mm long between the chain and tensioner.
29. Apply firm hand pressure behind the adjustment slot and tighten adjustment bolt first, followed by the pivot screw to 105 inch lbs. Remove the shim.
30. Install the chain guide making sure the tab on the guide fits into slot on the gear cover. Install nut/washer and tighten to 105 inch lbs.
31. Install the chain cover and tighten screws to 105 inch lbs.
32. Apply a 1.5mm diameter bead of RTV gasket material to retainer sealing surface. Install retainer assembly.
33. Install the crankshaft sprocket and timing belt. See Timing Belt Adjustment and Engine Timing Procedures.
34. Install the timing cover.

Silent Shafts

The 2.6L engine uses 2 counter shafts (silent shafts) in the cylinder block to reduce engine noise and vibration.

REMOVAL AND INSTALLATION

The following procedures to be performed with engine removed from vehicle.
1. Remove the timing chain case cover. Refer to Timing Chain Case Cover Removal procedures.
2. Remove the silent shaft chain assembly and timing chain assembly. Refer to Timing Chain Removal procedures.
3. Remove the silent shaft bolt (bolt directly above the silent chain sprocket).
4. Remove the oil pump bolts and pull the pump housing straight forward. Remove the gaskets and the oil pump backing plate.
5. Remove the right silent shaft.
6. Remove the left silent shaft thrust plate by screwing 2 8mm screws into tapped holes in thrust plate. Remove left silent shaft.
To install:
7. Install both silent shafts into cylinder block. Be careful not to damage inner bearings.
8. Install the left silent shaft thrust plate on the left silent shaft using a new O-ring.

9. Install the oil pump. Refer to Oil Pump Installation procedures.

10. Install the timing chain and silent chain assembly. Refer to Timing Chain Installation procedures.

11. Install the timing chain case cover. See Timing Chain Case Cover Installation procedures.

SILENT SHAFT CLEARANCE

1. Outer diameter to outer bearing clearance: 0.02-0.06mm.
2. Inner diameter to inner bearing clearance: 0.05-0.09mm.

Pistons and Connecting Rods

REMOVAL

The following procedures are performed with the engine removed from vehicle.

1. Remove the engine from the vehicle.
2. Remove the timing case cover, timing belt or chain and sprockets.
3. Remove the intake manifold.
4. Remove the cylinder head from engine.
5. Remove the engine oil pan.
6. Remove the oil pump.
7. Remove the balance shaft carrier (2.5L engine).

NOTE: Because the top piston ring does not travel to the very top of the cylinder bore, a ridge is built up between the end of the travel and the top of the cylinder walls. Pushing the piston and connecting rod assembly past the ridge is difficult and may cause damage to the piston. If new rings are installed and the ridge has not been removed, ring breakage and piston damage can occur.

Turn the crankshaft to position the piston at the bottom of the cylinder bore. Cover the top of the piston with a rag. Install a ridge reamer in the bore and follow the manufacturer's instructions to remove the ridge. Use caution, avoid cutting too deeply. Remove the rag and cuttings from the top of the piston. Remove the ridge from all cylinders.

8. Turn the crankshaft until the connecting rod is at the bottom of travel.
9. Number all connecting rod caps if not already labeled to aid during assembly. Remove connecting rod bearing cap nuts and remove caps. Keep all parts separated.
10. Take 2 pieces of rubber tubing and cover the rod bolts to prevent cylinder wall scoring.
11. Before removing the piston assembly from cylinder bore scribe a mark indicating front position, or take notice of manufacturer identification mark. Using a wooden hammer handle, carefully tap piston assembly away from crankshaft and remove from cylinder block. Care should be taken not to damage crankshaft connecting rod journals or threads on connecting rod cap bolts.
12. Remove all the pistons from cylinder block in similar fashion.

NOTE: It is not necessary to remove the crankshaft from cylinder block for piston service. If crankshaft service is necessary refer to Crankshaft Removal procedures.

CLEANING AND INSPECTION

1. Use a piston ring expander and remove the rings from the piston.
2. Clean the ring grooves using an appropriate cleaning tool, exercise care to avoid cutting too deeply.

RIDGE CAUSED BY CYLINDER WEAR

CYLINDER WALL / TOP OF PISTON

Cylinder bore ridge

USE A SHORT PIECE OF 3/8" HOSE AS A GUIDE

Use lengths of rubber tubing to protect the crankshaft journal and cylinder linings during piston and rod removal/installation

GAP OF LOWER SIDE RAIL

NO. 1 RING GAP

FRONT OF ENGINE

NO. 2 RING GAP AND SPACER EXPANDER GAP

GAP OF UPPER SIDE RAIL

Piston ring positioning

PISTON RING

FEELER GAUGE

RING GROOVE

Check the piston ring side clearance

Check the piston ring end gap

3. Clean all varnish and carbon from the piston with a safe solvent. Do not use a wire brush or caustic solution on the pistons.

4. Inspect the pistons for scuffing, scoring, cracks, pitting or excessive ring groove wear. If wear is evident, the piston must be replaced.

5. Have the piston and connecting rod assembly checked by a machine shop for correct alignment, piston pin wear and piston diameter. If the piston has collapsed it will have to be replaced or knurled to restore original diameter. Connecting rod bushing replacement, piston pin fitting and piston changing can be handled by the machine shop.

6. Check the cylinder bore diameter and cylinder bore for wear using a telescope gauge at 3 different levels. Cylinder bore out of round: 0.05mm maximum. Cylinder bore taper: 0.13mm maximum. Refer to General Engine Specification Chart for cylinder bore specification.

7. Check piston dimensions. Measure approximately 2mm above the bottom of the piston skirt and across the thrust face. Refer to Piston and Ring Specification Chart for piston diameter.

8. After recording cylinder bore measurement and piston diameter, subtract the low reading. The difference is Piston to Cylinder Wall Clearance: 0.02-0.04mm.

9. Check piston ring gap using a piston to position the ring at least 16mm from the bottom of cylinder bore. Measure clearance using a feeler gauge. Refer to Piston and Rings Specification Chart.

10. Check the piston ring to piston ring groove clearance using a feeler gauge.

11. Check the ring groove by rolling the new piston ring around the groove to check for burrs or carbon deposits. If any are found, remove with a fine file.

12. If all clearances and measurements are within specifications, honing or glaze breaking the cylinder bore is all that is required.

INSTALLATION

1. Start with the oil ring expander in the lower oil ring groove.

2. Install one oil rail at bottom of the oil ring expander and the other at top. The oil rails must be spaced 180 degrees apart from each other.

3. Using the ring expander install the intermediate piston ring.

4. Install the upper piston ring using the ring expander.

NOTE: Generally marks on the upper and intermediate piston rings must point toward the crown of piston. Consult the illustration with piston ring set instruction sheet for ring positioning.

RING COMPRESSOR

Piston Installation

5. Install a ring compressor and insert the piston and rod assembly into the engine with mark previously made or labeled mark on piston head toward timing chain end of cylinder block.

6. Rotate the crankshaft so that the connecting rod journal is on center of cylinder bore. Install a new connecting rod bearing in connecting rod and cap. Check the connecting rod bearing oil clearance using Plastigage. Follow the manufacturer procedures. Refer to Crankshaft and Connecting Rod Specification Chart.

7. Tighten the connecting rod cap nuts to specification. Refer to Torque Specification Chart.

8. Install the remaining piston and rod assemblies.

9. Using a feeler gauge, check connecting rod side clearance.

10. On 2.5L engine install the balance shaft carrier.

11. Install the oil pump and pick-up.

12. Install the cylinder head.

13. Install the intake manifold.

14. Install the timing chain or belt and sprockets.

15. Install the timing case cover.

16. Install the engine oil pan. Refer to Oil Pan Installation procedures.

Freeze Plugs

REMOVAL AND INSTALLATION

Freeze plugs can be removed with the engine in or out of the vehicle.

Using a blunt tool, such as a drift and hammer, strike the bottom edge of the plug. With the plug rotated, grasp it firmly with pliers and remove it. Do not drive the plug into the block as coolant flow restriction would occur.

When installing the replacement plug, thoroughly clean the plug bore, removing any old sealant. Coat the new plug with Loctite® Stud Mount, or equivalent. Position the plug on the block and drive it into the block so that the sharp edge is at least 0.020 in. (0.5mm) inside the chamfer. Check the plug for leaks after cooling system refilling.

Engine Block Heater

REMOVAL AND INSTALLATION

1. Disconnect the negative battery cable.

2. Drain the cooling system, including the engine block.

3. Detach the power cord plug from the block heater assembly.

4. Loosen the screw in the center of the heater and pull the heater from the block.

To install:

5. Clean the heater hole in the block and the heater seat.

6. Insert the heater with the element loop facing upward.

7. Tighten the heater retaining screw securely.

8. Refill the cooling system and pressurize the cooling system with a radiator pressure tool. Check for leaks before operating block heater.

Engine block heater system components

9. Connect the negative battery cable.

Rear Main Seal

REMOVAL AND INSTALLATION

2.2L and 2.5L Engines

1. With the engine or transaxle removed from vehicle, remove the flywheel or flexplate.
2. Pry out rear crankshaft oil seal from seal retainer. Be careful not to nick of damage crankshaft sealing surface or seal retainer.
3. Place Tool C-4681 or equivalent on the crankshaft.
4. Lubricate outer diameter with Loctite Stud N' Bearing Mount (PN. 4057987) or equivalent.
5. Lightly lubricate the seal lip with engine oil and tap in place with a plastic hammer.

6. Install the flywheel/flex plate and tighten bolts to 95 Nm (70 ft. lbs.).

2.6L Engine

1. With the engine or transaxle removed from vehicle, remove the flywheel or flex plate.
2. Remove the rear crankshaft seal retainer.
3. Remove the separator from retainer and remove seal.
4. Clean all old gasket material from the retainer and engine block surface.
5. Install a new gasket on the retainer.
6. Lightly lubricate the new seal lip with engine oil and install the separator making sure the oil hole is at the bottom of separator.
7. Install flywheel tighten bolts to 95 Nm (70 ft. lbs.).

Removing the rear main oil seal — 2.2L engine

Rear main oil seal installation — 2.6L engine

3.0L and 3.3L Engine

1. With the engine or transaxle removed from vehicle, remove the flywheel or flex plate.

2. Pry out the rear crankshaft oil seal from the seal retainer. Be careful not to nick or damage the crankshaft sealing surface or seal retainer.

3. Lightly lubricate the new seal lip with engine oil and install seal in retainer housing using Tool MD998718 or equivalent.

4. Install flywheel and tighten the bolts to 95 Nm (70 ft. lbs.).

Crankshaft and Main Bearings

Although, crankshaft service can be performed without removing the engine from the vehicle, it is far easier to work on the engine after it has been removed from the vehicle.

REMOVAL AND INSTALLATION

1. Remove the engine from vehicle. Refer to Engine Removal procedures.

2. Remove the timing case cover, timing belt or chain and sprockets.

3. Remove the flywheel.

4. Remove the engine oil pan.

5. Remove the front crankshaft seal retainer if used. On 3.0L and 3.3L engines the front crankshaft seal is located in the oil pump assembly.

6. Remove the oil pump assembly 3.0L and 3.3L engines.

7. On 2.5L engines, remove the balance shaft carrier assembly.

8. Remove the rear crankshaft oil seal retainer bolts and remove retainer.

9. Before removing the crankshaft check Crankshaft End

Remove the upper main bearing insert, using a roll out pin

Home made rollout pin

Home made roll out pin

Play. as follows:

a. Position a screwdriver between a main bearing cap and crankshaft. Move the crankshaft all the way to the rear of its travel.

b. Position a feeler gauge between the thrust bearing and crankshaft machined surface to determine end play. Refer to Crankshaft and Connecting Rod Specification Chart.

Use the following procedure if only crankshaft removal is necessary. If other engine repairs are being perform complete engine disassembly will be required.

10. Number all connecting rod caps if not already labeled to aid during assembly. Remove the connecting rod bearing caps nuts and remove caps.

11. Take 2 pieces of rubber tubing and cover the rod bolts to prevent crankshaft scoring.

12. Tap the piston assembly lightly away from crankshaft. Care should be taken not to damage crankshaft connecting rod journals or threads on connecting rod cap bolts.

13. Remove the main bearing cap bolts and remove caps. Remove crankshaft.

To install:

14. Install the main bearing shells with the lubrication groove in the cylinder block. Make certain the oil holes are in alignment, and bearing tabs seat in block.

15. Install the thrust bearing in journal No.3.

16. Oil the bearings and journals and install crankshaft.

17. Install the lower main bearing shells (without oil grooves) in lower bearing caps.

18. Check the main or connecting bearing oil clearance as followed:

a. Wipe oil from bearing shells.

b. Cut a piece of Plastigage to the same length as width of the bearing and place it in parallel with the journal.

c. Install the bearing cap and torque to specification.

NOTE: Do not rotate crankshaft or the Plastigage will be smeared.

d. Carefully remove the bearing cap and measure the width of the Plastigage at the widest part using the scale printed on

Installing the crankshaft mono-block main bearing — 3.0L engine. Tighten the bolts in the sequence shown.

the Plastigage package. Refer to Crankshaft and Connecting Rod Specification Chart.

19. Install all main bearing caps with arrows toward the timing chain end of cylinder block. Dip bolts in engine oil and install bolts finger tight then alternately torque each bolt. Refer to Torque Specification Chart.

20. Position the connecting rods with new bearing shells against crankshaft. Install lower caps.

21. Before installing the nuts oil the threads. Install the nut on each bolt finger tight, then alternately torque each nut to specification. Refer to Torque Specification Chart.

22. On 2.5L engine install balance shaft carrier assembly.

23. Install the front and rear crankshaft oil seal retainer assembly. Apply a 1.5mm diameter bead of RTV gasket material to retainers sealing surface.

24. Install the timing sprockets, timing belt and timing case cover. Refer to procedures previously outlined.

25. Install the engine oil pan. Refer to Oil Pan Installation procedures.

26. Install the flywheel. Refer to Torque Specifications.

CRANKSHAFT CLEANING AND INSPECTION

1. Inspect the main and connecting rod bearings replace if necessary.

2. Clean the crankshaft oil passages. Check the crankshaft main journals and connecting rod journals for wear or damage.

EXHAUST SYSTEM

Safety Precautions

For a number of reasons, exhaust system work can be the most dangerous type of work you can do on your car. Always observe the following precautions:

• Support the car extra securely. Not only will you often be working directly under it, but you'll frequently be using a lot of force, say, heavy hammer blows, to dislodge rusted parts. This can cause a car that's improperly supported to shift and possibly fall.

• Wear goggles. Exhaust system parts are always rusty. Metal chips can be dislodged, even when you're only turning rusted bolts. Attempting to pry pipes apart with a chisel makes the chips fly even more frequently.

• If you're using a cutting torch, keep it a great distance from either the fuel tank or lines. Stop what you're doing and feel the temperature of the fuel bearing pipes on the tank frequently. Even slight heat can expand and/or vaporize fuel, resulting in accumulated vapor, or even a liquid leak, near your torch.

• Watch where your hammer blows fall and make sure you hit squarely. You could easily tap a brake or fuel line when you hit an exhaust system part with a glancing blow. Inspect all lines and hoses in the area where you've been working.

——————— CAUTION ———————

Be very careful when working on or near the catalytic converter. External temperatures can reach 1,500°F (816°C) and more, causing severe burns. Removal or installation should be performed only on a cold exhaust system.

Special Tools

A number of special exhaust system tools can be rented from auto supply houses or local stores that rent special equipment. A common one is a tail pipe expander, designed to enable you to join pipes of identical diameter.

It may also be quite helpful to use solvents designed to loosen rusted bolts or flanges. Soaking rusted parts the night before you do the job can speed the work of freeing rusted parts considerably. Remember that these solvents are often flammable. Apply only to parts after they are cool!

Exhaust (Converter/Resonator) Pipe

REMOVAL AND INSTALLATION

1. Raise the vehicle and properly support on jackstands.

——————— CAUTION ———————

Be very careful when working on or near the catalytic converter! External temperatures can reach 1,500°F (816°C) and more, causing severe burns! Removal or installation should be performed only on a cold exhaust system.

2. Apply penetrating oil to clamp bolts, nuts and connecting points of system to be remove.
3. Remove the nuts and clamp assembly from exhaust pipe to muffler connecting point.
4. Remove the shoulder bolts, springs and nuts attaching exhaust pipe to exhaust manifold.

5. Remove the exhaust pipe/converter assembly from muffler.
6. Clean the exhaust manifold to exhaust pipe/converter assembly gasket mating surfaces and the end of muffler with a wire brush.
7. Install the exhaust pipe/converter assembly or resonator into muffler. Make certain the key on the converter or resonator pipe bottomed in slot of muffler.
8. Install a new gasket on the exhaust pipe and position exhaust pipe into exhaust manifold. Install springs, shoulder bolts and nuts. Tighten nuts to 21 ft. lbs.
9. Align parts and install a new clamp assembly at exhaust pipe and muffler connecting point tighten clamps nuts to 23 ft. lbs.

Tailpipe

REMOVAL AND INSTALLATION

1. Raise the vehicle and properly support on jackstands.
2. Apply penetrating oil to clamp bolts, nuts and connecting points of system to be remove.
3. Remove the support saddle type clamp assembly from the tail pipe to muffler connecting point.
4. Remove the U-nut and shoulder bolts from tail pipe mid-point and rear tail pipe bracket.
5. When removing the tail pipe, raise the rear of vehicle enough to provide clearance between pipe and rear axle parts.
6. Remove the tailpipe from muffler.
7. Clean the muffler mating surface with a wire brush.
8. Replace broken or worn insulators, supports or attaching parts.
9. Loosely assemble the tail pipe to muffler, mid-point support and tail pipe bracket. Make certain slot in tail pipe is keyed with key in muffler.
10. Align parts and install support saddle type clamp tighten nuts to 28 ft. lbs.

Muffler

REMOVAL AND INSTALLATION

1. Raise the vehicle and properly support on jackstands.
2. Apply penetrating oil to clamp bolts, nuts and connecting points of system to be remove.
3. Disconnect the tail pipe from the muffler assembly. Refer to Tail Pipe Removal procedures.
4. Remove nuts and clamp from exhaust pipe and muffler connection and remove the muffler.
5. Clean the exhaust pipe and tail pipe mating surfaces with a wire brush.
6. Replace broken or worn insulators, supports or attaching parts.
7. Loosely assemble the muffler to exhaust pipe and tail pipe. Make certain keys are bottomed in slots of muffler and pipes.
8. Align parts and install support saddle type clamp between tail pipe and muffler connecting point. Tighten nuts to 28 ft. lbs.
9. Install clamp assembly and nuts at exhaust pipe and muffler connecting point and tighten to 25 ft. lbs.

Exhaust system components

Special tools for exhaust system work

TORQUE SPECIFICATIONS

Component	English	Metric
Air intake plenum attaching bolts 3.0L engine:	115 inch lbs.	13 Nm
Alternator support bracket:	40 ft. lbs.	54 Nm
Alternator mounting bolts:	40 ft. lbs.	54 Nm
Automatic transmission oil cooler mounting bolts:	35 inch lbs.	4 Nm
Automatic transmission oil cooler lines-to-cooler clamps:	16 inch lbs.	2 Nm
Balance shaft bolt 2.5L engine:	21 ft. lbs.	29 Nm
Balance shafts carrier assembly-to-crankcase bolts 2.5L engine:	40 ft. lbs.	54 Nm
Cam sensor bolt 3.3L engine:	9 ft. lbs.	12 Nm

Camshaft bearing cap bolts
  2.2L and 2.5L Engines:
  2.6L and 3.0L Engines
    Step 1:
    Step 2:
	18 ft. lbs.
	
	85 inch lbs.
	15 ft. lbs.
		24 Nm
		
		10 Nm
		19 Nm

Camshaft sprocket bolt
  Except 3.3L engine:
  3.3L engine:
	40 ft. lbs.
	35 ft. lbs.
		54 Nm
		47 Nm

Camshaft thrust plate bolts 3.3L engine:	10 ft. lbs.	14 Nm
Carburetor air heater-to-manifold 2.6L engine:	80 inch lbs.	9 Nm
Catalytic converter-to-manifold 3.0L engine:	24 ft. lbs.	32 Nm

Combination Manifold
  2.2L and 2.5L Engines
    Exhaust manifold-to-cylinder head:
    Intake manifold-to-cylinder head:
	17 ft. lbs.
	19 ft. lbs.
		23 Nm
		26 Nm

Connecting rod bearing cap bolts
  2.2L, 2.5L and 3.3L engines
    Step 1:
    Step 2:
  2.6L engine:
  3.0L engine:
	40 ft. lbs.
	an additional 90° (¼) turn
	34 ft. lbs.
	38 ft. lbs.
		54 Nm
		
		46 Nm
		52 Nm

Crankshaft damper bolt
  2.2L and 2.5L engines:
  2.6L engine:
  3.0L engine:
  3.3L engine:
	50 ft. lbs.
	87 ft. lbs.
	110 ft. lbs.
	40 ft. lbs.
		68 Nm
		118 Nm
		150 Nm
		54 Nm

Crankshaft pulley bolt
  2.2L and 2.5L Engine:
  3.3L engine:
	20 ft. lbs.
	40 ft. lbs.
		27 Nm
		54 Nm

Crankshaft sprocket Torx® screws 2.5L engine:	11 ft. lbs.	15 Nm

TORQUE SPECIFICATIONS

Component	English	Metric
Cylinder Head		
2.2L and 2.5L Engines		
Step 1:	45 ft. lbs.	61 Nm
Step 2:	65 ft. lbs.	88 Nm
Step 3:	additional 90° (¼) turn.	
2.6L Engine		
Step 1:	34 ft. lbs.	40 Nm
Step 2:	69 ft. lbs.	94 Nm
3.0L Engine		
Step 1:	30 ft. lbs.	41 Nm
Step 2:	50 ft. lbs.	68 Nm
Step 3:	70 ft. lbs.	95 Nm
3.3L Engine		
8 shorter bolts first		
Step 1:	45 ft. lbs.	61 Nm
Step 2:	65 ft. lbs.	88 Nm
Step 3:	an additional 90° (¼) turn	
2 longer bolts next:	25 ft. lbs.	33 Nm
Distributor drive gear bolt		
2.6L engine:	40 ft. lbs.	54 Nm
EGR tube flange-to-intake plenum		
3.0L engine:	15 ft. lbs.	20 Nm
Engine-to-transaxle mounting bolts:	70 ft. lbs.	95 Nm
Exhaust crossover pipe-to-manifold		
3.0L engine:	51 ft. lbs.	69 Nm
Exhaust Manifold		
All exc. 2.6L engine:	17 ft. lbs.	23 Nm
2.6L Engine:	13 ft. lbs.	18 Nm
Exhaust pipe-to-manifold		
3.0L engine:	20 ft. lbs.	27 Nm
Exhaust pipe-to-exhaust manifold nuts:	21 ft. lbs.	29 Nm
Exhaust pipe-to-muffler clamp nuts:	23 ft. lbs.	31 Nm
Exhaust system saddle type clamp nuts:	28 ft. lbs.	38 Nm
Flywheel/flex plate bolts		
All Engines:	70 ft. lbs.	95 Nm
Front engine mount:	40 ft. lbs.	54 Nm
Fuel line-to-fuel rail clamps		
3.0L engine:	10 inch lbs.	1 Nm
Fuel pressure regulator hose clamps		
3.0L engine:	10 inch lbs.	1 Nm
Fuel pressure regulator mounting bolts		
3.0L engine:	95 inch lbs.	11 Nm
Fuel rail bracket screws		
2.2L and 2.5L engines:	21 ft. lbs.	28 Nm
Fuel supply and return tube holddown bolt		
3.0L engine:	95 inch lbs.	11 Nm
Heat shield-to-manifold		
2.6L engine:	80 inch lbs.	9 Nm
3.0L engine:	10 ft. lbs.	14 Nm
Idler pulley-to-engine bracket bolts		
3.3L engine:	40 ft. lbs.	54 Nm
Ignition coil mounting bolts:	105 inch lbs.	12 Nm
Injector rail attaching bolts		
3.0L engine:	115 inch lbs.	13 Nm

TORQUE SPECIFICATIONS

Component	English	Metric
Intake Manifold		
2.2L and 2.5L engines:	17 ft. lbs.	23 Nm
2.6L engine:	13 ft. lbs.	18 Nm
3.0L engine:	17 ft. lbs.	23 Nm
3.3L engine		
Step 1:	10 inch lbs.	1 Nm
Step 2:	17 ft. lbs.	23 Nm
Step 3:	17 ft. lbs.	23 Nm
Intake manifold end retainers		
3.3L engine:	105 inch lbs.	12 Nm
Intermediate shaft retainer screws		
2.2L and 2.5L engines:	105 inch lbs.	12 Nm
Main bearing cap bolts		
2.2L, 2.5L and 3.3L engines		
Step 1:	30 ft. lbs.	41 Nm
Step 2:	an additional 90° (¼) turn	
2.6L engine:	58 ft. lbs.	79 Nm
3.0L engine:	60 ft. lbs.	82 Nm
Oil Pan		
2.2L Engine:	15 ft. lbs.	21 Nm
2.5L Engine		
M8 screws:	15 ft. lbs.	21 Nm
M6 screws:	105 inch lbs.	12 Nm
2.6L Engine		
Oil pan-to-block:	60 inch lbs.	7 Nm
Oil pan-to-timing case:	53 inch lbs.	6 Nm
3.0L Engine:	50 inch lbs.	6 Nm
3.3L Engine:	17 ft. lbs.	23 Nm
Oil Pump attaching bolts		
2.2L and 2.5L Engines:	15 ft. lbs.	21 Nm
3.0L Engine:	10 ft. lbs.	14 Nm
3.3L Engine:	20 ft. lbs.	27 Nm
Oil pump cover screws		
3.3L engine:	10 ft. lbs.	12 Nm
Oil pump sprocket bolt		
2.6L engine:	25 ft. lbs.	34 Nm
Radiator mounting bolts:	105 inch lbs.	12 Nm
Radiator hose-to-thermostat housing:	35 inch lbs.	4 Nm
Radiator hose-to-radiator clamps:	to 35 inch lbs.	4 Nm
Right engine mount:	20 ft. lbs.	27 Nm
Rocker arm and shaft assembly bolts		
3.3L Engine:	21 ft. lbs.	28 Nm
Rocker (Valve) Cover		
2.2L Engine:	105 inch lbs.	12 Nm
2.5L Engine:	105 inch lbs.	12 Nm
2.6L Engine:	55 inch lbs.	6 Nm
3.0L Engine:	68 inch lbs.	7 Nm
3.3L Engine:	102 inch lbs.	11 Nm
Silent shaft chain tensioner bolt		
2.6L engine:	13 ft. lbs.	18 Nm
Thermostat housing		
All engines:	15 ft. lbs.	20 Nm
Throttle body-to-intake manifold screws		
2.2L and 2.5L Engines:	21 ft. lbs.	28 Nm
Timing belt cover screws		
3.0L engine:	10 ft. lbs.	14 Nm

TORQUE SPECIFICATIONS

Component	English	Metric
Timing belt tensioner lock nut		
2.2L and 2.5L engines:	45 ft. lbs.	61 Nm
3.0L Engine:	23 ft. lbs.	31 Nm
Timing chain case cover		
2.6L Engine:	13 ft. lbs.	18 Nm
Timing chain cover screws		
2.5L engine:	105 inch lbs.	12 Nm
Timing chain guide nut		
2.5L engine:	105 inch lbs.	12 Nm
Timing chain tensioner adjustment and pivot bolts		
2.5L engine:	105 inch lbs.	12 Nm
Torque converter-to-flex plate bolts:	40 ft. lbs.	54 Nm
Turbocharger-to-exhaust manifold:	40 ft. lbs.	54 Nm
Turbocharger articulated joint shoulder bolts:	21 ft. lbs.	28 Nm
Turbocharger connector tube clamps:	30 inch lbs.	41 Nm
Turbocharger inlet tube-to-throttle body tube clamp:	30 inch lbs.	3 Nm
Turbocharger inlet coolant tube-to-engine block:	30 ft. lbs.	41 Nm
Turbocharger mounting screws		
Block screw:	40 ft. lbs.	54 Nm
Housing screw:	20 ft. lbs.	27 Nm
Turbocharger oil feed line nuts:	10 ft. lbs.	14 Nm
Turbocharger oil drain-back hose clamps:	30 inch lbs.	3 Nm
Turbocharger outlet-to-exhaust manifold nuts:	30 ft. lbs.	41 Nm
Upper intake manifold bolts		
3.3L engine:	21 ft. lbs.	28 Nm
Upper intake manifold bracket and strut bolts		
3.3L engine:	40 ft. lbs.	54 Nm
Water Pump		
2.2L and 2.5L Engines		
3 upper bolts:	20 ft. lbs.	27 Nm
1 lower bolt:	50 ft. lbs.	68 Nm
2.6L and 3.0L Engines:	20 ft. lbs.	27 Nm
3.3L Engine:	21 ft. lbs.	30 Nm
Water pump pulley screws		
2.2L and 2.5L Engine:	105 inch lbs.	12 Nm

Exhaust system heat shield mounting

Emission Controls 4

QUICK REFERENCE INDEX

GENERAL INDEX

EMISSION CONTROLS

Vehicle Emission Control Information Label

All vehicles described in this Repair and Tune-Up Guide are equipped with a Vehicle Emission Control Information Label (VECI). The VECI label is located in the engine compartment and is permanently attached. No attempt should be made to remove the VECI label. The VECI label contains specific information for the vehicle to which it is attached. If the specifications on the VECI label differ from the information contain in this manual, those shown on the label should be followed.

Crankcase Ventilation System

The Positive Crankcase Ventilation System is described, and servicing procedures are detailed in the "General Information and Maintenance" section of this book.

1984-86 underhood label identification

1997-91 underhood label identification

Canister purge solenoid

Evaporative Emission Controls

The Evaporative Emission Control System prevents gasoline vapor emissions from the fuel system, from entering the atmosphere.

Evaporating fuel from the gas tank or carburetor, passes through vent hoses and tubes to a charcoal canister where they are temporarily stored until they can be drawn into the intake manifold and burned when the engine is running.

CHARCOAL CANISTER

The charcoal canister is a sealed, maintenance free unit which stores fuel vapors from the fuel tank and carburetor bowl. Although all carburetor bowls are vented internally, some models do not required venting to the canister. In cases where the carburetor is not vented to the canister, the bowl vent port on the canister will be capped. If the canister becomes damaged, replacement with a new unit is required. The hoses connecting the canister are of fuel resistant construction. Use only fuel resistant hoses if replacement is necessary.

DAMPING CANISTER

Some models are equipped with a damping canister that is connected in series with the charcoal canister. The damping canister cushions the effect of a sudden release of fuel rich vapors when the purge valve is signaled to open. The rich vapors are held momentarily and then gradually fed into the intake manifold to be burned.

CANISTER PURGE SOLENOID

All engines are equipped with a canister purge solenoid which is connected in series with the charcoal canister. The canister purge solenoid is electrically operated by the Single Module Engine Controller (SMEC) which grounds the solenoid if engine temperature is below 66°C. This prevents vacuum from reaching the charcoal canister. When the engine reaches operating temperature the SMEC de-energizes the solenoid and allows purge vapors from the canister to pass through the throttle body.

ROLLOVER VALVE

All vehicles pass a full 360° rollover without allowing fuel leakage. To accomplish this, fuel and vapor flow controls are needed for all fuel tank connections. A rollover valve is mounted in the top of the fuel tank to prevent leakage if the vehicle is involved in a rollover.

Pressure vacuum gas filler cap

Heated air intake system on 2.2L engine

GAS TANK FILLER CAP

The fuel tank is covered and sealed with a specially engineered pressure/vacuum relief gas cap. The built-in relief valve is a safety feature, and allows pressure to be relieved without separating the cap from the filler tube eliminating excessive tank pressure. If a replacement cap is required, a similar cap must be installed in order for the system to remain effective.

NOTE: Always remove the gas tank cap to release pressure whenever the fuel system requires servicing.

BOWL VENT VALVE

The bowl vent valve (carburetor equipped models) is connected to the carburetor fuel bowl, the charcoal canister, and the air pump discharge. When the engine is not running and no air pump pressure is applied, a direct connection between the carburetor and canister exists. When the engine is running, air pump pressure closes the connection between the canister and the fuel bowl. When the engine is shut off, air pressure in the valve bleeds down and the fuel bowl is allow to vent vapors into the canister.

Testing the vacuum diaphragm

Exhaust Emission Controls

HEATED INLET AIR SYSTEM

All TBI engines are equipped with a vacuum device located in the air cleaner air intake. A small door is operated by a vacuum diaphragm and a thermostatic spring. When the outside air temperature is below a specified level, the door will block off air entering from outside the air cleaner snorkel, and allow heated air channeled from the exhaust manifold area to enter the air cleaner assembly. With the engine warmed up and running the thermostatic spring allows the heat control door to draw outside air through the air cleaner snorkel.

On later models the air temperature in the air intake is monitored by a temperature sensor in the intake housing.

Testing the heated air inlet diaphragm

SERVICE PROCEDURES

NOTE: A malfunction in the heated air system will affect driveability and the emissions output of the vehicle.

2.2L Engine

1. Verify all vacuum hoses and the flexible heat pipe between the air cleaner and heat stove are properly attached and in good condition.

2. On a cold engine with an ambient temperature less than 19°C (65°F) the heat door valve plate in the snorkel should be in the up position (Heat On).

3. With the engine running at normal operating temperature, the heat door should be in the down position (Heat Off).

4. If the heat door valve plate does not respond to hot and cold temperatures, the door diaphragm or the sensor may need replacing.

5. To test the diaphragm, remove the air cleaner from the engine and allow it to cool down to 19°C (65°F).

6. Connect a hand operated vacuum pump to the vacuum diaphragm and apply 20 inches of vacuum. The diaphragm should not leak down more than 10 inches in 5 minutes. The control door should not lift from the bottom of the snorkel at less than 2

inches of vacuum and be in the full up position with no more than 4 inches of vacuum. If the vacuum test proves the diaphragm defective, replace the air cleaner.

7. If the vacuum test shows the diaphragm in proper working condition, replace the sensor.

8. Label the vacuum hoses at the sensor to aid during reassemble. Disconnect the vacuum hoses, remove the retaining clips with a screwdriver and discard. Remove the sensor and mounting gasket.

9. Position the new gasket on the sensor and install sensor. Support the sensor on the outer diameter, and install the retaining clips.

10. Reconnect vacuum hoses.

2.5L Engine

1. Verify all vacuum hoses and the flexible heat pipe between the air cleaner and heat stove are properly attached and in good condition.

2. On a cold engine with an ambient temperature less than 46°C (115°F) the heat door valve plate in the snorkel should be in the up position (Heat On).

3. With the engine running at normal operating temperature, the heat door should be in the down position (Heat Off).

4. If the heat door valve plate does not respond to hot and cold temperatures, the door diaphragm or the sensor may need replacing.

5. To test the diaphragm, remove the air cleaner from the engine and allow it to cool down to 46°C (115°F).

6. Connect a hand operated vacuum pump to the sensor and apply 20 inches of vacuum. The door valve should be in the up position (Heat On).

7. If the door does not raise to "Heat On" position, test the vacuum diaphragm for proper operation.

8. Apply 20 inches of vacuum with a hand operated vacuum pump to the vacuum diaphragm. The diaphragm should not leak down more than 10 inches in 5 minutes. The control door should not lift from the bottom of the snorkel at less than 2 inches of vacuum and be in the full up position with no more than 4 inches of vacuum. If the vacuum test proves the diaphragm defective, replace the air cleaner.

9. If the vacuum test shows the diaphragm in proper working condition, replace the sensor.

10. Label the vacuum hoses at the sensor to aid during assembly. Disconnect the vacuum hoses, remove the retaining clips with a screwdriver and discard. Remove the sensor and mounting gasket.

11. Position the new gasket on the sensor and install sensor. Support the sensor on the outer diameter, and install the retaining clips.

12. Connect the vacuum hoses.

2.6L Engine

1. Verify all vacuum hoses and the flexible heat pipe between the air cleaner and heat stove are properly attached and in good condition.

2. On a cold engine with an ambient temperature less than 30°C (84°F) the heat door valve plate in the snorkel should be in the up position (Heat On).

3. With the engine running at normal operating temperature, the heat door should be in the down position (Heat Off).

4. If the heat door valve plate does not respond to hot and cold temperatures, the door diaphragm or the sensor may need replacing.

5. To test the diaphragm, remove the air cleaner from the engine and allow it to cool down to 30°C (84°F).

6. Connect a hand operated vacuum pump to the sensor and apply 15 inches of vacuum. The valve should be in the up position (Heat On).

7. If the door does not raise to Heat On position, test the vacuum motor for proper operation.

Heated air intake system on the 2.6L engine

8. Apply 10 inches of vacuum to the vacuum motor with a hand operated vacuum pump, if the valve does not remain in the full up position replace the air cleaner body assembly.

9. If the door perform adequately with vacuum applied to the motor, replace the sensor.

HEATED AIR TEMPERATURE SENSOR REPLACEMENT

The heated air temperature sensor is located in the air cleaner housing and can be removed with the air filter removed from the housing.

1. Remove the top of the air cleaner housing, this can be done by releasing the clips.

2. Remove the air filter.

3. Disconnect the vacuum lines from the sensor.

4. Remove the sensor from the housing by prying it carefully out.

5. Install the new sensor in position using a new gasket. Make sure the sensor is firmly seated.

6. Reconnect the vacuum lines to the sensor and reinstall the air filter.

Installing the heated air temperature sensor — TBI engines

EGR system — late model 2.5L engines

EGR valve and Electric Transducer mounting — late model 2.5L engines

Exhaust Gas Recirculation (EGR) System

The EGR system reduces the oxides of nitrogen in the engine exhaust. The reduction of NOx is accomplished by allowing a predetermined amount of the hot exhaust gas to recirculate and dilute the incoming fuel and air mixture. This dilution reduces peak flame temperature during combustion.

SERVICE

2.2L Engine

The components of the EGR system on the 2.2L engine are; a Coolant Controlled Exhaust Gas Recirculation/Coolant Vacuum Switch Cold Closed (CVSCC) unit mounted in the thermostat housing, an EGR valve, and a EGR tube.

The CVSCC prevents vacuum from being supplied to the EGR system or other systems until the coolant temperature reaches a certain level. When a certain temperature is reached the CVSCC opens and vacuum is supplied as necessary.

To assure proper operation test the system as follows:

1. Inspect all passages and moving parts for free movement.

2. Inspect all hoses. If any are hardened, cracked or have faulty connection, replacement is necessary.

3. Allow the engine to reach normal operating temperature. Locate the EGR valve at the end of the intake manifold. Allow the engine to idle for about a minute, then abruptly accelerate to about 2000 rpm, but not over 3000 rpm. Visible movement of the EGR valve stem should be noticed. Movement of the stem indicates the valve is operating normally. If no movement is noticed. Remove the EGR valve and inspect it for deposits and wear.

4. If deposits around the poppet and seat are more than a film, apply some heat control solvent to the area to help soften the deposits. Apply vacuum to the valve with a hand operated vacuum pump. When the valve opens, scrap away the deposits from the poppet and seat. If the valve poppet does not open when vacuum is applied, replace the valve. If the stem or seat is worn replace the valve.

5. If the EGR valve is functioning properly, check the CVSCC.

6. Check condition of vacuum hoses at the CVSCC and properly routed (see vacuum hose under hood sticker).

7. Check engine coolant level.

8. Disconnect the vacuum hoses and remove the valve from the thermostat housing. Place the valve in an ice bath below 4.4°C (40°F) so that the threaded portion is covered. Attach a vacuum pump to the lower connection on the valve (the one connected to the vacuum hose showing a yellow stripe). Apply 10 inches of vacuum. Pressure should drop no more than one inch in one minute. If the vacuum drops more, replace the CVSCC.

2.6L Engine

With this system exhaust gases are partially recirculated from an exhaust port in the cylinder head into a port at the intake manifold below the carburetor. EGR flow is controlled by

EGR system on the 2.2L engine

Coolant vacuum switch

EGR system on the 2.6L engine

EGR valve — cut away view

Sub EGR valve assembly

A carburetor mounted Sub EGR valve is directly opened and closed by the throttle linkage in order to closely modulate the EGR flow controlled by the EGR control valve, in response to the throttle opening.

Two thermo valves connected to the EGR system, sense coolant temperature changes and open and close accordingly to control the vacuum flow to the EGR system.

Test the system as follows:

1. Check the vacuum hose for good condition and proper routing (see vacuum hose under hood sticker).

2. Engine must be cold. Cold start the engine and allow to idle.

3. Check to make sure that the fast idle does not cause the secondary EGR valve to operate. If the secondary EGR valve operates at cold start fast idle, replace the secondary EGR valve thermo valve.

4. Run the engine until the operating temperature exceeds 65°C (149°F). The secondary EGR valve should now be in operation. If if does not operate, inspect the EGR valve or thermo valve.

5. Disconnect the green stripped vacuum hose from the carburetor. Connect a hand vacuum pump to the hose and apply 6 inches of vacuum while opening the sub EGR valve by hand. If the idle speed becomes unstable, the secondary valve is operating properly. If the idle speed remains the same, replace the secondary EGR valve and thermo valve.

6. Connect the green stripped hose to the carburetor. Discon-

thermo valves, and a combination of a Dual EGR valve and Sub EGR valve.

The dual EGR valve consists of a primary and secondary valve which are controlled by a different carburetor vacuums in response to the throttle opening. EGR flow is halted at idle and wide open throttle operation. The primary valve controls the EGR flow at narrow throttle openings, while the secondary valve allows flow into the intake mixture at wider throttle openings. Vacuum to the dual EGR valve is controlled by thermo valves.

nect the yellow stripped hose from the carburetor and connect it to the hand vacuum pump. Hold the sub EGR valve opened and apply 6 inches of vacuum.

7. If the idle speed becomes unstable, the primary EGR valve is operating properly. If the idle speed remains unchanged, replace the primary EGR valve and thermo valve.

2.5L and 3.0L Engines

The EGR system for late model vehicles equipped with the 2.5L engines, is a back pressure type. A back pressure transducer measures the amount of exhaust gas back pressure on the exhaust side of the EGR valve and varies the strength of the vacuum signal applied to the EGR valve. The transducer uses this back pressure signal to provide the correct amount of exhaust gas recirculation under all conditions.

This utilizes an intake manifold mounted EGR valve and Electric EGR Transducer (EET). An EGR tube carries the exhaust gases from the intake manifold to the exhaust manifold. The EGR systems are solenoid controlled, using a manifold vacuum signal from the throttle body. The EGR solenoid is part of the EET. These systems do not allow EGR at idle. EGR systems operate at all temperatures above 60°F (16°C).

California vehicles with EGR have an on-board diagnostic system and a solenoid in series with the vacuum line to the EGR valve. The engine controller monitors EGR system performance and energized or de-energized the solenoid base on engine/driving conditions. If the system malfunction the engine controller will turn on the Check Engine light and a fault code will be stored in the diagnostic system.

Test the system as follows:

1. Inspect all passages and moving parts for free movement.

2. Inspect all hoses. If any are hardened, cracked or have faulty connection, replacement is necessary.

3. Warm the engine to normal operating temperature. Allow the engine to idle for about a minute, then abruptly accelerate to about 2000 rpm, but not over 3000 rpm. Visible movement of the groove on EGR valve stem should be noticed. Movement of the stem indicates the valve is operating normally. If no movement is noticed.

4. Disconnect the vacuum hoses from the EGR vacuum transducer, and attach a hand operated vacuum pump. Raise the engine to 2000 rpm and apply 10 inches of vacuum, while checking valve movement. If no valve movement occurs, replace the valve/transducer assembly.

NOTE: If the back-pressure EGR valve does not function satisfactory. Replace the entire Valve/Transducer assembly. No attempt should be made to clean the valve.

5. If movement occurs, check the diaphragm for leaks. Valve should remain open at least 30 seconds.

6. If the valve is functioning satisfactory, remove the throttle body and inspect port in throttle bore and associated passages. Apply some heat control solvent to the area to help soften any deposit.

7. Install the throttle body and recheck EGR operation.

Air Injection System

2.2L engines are equipped with an air injection system. This system is designed to supply a controlled amount of air to the exhaust gases, through exhaust ports, aiding in the oxidation of the gases and reduction of carbon monoxide and hydrocarbons to an appreciable level.

During engine warm-up air is injected into the base of the exhaust manifold. After the engine warms up, the air flow is switched (by a Coolant Vacuum Switch Cold Open or by a vacuum solenoid) to the 3-way catalyst where it further aids in the reduction of carbon monoxide and hydrocarbons in the exhaust system.

The system consists of a belt driven air pump, hoses, a switch/relief valve and a check valve to prevent the components within the system from high temperature exhaust gases.

NOTE: No repairs are possible on any of the air injection system components. All replacement parts must be serviced as a unit.

Air injection system on the 2.2L engine — Federal/Canadian shown

Coolant Vacuum Switch Cold Open

1. Locate the switch on the thermostat housing.
2. Label the hoses before removing. Remove hoses.
3. Remove the vacuum switch from housing.
4. Install a new vacuum switch and connect the vacuum hoses. (See under hood vacuum hose routing label).

Air Pump

NOTE: The air injection system is not completely noiseless. Do not assume the air pump is defective because it squeals. If the system creates excessive noise, remove the drive belt and operate the engine. If the noise ceases, check all hoses connection for proper tightening. Replace pump if necessary.

1. Remove all hoses and vacuum lines from the air pump and diverter valve or switch/relief valve (depending on how equipped).
2. Remove the air pump drive pulley shield.
3. Remove the air pump pivot bolt and remove air pump belt.
4. Remove the remaining mounting bolts and remove pump.
5. Remove the diverter valve or switch/relief valve from pump.
6. Clean all gasket material from valve and pump mounting surface.
7. Install the diverter valve or switch/relief valve using a new gasket, to the new pump.
8. Install the pump on the engine and loosely install pivot bolt.
9. Install drive belt and tighten pivot bolt.
10. Install air pump drive pulley shield.
11. Install all hoses and vacuum lines.

Switch/Relief Valve

If vacuum is apply to the valve and air injection is not upstream, or if air injection is in both upstream and downstream, the valve is faulty and must be replaced.

1. Remove all air hoses and vacuum hoses.
2. Remove the valve to pump mounting bolts, and remove valve.
3. Clean all gasket material from mounting surfaces.
4. Install the new valve to the pump with a new gasket.
5. Secure the valve with mounting bolts, tighten bolts to 14Nm (125 inch lbs.).
6. Reinstall all air hoses and vacuum hoses.

Relief Valve

The purpose of this valve is to control air pump pressure during high engine speeds. If the pump discharge pressure exceeds 9 PSI the valve will open and vent the excess pressure to the atmosphere.

1. Remove the air hoses from the valve.
2. Remove the valve mounting screws and remove valve.
3. Clean all gasket material from mounting surfaces.
4. Install a new gasket on valve and secure with mounting screws.
5. Reconnect air hoses.

Check Valve

The check valve is located in the injection tube which lead to the exhaust manifold and converter assembly. The valve has a one-way diaphragm to protect the pump and hoses from high exhaust system pressure if the belt or pump failed.

Remove the air hose from check valve inlet tube. If exhaust gas escapes from the inlet tube, the valve have failed and must be replaced.

1. Loosen clamp and remove inlet hose from the valve.
2. Remove the tube nut retaining the tube to the exhaust manifold or catalyst.
3. Loosen the starter motor mounting bolt and remove injection tube from engine.
4. Remove the catalyst injection tube mounting screws from catalyst flange and remove injection tube.
5. Position the injection tube to catalyst flange and secured with mounting screws.
6. Install the injection tube into fitting in exhaust manifold and bracket at starter motor.
7. Connect hoses to the check valve.

Pulse Air Feeder System

2.6L engines use a pulse air feeder system to promote oxidation of exhaust emissions in the rear catalytic converter. The system consists of a main reed valve and sub-reed valve. The main reed valve is controlled by a diaphragm which is activated by pressure pulses from the crankcase. The sub-reed valve is activated by pulsation in the exhaust system between the front and rear converters.

1. Remove the air duct from the right side of the radiator.
2. Remove the carburetor protector shield.

Pulse air feed system on the 2.6L engine

3. Remove the engine oil dipstick and tube.
4. Remove the pulse air feeder mounting bolts.
5. Raise and support the front of the vehicle on jackstands. Disconnect the pulse air feeder hoses and remove the feeder.
6. Install hoses on pulse air feeder.
7. Lower the vehicle and tighten feeder mounting bolts.
8. Check O-ring on lower end of the dipstick tube. Replace if damaged.
9. Install carburetor protector shield.
10. Install the air deflector on radiator.

Dual Air Aspirator System

2.6L engines use an air aspirator system which aids in reducing carbon monoxide (CO) and hydrocarbon emissions. The system uses pulsating exhaust pressure to draw fresh air from the air cleaner assembly. Failure of the aspirator valve will result in excess noise.

SYSTEM TEST

1. Check the aspirator tube/exhaust manifold assembly joint and hoses. If aspirator tube/exhaust manifold joint is leaking, retighten to 68 Nm (50 ft. lbs.). If hoses are harden, replace as necessary.
2. Disconnect the inlet hose from aspirator valve.
3. With engine at idle, the negative (vacuum) exhaust pulses should be felt at the valve inlet.
4. If hot exhaust gases escaped from the aspirator inlet, replace the valve.

REMOVAL AND INSTALLATION

1. Remove the air inlet hose from aspirator valve.
2. Remove screws from aspirator bracket, and remove tube assembly from engine.
3. Install tube and tighten nuts to 54 Nm (40 ft. lbs.).
4. Install tube bracket assembly and torque to 28 Nm (250 in.lbs.).
5. Connect the air hose to valve and air cleaner nipple, install clamps.

Electronic Feedback Carburetor (EFC) System

Some models are equipped with an Electronic Feedback Carburetor (EFC) System which is designed to convert Hydrocarbons(HC), Carbon Monoxide (CO) and Oxides of Nitrogen (NOx) into harmless substances. An exhaust gas oxygen sensor generates an electronic signal which is used by the Spark Control Computer to precisely control the air-fuel mixture ratio to the carburetor.

There are two operating modes in the EFC system:
1. OPEN LOOP-During cold engine operation the air-fuel ratio will be fixed to a richer mixture programmed into the computer by the manufacture.
2. CLOSED LOOP-The computer varies the air-fuel ratio based on information supplied by the oxygen sensor.

Oxygen Sensor

The oxygen sensor is a galvanic battery which produces electrical voltage after being heated by exhaust gases. The sensor monitors the oxygen content in the exhaust stream, convert it to an electrical voltage and transmit this voltage to the Spark Control Computer.

WARNING: Use care when working around the oxygen sensor as the exhaust manifold may be extremely hot. The sensor must be remove using Tool C-4907.

Oxygen sensor assembly

Oxygen feedback solenoid — cut away

When the sensor is removed, the exhaust manifold threads must be cleaned with an 18mm x 1.5 x 6E tap.

If the sensor is to be reinstalled, the sensor threads must be coated with an anti-seize compound such as Loctite 771-64 or equivalent. New sensors are coated with compound on the threads and no additional compound is required. The sensor should be torque to 27 Nm (20 ft. lbs.).

Heated Oxygen Sensor

The heated oxygen sensor is basically the same as the standard oxygen sensor, except that it is internally heated for faster switching during engine operation. Replacement of the heated oxygen sensor is the same as the standard sensor.

Oxygen Feedback Solenoid

In addition to the oxygen sensor, EFC uses an Oxygen Feedback Solenoid. It purpose is to regulate the fuel-air ratio of the feedback carburetor, along with a conventional fixed main metering jet, in response to the electrical signal generated by the Spark Control Computer.

With the feedback solenoid de-energized, the main metering orifice is fully uncovered and the richest condition exists within the carburetor.

With the feedback solenoid energized, the solenoid push rod seals the main metering orifice. This position offers the leanest condition within the carburetor.

Electric Choke Assembly

The electric choke system is a heater and switch assembly sealed within the choke housing. When the engine is running and the engine oil pressure is 2.7 kPa (4 psi) or above, the contacts in the oil pressure switch closes and feed current to the automatic choke system to open the choke and keep it open.

NOTE: The choke assembly must never be immersed in fluid as damage to the internal switch and heater assembly will result.

TESTING

1. Disconnect the electrical lead from choke heater assembly.
2. Connect direct battery voltage to choke heater connection.
3. The choke valve should reach the open position within five minutes.

WARNING: Operation of any type should be avoided if there is a loss of choke power. This condition cause a very rich mixture to burn and result in abnormally high exhaust system temperatures, which may cause damage to the catalyst or other underbody parts of the vehicle.

Emission Maintenance Light

All models have an Emission Maintenance Reminder (EMR) lamp, this lamp is illuminated when the ignition key is turned **ON**. The lamp is connected with the engine controller, which records the vehicle mileage and stores it into memory every 8 miles. At the time the mileage is stored, the controller checks for the 60,000, 82,500 and 120,000 mile trip points. When the current mileage matches one of these mileages, the EMR lamp is illuminated.

When the EMR lamp is illuminated some of the emission components are supposed to be changed. These components are: EGR valve, EGR tube and PCV valve at 60,000 miles and 120,000 miles. At 82,500 miles the oxygen sensor must also be replaced. The EMR lamp can then be reset using an appropriate DRB tester or equivalent.

CHRYSLER SELF DIAGNOSTIC SYSTEM

General Information

The Chrysler fuel injection systems combine electronic spark advance and fuel control. At the center of these systems is a digital, pre-programmed computer, known as an Single Module Engine Controller (SMEC), also referred to as the Single Board Engine Controller (SBEC). The SMEC/SBEC regulates ignition timing, air-fuel ratio, emission control devices, cooling fan, charging system idle speed and speed control. It has the ability to update and revise its commands to meet changing operating conditions.

Various sensors provide the input necessary for SMEC/SBEC to correctly regulate fuel flow at the injectors. These include the Manifold Absolute Pressure (MAP), Throttle Position Sensor (TPS), oxygen sensor, coolant temperature sensor, charge temperature sensor, and vehicle speed sensors.

In addition to the sensors, various switches are used to provide important information to the SMEC/SBEC. These include the neutral safety switch, air conditioning clutch switch, brake switch and speed control switch. These signals cause the SMEC/SBEC to change either the fuel flow at the injectors or the ignition timing or both.

The Single Module Engine Controller (SMEC) or Single Board Engine Controller (SBEC), are designed to test their own input and output circuits, If a fault is found in a major system, this information is stored in the SMEC/SBEC for eventual display to the technician. Information on this fault can be displayed to the technician by means of the instrument panel CHECK ENGINE light or by connecting a diagnostic read-out tester and reading a numbered display code, which directly relates to a general fault. Some inputs and outputs are checked continuously and others are checked under certain conditions.

If the problem is repaired or no longer exists, the SMEC/SBEC cancels the fault code after 50–100 key ON/OFF cycles.

When a fault code is detected, it appears as either a flash of the CHECK ENGINE light on the instrument panel or by watching the Diagnostic Readout Box II (DRB II). This indicates that an abnormal signal in the system has been recognized by the SMEC/SBEC. Fault codes do indicate the presence of a failure but they don't identify the failed component directly.

FAULT CODES

Fault codes are 2 digit numbers that tell the technician which

Diagnostic connector and relays — single and dual point fuel injection system

Pin	Circuit	Color	Function
1	N-6	OR	8 Volt Output
2	K-5	BK/WT	Signal Ground
3	K-14	DB/WT	FJ2 Output
4	J-2	DB	12-Volt
5	Y-1	GY/WT	Injector Control 2
6	J-9-A	BK	Power Ground
7	J-9-B	BK	Power Ground
8	K-16	VT/YL	Injector Control Signal
9	Y-11	WT	Injector Driver #1
10	Y-12	TN	Injector Driver 2
11	R-31	DG/OR	Voltage Regulator Signal
12	J-5	BK/YL	Ignition Coil Driver
13	K-15	YL	Anti Dwell Signal
14	R-3	DG	Regulator Control

TERMINAL SIDE

SMEC 14-way connector pin description

circuit is bad. Fault codes do indicate the presence of a failure but they don't identify the failed component directly. Therefore a fault code and a result are not always the reason for the problem.

INDICATOR CODES

Indicator codes are 2 digit numbers that tell the technician if particular sequences or conditions have occurred. Such a condition where the indicator code will be displayed is at the beginning or the end of a diagnostic test. Indicator codes will not generate a CHECK ENGINE light or engine running test code.

ACTUATOR TEST MODE (ATM) CODES

ATM test codes are 2 digit numbers that identify the various circuits used by the technician during the diagnosis procedure.

ENGINE RUNNING TEST CODES

Engine running test codes are 2 digit numbers. The codes are used to access sensor readouts while the engine is running and place the engine in particular operating conditions for diagnosis.

CHECK ENGINE LIGHT

The CHECK ENGINE light has 2 modes of operation: diagnostic mode and switch test mode.

If a DRB II diagnostic tester is not available, the SMEC/SBEC can show the technician fault codes by flashing the CHECK ENGINE light on the instrument panel in the diagnostic mode. In the switch test mode, after all codes are displayed, switch function can be confirmed. The light will turn on and off when a switch is turned **ON** and **OFF**.

Even though the light can be used as a diagnostic tool, it cannot do the following:

a. Once the light starts to display fault codes, it cannot be stopped. If the technician loses count, he must start the test procedure again.

b. The light cannot display all of the codes or any blank displays.

c. The light cannot tell the technician if the oxygen feed-

back system is lean or rich and if the idle motor and detonation systems are operational.

d. The light cannot perform the actuation test mode, sensor test mode or engine running test mode.

NOTE: Be advised that the CHECK ENGINE light can only perform a limited amount of functions and is not to be used as a substitute for a diagnostic tester. All diagnostic procedure described herein are intended for use with a Diagnostic Readout Box II (DRB II) or equivalent tool.

LIMP-IN MODE

The limp-in mode is the attempt by the SMEC/SBEC to compensate for the failure of certain components by substituting information from other sources. If the SMEC/SBEC senses incorrect data or no data at all from the MAP sensor, throttle position sensor or coolant temperature sensor, the system is placed into limp-in mode and the CHECK ENGINE light on the instrument panel is activated. This mode will keep the vehicle driveable until the customer can get it to a service facility.

TEST MODES

There are 5 modes of testing required for the proper diagnosis of the system. They are as follows:

Diagnostic Test Mode—This mode is used to access the fault codes from the SMEC's memory.

Circuit Actuation Test Mode (ATM Test)—This mode is used to turn a certain circuit on and off in order to test it. ATM test codes are used in this mode.

Switch Test Mode—This mode is used to determine if specific switch inputs are being received by the SMEC/SBEC.

Sensor Test Mode—This mode looks at the output signals of certain sensors as they are received by the SMEC/SBEC when the engine is not running. Sensor access codes are read in this mode. Also this mode is used to clear the SMEC/SBEC memory of stored codes.

Engine Running Test Mode—This mode looks at sensor output signals as seen by the SMEC/SBEC when the engine is running. Also this mode is used to determine some specific running conditions necessary for diagnosis.

ENTERING SELF-DIAGNOSTICS

NOTE: The following diagnostic and test procedures are intended for use with the Diagnostic Readout Box II (DRB II). Since each available diagnostic readout box may differ in its interpretation and display of the sensor results, refer to the instructional procedure that accompanies each tester unit.

Obtaining Fault Codes

1. Connect the readout box to the diagnostic connector located in the engine compartment near SMEC/SBEC.

2. Start the engine, if possible, cycle the transmission selector and the A/C switch if applicable. Shut off the engine.

3. On 1988 models, turn the ignition switch **ON, OFF, ON, OFF, ON** within 5 seconds. On 1989–91 models, simply turn the ignition switch **ON** to access the read fault code data. Record all the fault code messages displayed on the readout box.

4. Observe the CHECK ENGINE light on the instrument panel. The light should illuminate for 3 seconds and then go out.

Switch Test

The SMEC/SBEC only recognizes 2 switch input states—HI and LOW. For this reason the SMEC/SBEC cannot tell the difference between a selected switch position and an open circuit, short circuit or an open switch. However, if one of the switches is toggled, the controller does have the ability to respond to the change of state in the switch. If the change is displayed, it can be assumed that entire switch circuit to the SMEC/SBEC is operational.

1988 MODELS

After all codes have been shown and has indicated Code 55 end of message, actuate the following component switches. The digital display must change its numbers between 00 and 88 and the CHECK ENGINE light will blink when the following switches are activated and released:

    Brake pedal
    Gear shift selector
    A/C switch (if applicable)
    Electric backlite switch (if applicable).

1989–91 MODELS

To enter the switch test mode, activate read input states or equivalent function on the readout box for the following switch tests:

    Z1 Voltage Sense
    Speed Control Set
    Speed Control ON/OFF
    Speed Control Resume
    A/C Switch Sense
    Brake Switch
    Park/neutral Switch

Obtaining Circuit Actuation Test Mode (ATM Test)

The purpose of the circuit actuation mode test is to check for proper operation of the output circuits that the SMEC cannot internally recognize. The SMEC can attempt to activate these outputs and allow the technician to affirm proper operation. Most of the tests performed in this mode issue an audible click or visual indication of component operation (click of relay contacts, injector spray, etc.). Except for intermittent conditions, if a component functions properly when it is tested, it can be assumed that the component, attendant wiring and driving circuit are functioning properly.

1988 MODELS

1. Put the system into the diagnostic test mode and wait for Code 55 to appear on the display screen.
2. Press ATM button on the tool to activate the display. If a specific ATM test is desired, hold the ATM button down until the desired test code appears.
3. The computer will continue to turn the selected circuit on and off for as long as 5 minutes or until the ATM button is pressed again or the ignition switch is turned to the OFF position.
4. If the ATM button is not pressed again, the computer will continue to cycle the selected circuit for 5 minutes and then shut the system off. Turning the ignition to the OFF position will also turn the test mode off.

Actuator Test Display Codes:

    Code 01 – Spark activation – once every 2 seconds
    Code 02 – Injector activation – once every 2 seconds
    Code 03 – AIS activation – one step open, one step closed every 4 seconds
    Code 04 – Radiator fan relay – once every 2 seconds
    Code 05 – A/C WOT cutout relay – once every 2 seconds
    Code 06 – ASD relay activation – once every 2 seconds
    Code 07 – Purge solenoid activation – one toggle every 2 seconds (The A/C fan will run continuously and the A/C switch must be in the ON position to allow for actuation)
    Code 08 – Speed control activation – speed control vent and vacuum every 2 seconds (Speed control switch must be in the ON position to allow for activation)
    Code 09 – Alternator control field activation – one toggle every 2 seconds

    Code 10 – Shift indicator activation – one toggle every 2 seconds
    Code 11 – EGR diagnosis solenoid activation – one toggle every 2 seconds

1989–91 MODELS

To enter the ATM Mode, activate the actuate solenoid/relay or actuate outputs or equivalent functions on the readout box for the following test displays:

Actuate Solenoid/Relay
Stop all tests
Radiator fan relay
A/C clutch relay
Auto shutdown relay
Purge solenoid
S/C servo solenoids
PTU solenoid (auto trans only)
EGR solenoid
All solenoids and relays

Actuate Outputs
Stop all tests
Ignition coil
Fuel injector No. 1
Fuel injector No. 2
Fuel injector No. 3
AIS motor open/close
Alternator field
Tachometer output
Fuel monitor signal

Obtaining Sensor Read Test Mode Display Codes

The sensor mode allows the output of 7 sensors and the state of 3 switches to be displayed on the readout box while the engine is not running. This provides a vehicle for testing each individual sensor and switch including harness wiring and SMEC/SBEC circuitry.

1988 MODELS

1. Put the system into the diagnostic test mode and wait for Code 55 to appear on the display screen.
2. Press the ATM button on the diagnostic tool to activate the display. If a specific sensor read test is desired, hold the ATM button down until the desired test code appears.
3. Slide the READ/HOLD switch to the HOLD position to display the corresponding sensor output.

Sensor Read Test Display Codes:

    Code 01 – Battery temperature sensor; display voltage divided by 10 equals sensor temperature
    Code 02 – Oxygen sensor voltage; display number divided by 10 equals sensor voltage
    Code 03 – Charge temperature sensor voltage; display number divided by 10 equals sensor voltage
    Code 04 – Engine coolant temperature sensor; display number multiplied by 10 equals degrees of engine coolant sensor
    Code 05 – Throttle position sensor voltage; display number divided by 10 equals sensor voltage or temperature
    Code 06 – Peak knock sensor voltage; display number is sensor voltage
    Code 07 – Battery voltage; display number is battery voltage
    Code 08 – Map sensor voltage; display number divided by 10 equals sensor voltage
    Code 09 – Speed control switches:
        Display is blank – Cruise OFF
        Display shows 00 – Cruise ON
        Display shows 10 – Cruise SET
        Display shows 01 – Cruise RESUME
    Code 10 – Fault code erase routine; display will flash 0's for 4 seconds

1989–91 MODELS

To enter the sensor test mode, activate read sensor voltage or read sensor values or equivalent functions on the readout box for the following sensor displays:

Read Sensor Voltage
Battery temperature sensor
Oxygen sensor input
Throttle body temperature sensor
Coolant temperature sensor
Throttle position
Minimum throttle
Battery voltage
MAP sensor voltage

Read Sensor Values
Throttle body temperature
Coolant temperature
MAP gauge reading
AIS motor position
Added adaptive fuel
Adaptive fuel factor
Barometric pressure
Engine speed
Module spark advance
Vehicle speed
Oxygen sensor state

Engine Running Test Mode

1988 MODELS ONLY

The Engine Running Test Mode monitors the sensors on the vehicle which check operating conditions while the engine is running. The engine running test mode can be performed with the engine idling in **NEUTRAL** and with parking brake set or under actual driving conditions. With the diagnostic readout box READ/HOLD switch in the **READ** position, the engine running test mode is initiated after the engine is started.

Select a test code by switching the READ/HOLD switch to the **READ** position and pressing the actuator button until the desired code appears. Release actuator button and switch the READ/HOLD switch to the **HOLD** position. The logic module will monitor that system test and results will be displayed.

ENGINE RUNNING TEST DISPLAY CODES

Code 61—Battery temperature sensor; display number divided by 10 equals voltage

Code 62—Oxygen sensor; display number divided by 10 equals voltage

Code 63—Fuel injector temperature sensor; display number divided by 10 equals voltage

Code 64—Engine coolant temperature sensor; display number multiplied by 10 equals degrees F

Code 65—Throttle position sensor; display number divided by 10 equals voltage

Code 67—Battery voltage sensor; display is voltage

Code 68—Manifold vacuum sensor; display is in. Hg

Code 69—Minimum throttle position sensor; display number divided by 10 equals voltage

Code 70—Minimum airflow idle speed sensor; display number multiplied by 10 equals rpm (see minimum air flow check procedure)

Code 71—Vehicle speed sensor; display is mph

Code 72—Engine speed sensor; display number multiplied by 10 equals rpm

EXITING DIAGNOSTIC TEST

By turning the ignition switch to the **OFF** position, the test mode system is exited. With a Diagnostic Readout Box attached to the system and the ATM control button not pressed, the computer will continue to cycle the selected circuits for 5 minutes and then automatically shut the system down.

VACUUM DIAGRAMS

1984 Federal 2.2L vacuum hose routing

1984 California 2.2L vacuum hose routing

1984 Altitude 2.2L vacuum hose routing

1984 Federal 2.6L vacuum hose routing

1984 Canadian 2.2L vacuum hose routing

1984 California 2.6L vacuum hose routing

1984 Canadian 2.6L vacuum hose routing

1985 California 2.2L vacuum hose routing

1985 Federal 2.2L vacuum hose routing

1985 Altitude 2.6L vacuum hose routing

1985 Federal 2.6L vacuum hose routing

1986 Federal 2.2L vacuum hose routing

1985 California 2.6L vacuum hose routing

1986 California 2.2L vacuum hose routing

1986 Altitude 2.6L vacuum hose routing

1986 California 2.6L vacuum hose routing

1986 Federal 2.6L vacuum hose routing

1987 Federal 2.2L vacuum hose routing

1987 California 2.2L vacuum hose routing

1987 California 2.6L vacuum hose routing

1987 Federal 2.6L vacuum hose routing

1987 Canadian 2.6L vacuum hose routing

1988 Federal and Altitude 2.5L vacuum hose routing

1988 Federal and Altitude 3.0L vacuum hose routing

1988 California 2.5L vacuum hose routing

1988 California 3.0L vacuum hose routing

1988 Canadian 2.5L vacuum hose routing

1989 Federal, Altitude and Canadian 2.5L vacuum hose routing

1988 Canadian 3.0L vacuum hose routing

1989 California 2.5L vacuum hose routing

1989 Federal, California and Canadian 2.5L Turbo
vacuum hose routing

1990 Federal, Altitude and Canadian 2.5L vacuum
hose routing

1989 California, Federal and Canadian 3.0L vacuum
hose routing

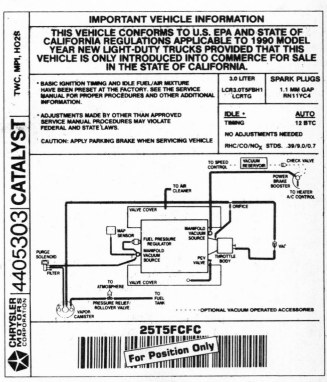

1990 Federal, Altitude and Canadian 3.0L vacuum
hose routing

1990 Federal, Altitude and Canadian 3.0L vacuum hose routing

1990 Federal, Altitude and Canadian 3.3L vacuum hose routing

1990 Federal, California, Canadian and Altitude 2.5L Turbo vacuum hose routing

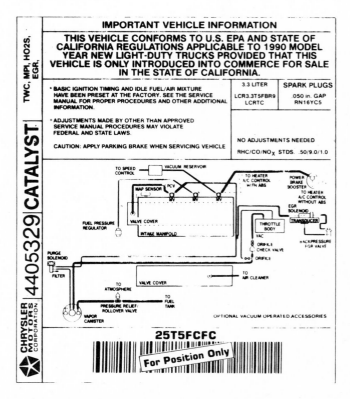

1990 California 3.3L vacuum hose routing

1991 Federal and Canadian 2.5L vacuum hose routing

1991 Federal, California and Canadian 3.0L vacuum hose routing

1991 California 2.5L vacuum hose routing

1991 Federal, California and Canadian 3.3L vacuum hose routing — front wheel drive

IMPORTANT VEHICLE INFORMATION

THIS VEHICLE CONFORMS TO U.S. EPA
REGULATIONS APPLICABLE TO 1991 MODEL YEAR
NEW LIGHT-DUTY TRUCKS AT ALL ALTITUDES.

- BASIC IGNITION TIMING AND IDLE FUEL/AIR MIXTURE HAVE BEEN PRESET AT THE FACTORY. SEE THE SERVICE MANUAL FOR PROPER PROCEDURES AND OTHER ADDITIONAL INFORMATION.
- ADJUSTMENTS MADE BY OTHER THAN APPROVED SERVICE MANUAL PROCEDURES MAY VIOLATE FEDERAL AND STATE LAWS.

CAUTION: APPLY PARKING BRAKE WHEN SERVICING VEHICLE

3.3 LITER
MCR3.3T5FCZI
MCRTG

SPARK PLUGS
.050 in. GAP
RN16YC5

NO ADJUSTMENTS NEEDED

FAMILY NOx EMISSION LIMIT 1.7

CHRYSLER CORPORATION — 4405254 — CATALYST

1991 Federal, California and Canadian 3.3L vacuum hose routing — all wheel drive

TORQUE SPECIFICATIONS

Component	English	Metric
Aspirator tube-to-exhaust manifold joint:	50 ft. lbs.	68 Nm
Aspirator tube bracket assembly:	21 ft. lbs.	28 Nm
Aspirator tube nuts:	40 ft. lbs.	54 Nm
Oxygen Sensor:	20 ft. lbs.	27 Nm
Switch/Relief Valve:	125 inch lbs.	14 Nm

Fuel System 5

QUICK REFERENCE INDEX

GENERAL INDEX

CARBURETED FUEL SYSTEM

Mechanical Fuel Pump

The 2.2L and 2.6L engine use a mechanical type fuel pump located on the side of the engine. The fuel pump is driven by an eccentric cam which is cast on the accessory drive shaft.

REMOVAL AND INSTALLATION

———————— CAUTION ————————
Don't smoke when working around gasoline, cleaning solvent or other flammable substances.

1. Remove the oil filter.
2. Disconnect the fuel lines from the pump.
3. Plug the lines to prevent fuel leakage.
4. Remove the fuel pump blocker strut from front engine mount to blocker assembly.
5. Remove the fuel pump mounting bolts.
6. Clean all gasket material from engine block mounting surface and spacer block.
7. Assemble the new gaskets and spacer block to fuel pump.
8. Install the fuel pump mounting bolts in pump mounting flange.
9. Position the pump assembly on engine block and torque bolts alternately to 250 inch lbs.
10. Connect the fuel lines to the pump.
11. Position the fuel pump blocker strut on blocker assembly and front engine mount. Tighten assembly.
12. Install the oil filter. Check and adjust oil level.
13. Start the engine and check fuel fittings for leaks.

TESTING

Volume Test

The fuel pump should supply 1 qt. of fuel in 1 minute or less at idle.

Pressure Test

1. Insert a T-fitting in the fuel line at the carburetor.

———————— CAUTION ————————
Never smoke when working around gasoline! Avoid all sources of sparks or ignition. Gasoline vapors are EXTREMELY volatile!

2. Connect a six inch piece of hose between the T-fitting and a pressure gauge. A longer piece of hose will result in an inaccurate reading.
3. Disconnect the inlet line to the carburetor at the fuel pump and vent the pump. Failure to vent the pump will result in low pressure reading. Reconnect the fuel line.
4. Connect a tachometer to the engine. Start the engine and allow to idle. The pressure gauge should show a constant 4½-6 psi reading. When the engine is turned off, the pressure should slowly drop to zero. An instant drop to zero indicates a leaky diaphragm or weak spring. If pressure is too high, the main spring is too strong or the air vent is plugged.
5. Proceed with vacuum test.

Vacuum Test

1. Remove the inlet and outlet fuel lines from the pump.

———————— CAUTION ————————
Never smoke when working around gasoline! Avoid all sources of sparks or ignition. Gasoline vapors are EXTREMELY volatile!

2. Plug the fuel line to the carburetor to prevent fuel leakage.
3. Connect a vacuum gauge to the fuel pump inlet fitting.
4. Using the starter motor, turn the engine over several times and observe the vacuum gauge. The fuel pump should develop a minimum of 11 inches of vacuum.
5. If the vacuum readings are below specification, replace the pump.

Carburetor

ADJUSTMENTS

Idle Speed/Solenoid Kicker Check — Holley

2.2L air conditioned vehicles are equipped with a solenoid kicker.
1. Start engine and run until operating temperature is reached.
2. Turn air conditioning switch on and set temperature control lever to the coldest position.
3. Notice the kicker solenoid for in and out movement as the compressor cycles on and off. If no movement occurred, check the kicker system for vacuum leaks. Check the operation of the vacuum solenoid. If no problems are found, replace the kicker.
4. If the kicker solenoid functions properly, turn off the air conditioning switch and shut engine off.

Solenoid Kicker Adjustment — Holley

1. Check ignition timing and adjust if necessary.
2. Disconnect and plug vacuum connector at the CVSCC.
3. Unplug connector at cooling fan and jumper harness so fan will run continuously.
4. Remove the PCV valve and allow it to draw underhood air.
5. Connect a tachometer to the engine.

Solenoid kicker system

6. Ground the carburetor switch with a jumper wire.

7. Disconnect the oxygen system test lead located on the left fender shield on vehicles equipped with 6520 carburetors.

8. Start the engine and run until normal operating temperature is reached.

9. Adjust idle speed screw to specification given in under hood label.

10. Reconnect PCV valve, oxygen connector and CVSCC vacuum connector.

11. Remove the jumper from carburetor switch.

12. Remove the jumper from radiator fan and reconnect harness.

NOTE: After Steps 10, 11 and 12 are completed, the idle speed may change slightly. This is normal and engine speed should not be readjusted.

Fast Idle — Holley

Before adjusting fast idle, check and adjust ignition timing.

1. Disconnect the electrical harness at the radiator fan and install a jumper wire so the fan will run continuously.

2. Remove the PCV valve and allow it to draw under hood air.

3. Disconnect and plug the vacuum connector at the CVSCC.

4. Install a tachometer.

5. Jumper the carburetor switch.

6. Disconnect oxygen system test connector located on the left fender shield by shock tower.

7. Start engine and allow to reach normal operating temperature.

8. Open throttle slightly and place adjustment screw on the lowest step of fast idle cam.

9. Adjust the fast idle screw to specification shown on under hood VECI label. Return engine to idle and repeat Step 8, readjust if necessary.

10. Stop engine, remove jumper wire from radiator fan harness and reconnect connector.

11. Reinstall PCV valve.

12. Reconnect oxygen system test connector, and vacuum connector at CVSCC.

Choke Vacuum Kick — Holley

1. Open the carburetor throttle and hold choke valve in closed position. While maintaining choke valve in closed position, release the throttle. Fast idle system should now be trapped at closed choke condition.

2. Disconnect carburetor vacuum source at carburetor.

3. Using light finger pressure, close choke valve to the smallest opening possible without disturbing linkage system.

4. Using the proper size drill or gauge, insert between choke valve and air horn wall at primary throttle end of carburetor. Refer to Choke Vacuum Kick Specification Chart.

5. Using an allen head screw in center of diaphragm housing, adjust by turning clockwise or counterclockwise to obtain correct setting.

6. Reconnect vacuum hose to carburetor vacuum source.

Mixture Adjustment (Propane Assisted)

NOTE: The following procedures require the use of a propane cylinder, vacuum hose and a special control valve to provide proper enrichment. Any adjustments made other than those in the following procedures, may violate Federal and State Laws.

1. Remove the concealment plug. Refer to Steps 18 through 20 under carburetor disassembling procedure.

2. Set the parking brake and place the transaxle in neutral position. Turn off all accessories. Start engine and allow to idle on second highest step of fast idle cam until normal operating temperature is reached. Return engine to idle.

Choke vacuum kick adjustment on 2.2L enigne

Fast idle adjustment on 2.2L engine

A/C kicker adjustment on 2.2L engine

Vacuum Kick Specifications

Carb Number	Setting
4288460	.07 in.
4288461	.07 in.
4288262	.07 in.
4288263	.07 in.
4288456	.08 in.
4288458	.08 in.
4288459	.08 in.

Vacuum kick adjustment specifications

3. Disconnect vacuum connector at CVSCC and plug. Disconnect the vacuum hose to the heated air door sensor at the three way connector, and in its place, install the supply hose from the propane bottle.

4. Unplug the radiator fan connector and jumper harness so the fan will run continuously. Remove PCV valve and allow it to draw under hood air. Connect a jumper wire between the carburetor switch and ground. On vehicles equipped with 6520 carburetors, disconnect the oxygen test lead located on the left fender shield.

5. With the air cleaner installed. Open the propane main valve. Slowly open the propane metering valve until maximum engine RPM idle is reached. If too much propane is added engine RPM will decrease. Adjust metering valve for the highest engine RPM.

6. With the propane still flowing, adjust the idle speed screw on top of the solenoid to obtain specified RPM on under hood label. Again adjust the propane metering valve to get the highest engine RPM. If the maximum RPM changes, readjust the idle speed screw to the specified propane RPM.

7. Shut off the propane main valve and allow the engine to stabilize. With the air cleaner still in place, slowly adjust the mixture screws to obtain the specified set RPM. Pause for a few seconds after each adjustment to allow engine speed to stabilized.

8. Again turn on the propane main valve and adjust the metering valve to obtain the highest engine RPM. If the maximum speed differs more than 25 RPM, repeat Steps 5 through 8.

9. Shut off both valves on propane cylinder. Disconnect the propane vacuum supply hose and connect the vacuum hose to the heated air door sensor at the three way connector.

10. Install concealment plug. Proceed with fast idle adjustment starting at Step 7.

Anti-Dieseling Adjustment — Holley

NOTE: Always check and adjust ignition timing before any idle speed adjustment is performed.

1. Warm engine to normal operating temperature. Place transaxle in neutral position and set parking brake.
2. Turn off all accessories. Jumper wire between carburetor switch and ground.
3. Remove the RED wire from the 6-Way connector (carburetor side).
4. Adjust the throttle stop speed screw to obtain 700 rpm.
5. Reconnect RED wire and remove jumper from carburetor switch.

Idle RPM — Mikuni Carburetor

1. Check and adjust ignition timing.
2. Set the parking brake and place transaxle in neutral. Turn off all accessories.
3. Disconnect the radiator fan.
4. Connect a tachometer to the engine.
5. Start engine and run until operating temperature is reached.
6. Disconnect cooling fan. Run engine at 2500 RPM for 10 seconds and return to idle.
7. Wait 2 minutes and record RPM. If RPM differs from VECI under hood specification label, turn idle speed adjusting screw until specification is obtained.
8. On air condition models, set the temperature lever to the coldest position and turn air conditioning switch on. With the air condition running, set the engine speed to 900 RPM using the idle-up adjustment screw.
9. Shut engine off. Connect the cooling fan and remove tachometer.

Fast Idle — Mikuni Carburetor

1. Connect a tachometer to the engine. Check and adjust ignition timing.
2. Set the parking brake and place transaxle in neutral. Turn off all accessories.
3. Start engine and run until operating temperature is reached.
4. Disconnect radiator fan. Remove and plug vacuum advance hose at distributor.
5. Open the throttle slightly and install Tool 4812-2C on cam follower pin.
6. Release throttle lever and adjust fast idle adjusting screw to specification shown on VECI under hood label.
7. Remove tool and shut engine off. Reconnect fan, unplug and reconnect vacuum hose, and remove tachometer.

Idle up adjustment on the Mikuni carburetor

Fast idle adjustment on the Mikuni carburetor

Installing tool C4812 on the Mikuni carburetor

Idle Mixture (Propane Assist)
Mikuni Carburetor

NOTE: The following procedures require the use of a propane cylinder, vacuum hose and a special control valve to provide proper enrichment. Any adjustments made other than those in the following procedures, may violate Federal and State Laws.

1. Remove concealment plug. Refer to Concealment Plug Removal procedure. Check and adjust ignition timing.
2. Set the parking brake and place transaxle in neutral. Turn off all accessories.
3. Disconnect the cooling fan.
4. Connect a tachometer to the engine.
5. Start engine and run until operating temperature is reached.
6. Disconnect cooling fan. Run engine at 2500 RPM for 10 seconds and return to idle. Allow engine to idle for 2 minutes.
7. Remove the air cleaner fresh air duct. Place the propane bottle in a safe location and in an upright position. Insert the propane supply hose approximately 4 inches into the air cleaner snorkel.
8. Open the propane bottle main valve. Slowly open the metering valve until the highest engine RPM is reached. If too much propane is added, the engine RPM will decrease. Fine Tune the propane metering valve to obtain the highest engine RPM.
9. With the propane still flowing, adjust the idle speed screw to the specified RPM shown on VECI under hood label. Again Fine Tune the propane metering valve to get the highest engine RPM. If the RPM increases, readjust the idle speed screw to specification.
10. Shut off the propane main valve and allow the engine speed to stabilize. Slowly adjust the carburetor mixture screws to obtain the specified idle RPM. Pause between each adjustment to allow engine speed to stabilize.
11. Again turn on the propane main valve, Fine Tune the metering valve to get the highest engine RPM. If the RPM changes, repeat Step 8 through 10.
12. Shut off the propane main valve and metering valve. Remove the propane supply hose. Install the air cleaner fresh air duct. Install the concealment plug and impact plate.

Concealment Plug Removal
Mikuni Carburetor

1. Remove the impact plate, if used.
2. Remove the vacuum connector from high altitude compensator (HAC) fitting on carburetor, if used.
3. With an eight inch long ¼″ diameter drill bit, drill out concealment plug at location show.
4. Remove concealment plug.

REMOVAL AND INSTALLATION

2.2L Engine

———————————— CAUTION ————————————
Never remove a carburetor from an engine that has just been road tested. Allow the engine to cool down to prevent accidental fuel ignition or personal injury.
——————————————————————————————————

1. Disconnect the negative battery cable.
2. Remove the air cleaner.
3. Remove the fuel tank filler cap to relieve fuel system pressure.
4. Disconnect all carburetor electrical wiring.

———————————— CAUTION ————————————
Never smoke when working around gasoline! Avoid all sources of sparks or ignition. Gasoline vapors are EXTREMELY volatile!
——————————————————————————————————

5. Disconnect the carburetor inlet line and block off line to prevent fuel leakage.
6. Disconnect the throttle linkage. Label and remove all vacuum hoses.
7. Remove the carburetor mounting nuts and remove carburetor.
8. Inspect the mating surfaces of the carburetor and isolator for nicks, burrs, dirt or other damage. It is not necessary to disturb the isolator to intake manifold mounting screws, unless the isolator is damage.
9. Carefully install carburetor on engine. Install nuts evenly and torque to 200 inch lbs. Make certain throttle plates and choke plate opens and closes properly when operated.
10. Connect the throttle linkage and fuel inlet line.
11. Connect the vacuum hoses.
12. Connect the negative battery cable.
13. Install the air cleaner and adjust the carburetor.

2.6L Engine

———————————— CAUTION ————————————
Never remove a carburetor from an engine that has just been road tested. Allow the engine to cool down to prevent accidental fuel ignition or personal injury.
——————————————————————————————————

1. Disconnect the negative battery cable.
2. Remove the air cleaner.
3. Remove the fuel tank filler cap.to relieve fuel system pressure.
4. Disconnect the carburetor protector and all carburetor electrical wiring.
5. Drain the cooling system. Label and remove the vacuum hoses and coolant hoses at carburetor.

———————————— CAUTION ————————————
When draining the coolant, keep in mind that cats and dogs are attracted by the ethylene glycol antifreeze, and are quite likely to drink any that is left in an uncovered container or in puddles on the ground. This will prove fatal in sufficient quantity. Always drain the coolant into a sealable container. Coolant should be reused unless it is contaminated or several years old.
——————————————————————————————————

6. Disconnect the carburetor inlet line and block off line to prevent fuel leakage.

———————————— CAUTION ————————————
Never smoke when working around gasoline! Avoid all sources of sparks or ignition. Gasoline vapors are EXTREMELY volatile!
——————————————————————————————————

7. Disconnect the throttle linkage.
8. Remove the carburetor mounting bolts and nuts and remove carburetor.
9. Inspect the mating surfaces of the carburetor and intake manifold for nicks, burrs, dirt or other damage.
10. Install a new gasket on intake manifold.
11. Carefully install the carburetor on the engine. Install mounting bolts and nuts. Tighten evenly and torque to 150 inch lbs. Make certain throttle plates and choke plate opens and closes properly when operated.
12. Connect the throttle linkage, fuel line and electrical connectors.
13. Install and tighten carburetor protector.
14. Fill the cooling system.
15. Connect the negative battery cable.
16. Install the air cleaner and adjust the carburetor.

OVERHAUL

Holley Model 5220/6520

1. Remove the carburetor from the engine as described in carburetor removal procedure.

2. Using a small screwdriver disconnect and remove choke valve operating rod and seal.

3. Remove the idle stop solenoid mounting screws and remove solenoid.

4. Remove the oxygen solenoid retaining screws and carefully remove the sensor.

5. Remove the retaining clip securing the vacuum diaphragm control rod, remove the vacuum diaphragm mounting screws and remove vacuum diaphragm assembly.

6. Make a mark for proper alignment during assembly, on the air conditioning wide open throttle cut-out switch, and remove switch and wiring assembly.

7. Remove the (5) air horn screws and separate the air horn from carburetor body.

8. Invert the air horn and remove the float pin, float and inlet needle.

9. Remove the fuel inlet needle and seat.

10. Notice the size and position of the secondary main metering jets, and remove jets.

11. Notice the size and position of the primary main metering jets, and remove jets.

12. Using a small screwdriver remove the secondary high speed bleed and secondary main well tube. Note the size and position so it can be reinstalled in its proper location.

13. Remove the primary high speed bleed and primary main well tube. Note the size and position so it can be reinstalled in its proper location.

14. Remove the pump discharge nozzle retaining screw, nozzle and gasket. Invert the carburetor and remove the pump discharge weight ball and check ball. (Both are the same size).

15. Remove the accelerator pump cover retaining screws, cover, pump diaphragm and spring.

16. Remove the choke diaphragm retaining screws and remove cover and spring.

17. Rotate the choke shaft and lever assembly counterclockwise. Rotate choke diaphragm assembly clockwise and remove from housing. Remove end of lower screw from housing. If the choke diaphragm need replacement, the diaphragm cover must also be replaced.

18. To remove concealment plug, center punch at a point ¼″ from the end of the mixture screw housing.

19. Drill through the outer housing with a ⅛ in. drill bit.

20. Pry out the concealment plug and save for reinstallation.

21. Remove the idle mixture screws from carburetor body.

CLEANING AND INSPECTION

Efficient carburetion depends greatly on careful cleaning and inspection during overhaul, since dirt, gum, water, or varnish in or on the carburetor parts are often responsible for poor performance. There are many commercial carburetor cleaning solvent which can give satisfactory results.

NOTE: Avoid placing any seals, O-rings, float, choke and vacuum diaphragm in cleaning solvent. Such components can be damage if immerse in cleaning solvent. Clean the external surfaces of these parts with a clean lint free cloth or brush.

Soak carburetor parts in cleaning solvent, but do not leave parts in solvent no longer than necessary to loosen deposits. Remove parts and rinse with clean hot water. Blow out all passages and jets with compressed air. Blow dry all parts.

Inspect the following:

1. Check the float needle and seat for wear. If wear is found, needle/seat assembly.

2. Check the float pin for wear and the float for damage. Replace if necessary.

3. Check the throttle and choke shaft bores for wear or an out-of-round condition. Damage or wear to the throttle arm, shaft, or shaft bore will often require replacement of the throt-

tle body. These parts require a close tolerance fit. Wear on these parts may allow air leakage, which could affect starting and idling.

4. Inspect the idle mixture adjusting needles for burrs or grooves, Any such condition requires replacement of the needle, since you will not be able to obtain a satisfactory idle.

5. Check the bowl cover for warped surfaces with a straight edge.

ASSEMBLY

1. Install the choke shaft, while rotating counterclockwise. Install the diaphragm with a clockwise motion. Position spring and cover over diaphragm, and install retaining screws. Be certain fast idle link has been properly installed.

2. Install the accelerator pump spring, diaphragm cover and screws.

--------- CAUTION ---------

Never smoke when working around gasoline! Avoid all sources of sparks or ignition. Gasoline vapors are EXTREMELY volatile!

3. Install the accelerator pump discharge check ball in discharge passage. Check the accelerator pump and seat operation before complete reassembling as follows:

a. Fill the fuel bowl with clean fuel.

b. Hold the discharge check ball down with a small brass rod and operate the pump plunger by hand. If the check ball and seat is leaking, no resistance will be felt when the plunger is operated. If the valve is leaking, use the old ball and carefully stake the ball using a suitable drift punch. Avoid damaging the bore containing the pump weight.

c. After staking the old ball, remove and replace with the new ball. Recheck for leaks.

Measuring the float drop on the 2.2L carburetor

Float drop adjustment on the 2.2L carburetor

4. Install a new gasket, discharge nozzle and nozzle retaining screw.

5. Install the primary main well tube and primary high speed bleed.

6. Install the secondary main well tube and secondary high speed bleed.

7. Install the primary main metering (smaller size number) jet.

8. Install the secondary main metering (larger size number) jet.

9. Install the needle and seat assembly with a new gasket.

10. Invert the air horn and install float, inlet needle and float lever pin. Reset "dry float setting" and "float drop." Refer to carburetor adjustment procedures.

11. Install a new gasket on air horn, and install choke rod seal and choke rod.

12. Carefully position the air horn on carburetor body.

13. Install a new retainer on choke shaft lever and fast idle cam pickup lever and connect choke rod.

14. Install air horn retaining screws and torque to 30 inch lbs.

15. Install idle stop solenoid, and reinstall anti-rattle spring.

16. Install the air conditioning wide open throttle cut-out switch and aligned with mark previously made. The switch must be position so that the air conditioning clutch circuit is open 10 before wide open throttle position.

17. Install the oxygen solenoid gasket on air horn. Install new O-ring seal on oxygen solenoid. Coat the new O-ring seal with petroleum jelly and install solenoid in carburetor body. Tighten solenoid mounting screws and secure wiring and clamps.

18. Install the vacuum solenoid.

19. Install the vacuum control valve.

Float Setting

1. Invert the air horn. With gasket remove, insert a 12.2mm gauge or drill between air horn and float.

2. To obtain proper dry float level bend adjusting tang with a small screwdriver.

Float Drop

1. With the air horn upright, check float drop with a depth gauge.

2. To obtain proper float drop adjustment, hold float assembly securely with one hand. Using a small screwdriver, carefully bend adjusting tang to obtain a float drop of 47.6mm.

Mikuni Carburetor

2.6L engines are equipped with a downdraft type two barrel carburetor, which can be identified with its black resin compound main body. The automatic choke is a thermowax type which is controlled by engine coolant temperature.

This carburetor also features a diaphragm type accelerator pump, bowl vent, fuel cut-off solenoid, air switching valve (ASV), sub-EGR valve, coasting air valve (CAV), jet air control valve (JACV) and a high altitude compensation (HAC) system. (California Only).

OVERHAUL

1. Grind head from screws of choke cover. Gently tap the remaining screw portions using a hammer and a pointed punch in a counterclockwise direction until screws are removed.

2. Take notice of the painted punch mark and scribed lines on choke pinion plate. During reassembly, these marks must be aligned.

3. Remove the E-clip from the throttle opener link. Remove the throttle opener mounting screws and set aside.

4. Remove the ground wire from the fuel cut-off solenoid, remove solenoid mounting screws, and remove solenoid.

5. Remove the throttle return spring and damper spring.

6. Remove the choke unloader E-clip from its link and remove choke unloader.

7. Remove vacuum hose and link from vacuum chamber. Remove vacuum chamber mounting screws and remove vacuum chamber.

8. Remove accelerator rod link from throttle lever.

9. Remove the air horn mounting screws (6) and carefully separate air horn from carburetor body.

10. Slide out float pivot pin and remove float assembly. Remove air horn gasket.

11. Unscrew needle/seat retainer, remove needle/seat, O-ring and screen.

12. Remove the primary and secondary venturi and O-rings. Mark both venturi for proper location during reassembly.

13. Remove primary and secondary main jets. Mark both jets for proper location during reassembly.

14. Remove primary and secondary pedestals and gaskets.

15. Remove bowl vent solenoid mounting screws, solenoid, bowl vent assembly, seal and gasket.

16. Remove the coasting air valve (CAV) mounting screws and remove valve assembly from air horn. (California and Altitude Models).

17. Remove enrichment valve mounting screws and remove enrichment valve assembly.

18. Remove air switching valve (ASV) mounting screws and remove air switching valve assembly from air horn.

19. Remove the primary and secondary pilot jet set screw and lock. Remove pilot jet set assembly.

20. Remove primary and secondary air bleed jets from top of air horn. Mark both jets for proper location during reassembly.

21. Invert the air horn, carefully drop out and note pump weight, check ball and hex nut.

22. Remove accelerator pump mounting screws and remove pump cover, diaphragm, spring, pump body and gasket.

23. Remove jet air control valve mounting screws and remove J.A.C.V. cover, spring, retainer and diaphragm seal.

24. Remove E-clip from sub-EGR lever. The sub-EGR valve is under pressure by a steel ball and spring. Care should be used when removing lever to prevent accidental lost of spring or ball. Carefully slide the pin from lever and sub-EGR valve. Remove the steel ball, spring, sub-EGR valve and boot seal.

CLEANING AND INSPECTION

Efficient carburetion depends greatly on careful cleaning and inspection during overhaul, since dirt, gum, water, or varnish in or on the carburetor parts are often responsible for poor performance. There are many commercial carburetor cleaning solvents which can give satisfactory results.

NOTE: Avoid placing any seals, O-rings, float, choke and vacuum diaphragm in cleaning solvent. Such components can be damage if immerse in cleaning solvent. Clean the external surfaces of these parts with a clean lint free cloth or brush.

Soak carburetor parts in cleaning solvent, but do not leave parts in solvent longer than necessary to loosen deposits. Remove parts and rinse with clean hot water. Blow out all passages and jets with compressed air. Blow dry all parts.
Inspect the following:

1. Check the float needle and seat for wear. If wear is found, needle/seat assembly.

2. Check the float pin for wear and the float for damage. Replace if necessary.

3. Check the throttle and choke shaft bores for wear or an out-of-round condition. Damage or wear to the throttle arm, shaft, or shaft bore will often require replacement of the throttle body. These parts require a close tolerance fit. Wear on these

parts may allow air leakage, which could affect starting and idling.

4. Inspect the idle mixture adjusting needles for burrs or grooves, Any such condition requires replacement of the needle, since you will not be able to obtain a satisfactory idle.

5. Check the bowl cover for warped surfaces with a straight edge.

ASSEMBLY

1. Install the sub-EGR valve to throttle valve and check for proper operation.

2. Assemble the jet air control valve to throttle body and secure with mounting screws.

3. Assemble the accelerator pump to throttle body and secure with mounting screws.

4. Install the primary and secondary air bleed jets. The secondary air bleed jet has the largest number.

5. Position new O-ring seals on primary and secondary pilot jet side. Slide assembly into place and install lock and screw.

6. Assemble the air switching valve to air horn and secure with mounting screws.

7. Assemble the enrichment valve to air horn.

8. Assemble the coasting air valve to air horn.

9. Position a new O-ring and gasket on bowl vent assembly and install on air horn.

10. Position a new gasket on air horn and install primary and secondary pedestals.

11. Install primary and secondary main jets in their pedestals. The secondary main jet has the largest number.

12. Position new O-rings on both primary and secondary venturi. Install primary and secondary venturi and retainers.

13. Position a new O-ring on needle seat. Install a new screen on needle seat. Install shim and needle seat into air horn. Install retainer and screw.

14. Position the float on air horn and install float pivot pin. Refer to Float Level Adjustment procedure.

15. Position a new gasket on throttle body. Install main body to throttle and install nut, check ball and weight in main body.

16. Position a new gasket on main body and carefully assemble air horn to main body.

17. Install vacuum hoses to air horn.

18. Connect accelerator rod link to throttle lever.

Measuring the float level on the Mikuni carburetor

19. Install vacuum chamber to air horn. Connect vacuum hose and secondary throttle lever link.

20. Connect choke unloader link and install E-clip.

21. Position a new O-ring on fuel cut-off solenoid. Install the solenoid to main body and connect ground wire.

22. Install throttle opener to air horn. Connect throttle opener link and install E-clip.

23. Replace tamper-proof choke cover screws. Align the punch mark with the painted mark on gear.

24. Install the choke cover and peen over screws. Tighten the remaining screw using a pointed punch and a small hammer.

25. Install the choke water hose and clamp.

Float Level

1. Remove air horn from carburetor main body.

2. Remove air horn gasket and invert air horn.

3. Using a gauge measure the distance from bottom of float to air horn surface. The distance should be 20mm ± 1mm. If distance is not within specification, the shim under the needle and seat must be changed. Shim pack MD606952 or equivalent has three shims: 0.3mm, 0.4mm, or 0.5mm. Adding or removing one shim will change the float level three its thickness.

CHRYSLER MULTI-POINT ELECTRONIC FUEL INJECTION

General Information

The turbocharged and non-turbocharged Multi-Point Electronic Fuel Injection (MPI) system combines an electronic fuel and spark advance control system with a turbocharged intake system or cross type intake system. At the center of this system is a digital computer containing a microprocessor known as a Single Module Engine Controller (SMEC) that regulates ignition timing, air/fuel ratio, emission control devices, idle speed, cooling fan, charging system, turbocharger waste gate (on turbo models) and speed control. This component has the ability to update and revise its programming to meet changing operating conditions.

Various sensors provide the input necessary for the SMEC to correctly regulate fuel flow at the fuel injectors. These include the manifold absolute pressure, throttle position, oxygen sensor, coolant temperature, charge temperature, vehicle speed (distance) sensors and detonation sensor. In addition to the sen-

Multi-point fuel injection system components — 3.0L engine

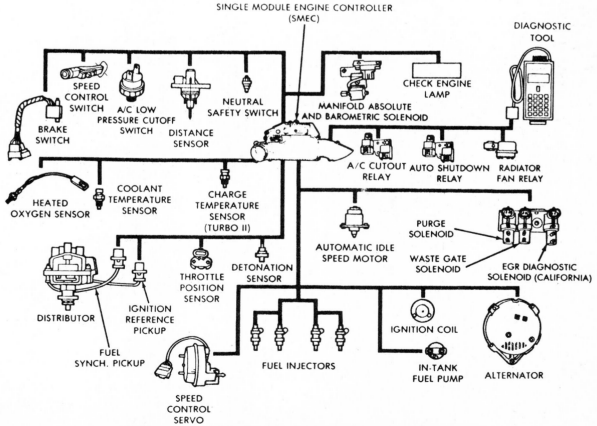

Multi-point fuel injection system components — 2.5L engine

Multi-point fuel injection system components — 3.3L engine

sors, various switches also provide important information. These include the neutral-safety, air conditioning clutch switch, brake switch and speed control switch.

SYSTEM COMPONENTS

Single Module Engine Controller (SMEC)

The SMEC contains the circuits necessary to drive the ignition coil, fuel injector and the alternator field. The SMEC is a digital computer containing a microprocessor. The module receives input signals from various switches and sensors. It then computes the fuel injector pulse width, spark advance, ignition dwell, idle speed, purge, cooling fan turn on and alternator charge rate.

NOTE: The Single Board Engine Controller (SBEC) is basically the same as the Single Module Engine Controller (SMEC) with the internal construction being different.

The Automatic Shut Down (ASD) relay is mounted externally, but is turned on and off by the SMEC. The distributor pickup signal goes to the SMEC. In the event of no distributor signal, the ASD relay is not activated and power is shut off to the fuel injector, fuel pump and ignition coil. The SMEC contains a voltage convertor which converts battery voltage to a regulated 9.0 volt output. This 9.0 volt output powers the distributor pickup. The internal 5 volt supply powers the MAP and TPS sensors.

The SMEC tests many of its own input and output circuits. If a fault is found in a major system, this information is stored in the SMEC memory. Information on this fault can be displayed to a technician by means of the instrument panel check engine

Single Module Engine Controller (SMEC) assembly

light or by connecting the Diagnostic Readout Box II (DRBII) and reading a numbered display code which directly relates to a general fault.

NOTE: Fault codes indicate the results of a failure but never identify the failed component directly.

Automatic Shut Down (ASD) Relay

The Automatic Shut Down (ASD) relay is powered and controlled through the SMEC. When there is no distributor signal present with the ignition key in the **RUN** position, there is no need for fuel delivery. When this condition occurs, the ASD relay interrupts power to the electric fuel pump, fuel injectors, ignition coil and oxygen sensor heater element.

Manifold Absolute Pressure (MAP) Sensor

The Manifold Absolute Pressure (MAP) sensor is a device

ASD relay location

Manifold Air Pressure sensor (MAP)

Oxygen sensor (heated)

which monitors manifold vacuum. It is mounted under the hood on the shock tower and is connected to a vacuum nipple on the intake plenum (through the baro read solenoid-turbo vehicles only) and electrically to the SMEC. The sensor transmits information on manifold vacuum conditions and barometric pressure (turbo vehicles only) to the SMEC. The MAP sensor data on engine load is used with data from other sensors to determine the correct air/fuel mixture.

Heated Oxygen Sensor (O2 Sensor)

The oxygen sensor is a device which produces an electrical voltage when exposed to the oxygen present in the exhaust gases. The oxygen sensor is electrically heated internally for faster switching when the engine is running. When there is a large amount of oxygen present (lean mixture), the sensor produces a low voltage. When there is a lesser amount present (rich mixture) it produces a higher voltage. By monitoring the oxygen content and converting it to electrical voltage, the sensor acts as a rich-lean switch. The voltage is transmitted to the SMEC which changes the fuel injection pulse. The sensor is mounted in the turbo outlet or rear exhaust manifold.

Charge Temperature Sensor

The charge temperature sensor is a device mounted in the intake manifold which measures the temperature of the air/fuel mixture. This information is used by the SMEC to modify air/fuel mixture.

Coolant Temperature Sensor

The coolant temperature sensor is a device which monitors coolant temperature (which is the same as engine operating temperature). It is mounted in the thermostat housing. This sensor provides data on engine operating temperature to the SMEC. This data along with data provided by the charge temperature sensor allows the SMEC to demand slightly richer air/fuel mixtures and higher idle speeds until normal operating temperatures are reached. The sensor is a variable resistor with a range of −40°F–265°F. On all models, this sensor is also used for cooling (radiator) fan control.

Switch Input

Various switches provide information to the SMEC. These include the neutral-safety, air conditioning clutch, speed control and brake light switches. If one or more of these switches is sensed as being in the on position, the SMEC adjusts engine operation.

Charge and coolant temperature sensors

NOTE: The state of these switch inputs (high-low) may be read in the "Read Switch Inputs" mode of the Diagnostic Readout Box II (DRBII).

Check Engine Light

The check engine light comes on each time the ignition key is turned **ON** and stays on for a few seconds as a bulb test. If the SMEC receives an incorrect signal or no signal from either the coolant temperature sensor, charge temperature sensor, manifold absolute pressure sensor, throttle position sensor, battery voltage sensor input or emission related system on California vehicles the check engine light on the instrument panel is illuminated.

This is a warning that the SMEC has gone into Limp In Mode in an attempt to keep the system operational. The light can also be used to display fault codes. Cycle the ignition switch **ON, OFF, ON, OFF, ON** within 5 seconds and any fault codes stored in the memory will be displayed.

Limp In Mode is the attempt by the SMEC to compensate for the failure of certain components by substituting information from other sources.

Canister Purge Solenoid

The canister purge solenoid is controlled by the engine controller. When energized, it blocks the flow of fuel vapor and increases fuel pressure. Depending upon data supplied by the coolant temperature sensor and charge temperature sensor at start up and for a specified time period after hot starts, the solenoid will be energized. The purge solenoid will also be energized during certain idle conditions, this is to update the fuel delivery calibration.

Wastegate Control Solenoid (Turbo Models)

The wastegate control solenoid is controlled by the SMEC. The SMEC adjusts maximum boost to varying engine conditions by varying the duty cycle of the wastegate solenoid.

Barometric Read Solenoid (Turbo Models)

The barometric read solenoid is controlled by the SMEC. The solenoid is in the MAP sensor vacuum line next to the MAP sensor. The solenoid controls whether manifold pressure or atmospheric pressure is supplied to the MAP sensor. Atmospheric pressure is periodically supplied to the MAP sensor to measure barometric pressure. This occurs at closed throttle, once per throttle closure but no more often than once every 3 minutes within a specified rpm. The barometric information is used primarily for boost control.

Air Conditioning Clutch Cutout Relay

The air conditioning clutch cutout relay is controlled by the SMEC and powered by the cooling fan relay, A/C switch and the SMEC. This relay is in the energized closed (on) position during engine operation when A/C switch is closed and blower switch is **ON**. When the SMEC senses wide open throttle through the throttle position sensor or low engine rpm, it will de-energize the relay, open its contacts and prevent air conditioning clutch engagement.

Canister purge solenoid mounting

Detonation (Knock) Sensor

The detonation sensor is a device that generates a signal when spark knock occurs in the combustion chamber(s). It is mounted at a position on the intake manifold where detonation in each cylinder can be detected. The sensor provides information used by the SMEC to modify spark advance and boost schedules in order to eliminate detonation.

Vehicle Distance (Speed) Sensor

The speed sensor is located in the transaxle extension housing to sense vehicle motion. This sensor generates 8 pulses per axle shaft revolution. These signals are interpreted, in conjunction with other sensor input by the SMEC to adjust engine operation.

Throttle Body

The throttle body assembly replaces a conventional carburetor air intake system. It is located between the turbocharger and intake manifold on Turbo I. It is located between the intercooler and intake manifold on Turbo II. It is located at the left end of the air intake plenum on 3.0L engine. The throttle body houses the throttle position sensor and the automatic idle speed motor. Air flow through the throttle body is controlled by a cable operated throttle blade located in the base of the throttle body.

Throttle body assembly — 2.5L turbo engine

Throttle body assembly — Multi-point fuel injection

Fuel Supply Circuit

Fuel is pumped to the fuel rail by an electrical pump which is mounted in the fuel tank. The pump inlet is fitted with filter to prevent water and other contaminants from entering the fuel supply circuit. Fuel pressure is controlled to a preset level above intake manifold pressure by a pressure regulator which is mounted near the fuel rail. The regulator uses intake manifold pressure at the vacuum tee as a reference.

Fuel Injectors and Fuel Rail Assembly

The fuel injectors are retained in the fuel rail by lock rings. The rail and injector assembly is then bolted in position with the injectors inserted in the recessed holes in the intake manifold.

Fuel Injector

The fuel injector is an electric solenoid powered by the SMEC. The SMEC determines when and how long the injector should

Fuel rail and injector assembly — 2.5L turbo engine

Fuel rail assembly — 3.0L/3.3L engines

operate. When an electric current is supplied to the injector, the armature and pintle move a short distance against a spring, opening a small orifice. Fuel is supplied to the inlet of the injector by the fuel pump, then passes through the injector, around the pintle, and out the orifice. Since the fuel is under high pressure a fine spray is developed in the shape of a hollow cone. The injector, through this spraying action, atomizes the fuel and distributes it into the air entering the combustion chamber.

Fuel Injectors — component view

Fuel pressure regulator assembly

Fuel Pressure Regulator

The pressure regulator is a mechanical device located downstream of the fuel injector on the throttle body. Its function is to maintain constant fuel pressure across the fuel injector tip, 55 psi (380 kPa) for turbo models and 48 psi (330 kPa) for non-turbo models. The regulator uses a spring loaded rubber diaphragm to uncover a fuel return port. When the fuel pump becomes operational, fuel flows past the injector into the regulator and is restricted from flowing any further by the blocked return port. When the specified operating fuel pressure reached it pushes on the diaphragm, compressing the spring and uncovers the fuel return port. The diaphragm and spring will constantly move from an open to closed position to keep the fuel pressure constant. An assist to the spring loaded diaphragm comes from vacuum in the throttle body above the throttle blade. As venturi vacuum increases less pressure is required to supply the same amount of fuel into the air flow. The vacuum assists in opening the fuel port during high vacuum conditions.

Fuel Reservoir

The fuel pump is mounted within a fuel reservoir in the fuel tank. The purpose of the reservoir is to provide fuel at the pump intake during all driving conditions. The fuel return line directs fuel into a cup on the side of a reservoir.

Throttle Position Sensor (TPS)

The Throttle Position Sensor (TPS) is an electric resistor which is activated by the movement of the throttle shaft. It is mounted on the throttle body and senses the angle of the throttle blade opening. The voltage that the sensor produces increases or decreases according to the throttle blade opening. This voltage is transmitted to the SMEC where it is used along with data from other sensors to adjust the air/fuel ratio to varying conditions and during acceleration, deceleration, idle, and wide open throttle operations.

Automatic Idle Speed (AIS) Motor

The Automatic Idle Speed (AIS) motor is operated by the SMEC. Data from the throttle position sensor, speed sensor,

coolant temperature sensor, and various switch operations, (neutral-safety, brake) are used by the SMEC to adjust engine idle to an optimum during all idle conditions. The AIS adjust the air portion of the air/fuel mixture through an air bypass in the throttle body. Basic (no load) idle is determined by the minimum air flow through the throttle body. The AIS opens or closes off the air bypass as an increase or decrease is needed due to engine loads or ambient conditions. The SMEC senses an air/fuel change and increases or decreases fuel proportionally to change engine idle. Deceleration die out is also prevented by increasing engine idle when the throttle is closed quickly after a driving (speed) condition.

SERVICE PRECAUTIONS

- When working around any part of the fuel system, take precautionary steps to prevent fire and/or explosion.
- Disconnect negative terminal from battery (except when testing with battery voltage is required).
- When ever possible, use a flashlight instead of a drop light.
- Keep all open flame and smoking material out of the work area.
- Use a shop cloth or similar to catch fuel when opening a fuel system.
- Always relieve fuel system pressure before servicing any part of the fuel system.
- Always use eye protection.
- Always keep a dry chemical (class B) fire extinguisher near the area.

Diagnosis and Testing

NOTE: For Self-Diagnostic System and Accessing Trouble Code Memory, see the diagnostic procedures in Section 4. These procedures require an extensive knowledge of electronic fuel injection systems, use extreme care when performing any of these procedures.

The SMEC has been programmed to monitor several different circuits of the fuel injection system. This monitoring is called On Board Diagnosis. If a problem is sensed with a monitored circuit, often enough to indicate an actual problem, its fault code is stored in the SMEC for eventual display to the service technician. If the problem is repaired or ceases to exist, the SMEC cancels the fault code after 50–100 ignition key **ON/OFF** cycles.

Fault codes are 2 digit numbers that identify which circuit is bad. In most cases, they DO NOT identify which component is bad in a circuit. When a fault code appears it indicates that the SMEC has recognized an abnormal signal in the system. Fault codes indicate the results of a failure but do not always identify the failed component directly.

DIAGNOSTIC CHARTS

1988 3.0L DIAGNOSTIC CHART—NO START TEST

TEST DR-21 | STEP C — CHECKING FOR LOW FUEL PRESSURE
COMPLETE TEST DR-21B BEFORE PROCEEDING

PROCEDURE	TEST INDICATION	ACTION REQUIRED
• DRB II connected. • Turn the ignition switch off. • Release pressure. • Install fuel pressure between filter and fuel rail. • Turn the ignition switch to the run position. • Press and hold the ATM Key on the DRB II	• Fuel pressure increases above operating pressure	• Replace pressure regulator valve
• **Very gently, squeeze fuel return line at throttle body and immediately let go.** **NOTE: Fuel pressure must not exceed 72 P.S.I. or damage to the regulator will result.**	• Fuel pressure does not increase	• Replace intank fuel pump. **NOTE:** Before replacing pump look for contamination in the fuel tank that may be plugging pump filter. Also make sure electrical connections are not corroded.

TEST DR-21 | STEP D — CHECKING FOR HIGH FUEL PRESSURE
COMPLETE TEST DR-21A BEFORE PROCEEDING

PROCEDURE	TEST INDICATION	ACTION REQUIRED
• DRB II connected. • Turn the ignition switch off. • Pressure gauge connected. • Remove fuel return hose (small one) from fuel rail. • Connect a suitable length of fuel hose to the fuel rail and put open end into an approved gasoline container (2-gallon size). • Turn the ignition switch to the run position. • Press and hold the ATM Key on the DRB II	• Fuel pressure is 55 psi ± 2	• Check fuel return lines for kinks or restrictions, including return line check valve inside fuel tank.
	• Fuel pressure is above 57 psi	• Replace pressure regulator valve.

TEST NS-1 | STEP A — CHECKING FOR SPARK AT SPARK PLUGS

PROCEDURE	TEST INDICATION	ACTION REQUIRED
• Disconnect any spark plug wire • Insert an insulated screwdriver in terminal • Hold screwdriver shaft (¼") near a good engine ground • Have someone crank the engine for at least 7 seconds. **NOTE:** Fault code erase and SMEC damage may occur if the spark plug wire is held more than ¼" from ground.	• There is a good spark between screwdriver and ground as long as the engine is cranking	• **Perform TEST NS-2.**
	• There is no spark **NOTE:** Handle 1 or 2 sparks as no spark.	• **Perform STEP B.**
	• There is good spark between screwdriver and ground as long as the engine is cranking but engine is hard to start or starts and stalls	• **Perform TEST NS-9.**

TEST NS-1 | STEP B — CHECKING FOR SPARK AT IGNITION COIL WIRE
COMPLETE TEST NS-1A BEFORE PROCEEDING

PROCEDURE	TEST INDICATION	ACTION REQUIRED
• Disconnect ignition coil wire from distributor cap. • Hold coil wire (¼") from a good engine ground. • Have someone crank the engine **NOTE:** Fault code erase and SMEC damage may occur if the spark plug wire is held more than ¼" from ground.	• There is a good spark between ignition coil wire and ground	• Repair secondary ignition system (distributor cap and/or rotor)
	• There is no spark **NOTE:** Handle 1 or 2 sparks as no spark	• **Perform STEP C.**

TEST DR-22 | STEP A — CHECKING THROTTLE BODY MINIMUM AIR FLOW
COMPLETE TEST DR-21A BEFORE PROCEEDING

PROCEDURE	TEST INDICATION	ACTION REQUIRED
• DRB II connected. • Start the engine and let it run until fully warm. • Put the system into **Engine Running Test 70**	• Tachometer is reading as follows: Low mileage (below 1,000 miles) 600-900 rpm Broken-in 650-900 rpm	• **Perform TEST DR-23.**
	• DRB II is not reading within above specifications.	• Replace the throttle body casting assembly.

TEST NO. DR-23

COMPLETE TEST DR-22A BEFORE PROCEEDING

AT THIS POINT IN THE DRIVEABILITY TEST PROCEDURE YOU HAVE DETERMINED THAT ALL OF THE ENGINE CONTROL SYSTEMS ARE OPERATING AS THEY WERE DESIGNED TO. THEREFORE THEY ARE **NOT THE CAUSE OF THE DRIVEABILITY PROBLEM.**

THE FOLLOWING ADDITIONAL ITEMS SHOULD BE CHECKED AS POSSIBLE CAUSES:

1. **ENGINE VACUUM** – MUST BE AT LEAST 13 INCHES IN NEUTRAL.
2. **ENGINE VALVE TIMING** – TO SPECIFICATIONS.
3. **ENGINE COMPRESSION** – TO SPECIFICATIONS.
4. **ENGINE EXHAUST SYSTEM** – MUST BE FREE OF ANY RESTRICTIONS.
5. **ENGINE PCV SYSTEM** – MUST FLOW FREELY.
6. **ENGINE DRIVE SPROCKETS** – CAM, CRANK AND INTERMEDIATE SHAFTS.
7. **TORQUE CONVERTOR STALL SPEED** – TO SPECIFICATIONS.
8. **POWER BRAKE BOOSTER** – NO INTERNAL VACUUM LEAKS.
9. **FUEL CONTAMINATION** – HIGH ALCOHOL AND WATER CONTENT.
10. **TECHNICAL SERVICE BULLETINS** – ANY THAT MAY APPLY TO VEHICLE.

ANY ONE OR MORE OF THESE ITEMS CAN CREATE A DRIVEABILITY RELATED PROBLEM. THEY CANNOT BE OVERLOOKED AS POSSIBLE CAUSES.

TEST NS-1 | STEP C — CHECKING VOLTAGE SUPPLY FROM THE ASD RELAY (Z1 CIRCUIT)
COMPLETE TEST NS-1B BEFORE PROCEEDING

PROCEDURE	TEST INDICATION	ACTION REQUIRED
• Connect a voltmeter to the Z1 (DG/BK) wire of the ignition coil positive terminal and ground. • Crank the engine for at least 7 seconds.	• Voltmeter is reading within one volt of cranking voltage as long as the engine is cranking.	• **Perform TEST NS-6.**
	• Voltmeter is reading 0 volts or cranking voltage for about 1 second.	• **Perform TEST NS-12.**

TEST NS-2 | STEP A — CHECKING FUEL SUPPLY PRESSURE
COMPLETE TEST NS-1A BEFORE PROCEEDING

PROCEDURE	TEST INDICATION	ACTION REQUIRED
• Install pressure gauge (Tool C3292) with (C4799 adapter) in fuel supply hose at throttle body. **CAUTION:** Fuel is under high pressure • Crank the engine for at least 7 seconds	• Fuel pressure is reading at least 40 psi	• Fuel pressure okay, Perform **STEP B.**
	• Fuel pressure is 0.	• **Perform TEST NS-5.**

1988 3.0L DIAGNOSTIC CHART—NO START TEST

TEST NS-2 | STEP B | CHECKING THROTTLE POSITION SENSOR
COMPLETE TEST NS-2A BEFORE PROCEEDING

PROCEDURE		TEST INDICATION	ACTION REQUIRED
• Connect DRB II to the engine harness connector. • Put the system into Sensor Test 05.		• Display on the readout box is reading between ½ and 1½ volts	• Perform STEP C.
		• Display on the DRB II is more than 1½ volts	• Replace the throttle position sensor
		• System will not go into the sensor test mode (no code 88)	• Replace the SMEC

TEST NS-2 | STEP C | CHECKING VOLTAGE SUPPLY TO THE INJECTORS FROM THE AUTO SHUTDOWN RELAY (Z1 CIRCUIT)
COMPLETE TEST NS-2B BEFORE PROCEEDING

PROCEDURE		TEST INDICATION	ACTION REQUIRED
• DRB II connected to the engine harness connector. • Connect a voltmeter to the Z1 (DG/BK) wire of the injector harness. 4-way connector and ground. • Put the system in ATM Test 02.		• Voltmeter reads battery voltage	• Perform TEST NS-3.
		• Voltmeter is reading 0 volts.	• Repair the Z1 (DG/BK) wire of the injector harness connector for an open circuit to the wiring harness splice

TEST NS-4 | STEP B | CHECKING ENGINE TIMING
COMPLETE TEST NS-4A BEFORE PROCEEDING

PROCEDURE		TEST INDICATION	ACTION REQUIRED
• Timing device connected to engine. • Set timing to 10° BTC during cranking.		• Engine starts.	• Reset timing to specifications.
		• Engine does not start.	• Remove distributor cap, crank engine to make sure rotor is turning and is indexed correctly. • Check compression and valve timing.

TEST NS-5 | STEP A | CHECKING FUEL PUMP
COMPLETE TEST NS-2A BEFORE PROCEEDING

PROCEDURE		TEST INDICATION	ACTION REQUIRED
• Connect the DRB II to the engine harness connector. • Put the system into the Diagnostic Test Mode. • Press and hold the ATM key on the DRB II.		• The fuel pump is running.	• Check the following: a) all fuel lines for kinks, restrictions, or leaks b) a plugged fuel filter If all okay remove the pump for inspection and check for fuel contamination.
		• The fuel pump is not running.	• Perform STEP B.

TEST NS-3 | STEP A | CHECKING FOR FUEL FOULED SPARK PLUGS
COMPLETE TEST NS-2C BEFORE PROCEEDING

PROCEDURE		TEST INDICATION	ACTION REQUIRED
• Remove spark plugs. • Look at tips for wet fuel		• Spark plug tips are not wet with fuel NOTE: It is normal for spark plugs to be black after engine is started cold	• Perform TEST NS-4.
		• Spark plugs are wet with fuel	• Clean and reinstall. Do not replace spark plugs. • Attempt restart.

LOOK FOR WET FUEL

TEST NS-4 | STEP A | CHECKING ENGINE TIMING
COMPLETE TEST NS-3A BEFORE PROCEEDING

PROCEDURE		TEST INDICATION	ACTION REQUIRED
• Connect timing device to engine. • Have someone crank engine while you look at the timing marks.		• Timing is between 0°-16° BTC.	• Remove distributor cap, crank engine to make sure rotor is turning and is indexed correctly. • Check compression and valve timing.
		• Timing is not between 0°-16° BTC.	• Perform STEP B.

TEST NS-5 | STEP B | CHECKING FUEL PUMP WIRES (Z1 AND Y2 CIRCUITS)
COMPLETE TEST NS-5A BEFORE PROCEEDING

PROCEDURE		TEST INDICATION	ACTION REQUIRED
• DRB II connected to the engine harness connector. • System in Diagnostic Test Mode. • Raise the car on a hoist. • Disconnect the intank fuel pump connector. • Connect the positive lead of a voltmeter to the Z1 (DG/BK) wire of the connector. • Connect the negative lead of the voltmeter to the X2 (GY) wire of the connector. • Press and hold the ATM key on the DRB II.	VOLTMETER GY DG/BK IN TANK FUEL PUMP CONNECTOR	• Voltmeter is reading within one volt of battery voltage.	• Replace the fuel pump
		• Voltmeter reads 0.	• Move negative lead of voltmeter to a good engine ground and press the ATM key on the DRB II. • If voltage is now okay repair gray wire of connector for an open circuit. • If voltage is still 0, repair the dark green with black tracer wire for an open circuit

TEST NS-6 | STEP A | CHECKING IGNITION CONTROL SYSTEM FOR FAULT CODES
COMPLETE TEST NS-1C BEFORE PROCEEDING

PROCEDURE		TEST INDICATION	ACTION REQUIRED
• Connect DRB II to the engine harness connector. • Put the system in the Diagnostic Test Mode. • Record all codes		88-12-55 No fault codes	Perform TEST NS-7.
		88-12-43-55 Spark control circuit	Perform TEST NS-8.

1988 3.0L DIAGNOSTIC CHART—NO START TEST

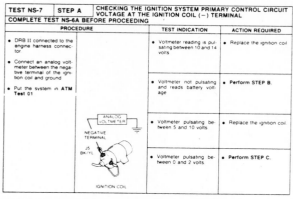

TEST NS-7	STEP A	CHECKING THE IGNITION SYSTEM PRIMARY CONTROL CIRCUIT VOLTAGE AT THE IGNITION COIL (−) TERMINAL

COMPLETE TEST NS-6A BEFORE PROCEEDING

PROCEDURE	TEST INDICATION	ACTION REQUIRED
• DRB II connected to the engine harness connector. • Connect an analog voltmeter between the negative terminal of the ignition coil and ground. • Put the system in ATM Test 01.	• Voltmeter reading is pulsating between 10 and 14 volts.	• Replace the ignition coil.
	• Voltmeter not pulsating and reads battery voltage.	• Perform STEP B.
	• Voltmeter pulsating between 5 and 10 volts.	• Replace the ignition coil.
	• Voltmeter pulsating between 0 and 2 volts.	• Perform STEP C.

TEST NS-7	STEP C	CHECKING THE IGNITION COIL PRIMARY WINDINGS FOR A SHORT CIRCUIT

COMPLETE TEST NS-7A BEFORE PROCEEDING

PROCEDURE	TEST INDICATION	ACTION REQUIRED
• DRB II connected to the engine harness connector. • Turn the ignition switch off. • Disconnect the wire from the negative side (−) of the ignition coil. • Connect the voltmeter to the negative (−) terminal of the ignition coil and ground. • Put the system in ATM Test 01.	• Voltmeter is reading above 10 volts.	• Perform STEP D.
	• Voltmeter reads between 0 and 2 volts.	• Replace the ignition coil.

TEST NS-7	STEP B	CHECKING THE IGNITION SYSTEM PRIMARY CONTROL CIRCUIT FOR AN OPEN CIRCUIT (J5 CIRCUIT)

COMPLETE TEST NS-7A BEFORE PROCEEDING

PROCEDURE	TEST INDICATION	ACTION REQUIRED
• Turn the ignition switch off. • Disconnect the 14-way connector from the SMEC. • Connect an ohmmeter between the negative (−) terminal of the ignition coil and cavity No. 12 of the 14-way connector.	• Ohmmeter is showing continuity.	• Defective power board. Replace the SMEC. CAUTION: Before replacing the SMEC, check the J5 terminal in cavity No. 12 of the 14-way connector to make sure that it is not spread apart causing a poor connection.
	• Ohmmeter is not showing continuity.	• Repair the J5 (BK/YL) wire of cavity No. 12 for an open circuit.

TEST NS-7	STEP D	CHECKING THE IGNITION SYSTEM PRIMARY CIRCUIT FOR A SHORT CIRCUIT TO GROUND (J5 CIRCUIT)

COMPLETE TEST NS-7C BEFORE PROCEEDING

PROCEDURE	TEST INDICATION	ACTION REQUIRED
• Ignition coil negative (−) wire disconnected. • Turn the ignition switch off. • Disconnect the 14-way connector from the SMEC. • Connect an ohmmeter between cavity No. 12 of the 14-way connector and ground.	• Ohmmeter is not showing continuity.	• Defective power board. Replace the SMEC.
	• Ohmmeter is showing continuity.	• Repair the J5 (BK/YL) wire of cavity No. 12 for a short circuit to ground.

TEST NS-8	STEP A	CHECKING FOR FAULT CODE 43 — SPARK CONTROL CIRCUIT

COMPLETE TEST NS-6A BEFORE PROCEEDING

PROCEDURE		TEST INDICATION	ACTION REQUIRED
• DRB II connected to the engine harness connector. • Put the System in Diagnostic Test Mode. • Turn the ignition switch off. • Disconnect the ignition coil wire at the distributor and place it near a good engine ground so there is a ¼ inch gap. • Disconnect the 60-way connector from the (SMEC) and connect one end of a jumper wire to cavity No. 34. • Turn the ignition switch on, press and hold the ATM key on the DRB II.	• Touch the other end of the jumper to a good ground. Make and break this connection several times while looking at the ignition coil wire. VIEW FROM TERMINAL END	• There is spark at the ignition coil wire as you make and break the connection.	• Defective logic board. Replace the SMEC. CAUTION: Before replacing the SMEC, check the K15 terminal in cavity No. 34 of the 60-way connector to make sure it is not damaged causing a poor connection.
		• There is no spark at the ignition coil wire as you make and break the connection.	• Perform STEP B.

TEST NS-9	STEP A	CHECKING INJECTOR CONTROL SYSTEM FOR FAULT CODES

COMPLETE TEST NS-1A BEFORE PROCEEDING

PROCEDURE	TEST INDICATION	ACTION REQUIRED
• Connect DRB II to the engine harness connector. • Put the system into the Diagnostic Test Mode. • Record all codes.	No fault codes	• Perform Driveability TEST DR-1.
	88-12-26-55 Injector driver circuits	• Perform TEST NS-10.
	88-12-27-55 Injector control circuits	• Perform TEST NS-11.

TEST NS-8	STEP B	CHECKING THE SPARK CONTROL WIRE FOR AN OPEN CIRCUIT (K15 CIRCUIT)

COMPLETE TEST NS-6A BEFORE PROCEEDING

PROCEDURE		TEST INDICATION	ACTION REQUIRED
• SMEC 60-way connector disconnected. • Turn the ignition switch off. • Remove the jumper wire from cavity No. 34 of the SMEC 60-way connector. • Disconnect the 14-way connector from the SMEC. • Connect one lead of an ohmmeter to cavity No. 34 of the SMEC 60-way connector. • Connect the other lead of the ohmmeter to cavity No. 13 of the SMEC 14-way connector.	VIEW FROM TERMINAL END	• Ohmmeter is showing continuity.	• Defective power board. Replace the SMEC. CAUTION: Before replacing the SMEC, check the K15 terminal in cavity No. 13 of the 14-way connector to make sure it is not spread apart causing a poor connection.
		• Ohmmeter is not showing continuity.	• Repair the K15 (YL) wire for an open circuit

TEST NS-10	STEP A	CHECKING THE VOLTAGE SUPPLY CIRCUIT TO EACH INJECTOR (Z1 CIRCUIT)

COMPLETE TEST NS-9A BEFORE PROCEEDING

PROCEDURE	TEST INDICATION	ACTION REQUIRED
• DRB II connected to the engine harness connector. • Remove air intake plenum. • Disconnect all injectors. • Put the system in ATM Test 02. • Connect the negative lead of a voltmeter to ground and touch the positive lead to the Z1 (DG/BK) wire of each injector connector.	• Voltmeter shows battery voltage at each connector.	• Perform STEP B.
	• Voltmeter shows 0 volts at one or more of the connectors.	• Repair the Z1 (DG/BK) wire of the injector harness for an open circuit to the injector connector.

1988 3.0L DIAGNOSTIC CHART—NO START TEST

TEST NS-10	STEP B	CHECKING INJECTOR NO. 1 CIRCUIT (Y13 CIRCUIT)	
COMPLETE TEST NS-10A BEFORE PROCEEDING			
PROCEDURE		TEST INDICATION	ACTION REQUIRED
• DRB II connected to the engine harness connector		• Injector number 1 clicks	• Perform STEP H.
• Air intake plenum removed			
• All injectors disconnected			
• System in ATM Test 02			
• Connect injector connector number 1 to injector number 1		• Injector number 1 does not click	• Perform STEP C NOTE: Make sure ATM Test 02 has not timed out before proceeding to STEP C.
• Leave connected for 10 seconds and listen for a click			

TEST NS-10	STEP D	CHECKING INJECTORS 1 AND 6	
COMPLETE TEST NS-10C BEFORE PROCEEDING			
PROCEDURE		TEST INDICATION	ACTION REQUIRED
• DRB II connected to the engine harness connector	• Disconnect injector connector number 2 from injector number 1	• Injectors 1 and 6 do not click	• Replace injectors number 1 and 6
• Air intake plenum removed	• Connect injector connector number 4 to injector number 6		
• All injectors except injector for cylinder number 6 disconnected	• Leave connected for 10 seconds and listen for a click	• One injector either 1 or 6 clicks and the other doesn't	• Replace injector which failed to click
• System in ATM Test 02			
• Disconnect injector connector number 6 from injector			
• Connect injector connector number 2 to injector number 1		• Both injector 1 and 6 click	• Perform STEP E.
• Leave connected for 10 seconds and listen for a click			

TEST NS-10	STEP C	CHECKING INJECTOR NO. 6 CIRCUIT	
COMPLETE TEST NS-10B BEFORE PROCEEDING			
PROCEDURE		TEST INDICATION	ACTION REQUIRED
• DRB II connected to the engine harness connector		• Injector number 6 clicks	• Perform STEP G
• Air intake plenum removed			
• All injectors except injector for cylinder number 1 disconnected			
• System in ATM Test 02			
• Disconnect injector connector number 1 from injector		• Injector number 6 does not click	• Perform STEP D
• Connect injector connector number 6 to injector number 6			
• Leave connected for 10 seconds and listen for a click			

TEST NS-10	STEP E	CHECKING 1 AND 6 CONTROL WIRE FOR A SHORT TO GROUND	
COMPLETE TEST NS-10D BEFORE PROCEEDING			
PROCEDURE		TEST INDICATION	ACTION REQUIRED
• Turn the ignition switch off		• Ohmmeter is showing continuity	• Repair the Y13 (YL/WT) wire of cavity No. 5 of the 14-way connector for a short to ground
• Disconnect the 14-way connector from the SMEC			
• Connect an ohmmeter between the Y13 (YL/WT) wire in cavity No. 5 of the 14-way connector and ground		• Ohmmeter is showing open	• Perform STEP F.

TEST NS-10	STEP F	CHECKING 1 AND 6 CONTROL WIRE FOR AN OPEN CIRCUIT TO THE ENGINE CONTROL MODULE	
COMPLETE TEST NS-10E BEFORE PROCEEDING			
PROCEDURE		TEST INDICATION	ACTION REQUIRED
• Ignition switch turned off		• Ohmmeter is showing continuity	• Defective power board Replace the SMEC CAUTION: Before replacing the SMEC, check the Y13 terminal in cavity No. 5 of the 14-way connector to make sure it is not spread apart causing a poor connection
• 14-way connector disconnected from the SMEC			
• Connect an ohmmeter between the Y13 (YL/WT) wire in cavity No. 5 of the 14-way connector and the Y13 (YL/WT) wire of injector connectors 1 and 6		• Ohmmeter is not showing continuity	• Repair the Y13 (YL/WT) wire of cavity No. 5 of the 14-way connector for an open circuit to the injector connector

TEST NS-10	STEP H	CHECKING INJECTOR NO. 6 CIRCUIT	
COMPLETE TEST NS-10B BEFORE PROCEEDING			
PROCEDURE		TEST INDICATION	ACTION REQUIRED
• DRB II connected to the engine harness connector		• Injector No. 6 clicks	• Perform STEP J
• Air intake plenum removed			
• All injectors except injector No. 1 disconnected			
• System in ATM Test 02			
• Disconnect injector connector No. 1 from injector		• Injector No. 6 does not click	• Perform STEP I
• Connect injector connector No. 6 to injector No. 6			
• Leave connected for 10 seconds and listen for a click			

TEST NS-10	STEP G	CHECKING INJECTOR NUMBER 1 CONTROL WIRE FOR AN OPEN CIRCUIT IN INJECTOR HARNESS (Y13 CIRCUIT)	
COMPLETE TEST NS-10B BEFORE PROCEEDING			
PROCEDURE		TEST INDICATION	ACTION REQUIRED
• Turn the ignition switch off		• Ohmmeter is showing continuity	• Replace injector No. 1
• Disconnect injector connector No. 6 from injector			
• Disconnect injector harness 4-way connector from the engine harness connector			
• Connect an ohmmeter between the Y13 (YL/WT) wire at injector No. 1 and the Y13 (YL/WT) wire at the injector harness 4-way connector		• Ohmmeter is not showing continuity	• Repair the Y13 (YL/WT) wire for an open circuit in the injector harness

TEST NS-10	STEP I	CHECKING INJECTOR NUMBER 6 CONTROL WIRE FOR AN OPEN CIRCUIT IN INJECTOR HARNESS (Y13 CIRCUIT)	
COMPLETE TEST NS-10H BEFORE PROCEEDING			
PROCEDURE		TEST INDICATION	ACTION REQUIRED
• Turn the ignition switch off		• Ohmmeter is showing continuity	• Replace injector No. 6
• Disconnect injector connector No. 6 from injector			
• Disconnect injector harness 4-way connector from the engine harness			
• Connect an ohmmeter between the Y13 (YL/WT) wire at injector No. 6 connector and the Y13 (YL/WT) wire at the 4-way injector harness connector		• Ohmmeter is not showing continuity	• Repair the Y13 (YL/WT) wire for an open circuit in the injector harness

1988 3.0L DIAGNOSTIC CHART—NO START TEST

TEST NS-10 | STEP J | CHECKING INJECTOR NO. 2 CIRCUIT (Y12 CIRCUIT)

COMPLETE TEST NS-10H BEFORE PROCEEDING

PROCEDURE	TEST INDICATION	ACTION REQUIRED
• DRB II connected to the engine harness connector • Air intake plenum removed • All injectors except injector for cylinder No. 6 disconnected • System in ATM Test 02 • Disconnect injector connector No. 6 from injector • Connect injector connector No. 2 to injector No. 2 • Leave connected for 10 seconds and listen for a click	• Injector No. 2 clicks	• Perform STEP P
	• Injector No. 2 does not click	• Perform STEP K NOTE: Make sure ATM Test 02 has not timed out before proceeding to STEP K.

TEST NS-10 | STEP K | CHECKING INJECTOR CIRCUIT NO. 3

COMPLETE TEST NS-10J BEFORE PROCEEDING

PROCEDURE	TEST INDICATION	ACTION REQUIRED
• DRB II connected to the engine harness connector • Air intake plenum removed • All injectors except injector for cylinder No. 2 disconnected • System in ATM Test 02 • Disconnect injector connector No. 2 from injector • Connect injector connector No. 3 to injector No. 3 • Leave connected for 10 seconds and listen for a click	• Injector No. 3 clicks	• Perform STEP O.
	• Injector No. 3 does not click	• Perform STEP L.

TEST NS-10 | STEP N | CHECKING 2 AND 3 CONTROL WIRE FOR AN OPEN CIRCUIT TO THE ENGINE CONTROL MODULE (Y12 CIRCUIT)

COMPLETE TEST NS-10M BEFORE PROCEEDING

PROCEDURE	TEST INDICATION	ACTION REQUIRED
• Ignition switch turned off • 14 way connector disconnected from the SMEC • Connect an ohmmeter between the Y12 (TN) wire in cavity No. 10 of the 14 way connector and the Y12 (TN) wire of injector connectors 2 and then 3	• Ohmmeter is showing continuity	• Defective power board. Replace the SMEC. CAUTION: Before replacing the SMEC, check the Y12 terminal in cavity No. 10 of the 14 way connector to make sure it is not spread apart causing a poor connection
	• Ohmmeter is not showing continuity	• Repair the Y12 (TN) wire of cavity No. 10 of the 14 way connector for an open circuit to the injector harness connector

TEST NS-10 | STEP O | CHECKING INJECTOR NO. 2 CONTROL WIRE FOR AN OPEN CIRCUIT IN INJECTOR HARNESS (Y12 CIRCUIT)

COMPLETE TEST NS-10K BEFORE PROCEEDING

PROCEDURE	TEST INDICATION	ACTION REQUIRED
• Turn the ignition switch off • Disconnect injector connector for cylinder No. 3 from injector • Disconnect injector harness 4 way connector from the engine harness connector • Connect an ohmmeter between the Y12 (TN) wire at injector No. 2 connector and the Y12 (TN) wire at the injector harness 4 way connector	• Ohmmeter is showing continuity	• Replace injector No. 2
	• Ohmmeter is not showing continuity	• Repair the Y12 (TN) wire for an open circuit in the injector harness

TEST NS-10 | STEP L | CHECKING INJECTORS 2 AND 3

COMPLETE TEST NS-10K BEFORE PROCEEDING

PROCEDURE	TEST INDICATION	ACTION REQUIRED
• DRB II connected to the engine harness connector • Air intake plenum removed • All injectors, except injector for cylinder No. 3 disconnected • System in ATM Test 02 • Disconnect injector connector No. 3 from injector • Connect injector connector No. 1 to injector No. 2 • Leave connected for 10 seconds and listen for a click	• Disconnect injector connector No. 1 from injector No. 2 • Connect injector connector No. 1 to injector No. 3 • Leave connected for 10 seconds and listen for a click	• Injectors No. 2 and 3 do not click	• Replace injectors No. 2 and 3
		• One injector, either 2 or 3, clicks and the other doesn't	• Replace injector which failed to click
		• Both injectors 2 and 3 click	• Perform STEP M.

TEST NS-10 | STEP M | CHECKING 2 AND 3 CONTROL WIRE FOR A SHORT TO GROUND (Y12 CIRCUIT)

COMPLETE TEST NS-10L BEFORE PROCEEDING

PROCEDURE	TEST INDICATION	ACTION REQUIRED
• Turn the ignition switch off • Disconnect the 14-way connector from the SMEC • Connect an ohmmeter between the Y12 (TN) wire in cavity No. 10 of the 14-way connector and ground	• Ohmmeter is showing continuity	• Repair the Y12 (TN) wire of cavity No. 10 of the 14-way connector for a short to ground
	• Ohmmeter is showing no continuity	• Perform STEP N.

TEST NS-10 | STEP P | CHECKING INJECTOR NO. 3 CIRCUIT

COMPLETE TEST NS-10J BEFORE PROCEEDING

PROCEDURE	TEST INDICATION	ACTION REQUIRED
• DRB II connected to the engine harness connector • Air intake plenum removed • All injectors except injector No. 2 disconnected • System in ATM Test 02 • Disconnect injector connector No. 2 • Connect injector connector No. 3 to injector No. 3 • Leave connected for 10 seconds and listen for a click	• Injector No. 3 clicks	• Perform STEP R.
	• Injector No. 3 does not click	• Perform STEP Q.

TEST NS-10 | STEP Q | CHECKING INJECTOR NO. 3 CONTROL WIRE FOR AN OPEN CIRCUIT IN INJECTOR HARNESS (Y12 CIRCUIT)

COMPLETE TEST NS-10P BEFORE PROCEEDING

PROCEDURE	TEST INDICATION	ACTION REQUIRED
• Turn the ignition switch off • Disconnect injector connector No. 3 from injector • Disconnect injector harness 4 way connector from the engine harness • Connect an ohmmeter between the Y12 (TN) wire at injector No. 3 connector and the Y12 (TN) wire at the injector harness 4 way connector	• Ohmmeter is showing continuity	• Replace injector No. 1
	• Ohmmeter is not showing continuity	• Repair the Y12 (TN) wire for an open circuit in the injector harness

1988 3.0L DIAGNOSTIC CHART—NO START TEST

TEST NS-10	STEP R	CHECKING INJECTOR NO. 4 CIRCUIT (Y11 CIRCUIT)	
COMPLETE TEST NS-10Q BEFORE PROCEEDING			
PROCEDURE		TEST INDICATION	ACTION REQUIRED
• DRB II connected to the engine harness connector • Air intake plenum removed • All injectors except injector for cylinder No 3 disconnected • System in ATM Test 02 • Disconnect injector connector No 3 from injector • Connect injector connector No 4 to injector for cylinder No 4 • Leave connected for 10 seconds and listen for a click		• Injector No 4 clicks	• Perform STEP X.
		• Injector No 4 does not click	• Perform STEP S. NOTE: Make sure ATM Test 02 has not timed out before proceeding to Step S

TEST NS-10	STEP T	CHECKING INJECTORS 4 AND 5	
COMPLETE TEST NS-10S BEFORE PROCEEDING			
PROCEDURE		TEST INDICATION	ACTION REQUIRED
• DRB II connected to the engine harness connector • Air intake plenum removed • All injectors except injector for cylinder No 5 disconnected • System in ATM Test 02 • Disconnect injector connector No 5 from injector • Connect injector connector No 6 to injector No 4 • Leave connected for 10 seconds and listen for a click • Disconnect injector connector No 6 from injector No 4		• Injectors No 4 and 5 do not click	• Replace injectors No 4 and 5
		• One injector either 4 or 5 clicks and the other doesn't	• Replace injector which failed to click
		• Both injectors 4 and 5 click	• Perform STEP U.

TEST NS-10	STEP S	CHECKING INJECTOR NO. 5 CIRCUIT	
COMPLETE TEST NS-10R BEFORE PROCEEDING			
PROCEDURE		TEST INDICATION	ACTION REQUIRED
• DRB II connected to the engine harness connector • Air intake plenum removed • All injectors except injector for cylinder No 4 disconnected • System in ATM Test 02 • Disconnect injector connector No 4 from injector • Connect injector connector No 5 to injector for cylinder No 5 • Leave connected for 10 seconds and listen for a click		• Injector No 5 clicks	• Perform STEP W
		• Injector No 5 does not click	• Perform STEP T

TEST NS-10	STEP U	CHECKING 4 AND 5 CONTROL WIRE FOR A SHORT TO GROUND (Y11 CIRCUIT)	
COMPLETE TEST NS-10T BEFORE PROCEEDING			
PROCEDURE		TEST INDICATION	ACTION REQUIRED
• Turn the ignition switch off • Disconnect the 14 way connector from the SMEC • Connect an ohmmeter between the Y11 (WT) wire in cavity No 9 of the 14 way connector and ground		• Ohmmeter is showing continuity	• Repair the Y11 (WT) wire of cavity No 9 of the 14 way connector for a short to ground
		• Ohmmeter is showing no continuity	• Perform STEP V

TEST NS-10	STEP V	CHECKING INJECTOR NO. 5 CONTROL WIRE FOR AN OPEN CIRCUIT (Y11 CIRCUIT)	
COMPLETE TEST NS-10U BEFORE PROCEEDING			
PROCEDURE		TEST INDICATION	ACTION REQUIRED
• Ignition switch turned off • 14 way connector disconnected from the SMEC • Connect an ohmmeter between the Y11 (WT) wire in cavity No 9 of the 14 way connector and the Y11 (WT) wire of injector connectors 4 and 5		• Ohmmeter is showing continuity	• Defective power board Replace the SMEC. CAUTION: Before replacing the SMEC check the Y11 terminal in cavity No 9 of the 14 way connector to make sure it is not spread apart causing a poor connection
		• Ohmmeter is not showing continuity	• Repair the Y11 (WT) wire of cavity No 9 of the 14 way connector for an open circuit to the injector connectors

TEST NS-10	STEP X	CHECKING INJECTOR NO. 5 CONTROL WIRE FOR AN OPEN CIRCUIT IN INJECTOR HARNESS (Y11 CIRCUIT)	
COMPLETE TEST NS-10R BEFORE PROCEEDING			
PROCEDURE		TEST INDICATION	ACTION REQUIRED
• Turn the ignition switch off • Disconnect injector connector No 4 from injector • Disconnect injector harness 4 way connector from engine harness connector • Connect an ohmmeter between the Y11 (WT) wire at injector No 5 and the Y11 (WT) wire at the injector harness 4 way connector		• Ohmmeter is showing continuity	• Replace injector No 5
		• Ohmmeter is not showing continuity	• Repair the Y11 (WT) wire for an open circuit in the injector harness

TEST NS-10	STEP W	CHECKING INJECTOR NO. 4 CONTROL WIRE FOR AN OPEN CIRCUIT IN INJECTOR HARNESS (Y11 CIRCUIT)	
COMPLETE TEST NS-10S BEFORE PROCEEDING			
PROCEDURE		TEST INDICATION	ACTION REQUIRED
• Turn the ignition switch off • Disconnect injector connector No 5 from injector • Disconnect injector harness 4 way connector from the engine harness connector • Connect an ohmmeter between the Y11 (WT) wire at injector No 4 and the Y11 (WT) wire at the injector harness 4 way connector		• Ohmmeter is showing continuity	• Replace injector No 4
		• Ohmmeter is not showing continuity	• Repair the Y11 (WT) wire for an open circuit in the injector harness

TEST NS-11	STEP A	CHECKING FOR FAULT CODE 27 - FUEL CONTROL CIRCUIT (INJECTORS 4 AND 5 CONTROL CIRCUIT)	
COMPLETE TEST NS-9A BEFORE PROCEEDING			
PROCEDURE		TEST INDICATION	ACTION REQUIRED
• DRB II connected to the engine harness connector • Put the system in Diagnostic Test Mode • Turn the ignition switch off • Disconnect the 60 way connector • Connect one end of a jumper wire to the K16 (VT-YL) wire in cavity No 33 of the 60 way connector • Turn ignition switch to the run position • Press and hold the ATM key on DRB II and touch the other end of the jumper wire to the positive post of the battery	VIEW FROM TERMINAL END BATTERY POSITIVE	• Injectors 4 and 5 click	• Perform STEP C
		• Injectors 4 and 5 do not click	• Perform STEP B

TEST NS-11 | **STEP B** | CHECKING INJECTORS 4 AND 5 CONTROL WIRE FOR AN OPEN CIRCUIT

COMPLETE TEST NS-11A BEFORE PROCEEDING

PROCEDURE	TEST INDICATION	ACTION REQUIRED
• (illegible) •Turn the ignition switch ... •Disconnect the 14 way connector from the SMEC •Connect an ohmmeter between ...	• Ohmmeter is showing continuity	• Defective power board. Replace the SMEC. CAUTION: Before replacing the SMEC check the K1N terminal in cavity No 8 of the 14 way connector to make sure it is not spread apart causing a poor connection
	• Ohmmeter is not showing continuity	• Repair the K1N (VT) wire for an open circuit between the 14 and two way connectors

14 way connector (view)

TEST NS-11 | **STEP C** | CHECKING INJECTORS 2 AND 3 CONTROL CIRCUIT

COMPLETE TEST NS-11A BEFORE PROCEEDING

PROCEDURE	TEST INDICATION	ACTION REQUIRED
• DRB II connected to the engine harness connector • System in Diagnostic Test Mode • 60 way connector disconnected from the SMEC • Disconnect the 14 way connector from the SMEC • Remove the SMEC • Remove the cover from the SMEC • Disconnect the 2 way connector located between the logic and power boards • Connect one end of a jumper wire to the 14 way connector to the power board	• Connect one end of a jumper wire to the male terminal of the 2 way connector of the power board • Turn the ignition switch to the run position • Press and hold the ATM key on the DRB II and touch the other end of the jumper wire to the positive post of the battery	• Injectors 2 and 3 click	• Perform STEP D
	• Injectors 2 and 3 do not click	• Defective power board. Replace the SMEC.

METER (view)

TEST NS-13 | **STEP A** | CHECKING FOR THE 5 VOLT SUPPLY (K8 CIRCUIT)

COMPLETE TEST NS-12A BEFORE PROCEEDING

PROCEDURE	TEST INDICATION	ACTION REQUIRED
• Turn the ignition switch off • Disconnect the throttle position sensor connector • Turn the ignition switch on • Connect a voltmeter to the K8 (VT/WT) wire at the throttle position sensor connector and ground	• Voltmeter is reading at least 4.5 volts	• Perform STEP B
	• Voltmeter is reading 0 volts	• Perform STEP C

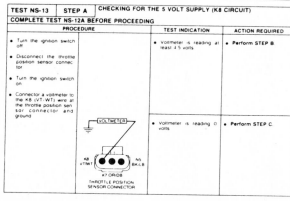

VOLTMETER

K8 VT/WT   N5 BK/LB
K7 OR/DB
THROTTLE POSITION SENSOR CONNECTOR

TEST NS-13 | **STEP B** | CHECKING THE SMEC GROUND CIRCUIT (K9 CIRCUIT)

COMPLETE TEST NS-13A BEFORE PROCEEDING

PROCEDURE	TEST INDICATION	ACTION REQUIRED
• Turn the ignition switch off • Disconnect the 60 way connector from the SMEC • Connect one lead of an ohmmeter to the system ground eyelet • Touch the other end of the ohmmeter to cavity No 15 and 16 of the 60-way connector	• Ohmmeter is showing continuity with less than ½ ohm of resistance in both wires	• Defective logic board. Replace the SMEC.
	• Ohmmeter is not showing continuity	• Repair the K9 (BK) wires for an open circuit to the wiring harness splice • Replace the SMEC
	• Ohmmeter is showing more than ½ ohm of resistance at one or both wires	• Repair K9 ground circuit for high resistance to system ground eyelet

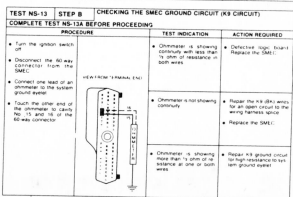

VIEW FROM TERMINAL END

OHMMETER

TEST NS-11 | **STEP D** | CHECKING INJECTORS 1 AND 6 CONTROL CIRCUIT

COMPLETE TEST NS-11C BEFORE PROCEEDING

PROCEDURE	TEST INDICATION	ACTION REQUIRED
• DRB II connected • System in Diagnostic Test Mode • Ignition switch in the run position • 60 way connector disconnected • SMEC removed, opened and the 2 way connector located between the logic and power board disconnected • 14 way connector connected to the SMEC • Connect one end of a jumper wire to the female terminal of the 2-way connector of the power board	• Press and hold the ATM key on the DRB II and touch the other end of the jumper wire to the positive post of the battery	• Injectors 1 and 6 clicking	• Defective power board. Replace the SMEC
	• Injectors 1 and 6 not clicking	• Defective logic board. Replace the SMEC

JUMPER

BATTERY POSITIVE

POWER BOARD INTERNAL CONNECTOR

TEST NS-12 | **STEP A** | CHECKING SYSTEM FOR FAULT CODES

COMPLETE TEST NS-1C BEFORE PROCEEDING

PROCEDURE	TEST INDICATION	ACTION REQUIRED
• Connect the DRB II to the engine harness connector • Erase fault codes • Crank the engine for 7 seconds and then turn the ignition switch to the run position for 5 seconds before turning to off • Put the system in the Diagnostic Mode • Record all codes	88-12-55 No Fault Codes	• Repair Z1 (DG/BK) wire of the auto shutdown relay for an open circuit
	No Code 88 or 00 System Power Circuits	• Perform TEST NS-13.
	88-11-12-55 Distributor pickup circuit	• Perform TEST NS-14.
	88-12-42-55 Auto shutdown relay pull in coil circuit	• Perform TEST NS-15.
	88-12-44-55 Fused J2	• Perform TEST NS-16.
	88-12-14-22-24-55 88-12-14-22-23-24-55	• Repair the N5 (BK/LB) wire in cavity No 4 of the SMEC 60-way connector for an open circuit

DRB II (view)

TEST NS-13 | **STEP C** | CHECKING FOR A SHORTED MAP SENSOR

COMPLETE TEST NS-13A BEFORE PROCEEDING

PROCEDURE	TEST INDICATION	ACTION REQUIRED
• Ignition switch turned on • Throttle position sensor connector disconnected • Negative lead of a voltmeter connected to ground • Disconnect the MAP sensor connector • Touch the positive lead of a voltmeter to the K8 (VT/WT) wire at the throttle position sensor connector	• Voltmeter is reading at least 4.5 volts	• Replace the MAP sensor
	• Voltmeter is reading 0 volts	• Perform STEP D.

VOLTMETER

K8 VT/WT   N5 BK/LB
K7 OR/DB
THROTTLE POSITION SENSOR CONNECTOR

TEST NS-13 | **STEP D** | CHECKING FOR THE 8 VOLT SUPPLY (N6 CIRCUIT)

COMPLETE TEST NS-13C BEFORE PROCEEDING

PROCEDURE	TEST INDICATION	ACTION REQUIRED
• Turn the ignition switch off • Disconnect the 60-way connector from the SMEC • Connect the negative lead of a voltmeter to ground • Turn the ignition switch on • Touch the positive lead of the voltmeter to the N6 (OR) wire in cavity No 52 of the SMEC 60-way connector	• Voltmeter is reading at least 8 volts	• Defective logic board. Replace the SMEC. CAUTION: Before replacing the SMEC check the N6 terminal in cavity No 52 to make sure it is not damaged causing a poor connection
	• Voltmeter is reading 0 volts	• Perform STEP E.

VIEW FROM TERMINAL END

N6 OR   52

VOLTMETER

1988 3.0L DIAGNOSTIC CHART—NO START TEST

TEST NS-13	STEP E	CHECKING FOR A SHORTED DISTRIBUTOR PICKUP

COMPLETE TEST NS-13D BEFORE PROCEEDING

PROCEDURE		TEST INDICATION	ACTION REQUIRED
• 60-way connector disconnected. • Ignition switch turned on. • The negative lead of a voltmeter connected to ground. • Disconnect the distributor pickup harness connector. • Touch the positive lead of the voltmeter to the N6 (OR) wire in cavity No. 52 of the SMEC 60-way connector.		• Voltmeter is reading at least 8 volts.	• Replace the distributor pickup
		• Voltmeter is reading 0 volts.	• Perform STEP F.

TEST NS-13	STEP F	CHECKING THE 8 VOLT SUPPLY WIRE FOR AN OPEN CIRCUIT (N6 CIRCUIT)

COMPLETE TEST NS-13E BEFORE PROCEEDING

PROCEDURE		TEST INDICATION	ACTION REQUIRED
• 60-way connector disconnected. • Distributor pickup connector disconnected. • Turn the ignition switch off. • Connect one lead of an ohmmeter to the N6 (OR) wire in cavity No. 52 of the 60-way connector and the other lead to the N6 (OR) wire in the distributor harness connector.		• Ohmmeter is showing continuity.	• Perform STEP G.
		• Ohmmeter is not showing continuity.	• Repair the N6 (OR) wire of cavity No. 52 of the 60-way connector for an open circuit to the wiring harness splice.

TEST NS-14	STEP A	CHECKING FOR FAULT CODE 11 - DISTRIBUTOR REFERENCE PICKUP CIRCUIT

COMPLETE TEST NS-12A BEFORE PROCEEDING

PROCEDURE		TEST INDICATION	ACTION REQUIRED
• Turn ignition switch off. • Disconnect distributor pickup connector. • Remove coil wire from distributor and place it (¼ inch) near a good engine ground. • Turn ignition switch to the run position. • Connect a jumper wire between the N7 (GY/BK) and the N5 (BK/LB) wires at the distributor harness connector. • Make and break this connection several times while looking at the coil wire.		• There is spark at the coil wire.	• Perform STEP B.
		• There is no spark at the coil wire.	• Perform STEP D.

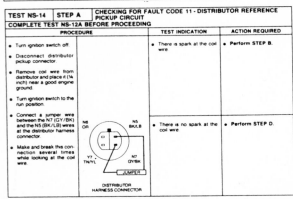

TEST NS-14	STEP B	CHECKING FOR THE 8 VOLT POWER SUPPLY TO THE DISTRIBUTOR PICKUP (N6 CIRCUIT)

COMPLETE TEST NS-14A BEFORE PROCEEDING

PROCEDURE		TEST INDICATION	ACTION REQUIRED
• Ignition switch in the run position. • Distributor pickup coil connector disconnected. • Connect a voltmeter between the N6 (OR) wire of the distributor harness and ground.		• Voltmeter is reading at least 7 volts.	• Perform STEP C.
		• Voltmeter reads 0 volts.	• Repair the N6 (OR) wire of the distributor harness connector for an open circuit to the wiring harness splice.

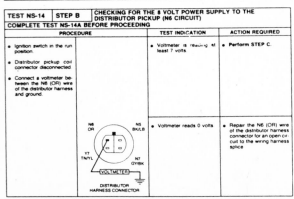

TEST NS-13	STEP G	CHECKING THE IGNITION SWITCH SUPPLY VOLTAGE (J2 CIRCUIT)

COMPLETE TEST NS-13F BEFORE PROCEEDING

PROCEDURE		TEST INDICATION	ACTION REQUIRED
• Ignition switch off. • Disconnect the 14-way connector from the SMEC. • Connect the negative lead of a voltmeter to ground. • Turn the ignition switch on. • Touch the positive lead of a voltmeter to the J2 (DB) wire in cavity No. 4 of the SMEC 14-way connector.		• Voltmeter is reading within one volt of battery voltage	• Perform STEP H.
		• Voltmeter is not reading within one volt of battery voltage	• Repair the J2 (DB) wire in cavity No. 4 of the 14-way connector for an open circuit to the wiring harness splice

TEST NS-13	STEP H	CHECKING POWER MODULE GROUND WIRES FOR AN OPEN CIRCUIT (J9 CIRCUIT)

COMPLETE TEST NS-13G BEFORE PROCEEDING

PROCEDURE		TEST INDICATION	ACTION REQUIRED
• 14-way connector disconnected. • Turn the ignition switch off. • Connect one lead of an ohmmeter to the system ground eyelet. • Connect the other lead of the ohmmeter to cavities 6 and 7 of the 14-way connector		• Ohmmeter is showing continuity at both cavities with less than ½ ohm of resistance	• Defective power board Replace the SMEC. NOTE: Before replacing the SMEC, check the J9 terminals in cavities No. 6 and 7 to make sure they are not spread apart causing a poor connection
		• Ohmmeter is not showing continuity at cavities No 6 and 7.	• Repair the J9 (BLK) wires in cavities No. 6 and 7 of the 14-way connector for an open circuit to the wiring harness splice • Replace the SMEC
		• Ohmmeter is showing continuity with resistance higher than ½ ohm	• Repair J9 ground circuit for high resistance to system ground eyelet

TEST NS-14	STEP C	CHECKING DISTRIBUTOR MECHANICAL OPERATION

COMPLETE TEST NS-14B BEFORE PROCEEDING

PROCEDURE		TEST INDICATION	ACTION REQUIRED
• Turn the ignition switch off • Remove the distributor cap • Crank engine while watching rotor		• The rotor is turning as the engine is cranked	• Replace the distributor pickup plate NOTE: Before replacing the pickup plate, check the terminals in the distributor harness connector to make sure they are not damaged causing a poor connection
		• The rotor is not turning as the engine is cranked	• Determine cause and repair engine or distributor as required

TEST NS-14	STEP D	CHECKING THE DISTRIBUTOR PICKUP SIGNAL GROUND FOR AN OPEN CIRCUIT AT THE DISTRIBUTOR (N5 CIRCUIT)

COMPLETE TEST NS-14A BEFORE PROCEEDING

PROCEDURE		TEST INDICATION	ACTION REQUIRED
• Ignition switch in the run position • Distributor pickup connector disconnected • Coil wire removed from distributor and placed (¼ inch) near a good engine ground • Connect a jumper wire between the N7 (GY) wire of the distributor harness connector and a good engine ground		• There is spark at the coil wire	• Repair the N5 (BK/LB) wire of the distributor harness connector for an open circuit to the wiring harness splice
		• There is no spark at the coil wire	• Perform STEP E

1988 3.0L DIAGNOSTIC CHART—NO START TEST

TEST NS-14	STEP E	CHECKING REFERENCE PICKUP SIGNAL WIRE FOR AN OPEN CIRCUIT TO THE SMEC (N7 CIRCUIT)
COMPLETE TEST NS-14D BEFORE PROCEEDING		

PROCEDURE	TEST INDICATION	ACTION REQUIRED
• Distributor pickup connector disconnected • Disconnect the 60-way connector from the SMEC • Connect an ohmmeter between the N7 (GY/BK) wire in cavity No 47 of the 60-way connector and the N7 (GY/BK) wire at the distributor harness connector	• Ohmmeter is showing continuity	• Defective logic board Replace the SMEC CAUTION: Before replacing the SMEC, check the N7 terminal in cavity No 47 to make sure it is not damaged causing a poor connection
	• Ohmmeter is not showing continuity	NOTE: Repair the N7 (G7/BK) wire in cavity No 47 of the 60-way connector for an open circuit to the distributor.

TEST NS-15	STEP A	CHECKING FOR FAULT CODE 42 - AUTO SHUTDOWN RELAY
COMPLETE TEST NS-12A BEFORE PROCEEDING		

PROCEDURE	TEST INDICATION	ACTION REQUIRED
• DRB II connected to the engine harness connector • Connect a voltmeter to the K19 (DB/YL) wire of the auto shutdown relay 4-way connector and ground • Put the sytem in ATM Test 06.	• Voltmeter pulsates between 0 and 12 volts while system is in ATM Test 06.	• Perform STEP B.
	• The voltmeter reading is within 1 volt of battery voltage and the system cannot be put into ATM Test 06.	• Perform STEP F.
	• The voltmeter reading is 0-1 volt steady and the system cannot be put into ATM Test 06	• Perform STEP D.

TEST NS-15	STEP D	CHECKING FOR FJ2 SUPPLY VOLTAGE TO THE AUTO SHUTDOWN RELAY PULL IN COIL (K14 CIRCUIT)
COMPLETE TEST NS-15A BEFORE PROCEEDING		

PROCEDURE	TEST INDICATION	ACTION REQUIRED
• Negative lead of a voltmeter connector to ground • Turn the ignition switch off • Connect a voltmeter to the K14 (DB/WT) wire of the auto shutdown relay 4-way connector and ground • Turn the ignition switch on	• The voltmeter reading is within one volt of battery voltage	• Replace the auto shutdown relay
	• The voltmeter is reading 0 volts	• Perform STEP E.

TEST NS-15	STEP E	CHECKING THE FJ2 VOLTAGE SUPPLY WIRE FOR AN OPEN CIRCUIT (K14 CIRCUIT)
COMPLETE TEST NS-15D BEFORE PROCEEDING		

PROCEDURE	TEST INDICATION	ACTION REQUIRED
• Turn the ignition switch off • Disconnect the 14-way connector from the SMEC • Connect an ohmmeter between cavity No. 3 of the 14-way connector and the K14 (DB/WT) wire of the auto shutdown relay 4-way connector	• Ohmmeter does not show continuity	• Repair the K14 (DB/WT) wire in cavity No. 3 of the 14-way connector for an open circuit to the auto shutdown relay
	• Ohmmeter show continuity	• Defective power board CAUTION: Before replacing the SMEC, check the K14 terminal in cavity No 3 to make sure it is not spread apart causing a poor connection

TEST NS-15	STEP B	CHECKING FOR BATTERY SUPPLY VOLTAGE TO THE AUTO SHUTDOWN RELAY CONTACT POINTS (INPUT SIDE) (J1 CIRCUIT)
COMPLETE TEST NS-15A BEFORE PROCEEDING		

PROCEDURE	TEST INDICATION	ACTION REQUIRED
• Connect a voltmeter to the J1 (RD) wire of the auto shutdown relay 4-way connector and ground.	• The voltmeter reading is within 1 volt of battery voltage.	• Perform STEP C.
	• The voltmeter reading is 0 volts	• Repair the J1 (RD) wire of the auto shutdown relay connector for an open circuit to the wiring harness splice.

TEST NS-15	STEP C	CHECKING THE AUTO SHUTDOWN RELAY CONTACTS (OUTPUT SIDE) (Z1 CIRCUIT)
COMPLETE TEST NS-15B BEFORE PROCEEDING		

PROCEDURE	TEST INDICATION	ACTION REQUIRED
• Turn the ignition switch off. • Connect one lead of a jumper wire to the Z1 (DG/BK) wire of the auto shutdown relay 4-way connector • Touch the other end of the jumper wire to the red wire of the auto shutdown relay 4-way connector.	• The fuel pump turns on.	• Replace the auto shutdown relay.
	• The fuel pump does not turn on.	• Repair the Z1 (DG/BK) wire of the auto shutdown relay connector for an open circuit to the wiring harness splice.

TEST NS-15	STEP F	CHECKING THE AUTO SHUTDOWN RELAY CONTROL WIRE FOR AN OPEN CIRCUIT (K19 CIRCUIT)
COMPLETE TEST NS-15A BEFORE PROCEEDING		

PROCEDURE	TEST INDICATION	ACTION REQUIRED
• Turn the ignition switch off • Disconnect the 60-way connector from the SMEC • Connect a voltmeter to the K19 (DB/YL) wire in cavity No. 58 of the 60-way connector and ground • Turn the ignition switch on	• Voltmeter is reading within 1 volt of battery voltage	• Defective logic board Replace the SMEC CAUTION: Before replacing the SMEC, check the K19 terminal in cavity No 58 of the 60-way connector to make sure it is not damaged causing a poor connection
	• Voltmeter is reading 0 volts	• Repair the K19 (DB/YL) wire in cavity No 58 of the 60-way connector for an open circuit to the auto shutdown relay

TEST NS-16	STEP A	CHECKING FOR FAULT CODE 44 - FUSED J2 CIRCUIT
COMPLETE TEST NS-12A BEFORE PROCEEDING		

PROCEDURE	TEST INDICATION	ACTION REQUIRED
• Turn the ignition switch off • Disconnect the 14-way connector from the SMEC • Connect an ohmmeter between the K14 (DB/WT) wire of the auto shutdown relay 4-way connector and cavity No 3 of the 14-way connector	• Ohmmeter show continuity	• Defective power board, replace the SMEC. NOTE: Before replacing the SMEC, check the K14 terminal in cavity No 3 of the 14-way connector to make sure it is not spread apart causing a poor connection.
	• Ohmmeter does not show continuity	• Repair the K14 (DB/WT) wire of cavity No 3 for an open circuit to the wiring harness splice

1988 3.0L DIAGNOSTIC CHART—DRIVEABILITY TEST

TEST DR-1	STEP A	CHECKING SYSTEM FOR FAULT CODES

PROCEDURE	TEST INDICATION	CIRCUIT	ACTION REQUIRED
● Connect DRB II		No fault codes	Perform STEP B
● Put the system in Diagnostic Test Mode.	88-12-55 88-12-13-55 88-12-14-55 88-12-13-14-55	MAP sensor	Perform TEST DR-2
	88-12-15-55	Speed sensor	Perform TEST DR-3
● Turn ignition switch on-off-on-off-on within 5 seconds	88-11-12-16-55	Battery voltage sense/SMEC memory circuit	Check charging system TEST CH-3A
	88-12-17-55	Engine running too cool	Check engine cooling system for a bad thermostat
● RECORD ALL CODES	88-12-21-55	Oxygen sensor	Perform TEST DR-4
NOTE: If fault codes 15-17-21-33-51 or 52 appear at this time proceed to test indication.	88-12-22-55 88-12-17-22-55	Engine coolant sensor	Perform TEST DR-5
	88-12-23-55	Charge temperature sensor	Perform TEST DR-6
	88-12-24-55	Throttle position sensor	Perform TEST DR-7
● Erase fault codes	88-12-25-55	Idle motor	Perform TEST DR-8
	88-12-26-55	Injector driver	Perform No Start TEST NS-9
● Start engine	88-12-27-55	Injector interface	Perform No Start TEST NS-9
CAUTION: Do not depress accelerator to start engine	88-12-31-55	Canister purge solenoid	Perform TEST DR-9
	88-12-32-55 California Only	EGR system	Perform TEST DR-10
● Raise engine speed to 2,000 rpm for 10 seconds and then return to idle	88-12-33-55	A/C cutout relay	Perform TEST DR-11
		NOTE: Fault code 33 will be displayed if the vehicle is not equipped with A/C.	
● Cycle transmission gear selector	88-12-35-55	Radiator fan relay	Perform TEST DR-12
● If so equipped, press A/C button on and off	88-12-37-55	Transmission lock-up solenoid	Perform TEST DR-13
● Turn engine off	88-12-42-55	Auto shutdown relay	Repair the Z1 (DG/BK) wire of cavity No. 10 of the SMEC 60-way connector for an open circuit to the wiring harness splice
● Put the system in Diagnostic Test Mode.	88-12-44-55	Fused J2 (K14)	Perform TEST DR-14
● RECORD ALL CODES	88-12-51-55	Oxygen feedback system locked lean	Perform TEST DR-18
If the same code appears before and after the engine is started, the problem still exists. Proceed to test indications.	88-12-52-55	Oxygen feedback system locked rich	
	88-12-53-55		Replace the SMEC
	88-12-54-55	Distributor sync pickup	Perform TEST DR-15
If a code does not reappear after the engine is started, the problem no longer exists. Perform STEP N.			

TEST DR-1	STEP B	CHECKING THE OUTPUT CIRCUITS OF THE SMEC CONTROLLED COMPONENTS
COMPLETE TEST DR-1A BEFORE PROCEEDING		

PROCEDURE	TEST INDICATION	CIRCUIT	ACTION REQUIRED
REMINDERS		**Test Code 04**	● Radiator fan is turning on and off press and hold the ATM key as follows
● DRB II connected to the engine harness connector		● The radiator fan should be turning on and off every two seconds	**Without A/C** until Test Code 07 appears
● Put the system into **ATM Test 04.**			**With A/C** until Test Code 05 appears
			● If fan does not turn on and off, is the relay clicking? If it is, repair the circuit to the radiator fan motor as required
			● If the relay does not click, replace it
		Test Code 05	● A/C relay clicking, press and hold the ATM button until Test Code 07 appears
		● Press the A/C button on	
		● You should hear the A/C cutout relay clicking every two seconds	● If the A/C relay is not clicking replace it
		CAUTION: A/C compressor clutch will also cycle every two seconds and A/C condenser fan will run continuously	
		Test Code 07	● Canister purge solenoid clicking
		● You should hear the canister purge solenoid clicking	● Perform STEP C.
			● If the canister purge solenoid is not clicking replace it

TEST DR-1	STEP C	CHECKING SWITCH INPUTS TO THE SMEC
COMPLETE TEST DR-1B BEFORE PROCEEDING		

PROCEDURE		TEST INDICATION	ACTION REQUIRED
● DRB II connected.		● Display on the DRB II changes as each switch is activated	● Perform STEP H.
● Put the system into the **Switch Test Mode.**		NOTE: It is not important what display changes to. Just make sure it changes	
● Check switch inputs as follows:			
a) press down on brake pedal			
b) move gear selector from park to reverse to neutral to drive		● Display on the DRB II does not change when one or more of the switches are activated	● Perform STEPS as follows: Brake Switch w/o speed control **STEP D** with speed control **STEP E** Park/Neutral Switch **STEP F** A/C Button **STEP G**
c) with heater blower motor turned on, press the A/C button.			

TEST DR-1	STEP E	CHECKING BRAKE SWITCH INPUT CIRCUIT TO THE SMEC - WITH SPEED CONTROL (D40 CIRCUIT)
COMPLETE TEST DR-1C BEFORE PROCEEDING		

PROCEDURE		TEST INDICATION	ACTION REQUIRED
● Turn the ignition switch off	VIEW FROM TERMINAL END	● Ohmmeter shows open when brake pedal is pressed down and continuity when released	● Defective logic board Replace the SMEC
● Disconnect the 60-way connector from the SMEC.			**CAUTION:** Before replacing the SMEC, check the D40 terminal in cavity No. 29 of the 60-way connector to make sure it is not damaged causing a poor connection
● Connect an ohmmeter between the D40 wire (WT/PK) at cavity No 29 of the 60-way connector and ground	N31 VT 29		
● Press down on brake pedal then and release		● Ohmmeter does not read as above	● Check D40 (WT/PK) wire of cavity No 29 for an open circuit to the brake switch
			● Check for a bad brake switch
			● Check for an open circuit to the stop lamp bulbs

TEST DR-1	STEP D	CHECKING BRAKE SWITCH INPUT CIRCUIT TO THE SMEC - WITHOUT SPEED CONTROL (D40 CIRCUIT)
COMPLETE TEST DR-1C BEFORE PROCEEDING		

PROCEDURE		TEST INDICATION	ACTION REQUIRED
● Turning ignition switch off	VIEW FROM TERMINAL END	● Voltmeter is reading within one volt of battery voltage	● Defective logic board Replace the SMEC
● Disconnect the 60-way connector from the SMEC.			**CAUTION:** Before replacing the SMEC, check the D40 terminal in cavity No 29 of the 60-way connector to make sure it is not damaged causing a poor connection
● Connect voltmeter to the D40 (WT/PK) wire in cavity No. 29 of the 60-way connector and ground.	D40 WT/PK		
● Turn ignition switch to the run position.	29	● Voltmeter reads 0	● Check the D40 (WT/PK) wire of cavity No 29 for open circuit to brake switch.
● Press brake pedal down			● Check for a bad brake switch
			● Check voltage supply circuit to the brake switch

TEST DR-1	STEP F	CHECKING PARK/NEUTRAL SWITCH INPUT TO THE SMEC (S4 CIRCUIT)
COMPLETE TEST DR-1C BEFORE PROCEEDING		

PROCEDURE		TEST INDICATION	ACTION REQUIRED
● Turn ignition switch off.	VIEW FROM TERMINAL END	● Ohmmeter shows continuity in all positions of the gear selector	● Check S4 (BR/YL) wire of cavity No 30 for a short circuit to ground
● Disconnect the 60-way connector from the SMEC.			● Check for a bad safety neutral switch
● Connect an ohmmeter between the S4 (BR/YL) wire in cavity No. 30 of the 60-way connector and ground.		● Ohmmeter shows open in all positions in gear selector	● Repair S4 (BR/YL) wire of cavity No. 30 for an open circuit to the safety neutral switch
● **Disconnect the battery quick disconnect.**			● Check for bad safety neutral switch
● If column shift, turn the ignition switch to the run position.	30	● Ohmmeter reads as follows: **Park** - Continuity **Reverse** - No Continuity **Neutral** - Continuity **Drive** - No Continuity	● Defective logic board Replace the SMEC
● Put gear selector in park, reverse, neutral, and drive and observe ohmmeter in each position.		NOTE: Disregard any resistance readings. Just make sure there is continuity	**CAUTION:** Before replacing the SMEC, check the S4 terminal in cavity No 30 of the 60-way connector to make sure it is not damaged causing a poor connection

1988 3.0L DIAGNOSTIC CHART—DRIVEABILITY TEST

TEST DR-1	STEP G	CHECKING A/C PUSH BUTTON SWITCH INPUT TO THE SMEC (C20 CIRCUIT)
COMPLETE TEST DR-1C BEFORE PROCEEDING		

PROCEDURE	TEST INDICATION	ACTION REQUIRED
• Turn ignition switch off • Disconnect the 60-way connector from the SMEC. • Connect an ohmmeter to the C20 (BR) wire in cavity No 45 of the 60-way connector and ground • Press the A/C button, turn blower motor switch on and then turn the blower motor switch off **NOTE:** The A/C system must have an adequate freon charge for this test to work	• Ohmmeter shows continuity when A/C button is pressed and open when the blower motor switch is turned off	• Defective logic board Replace the SMEC **CAUTION:** Before replacing the SMEC, check the C20 terminal in cavity No 45 of the 60-way connector to make sure it is not damaged causing a poor connection
	• Ohmmeter reading is not as described above	• Repair the C20 (BN) wire in cavity No 45 for an open or short circuit to the wiring harness splice

TEST DR-1	STEP I	CHECKING AUTOMATIC IDLE SPEED MOTOR SIGNAL FROM THE SMEC (N1 AND N3 CIRCUITS)
COMPLETE TEST DR-1H BEFORE PROCEEDING		

PROCEDURE	TEST INDICATION	ACTION REQUIRED
• Turn the engine off • DRB II connected • Disconnect the automatic idle speed motor connector • Connect a voltmeter between N1 (GY/RD) wire in cavity No 1 and the N8 (VT/BK) wire in cavity No 4 of the AIS motor connector • Put the system into ATM Test 03.	• Voltmeter is pulsating between 0 and 12 volts every two seconds	• **Perform STEP J.**
	• Voltmeter does not pulsate.	• **Perform STEP K.**

DIGITAL VOLTMETER SET TO A C POSITION

1 2 3 4

TEST DR-1	STEP H	CHECKING AUTOMATIC IDLE SPEED MOTOR OPERATION
COMPLETE TEST DR-1C BEFORE PROCEEDING		

PROCEDURE	TEST INDICATION	ACTION REQUIRED
• Connect DRB II **NOTE:** Make sure **Read** is displayed • Connect a tachometer to the engine • Start the engine • Disconnect the coolant sensor • Press the **Read/Hold** key on the DRB II so **Hold** is displayed • Press the **Read/Hold** key on the DRB II so **Read** is displayed	• Engine speed increases to approximately 1,500 rpm when **Hold** is displayed on the DRB II • Engine returns to idle when **Read** is displayed on the DRB II	• **Perform STEP M.**
	• Engine speed does not increase when hold key is pressed or engine speed does not return to idle when read switch is keyed	• **Perform STEP I.**

TEST DR-1	STEP J	CHECKING AUTOMATIC IDLE SPEED MOTOR SIGNAL FROM THE SMEC (N2 AND N4 CIRCUITS)
COMPLETE TEST DR-1I BEFORE PROCEEDING		

PROCEDURE	TEST INDICATION	ACTION REQUIRED
• DRB II connected • Automatic idle speed motor disconnected • System in ATM Test Mode 03 • Connect voltmeter between the N2 (BR/WT) wire in cavity No 2 and the N4 (YL/BK) wire in cavity No 3 of the AIS motor connector	• Voltmeter is pulsating between 0 and 12 volts every two seconds	• Replace the automatic idle speed motor. **CAUTION:** Before replacing the idle motor, check the terminals of the connector to make sure they are not damaged causing a poor connection.
	• Voltmeter does not pulsate.	• **Perform STEP L.**

DIGITAL VOLTMETER SET TO A C POSITION

1 2 3 4

TEST DR-1	STEP K	CHECKING AUTOMATIC IDLE SPEED MOTOR CIRCUIT AT THE SMEC 60-WAY CONNECTOR (N1 AND N3 CIRCUITS)
COMPLETE TEST DR-1I BEFORE PROCEEDING		

PROCEDURE	TEST INDICATION	ACTION REQUIRED
• Turn the ignition switch off • Connect the AIS motor connector • Disconnect the 60-way connector from the SMEC. • Connect an ohmmeter between the N1 (GY/RD) wire in cavity No 19 and the N3 (VT/BK) wire in cavity No 20 of the 60-way connector.	• Ohmmeter is showing continuity	• Defective logic board Replace the SMEC. **CAUTION:** Before replacing the SMEC, check the N1 and N3 terminals in cavity No 19 of the 60-way connector to make sure they are not damaged causing a poor connection.
	• Ohmmeter is not showing continuity.	• Repair N1 (GY/RD) or N3 (VT/BK) wires for an open circuit to the automatic idle speed motor connector.

VIEW FROM TERMINAL END

20
19

VOLTMETER

TEST DR-1	STEP M	CHECKING THE SMEC GROUND CIRCUITS
COMPLETE TEST DR-1H BEFORE PROCEEDING		

PROCEDURE	TEST INDICATION	ACTION REQUIRED
• Turn the ignition switch off. • Disconnect both SMEC connectors. • Connect one lead of a digital ohmmeter to ground. • Connect the other lead of ohmmeter as follows. 14-way connector cavities No 2 (K5 BK/WT), 6 (J9 BK), and 7 (J9 BK) 60-way connector cavities No 5 (K5 BK/WT), 15 (K9 LB/RD) and 16 (K9 LB/RD)	• Ohmmeter is showing continuity with less than ½ ohm of resistance at all cavities of the connectors.	• Grounds are OK, Perform TESTS as follows: If a cold problem **TEST DR-16.** If a warm problem **TEST DR-18.**
	• Ohmmeter is showing open at one or more cavities of the connectors.	• Defective ground wire. Repair the wire for an open circuit to the wiring harness connector. • Replace the SMEC
	• Ohmmeter is showing more than ½ ohm of resistance at one or more cavities of the connectors.	• Ground circuit has excessive resistance. Repair circuit for high resistance to system ground eyelet.

VIEW FROM TERMINAL END

16
15
5

OHMMETER

14-WAY CONNECTOR
GROUND EYELET ON CYLINDER HEAD

TEST DR-1	STEP L	CHECKING AUTOMATIC IDLE SPEED MOTOR CIRCUIT AT THE SMEC 60-WAY CONNECTOR (N2 AND N4 CIRCUITS)
COMPLETE TEST DR-1J BEFORE PROCEEDING		

PROCEDURE	TEST INDICATION	ACTION REQUIRED
• Turn the ignition switch off. • Connect the AIS motor connector. • Disconnect the 60-way connector from the SMEC. • Connect an ohmmeter between the N2 (BR/WT) wire in cavity No 17 and the N4 (YL/BK) wire in cavity No 18 of the 60-way connector.	• Ohmmeter is showing continuity	• Defective logic board Replace the SMEC. **CAUTION:** Before replacing the SMEC, check the N2 and N4 terminals in cavities No 17 and 18 of the 60-way connector to make sure they are not damaged causing a poor connection
	• Ohmmeter is not showing continuity.	• Repair the N2 (BR/WT) or N4 (YL/BK) wires for an open circuit to the automatic idle speed motor

5 FUEL SYSTEM

1988 3.0L DIAGNOSTIC CHART—DRIVEABILITY TEST

TEST 1	STEP N	CHECKING FOR INTERMITTENT FAILURES CAUSED BY WIRING AND/OR CONNECTORS

The majority of intermittent failures are caused by wiring and connections. One way to find them is to try and duplicate the problem. Since the SMEC can remember where they are, the ATM and Sensor Test Modes can be used in an attempt to locate them.

- If the following fault code does not reappear, use the **ATM Test** as indicated.

Fault Code	ATM Test
25	03
26	02
27	02
31	07
35	04
37	10
42	06
43	01

Once in the correct test mode, wiggle all the connectors and wires in the circuit. When the bad connection or wire is located, the ATM test will be interrupted.

- If the following fault codes do not reappear, use the **Sensor Test** as indicated.

Fault Code	Sensor Test
14**	08
22	04
23	03
24	05

** When checking the M.A.P. sensor circuit, (fault code 14) apply 10 inches of vacuum to the M.A.P. sensor before testing.

Once in the correct test mode, wiggle all the connectors and wires in the circuit. When the bad connection or wire is located, the display on the DRB II will change.

TEST DR-2	STEP A	CHECKING FOR FAULT CODES 13 AND/OR 14— M.A.P. SENSOR CIRCUIT

COMPLETE TEST DR-1A BEFORE PROCEEDING

PROCEDURE	TEST INDICATION	ACTION REQUIRED
• Turn ignition switch off • Tee a vacuum gauge into the vacuum line at the M.A.P. sensor • Start the engine and look at the vacuum gauge with the engine idling • Look at the vacuum gauge while snapping the throttle open and closed	• Vacuum gauge is reading manifold vacuum with the engine idling • Vacuum gauge reading immediately drops to 0 when the throttle is snapped open	• Perform STEP B.
	• Vacuum gauge reads 0 at idle	• Repair hole in vacuum line to throttle body
	• Vacuum gauge reading slowly drops to 0 when the throttle is snapped open	• Repair restriction in vacuum supply line to M.A.P. sensor

VACUUM GAUGE

TEST DR-2	STEP B	CHECKING THE M.A.P. SENSOR CIRCUIT IN THE SMEC

COMPLETE TEST DR-2A BEFORE PROCEEDING

PROCEDURE	TEST INDICATION	ACTION REQUIRED
• DRB II connected • Disconnect the M.A.P. sensor connector • Put the system in **Sensor Test 08.**	• Display on the DRB II is reading at least 4 volts	• Perform STEP C.
	• Display on the DRB II is reading 0 volts	• Replace the SMEC **NOTE:** Before replacing the SMEC, make sure the K4 (DG/RD) wire of cavity No. 1 of the 60-way connector is not shorted to ground

DISCONNECT

TEST DR-2	STEP C	CHECKING THE M.A.P. SENSOR SIGNAL TO THE SMEC (K4 CIRCUIT)

COMPLETE TEST DR-2B BEFORE PROCEEDING

PROCEDURE	TEST INDICATION	ACTION REQUIRED
• DRB II connected • System in Sensor Test 08 • M.A.P. sensor connector disconnected • Connect a jumper wire between the K4 (DG/RD) wire and the N5 (BK/LB) wire of the M.A.P. sensor harness connector	• Display on the DRB II is reading 0 volts	• Perform STEP E.
	• Display on the DRB II is not reading 0 volts	• Perform STEP D.

JUMPER
DISCONNECT
N5 BK/LB K8 VT/WT
K4 DG/RD
MAP SENSOR HARNESS CONNECTOR

TEST DR-2	STEP E	CHECKING THE 5 VOLT SUPPLY TO THE M.A.P. SENSOR (K8 CIRCUIT)

COMPLETE TEST DR-2C BEFORE PROCEEDING

PROCEDURE	TEST INDICATION	ACTION REQUIRED
• Ignition switch in the run position • M.A.P. sensor connector disconnected • Connect a digital voltmeter between the K8 (VT/WT) wire of the M.A.P. sensor harness connector and ground	• Voltmeter is reading at least 4 volts	• Replace the M.A.P. sensor **NOTE:** Before replacing the M.A.P. sensor, check the terminals in the harness connector to make sure they are not defective causing a poor connection.
	• Voltmeter is reading 0 volts	• Repair the K8 (VT/WT) wire for an open circuit to the wiring harness splice

DIGITAL VOLTMETER
N5 BK/LB   K8 VT/WT
K4 DG/RD
MAP SENSOR HARNESS CONNECTOR

TEST DR-2	STEP D	CHECKING THE M.A.P. SENSOR WIRE TO THE SMEC FOR AN OPEN CIRCUIT (K4 CIRCUIT)

COMPLETE TEST DR-2C BEFORE PROCEEDING

PROCEDURE	TEST INDICATION	ACTION REQUIRED
• DRB II connected • System in Sensor Test 08 • M.A.P. sensor disconnected • Connect one end of a jumper wire to the negative terminal of the battery • Connect the other end of the jumper wire to the K4 (DG/RD) wire terminal of the M.A.P. sensor harness connector	• Display on the DRB II is reading 0 volts	• Repair the N5 (BK/LB) wire of the M.A.P. sensor connector for an open circuit to the wiring harness splice
	• Display on the DRB II is reading 5 volts	• Repair the K4 (DG/RD) wire of the M.A.P. sensor connector for an open circuit to the SMEC

JUMPER
N5 BK/LB   K8 VT/WT
K4 DG/RD
MAP SENSOR HARNESS CONNECTOR

TEST DR-3	STEP A	CHECKING FOR FAULT CODE 15 — SPEED SENSOR

COMPLETE TEST DR-1A OR SC-1B BEFORE PROCEEDING

PROCEDURE	TEST INDICATION	ACTION REQUIRED
• DRB II connected • Start the engine • Disconnect the speed sensor connector • Put the system in the **Engine Running Test 71.** • Connect a jumper wire between the T9 (BK) and the G7 (WT/OR) terminals of the speed sensor harness connector • Make and break this connection	• As you make and break this connection the display on the DRB II changes	• Replace the speed sensor
	• As you make and break this connection the display on the DRB II does not change	• Perform STEP B.

JUMPER
N5 BK/LB   G7 WT/OR
SPEED SENSOR CONNECTOR

5–26

1988 3.0L DIAGNOSTIC CHART—DRIVEABILITY TEST

TEST DR-3	STEP B	CHECKING THE SPEED SENSOR SIGNAL WIRE TO THE SMEC FOR AN OPEN CIRCUIT (G7 CIRCUIT)

COMPLETE TEST DR-3A BEFORE PROCEEDING

PROCEDURE	TEST INDICATION	ACTION REQUIRED
• Turn the engine off • Speed sensor connector disconnected • Disconnect the 60-way connector from the SMEC • Connect an ohmmeter between the G7 (WT/OR) wire at cavity No 48 of the 60-way connector and the G7 (WT/OR) wire terminal of the speed sensor harness connector	• Ohmmeter shows continuity	• **Perform STEP C.**
	• Ohmmeter is not showing continuity	• Repair the G7 (WT/OR) wire in cavity No 48 of the 60-way connector for an open circuit to the speed sensor connector

TEST DR-4	STEP A	CHECKING FOR FAULT CODE 21 — OXYGEN SENSOR

COMPLETE TEST DR-1A BEFORE PROCEEDING

PROCEDURE	TEST INDICATION	ACTION REQUIRED
• DRB II connected. • Turn the ignition switch off. • Disconnect the oxygen sensor connector. • Put the system into **Sensor Test 02**.	• Display on the DRB II is reading at least .4 volt, (4 tenths).	• **Perform STEP B.**
	• Display on the DRB II is reading 0.	• Replace the SMEC. **NOTE:** Before replacing the SMEC, make sure the N11 (BK/DG) wire at cavity No. 23 of the SMEC 60-way connector is not shorted to ground.

HEATED OXYGEN SENSOR 3-WAY CONNECTOR

TEST DR-3	STEP C	CHECKING THE SPEED SENSOR GROUND WIRE TO THE SMEC FOR AN OPEN CIRCUIT (T9 AND N5 CIRCUITS)

COMPLETE TEST DR-3B BEFORE PROCEEDING

PROCEDURE	TEST INDICATION	ACTION REQUIRED
• Engine off • Speed sensor connector disconnected • 60-way connector disconnected • Connect an ohmmeter between the N5 (BK/LB) wire at cavity No 4 of the 60-way connector and the T9 (BK) wire terminal of the speed sensor harness connector	• Ohmmeter shows continuity	• Defective logic board Replace the SMEC. **CAUTION:** Before replacing the SMEC, check the G7 terminal in cavity No 48 and the N5 terminal in cavity No 4 of the 60-way connector to make sure they are not damaged causing a poor connection
	• Ohmmeter is not showing continuity	• Repair the N5 (BK/LB) or T9 (BK) wire of the speed sensor harness connector for an open circuit to the wiring harness splice

TEST DR-4	STEP B	CHECKING THE OXYGEN SENSOR WIRE TO THE SMEC FOR AN OPEN CIRCUIT (N11 CIRCUIT)

COMPLETE TEST DR-4A BEFORE PROCEEDING

PROCEDURE	TEST INDICATION	ACTION REQUIRED
• System in Sensor Test 02. • Oxygen sensor connector disconnected. • Connect one end of a jumper wire to the N11 (BK/DG) wire of the oxygen sensor harness connector. • Connect the other end of the jumper wire to the battery positive post.	• Display on the DRB II is reading at least 5 volts.	• Replace the oxygen sensor.
	• Display on the DRB II is reading .4 volts, (4 tenths).	• Repair the N11 (BK/DG) wire of the oxygen sensor connector for an open circuit to the SMEC.

HEATED OXYGEN SENSOR HARNESS CONNECTOR

JUMPER

BATTERY

TEST DR-5	STEP A	CHECKING FOR FAULT CODE 22 — COOLANT SENSOR

COMPLETE TEST DR-1A BEFORE PROCEEDING

PROCEDURE	TEST INDICATION	ACTION REQUIRED
• DRB II connected • Turn the ignition switch off • Disconnect the coolant sensor connector • Put the system in **Sensor Test 04**.	• Display on the DRB II is reading 00°.	• **Perform STEP B.**
	• Display on the DRB II is reading 260°.	• Defective logic board Replace the SMEC. **NOTE:** Before replacing the SMEC, make sure the K10 (TN/WT) wire at cavity No 3 of the SMEC 60-way connector is not shorted to ground.

COOLANT TEMPERATURE SENSOR

TEST DR-5	STEP C	CHECKING THE COOLANT SENSOR WIRES TO THE SMEC FOR AN OPEN CIRCUIT (K10 AND N5 CIRCUITS)

COMPLETE TEST DR-5B BEFORE PROCEEDING

PROCEDURE	TEST INDICATION	ACTION REQUIRED
• DRB II connected • System in Sensor Test 04 • Coolant sensor disconnected • Connect one end of a jumper wire to ground. • Connect the other end of the jumper wire to the K10 (TN/WT) wire terminal of the coolant sensor harness connector.	• Display on the DRB II is reading 260°	• Repair the N5 (BK/LB) wire of the coolant sensor harness connector for an open circuit to the wiring harness splice
	• Display on the DRB II is reading 00°	• Repair the K10 (TN/WT) wire of the coolant sensor harness connector for an open circuit to the SMEC

JUMPER

K10 TN/WT N5 BK/LB

COOLANT SENSOR CONNECTOR

TEST DR-5	STEP B	CHECKING THE COOLANT SENSOR WIRE TO THE SMEC (K10 CIRCUIT)

COMPLETE TEST DR-5A BEFORE PROCEEDING

PROCEDURE	TEST INDICATION	ACTION REQUIRED
• DRB II connected • System in Sensor Test 04 • Coolant sensor connector disconnected • Connect a jumper wire between the K10 (TN/WT) and the N5 (BK/LB) terminals of the coolant sensor connector	• Display on the DRB II is reading 260°	• Replace the coolant sensor
	• Display on the DRB II is reading 00°	• **Perform STEP C.**

JUMPER

K10 TN/WT N5 BK/LB

COOLANT SENSOR CONNECTOR

TEST DR-6	STEP A	CHECKING FOR FAULT CODE 23 – CHARGE TEMPERATURE SENSOR

COMPLETE TEST DR-1A BEFORE PROCEEDING

PROCEDURE	TEST INDICATION	ACTION REQUIRED
• DRB II connected • Disconnect the charge temperature sensor connector • Put the system in **Sensor Test 03**.	• Display on the DRB II is reading 5 volts	• **Perform STEP B.**
	• Display on the DRB II is reading 0 volts or 0 volts and then increases	• Replace the SMEC. **CAUTION:** Before replacing the SMEC, make sure the K13 wire of the 60-way connector is not shorted to ground

CHARGE TEMPERATURE SENSOR

5 FUEL SYSTEM

1988 3.0L DIAGNOSTIC CHART—DRIVEABILITY TEST

TEST DR-6	STEP B	CHECKING THE CHARGE TEMPERATURE SENSOR SIGNAL TO THE SMEC (K13 CIRCUIT)
COMPLETE TEST DR-6A BEFORE PROCEEDING		

PROCEDURE	TEST INDICATION	ACTION REQUIRED
• DRB II connected. • System in Sensor Test 03. • Charge temperature sensor connector disconnected. • Connect a jumper wire between the K13 (BK/RD) and N5 (BK/LB) terminals of the charge temperature sensor connector.	• Display on the DRB II is reading 0 volts	• Replace the charge temperature sensor
	• Display on the DRB II is reading 5 volts	• Perform STEP C.

TEST DR-7	STEP A	CHECKING FOR FAULT CODE 24 – THROTTLE POSITION SENSOR
COMPLETE TEST DR-1A BEFORE PROCEEDING		

PROCEDURE	TEST INDICATION	ACTION REQUIRED
• DRB II connected. • Disconnect the throttle position sensor. • Put the system in Sensor Test 05.	• Display on the DRB II is reading between 4 and 5 volts	• Perform STEP B.
	• Display on the DRB II is reading 0 volts	• Defective logic board Replace the SMEC NOTE: Before replacing the SMEC, make sure the K7 (OR/DB) wire at cavity No. 22 of the SMEC 60-way connector is not shorted to ground

TEST DR-6	STEP C	CHECKING THE CHARGE TEMPERATURE SENSOR WIRES TO THE SMEC FOR AN OPEN CIRCUIT (K13 AND N5 CIRCUITS)
COMPLETE TEST DR-6B BEFORE PROCEEDING		

PROCEDURE	TEST INDICATION	ACTION REQUIRED
• DRB II connected. • System in Sensor Test 03. • Charge temperature sensor connector disconnected. • Connect one end of a jumper wire to ground. • Connect the other end of the jumper wire to the K13 (BK/RD) wire terminal of the throttle body temperature sensor connector.	• Display on the DRB II is reading 0 volts	• Repair the N5 (BK/LB) wire of the charge temperature sensor connector for an open circuit to the wiring harness splice
	• Display on the DRB II is reading 5 volts	• Repair the wire of the charge temperature sensor connector for an open circuit to the SMEC.

TEST DR-7	STEP B	CHECKING THE THROTTLE POSITION SENSOR SIGNAL WIRE (K7 CIRCUIT) TO THE SMEC
COMPLETE TEST DR-7A BEFORE PROCEEDING		

PROCEDURE	TEST INDICATION	ACTION REQUIRED
• DRB II connected. • System in Sensor Test 05. • Throttle position sensor disconnected. • Connect a jumper wire between the K7 (OR/DB) wire and the N5 (BK/LB) wire of the throttle position sensor connector.	• Display on the DRB II is reading 0 volts	• Perform STEP D.
	• Display on the DRB II is reading 5 volts	• Perform STEP C.

TEST DR-7	STEP C	CHECKING THE THROTTLE POSITION SENSOR WIRES TO THE SMEC FOR AN OPEN CIRCUIT (K7 AND N5 CIRCUITS)
COMPLETE TEST DR-7B BEFORE PROCEEDING		

PROCEDURE	TEST INDICATION	ACTION REQUIRED
• DRB II connected. • System in Sensor Test 05. • Throttle position sensor connector disconnected. • Connect one end of a jumper wire to ground. • Connect the other end of the jumper wire to the K7 (OR/DB) wire terminal of the throttle position sensor harness connector.	• Display on the DRB II is reading 0 volts	• Repair the N5 (BK/LB) wire of the throttle position sensor connector for an open circuit to the wiring harness splice
	• Display on the DRB II is reading 5 volts	• Repair the K7 (OR/DB) wire of the throttle position sensor connector for an open circuit to the SMEC.

TEST DR-8	STEP A	CHECKING FOR FAULT CODE 25 – AUTOMATIC IDLE SPEED MOTOR FOR A SHORT (N2 AND N4 CIRCUITS)
COMPLETE TEST DR-1A BEFORE PROCEEDING		

PROCEDURE	TEST INDICATION	ACTION REQUIRED
• Turn the ignition switch off. • Disconnect the 60-way connector from the SMEC. • Connect an ohmmeter between the N2 (BN/WT) wire in cavity No. 17 and the N4 (YL/BK) wire in cavity No. 18 of the 60-way connector.	• Ohmmeter is showing some resistance NOTE: The amount of resistance is not important. Just make sure there is some	• Perform STEP B.
	• Ohmmeter is showing 0 resistance	• Perform STEP C.

TEST DR-7	STEP D	CHECKING THE 5 VOLT SUPPLY TO THE THROTTLE POSITION SENSOR (K8 CIRCUIT)
COMPLETE TEST DR-7B BEFORE PROCEEDING		

PROCEDURE	TEST INDICATION	ACTION REQUIRED
• Ignition switch in the run position. • Throttle position sensor connector disconnected. • Connect a digital voltmeter between the K8 (VT/WT) wire of the throttle position sensor harness connector and ground.	• Voltmeter is reading at least 4 volts.	• Replace the throttle position sensor.
	• Voltmeter reads 0.	• Repair the K8 (VT/WT) wire for an open circuit to the wiring harness splice.

TEST DR-8	STEP B	CHECKING AUTOMATIC IDLE SPEED MOTOR CIRCUIT FOR A SHORT (N1 AND N3 CIRCUITS)
COMPLETE TEST DR-8A BEFORE PROCEEDING		

PROCEDURE	TEST INDICATION	ACTION REQUIRED
• Ignition switch off. • 60-way connector disconnected. • Connect an ohmmeter between the N1 (GY/RD) wire in cavity No. 19 and the N3 (VT/BK) wire in cavity No. 20 of the 60-way controller.	• Ohmmeter is showing some resistance NOTE: The amount of resistance is not important. Just make sure there is some	• Defective logic board Replace the SMEC
	• Ohmmeter is showing 0 resistance	• Perform STEP C.

1988 3.0L DIAGNOSTIC CHART—DRIVEABILITY TEST

TEST DR-8 | STEP C | CHECKING AUTOMATIC IDLE SPEED MOTOR CONTROL WIRES FOR A SHORT
COMPLETE TEST DR-8B BEFORE PROCEEDING

PROCEDURE	TEST INDICATION	ACTION REQUIRED
• Ignition switch off • 60-way connector disconnected • Ohmmeter connected to the 60-way connector as instructed in STEP A and B • Disconnect the AIS motor connector	• Ohmmeter is not showing continuity	• Replace the automatic idle speed motor
VIEW FROM TERMINAL END	• Ohmmeter is showing 0 resistance	• Repair the wires to the idle motor for a short circuit to each other

TEST DR-9 | STEP B | CHECKING PURGE CONTROL WIRE FOR AN OPEN CIRCUIT (K1 CIRCUIT)
COMPLETE TEST NS-10C BEFORE PROCEEDING

PROCEDURE	TEST INDICATION	ACTION REQUIRED
• Turn the ignition switch off. • Disconnect the 60-way connector from the SMEC. • Connect voltmeter between the K1 (PK/BK) wire in cavity No. 54 of the 60-way connector and ground. • Turn the ignition switch to the run position.	• Voltmeter reads battery voltage.	• Replace SMEC. CAUTION: Before replacing the SMEC check the K1 terminal in cavity No. 54 of the 60-way connector to make sure it is not damaged causing a poor connection.
VIEW FROM TERMINAL END	• Voltmeter reads 0 volts.	• Repair the K1 (PK/BK) wire of cavity No. 54 for an open circuit to the canister purge solenoid.

TEST DR-9 | STEP A | CHECKING FOR FAULT CODE 31 - CANISTER PURGE SOLENOID
COMPLETE TEST DR-1A BEFORE PROCEEDING

PROCEDURE	TEST INDICATION	ACTION REQUIRED
• Connect a voltmeter between the K1 (PK/BK) wire of the canister purge solenoid connector and ground	• Voltmeter reads battery voltage.	• Perform STEP B.
	• Voltmeter reads 0 volts.	• Perform STEP C.

TEST DR-9 | STEP C | CHECKING CANISTER PURGE SOLENOID SUPPLY VOLTAGE (J2 CIRCUIT)
COMPLETE TEST DR-9A BEFORE PROCEEDING

PROCEDURE	TEST INDICATION	ACTION REQUIRED
• Ignition switch in the run position. • Connect voltmeter between the J2 (DB) wire of the canister purge solenoid connector and ground.	• Voltmeter reads battery voltage.	• Perform STEP D.
	• Voltmeter reads 0 volts.	• Repair the J2 (DB) wire for an open circuit to the harness splice.

TEST DR-9 | STEP D | CHECKING CANISTER PURGE SOLENOID CIRCUIT FOR A SHORT IN THE SMEC (K1 CIRCUIT)
COMPLETE TEST DR-9C BEFORE PROCEEDING

PROCEDURE	TEST INDICATION	ACTION REQUIRED
• Turn the ignition switch off. • Connect a voltmeter between the K1 (PK/BK) wire at the canister purge solenoid connector and ground. • Disconnect the 60-way connector from the SMEC. • Turn the ignition switch to the run position.	• Voltmeter reads battery voltage.	• Defective logic board, replace the SMEC. NOTE: Before replacing the SMEC, make sure the K1 (PK/BK) wire is not shorted to ground.
	• Voltmeter reads 0.	• Replace the canister purge solenoid.

TEST DR-10 | STEP B | CHECKING THE EGR SOLENOID CONTROL WIRE FOR AN OPEN CIRCUIT (S6 CIRCUIT)
COMPLETE TEST DR-10A BEFORE PROCEEDING

PROCEDURE	TEST INDICATION	ACTION REQUIRED
• Turn ignition switch off. • Disconnect 60-way connector from the SMEC. • Connect voltmeter between the S6 (GY/YL) wire in cavity No. 40 of the 60-way connector and ground. • Turn the ignition switch to the run position.	• Voltmeter reads battery voltage.	• Replace the SMEC. CAUTION: Before replacing the SMEC, check the S6 terminal in cavity No. 40 of the 60-way connector to make sure it is not damaged causing a poor connection.
VIEW FROM TERMINAL END	• Voltmeter reads 0 volts.	• Repair the S6 (GY/YL) wire of cavity No. 40 for an open circuit to the solenoid connector.

TEST DR-10 | STEP A | CHECKING FOR FAULT CODE 32 - EGR SYSTEM (CALIFORNIA ONLY)
COMPLETE TEST DR-1A BEFORE PROCEEDING

PROCEDURE	TEST INDICATION	ACTION REQUIRED
• DRB II connected. • Analog voltmeter positive lead connected to the S6 (GY/YL) wire of the 4-way EGR/purge solenoid connector. • Voltmeter negative lead connected to ground. • Put system in ATM Test 11.	• Voltmeter reads battery voltage and is not pulsating. Solenoid does not click.	• Perform STEP B.
	• Voltmeter reads 0 volts. Solenoid does not click.	• Perform STEP C.
	• Voltmeter reading pulsates between one and battery voltage. Solenoid does not click.	• Replace EGR solenoid.
	• Voltmeter reading pulsates between one and battery voltage. Solenoid clicks.	• Perform STEP E.

TEST DR-10 | STEP C | CHECKING FOR SUPPLY VOLTAGE TO THE EGR SOLENOID (J2 CIRCUIT)
COMPLETE TEST DR-10A BEFORE PROCEEDING

PROCEDURE	TEST INDICATION	ACTION REQUIRED
• Turn the ignition switch off. • Connect a voltmeter between the J2 (DB) wire of the EGR/purge solenoid 4-way connector and ground. • Turn the ignition switch to the run position.	• Voltmeter reads 0 volts.	• Repair J2 (DB) wire for an open to the wiring harness splice.
	• Voltmeter reads battery voltage.	• Perform STEP D.

1988 3.0L DIAGNOSTIC CHART—DRIVEABILITY TEST

TEST DR-10	STEP D	CHECKING THE EGR SOLENOID CONTROL WIRE FOR A SHORT TO GROUND (S6 CIRCUIT)
COMPLETE TEST DR-10C BEFORE PROCEEDING		

PROCEDURE		TEST INDICATION	ACTION REQUIRED
• Turn the ignition switch off. • Disconnect the 60-way connector from the SMEC. • Connect a voltmeter between the S6 (GY/YL) wire at cavity No. 40 of the 60-way connector and ground. • Turn the ignition switch to the run position.	VIEW FROM TERMINAL END S6 GY/YL 40	• Voltmeter reads battery voltage.	• Defective logic board. Replace SMEC.
		• Voltmeter reads 0 volts.	• Replace the EGR solenoid.

TEST DR-10	STEP E	CHECKING THE EGR SYSTEM — VACUUM SUPPLY FROM THE THROTTLE BODY TO THE EGR BACKPRESSURE VALVE
COMPLETE TEST DR-10A BEFORE PROCEEDING		

PROCEDURE		TEST INDICATION	ACTION REQUIRED
• Disconnect the vacuum line at the EGR back-pressure valve that comes from the throttle body or solenoid. • Connect a vacuum gauge to this line. • Start the engine. • Disconnect idle speed motor. • Raise engine speed to 2,500 rpm. NOTE: Engine must be at normal operating temperature	CONNECT VACUUM GAUGE BACK PRESSURE VALVE EGR VALVE	• Vacuum gauge is reading at least 5 inches.	• Remember what it is and Perform STEP F.
		• No vacuum or vacuum below 5 inches.	• Repair vacuum supply from throttle body or solenoid. • If vacuum supply lines are OK, replace the EGR solenoid.

TEST DR-10	STEP H	CHECKING THE EGR VALVE VACUUM CHAMBER FOR LEAKS
COMPLETE TEST DR-10H BEFORE PROCEEDING		

PROCEDURE		TEST INDICATION	ACTION REQUIRED
• Vacuum line disconnected from the EGR valve. • Auxiliary vacuum supply connected to the EGR valve. • Engine running at idle speed. • Reconnect the automatic idle speed motor. • Apply 10 inches of vacuum to EGR valve.	CONNECT AUXILIARY VACUUM SUPPLY EGR VALVE	• Vacuum should hold without bleeding for at least 10 seconds.	• Perform TEST DR-18.
		• Vacuum does not hold or bleeds down before 10 seconds.	• Replace EGR/backpressure valve assembly.

TEST DR-11	STEP A	CHECKING FOR FAULT CODE 33 — A/C CUTOUT RELAY
COMPLETE TEST DR-1A BEFORE PROCEEDING		

PROCEDURE		TEST INDICATION	ACTION REQUIRED
NOTE: In order for the A/C cutout relay to operate the radiator fan relay (condenser fan relay on mini vans) must be operating correctly. Do not proceed with test unless they are. If they are not working, disregard fault code 33. • Connect a voltmeter to N13 (DB/OR) wire of the A/C cutout relay single connector and ground. • Turn ignition switch to the run position. • Turn the blower motor on and press the A/C button to the on position. Make sure the radiator fan is running.	VOLTMETER N13 DB/OR A/C CUT-OUT RELAY	• Voltmeter reads battery voltage.	• Perform STEP B.
		• Voltmeter reads 0-1 volts.	• Perform STEP C.

TEST DR-10	STEP F	CHECKING THE VACUUM SUPPLY FROM THE BACKPRESSURE VALVE TO THE EGR VALVE
COMPLETE TEST DR-10F BEFORE PROCEEDING		

PROCEDURE		TEST INDICATION	ACTION REQUIRED
• Engine running. • Disconnect the vacuum gauge from the vacuum line and reconnect the vacuum line to the back-pressure valve. • Disconnect the vacuum line from the EGR valve and connect a vacuum gauge to it. • Disconnect idle speed motor. • Raise engine speed to 2,500 rpm.	CONNECT VACUUM GAUGE EGR VALVE	• Vacuum gauge is reading the same or near the same as seen in STEP E.	• Perform STEP G.
		• Vacuum gauge is not reading the same or near the same as seen in STEP E.	• Replace EGR/backpressure valve assembly.

TEST DR-10	STEP G	CHECKING THE EGR VALVE OPERATION
COMPLETE TEST DR-10G BEFORE PROCEEDING		

PROCEDURE		TEST INDICATION	ACTION REQUIRED
• Vacuum line disconnected from the EGR valve. • Engine running. • Connect an auxiliary vacuum supply to the EGR valve. • Disconnect the automatic idle speed motor. • With engine running at idle speed, slowly apply vacuum.	CONNECT AUXILIARY VACUUM SUPPLY EGR VALVE	• Engine speed begins to drop when applied vacuum reaches 2½ to 3½ inches.	• Perform STEP H.
		• Engine speed does not drop.	• Replace EGR/backpressure valve assembly.

TEST DR-11	STEP B	CHECKING THE A/C CUTOUT RELAY CONTROL WIRE FOR AN OPEN CIRCUIT TO THE SMEC (N13 CIRCUIT)
COMPLETE TEST DR-11A BEFORE PROCEEDING		

PROCEDURE		TEST INDICATION	ACTION REQUIRED
• Turn the ignition switch off. • Disconnect the 60-way connector from the SMEC. • Connect a voltmeter between the N13 (DB/OR) wire in cavity No. 56 of the 60-way connector and ground. • Connect a jumper wire between cavity No. 57 on C-Body, cavity No. 45 on S-Body of the 60-way connector and ground. • Turn the ignition switch to the run position. CAUTION: The radiator or condenser fan will turn on	VIEW FROM TERMINAL END 57 56 VOLTMETER JUMPER 45	• Voltmeter reads battery voltage.	• Defective logic board. Replace the SMEC. CAUTION: Before replacing the SMEC, check N13 terminal in cavity No. 56 of the 60-way connector to make sure it is not damaged causing a poor connection.
		• Voltmeter reads 0.	• Repair the N13 (DB/OR) wire of cavity No. 56 for an open circuit to the A/C cutout relay. NOTE: This wire has a diode in it. Make sure it is not failed causing an open circuit.

TEST DR-11	STEP C	CHECKING A/C CUTOUT RELAY PULL-IN COIL CIRCUIT FOR A SHORT IN THE SMEC (N13 CIRCUIT)
COMPLETE TEST DR-11A BEFORE PROCEEDING		

PROCEDURE		TEST INDICATION	ACTION REQUIRED
• Turn the ignition switch off. • Voltmeter connected to the N13 (DB/OR) wire of the A/C cutout relay single connector. • Disconnect the 60-way connector from the SMEC. • Connect a jumper wire between cavity No. 57 on C-Body, cavity No. 45 on S-Body of the 60-way connector and ground. • Turn the ignition switch to the run position. CAUTION: The radiator or condenser fan will turn on	VOLTMETER J2 DB RADIATOR FAN RELAY	• Voltmeter reads battery voltage.	• Replace the SMEC.
		• Voltmeter reads 0.	• Perform STEP D.

1988 3.0L DIAGNOSTIC CHART—DRIVEABILITY TEST

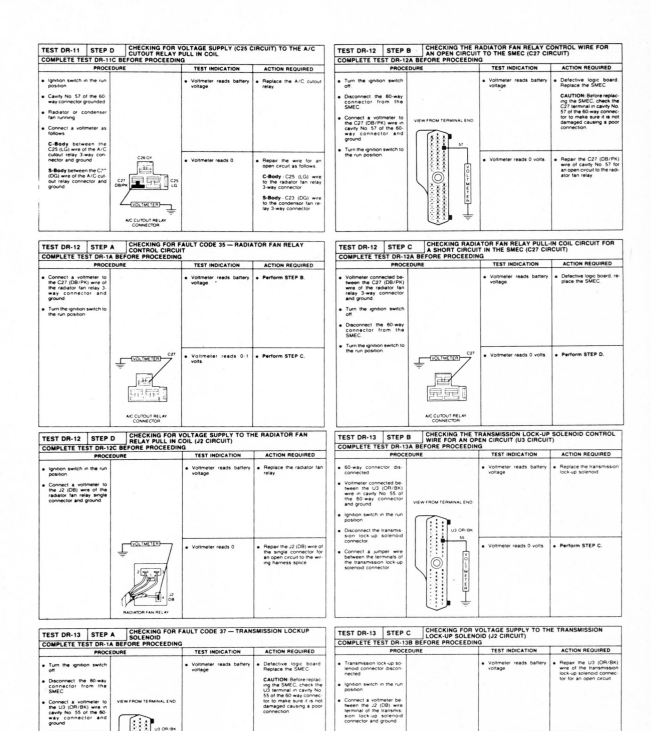

TEST DR-11 | STEP D | CHECKING FOR VOLTAGE SUPPLY (C25 CIRCUIT) TO THE A/C CUTOUT RELAY PULL IN COIL

COMPLETE TEST DR-11C BEFORE PROCEEDING

PROCEDURE	TEST INDICATION	ACTION REQUIRED
• Ignition switch in the run position • Cavity No. 57 of the 60-way connector grounded • Radiator or condenser fan running • Connect a voltmeter as follows **C-Body** between the C25 (LG) wire of the A/C cutout relay 3-way connector and ground **S-Body** between the C23 (DG) wire of the A/C cutout relay connector and ground	• Voltmeter reads battery voltage	• Replace the A/C cutout relay
	• Voltmeter reads 0.	• Repair the wire for an open circuit as follows: **C-Body** - C25 (LG) wire to the radiator fan relay 3-way connector **S-Body** - C23 (DG) wire to the condensor fan relay 3-way connector

A/C CUTOUT RELAY CONNECTOR

TEST DR-12 | STEP B | CHECKING THE RADIATOR FAN RELAY CONTROL WIRE FOR AN OPEN CIRCUIT TO THE SMEC (C27 CIRCUIT)

COMPLETE TEST DR-12A BEFORE PROCEEDING

PROCEDURE	TEST INDICATION	ACTION REQUIRED
• Turn the ignition switch off • Disconnect the 60-way connector from the SMEC • Connect a voltmeter to the C27 (DB/PK) wire in cavity No. 57 of the 60-way connector and ground • Turn the ignition switch to the run position.	• Voltmeter reads battery voltage.	• Defective logic board. Replace the SMEC. CAUTION: Before replacing the SMEC, check the C27 terminal in cavity No. 57 of the 60-way connector to make sure it is not damaged causing a poor connection.
	• Voltmeter reads 0 volts.	• Repair the C27 (DB/PK) wire of cavity No. 57 for an open circuit to the radiator fan relay

VIEW FROM TERMINAL END

TEST DR-12 | STEP A | CHECKING FOR FAULT CODE 35 — RADIATOR FAN RELAY CONTROL CIRCUIT

COMPLETE TEST DR-1A BEFORE PROCEEDING

PROCEDURE	TEST INDICATION	ACTION REQUIRED
• Connect a voltmeter to the C27 (DB/PK) wire of the radiator fan relay 3-way connector and ground. • Turn the ignition switch to the run position	• Voltmeter reads battery voltage.	• Perform STEP B.
	• Voltmeter reads 0-1 volts.	• Perform STEP C.

A/C CUTOUT RELAY CONNECTOR

TEST DR-12 | STEP C | CHECKING RADIATOR FAN RELAY PULL-IN COIL CIRCUIT FOR A SHORT CIRCUIT IN THE SMEC (C27 CIRCUIT)

COMPLETE TEST DR-12A BEFORE PROCEEDING

PROCEDURE	TEST INDICATION	ACTION REQUIRED
• Voltmeter connected between the C27 (DB/PK) wire of the radiator fan relay 3-way connector and ground. • Turn the ignition switch off. • Disconnect the 60-way connector from the SMEC. • Turn the ignition switch to the run position.	• Voltmeter reads battery voltage	• Defective logic board, replace the SMEC
	• Voltmeter reads 0 volts.	• Perform STEP D.

A/C CUTOUT RELAY CONNECTOR

TEST DR-12 | STEP D | CHECKING FOR VOLTAGE SUPPLY TO THE RADIATOR FAN RELAY PULL IN COIL (J2 CIRCUIT)

COMPLETE TEST DR-12C BEFORE PROCEEDING

PROCEDURE	TEST INDICATION	ACTION REQUIRED
• Ignition switch in the run position • Connect a voltmeter to the J2 (DB) wire of the radiator fan relay single connector and ground.	• Voltmeter reads battery voltage	• Replace the radiator fan relay
	• Voltmeter reads 0	• Repair the J2 (DB) wire of the single connector for an open circuit to the wiring harness splice

RADIATOR FAN RELAY

TEST DR-13 | STEP B | CHECKING THE TRANSMISSION LOCK-UP SOLENOID CONTROL WIRE FOR AN OPEN CIRCUIT (U3 CIRCUIT)

COMPLETE TEST DR-13A BEFORE PROCEEDING

PROCEDURE	TEST INDICATION	ACTION REQUIRED
• 60-way connector disconnected • Voltmeter connected between the U3 (OR/BK) wire in cavity No. 55 of the 60-way connector and ground • Ignition switch in the run position • Disconnect the transmission lock-up solenoid connector • Connect a jumper wire between the terminals of the transmission lock-up solenoid connector	• Voltmeter reads battery voltage	• Replace the transmission lock-up solenoid
	• Voltmeter reads 0 volts.	• Perform STEP C.

VIEW FROM TERMINAL END

TEST DR-13 | STEP A | CHECKING FOR FAULT CODE 37 — TRANSMISSION LOCKUP SOLENOID

COMPLETE TEST DR-1A BEFORE PROCEEDING

PROCEDURE	TEST INDICATION	ACTION REQUIRED
• Turn the ignition switch off • Disconnect the 60-way connector from the SMEC • Connect a voltmeter to the U3 (OR/BK) wire in cavity No. 55 of the 60-way connector and ground • Turn the ignition switch to the run position	• Voltmeter reads battery voltage	• Defective logic board. Replace the SMEC. CAUTION: Before replacing the SMEC, check the U3 terminal in cavity No. 55 of the 60-way connector to make sure it is not damaged causing a poor connection
	• Voltmeter reads 0	• SMEC OK Perform STEP B.

VIEW FROM TERMINAL END

TEST DR-13 | STEP C | CHECKING FOR VOLTAGE SUPPLY TO THE TRANSMISSION LOCK-UP SOLENOID (J2 CIRCUIT)

COMPLETE TEST DR-13B BEFORE PROCEEDING

PROCEDURE	TEST INDICATION	ACTION REQUIRED
• Transmission lock-up solenoid connector disconnected • Ignition switch in the run position • Connect a voltmeter between the J2 (DB) wire terminal of the transmission lock-up solenoid connector and ground	• Voltmeter reads battery voltage	• Repair the U3 (OR/BK) wire of the transmission lock-up solenoid connector for an open circuit
	• Voltmeter reads 0 volts	• Repair the J2 (DB) wire of the transmission lock-up solenoid connector for an open circuit to the wiring harness splice

TRANSMISSION LOCK-UP SOLENOID CONNECTOR

1988 3.0L DIAGNOSTIC CHART—DRIVEABILITY TEST

TEST DR-14	STEP A	CHECKING FOR FAULT CODE 44 - FUSED J2
COMPLETE TEST DR-1A BEFORE PROCEEDING		

PROCEDURE		TEST INDICATION	ACTION REQUIRED
• Turn the ignition switch off. • Disconnect the 60-way connector. • Connect a voltmeter to the K14 (DB/WT) wire in cavity No. 12 of the 60-way connector and ground. • Turn the ignition switch to the run position.	VIEW FROM TERMINAL END	• Voltmeter reads battery voltage	• Defective logic board. Replace SMEC. CAUTION: Before replacing the SMEC, make sure the K14 terminal in cavity No. 12 of the 60-way connector is not damaged causing a poor connection
		• Voltmeter reads 0 volts	• Repair the K14 (DB/WT) wire of cavity No. 12 for an open circuit to the wiring harness splice.

TEST DR-15	STEP B	CHECKING THE DISTRIBUTOR SYNC PICKUP SIGNAL WIRE FOR AN OPEN CIRCUIT TO THE SMEC (Y7 CIRCUIT)
COMPLETE TEST DR-15A BEFORE PROCEEDING		

PROCEDURE		TEST INDICATION	ACTION REQUIRED
• Distributor pickup connector disconnected. • Turn the ignition switch off. • Disconnect the 60-way connector from the SMEC. • Connect an ohmmeter between the Y7 (TN/YL) wire in cavity No. 49 of the 60-way connector and the Y7 (TN/YL) wire in the distributor harness connector.		• Ohmmeter is showing continuity	• Defective logic board, replace the SMEC CAUTION: Before replacing the SMEC, check the Y7 terminal in cavity No. 49 of the 60-way connector to make sure it is not damaged causing a poor connection
		• Ohmmeter is not showing continuity	• Repair the Y7 (TN/YL) wire in cavity No. 49 of the 60-way connector for an open circuit to the distributor harness connector

TEST DR-15	STEP A	CHECKING FOR FAULT CODE 54 — DISTRIBUTOR SYNC PICKUP
COMPLETE TEST DR-1A BEFORE PROCEEDING		

PROCEDURE		TEST INDICATION	ACTION REQUIRED
• Turn the ignition switch off. • Disconnect the distributor connector. • Connect a voltmeter to the Y7 (TN/YL) wire of the distributor harness connector and ground. • Turn the ignition switch to the run position.		• Voltmeter is reading at least 4 volts	• Replace the distributor pickup assembly
		• Voltmeter is reading 0	• Perform STEP B.

THE FOLLOWING TEST MUST BEGIN WITH A COLD ENGINE

TEST DR-16	STEP A	CHECKING SENSOR CALIBRATIONS (ENGINE COOLANT TEMPERATURE SENSOR)
COMPLETE TEST DR-1N BEFORE PROCEEDING		

PROCEDURE		TEST INDICATION	ACTION REQUIRED
• DRB II connected. • Engine cold. • Put the system in Engine Running Test 64		• Display on the DRB II is reading ambient temperature ± 10°F	• Perform STEP B.
		• Display on the DRB II is reading more than 10°F above or below ambient temperature	• Replace the coolant sensor

TEST DR-16	STEP B	CHECKING SENSOR CALIBRATIONS (THROTTLE POSITION SENSOR)
COMPLETE TEST DR-16A BEFORE PROCEEDING		

PROCEDURE	TEST INDICATION	ACTION REQUIRED
• DRB II connected. • Engine cold. • Turn the engine off. • Put the system in Sensor Test 05	• Display on DRB II reads as follows **Throttle Fully Closed** 1 volt ± ½ volt NOTE: Make sure the cables attached to the throttle body are not misadjusted holding the throttle open. **In Between Closed and Open** You should see an uninterrupted change of voltage between closed and open throttle **Throttle Wide Open** at least 3½ volts	• If the voltage readings are within specifications throttle pot is OK. Perform STEP C. • If the voltage readings are not within specifications, replace the throttle position sensor

TEST DR-16	STEP D	CHECKING SENSOR CALIBRATION (THROTTLE POSITION SENSOR)
COMPLETE TEST DR-16C BEFORE PROCEEDING		

PROCEDURE	TEST INDICATION	ACTION REQUIRED
• DRB II connected. • Engine running at idle. • Put the system into Engine Running Test 69	• Display on the DRB II is between 00 and 1 (one tenth) volt	• Perform STEP E.
	• Display on the DRB II is reading more than 1 (one tenth) volt	• Replace the throttle position sensor

TEST DR-16	STEP C	CHECKING SENSOR CALIBRATION (THROTTLE POSITION SENSOR)
COMPLETE TEST DR-16B BEFORE PROCEEDING		

PROCEDURE	TEST INDICATION	ACTION REQUIRED
• DRB II connected. • Start the engine. • Put the system into Engine Running Test 65 • Slowly increase engine speed to 2,000 rpm.	• As engine speed increases the voltage displayed on the DRB II also increases.	• Perform STEP D.
	• As engine speed increases the voltage displayed on the DRB II is not increasing.	• Replace the throttle position sensor

TEST DR-16	STEP E	CHECKING SENSOR CALIBRATION (M.A.P. SENSOR)
COMPLETE TEST DR-16D BEFORE PROCEEDING		

PROCEDURE	TEST INDICATION	ACTION REQUIRED
• DRB II connected. • Tee a vacuum gauge into the vacuum line at the M.A.P. sensor. • Start the engine. • Put the system into Engine Running Test 68	• Vacuum displayed on the DRB II is within 1 inch of vacuum shown on the vacuum gauge	• Perform STEP G.
	• Vacuum displayed on the DRB II is not within 1 inch of vacuum shown on the vacuum gauge	• Perform STEP F.

1988 3.0L DIAGNOSTIC CHART — DRIVEABILITY TEST

TEST DR-16	STEP F	CHECKING SENSOR CALIBRATION (M.A.P. SENSOR)
COMPLETE TEST DR-16E BEFORE PROCEEDING		

PROCEDURE	TEST INDICATION	ACTION REQUIRED
• DRB II connected. • Engine cold • Put the system in **Sensor Test 08** • Disconnect the vacuum hose from the M.A.P. sensor. • Connect an auxiliary vacuum supply to the M.A.P. sensor • Apply 5 inches of vacuum and record the voltage displayed on the DRB II • Slowly apply vacuum to 20 inches and watch display on DRB II	• Record the voltage displayed on DRB II at 20 inches. • Subtract the voltage recorded at 20 inches from the voltage recorded at 5 inches **Example** Voltage at 5 in. 3.8 Voltage at 20 in. 1.1 Difference 2.7	• The DRB II is showing an uninterrupted change of voltage between 5 and 20 inches of vacuum • The voltage difference is between 2.3 and 2.9 volts	• Repair vacuum line to the M.A.P. sensor for a restriction
		• The DRB II is showing an interrupted change of voltage between 5 and 20 inches of vacuum • The voltage difference is not between 2.3 and 2.9 volts	• Replace the M.A.P. sensor

TEST DR-17	STEP A	CHECKING FOR FUEL FOULED SPARK PLUGS
COMPLETE TEST DR-16D OR 16G BEFORE PROCEEDING		

PROCEDURE	TEST INDICATION	ACTION REQUIRED
• Remove the spark plugs.	• Spark plugs are dry. **NOTE:** It is normal for spark plugs to be black after an engine has been started cold.	• Spark plugs OK. **Perform TESTS** as follows: Federal **TEST DR-19** California **TEST DR-20**
LOOK FOR WET FUEL	• Spark plugs are wet with fuel.	• Clean and reinstall. Do not install new spark plugs. • Check for gasoline in the crankcase. Change oil and filter if required.

TEST DR-16	STEP G	CHECKING SENSOR CALIBRATION CHARGE TEMPERATURE SENSOR
COMPLETE TEST DR-16E BEFORE PROCEEDING		

PROCEDURE	TEST INDICATION	ACTION REQUIRED
• DRB II connected • Engine cold • Start the engine • Put the system in **Engine Running Test 63**	• Display on the DRB II reading between 3 and 5 volts.	• Charge temperature sensor circuit is OK. **Perform TEST DR-17.**
	• Display on the DRB II is not reading between 3 and 5 volts.	• Replace the charge temperature sensor.

THE FOLLOWING TEST MUST BEGIN WITH A WARM ENGINE

TEST DR-18	STEP A	CHECKING SENSOR CALIBRATION (ENGINE COOLANT TEMPERATURE SENSOR)
COMPLETE TEST DR-1A OR DR-1N BEFORE PROCEEDING		

PROCEDURE	TEST INDICATION	ACTION REQUIRED
• DRB II connected. • Start the engine. • Put the system in **Engine Running Test 64**	• Display on the DRB II is reading between 180° and 250°.	• **Perform STEP B.**
	• Display on the DRB II is not reading between 180° and 250°.	• Replace the coolant sensor.

TEST DR-18	STEP B	CHECKING SENSOR CALIBRATIONS (THROTTLE POSITION SENSOR)
COMPLETE TEST DR-18A BEFORE PROCEEDING		

PROCEDURE	TEST INDICATION	ACTION REQUIRED
• DRB II connected. • Engine warm • Put the system in **Sensor Test 05**	• Display on DRB II should read as follows: **Throttle Fully Closed** 1 volt ± ½ volt **NOTE:** Make sure the cables attached to the throttle body are not misadjusted holding the throttle open. **In Between Closed and Open** You should see an uninterrupted change of voltage between closed and open throttle. **Throttle Wide Open** at least 3½ volts	• If the voltage readings are within specifications the throttle pot is OK. **Perform STEP C.** • If the voltage readings are not within specifications, replace the throttle position sensor.

TEST DR-18	STEP D	CHECKING SENSOR CALIBRATION (THROTTLE POSITION SENSOR)
COMPLETE TEST DR-18C BEFORE PROCEEDING		

PROCEDURE	TEST INDICATION	ACTION REQUIRED
• DRB II connected. • Start and stop the engine 5 times then start the engine and let it idle. • Put the system into **Engine Running Test 69**	• Display on the DRB II is reading between 00 and .1 (one tenth) volt.	• **Perform STEP E.**
	• Display on the DRB II is reading more than .1 (one tenth) volt.	• Replace the throttle position sensor.

TEST DR-18	STEP C	CHECKING SENSOR CALIBRATION (THROTTLE POSITION SENSOR)
COMPLETE TEST DR-18B BEFORE PROCEEDING		

PROCEDURE	TEST INDICATION	ACTION REQUIRED
• DRB II connected. • Put the system into **Engine Running Test 65** • Slowly increase engine speed to 2,000 rpm.	• As engine speed increases the voltage displayed on the DRB II also increases.	• **Perform STEP D.**
	• As engine speed increases the voltage displayed on the DRB II is not increasing.	• Replace the throttle position sensor.

TEST DR-18	STEP E	CHECKING SENSOR CALIBRATION (M.A.P. SENSOR)
COMPLETE TEST DR-18D BEFORE PROCEEDING		

PROCEDURE	TEST INDICATION	ACTION REQUIRED
• DRB II connected. • Tee a vacuum gauge into the vacuum line at the M.A.P. sensor. • Start the engine. • Put the system into **Engine Running Test 68**	• Vacuum displayed on the DRB II is within 1 inch of vacuum shown on the vacuum gauge.	• **Perform STEP G.**
VACUUM GAUGE	• Vacuum displayed on the DRB II is not within 1 inch of vacuum shown on the vacuum gauge.	• **Perform STEP F.**

1988 3.0L DIAGNOSTIC CHART—DRIVEABILITY TEST

TEST DR-18	STEP F	CHECKING SENSOR CALIBRATION (M.A.P. SENSOR)

COMPLETE TEST DR-18E BEFORE PROCEEDING

PROCEDURE		TEST INDICATION	ACTION REQUIRED
• DRB II connected. • Engine warm. • Put the system in **Sensor Test 06**. • Disconnect the vacuum hose from the M.A.P. sensor. • Connect an auxiliary vacuum supply to the M.A.P. sensor. • Apply 5 inches of vacuum and record the voltage displayed on the DRB II. • Slowly apply vacuum to 20 inches and watch display on DRB II.	• Record the voltage displayed on the DRB II at 20 inches. • Subtract the voltage recorded at 20 inches from the voltage recorded at 5 inches. **Example** Voltage at 5 in. 1.9 Voltage at 20 in. −0.6 Difference 1.3	• The DRB II is showing an uninterrupted change of voltage between 5 and 20 inches of vacuum. • The voltage difference is between 1.1 and 1.4 volts.	• Repair vacuum line to the M.A.P. sensor for a restriction.
		• The DRB II is showing an interrupted change of voltage between 5 and 20 inches of vacuum. • The voltage difference is not between 1.1 and 1.4 volts.	• Replace the M.A.P. sensor.

TEST DR-19	STEP A	CHECKING THE EGR SYSTEM - VACUUM SUPPLY FROM THE THROTTLE BODY TO THE EGR BACKPRESSURE VALVE

COMPLETE TEST DR-18A BEFORE PROCEEDING

PROCEDURE		TEST INDICATION	ACTION REQUIRED
• Disconnect the vacuum line at the EGR backpressure valve that comes from the throttle body. • Connect a vacuum gauge to this line. • Start the engine. • Disconnect idle speed motor. • Raise engine speed to 2,500 rpm.		• Vacuum gauge is reading at least 5 inches.	• Remember what it is, and **Perform STEP B.**
		• No vacuum or vacuum below 5 inches.	• Repair vacuum supply or vacuum from throttle body or solenoid.

TEST DR-18	STEP G	CHECKING SENSOR CALIBRATION (CHARGE TEMPERATURE SENSOR)

COMPLETE TEST DR-18E BEFORE PROCEEDING

PROCEDURE		TEST INDICATION	ACTION REQUIRED
• DRB II connected. • Start the engine. • Put the system in **Engine Running Test 63**.		• Display on the DRB II is reading between 1 and 4 volts.	• Perform TESTS as follows. Federal TEST DR-19 California TEST DR-20
		• Display on the DRB II is not reading between 1 and 4 volts.	• Replace the charge temperature sensor.

TEST DR-19	STEP B	CHECKING THE VALVE SUPPLY FROM THE BACKPRESSURE VALVE TO THE EGR VALVE

COMPLETE TEST DR-19A BEFORE PROCEEDING

PROCEDURE		TEST INDICATION	ACTION REQUIRED
• Engine running. • Idle speed motor disconnected. • Disconnect the vacuum gauge from the vacuum line and reconnect the vacuum line to the backpressure valve. • Disconnect the vacuum line from the EGR valve and connect a vacuum gauge to it. • Raise the engine speed to 2,500 rpm.		• Vacuum gauge is reading the same or near the same as seen in **STEP A**.	• **Perform STEP C.**
		• Vacuum gauge is not reading the same or near the same as seen in **STEP A**.	• Replace EGR/backpressure valve assembly.

TEST DR-19	STEP C	CHECKING THE EGR VALVE OPERATION

COMPLETE TEST DR-19B BEFORE PROCEEDING

PROCEDURE		TEST INDICATION	ACTION REQUIRED
• Vacuum line disconnected from the EGR valve. • Engine running. • Idle speed motor disconnected. • Connect an auxiliary vacuum supply to the EGR valve. • With engine running at idle speed slowly apply vacuum.		• Engine speed begins to drop when applied vacuum reaches 2½ to 3½ inches.	• **Perform STEP D.**
		• Engine speed does not drop.	• Replace EGR/backpressure valve assembly

TEST DR-20	STEP A	CHECKING SECONDARY IGNITION SYSTEM

COMPLETE TEST DR-18G OR DR-19D BEFORE PROCEEDING

PROCEDURE		TEST INDICATION	ACTION REQUIRED
• Connect suitable engine analyzer to engine. • Start engine and let engine speed stabilize for two minutes.		• Follow equipment manufacturer's procedure for secondary ignition testing and pattern analysis. **CAUTION: Make sure ignition coil output is checked in this testing. Open circuit secondary voltage should be at least 25,000 volts.**	• Secondary pattern OK. Perform TEST DR-21.
		• Secondary ignition not to specs	• Repair as required

TEST DR-19	STEP D	CHECKING THE EGR VALVE VACUUM CHAMBER FOR LEAKS

COMPLETE TEST DR-19C BEFORE PROCEEDING

PROCEDURE		TEST INDICATION	ACTION REQUIRED
• Vacuum line disconnected from the EGR valve. • Auxiliary vacuum supply connected to the EGR valve. • Apply 10 inches of vacuum to EGR valve.		• Vacuum should hold without bleeding for at least 10 seconds.	• EGR diaphragm is OK **Perform TEST DR-20.**
		• Vacuum does not hold or bleeds down before 10 seconds.	• Replace EGR/backpressure valve assembly

TEST DR-21	STEP A	CHECKING BASIC IGNITION TIMING

COMPLETE TEST DR-20A BEFORE PROCEEDING

PROCEDURE		TEST INDICATION	ACTION REQUIRED
• Connect a tachometer to engine. • Connect a power timing light to engine. • Start and run engine until operating temperature is reached. • Disconnect the engine coolant sensor connector and do not reconnect it. **NOTE:** The check engine lamp on the instrument panel must come on.		• Basic timing is within 2° of specification as shown on the emission label	• **Perform STEP B.**
		• Basic timing is not within 2° of specification as shown on the emission label	• Adjust following basic ignition timing procedure.

1988 3.0L DIAGNOSTIC CHART—DRIVEABILITY TEST

TEST DR-21	STEP B	CHECKING SPARK ADVANCE
COMPLETE TEST DR-21A BEFORE PROCEEDING		
PROCEDURE	TEST INDICATION	ACTION REQUIRED
• Tachometer connected to engine • Timing light connected to engine • Air cleaner removed (if necessary) • Engine at operating temperature • Reconnect the coolant sensor connector **NOTE:** Check engine lamp will not turn off until the engine is restarted. • Raise engine speed to 2,000 rpm	• Timing is between 26° and 34° before top dead center	• **Perform TEST DR-22.**
	• Spark advance not within minimum specification	• Defective logic board Replace the SMEC.

TEST DR-22	STEP A	CHECKING FUEL SUPPLY AND RETURN SYSTEM
COMPLETE TEST DR-21B BEFORE PROCEEDING		
PROCEDURE	TEST INDICATION	ACTION REQUIRED
• DRB II connected. • Install pressure gauge (Tool C3292) with C4799 adapter in the fuel supply hose at the fuel rail. **CAUTION:** Fuel is under high pressure. • Put system in **Diagnostic Test Mode.** • Press and hold the ATM key on the DRB II	• Fuel pressure is 48 psi ± 1.	• **Perform TEST DR-23.**
	• Fuel pressure below 47 psi, record what it is	• **Perform STEP B.**
	• Fuel pressure above 49 psi	• **Perform STEP D.**

TEST DR-22	STEP D	CHECKING FOR HIGH FUEL PRESSURE
COMPLETE TEST DR-22A BEFORE PROCEEDING		
PROCEDURE	TEST INDICATION	ACTION REQUIRED
• DRB II connected • Turn the ignition switch off • Pressure gauge connected. • Remove fuel return hose (small one) from fuel rail • Connect a suitable length of fuel hose to the fuel rail and put open end into an approved gasoline container (2-gallon size) • Turn the ignition switch to the run position • Press and hold the ATM key on the DRB II	• Fuel pressure is 48 psi ± 1	• Check fuel return lines for kinks or restrictions, including return line check valve inside fuel tank
	• Fuel pressure is above 49 psi	• Replace pressure regulation valve

TEST DR-23	STEP A	CHECKING THROTTLE BODY MINIMUM AIR FLOW
COMPLETE TEST DR-22A BEFORE PROCEEDING		
PROCEDURE	TEST INDICATION	ACTION REQUIRED
• Connect DRB II to the engine harness connector • Connect a tachometer to the engine • Disconnect the hose from the PCV valve • Install Tool C5004 (.125" orifice) into the PCV vacuum supply hose • Start the engine and let it run until the radiator cooling fan cycles then off. With the radiator fan not running, put the system into **Engine Running Test 70**	• Tachometer is reading between 850 and 1,050 rpm **NOTE:** If vehicle has less than 1,000 miles specification is between 725 and 1,050 rpm	• **Perform TEST DR-24.**
	• Tachometer is not reading within above specifications	• Replace the throttle body

TEST DR-22	STEP B	CHECKING FOR LOW FUEL PRESSURE
COMPLETE TEST DR-22A BEFORE PROCEEDING		
PROCEDURE	TEST INDICATION	ACTION REQUIRED
• DRB II connected. • Turn the ignition switch off. • Install pressure gauge between in-tank pump and fuel filter. Use adapter C4799. • Turn the ignition switch to the run position. • Press and hold the ATM key on the DRB II.	• Fuel pressure is 5 psi higher than previously recorded pressure.	• Replace filter.
	• Fuel pressure still below 47 psi.	• **Perform STEP C.**

TEST DR-22	STEP C	CHECKING FOR LOW FUEL PRESSURE
COMPLETE TEST DR-22B BEFORE PROCEEDING		
PROCEDURE	TEST INDICATION	ACTION REQUIRED
• DRB II connected. • Turn the ignition switch off. • Release pressure. • Install fuel pressure between filter and fuel rail. • Turn the ignition switch to the run position. • Press and hold the ATM key on the DRB II. • Very gently, squeeze fuel return line at throttle body and immediately let go. **NOTE: Fuel pressure must not exceed 72 P.S.I. or damage to the regulator will result.**	• Fuel pressure increases above operating pressure.	• Replace pressure regulator valve.
	• Fuel pressure does not increase.	• Replace intank fuel pump. **NOTE:** Before replacing pump look for contamination in the fuel tank that may be plugging pump filter. Also make sure electrical connections are not corroded.

TEST NO. DR-24

AT THIS POINT IN THE DRIVEABILITY TEST PROCEDURE YOU HAVE DETERMINED THAT ALL OF THE ENGINE CONTROL SYSTEMS ARE OPERATING AS THEY WERE DESIGNED TO. THEREFORE THEY ARE **NOT THE CAUSE OF THE DRIVEABILITY PROBLEM.**

THE FOLLOWING ADDITIONAL ITEMS SHOULD BE CHECKED AS POSSIBLE CAUSES:

1. **ENGINE VACUUM** – MUST BE AT LEAST 13 INCHES IN NEUTRAL.

2. **ENGINE VALVE TIMING** – TO SPECIFICATIONS.

3. **ENGINE COMPRESSION** – TO SPECIFICATIONS.

4. **ENGINE EXHAUST SYSTEM** – MUST BE FREE OF ANY RESTRICTIONS.

5. **ENGINE PCV SYSTEM** – MUST FLOW FREELY.

6. **ENGINE DRIVE SPROCKETS** – CAM AND CRANK SHAFTS.

7. **TORQUE CONVERTOR STALL SPEED** – TO SPECIFICATIONS.

8. **POWER BRAKE BOOSTER** – NO INTERNAL VACUUM LEAKS.

9. **FUEL CONTAMINATION** – HIGH ALCOHOL AND WATER CONTENT.

10. **FUEL INJECTORS** - ROUGH IDLE MAY BE CAUSED BY INJECTOR CONTROL WIRES NOT CONNECTED TO THE CORRECT INJECTOR.

ANY ONE OR MORE OF THESE ITEMS CAN GIVE A DRIVEABILITY RELATED PROBLEM. THEY CANNOT BE OVERLOOKED AS POSSIBLE CAUSES.

5 FUEL SYSTEM

2.5L TURBO DIAGNOSTIC CHART—NO START TEST

2.5L TURBO DIAGNOSTIC CHART — NO START TEST

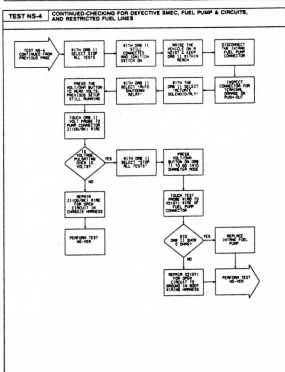

5 FUEL SYSTEM

2.5L TURBO DIAGNOSTIC CHART—NO START TEST

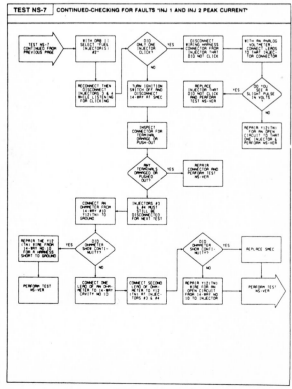

2.5L TURBO DIAGNOSTIC CHART — NO START TEST

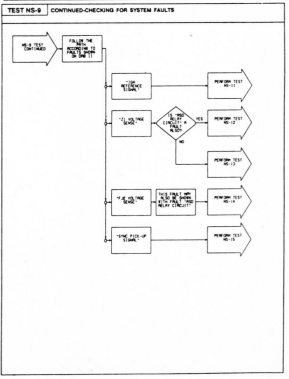

2.5L TURBO DIAGNOSTIC CHART — NO START TEST

2.5L TURBO DIAGNOSTIC CHART—NO START TEST

2.5L TURBO DIAGNOSTIC CHART—NO START TEST

2.5L TURBO DIAGNOSTIC CHART—DRIVEABILITY TEST

2.5L TURBO DIAGNOSTIC CHART — DRIVEABILITY TEST

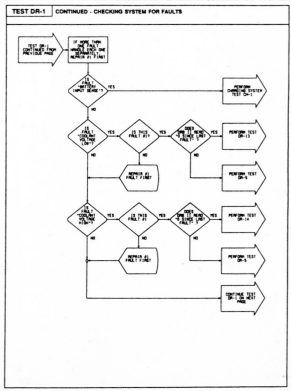

2.5L TURBO DIAGNOSTIC CHART — DRIVEABILITY TEST

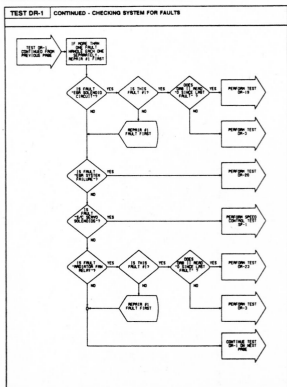

2.5L TURBO DIAGNOSTIC CHART—DRIVEABILITY TEST

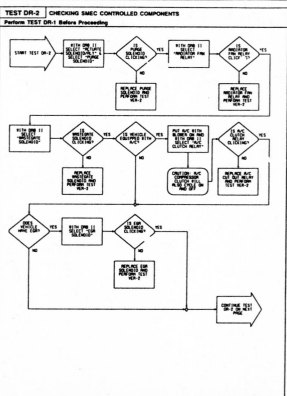

2.5L TURBO DIAGNOSTIC CHART—DRIVEABILITY TEST

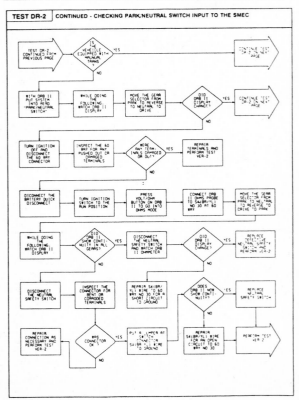

2.5L TURBO DIAGNOSTIC CHART—DRIVEABILITY TEST

TEST DR-2 CONTINUED - CHECKING THE A/C PUSH BUTTON SWITCH INPUT TO THE SMEC

TEST DR-2 CONTINUED - CHECKING THE 5 VOLT SUPPLY TO MAP SENSOR

TEST DR-2 CONTINUED - CHECKING THE AUTOMATIC IDLE SPEED MOTOR OPERATION

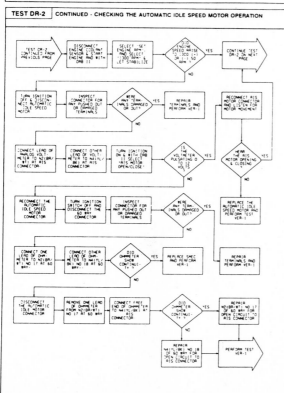

TEST DR-2 CONTINUED - CHECKING THE AUTOMATIC IDLE SPEED MOTOR OPERATION

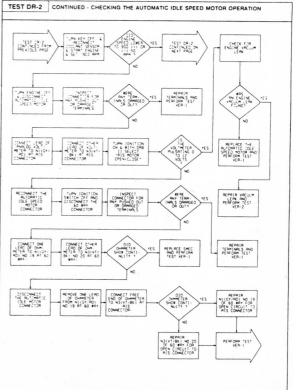

2.5L TURBO DIAGNOSTIC CHART – DRIVEABILITY TEST

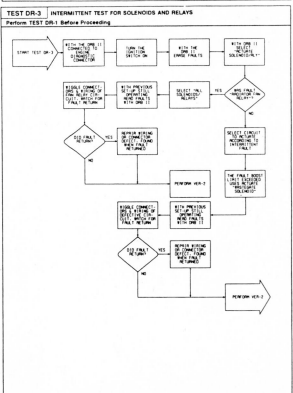

2.5L TURBO DIAGNOSTIC CHART—DRIVEABILITY TEST

2.5L TURBO DIAGNOSTIC CHART—DRIVEABILITY TEST

TEST DR-8 | CHECKING FOR FAULT MESSAGE · MAP PNEUMATIC CHANGE
Perform TEST DR-1 Before Proceeding

TEST DR-9 | CHECKING FOR FAULT MESSAGE · MAP VOLTAGE LOW
Perform TEST DR-1 Before Proceeding

TEST DR-10 | CHECKING FOR FAULT MESSAGE · MAP VOLTAGE TOO HIGH
Perform TEST DR-1 Before Proceeding

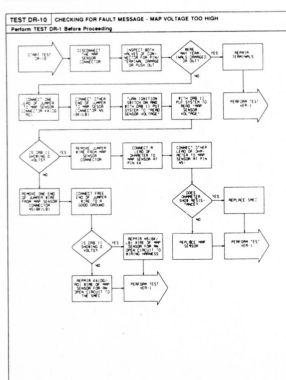

TEST DR-11 | CHECKING FOR FAULT MESSAGE · VEHICLE SPEED SIGNAL
Perform TEST DR-1 Before Proceeding

2.5L TURBO DIAGNOSTIC CHART—DRIVEABILITY TEST

TEST DR-11 CONTINUED - CHECKING FOR FAULT MESSAGE - VEHICLE SPEED SIGNAL

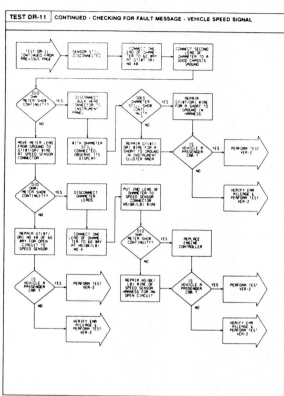

TEST DR-12 CHECKING FOR FAULT MESSAGE - OXYGEN SENSOR SIGNAL

Perform TEST DR-1 Before Proceeding

TEST DR-13 CHECKING FOR FAULT MESSAGE - COOLANT VOLTAGE LOW

Perform TEST DR-1 Before Proceeding

TEST DR-14 CHECKING FOR FAULT MESSAGE - COOLANT VOLTAGE HIGH

Perform TEST DR-1 Before Proceeding

2.5L TURBO DIAGNOSTIC CHART—DRIVEABILITY TEST

2.5L TURBO DIAGNOSTIC CHART—DRIVEABILITY TEST

2.5L TURBO DIAGNOSTIC CHART—DRIVEABILITY TEST

2.5L TURBO DIAGNOSTIC CHART—DRIVEABILITY TEST

2.5L TURBO DIAGNOSTIC CHART—DRIVEABILITY TEST

2.5L TURBO DIAGNOSTIC CHART—DRIVEABILITY TEST

TEST DR-30	CHECKING SPARK PLUGS

Perform TEST DR-29 Before Proceeding

TEST DR-31	THE FOLLOWING TEST MUST BEGIN WITH WARM ENGINE CHECKING SENSOR CALIBRATIONS

Perform TEST DR-29 Before Proceeding

TEST DR-31	CONTINUED · CHECKING SENSOR CALIBRATIONS

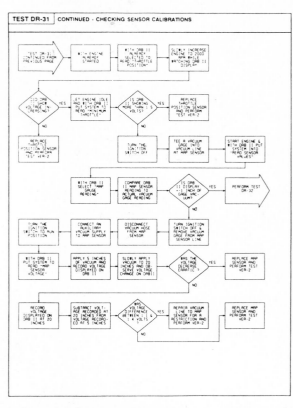

TEST DR-32	CHECKING SECONDARY IGNITION SYSTEM

Perform TEST DR-30 and DR-31 Before Proceeding

TEST DR-33	CHECKING BASIC TIMING AND FUEL SYSTEM

Perform TEST DR-32 Before Proceeding

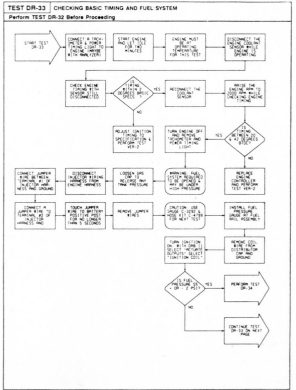

5 FUEL SYSTEM

2.5L TURBO DIAGNOSTIC CHART—DRIVEABILITY TEST

2.5L TURBO DIAGNOSTIC CHART—DRIVEABILITY TEST

TEST DR-34 | CONTINUED - CHECKING THE OXYGEN SENSOR FUNCTION

TEST DR-35 | CHECKING THROTTLE BODY MINIMUM AIR FLOW
Perform TEST DR-34 Before Proceeding

TEST DR-36 | OTHER POSSIBLE CAUSES OF DRIVEABILITY RELATED PROBLEMS
Perform TEST DR-35 Before Proceeding

AT THIS POINT IN THE DRIVEABILITY TEST PROCEDURE YOU HAVE DETERMINED THAT ALL OF THE ENGINE CONTROL SYSTEMS ARE OPERATING AS THEY WERE DESIGNED. THEREFORE, THEY ARE **NOT THE CAUSE OF THE DRIVEABILITY PROBLEM.**

THE FOLLOWING ADDITIONAL ITEMS SHOULD BE CHECKED AS POSSIBLE CAUSES:

1. **ENGINE VACUUM** - MUST BE AT LEAST 13 INCHES IN NEUTRAL.
2. **ENGINE VALVE TIMING** - TO SPECIFICATIONS.
3. **ENGINE COMPRESSION** - TO SPECIFICATIONS.
4. **ENGINE EXHAUST SYSTEM** - MUST BE FREE OF ANY RESTRICTIONS.
5. **ENGINE PCV SYSTEM** - MUST FLOW FREELY.
6. **ENGINE DRIVE SPROCKETS** - CAM, CRANK AND INTERMEDIATE SHAFTS.
7. **TORQUE CONVERTOR STALL SPEED** - TO SPECIFICATIONS.
8. **POWER BRAKE BOOSTER** - NO INTERNAL VACUUM LEAKS.
9. **FUEL CONTAMINATION** - HIGH ALCOHOL AND WATER CONTENT.
10. **TECHNICAL SERVICE BULLETINS** - ANY THAT MAY APPLY TO VEHICLE.

ANY ONE OR MORE OF THESE ITEMS CAN CREATE A DRIVEABILITY RELATED PROBLEM. THEY CAN NOT BE OVERLOOKED AS POSSIBLE CAUSES.

VER-1 | DRIVEABILITY VERIFICATION

2.5L TURBO DIAGNOSTIC CHART — SPEED CONTROL SYSTEM TEST

2.5L TURBO DIAGNOSTIC CHART—SPEED CONTROL SYSTEM TEST

2.5L TURBO DIAGNOSTIC CHART—SPEED CONTROL SYSTEM TEST

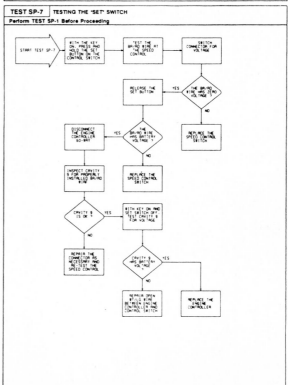

2.5L TURBO DIAGNOSTIC CHART — CHARGING SYSTEM TEST

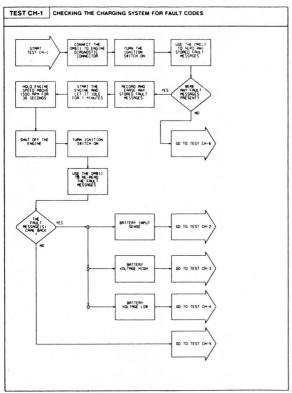

TEST CH-1 | CHECKING THE CHARGING SYSTEM FOR FAULT CODES

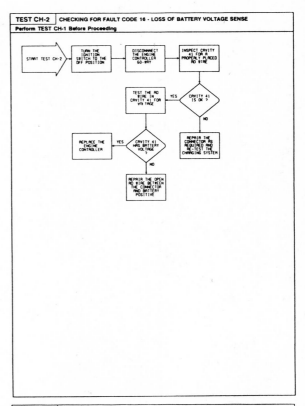

TEST CH-2 | CHECKING FOR FAULT CODE 16 - LOSS OF BATTERY VOLTAGE SENSE
Perform TEST CH-1 Before Proceeding

TEST CH-3 | CHECKING FOR FAULT CODE 46 - BATTERY VOLTAGE TOO HIGH
Perform TEST CH-1 Before Proceeding

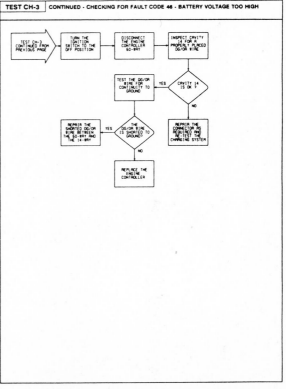

TEST CH-3 | CONTINUED - CHECKING FOR FAULT CODE 46 - BATTERY VOLTAGE TOO HIGH

5 FUEL SYSTEM

2.5L TURBO DIAGNOSTIC CHART—CHARGING SYSTEM TEST

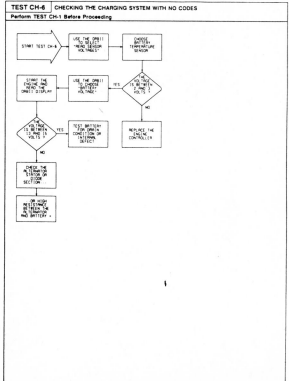

1989-91 3.0L/3.3L DIAGNOSTIC CHART—NO START TEST

1989-91 3.0L/3.3L DIAGNOSTIC CHART—NO START TEST

1989-91 3.0L/3.3L DIAGNOSTIC CHART—NO START TEST

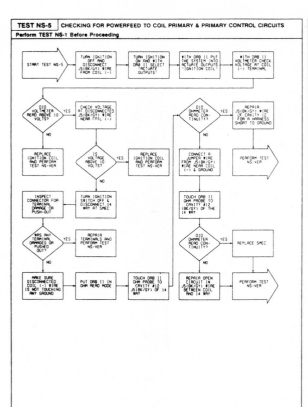

TEST NS-5 CHECKING FOR POWERFEED TO COIL PRIMARY & PRIMARY CONTROL CIRCUITS

Perform TEST NS-1 Before Proceeding

TEST NS-6 CHECKING SPARK CONTROL CIRCUITRY

Perform TEST NS-5 Before Proceeding

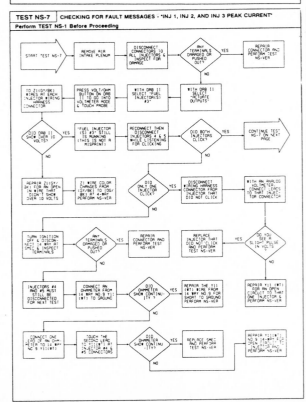

TEST NS-7 CHECKING FOR FAULT MESSAGES - "INJ 1, INJ 2, AND INJ 3 PEAK CURRENT"

Perform TEST NS-1 Before Proceeding

TEST NS-7 CONTINUED - CHECKING FOR FAULT MESSAGES - "INJ 1, INJ 2, AND INJ 3 PEAK CURRENT"

1989-91 3.0L/3.3L DIAGNOSTIC CHART—NO START TEST

1989-91 3.0L/3.3L DIAGNOSTIC CHART—NO START TEST

1989-91 3.0L/3.3L DIAGNOSTIC CHART—NO START TEST

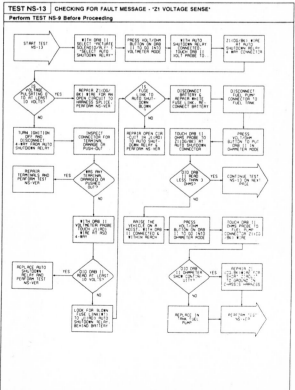

1989-91 3.0L/3.3L DIAGNOSTIC CHART—NO START TEST

1989-91 3.0L/3.3L DIAGNOSTIC CHART—DRIVEABILITY TEST

1989-91 3.0L/3.3L DIAGNOSTIC CHART—DRIVEABILITY TEST

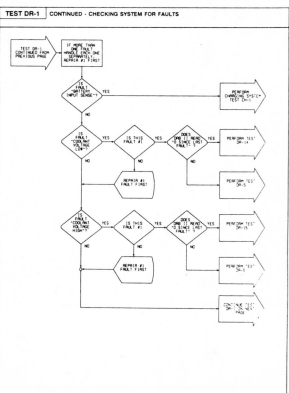

1989-91 3.0L/3.3L DIAGNOSTIC CHART—DRIVEABILITY TEST

5 FUEL SYSTEM

1989-91 3.0L/3.3L DIAGNOSTIC CHART—DRIVEABILITY TEST

1989-91 3.0L/3.3L DIAGNOSTIC CHART—DRIVEABILITY TEST

TEST DR-2 | CONTINUED - CHECKING LOCK-UP SOLENOID CIRCUIT

TEST DR-2 | CONTINUED - CHECKING BRAKE SWITCH INPUT CIRCUIT TO ENGINE CONTROLLER

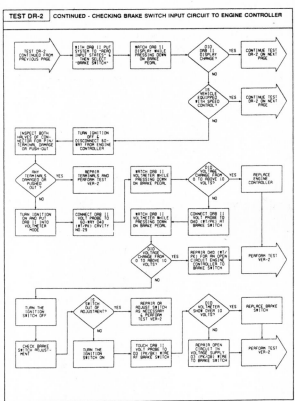

TEST DR-2 | CONTINUED - CHECKING BRAKE SWITCH INPUT CIRCUIT TO ENGINE CONTROLLER

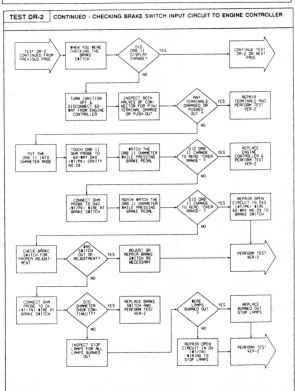

TEST DR-2 | CONTINUED - CHECKING PARK/NEUTRAL SWITCH INPUT TO THE SMEC

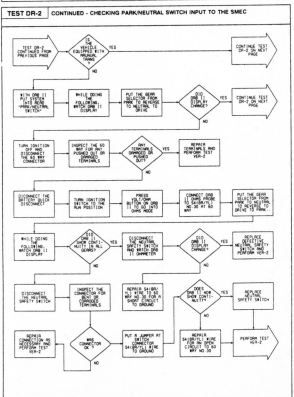

1989-91 3.0L/3.3L DIAGNOSTIC CHART—DRIVEABILITY TEST

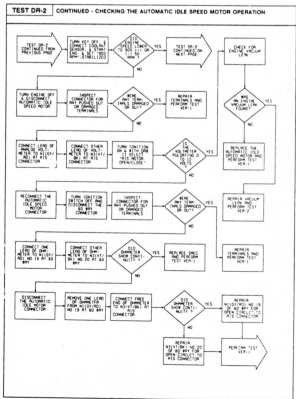

1989-91 3.0L/3.3L DIAGNOSTIC CHART — DRIVEABILITY TEST

5 FUEL SYSTEM

1989-91 3.0L/3.3L DIAGNOSTIC CHART—DRIVEABILITY TEST

1989-91 3.0L/3.3L DIAGNOSTIC CHART — DRIVEABILITY TEST

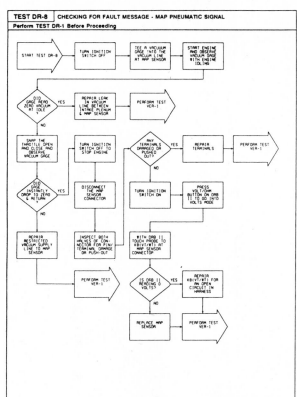

TEST DR-8 | CHECKING FOR FAULT MESSAGE - MAP PNEUMATIC SIGNAL
Perform TEST DR-1 Before Proceeding

TEST DR-9 | CHECKING FOR FAULT MESSAGE - MAP PNEUMATIC CHANGE
Perform TEST DR-1 Before Proceeding

TEST DR-10 | CHECKING FOR FAULT MESSAGE - MAP VOLTAGE LOW
Perform TEST DR-1 Before Proceeding

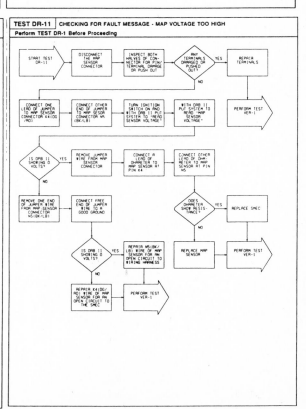

TEST DR-11 | CHECKING FOR FAULT MESSAGE - MAP VOLTAGE TOO HIGH
Perform TEST DR-1 Before Proceeding

1989-91 3.0L/3.3L DIAGNOSTIC CHART—DRIVEABILITY TEST

1989-91 3.0L/3.3L DIAGNOSTIC CHART—DRIVEABILITY TEST

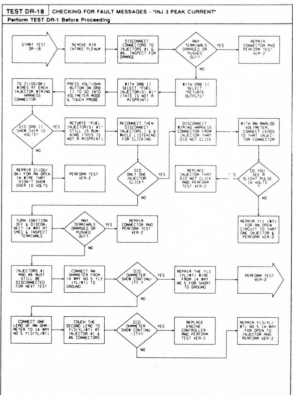

1989-91 3.0L/3.3L DIAGNOSTIC CHART—DRIVEABILITY TEST

1989-91 3.0L/3.3L DIAGNOSTIC CHART — DRIVEABILITY TEST

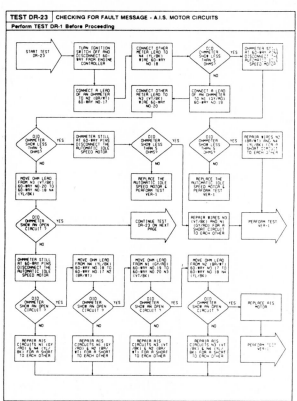

TEST DR-23 | CHECKING FOR FAULT MESSAGE - A.I.S. MOTOR CIRCUITS

Perform TEST DR-1 Before Proceeding

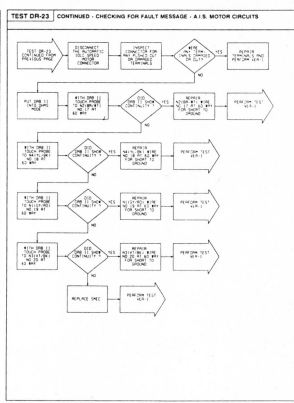

TEST DR-23 | CONTINUED - CHECKING FOR FAULT MESSAGE - A.I.S. MOTOR CIRCUITS

TEST DR-24 | CHECKING FOR FAULT MESSAGE - PURGE SOLENOID CIRCUIT

Perform TEST DR-1 Before Proceeding

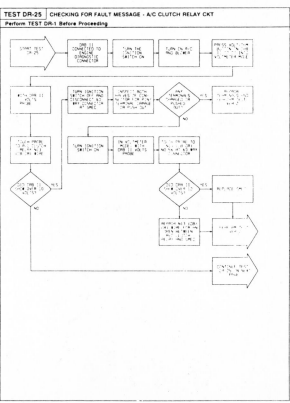

TEST DR-25 | CHECKING FOR FAULT MESSAGE - A/C CLUTCH RELAY CKT

Perform TEST DR-1 Before Proceeding

1989-91 3.0L/3.3L DIAGNOSTIC CHART—DRIVEABILITY TEST

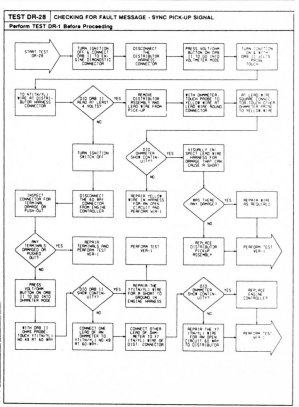

1989-91 3.0L/3.3L DIAGNOSTIC CHART—DRIVEABILITY TEST

5 FUEL SYSTEM

1989-91 3.0L/3.3L DIAGNOSTIC CHART—DRIVEABILITY TEST

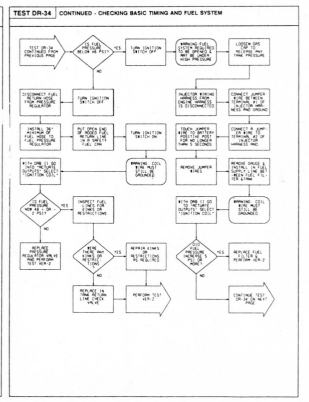

1989-91 3.0L/3.3L DIAGNOSTIC CHART—DRIVEABILITY TEST

1989-91 3.0L/3.3L DIAGNOSTIC CHART—DRIVEABILITY TEST

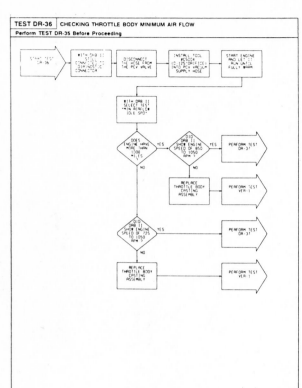

TEST DR-36 CHECKING THROTTLE BODY MINIMUM AIR FLOW
Perform TEST DR-35 Before Proceeding

TEST DR-37 OTHER POSSIBLE CAUSES OF DRIVEABILITY RELATED PROBLEMS
Perform TEST DR-36 Before Proceeding

AT THIS POINT IN THE DRIVEABILITY TEST PROCEDURE YOU HAVE DETERMINED THAT ALL OF THE ENGINE CONTROL SYSTEMS ARE OPERATING AS THEY WERE DESIGNED. THEREFORE, THEY ARE NOT THE CAUSE OF THE DRIVEABILITY PROBLEM.

THE FOLLOWING ADDITIONAL ITEMS SHOULD BE CHECKED AS POSSIBLE CAUSES.

1. ENGINE VACUUM - MUST BE AT LEAST 13 INCHES IN NEUTRAL.
2. ENGINE VALVE TIMING - TO SPECIFICATIONS.
3. ENGINE COMPRESSION - TO SPECIFICATIONS.
4. ENGINE EXHAUST SYSTEM - MUST BE FREE OF ANY RESTRICTIONS
5. ENGINE PCV SYSTEM - MUST FLOW FREELY
6. ENGINE DRIVE SPROCKETS - CAM, CRANK AND INTERMEDIATE SHAFTS
7. TORQUE CONVERTOR STALL SPEED - TO SPECIFICATIONS.
8. POWER BRAKE BOOSTER - NO INTERNAL VACUUM LEAKS.
9. FUEL CONTAMINATION - HIGH ALCOHOL AND WATER CONTENT.
10. FUEL INJECTORS - ROUGH IDLE MAY BE CAUSED BY INJECTOR CONTROL WIRES NOT CONNECTED TO THE CORRECT INJECTOR.

ANY ONE OR MORE OF THESE ITEMS CAN CREATE A DRIVEABILITY RELATED PROBLEM. THEY CAN NOT BE OVERLOOKED AS POSSIBLE CAUSES

VER-1 DRIVEABILITY VERIFICATION

VER-2 DRIVEABILITY VERIFICATION

1989-91 3.0L/3.3L DIAGNOSTIC CHART — SPEED CONTROL SYSTEM TEST

1989-91 3.0L/3.3L DIAGNOSTIC CHART—SPEED CONTROL SYSTEM TEST

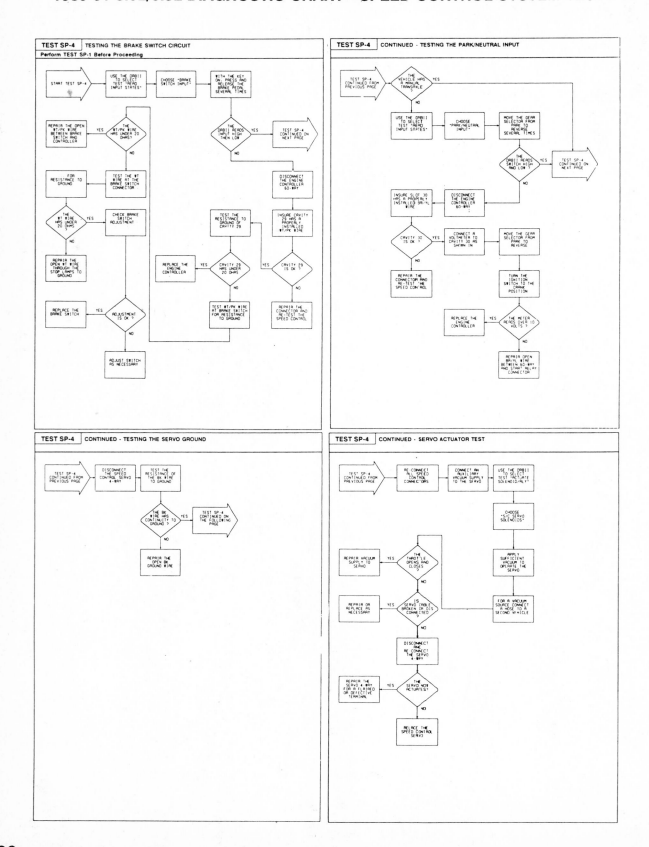

1989-91 3.0L/3.3L DIAGNOSTIC CHART—SPEED CONTROL SYSTEM TEST

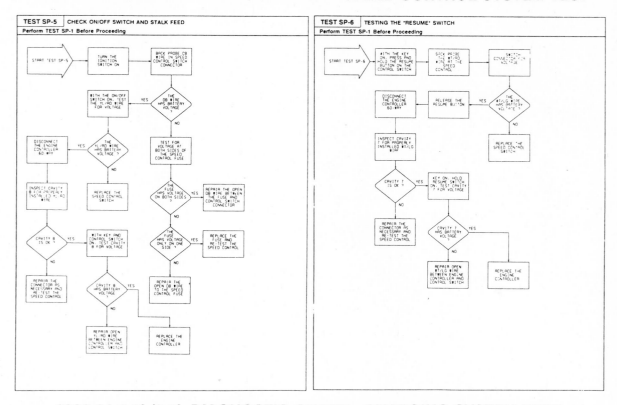

1989-91 3.0L/3.3L DIAGNOSTIC CHART—CHARGING SYSTEM TEST

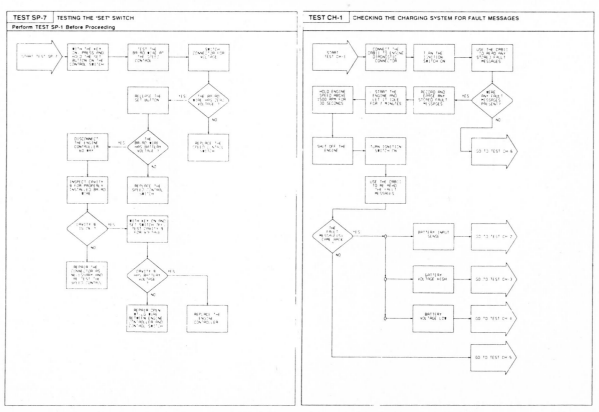

1989-91 3.0L/3.3L DIAGNOSTIC CHART—CHARGING SYSTEM TEST

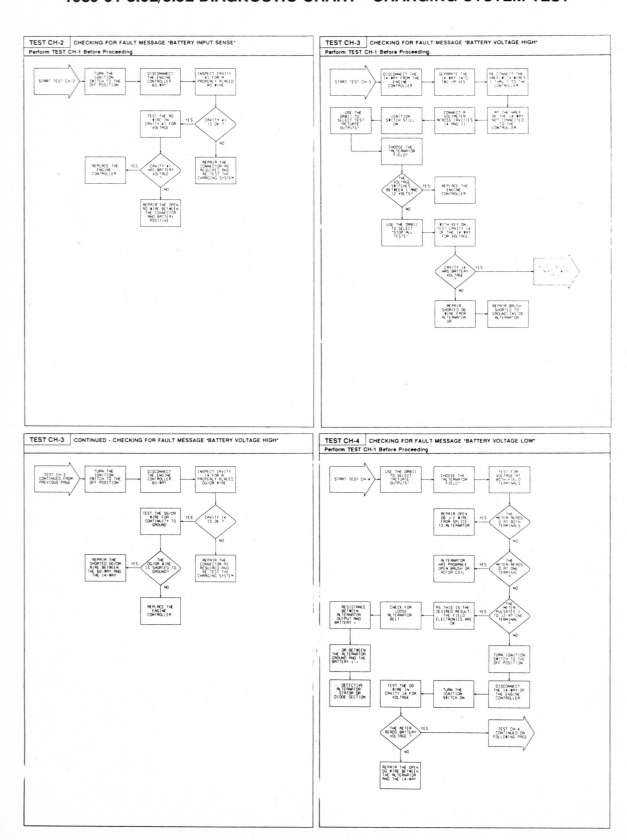

1989-91 3.0L/3.3L DIAGNOSTIC CHART—CHARGING SYSTEM TEST

CONNECTOR PINOUTS

CONNECTOR PINOUTS

ENGINE CONTROLLER
60-WAY CONNECTOR

ENGINE CONTROLLER
14-WAY CONNECTOR

CAV.	COLOR	FUNCTION
*1	N6 OR	8 Volt (Output)
2	K5 BK/WT	Signal Ground
*3	K14 DB/WT	Fused J2 Output
4	J2 DB	Battery Voltage from Ignition Switch
5	Y13 YL/WT	Injector Driver 3
6	J9 BK	Ground
7	J9 BK	Ground
*8	K16 VT/YL	Injector Control 1
9	Y11 WT/DB	Injector Driver 1
10	Y12 TN	Injector Driver 2
*11	R31 DG/OR	Charging System Interface
12	J5 BK/GY	Ignition Coil Driver
*13	K15 YL	Dwell Control
14	R3 DG	Alternator Field Control

* Interconnection through wiring harness between the 60 and 14-way connectors.

CAV.	COLOR	FUNCTION		CAV.	COLOR	FUNCTION
1	K4 DG/RD	Map Sensor		31	DK20 LG	Diagnostic Connector
2				32		
3	K10 TN/WT	Coolant Sensor		*33	K16 VT/YL	Injector Control
4	N5 BK/LB	Sensor Ground		*34	K15 YL	Dwell Control
5	K5 BK/WT	Signal Ground		35		
† 6	MX1 BK/VT	CCD Bus (+)		36		
7	X33 WT/LG	Speed Control Resume		37	G29 GY/PK	EMR Lamp
8	X32 YL/RD	Speed Control On/Off		38		
9	X31 BR/RD	Speed Control Set		39		
10	Z1 DG/BK	ASD Output		40		
11				41	J11 RD	Direct Battery Voltage
*12	K14 DB/WT	Fused J2 (Input)		42		
13	K8 VT/WT	5 Volt Supply to Sensors		43		
*14	R31 DG/OR	Alternator Field Control		44		
15	Y9A LB/RD	Power Ground		45	C20 BR	A/C Clutch Sensing
16	K9B LB/RD	Power Ground		† 46	MX2 WT/BK	CCD Bus (-)
17	N2 BR/WT	Automatic Idle Speed Motor		47	N7 GY/BK	Distributor Reference
18	N4 YL/BK	Automatic Idle Speed Motor		48	G7A WT/OR	Speed Sensor
19	N1 GY/RD	Automatic Idle Speed Motor		49	Y7 TN/YL	Dist. Sync
20	N3 VT/BK	Automatic Idle Speed Motor		50	T1 GY/LB	Tachometer Signal
21				51	DK21 PK	Diagnostic Connector
22	K7 OR/DB	Throttle Position Sensor		*52	N6 OR	8 Volt Input from 14-Way Conn.
23	N11 BK/DG	Oxygen Sensor		53	X36 TN/RD	Speed Control Vacuum Solen.
24				54	K1 PK/BK	Canister Purge Solenoid
25				‡ 55	U3 OR/BK	Part Throttle Unlock Solenoid
26				56	N13 DB/OR	A/C Cutout Relay Control
27				57	C27 DB/PK	Radiator Fan Relay
28				58	K19 DB/YL	Auto Shutdown Relay Control
29	D40 WT/PK	Brake Switch		59	K3 BK/PK	Check Engine Light
30	S4A BR/YL	Park/Neutral Switch		60	X35 LG/RD	Speed Control Vent Solenoid

* Interconnection through wiring harness between the 60 and 14-way connectors.
† With electronic transmission.
‡ Without electronic transmission.

FUEL PRESSURE

Release

ALL ENGINES

──────────── CAUTION ────────────
The fuel injection system is under a constant pressure. Before servicing any part of the fuel system, the system pressure must be relieved.

1. Loosen the fuel filler cap to release the pressure.
2. Remove the wiring harness connector from the injector.
3. Connect a jumper wire to the No. 1 terminal of the injector harness connector and to engine ground.
4. Connect a jumper wire to the positive terminal No. 2 of the injector harness and touch battery positive post for no longer than 5 seconds. This releases system pressure.
5. Remove test equipment and continue fuel system service.

Testing

2.5L TURBO ENGINES

1. Release fuel system pressure.
2. Remove the protective cover from the service valve on the fuel rail.
3. Connect a suitable fuel pressure gauge to fuel rail service valve.
4. Using the DRBII tester, with the key in the **RUN** position, use "Actuate Outputs Test-Auto Shutdown Relay" this will activate the fuel pump for 1.5 seconds to pressurize the system.
5. If the gauge reads 53–57 psi fuel pressure is correct and no further testing is necessary. Remove all test equipment.
6. If pressure is not correct, record the pressure and continue with the test procedure.
7. If the fuel pressure is below specifications, install the fuel pressure gauge in the fuel supply line, between the fuel tank and fuel filter at the rear of the vehicle.
8. Repeat test. If pressure is 5 psi higher than recorded pressure replace the fuel filter. If no change in pressure is observed, gently squeeze the return hose. If the pressure increases replace the pressure regulator. If no change is observed check for a defective fuel pump or plugged filter sock.

NOTE: The test (Step 9) should be performed when fuel tank is a least ½–¾ full.

9. If the fuel pressure is above specifications, remove the fuel return line hose from the chassis line at fuel tank and connect a 3 foot piece of fuel hose to the return line. Position the other end in suitable container (2 gallons or more). Repeat test and, if pressure is now correct, check in-tank return hose for kinking.
10. Replace the fuel tank assembly if the in-tank reservoir check valve or the aspirator jet is blocked.
11. If the pressure is still above specifications, remove fuel return hose from fuel pressure regulator. Connect a suitable hose to the fuel pressure regulator nipple and place the other in a suitable container. Repeat test. If pressure is now correct, check for restricted fuel line. If no change is observed, replace fuel pressure regulator.

3.0L AND 3.3L ENGINE

1. Release fuel system pressure.
2. Disconnect the fuel supply hose from the engine fuel line assembly. Connect a suitable fuel pressure gauge between fuel supply hose and engine fuel line assembly.
3. Using the DRBII tester, with the key in the **RUN** position, use "Actuate Outputs Test-Auto Shutdown Relay" this will activate the fuel pump for 1.5 seconds to pressurize the system.
4. If the gauge reads 46–50 psi fuel pressure is correct and no further testing is necessary. Remove all test equipment.
5. If pressure is not correct, record the pressure and continue with the test procedure.

6. If the fuel pressure is below specifications, install the fuel pressure gauge in the fuel supply line, between the fuel tank and fuel filter at the rear of the vehicle.
7. Repeat test. If pressure is 5 psi higher than recorded pressure replace the fuel filter. If no change in pressure is observed, gently squeeze the return hose. If the pressure increases replace the pressure regulator. If no change is observed check for a defective fuel pump or plugged filter sock.

NOTE: The test (Step 8) should be performed when fuel tank is a least ½–¾ full.

8. If the fuel pressure is above specifications, remove the fuel return line hose from the chassis line at fuel tank and connect a 3 foot piece of fuel hose to the return line. Position the other end in suitable container (2 gallons or more). Repeat test and, if pressure is now correct, check in-tank return hose for kinking.
9. Replace the fuel tank assembly if the in-tank reservoir check valve or the aspirator jet is blocked.
10. If the pressure is still above specifications, remove fuel return hose from fuel pressure regulator. Connect a suitable hose to the fuel return line and place the other end in a suitable container. Repeat the test. If the pressure is now correct, check for restricted fuel line. If no change has occured, replace the fuel pressure regulator.

WASTEGATE CALIBRATION

Check

2.5L Turbo Engines

1. Disconnect the vacuum hose from the wategate diaphragm.
2. Connect a cooling system pressure tester or equivalent to the wastegate diaphragm.
3. Slowly apply pressure while watching the actuator rod.
4. If the wastegate actuator rod moves more than 0.015 inch before 2–4 psi (4 psi on Turbo II) or does not move after 5 psi is applied the wastegate is faulty.
5. Service faulty component as necessary.

Component Replacement

THROTTLE BODY

Removal and Installation

When servicing the fuel portion of the throttle body, it will be necessary to bleed fuel pressure before opening any hoses refer to Fuel Pressure Release procedure. Always reassemble throttle body components with new O-rings and seals where applicable. Use care when removing fuel hoses to prevent damage to hose or hose nipple. Always use new hose clamps of the correct type when reassembling and torque hose clamps to 10 inch lbs. (1 Nm).

1. Drain engine coolant, if necessary, and release fuel pressure. Disconnect negative battery cable.
2. Remove air cleaner to throttle body screws (or nuts), loosen hose clamp and remove air cleaner adaptor.

NOTE: When removing accelerator cable, note position or adjustment for correct installation.

3. Remove accelerator, speed control and transaxle kickdown cables and return spring.
4. Remove throttle cable bracket from throttle body.
5. Disconnect all necessary electrical connector(s).
6. Disconnect vacuum hoses from throttle body.
7. Loosen throttle body-to-turbocharger hose clamp if so equipped.

8. Remove throttle body-to-intake manifold or adapter screws (or nuts). Always note position of retaining bolts as some may be different in length.

9. Remove throttle body and gasket.

10. Reverse the above procedure for installation.

NOTE: If fuel system hoses are to be replaced, only hoses marked EFI/EFM may be used.

THROTTLE POSITION SENSOR

Removal and Installation

1. Disconnect negative battery cable and 3-way throttle position sensor wiring connector.

2. Remove 2 screws, mounting throttle position sensor to throttle body.

3. Lift throttle position sensor off throttle shaft.

4. To install, reverse removal procedure and torque screws to 17 inch lbs. (2 Nm).

AUTOMATIC IDLE SPEED (AIS) MOTOR

Removal and Installation

1. Disconnect negative battery cable and 4-way AIS motor wiring connector.

2. Remove 2 screws that mount AIS motor to throttle body.

Automatic Idle Speed (AIS) motor servicing — 2.5L turbo engine

Automatic Idle Speed (AIS) motor servicing — 3.0L/3.3L engine

Throttle position sensor servicing — 3.0L/3.3L engines

Throttle position sensor servicing — 2.5L turbo engine

3. Remove AIS motor from throttle body. Make certain that the O-ring is on the AIS motor.

4. To install, place new O-ring on AIS motor. If pintle measures more than 1 inch, it must be retracted by using the AIS Motor Test in the Actuate Outputs mode of the DRBII. (Battery must be reconnected for this operation.)

5. Carefully place AIS motor into throttle body.

6. Install 2 mounting screws and torque to 17 inch lbs. (2 Nm).

7. Connect 4 way wiring connector to AIS motor and reconnect negative battery cable.

FUEL INJECTOR RAIL ASSEMBLY

Removal and Installation

2.5L TURBO ENGINES

1. Perform fuel system pressure release procedure.

2. Disconnect negative battery cable.

3. Remove air cleaner assembly.

4. Disconnect detonation (knock) sensor and fuel injector wiring connectors.

5. Loosen fuel supply hose clamp at fuel rail inlet and remove hose. Wrap a shop towel around hose to absorb any fuel spillage which may occur when removing.

6. Loosen fuel return hose clamp at the fuel pressure regula-

tor and remove the hose. Wrap a shop towel around the hose to absorb any fuel spillage, which may occur when removing the hose.

7. Disconnect the vacuum hose from the fuel pressure regulator.

8. Remove the fuel pressure regulator mounting bolts from the fuel rail.

9. Remove the fuel pressure regulator from the fuel rail.

10. Remove the PCV vacuum harness and vacuum vapor harness from the intake manifold.

11. Remove the fuel rail to the valve cover bracket screw. Remove the knock sensor connector from the sensor.

12. Remove the fuel rail to intake manifold mounting bolts.

13. Remove fuel rail and injector assembly by pulling rail so that injectors come straight out of there ports.

14. Be careful not to damage rubber injector O-ring upon removal from ports.

15. Remove fuel rail assembly from vehicle.

16. Do not remove fuel injectors until fuel rail assembly has been completely removed from vehicle.

To install:

17. To install, be sure injectors are seated into receiver cup, with lock ring in place.

18. Install injector wiring harness to injectors and fasten into wiring clips.

19. Make sure injector holes are clean and all plugs have been removed.

20. Lube injector O-ring with a drop of clean engine oil to ease installation.

21. Put tip of each injector into respective ports. Push assembly into place until injectors are seated in ports.

22. Install attaching bolts and ground eyelet. Torque bolts to 250 inch lbs. (28 Nm).

23. Connect detonation (knock) sensor wire connector to sensor. Install fuel rail to valve cover bracket screw.

24. Lube fuel pressure O-ring with a drop of clean engine oil and install into receiver cup on fuel rail.

25. Install attaching nuts and torque to 65 inch lbs. (7 Nm).

26. Install the PCV system hose harness and vacuum hose harness.

27. Reconnect vacuum hose from fuel pressure regulator.

28. Connect fuel return hose to fuel pressure regulator tighten hose clamp.

29. Connect fuel supply hose to fuel rail inlet and tighten hose clamp.

30. Connect fuel injector and detonation (knock) sensor wiring connector.

31. Install air cleaner assembly.

32. Connect negative battery cable.

33. Use ATM tester to test for leaks.

3.0L ENGINE

1. Perform fuel system pressure release procedure.

2. Disconnect negative battery cable.

3. Remove air cleaner to throttle body hose.

4. Remove throttle cable and transaxle kickdown linkage.

5. Remove Automatic Idle Speed (AIS) motor and Throttle Position Sensor (TPS) wiring connectors from throttle body.

6. Remove vacuum hose harness from throttle body.

7. Remove PCV and brake booster hoses from air intake plenum.

8. If equipped, remove EGR tube flange from intake plenum.

9. Remove wiring connectors from charge temperature sensor and coolant temperature sensor.

10. Remove vacuum connections from air intake plenum vacuum connector.

11. Remove fuel hoses from fuel rail. Wrap a shop towel around hose to absorb any fuel spillage which may occur when removing.

12. Remove fasteners from air intake plenum to intake manifold.

Removing the air intake plenum — 3.0L engine

Fuel rail assembly — 3.0L engine

Fuel rail assembly — 3.3L engine

13. Remove air intake plenum.

14. Cover intake manifold with suitable cover when servicing.

15. Remove vacuum hoses from fuel rail and fuel pressure regulator.

16. Disconnect fuel injector wiring harness from engine wiring harness.

17. Remove the fuel pressure regulator attaching bolts. Loosen the hose clamps and remove the fuel pressure regulator from the fuel rail.
18. Remove the fuel rail attaching bolts and lift the fuel rail from the intake manifold.
19. Be careful not to damage the injector ports when removing.
20. Remove the fuel rail assembly from the vehicle.
21. Do not remove the injectors until the fuel rail has been completely removed from the vehicle.

To install:

22. Make sure the injectors are completely seated with the lockring in place.
23. Make sure the injector holes are clean and that all plugs have been removed.
24. Lube injector O-ring with a drop of clean engine oil to ease installation.
25. Put tip of each injector into respective ports. Push assembly into place until injectors are seated in ports.
26. Install fuel rail attaching bolts. Torque bolts to 115 inch lbs. (13 Nm).
27. Install fuel pressure regulator and hose assembly onto fuel rail. Install attaching bolts to intake manifold. Torque to 77 inch lbs. (8.7 Nm).
28. Install fuel supply and return tube hold-down bolt and vacuum crossover tube hold-down bolt. Torque to 95 inch lbs. (10 Nm).
29. Tighten fuel pressure regulator hose clamps.
30. Connect fuel injector wiring harness to engine wiring harness.
31. Connect vacuum harness to fuel pressure regulator and fuel rail assembly.
32. Remove covering from lower intake manifold and clean surface.
33. Place intake manifold gaskets, with beaded sealer up, on lower manifold. Put air intake in place. Install attaching fasteners and torque to 115 inch lbs. (13 Nm).
34. Connect fuel line to fuel rail and tighten.
35. Connect vacuum harness to air intake plenum.
36. Connect charge temperature sensor and coolant temperature sensor electrical connectors to sensors.
37. If equipped, connect EGR tube flange to intake plenum and torque to 200 inch lbs. (22 Nm).
38. Connect PCV and brake booster supply hose to intake plenum.
39. Connect Automatic Idle Speed (AIS) motor and Throttle Position Sensor (TPS) electrical connectors.
40. Connect vacuum vapor harness to throttle body.
41. Install throttle cable and transaxle kickdown linkage.
42. Install air inlet hose assembly.
43. Connect negative battery cable.
44. Use ATM tester to test for leaks.

3.3L ENGINE

1. Relieve the fuel pressure.
2. Disconnect the negative battery cable.
3. Remove the air cleaner and hose assembly.
4. Disconnect the throttle cable. Remove the wiring harness from the throttle cable bracket and intake manifold water tube.
5. Remove the vacuum hose harness from the throttle body.
6. Remove the PCV and brake booster hoses from the air intake plenum.
7. Remove the EGR tube flange from the intake plenum, if equipped.
8. Unplug the charge temperature sensor and unplug all vacuum hoses from the intake plenum.
9. Remove the cylinder head to intake plenum strut.
10. Disconnect the MAP sensor and oxygen sensor connector. Remove the engine mounted ground strap.

11. Release the fuel hose quick disconnect fittings and remove the hoses from the fuel rail. Plug the hoses.
12. Remove the Direct Ignition System (DIS) coils and the alternator bracket to intake manifold bolt.
13. Remove the intake manifold bolts and rotate the manifold back over the rear valve cover. Cover the intake manifold.
14. Remove the vacuum harness from the pressure regulator.
15. Remove the fuel tube retainer bracket screw and the fuel rail attaching bolts. Spread the retainer bracket to allow for clearance when removing the fuel tube.
16. Remove the fuel rail injector wiring clip from the alternator bracket.
17. Disconnect the camshaft sensor, coolant temperature sensor and engine temperature sensor.
18. Remove the fuel rail.
19. Position the fuel rail on a work bench, so that the injectors are easy to get at.
20. Remove the small connector retaining clip and unplug the injector. Remove the injector clip from the fuel rail and injector. Pull the injector straight off of the rail.

To install:

21. Lubricate the rubber O-ring with clean oil and install to the rail receiver cap. Install the injector clip to the slot in the injector, plug in the connector and install the connector clip.
22. Install the fuel rail.
23. Connect the cam sensor, coolant temperature sensor and engine temperature sensor.
24. Install the fuel rail injector wiring clip to the alternator bracket.
25. Install the fuel rail attaching bolts and fuel tube retainer bracket screw.
26. Install the vacuum harness to the pressure regulator.
27. Install the intake manifold with a new gasket. Install the bolts only fingertight. Install the alternator bracket to intake manifold bolt and the cylinder head to intake manifold strut and bolts. Torque the intake manifold mounting bolts to 21 ft. lbs. (28 Nm) starting from the middle and working outward. Torque the bracket and strut bolts to 40 ft. lbs. (54 Nm).
28. Install or connect all items that were removed or disconnected from the intake manifold and throttle body.
29. Connect the fuel hoses to the rail. Push the fittings in until they click in place.
30. Install the air cleaner assembly.
31. Connect the negative battery cable and check for leaks using the DRB I or II to activate the fuel pump.

FUEL INJECTOR

Removal and Installation

1. Remove fuel rail.
2. Disconnect injector wiring connector from injector.
3. Position fuel rail assembly so that fuel injectors are easily accessible.
4. Remove injector clip off fuel rail and injector. Pull injector straight out of fuel rail receiver cup.
5. Check injector O-ring for damage. If O-ring is damaged, it must be replaced. If injector is to be reused, a protective cap must be installed on injector tip to prevent damage while injector is out for service.
6. Repeat for remaining injectors.
7. Before installing an injector, the rubber O-ring must be lubricated with a drop of clean engine oil to aid in installation.
8. Install injector top end into fuel rail receiver cup. Be careful not to damage O-ring during installation.
9. Install injector clip by sliding open end into top slot of injector and onto receiver cup ridge into side slots of clip.
10. Repeat steps for remaining injectors.

FUEL PRESSURE REGULATOR

Removal and Installation

1. Perform fuel system pressure release procedure.
2. Disconnect negative battery cable.
3. Remove vacuum hose from fuel pressure regulator.
4. Loosen fuel supply hose clamp at fuel rail inlet and remove hose. Wrap a shop towel around hose to absorb any fuel spillage which may occur when removing hose.
5. Loosen fuel return hose clamp at fuel pressure regulator and remove hose. Wrap a shop towel around hose to absorb any fuel spillage which may occur when removing hose.
6. Remove the fuel pressure regulator attaching nuts. Remove the fuel pressure regulator from the fuel rail.

To install:

7. Lubricate the O-ring for the fuel pressure regulator with a drop of clean engine oil and install it into the receiver cup, on the fuel rail.
8. Install the attaching nuts and torque to 65 inch lbs. (7 Nm).
9. Connect the fuel return hose to the pressure regulator.
10. Connect the fuel supply hose to the fuel rail.
11. Install the vacuum hose to the pressure regulator.
12. Connect the negative battery cable. Using the DRBII tester or equivalent, use the Actuate Outputs Test-Auto Shutdown Relay to pressurize the system and check for leaks.

FUEL PRESSURE DAMPENER

Removal and Installation

1. Perform fuel system pressure release procedure.
2. Remove PCV system hose assembly from intake manifold and valve cover.
3. Place a shop towel under fuel pressure dampener to absorb any fuel spillage.
4. Using 2 open end wrenches, 1 on the flats of fuel rail and the other on fuel pressure dampener. Remove fuel pressure dampener and copper washer.
5. To install, place a new copper washer on fuel rail and install fuel pressure dampener torque to 30 ft. lbs. (41 Nm) using a wrench to hold fuel rail while tightening fuel pressure dampener.
6. Connect fuel injector wiring harness reinstall PCV system hose assembly.
7. Using the DRBII tester use the Actuate Outputs Test—Auto Shutdown Relay to pressurize system to check for leaks.

SINGLE MODULE ENGINE CONTROLLER (SMEC)

Removal And Installation

1. Remove the air cleaner duct from the SMEC.
2. Remove the battery.
3. Remove 2 module mounting screws. Remove the 14 and 60 way wiring connectors from the module and remove the module.
4. Reverse the above procedure for installation.

HEATED OXYGEN SENSOR

Removal and Installation

Removing the oxygen sensor from the exhaust manifold may be difficult if the sensor was overtorqued during installation. Use tool C–4907 or equivalent, to remove the sensor. The

Fuel Injector installation — 2.5L turbo engine

Fuel pressure regulator installation — 2.5L turbo engine

Fuel injector dampener — servicing

threads in the exhaust manifold must be cleaned with an 18mm × 1.5 × 6E tap. If the same sensor is to be reinstalled, the threads must be coated with an anti-seize compound such as Loctite® 771–64 or equivalent. New sensors are packaged with anti-seize compound on the threads and no additional compound is required. Sensors must be torqued to 20 ft. lbs. (27 Nm).

CHRYSLER SINGLE POINT FUEL INJECTION SYSTEM

General Information

The electronic fuel injection system is a computer regulated single point fuel injection system that provides precise air/fuel ratio for all driving conditions. At the center of this system is a digital pre-programmed computer known as a Single Module Engine Controller (SMEC) that regulates ignition timing, air/fuel ratio, emission control devices, idle speed and cooling fan and charging system. This component has the ability to update and revise its programming to meet changing operating conditions.

Various sensors provide the input necessary for the SMEC to correctly regulate the fuel flow at the fuel injector. These include the manifold absolute pressure, throttle position, oxygen sensor, coolant temperature, vehicle speed (distance) sensors and throttle body temperature. In addition to the sensors, various switches also provide important information. These include the neutral-safety switch, air conditioning clutch relay, and auto shut-down relay.

All inputs to the SMEC are converted into signals which are used by the computer. Based on these inputs, air-fuel ratio, ignition timing or other controlled outputs are adjusted accordingly.

The SMEC tests many of its own input and output circuits. If a fault is found in a major system this information is stored in the memory. Information on this fault can be displayed to a technician by means of the instrument panel check engine light or by connecting a diagnostic read out and reading a numbered display code which directly relates to a specific fault.

COMPONENTS AND OPERATION

Single Module Engine Controller (SMEC)

The SMEC contains the circuits necessary to drive the ignition coil, fuel injector, and the alternator field. The SMEC is digital computer containing a microprocessor. The module receives input signals from various switches and sensors. These are high current devices and have been isolated to minimize any electrical noise in the passenger compartment.

The Automatic Shut Down (ASD) relay is mounted externally, but is turned on and off by the SMEC. Distributor pick-up signal goes to the SMEC. In the event of no distributor signal, the ASD relay is not activated and power is shut off from the fuel injector and ignition coil. The SMEC contains a voltage convertor which converts battery voltage to a regulated 9.0 volt output. This 9.0 volt output powers the distributor pick-up. The internal 5 volt supply which, in turn, powers the MAP sensor and TPS.

The SMEC is a digital computer containing a microprocessor. The module receives input signals from various switches and sensors. It then computes the fuel injector pulse width, spark advance, ignition coil dwell, idle speed, purge and cooling fan turn on and alternator charge rate.

The SMEC tests many of its input and output circuits. If a fault is found in a major system, this information is stored in the SMEC. Information on this fault can be displayed to a technician by means of the instrument panel check engine light or by connecting the diagnostic read out tool and reading a numbered display code which directly relates to a general fault.

Manifold Absolute Pressure (MAP) Sensor

The manifold absolute pressure (MAP) sensor is a device which monitors manifold vacuum. It is connected to a vacuum nipple on the throttle body and electrically to the SMEC. The sensor transmits information on manifold vacuum conditions and barometric pressure to the SMEC. The MAP sensor data on

engine load is used with data from other sensors to determine the correct air/fuel mixture. It is located as follows:

All Pre 1989 Models—Mounted under hood on the dash panel

All 1989 and later Models—Mounted under hood on the shock tower

Heated Oxygen Sensor (O2 Sensor)

The oxygen sensor (O2 sensor) is a device which produces an electrical voltage when exposed to the oxygen present in the exhaust gases. The sensor is mounted in the exhaust manifold and is electrically heated internally for faster switching when the engine is running. When there is a large amount of oxygen present (lean mixture), the sensor produces a low voltage. When there is a lesser amount present (rich mixture) it produces a higher voltage. By monitoring the oxygen content and converting it to electrical voltage, the sensor acts as a rich-lean switch. The voltage is transmitted to the SMEC which changes the fuel injector's pulse width. The injector changes the mixture.

Coolant temperature sensor location — Single Point fuel injection

Fuel injector cutaway view — Single Point fuel injection

Fuel pressure regulator — Single Point fuel injection

Coolant Temperature Sensor

The coolant temperature sensor is a device that monitors coolant temperature (which is the same as engine operating temperature). It is mounted in the thermostat housing. This sensor provides data on engine operating temperature to the SMEC. This allows the SMEC to demand slightly richer air/fuel mixtures and higher idle speeds until normal operating temperatures are reached. This sensor is also used for cooling fan control.

Switch Input

Various switches provide information to the SMEC. These include the neutral safety, air conditioning clutch, speed control and brake light switches. If one or more of these switches is sensed as being in the **ON** position, the SMEC signals the automatic idle speed motor to increase idle speed to a scheduled rpm.

Check Engine Light

The light comes on each time the ignition key is turned **ON** and stays on for a few seconds as a bulb test. If the SMEC receives an incorrect signal or no signal from certain sensors, or emission related systems (California vehicles only) the light on the instrument panel is illuminated. This is a warning that the

Throttle body assembly — Single Point fuel injection

SMEC has gone into limp-in mode in an attempt to keep the system operating. It signals an immediate need for service.

The light can also be used to display fault codes. Cycle the ignition switch **ON, OFF, ON, OFF, ON,** within 5 seconds and any fault code stored in the memory will be displayed.

Canister Purge Solenoid

The purge solenoid is controlled by the SMEC. During warm-up and for a specified time period after hot starts, the SMEC grounds the purge solenoid causing it to energized. This prevents vacuum from reaching the charcoal canister valve. When the engine reaches a specified operating temperature and the time delay interval has occurred, the solenoid is de energized by turning off the ground. Once this occurs vacuum will flow to the canister purge valve and purge fuel vapors through the throttle body. The purge solenoid will also be energized during certain idle conditions. This is to update the fuel delivery calibration.

Air Conditioning Cutout Relay

The air conditioning cutout relay is connected, in series, electrically with the A/C damped pressure switch, the A/C switch and, on some models, the A/C fan relay. This relay is in the energized, closed (on), position during engine operation. When the module senses low idle speeds and wide open throttle through the throttle position sensor, it will de energize the relay, open its contacts and prevent air conditioning clutch engagement.

Throttle Body

The throttle body assembly replaces a conventional carburetor and is mounted on top of the intake manifold. The throttle body houses the fuel injector(s), pressure regulator, throttle position sensor, automatic idle speed motor and throttle body temperature sensor. Air flow through the throttle body is controlled by a cable operated throttle blade located in the base of the throttle body. The throttle body itself provides the chamber for metering atomizing and distributing fuel throughout the air entering the engine.

Fuel Injector(s)

The fuel injector(s) is an electric solenoid driven by the SMEC. The SMEC, based on sensor inputs, determines when and how long the fuel injector(s) should operate. When an electric current is supplied to the injector, a spring loaded ball is lifted from it's seat. This allows fuel to flow through 6 spray orifices and deflects off the sharp edge of the injector nozzle. This action causes the fuel to form a 45 degree cone shaped spray pattern before entering the air stream in the throttle body.

Fuel is supplied to the injector constantly at regulated 14.5 psi; the unused fuel is returned to the fuel tank.

Fuel Pressure Regulator

The pressure regulator is a mechanical device located downstream of the fuel injector on the throttle body. Its function is to maintain a constant 14.5 psi (100 kPa) across the fuel injector tip. The regulator uses a spring loaded rubber diaphragm to uncover a fuel return port. When the fuel pump becomes operational, fuel flows past the injector into the regulator, and is restricted from flowing any further by the blocked return port. When fuel pressure reaches the predetermined setting, it pushes on the diaphragm, compressing the spring, and uncovers the fuel return port. The diaphragm and spring will constantly move from an open to closed position to keep the fuel pressure constant.

Throttle Position Sensor (TPS)

The Throttle Position Sensor (TPS) is an electric resistor which is activated by the movement of the throttle shaft. It is mounted on the throttle body and senses the angle of the throttle blade opening. The voltage that the sensor produces increases or decreases according to the throttle blade opening. This voltage is transmitted to the SMEC, where it is used along with data from other sensors to adjust the air/fuel ratio to varying conditions and during acceleration, deceleration, idle, and wide open throttle operations.

Automatic Idle Speed (AIS) Motor

The Automatic Idle Speed (AIS) motor is operated by the SMEC. Data from the throttle position sensor, speed sensor, coolant temperature sensor, and various switch operations, (safety/neutral, brake) are used by the module to adjust engine idle to an optimum during all idle conditions. The AIS adjusts the air portion of the air/fuel mixture through an air bypass on the back of the throttle body. Basic (no load) idle is determined by the minimum air flow through the throttle body. The AIS opens or closes off the air bypass as an increase or decrease is needed due to engine loads or ambient conditions. The module senses an air/fuel change and increases or decreases fuel proportionally to change engine idle. Deceleration die out is also prevented by increasing engine idle when the throttle is closed quickly after a driving (speed) condition.

Throttle Body Temperature Sensor

The throttle body temperature sensor is a device that monitors throttle body temperature which is the same as fuel temperature. It is mounted in the throttle body. This sensor provides information on fuel temperature which allows the SMEC, to provide the correct air/fuel mixture for a hot restart condition.

Fuel Pump

The fuel pump used in this system is a positive displacement, roller vane immersible pump with a permanent magnet electric motor. The fuel is drawn in through a filter sock and pushed through the electric motor to the outlet. The pump contains 2 check valves. One valve is used to relieve internal fuel pump pressure and regulate maximum pump output. The other check valve, located near the pump outlet, restricts fuel movement in either direction when the pump is not operational. Voltage to operate the pump is supplied through the Auto Shutdown relay (ASD).

SERVICE PRECAUTIONS

When working around any part of the fuel system, take precautionary steps to prevent possible fire and/or explosion:
- Disconnect the negative battery terminal, except when testing with battery voltage is required.
- Whenever possible, use a flashlight instead of a drop light to inspect fuel system components or connections.
- Keep all open flames and smoking material out of the area and make sure there is adequate ventilation to remove fuel vapors.
- Use a clean shop cloth to catch fuel when opening a fuel system. Dispose of gasoline-soaked rags properly.
- Relieve the fuel system pressure before any service procedures are attempted that require disconnecting a fuel line.
- Use eye protection.
- Always keep a dry chemical (class B) fire extinguisher near the area.

Diagnosis and Testing

NOTE: Mechanical malfunctions are more difficult to diagnose with the EFI system. The SMEC has been programmed to compensate for some mechanical malfunctions such as incorrect cam timing, vacuum leaks, etc. If

engine performance problems are encountered, and no fault codes are displayed, the problem may be mechanical rather than electronic.

VISUAL INSPECTION

A visual inspection for loose, disconnected or misrouted wires and hoses should be made before attempting to diagnose or service the fuel injection system. A visual check will help spot these faults and save unnecessary test and diagnostic time. A thorough visual inspection will include the following checks:
1. Check that vacuum connections on rear and/or front of throttle body are secure and not leaking.
2. Check that vacuum connection(s) at EGR and/or purge solenoid is secure and not leaking.
3. Check that hoses are securely attached to vapor canister.
4. Check that hose from PCV valve is securely attached to the intake manifold vacuum port.
5. Check that hoses are attached to back pressure transducer.
6. Check that alternator wiring and belt are correctly installed and tight.
7. Check that heated air door vacuum connection is connected and not leaking.
8. Check vacuum connections at MAP sensor.
9. Check that hose and wiring connections at the fuel pump are tight and wires are making contact with the terminals on pump.
10. Check power brake and speed control vacuum connections are tight.
11. Check that the following electrical connections are clean, tight and have good contact:
   a. Connectors to the Single Module Engine Controller (SMEC)
   b. Connector at EGR solenoid and/or purge solenoid
   c. Connector at speed (distance) sensor
   d. Connector at cooling fan relay
   e. Connector to oxygen sensor
   f. Connector at fuel injector(s)
   g. Connector at automatic idle speed (AIS) and throttle position sensor (TPS)
   h. Connector at coolant temperature sensor
   i. Connector at throttle body temperature sensor
   j. Connector to distributor
   k. Connectors for engine-to-main harness
   l. Connectors for all relays
   m. Connector to neutral safety switch (automatic only)
   n. All ignition cables are in order and seated
   o. Ground straps to engine and dash panel
   p. Connection to battery

ON-BOARD DIAGNOSTICS

The SMEC has been programmed to monitor several different circuits of the fuel injection system. This monitoring is called On-Board Diagnosis. If a problem is sensed with a monitored circuit, often enough to indicate an actual problem, its fault code is stored in the module for eventual display to the service technician. If the problem is repaired or ceases to exist, the SMEC cancels the fault code after 50–100 ignition key **ON/OFF** cycles.

Fault Codes

Fault codes are 2 digit numbers that identify the suspected circuit. In most cases, they do not identify which component is bad in a circuit. When a fault code appears, either by flashes of the check engine light or by watching the diagnostic read out tool, it indicates that the SMEC has recognized an abnormal signal in the system. Fault codes indicate the results of a failure but do not always identify the failed component directly.

Chrysler Diagnostic Readout Box II

Accessing Trouble Code Memory

There are 2 methods used in accessing trouble codes. The first method is the use of a diagnostic readout box tool, the second method is observing the check engine light.

The diagnostic readout box is used to put the system into a Diagnostic Test Mode, Circuit Actuation Test Mode, Switch Test Mode, Engine Running Test Mode and, Sensor Test Mode. Four of these modes of testing are called for at certain points of the driveability test procedure. A fifth test mode is available with the engine running. The following is a description of each test mode:
• Diagnostic Test Mode—This mode is used to see is there are any fault codes stored in the on-board diagnostic system memory.
• Circuit Actuation Test Mode (ATM Test)—This mode is used to turn a specific circuit on and off in order to check it. ATM test codes are used in this mode.
• Switch Test Mode—This mode is used to determine if specific switch inputs are being received by the SMEC.
• Sensor Test Mode—This mode is used to see the output signals of certain sensors as received by the SMEC.
  Engine Running Test Mode—This mode is used to determine if the oxygen feedback system is switching from rich to lean and lean to rich.

DIAGNOSIS USING READOUT BOX

The diagnostic readout box is used to put the on-board diagnostic system in 4 different modes of testing as called for in the driveability test procedure.
1. Connect the diagnostic tool to the diagnostic connector located in the engine compartment near the SMEC.
2. Start the engine (if possible), cycle the transmission selector and the A/C switch (if equipped). Turn the ignition switch **OFF**.
3. Turn the ignition switch **ON-OFF-ON-OFF-ON** within 5 seconds.
4. Record all codes.

DIAGNOSIS USING CHECK ENGINE LIGHT

If for some reason the diagnostic readout box is not available, the SMEC can show fault codes by means of flashing the CHECK ENGINE light on the instrument panel.

To activate this function, turn the ignition key **ON-OFF-ON-OFF-ON** within 5 seconds. The CHECK ENGINE light will then come on for 2 seconds as a bulb check. Immediately following this it will display a fault code by flashing on and off. There is a short pause between flashes and a longer pause between digits. All codes displayed are 2 digit numbers with a 4 second pause between codes.

1. Light on for 2 seconds, then turns off.
2. Light flashes 5 pauses and then flashes once.
3. Light pauses for 4 seconds, flashes 5 times, pauses and then flashes 5 times.

The 2 codes are 51 and 55. Any number of codes can be displayed as long as they are in memory. The lamp will flash until all of them are displayed.

NOTE: In some cases, proper diagnostic cannot be determined by only using fault codes. Remember, they are only the result, not necessarily the reason for the problem. This driveability test procedure is designed for use with the Diagnostic Readout Box not the flashing CHECK ENGINE light.

Additional Information From CHECK ENGINE Light

Switch Test—After all codes are displayed, switch function can be verified. The light will turn on or off when a switch is turned **ON** or **OFF**.

Unlike the diagnostic readout box, the CHECK ENGINE light cannot do the following:

a. Once the light begins to display fault codes, it can not be stopped. If code count is forgotten or lost, it is necessary to start over.

b. The light can not display any codes related to 88 diagnostic or blank displays.

c. The light can not show if the oxygen feedback system is switching (lean/rich).

d. The light can not perform the actuation test, sensor read test or engine running test modes.

DIAGNOSTIC PROCEDURE CHARTS

When using the Test Procedure, some guidelines should be followed:

1. Start from the first test of the category. Starting from any other test will give incorrect results.

2. Tests are made up of many steps. Only perform the steps which are required. Performing all steps will give incorrect results.

3. Some steps within a test have reminders. These are to inform that previous instructions are still required.

4. At the end of each test, reconnect all wires and hoses, turn engine off, if required, and reinstall any components that were removed for testing.

5. The vehicle being tested must have a fully charged battery, specific gravity 1.220 temperature corrected.

6. To perform the cold test, the engine must not be started for at least 7 hours.

7. To perform the warm test, the engine must be at normal operating temperature.

TOOLS AND EQUIPMENT

Make sure the following equipment is on hand:
1. Volt/ohm meter
2. Jumper wires
3. Auxiliary vacuum supply (hand-held vacuum pump)
4. Fuel pressure gauge
5. Tachometer
6. Timing light
7. Oscilloscope
8. Vacuum gauge
9. High pressure gauge (Tool C–3292 or equivalent)
10. High pressure gauge adapter hoses (Tool C–4799 or equivalent)
11. Two gallon gasoline can
12. Diagnostic readout box (Tool C–4805 or equivalent)

1987–88 2.5L DIAGNOSTIC TROUBLE CODE CHART

Code	Type	Check Engine Lamp	Circuit	When Monitored By The SMEC	When Put Into Memory	ATM Test Code	Sensor Access Code	Engine Running Test Code
11	Fault	No	Distributor Pickup Signal	Only during cranking	If no distributor pickup signal is present since the single module engine controller (SMEC) memory was cleared	None	None	None
12	Indication	No	Battery Feed to the Single Module Engine Controller (SMEC)	All the time when the ignition switch is on	If the memory of the single module engine controller (SMEC) has been cleared within the last 50-100 engine starts	None	None	None
13	Fault	Yes	M.A.P. Sensor (Vacuum)	During engine running between 800 and 1,500 rpm and M.A.P. signal is within electrical range	If no variance in the M.A.P. signal is detected between ignition pulses	None	None	64
14	Fault	Yes	M.A.P. Sensor (Electrical)	At engine speeds between 400 and 1,500 rpm	If the M.A.P. sensor signal is below .02 or above 4.7 volts	None	06	None
15	Fault	Yes	Vehicle Speed Sensor	At engine speeds greater than 1,800 rpm and vehicle speeds less than 10 inches	If no speed sensor signal is detected over an 13 second period	None	None	11
16	Fault	Yes	Battery voltage Sensing (Charging System)	All the time after one minute from when the engine starts	If the battery sensing voltage drops below 4 volts for more than 14 seconds	None	07	67
17	Fault	No	Engine Cooling System	After 12 minutes from when the engine starts	If engine coolant temperature does not reach 174°F within 8 minutes of vehicle speeds greater than 28 mph	None	None	None
21	Fault	Yes	Oxygen Sensor	Engine temperature above 170°F and engine rpm above 1,500	If no lean or rich condition is indicated for a 2 minute time period	None	02	62
22	Fault	Yes	Engine Coolant Sensor	All the time when the ignition switch is on	If the coolant sensor voltage is above 4.96 volts when the engine is cold or below .51 volts when the engine is warm	None	04	64
23	Fault	No	Throttle Body Temperature Sensor	During cranking	If the throttle body temperature sensor voltage is below .51 or above 4.96 when engine coolant temperature is above 77°F	None	03	63
24	Fault	Yes	Throttle Position Sensor	All the time when the ignition switch is on	If the throttle position sensor signal is below .16 or above 4.7 volts	None	05	65 / 69
25	Fault	Yes	Automatic Idle Speed Motor (AIS)	Only when the AIS system is required to control the engine speed	If proper voltage in the AIS system is not present NOTE: Open circuit will not activate code	03	None	None
26	Fault	Yes	Fuel Injector Driver	All the time when the ignition switch is on	If the current through the fuel injector does not reach its proper peak level	02	None	None
27	Fault	No	Fuel Control	At engine speeds below 2,000 rpm	If the fuel control interface fails to switch properly	None	None	None
31	Fault	Yes	Canister Purge Solenoid	All the time when the ignition switch is on	If the solenoid does not turn on and off when it should	07	None	None
32	Fault	Yes	EGR System	Fixed times with engine warm and off idle	If the system fails 8 self checks	11	None	None
33	Fault	No	A.C. Cutout Relay	All the time when the Radiator fan (condensor fan relay (on Caravan/Voyager)	If the relay does not turn on and off when it should	05	None	None
34	Fault	No	Speed Control Servo Circuit	All the time when the speed control switch is on and the brake is not applied, in drive and vehicle speed above 35 mph	If the servo does not turn on and off when it should	08	None	None
35	Fault	No	Radiator Fan Relay Circuit	All the time when the ignition switch is on when it should	If the relay does not turn on and off when it should	04	None	None
37	Fault	No	Transmission lock up solenoid	All the time when the ignition switch is on	If the lock up solenoid does not turn on and off when it should	10	None	None
41	Fault	No	Alternator Field Control (Charging System)	All the time when the ignition switch is on	If the field control interface fails to switch properly	09	None	None
42	Fault	No	Auto Shutdown	All the time when the ignition switch is on	If the relay does not turn on and off when it should	06	None	None
43	Fault	No	Spark Control	During cranking only	If the spark control interface fails to switch properly	01	None	None
44	Fault	No	Fused J2	All the time when the ignition key is on	If fused J2 is not present in the logic board of the single module engine controller	None	None	None
46	Fault	Yes	Battery Voltage Sensing (Charging System)	All the time when the engine is running	If the battery sense voltage is more than 1 volt above the desired control voltage for more than 20 seconds	None	07	67
47	Fault	No	Battery Voltage Sensing (Charging System)	When the engine has been running for more than 6 minutes, engine temperature above 160°F and engine rpm above 1,500 rpm	If the battery sense voltage is more than 1 volt below the desired control voltage for more than 35 seconds	None	07	67
51	Fault	Yes*	Oxygen Feedback System	During all closed loop conditions	If the O2 sensor indicates a lean condition for more than 3 minutes	None	None	01 Switching
52	Fault	Yes*	Oxygen Feedback System	During all closed loop conditions	If the O2 sensor indicates a rich condition for more than 3 minutes	None	None	01 Switching
53	Fault	No	Single module engine controller (SMEC)	When the ignition key is initially turned to the on position	If the logic board fails its self test	None	None	None
55	Indication	No			Indicates end of diagnostic mode			
88	Indication	No			Indicates start of diagnostic mode NOTE: This code must appear first in the diagnostic mode or fault codes will be inaccurate			
0	Indication	No			Indicates oxygen feedback system is lean with the engine running			
1	Indication	No			Indicates oxygen feedback system is rich with the engine running			

* California only

1987–88 2.5L DIAGNOSTIC CHART—NO START TEST

TEST NS-1	STEP A	CHECKING FOR SPARK AT SPARK PLUGS

PROCEDURE	TEST INDICATION	ACTION REQUIRED
• Disconnect any spark plug wire. • Insert an insulated screw driver in terminal. • Hold screwdriver shaft (¼") near a good engine ground. • Have someone crank the engine. NOTE: Fault code erase and SMEC damage may occur if the spark plug wire is held more than 1/4" from ground.	• There is a good spark between screwdriver and ground as long as the engine is cranking.	• Perform TEST NS-2.
	• There is no spark. NOTE: Handle 1 or 2 sparks as no spark.	• Perform STEP B.

TEST NS-1	STEP C	CHECKING FOR FUEL FROM INJECTOR
COMPLETE TEST NS-1B BEFORE PROCEEDING		

PROCEDURE	TEST INDICATION	ACTION REQUIRED
• Remove the air cleaner • Disconnect ignition coil wire from distributor and secure it to a good engine ground • Have someone crank the engine while you look for a fuel spray from the injector	• There is fuel spraying from the injector.	• Perform TEST NS-6.
LOOK FOR FUEL SPRAY	• There is no fuel spraying from the injector.	• Perform TEST NS-14.

TEST NS-1	STEP B	CHECKING FOR SPARK AT IGNITION COIL WIRE
COMPLETE TEST NS-1A BEFORE PROCEEDING		

PROCEDURE	TEST INDICATION	ACTION REQUIRED
• Disconnect ignition coil wire from distributor cap. • Hold coil wire (¼") near a good engine ground. CAUTION: Fault code erasure and SMEC damage may occur if the spark plug wire gap is more than ¼" gap between the coil wire and ground. • Have someone crank the engine.	• There is a good spark between ignition coil wire and ground.	• Repair secondary ignition system (distributor cap and/or rotor).
IGNITION COIL WIRE	• There is no spark. NOTE: Handle 1 or 2 sparks as no spark.	• Check ignition coil wire. If okay, Perform STEP C.

TEST NS-2	STEP A	CHECKING FOR FUEL FROM INJECTOR
COMPLETE TEST NS-1A BEFORE PROCEEDING		

PROCEDURE	TEST INDICATION	ACTION REQUIRED
• Remove the air cleaner. • Ignition coil wire removed from distributor and secured to a good engine ground. • Have someone crank the engine while you look for a fuel spray from the injector.	• There is a slow steady stream of fuel from the injector.	• Perform TEST NS-3A.
	• There is no fuel spray.	• Perform TEST NS-9A.
LOOK FOR FUEL SPRAY	• Injector is spraying an excessive amount of fuel.	• Perform TEST NS-13A.

1987–88 2.5L DIAGNOSTIC CHART — NO START TEST

TEST NS-3	STEP A	CHECKING THE SMEC

COMPLETE TEST NS-2A BEFORE PROCEEDING

PROCEDURE	TEST INDICATION	ACTION REQUIRED
• Connect DRB II to engine harness connector. • Put the system into the **Diagnostic Test Mode.**	• Code 88 appears on the DRB II display.	• **Perform TEST NS-4.**
	• Code 88 does not appear on the DRB II display	• Defective logic board. Replace the SMEC. **CAUTION:** Before replacing the SMEC, make sure your DRB II is operational and there is not an open circuit in the wires between the SMEC and diagnostic connector.

TEST NS-5	STEP A	CHECKING ENGINE TIMING

COMPLETE TEST NS-4A BEFORE PROCEEDING

PROCEDURE	TEST INDICATION	ACTION REQUIRED
• Connect timing device to engine. • Have someone crank engine while you look at the timing marks.	• Timing is between 0°-16° BTC	• Check compression and valve timing.
	• Timing is not between 0°-16° BTC.	• **Perform STEP B.**

TEST NS-4	STEP A	CHECKING FOR FUEL FOULED SPARK PLUGS

COMPLETE TEST NS-3A BEFORE PROCEEDING

PROCEDURE	TEST INDICATION	ACTION REQUIRED
• Remove spark plugs. • Look at tips for wet fuel.	• Spark plug tips are not wet with fuel. **NOTE:** It is normal for spark plugs to be black after engine is started cold.	• **Perform TEST NS-5.**
LOOK FOR WET FUEL	• Spark plugs are wet with fuel.	• Clean and reinstall. **Do not replace spark plugs.** • Attempt restart.

TEST NS-5	STEP B	CHECKING ENGINE TIMING

COMPLETE TEST NS-5A BEFORE PROCEEDING

PROCEDURE	TEST INDICATION	ACTION REQUIRED
• Timing device connected to engine. • Set timing to 10° BTC during cranking.	• Engine starts.	• Set timing to specifications. Check camshaft and intermediate shaft timing.
	• Engine does not start.	• Check compression and valve timing.

TEST NS-6	STEP A	CHECKING IGNITION CONTROL SYSTEM FOR FAULT CODES

COMPLETE TEST NS-1C BEFORE PROCEEDING

PROCEDURE	TEST INDICATION	ACTION REQUIRED
• Connect DRB II • Put the system in the Diagnostic Mode. • Record all codes.	88-12-55 No fault codes	Perform TEST NS-7.
	88-12-43-55 Spark control circuit	Perform TEST NS-8.

TEST NS-7	STEP B	CHECKING THE IGNITION SYSTEM PRIMARY CONTROL CIRCUIT VOLTAGE AT THE IGNITION COIL (−) TERMINAL (J5 CIRCUIT)

COMPLETE TEST NS-7A BEFORE PROCEEDING

PROCEDURE	TEST INDICATION	ACTION REQUIRED
• DRB II connected. • System in ATM Test 01. • Connect an analog voltmeter to the J5 (BK/YL) wire at the negative terminal of the ignition coil and ground.	• Voltmeter reading is pulsating slightly between 10 and 14 volts.	• Replace the ignition coil.
	• Voltmeter not pulsating but reads above 10 volts.	• **Perform STEP C.**
ANALOG VOLTMETER / NEGATIVE TERMINAL / IGNITION COIL	• Voltmeter pulsating between 5 and 10 volts.	• Replace the ignition coil.
	• Voltmeter pulsating between 0 and 2 volts.	• **Perform STEP D.**

TEST NS-7	STEP A	CHECKING FOR THE VOLT. SUPPLY TO THE IGN. COIL POSITIVE TERMINAL FROM THE AUTO SHUTDOWN RELAY (Z1 CIRCUIT)

COMPLETE TEST NS-6A BEFORE PROCEEDING

PROCEDURE	TEST INDICATION	ACTION REQUIRED
• DRB II connected. • Connect an analog voltmeter between the Z1 (DG/BK) wire at the positive terminal of the ignition coil and ground. • Put the system in the **ATM Test 01.**	• Voltmeter reads battery voltage.	• **Perform STEP B.**
ANALOG VOLTMETER / POSITIVE TERMINAL / IGNITION COIL	• Voltmeter reads 0.	• Repair the Z1 (DG/BK) wire of coil positive terminal for open circuit to the wiring harness splice.

TEST NS-7	STEP C	CHECKING THE IGNITION SYSTEM PRIMARY CONTROL CIRCUIT FOR AN OPEN CIRCUIT (J5 CIRCUIT)

COMPLETE TEST NS-7B BEFORE PROCEEDING

PROCEDURE	TEST INDICATION	ACTION REQUIRED
• Turn the ignition switch off. • Disconnect the 14-way connector from the SMEC. • Connect an ohmmeter between the J5 (BK/YL) wire at the negative (−) terminal of the ignition coil and the J5 (BK/YL) wire at cavity No. 12 of the 14-way connector.	• Ohmmeter shows continuity.	• Defective power board. Replace the SMEC. **CAUTION:** Before replacing the SMEC, check the J5 terminal in cavity No. 12 of the 14-way connector to make sure that it is not spread apart causing a poor connection.
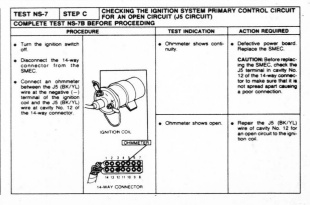 IGNITION COIL / OHMMETER / 14-WAY CONNECTOR	• Ohmmeter shows open.	• Repair the J5 (BK/YL) wire of cavity No. 12 for an open circuit to the ignition coil.

1987–88 2.5L DIAGNOSTIC CHART—NO START TEST

TEST NS-7 | STEP D | CHECKING THE IGNITION COIL PRIMARY WINDINGS FOR A SHORT CIRCUIT
COMPLETE TEST NS-7B BEFORE PROCEEDING

PROCEDURE	TEST INDICATION	ACTION REQUIRED
• Turn the ignition switch off. • DRB II connected. • Disconnect the J5 (BK/YL) wire from the negative side (−) of the ignition coil. • Connect the analog voltmeter to the negative (−) terminal of the ignition coil and ground. • Put the system in the **ATM Test 01**. (Refer to introduction)	• Voltmeter is reading above 10 volts.	• Perform STEP E.
	• Voltmeter reads between 0 and 2 volts.	• Replace the ignition coil.

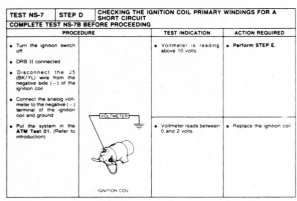

TEST NS-7 | STEP E | CHECKING THE IGNITION SYSTEM PRIMARY CIRCUIT FOR A SHORT CIRCUIT TO GROUND (J5 CIRCUIT)
COMPLETE TEST NS-7D BEFORE PROCEEDING

PROCEDURE	TEST INDICATION	ACTION REQUIRED
• Turn the ignition switch off. • Ignition coil negative (−) wire disconnected. • Disconnect the 14-way connector from the SMEC. • Connect an ohmmeter between the J5 (BK/YL) wire at cavity No. 12 of the 14-way connector and ground.	• Ohmmeter shows open.	• Defective power board. Replace the SMEC.
	• Ohmmeter shows continuity.	• Repair the J5 (BK/YL) wire of cavity No. 12 for a short circuit to ground.

TEST NS-9 | STEP A | CHECKING FUEL CONTROL SYSTEM FOR FAULT CODES
COMPLETE TEST NS-2A BEFORE PROCEEDING

PROCEDURE	TEST INDICATION	ACTION REQUIRED
• Connect DRB II • Put the system in the Diagnostic Mode • Record all codes.	88-12-55 No fault codes	Perform TEST NS-10.
	88-12-26-55 Fuel injector driver circuit	
	88-12-27-55 Fuel control circuit	Perform TEST NS-12.

TEST NS-10 | STEP A | CHECKING FOR PRESSURE IN FUEL SUPPLY SYSTEM
COMPLETE TEST NS-9A BEFORE PROCEEDING

PROCEDURE	TEST INDICATION	ACTION REQUIRED
• Turn the ignition switch off. • DRB II connected. • Install fuel pressure gauge (Tool C-3292) in fuel supply hose at the throttle body. **CAUTION:** Fuel may be under high pressure in the supply hose. Refer to the service manual for instructions on how to bleed the pressure. • Put system in **Diagnostic Test Mode.** • Press and hold the ATM key on the DRB II.	• Fuel gauge is reading 14½ psi ± 1	• Perform STEP B.
	• Fuel gauge is not reading 14½ psi ± 1	• Perform STEP C.

TEST NS-8 | STEP A | CHECKING FOR FAULT CODE 43 — SPARK CONTROL CIRCUIT
COMPLETE TEST NS-6A BEFORE PROCEEDING

PROCEDURE	TEST INDICATION	ACTION REQUIRED
• DRB II connected • Put the system in Diagnostic Test Mode • Turn the ignition switch off • Disconnect the ignition coil wire at the distributor and place it 1/4" from ground. • Disconnect the 60-way connector and connect one end of a jumper wire to the K15 (YL) wire at cavity No. 34. • Turn the ignition switch on, press and hold the ATM key on the DRB II. • Touch the other end of the jumper to a good ground. Make and break this connection several times while looking at the ignition coil wire.	• There is spark at the ignition coil wire as you make and break the connection.	• Defective logic board. Replace the SMEC. **CAUTION:** Before replacing the SMEC, check the K15 terminal in cavity No. 34 of the 60-way connector to make sure it is not damaged causing a poor connection.
	• There is no spark at the ignition coil wire as you make and break the connection.	• Perform STEP B.

VIEW FROM TERMINAL END

TEST NS-8 | STEP B | CHECKING THE SPARK CONTROL WIRE BETWEEN THE LOGIC AND POWER BOARDS FOR AN OPEN CIRCUIT (K15 CIRCUIT)
COMPLETE TEST NS-8A BEFORE PROCEEDING

PROCEDURE	TEST INDICATION	ACTION REQUIRED
• Turn the ignition switch off. • SMEC 60-way connector disconnected. • Disconnect the SMEC 14-way connector. • Connect one lead of an ohmmeter to the K15 (YL) wire at cavity No. 34 of the SMEC 60-way connector. • Connect the other lead of the ohmmeter to the K15 (YL) wire at cavity No. 13 of the SMEC 14-way connector.	• Ohmmeter shows continuity.	• Defective power board. Replace the SMEC. **CAUTION:** Before replacing the SMEC, check the K15 terminal in cavity No. 13 of the 14-way connector to make sure it is not spread apart causing a poor connection.
	• Ohmmeter shows open.	• Repair the K15 (YL) wire for an open circuit.

VIEW FROM TERMINAL END

TEST NS-10 | STEP B | CHECKING THE THROTTLE POSITION SENSOR
COMPLETE TEST NS-10A BEFORE PROCEEDING

PROCEDURE	TEST INDICATION	ACTION REQUIRED
• DRB II connected • Put the system into the **Sensor Test 05.**	• Display on DRB II is reading between ½ and 1½ volts	• Perform TEST NS-11.
	• Display on the DRB II reads more than 1½ volts	• Throttle position sensor defective, replace the sensor

TEST NS-10 | STEP C | CHECKING INTAKE FUEL PUMP
COMPLETE TEST NS-10A BEFORE PROCEEDING

PROCEDURE	TEST INDICATION	ACTION REQUIRED
• System in Diagnostic Test Mode • Press and hold the ATM key on the DRB II • Listen for intake fuel pump noise at rear of vehicle	• The fuel pump is running	• Check fuel supply line and hoses between fuel tank and throttle body for restrictions • Check for a plugged fuel filter • Check for a plugged in-tank fuel filter
	• The fuel pump is not running	• Perform STEP D.

1987–88 2.5L DIAGNOSTIC CHART—NO START TEST

TEST NS-10 | STEP D | CHECKING VOLTAGE SUPPLY TO INTANK PUMP (Z1 CIRCUIT)
COMPLETE TEST NS-10C BEFORE PROCEEDING

PROCEDURE	TEST INDICATION	ACTION REQUIRED
• System in Diagnositc Test Mode. • Raise car on hoist. • Disconnect the intank fuel pump connector. • Connect voltmeter to the Z1 (DG/BK) wire of connector and ground. • Press and hold the ATM key on DRB II.	• Voltmeter is reading battery voltage.	• Perform STEP E.
	• Voltmeter is reading 0.	• Repair Z1 circuit (DG/BK) wire for open circuit to wiring harness splice

TEST NS-11 | STEP A | CHECKING FUEL INJECTOR DRIVER CIRCUITS (Z1 AND Y11)
COMPLETE TEST NS-10B BEFORE PROCEEDING

PROCEDURE	TEST INDICATION	ACTION REQUIRED
• DRB II connected • System in the Diagnostic Test Mode. • Disconnect the fuel injector connector • Connect an analog voltmeter between the Z1 (DG/BK) and the Y11 (WT) terminals of the fuel injector connector. • Select the lowest voltage scale available on your voltmeter, 4 volt is recommended. • Put the system in the ATM Test 02.	• Voltmeter reading is pulsating between 0 and 1 volt. NOTE: If voltmeter is showing a negative voltage, reverse its leads at the injector connector and repeat the test	• Perform STEP D.
	• Voltmeter reading is not pulsating.	• Perform STEP B.

TEST NS-10 | STEP E | CHECKING INTANK PUMP GROUND (X2 CIRCUIT)
COMPLETE TEST NS-10D BEFORE PROCEEDING

PROCEDURE	TEST INDICATION	ACTION REQUIRED
• Car raised on hoist. • Intank fuel pump connector disconnected. • Connect ohmmeter between the X2 (GY) wire of fuel pump connector and ground.	• Ohmmeter shows continuity.	• Replace the intank fuel pump
	• Ohmmeter shows open.	• Repair the X2 (GY) wire for open circuit to body ground connection

TEST NS-11 | STEP B | CHECKING FOR VOLTAGE SUPPLY TO THE INJECTOR (Z1 CIRCUIT)
COMPLETE TEST NS-11A BEFORE PROCEEDING

PROCEDURE	TEST INDICATION	ACTION REQUIRED
• Injector connector disconnected. • System in ATM Test 02 • Connect a voltmeter to the Z1 (DG/BK) wire of the injector harness connector and ground.	• Voltmeter reads battery voltage	• Perform STEP C.
	• Voltmeter reads 0	• Repair the Z1 (DG BK) wire of the injector harness connector for an open circuit to the wiring harness splice

TEST NS-11 | STEP C | CHECKING FUEL INJECTOR CONTROL WIRE TO THE SMEC FOR AN OPEN CIRCUIT (Y11 CIRCUIT)
COMPLETE TEST NS-11B BEFORE PROCEEDING

PROCEDURE	TEST INDICATION	ACTION REQUIRED
• Turn the ignition switch off • Injector connector disconnected. • Turn the ignition switch off • Disconnect the 14-way connector from the SMEC • Connect ohmmeter between the Z1 (DG/BK) wire in cavity No 9 of 14-way connector and the Y11 (WT) wire of the injector harness connector	• Ohmmeter shows continuity.	• Defective power board Replace SMEC CAUTION: Before replacing the SMEC, check the Y11 terminal in cavity No 9 of the 14-way connector to make sure it is not spread apart causing a poor connection
	• Ohmmeter shows open	• Repair the Y11 (WT) wire of cavity No 9 of the 14-way connector for open circuit to injector connector

TEST NS-12 | STEP A | CHECKING FOR FAULT CODE 27 — FUEL CONTROL CIRCUIT
COMPLETE TEST NS-9A BEFORE PROCEEDING

PROCEDURE		TEST INDICATION	ACTION REQUIRED
• DRB II connected • Air cleaner removed • Put the system into Diagnostic Test Mode. • Turn the ignition switch off • Disconnect the 60-way connector • Connect one end of a jumper wire to the K16 (VT/YL) wire in cavity No 33 of the 60-way connector • Turn the ignition switch to the run position • Press and hold the ATM key on the DRB II • Very quickly connect and disconnect the other end of the jumper wire to the battery positive post	VIEW FROM TERMINAL END	• Fuel is spraying from injector	• Defective logic board Replace the SMEC CAUTION: Before replacing the SMEC check the K16 terminal in cavity No 33 of the 60-way connector to make sure it is not damaged causing a poor connection
		• There is no fuel spraying from the injector	• Perform STEP B.

TEST NS-11 | STEP D | CHECKING FUEL INJECTOR CAP AND WIRING HARNESS ASSEMBLY (Z1 AND Y11 CIRCUITS)
COMPLETE TEST NS-11A BEFORE PROCEEDING

PROCEDURE	TEST INDICATION	ACTION REQUIRED
• DRB II connected • System in the Diagnostic Test Mode • Remove the air cleaner assembly • Connect the fuel injector connector • Remove screw and lift cap from top of injector • Connect an analog voltmeter between the terminals of the fuel injector cap • Select the lowest voltage scale available on your voltmeter, 4 volt is recommended. • Put the system in the ATM Test 02.	• Voltmeter reading is pulsating between 0 and 1 volt. NOTE: If voltmeter is showing a negative voltage, reverse its leads at the injector cap, and repeat the test	• Replace the fuel injector CAUTION: Before replacing the injector, check the Z1 and Y11 terminals in the injector cap to make sure they are not damaged causing a poor connection
	• Voltmeter reading is not pulsating	• Replace the fuel injector cap and wiring harness assembly CAUTION: Before replacing the injector cap and wiring harness assembly, check the Z1 and Y11 terminals in the injector cap to make sure they are not damaged causing a poor connection

TEST NS-12 | STEP B | CHECKING THE FUEL CONTROL WIRE FOR AN OPEN CIRCUIT (K16 CIRCUIT)
COMPLETE TEST NS-12A BEFORE PROCEEDING

PROCEDURE		TEST INDICATION	ACTION REQUIRED
• Turn the ignition switch off • 60-way connector disconnected • Disconnect the 14-way connector • Connect an ohmmeter between the K16 (VT/YL) wire in cavity No 33 of the 60-way connector and the K16 (VT/YL) wire in cavity No 8 of the 14-way connector	VIEW FROM TERMINAL END	• Ohmmeter shows continuity	• Defective power board Replace the SMEC CAUTION: Before replacing the SMEC, check the K16 terminal in cavity No 8 of the 14-way connector to make sure it is not spread apart causing a poor connection
		• Ohmmeter shows open.	• Repair K16 (VT/YL) wire in cavity No 8 of the 14-way connector for an open circuit to the 60-way connector

1987–88 2.5L DIAGNOSTIC CHART—NO START TEST

TEST NS-13 | STEP A | CHECKING FOR A FLOODING INJECTOR
COMPLETE TEST NS-2A BEFORE PROCEEDING

PROCEDURE		TEST INDICATION	ACTION REQUIRED
• Connect DRB II. • Put the system in Diagnostic Test Mode. • Remove air cleaner assembly. • Disconnect injector harness connector. • Press and hold the ATM key on DRB II.		• There is fuel spraying from injector.	• Remove injector and inspect lower O ring seal for damage or misinstallation. If O ring is okay, replace injector.
		• There is no fuel spraying from injector.	• Perform STEP B.

TEST NS-14 | STEP A | CHECKING SYSTEM FOR FAULT CODES
COMPLETE TEST NS-1C BEFORE PROCEEDING

PROCEDURE		TEST INDICATION	ACTION REQUIRED
• Connect DRB II. • Erase fault codes. • Turn the ignition switch to the run position for 5 seconds. • Crank the engine for 7 seconds and then turn the ignition switch to the run position for 5 seconds. • Put the system in the Diagnostic Test Mode. • Record all codes.		No Code 88 or 00 System Power Circuits	Perform TEST NS-15.
		88-11-12-55 Distributor pickup circuit	Perform TEST NS-16.
		88-42-55 Auto shutdown relay pull in coil circuit	Perform TEST NS-17.
		88-12-14-22-24-55 88-12-14-22-23-24-55	Repair N5 (BK/LB) wire in cavity No. 4 of the SMEC 60-way connector for an open circuit.
		88-12-44-55 Fused J2 Circuit	Perform TEST NS-18.
		88-12-55 No fault codes	Perform TEST NS-19.

TEST NS-13 | STEP B | CHECKING THE FUEL CONTROL CIRCUIT TO THE SMEC
COMPLETE TEST NS-13A BEFORE PROCEEDING

PROCEDURE		TEST INDICATION	ACTION REQUIRED
• Turn the ignition switch off. • Air cleaner removed. • DRB II connected. • System in Diagnostic Test Mode. • Disconnect the 60-way connector. • Reconnect the injector connector. • Press and hold the ATM key on the DRB II.		• There is fuel spraying from injector.	• Defective power board. Replace the SMEC. NOTE: Before replacing the SMEC, check Y11 (WT) wire for a short to ground.
		• There is no fuel spraying from injector.	• Defective logic board. Replace the SMEC.

TEST NS-15 | STEP A | CHECKING FOR NO CODE 88 – 5 VOLT SUPPLY (K8 CIRCUIT)
COMPLETE TEST NS-14A BEFORE PROCEEDING

PROCEDURE		TEST INDICATION	ACTION REQUIRED
• Turn the ignition switch off. • Disconnect the throttle position sensor connector. • Turn the ignition switch on. • Connect a voltmeter to the K8 (VT/WT) wire at the throttle position sensor connector and ground.		• Voltmeter is reading at least 4.5 volts.	• Perform STEP B.
		• Voltmeter is reading 0 volts.	• Perform STEP C.

TEST NS-15 | STEP B | CHECKING THE SMEC GROUND (K9 CIRCUIT)
COMPLETE TEST NS-15A BEFORE PROCEEDING

PROCEDURE		TEST INDICATION	ACTION REQUIRED
• Turn the ignition switch off. • Disconnect the 60-way connector. • Connect one lead of an ohmmeter to the system ground eyelet. • Connect the other end of the ohmmeter to the K9 (LB/RD) wire in cavity No. 15 and 16 of the 60-way connector. NOTE: Refer to introduction for information on using digital volt/ohmmeter to check resistance.		• Ohmmeter is showing continuity with less than ½ ohm of resistance in both wires.	• Defective logic board. Replace the SMEC.
		• Ohmmeter shows open.	• Repair the K9 (LB/RD) wire for an open circuit to the wiring harness splice. • Replace the SMEC.
		• Ohmmeter is showing more than ½ ohm of resistance at one or both wires.	• Repair K9 (LB/RD) wire for high resistance to system ground eyelet.

TEST NS-15 | STEP D | CHECKING FOR THE 8 VOLT SUPPLY (N6 CIRCUIT)
COMPLETE TEST NS-15C BEFORE PROCEEDING

PROCEDURE		TEST INDICATION	ACTION REQUIRED
• Turn the ignition switch off. • Disconnect the 60-way connector. • Connect the negative lead of a voltmeter to ground. • Turn the ignition switch on. • Touch the positive lead of the voltmeter to the N6 (OR) wire at cavity No. 52 of the SMEC 60-way connector.		• Voltmeter is reading at least 8 volts.	• Defective logic board. Replace the SMEC. CAUTION: Before replacing the SMEC check the N6 terminal in cavity No. 52 to make sure it is not damaged causing a poor connection.
		• Voltmeter is reading 0 volts.	• Perform STEP E.

TEST NS-15 | STEP C | CHECKING FOR A SHORTED MAP SENSOR (K8 CIRCUIT)
COMPLETE TEST NS-15A BEFORE PROCEEDING

PROCEDURE		TEST INDICATION	ACTION REQUIRED
• Ignition switch turned on. • Throttle position sensor connector disconnected. • Negative lead of a voltmeter connected to ground. • Disconnect the MAP sensor connector. • Connect the positive lead of a voltmeter to the K8 (VT/WT) wire at the throttle position sensor connector.		• Voltmeter is reading at least 4.5 volts.	• Replace the MAP sensor.
		• Voltmeter is reading 0 volts.	• Perform STEP D.

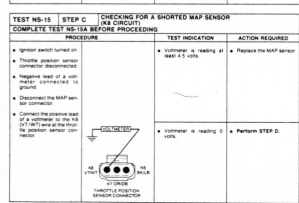

TEST NS-15 | STEP E | CHECKING FOR A SHORTED DISTRIBUTOR PICKUP (N6 CIRCUIT)
COMPLETE TEST NS-15D BEFORE PROCEEDING

PROCEDURE		TEST INDICATION	ACTION REQUIRED
• 60-way connector disconnected. • Ignition switch turned on. • The negative lead of a voltmeter connected to ground. • Disconnect the distributor pickup harness connector. • Touch the positive lead of the voltmeter to the N6 (OR) wire at cavity No. 52 of the SMEC 60-way connector.		• Voltmeter is reading at least 8 volts.	• Replace the distributor pickup.
		• Voltmeter is reading 0 volts.	• Perform STEP F.

1987–88 2.5L DIAGNOSTIC CHART — NO START TEST

TEST NS-15 | **STEP F** | CHECKING THE 8 VOLT SUPPLY WIRE FOR AN OPEN CIRCUIT BETWEEN THE LOGIC BOARD AND THE SPLICE (N6 CIRCUIT)

COMPLETE TEST NS-15E BEFORE PROCEEDING

PROCEDURE		TEST INDICATION	ACTION REQUIRED
• 60-way connector disconnected • Distributor pickup connector disconnected • Turn the ignition switch off • Connect an ohmmeter between the N6 (OR) wire in cavity No. 52 of the 60-way connector and the N6 (OR) wire in cavity No. 1 of the distributor harness connector	VIEW FROM TERMINAL END N6 OR 52 OHMMETER 3 1 2 DISTRIBUTOR PICKUP HARNESS CONNECTOR	• Ohmmeter shows continuity.	• Perform STEP G.
		• Ohmmeter shows open.	• Repair the N6 (OR) wire of cavity No. 52 of the 60-way connector for an open circuit to the distributor harness connector

---

TEST NS-15 | **STEP H** | CHECKING THE SMEC GROUND WIRES FOR AN OPEN CIRCUIT

COMPLETE TEST NS-15G BEFORE PROCEEDING

PROCEDURE		TEST INDICATION	ACTION REQUIRED
• 14-way connector disconnected • Turn the ignition switch off • Connect one lead of an ohmmeter to the system ground eyelet • Connect the other lead of the ohmmeter to the J9 (BK) wire in cavities No. 6 and 7 of the 14-way connector	OHMMETER 1 2 3 4 5 6 7 14 13 12 11 10 9 8 14 WAY CONNECTOR	• Ohmmeter is showing continuity at both cavities with less than ½ ohm of resistance	• Defective power board Replace the SMEC. CAUTION: Before replacing the SMEC, check the J9 terminals in cavities No. 6 and 7 to make sure they are not spread apart causing a poor connection
		• Ohmmeter is showing open at cavities No. 6 and 7	• Repair the J9 (BK) wires in cavities No. 6 and 7 of the 14-way connector for an open circuit to the wiring harness splice • Replace the SMEC
		• Ohmmeter is showing continuity with resistance higher than ½ ohm	• Repair J9 (BK) ground circuit for high resistance to system ground eyelet

---

TEST NS-15 | **STEP G** | CHECKING THE IGNITION SWITCH SUPPLY VOLTAGE TO THE SMEC

COMPLETE TEST NS-15F BEFORE PROCEEDING

PROCEDURE		TEST INDICATION	ACTION REQUIRED
• Ignition switch off • Disconnect the 14-way connector • Connect the negative lead of a voltmeter to ground • Turn the ignition switch on • Touch the positive lead of a voltmeter to the J2 (DB) wire at cavity No. 4 of the SMEC 14-way connector	VOLTMETER 1 2 3 4 5 6 7 14 13 12 11 10 9 8 14 WAY CONNECTOR	• Voltmeter is reading battery voltage	• Perform STEP H.
		• Voltmeter is not reading battery voltage	• Repair the J2 (DB) wire in cavity No. 4 of the 14-way connector for an open circuit to the wiring harness splice

---

TEST NS-16 | **STEP A** | CHECKING FOR FAULT CODE 11 – DISTRIBUTOR PICKUP CIRCUIT

COMPLETE TEST NS-14A BEFORE PROCEEDING

PROCEDURE		TEST INDICATION	ACTION REQUIRED
• Turn ignition switch off • Disconnect distributor pickup harness connector • Remove coil wire from distributor and place it (¼ inch) near a good engine ground. • Turn ignition switch to the run position. • Connect a jumper wire to the N7 (GY/BK) wire and the N5 (BK/LB) wire at the distributor pickup harness connector cavity No. 2 and 3 • Make and break this connection several times while looking at coil wire	JUMPER N6 OR 1 N7 GY/BK 3 N5 BK/LB 2 DISTRIBUTOR PICKUP HARNESS CONNECTOR	• There is spark at the coil wire	• Perform STEP B.
		• There is no spark at the coil wire.	• Perform STEP C.

TEST NS-16 | **STEP B** | CHECKING FOR THE 8 VOLT POWER SUPPLY TO THE DISTRIBUTOR PICKUP FROM THE SMEC (N6 CIRCUIT)

COMPLETE TEST NS-16A BEFORE PROCEEDING

PROCEDURE		TEST INDICATION	ACTION REQUIRED
• Distributor pickup harness connector disconnected. • Ignition switch in the run position. • Connect a voltmeter to the N6 (OR) wire at cavity No. 1 of the distributor pickup harness connector and ground.	VOLTMETER N6 OR N7 GY/BK 3 N5 BK/LB 2 DISTRIBUTOR PICKUP HARNESS CONNECTOR	• Voltmeter is reading at least 7 volts.	• Replace the distributor pickup CAUTION: Before replacing the pickup, check all the terminals in the distributor harness connector to make sure they are not spread apart causing a poor connection. Also make sure distributor rotor turns while cranking the engine.
		• Voltmeter reads 0.	• Repair N6 (OR) wire of cavity No. 1 for open circuit to wiring harness splice.

TEST NS-16 | **STEP D** | CHECKING THE DISTRIBUTOR PICKUP HARNESS GROUND (N5 CIRCUIT)

COMPLETE TEST NS-16C BEFORE PROCEEDING

PROCEDURE		TEST INDICATION	ACTION REQUIRED
• Distributor pickup harness connector disconnected. • Ignition switch in the run position. • Positive lead of voltmeter connected to the N7 (GY/BK) wire in cavity No. 3 of the distributor pickup harness connector. • Connect the negative lead of the voltmeter to a good engine ground.	VOLTMETER N6 OR N7 GY/BK 3 N5 BK/LB 2 DISTRIBUTOR PICKUP HARNESS CONNECTOR	• Voltmeter is reading at least 4 volts.	• Repair N5 (BK/LB) wire in cavity No. 2 of the distributor pickup harness connector for an open circuit to the wiring harness splice.
		• Voltmeter reads 0.	• Perform STEP E.

TEST NS-16 | **STEP C** | CHECKING FOR THE DISTRIBUTOR PICKUP SIGNAL VOLTAGE FROM THE SMEC (N7 CIRCUIT)

COMPLETE TEST NS-16A BEFORE PROCEEDING

PROCEDURE		TEST INDICATION	ACTION REQUIRED
• Distributor pickup harness connector disconnected. • Ignition switch in the run position. • Connect the positive lead of the voltmeter to the N7 (GY/BK) wire in cavity No. 3 of the distributor pickup harness connector. • Connect the negative lead of the voltmeter to the N5 (BK/LB) wire at cavity No. 2 of the distributor pickup harness connector.	VOLTMETER N6 OR N7 GY/BK 3 N5 BK/LB 2 DISTRIBUTOR PICKUP HARNESS CONNECTOR	• Voltmeter is reading at least 4 volts.	• Replace the SMEC.
		• Voltmeter reads 0.	• Perform STEP D.

TEST NS-16 | **STEP E** | CHECKING THE DISTRIBUTOR PICKUP HARNESS CONTROL (N7 CIRCUIT)

COMPLETE TEST NS-16D BEFORE PROCEEDING

PROCEDURE		TEST INDICATION	ACTION REQUIRED
• Distributor pickup harness connector disconnected. • Turn ignition switch off. • Disconnect the 60-way connector. • Connect an ohmmeter between the N7 (GY/BK) wire in cavity No. 3 of the distributor pickup harness connector to the N7 (GY/BK) wire in cavity No. 47 of the 60-way connector.	VIEW FROM TERMINAL END 47 OHMMETER N7 GY/BK 3 DISTRIBUTOR PICKUP HARNESS CONNECTOR	• Ohmmeter shows open.	• Repair the N7 (GY/BK) wire in cavity No. 47 of the 60-way connector for an open circuit to the distributor pickup harness connector.
		• Ohmmeter shows continuity.	• Defective logic board. Replace the SMEC. NOTE: Before replacing the SMEC, check the N7 terminals in cavity No. 47 of the 60-way connector to make sure it is not damaged causing a poor connection.

1987–88 2.5L DIAGNOSTIC CHART—NO START TEST

TEST NS-17	STEP A	CHECKING FOR FAULT CODE 42 - AUTO SHUTDOWN RELAY (K19 CIRCUIT)
COMPLETE TEST NS-14A BEFORE PROCEEDING		

PROCEDURE	TEST INDICATION	ACTION REQUIRED
• DRB II connected. • Connect a voltmeter to the K19 (DB/YL) wire of the auto shutdown relay 4-way connector and ground.	• The voltmeter reading is within 1 volt of battery voltage.	• Perform STEP B.
	• The voltmeter reading is 0-1 volt steady.	• Perform STEP C.

TEST NS-17	STEP C	CHECKING FOR SUPPLY VOLTAGE TO THE AUTO SHUTDOWN RELAY PULL IN COIL (K14 CIRCUIT)
COMPLETE TEST NS-17B BEFORE PROCEEDING		

PROCEDURE	TEST INDICATION	ACTION REQUIRED
• Turn the ignition switch off. • Disconnect the 4-way connector from the auto shutdown relay. • Connect a voltmeter to the K14 (DB/WT) wire of the auto shutdown relay 4-way wire connector and ground. • Turn the ignition switch on	• The voltmeter reads battery voltage.	• Replace the auto shutdown relay
	• The voltmeter reads 0 volts	• Repair the K14 (DB/WT) wire of the auto shutdown relay 4-way connector for an open circuit to the wiring harness splice

TEST NS-17	STEP B	CHECKING THE AUTO SHUTDOWN RELAY CONTROL WIRE FOR AN OPEN CIRCUIT TO THE SMEC (K19 CIRCUIT)
COMPLETE TEST NS-17A BEFORE PROCEEDING		

PROCEDURE	TEST INDICATION	ACTION REQUIRED
• Turn the ignition switch off. • Disconnect the 60-way connector from the SMEC. • Connect a voltmeter to the K19 (DB/YL) wire in cavity No. 58 of the 60-way connector and ground. • Turn the ignition switch on.	• Voltmeter reads battery voltage.	• Defective logic board. Replace the SMEC. CAUTION: Before replacing the SMEC, check the K19 terminal in cavity No. 58 of the 60-way connector to make sure it is not damaged causing a poor connection.
	• Voltmeter is reading 0 volts.	• Repair the K19 (DB/YL) wire in cavity No. 58 of the 60-way connector for an open circuit to the auto shutdown relay.

TEST NS-18	STEP A	CHECKING FOR FAULT CODE 44 – FUSED J2 CIRCUIT (K14)
COMPLETE TEST NS-14A BEFORE PROCEEDING		

PROCEDURE	TEST INDICATION	ACTION REQUIRED
• Turn the ignition switch off. • Disconnect the 14-way connector from the SMEC. • Connect an ohmmeter between the K14 (DB/WT) wire of the auto shutdown relay 4-way connector and the K14 (DB/WT) wire in cavity No 3 of the 14-way connector	• Ohmmeter shows continuity	• Defective power board replace the SMEC NOTE: Before replacing the SMEC, check the K14 terminal in cavity No. 3 of the 14-way connector to make sure it is not spread apart causing a poor connection
	• Ohmmeter does not show continuity	• Repair the K14 (DB/WT) wire of cavity No. 3 for an open circuit to the wiring harness splice

1988 2.2L AND 2.5L NO START DIAGNOSTIC CHART

TEST NS-19	STEP A	CHECKING THE AUTO SHUTDOWN RELAY CONTACTS (OUTPUT SIDE Z1 CIRCUIT)
COMPLETE TEST NS-17B BEFORE PROCEEDING		

PROCEDURE	TEST INDICATION	ACTION REQUIRED
• Turn the ignition switch off • Connect one lead of a jumper wire to the Z1 (DG/BK) wire of the auto shutdown relay 4-way connector • Touch the other end of the jumper wire to the J1 (RD) wire of the auto shutdown relay 4-way connector	• The fuel pump turns on	• Replace the auto shutdown relay
	• The fuel pump does not turn on	• Repair the Z1 (DG/BK) wire of the 4-way connector for an open circuit to the wiring harness splice

TEST NS-19	STEP B	CHECKING FOR BATTERY SUPPLY VOLTAGE TO THE AUTO SHUTDOWN RELAY CONTACT POINTS (INPUT SIDE J1 CIRCUIT)
COMPLETE TEST NS-14A BEFORE PROCEEDING		

PROCEDURE	TEST INDICATION	ACTION REQUIRED
• Connect a voltmeter to the J1 (R) wire in the auto shutdown relay 4-way connector and ground	• The voltmeter reads battery voltage	• Perform STEP C.
	• The voltmeter reads 0 volts	• Repair the J1 (RD) wire of the 4-way connector for an open circuit to the wiring harness splice

1988 2.2L AND 2.5L DRIVEABILITY DIAGNOSTIC CHART

TEST DR-1	STEP A	CHECKING SYSTEM FOR FAULT CODES

PROCEDURE	TEST INDICATION	CIRCUIT	ACTION REQUIRED
• Connect DRBII • Put the system in Diagnostic Test Mode. • RECORD ALL CODES NOTE: If fault codes 15-17-21-33-51 or 52 appear at this time proceed to test indication. • Erase fault codes • Start engine. CAUTION: Do not depress accelerator to start engine. • Raise engine speed to 2,000 rpm for 10 seconds and then return to idle. • Cycle transmission gear selector. • If equipped, press A/C button on and off • Turn engine off • Put system in Diagnostic Test Mode. • RECORD ALL CODES If the same code appears before and after the engine is started, the problem still exists. Proceed to test indications If a code does not reappear after the engine is started, the problem no longer exists. Perform Driveability TEST 1 STEP O.	88-12-55	No fault codes	Perform STEP B
	88-12-13-55 88-12-14-55 88-12-13-14-55	M A P sensor	Perform TEST DR-2
	88-12-15-55	Speed sensor	Perform TEST DR-3
	88-11-12-16-55	Battery voltage sense/ SMEC memory circuit	Perform charging system TEST NO. CH-3
	88-12-17-55	Engine running too cool	Check engine cooling system for a bad thermostat
	88-12-21-55	Oxygen sensor	Perform TEST DR-4
	88-12-22-55 88-12-17-22-55	Engine coolant sensor	Perform TEST DR-5
	88-12-23-55	Throttle body temperature sensor	Perform TEST DR-6
	88-12-24-55	Throttle position sensor	Perform TEST DR-7
	88-12-25-55	Idle motor	Perform TEST DR-8
	88-12-31-55	Purge solenoid	Perform TEST DR-9
	88-12-32-55 (California only)	EGR system	Perform TEST DR-10
	88-12-33-55	A/C cutout relay	Perform TEST DR-11
	88-12-35-55	Radiator fan relay	Perform TEST DR-12
	88-12-37-55	Transmission lock-up solenoid circuit.	Perform TEST DR-13
	88-12-44-55	Fused J2	Perform TEST DR-14
	88-12-51-55	Oxygen feedback system locked lean	Perform TEST DR-17
	88-12-52-55	Oxygen feedback system locked rich	
	88-12-53-55		Replace the SMEC

1987–88 2.5L DIAGNOSTIC CHART—DRIVEABILITY TEST

TEST DR-1	STEP B	CHECKING THE OUTPUT CIRCUITS OF THE SMEC CONTROLLED COMPONENTS
COMPLETE TEST DR-1A BEFORE PROCEEDING			

PROCEDURE	TEST INDICATION	ACTION REQUIRED
• DRB II connected. • Put the system into the **ATM Test 04.**	**Test Code 04** • The radiator fan should be turning on and off every two seconds.	• Radiator fan is turning on and off, press and hold the ATM key as follows: **Without A/C** until Test Code 07 appears. **With A/C** until Test Code 05 appears.
		• If fan does not turn on and off, is the relay clicking? If it is, repair the circuit to the radiator fan motor as required. • If the relay does not click, replace the relay.
	Test Code 05 • You should hear the A/C cutout relay clicking every two seconds. **CAUTION:** A/C compressor clutch will also cycle every two seconds and the cooling fan runs continuously.	• A/C relay clicking, press and hold the ATM key until Test Code 07 appears. • If the A/C relay is not clicking replace it.
	Test Code 07 • You should hear the canister purge solenoid clicking.	• Canister purge solenoid clicking. **With Manual Transmission** press and hold the ATM key until Test Code 10 appears. **With Automatic Transmission Perform STEP D.** • If the canister purge solenoid is not clicking replace it.
	Test Code 10 Manual Trans • You should see the shift indicator lamp on the instrument panel turning on and off	• If the shift indicator lamp is turning on and off, **Perform STEP D.** • If the shift indicator lamp is not turning on and off, **Perform STEP C.**

TEST DR-1	STEP C	CHECKING SHIFT INDICATOR LAMP CIRCUIT
COMPLETE TEST DR-1B BEFORE PROCEEDING			

PROCEDURE	VIEW FROM TERMINAL END	TEST INDICATION	ACTION REQUIRED
• Turn ignition switch off. • Disconnect the 60-way connector. • Connect one end of a jumper wire to the U3 (OR/BK) wire in cavity No. 55 of the 60-way connector. • Turn ignition switch on. • Touch the other end of the jumper wire to battery negative post.	U3 OR/BK 55	• Shift indicator lamp is on.	• Defective logic board. Replace the SMEC. **CAUTION:** Before replacing the SMEC, check the U3 terminal in cavity No. 55 to make sure it is not damaged causing a poor connection.
		• Shift indicator lamp is off.	• Repair U3 (OR/BK) wire in cavity No. 55 for an open circuit, check for a burned out bulb, or check for ignition feed voltage to lamp

TEST DR-1	STEP D	CHECKING SWITCH INPUTS TO THE SMEC
COMPLETE TEST DR-1B BEFORE PROCEEDING			

PROCEDURE	TEST INDICATION	ACTION REQUIRED
• DRB II connected. • Put the system into the **Switch Test Mode.** • Check switch inputs as follows: a) press down on brake pedal b) move gear selector from park to reverse to neutral to drive c) with A/C, turn the blower switch on and press the A/C button	• Display on the DRB II box changes as each switch is activated. **NOTE:** It is not important what display changes to. Just make sure it changes	• Switch inputs OK **Perform STEP I.**
	• Display on the DRB II does not change when one or more of the switches are activated	• Switch input malfunction **Perform STEPS** as follows: Brake Switch w/o Speed Control **STEP E** With Speed Control **STEP F** Park/Neutral Switch **STEP G** A/C Button **STEP H**

TEST DR-1	STEP E	CHECKING BRAKE SWITCH INPUT CIRCUIT TO THE SMEC – WITHOUT SPEED CONTROL (D40 CIRCUIT)
COMPLETE TEST DR-1D BEFORE PROCEEDING			

PROCEDURE	VIEW FROM TERMINAL END	TEST INDICATION	ACTION REQUIRED
• Turn ignition switch off • Disconnect the 60-way connector from the SMEC • Connect voltmeter to the D40 (WT/PK) D4 (WT/TN Omni/Horizon) wire in cavity No. 29 of the 60-way connector and ground • Turn ignition switch to the run position • Press brake pedal down	D40 WT/PK 29 — VOLTMETER — D4 (WT/TN) OMNI/HORIZON ONLY	• Voltmeter is reading within one volt of battery voltage	• Defective logic board. Replace the SMEC. **CAUTION:** Before replacing the SMEC, check the D40 terminal in cavity No. 29 of the 60-way connector to make sure it is not damaged causing a poor connection
		• Voltmeter reads 0	• Check the D40 (WT/PK) wire of cavity No. 29 for open circuit to brake switch • Check for a bad brake switch • Check voltage supply circuit to the brake switch

TEST DR-1	STEP G	CHECKING PARK/NEUTRAL SWITCH INPUT CIRCUIT TO THE SMEC (S4 CIRCUIT)
COMPLETE TEST DR-1D BEFORE PROCEEDING			

PROCEDURE	VIEW FROM TERMINAL END	TEST INDICATION	ACTION REQUIRED
• Turn ignition switch off • Disconnect the 60-way connector from the SMEC • Connect an ohmmeter between the S4 (BN/YL) wire in cavity No. 30 of the 60-way connector and ground • **Disconnect the battery quick disconnect.** • Turn the ignition switch to the run position • Put gear selector in park, reverse, neutral, and drive and observe ohmmeter in each position	30 — OHMMETER	• Ohmmeter shows continuity in all positions of the gear selector	• Check S4 (BN/YL) wire of cavity No. 30 for a short circuit to ground • Check for a bad safety neutral switch
		• Ohmmeter shows open in all positions of the gear selector	• Repair S4 (BN/YL) wire of cavity No. 30 for an open circuit to the safety neutral switch. • Check for bad safety neutral switch
		• Ohmmeter reads as follows: Park – Continuity Reverse – No Continuity Neutral – Continuity Drive – No Continuity **NOTE:** Disregard any resistance readings. Just make sure there is continuity	• Defective logic board. Replace the SMEC. **CAUTION:** Before replacing the SMEC, check the S4 terminal in cavity No. 30 of the 60-way connector to make sure it is not damaged causing a poor connection

TEST DR-1	STEP F	CHECKING BRAKE SWITCH INPUT CIRCUIT TO THE SMEC – WITH SPEED CONTROL (D40 CIRCUIT)
COMPLETE TEST DR-1D BEFORE PROCEEDING			

PROCEDURE	VIEW FROM TERMINAL END	TEST INDICATION	ACTION REQUIRED
• Turn the ignition switch off • Disconnect the 60-way connector from the SMEC • Connect an ohmmeter between the D40 wire (WT/PK) at cavity No. 29 of the 60-way connector and ground • Press down on brake pedal then release	N31 VT 29 — OHMMETER	• Ohmmeter shows open when brake pedal is pressed down and continuity when released	• Defective logic board. Replace the SMEC. **CAUTION:** Before replacing the SMEC, check the D40 terminal in cavity No. 29 of the 60-way connector to make sure it is not damaged causing a poor connection
		• Ohmmeter does not read as above	• Check D40 (WT/PK) wire of cavity No. 29 for an open circuit to the brake switch • Check for a bad brake switch • Check for an open circuit to the stop lights including to the bulbs

TEST DR-1	STEP H	CHECKING A/C PUSH BUTTON SWITCH INPUT CIRCUIT TO THE SMEC
COMPLETE TEST DR-1D BEFORE PROCEEDING			

PROCEDURE	VIEW FROM TERMINAL END	TEST INDICATION	ACTION REQUIRED
• Turn ignition switch off • Disconnect the 60-way connector from the SMEC • Connect an ohmmeter between the C20 (BN) wire in cavity No. 45 of the 60-way connector and ground • Turn the blower switch on and press the A/C button and then the off button. **NOTE:** The A/C system must have an adequate freon charge for this test to work.	C20 BR 45 — OHMMETER	• Ohmmeter shows continuity when A/C button is pressed, and open when off button is pressed	• Defective logic board. Replace the SMEC. **CAUTION:** Before replacing the SMEC, check the C20 terminal in cavity No. 45 of the 60-way connector to make sure it is not damaged causing a poor connection.
		• Ohmmeter reading is not as described above	• Repair the C20 (BN) wire in cavity No. 45 for an open or short circuit to the wiring harness splice

1987–88 2.5L DIAGNOSTIC CHART—DRIVEABILITY TEST

TEST DR-1	STEP I	CHECKING AUTOMATIC IDLE SPEED MOTOR OPERATION

COMPLETE TEST DR-1D BEFORE PROCEEDING

PROCEDURE	TEST INDICATION	ACTION REQUIRED
• Connect DRB II NOTE: Make sure Read is displayed. • Connect a tachometer to the engine. • Start the engine. • Disconnect the coolant sensor. • Press the read/hold key on the DRB II so Hold is displayed. • Press the read/hold key on the DRB II so Read is displayed.	• Engine speed increases to approximately 1,500 rpm when Hold is displayed on the DRB II. • Engine returns to idle when Read is displayed on the DRB II.	• Perform STEP N.
	• Engine speed does not increase and decrease as described above	• Perform STEP J.

TEST DR-1	STEP K	CHECKING AUTOMATIC IDLE SPEED MOTOR SIGNAL AT THE SMEC (N2 AND N3 CIRCUITS)

COMPLETE TEST DR-1J BEFORE PROCEEDING

PROCEDURE	TEST INDICATION	ACTION REQUIRED
• DRB II connected • Automatic idle speed motor disconnected • Connect a voltmeter between the N2 (BR/WT) wire and the N4 (YL/BK) wire at terminal 3 and 2 of the AIS connector. • System in ATM Test 03.	• Voltmeter is pulsating between 0 and 12 volts every two seconds.	• Replace the automatic idle speed motor. CAUTION: Before replacing the idle motor check the terminals of the connector to make sure they are not damaged causing a poor connection.
	• Voltmeter does not pulsate.	• Perform STEP M

TEST DR-1	STEP J	CHECKING AUTOMATIC IDLE SPEED MOTOR SIGNAL FROM THE SMEC (N1 AND N4 CIRCUITS)

COMPLETE TEST DR-1I BEFORE PROCEEDING

PROCEDURE	TEST INDICATION	ACTION REQUIRED
• Turn the engine off. • DRB II connected. • Disconnect the automatic idle speed motor connector. • Connect a voltmeter between N1 (GY/RD) wire at terminal 1 and the N3 (VT/BK) wire at terminal 4 of the idle speed motor. • Put the system into ATM Test 03.	• Voltmeter is pulsating between 0 and 12 volts every two seconds.	• Perform STEP K.
	• Voltmeter does not pulsate.	• Perform STEP L.

TEST DR-1	STEP L	CHECKING AUTOMATIC IDLE SPEED MOTOR CIRCUIT AT THE SMEC 60-WAY CONNECTOR (N1 AND N3 CIRCUITS)

COMPLETE TEST DR-1J BEFORE PROCEEDING

PROCEDURE	TEST INDICATION	ACTION REQUIRED
• Turn the ignition switch off. • Reconnect the automatic idle speed motor connector. • Disconnect the 60-way connector. • Connect an ohmmeter between the N1 (GY/RD) wire at cavity No. 19 and the N3 (VT/BK) wire at cavity No. 20 of the 60-way connector.	• Ohmmeter shows continuity.	• Defective logic board. Replace the SMEC. CAUTION: Before replacing the SMEC, check the N1 and N3 terminals in cavities No. 19 and 20 of the 60-way connector to make sure they are not damaged causing a poor connection.
	• Ohmmeter is not showing continuity	• Repair N1 (GY/RD) wire at cavity 19 or the N3 (VT/BK) wire at cavity No. 20 of the 60-way for an open circuit to the automatic idle speed motor

TEST DR-1	STEP M	CHECKING AUTOMATIC IDLE SPEED MOTOR CIRCUIT AT THE SMEC 60-WAY CONNECTOR (N2 AND N4 CIRCUITS)

COMPLETE TEST DR-1K BEFORE PROCEEDING

PROCEDURE	TEST INDICATION	ACTION REQUIRED
• Turn the ignition switch off. • Reconnect the automatic idle speed motor connector. • Disconnect the 60-way connector from the SMEC. • Connect an ohmmeter between the N2 (BN/WT) wire at cavity No. 17 and the N4 (YL/BK) wire at cavity No. 18 of the 60-way connector.	• Ohmmeter shows continuity.	• Defective logic board. Replace the SMEC. CAUTION: Before replacing the SMEC, check the N2 and N4 terminals in cavities 17 and 18 of the 60-way connector to make sure they are not damaged causing a poor connection
	• Ohmmeter is not showing continuity	• Repair the N2 (BN/WT) wire of cavity No. 17 or the N4 (YL/BK) wire of cavity No. 18 for an open circuit to the automatic idle speed motor

TEST DR-1	STEP O	CHECKING FOR INTERMITTENT FAILURES CAUSED BY WIRING AND/OR CONNECTORS

COMPLETE TEST DR-1A BEFORE PROCEEDING

The majority of intermittent failures are caused by wiring and connections. One way to find them is to duplicate the problem. Since the SMEC can remember where they are, the ATM and Sensor Tests can be used in an attempt to locate them.

• If the following fault codes do not reappear use the **ATM TEST** as indicated.

Fault Code	ATM Test
25	03
26	02
27	02
31	07
32	11
35	04
42	06
43	01

Once in the correct test mode, wiggle all the connectors and wires in the circuit. When the bad connection or wire is located the ATM test will be interrupted.

• If the following fault codes do not reappear use the **Sensor Test** as indicated.

Fault Code	Sensor Test
14**	08
22	04
23	03
24	05

** When checking the M.A.P. sensor circuit, (fault code 14) apply 10 inches of vacuum to the M.A.P. sensor before testing.

Once in the correct test mode, wiggle all the connectors and wires in the circuit. When the bad connection or wire is located the display on the DRB II will change.

TEST DR-1	STEP N	CHECKING THE SMEC GROUND CIRCUITS

COMPLETE TEST DR-1I BEFORE PROCEEDING

PROCEDURE	TEST INDICATION	ACTION REQUIRED
• Turn the ignition switch off. • Disconnect both SMEC connectors. • Connect one lead of a digital ohmmeter to the system ground eyelet on cylinder head. • Connect the other lead of ohmmeter as follows: 14-way connector cavities No. 2 K5 (BK/WT), 6 and 7 J9 (BK). 60-way connector cavities K5 (BK/WT), 15 and 16 K9 (LB/RD). NOTE: Refer to introduction for information when using a digital volt/ohmmeter to measure resistance.	• Ohmmeter is showing continuity with less than ½ ohm of resistance at all cavities of the connectors.	• Perform TESTS as follows. If a cold problem TEST DR-15. If a warm problem TEST DR-17.
	• Ohmmeter is showing open at one or more cavities of the connectors.	• Defective ground wire. Repair the wire for an open circuit to the wiring harness connector.
	• Ohmmeter is showing more than ½ ohm of resistance at one or more cavities of the connectors.	• Ground circuit has excessive resistance. Repair circuit for high resistance to system ground eyelet.

1987–88 2.5L DIAGNOSTIC CHART—DRIVEABILITY TEST

TEST DR-2	STEP A	CHECKING FOR FAULT CODES 13 AND/OR 14—M.A.P. SENSOR CIRCUIT
COMPLETE TEST DR-1A BEFORE PROCEEDING		

PROCEDURE	TEST INDICATION	ACTION REQUIRED
• Turn ignition switch off • Tee a vacuum gauge into the vacuum line at the M.A.P. sensor • Start the engine and look at the vacuum gauge with the engine idling • Look at the vacuum gauge while snapping the throttle open and closed	• Vacuum gauge is reading manifold vacuum with the engine idling • Vacuum gauge reading immediately drops to 0 when the throttle is snapped open	• **Perform STEP B.**
	• Vacuum gauge reads 0 at idle	• Repair hole in vacuum line to throttle body
	• Vacuum gauge reading slowly drops to 0 when the throttle is snapped open	• Repair restriction in vacuum supply line to M.A.P. sensor

VACUUM GAUGE

TEST DR-2	STEP B	CHECKING THE M.A.P. SENSOR CIRCUIT IN THE SMEC
COMPLETE TEST DR-2A BEFORE PROCEEDING		

PROCEDURE	TEST INDICATION	ACTION REQUIRED
• DRB II connected. • Disconnect the M.A.P. sensor connector. • Put the system in **Sensor Test 08.**	• Display on the DRB II is reading at least 4 volts.	• SMEC is OK, **Perform STEP C.**
	• Display on the DRB II is reading 0 volts.	• Defective logic board. Replace the SMEC. **NOTE:** Before replacing the SMEC, make sure the EP1 wire of cavity No. 11 of the 60-way connector is not shorted to ground.

DISCONNECT

TEST DR-2	STEP E	CHECKING THE 5 VOLT SUPPLY TO THE M.A.P. SENSOR
COMPLETE TEST DR-2C BEFORE PROCEEDING		

PROCEDURE	TEST INDICATION	ACTION REQUIRED
• Ignition switch in the run position. • M.A.P. sensor connector disconnected. • Connect a digital voltmeter to the K8 (VT/WT) wire of the M.A.P. sensor harness connector and ground.	• Voltmeter is reading at least 4 volts.	• Replace the M.A.P. sensor **NOTE:** Before replacing the M.A.P. sensor, check the terminals in the harness connector to make sure they are not defective causing a poor connection.
	• Voltmeter is reading 0 volts.	• Repair the K8 (VT/WT) wire for an open circuit to the wiring harness splice.

DIGITAL VOLTMETER

N5 BK/LB — K8 VT/WT
 K4 DG/RD
 MAP SENSOR HARNESS CONNECTOR

TEST DR-3	STEP A	CHECKING FOR FAULT CODE 15 — SPEED SENSOR CIRCUIT
COMPLETE TEST DR-1A OR SC-1B BEFORE PROCEEDING		

PROCEDURE	TEST INDICATION	ACTION REQUIRED
• DRB II connected. • Start the engine. • Disconnect the speed sensor connector. • Put the system in the **Engine Running Test 71.** • Connect a jumper wire between the N5 (BK) and the G7 (WT/OR) terminals of the speed sensor harness connector. • Make and break this connection.	• As you make and break this connection the display on the DRB II changes.	• Replace the speed sensor.
	• As you make and break this connection the display on the DRB II does not change.	• **Perform STEP B.**

JUMPER

N5 BK — G7 WT/OR
 SPEED SENSOR CONNECTOR

TEST DR-2	STEP C	CHECKING THE M.A.P. SENSOR SIGNAL CIRCUIT TO THE SMEC (K4 CIRCUIT)
COMPLETE TEST DR-2B BEFORE PROCEEDING		

PROCEDURE	TEST INDICATION	ACTION REQUIRED
• DRB II connected. • System in Sensor Test 08 • M.A.P. sensor connector disconnected. • Connect a jumper wire between the K4 (DG/RD) wire and the N5 (BK/LB) wire of the M.A.P. sensor harness connector.	• Display on the DRB II is reading 0 volts.	• **Perform STEP E.**
	• Display on the DRB II is not reading 0 volts.	• Perform STEP D.

JUMPER

N5 BK/LB — K8 VT/WT
 K4 DG/RD
 MAP SENSOR HARNESS CONNECTOR

TEST DR-2	STEP D	CHECKING THE M.A.P. SENSOR WIRES TO THE SMEC FOR AN OPEN CIRCUIT (K4 AND N5 CIRCUITS)
COMPLETE TEST DR-2C BEFORE PROCEEDING		

PROCEDURE	TEST INDICATION	ACTION REQUIRED
• DRB II connected. • System in Sensor Test 08. • M.A.P. sensor disconnected. • Connect one end of a jumper wire to the negative terminal of the battery. • Connect the other end of the jumper wire to the K4 (DG/RD) wire terminal of the M.A.P. sensor harness connector.	• Display on the DRB II is reading 0 volts.	• Repair the N5 (BK/LB) wire of the M.A.P. sensor connector for an open circuit to the wiring harness splice.
	• Display on the DRB II is reading 5 volts.	• Repair the K4 (DG/RD) wire of the M.A.P. sensor connector for an open circuit to the SMEC.

JUMPER

N5 BK/LB — K8 VT/WT
 K4 DG/RD
 MAP SENSOR HARNESS CONNECTOR

TEST DR-3	STEP B	CHECKING THE SPEED SENSOR SIGNAL WIRE TO THE SMEC FOR AN OPEN CIRCUIT (G7 CIRCUIT)
COMPLETE TEST DR-3A BEFORE PROCEEDING		

PROCEDURE	TEST INDICATION	ACTION REQUIRED
• Speed sensor connector disconnected. • Turn the engine off. • Disconnect the 60-way connector from the SMEC. • Connect an ohmmeter between the G7 (WT/OR) wire at cavity No. 48 of the 60-way connector and the G7 (WT/OR) wire terminal of the speed sensor harness connector.	VIEW FROM TERMINAL END • Ohmmeter shows continuity.	• **Perform STEP C.**
	• Ohmmeter is not showing continuity.	• Repair the G7 (WT/OR) wire in cavity No. 48 of the 60-way connector for an open circuit to the speed sensor connector.

N5 BK/LB — G7 WT/OR
 SPEED SENSOR CONNECTOR

TEST DR-3	STEP C	CHECKING THE SPEED SENSOR GROUND WIRE TO THE SMEC FOR AN OPEN CIRCUIT (N5 CIRCUIT)
COMPLETE TEST DR-3B BEFORE PROCEEDING		

PROCEDURE	TEST INDICATION	ACTION REQUIRED
• Engine off. • Speed sensor connector disconnected. • 60-way connector disconnected. • Connect an ohmmeter between the N5 (BK/LB) wire at cavity No. 4 of the 60-way connector and the N5 (BK) wire terminal of the speed sensor harness connector.	VIEW FROM TERMINAL END • Ohmmeter shows continuity.	• Defective logic board. Replace the SMEC. **CAUTION:** Before replacing the SMEC, check the G7 terminal in cavity No. 48 of the 60-way connector to make sure they are not damaged causing a poor connection.
	• Ohmmeter is not showing continuity.	• Repair the N5 (BK/LB) wire of the speed sensor connector for an open circuit to the wiring harness splice.

N5 BK/LB — G7 WT/OR
 SPEED SENSOR CONNECTOR

1987–88 2.5L DIAGNOSTIC CHART—DRIVEABILITY TEST

TEST DR-4 | **STEP A** | CHECKING FOR FAULT CODE 21 — OXYGEN SENSOR CIRCUIT

COMPLETE TEST DR-1A BEFORE PROCEEDING

PROCEDURE	TEST INDICATION	ACTION REQUIRED
• Turn the ignition switch off. • DRB II connected. • Disconnect the oxygen sensor connector. • Turn key on. • Put the system into Sensor Test 02.	• Display on the DRB II is reading at least .4 volts. (4 tenths)	• Perform STEP B.
	• Display on the DRB II is reading 0.	• Defective logic board. Replace the SMEC. **NOTE:** Before replacing the SMEC, make sure the N11 (BK/DG) wire at cavity No. 23 of the SMEC 60-way connector is not shorted to ground.

TEST DR-4 | **STEP B** | CHECKING THE OXYGEN SENSOR TO THE SMEC FOR AN OPEN CIRCUIT (N11 CIRCUIT)

COMPLETE TEST DR-4A BEFORE PROCEEDING

PROCEDURE	TEST INDICATION	ACTION REQUIRED
• System in Sensor Test 02. • Oxygen sensor connector disconnected. • Connect one end of a jumper wire to the N11 (BK/DG) wire of the oxygen sensor harness connector. • Connect the other end of the jumper wire to the battery positive post.	• Display on the DRB II is reading at least 5 volts.	• Replace the oxygen sensor.
	• Display on the DRB II is reading .4 volts, (4 tenths).	• Repair the N11 (BK/DG) wire of the oxygen sensor connector for an open circuit to the SMEC.

TEST DR-5 | **STEP C** | CHECKING THE COOLANT SENSOR WIRES TO THE SMEC FOR AN OPEN CIRCUIT (K10 AND N5 CIRCUITS)

COMPLETE TEST DR-5B BEFORE PROCEEDING

PROCEDURE	TEST INDICATION	ACTION REQUIRED
• DRB II connected • System in Sensor Test 04 • Coolant sensor disconnected • Connect one end of a jumper wire to ground • Connect the other end of the jumper wire to the K10 (TN/WT) terminal of the coolant sensor harness connector	• Display on the DRB II is reading 260°	• Repair the N5 (BK/LB) wire of the coolant sensor harness connector for an open circuit to the wiring harness splice
	• Display on the DRB II is reading 00°	• Repair the K10 (TN/WT) wire of the coolant sensor harness connector for an open circuit to the SMEC

TEST DR-6 | **STEP A** | CHECKING FOR FAULT CODE 23 – THROTTLE BODY TEMPERATURE SENSOR

COMPLETE TEST DR-1A BEFORE PROCEEDING

PROCEDURE	TEST INDICATION	ACTION REQUIRED
• DRB II connected. • Disconnect the throttle body temperature sensor connector. • Put the system in Sensor Test 03.	• Display on the DRB II is reading 5 volts.	• Perform STEP B.
	• Display on the DRB II is reading 0 volts or 0 volts and then increases.	• Replace the SMEC. **CAUTION:** Before replacing the SMEC, make sure the K13 (BK/RD) wire of cavity No. 21 of the 60-way connector is not shorted to ground.

TEST DR-5 | **STEP A** | CHECKING FOR FAULT CODE 22 — COOLANT SENSOR CIRCUIT

COMPLETE TEST DR-1A BEFORE PROCEEDING

PROCEDURE	TEST INDICATION	ACTION REQUIRED
• DRB II connected • Turn the ignition switch off. • Disconnect the coolant sensor connector • Put the system in Sensor Test 04.	• Display on the DRB II is reading 00°	• Perform STEP B.
	• Display on the DRB II is reading 260°	• Defective logic board. Replace the SMEC. **NOTE:** Before replacing the SMEC, make sure the K10 (TN/WT) wire at cavity No. 3 of the 60-way connector is not shorted to ground

TEST DR-5 | **STEP B** | CHECKING THE COOLANT SENSOR CIRCUIT TO THE SMEC (K10 CIRCUIT)

COMPLETE TEST DR-5A BEFORE PROCEEDING

PROCEDURE	TEST INDICATION	ACTION REQUIRED
• DRB II connected • System in Sensor Test 04 • Coolant sensor connector disconnector • Connect a jumper wire between the K10 (TN/WT) and the N5 (BK/LB) terminals of the coolant sensor connector.	• Display on the DRB II is reading 260°	• Replace the coolant sensor
	• Display on the DRB II is reading 00°	• Perform STEP C.

TEST DR-6 | **STEP B** | CHECKING THE THROTTLE BODY TEMPERATURE SENSOR SIGNAL CIRCUIT TO THE SMEC

COMPLETE TEST DR-6A BEFORE PROCEEDING

PROCEDURE	TEST INDICATION	ACTION REQUIRED
• DRB II connected • System in Sensor Test 03 • Throttle body temperature sensor connector disconnected • Connect a jumper wire between the terminals of the throttle body temperature sensor connector	• Display on the DRB II is reading 0 volts	• Replace the throttle body temperature sensor
	• Display on the DRB II is reading 5 volts	• Possible open circuit in K13 or N5. Perform STEP C.

TEST DR-6 | **STEP C** | CHECKING THE THROTTLE BODY TEMPERATURE SENSOR SIGNAL WIRE TO THE SMEC FOR AN OPEN CIRCUIT (K13 CIRCUIT)

COMPLETE TEST DR-6B BEFORE PROCEEDING

PROCEDURE	TEST INDICATION	ACTION REQUIRED
• DRB II connected • System in Sensor Test 03 • Throttle body temperature sensor connector disconnected • Connect one end of a jumper wire to the negative terminal of the battery • Connect the other end of the jumper wire to the K13 (BK/RD) terminal of the throttle body temperature sensor connector	• Display on the DRB II is reading 0 volts	• Repair the N5 (BK/LB) wire of the throttle body temperature sensor connector for an open circuit to the wiring harness splice
	• Display on the DRB II is reading 5 volts	• Repair the K13 (BK/RD) wire of the throttle body temperature sensor connector for an open circuit to the SMEC

1987–88 2.5L DIAGNOSTIC CHART—DRIVEABILITY TEST

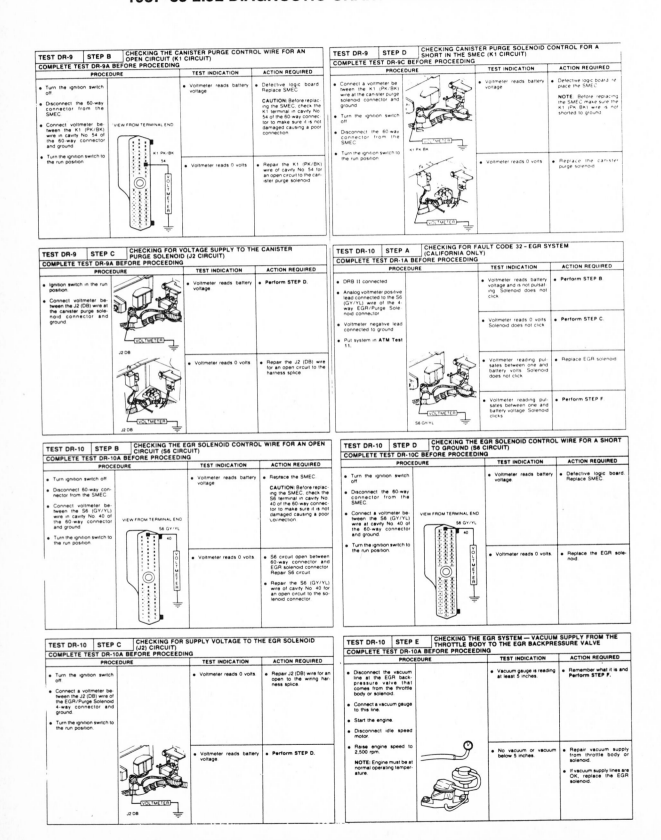

TEST DR-9	STEP B	CHECKING THE CANISTER PURGE CONTROL WIRE FOR AN OPEN CIRCUIT (K1 CIRCUIT)
COMPLETE TEST DR-9A BEFORE PROCEEDING		

PROCEDURE	TEST INDICATION	ACTION REQUIRED
• Turn the ignition switch off. • Disconnect the 60-way connector from the SMEC. • Connect voltmeter between the K1 (PK/BK) wire in cavity No 54 of the 60-way connector and ground. • Turn the ignition switch to the run position.	• Voltmeter reads battery voltage.	• Defective logic board Replace SMEC. CAUTION: Before replacing the SMEC, check the K1 terminal in cavity No. 54 of the 60-way connector to make sure it is not damaged causing a poor connection.
	• Voltmeter reads 0 volts.	• Repair the K1 (PK/BK) wire of cavity No 54 for an open circuit to the canister purge solenoid.

TEST DR-9	STEP D	CHECKING CANISTER PURGE SOLENOID CONTROL FOR A SHORT IN THE SMEC (K1 CIRCUIT)
COMPLETE TEST DR-9C BEFORE PROCEEDING		

PROCEDURE	TEST INDICATION	ACTION REQUIRED
• Connect a voltmeter between the K1 (PK/BK) wire at the canister purge solenoid connector and ground. • Turn the ignition switch off. • Disconnect the 60-way connector from the SMEC. • Turn the ignition switch to the run position.	• Voltmeter reads battery voltage.	• Defective logic board, replace the SMEC. NOTE: Before replacing the SMEC make sure the K1 (PK/BK) wire is not shorted to ground.
	• Voltmeter reads 0 volts.	• Replace the canister purge solenoid.

TEST DR-9	STEP C	CHECKING FOR VOLTAGE SUPPLY TO THE CANISTER PURGE SOLENOID (J2 CIRCUIT)
COMPLETE TEST DR-9A BEFORE PROCEEDING		

PROCEDURE	TEST INDICATION	ACTION REQUIRED
• Ignition switch in the run position. • Connect voltmeter between the J2 (DB) wire at the canister purge solenoid connector and ground.	• Voltmeter reads battery voltage.	• Perform STEP D.
	• Voltmeter reads 0 volts.	• Repair the J2 (DB) wire for an open circuit to the harness splice.

TEST DR-10	STEP A	CHECKING FOR FAULT CODE 32 – EGR SYSTEM (CALIFORNIA ONLY)
COMPLETE TEST DR-1A BEFORE PROCEEDING		

PROCEDURE	TEST INDICATION	ACTION REQUIRED
• DRB II connected • Analog voltmeter positive lead connected to the S6 (GY/YL) wire of the 4-way EGR/Purge Solenoid connector. • Voltmeter negative lead connected to ground. • Put system in ATM Test 11.	• Voltmeter reads battery voltage and is not pulsating. Solenoid does not click	• Perform STEP B.
	• Voltmeter reads 0 volts. Solenoid does not click	• Perform STEP C.
	• Voltmeter reading pulsates between one and battery volts. Solenoid does not click	• Replace EGR solenoid.
	• Voltmeter reading pulsates between one and battery voltage. Solenoid clicks	• Perform STEP F.

TEST DR-10	STEP B	CHECKING THE EGR SOLENOID CONTROL WIRE FOR AN OPEN CIRCUIT (S6 CIRCUIT)
COMPLETE TEST DR-10A BEFORE PROCEEDING		

PROCEDURE	TEST INDICATION	ACTION REQUIRED
• Turn ignition switch off. • Disconnect 60-way connector from the SMEC. • Connect voltmeter between the S6 (GY/YL) wire in cavity No. 40 of the 60-way connector and ground. • Turn the ignition switch to the run position.	• Voltmeter reads battery voltage.	• Replace the SMEC. CAUTION: Before replacing the SMEC, check the S6 terminal in cavity No. 40 of the 60-way connector to make sure it is not damaged causing a poor connection.
	• Voltmeter reads 0 volts.	• S6 circuit open between 60-way connector and EGR solenoid connector Repair S6 circuit. • Repair the S6 (GY/YL) wire of cavity No 40 for an open circuit to the solenoid connector

TEST DR-10	STEP D	CHECKING THE EGR SOLENOID CONTROL WIRE FOR A SHORT TO GROUND (S6 CIRCUIT)
COMPLETE TEST DR-10C BEFORE PROCEEDING		

PROCEDURE	TEST INDICATION	ACTION REQUIRED
• Turn the ignition switch off. • Disconnect the 60-way connector from the SMEC. • Connect a voltmeter between the S6 (GY/YL) wire at cavity No. 40 of the 60-way connector and ground. • Turn the ignition switch to the run position.	• Voltmeter reads battery voltage.	• Defective logic board. Replace SMEC.
	• Voltmeter reads 0 volts.	• Replace the EGR solenoid.

TEST DR-10	STEP C	CHECKING FOR SUPPLY VOLTAGE TO THE EGR SOLENOID (J2 CIRCUIT)
COMPLETE TEST DR-10A BEFORE PROCEEDING		

PROCEDURE	TEST INDICATION	ACTION REQUIRED
• Turn the ignition switch off. • Connect a voltmeter between the J2 (DB) wire of the EGR/Purge Solenoid 4-way connector and ground. • Turn the ignition switch to the run position.	• Voltmeter reads 0 volts.	• Repair J2 (DB) wire for an open to the wiring harness splice.
	• Voltmeter reads battery voltage.	• Perform STEP D.

TEST DR-10	STEP E	CHECKING THE EGR SYSTEM — VACUUM SUPPLY FROM THE THROTTLE BODY TO THE EGR BACKPRESSURE VALVE
COMPLETE TEST DR-10A BEFORE PROCEEDING		

PROCEDURE	TEST INDICATION	ACTION REQUIRED
• Disconnect the vacuum line at the EGR backpressure valve that comes from the throttle body or solenoid. • Connect a vacuum gauge to this line. • Start the engine. • Disconnect idle speed motor. • Raise engine speed to 2,500 rpm. NOTE: Engine must be at normal operating temperature.	• Vacuum gauge is reading at least 5 inches.	• Remember what it is and Perform STEP F.
	• No vacuum or vacuum below 5 inches.	• Repair vacuum supply from throttle body or solenoid. • If vacuum supply lines are OK, replace the EGR solenoid.

1987–88 2.5L DIAGNOSTIC CHART — DRIVEABILITY TEST

TEST DR-10	STEP F	CHECKING THE VACUUM SUPPLY FROM THE BACKPRESSURE VALVE TO THE EGR VALVE
COMPLETE TEST DR-10F BEFORE PROCEEDING		

PROCEDURE	TEST INDICATION	ACTION REQUIRED
• Engine running • Disconnect the vacuum gauge from the vacuum line and reconnect the vacuum line to the backpressure valve • Disconnect the vacuum line from the EGR valve and connect a vacuum gauge to it • Disconnect idle speed motor • Raise engine speed to 2,500 rpm	• Vacuum gauge is reading the same or near the same as seen in STEP E.	• Perform STEP G.
	• Vacuum gauge is not reading the same or near the same as seen in STEP E.	• Replace EGR/backpressure valve assembly

TEST DR-10	STEP H	CHECKING THE EGR VALVE VACUUM CHAMBER FOR LEAKS
COMPLETE TEST DR-10H BEFORE PROCEEDING		

PROCEDURE	TEST INDICATION	ACTION REQUIRED
• Vacuum line disconnected from the EGR valve • Auxiliary vacuum supply connected to the EGR valve • Engine running at idle speed • Reconnect the automatic idle speed motor • Apply 10 inches of vacuum to EGR valve	• Vacuum should hold without bleeding for at least 10 seconds	• Perform TEST DR-17.
	• Vacuum does not hold or bleeds down before 10 seconds	• Replace EGR/backpressure valve assembly

AUXILIARY VACUUM

TEST DR-10	STEP G	CHECKING THE EGR VALVE OPERATION
COMPLETE TEST DR-10G BEFORE PROCEEDING		

PROCEDURE	TEST INDICATION	ACTION REQUIRED
• Vacuum line disconnected from the EGR valve • Engine running • Connect an auxiliary vacuum supply to the EGR valve • Disconnect the automatic idle speed motor • With engine running at idle speed, slowly apply vacuum	• Engine speed begins to drop when applied vacuum reaches 2½ to 3½ inches	• Perform STEP H.
	• Engine speed does not drop	• Replace EGR/backpressure valve assembly

AUXILIARY VACUUM

TEST DR-11	STEP A	CHECKING FOR FAULT CODE 33 — A/C CUTOUT RELAY
COMPLETE TEST DR-1A BEFORE PROCEEDING		

PROCEDURE	TEST INDICATION	ACTION REQUIRED
NOTE: In order for the A/C cutout relay to operate the radiator fan relay on passenger cars or the A/C condensor fan relay on mini vans must be operating correctly. Do not proceed with test unless they are. If they are not working disregard fault code 33. • Connect a voltmeter to N13 (DB/OR) wire of the A/C cutout relay single connector and ground • Turn ignition switch to the run position • Turn the blower switch on and press the A/C button to the ''on'' position. Make sure the radiator or condensor fan is running	• Voltmeter reads battery voltage	• Perform STEP B.
	• Voltmeter reads 0–1 volts.	• Perform STEP C.

VOLTMETER

N13 DB/OR

A/C CUT-OUT RELAY

TEST DR-11	STEP B	CHECKING THE A/C CUTOUT RELAY CONTROL WIRE FOR AN OPEN CIRCUIT TO THE SMEC (N13 CIRCUIT)
COMPLETE TEST DR-11A BEFORE PROCEEDING		

PROCEDURE	TEST INDICATION	ACTION REQUIRED
• Turn the ignition switch off. • Disconnect the 60-way connector from the SMEC. • Connect a jumper wire between cavity No. 57 of the 60-way connector and ground. • Connect a voltmeter to the N13 (DB/OR) wire in cavity No. 56 of the 60-way connector and ground. • Turn the ignition switch to the run position. **CAUTION:** The radiator or condensor fan will turn on.	• Voltmeter reads battery voltage.	• Defective logic board. Replace the SMEC. **CAUTION:** Before replacing the SMEC, check N13 terminal in cavity No. 56 of the 60-way connector to make sure it is not damaged causing a poor connection.
	• Voltmeter reads 0.	• Repair the N13 (DB/OR) wire of cavity No. 56 for an open circuit to the A/C cutout relay. **NOTE:** This wire has a diode in it. Make sure it is not failed causing an open circuit.

VIEW FROM TERMINAL END

57

56

JUMPER / VOLTMETER

TEST DR-11	STEP D	CHECKING FOR VOLTAGE SUPPLY TO THE A/C CUTOUT RELAY PULL IN COIL (C25 CIRCUIT)
COMPLETE TEST DR-11C BEFORE PROCEEDING		

PROCEDURE	TEST INDICATION	ACTION REQUIRED
• Ignition switch in the run position • Cavity No. 57 of the 60-way connector grounded • Radiator or condensor fan running • Connect a voltmeter to the C25 (LG) wire of the A/C cutout relay 3-way connector and ground.	• Voltmeter reads battery voltage	• Replace the A/C cutout relay
	• Voltmeter reads 0	• Repair the C25 (LG) wire to the radiator fan relay for passenger cars or the condensor fan relay for mini vans.

VOLTMETER

C26 GY

C2 DB/BK   C25 LG

A/C CUTOUT RELAY CONNECTOR

TEST DR-11	STEP C	CHECKING A/C CUTOUT RELAY PULL IN COIL CIRCUIT FOR A SHORT TO THE SMEC (N13 CIRCUIT)
COMPLETE TEST DR-11A BEFORE PROCEEDING		

PROCEDURE	TEST INDICATION	ACTION REQUIRED
• Voltmeter connected to the N13 (DB/OR) wire of the A/C cutout relay single connector. • Turn the ignition switch off. • Disconnect the 60-way connector from the SMEC. • Connect a jumper wire between cavity No. 57 of the 60-way connector and ground. • Turn the ignition switch to the run position. **CAUTION:** The radiator or condensor fan will turn on.	• Voltmeter reads battery voltage.	• Replace the SMEC.
	• Voltmeter reads 0.	• Perform STEP D.

VOLTMETER

N13 DB/OR

A/C CUT-OUT RELAY

TEST DR-12	STEP A	CHECKING FOR FAULT CODE 35 — RADIATOR FAN RELAY CONTROL CIRCUIT
COMPLETE TEST DR-1A BEFORE PROCEEDING		

PROCEDURE	TEST INDICATION	ACTION REQUIRED
• Connect a voltmeter to the C27 (DB/PK) wire of the radiator fan relay 3-way connector and ground. • Turn the ignition switch to the run position.	• Voltmeter reads battery voltage	• Perform STEP B.
	• Voltmeter reads 0–1 volts.	• Perform STEP C.

VOLTMETER

C27 DB/PK   LG

DB

RADIATOR FAN RELAY

1987–88 2.5L DIAGNOSTIC CHART—DRIVEABILITY TEST

TEST DR-12 | STEP B — CHECKING THE RADIATOR FAN RELAY CONTROL WIRE FOR AN OPEN CIRCUIT TO THE SMEC (C27 CIRCUIT)
COMPLETE TEST DR-12A BEFORE PROCEEDING

PROCEDURE	TEST INDICATION	ACTION REQUIRED
• Turn the ignition switch off. • Disconnect the 60-way connector from the SMEC. • Connect a voltmeter to the C27 (DB/PK) wire in cavity NO. 57 of the 60-way connector and ground. • Turn the ignition switch to the run position.	• Voltmeter reads battery voltage	• Defective logic board. Replace the SMEC. CAUTION: Before replacing the SMEC, check the C27 terminal in cavity No. 57 of the 60-way connector to make sure it is not damaged causing a poor connection
	• Voltmeter reads 0 volts	• Repair the C27 (DB/PK) wire of cavity No. 57 for an open circuit to the radiator fan relay

TEST DR-12 | STEP D — CHECKING FOR VOLTAGE SUPPLY TO THE RADIATOR FAN RELAY PULL IN COIL (J2 CIRCUIT)
COMPLETE TEST DR-1B BEFORE PROCEEDING

PROCEDURE	TEST INDICATION	ACTION REQUIRED
• Ignition switch in the run position. • Connect a voltmeter to the J2 (DB) wire of the radiator fan relay single connector and ground.	• Voltmeter reads battery voltage	• Replace the radiator fan relay
	• Voltmeter reads 0	• Repair the J2 (DB) wire of the single connector for an open circuit to the wiring harness splice

TEST DR-12 | STEP C — CHECKING RADIATOR FAN RELAY PULL IN COIL CIRCUIT FOR A SHORT CIRCUIT IN THE SMEC (C27 CIRCUIT)
COMPLETE TEST DR-12A BEFORE PROCEEDING

PROCEDURE	TEST INDICATION	ACTION REQUIRED
• Voltmeter connected to the C27 (DB/PK) wire of the radiator fan relay 3-way connector and ground. • Turn the ignition switch off. • Disconnect the 60-way connector from the SMEC. • Turn the ignition switch to the run position.	• Voltmeter reads battery voltage.	• Defective logic board, replace the SMEC.
	• Voltmeter reads 0 volts	• Perform STEP D.

TEST DR-13 | STEP A — CHECKING FOR FAULT CODE 37 – TRANSMISSION LOCKUP SOLENOID
COMPLETE TEST DR-1A BEFORE PROCEEDING

PROCEDURE	TEST INDICATION	ACTION REQUIRED
• Turn the ignition switch off. • Disconnect the 60-way connector from the SMEC. • Connect a voltmeter to the U3 (OR/BK) wire in cavity No. 55 of the 60-way connector and ground. • Turn the ignition switch to the run position.	• Voltmeter reads battery voltage	• Defective logic board. Replace the SMEC. CAUTION: Before replacing the SMEC, check the U3 terminal in cavity No. 55 of the 60-way connector to make sure it is not damaged causing a poor connection
	• Voltmeter reads 0	• Perform STEP B

TEST DR-13 | STEP B — CHECKING THE TRANSMISSION LOCKUP SOLENOID CONTROL WIRE FOR AN OPEN CIRCUIT (U3 CIRCUIT)
COMPLETE TEST DR-13A BEFORE PROCEEDING

PROCEDURE	TEST INDICATION	ACTION REQUIRED
• 60-way connector disconnected. • Voltmeter connected between the U3 (OR/BK) wire in cavity No. 55 of the 60-way connector and ground. • Ignition switch in the run position. • Disconnect the transmission lockup solenoid connector. • Connect a jumper wire between the terminals of the transmission lockup solenoid connector.	• Voltmeter reads battery voltage	• Replace the transmission lockup solenoid
	• Voltmeter reads 0 volts	• Perform STEP C.

TEST DR-14 | STEP A — CHECKING FOR FAULT CODE 44 — FUSED J2
COMPLETE TEST DR-1A BEFORE PROCEEDING

PROCEDURE	TEST INDICATION	ACTION REQUIRED
• Turn the ignition switch off. • Disconnect the 60-way connector from the SMEC. • Connect a voltmeter between the K14 (DB/WT) wire in cavity No. 12 of the 60-way connector and ground. • Turn the ignition switch to the run position.	• Voltmeter reads battery voltage	• Defective logic board. Replace SMEC. CAUTION: Before replacing the SMEC, make sure the K14 terminal in cavity No. 12 of the 60-way connector is not damaged causing a poor connection.
	• Voltmeter reads 0 volts.	• Repair the K14 (DB/WT) wire of cavity No. 12 for an open circuit to the wiring harness splice.

TEST NS-13 | STEP C — CHECKING FOR VOLTAGE SUPPLY TO THE TRANSMISSION LOCKUP SOLENOID (J2 CIRCUIT)
COMPLETE TEST NR-13B BEFORE PROCEEDING

PROCEDURE	TEST INDICATION	ACTION REQUIRED
• Transmission lockup solenoid connector disconnected. • Ignition switch in the run position. • Connect a voltmeter between the J2 (DB) wire terminal of the transmission lockup solenoid connector and ground.	• Voltmeter reads battery voltage	• Repair the U3 (OR/BK) wire of the transmission lockup solenoid connector for an open circuit.
	• Voltmeter reads 0 volts	• Repair the J2 (DB) wire of the transmission lockup solenoid connector for an open circuit to the wiring harness splice

THE FOLLOWING TEST MUST BEGIN WITH A COLD ENGINE

TEST DR-15 | STEP A — CHECKING SENSOR CALIBRATIONS (ENGINE COOLANT TEMPERATURE SENSOR)
COMPLETE TEST DR-1N BEFORE PROCEEDING

PROCEDURE	TEST INDICATION	ACTION REQUIRED
• DRB II connected. • Engine cold. • Put the system in Engine Running Test 64.	• Display on the DRB II is reading approximately ambient temperature ± 10°F	• Perform STEP B.
	• Display on the DRB II is reading more than 10°F above or below ambient temperature	• Replace the coolant sensor

1987–88 2.5L DIAGNOSTIC CHART—DRIVEABILITY TEST

TEST DR-15 | STEP B | CHECKING SENSOR CALIBRATIONS (THROTTLE POSITION SENSOR)

COMPLETE TEST DR-15A BEFORE PROCEEDING

PROCEDURE		TEST INDICATION	ACTION REQUIRED
• DRB II connected. • Engine cold. • Turn the engine off. • Put the system in **Sensor Test 05.**		• Display on DRB II reads as follows: **Throttle Fully Closed** 1 volt ± ½ volt NOTE: Make sure the cables attached to the throttle body are not misadjusted holding the throttle open. **In Between Closed and Open** You should see an uninterrupted change of voltage between closed and open throttle. **Throttle Wide Open** at least 3½ volts	• If the voltage readings are within specifications. Perform STEP C. • If the voltage readings are not within specifications, replace the throttle position sensor.

TEST DR-15 | STEP C | CHECKING SENSOR CALIBRATION (THROTTLE POSITION SENSOR)

COMPLETE TEST DR-15B BEFORE PROCEEDING

PROCEDURE		TEST INDICATION	ACTION REQUIRED
• DRB II connected. • Start the engine. • Put the system into **Engine Running Test 65.** • Slowly increase engine speed to 2,000 rpm.		• As engine speed increases the voltage displayed on the DRB II also increases. • As engine speed increases the voltage displayed on the DRB II is not increasing	• **Perform STEP D.** • Replace the throttle position sensor

---

TEST DR-15 | STEP F | CHECKING SENSOR CALIBRATION (M.A.P. SENSOR)

COMPLETE TEST DR-15E BEFORE PROCEEDING

PROCEDURE		TEST INDICATION	ACTION REQUIRED
• DRB II connected. • Engine cold. • Put the system in **Sensor Test 08.** • Disconnect the vacuum hose from the M.A.P. sensor. • Connect an auxiliary vacuum supply to the M.A.P. sensor. • Apply 5 inches of vacuum and record the voltage displayed on the DRB II • Slowly apply vacuum to 20 inches and watch display on DRB II	• Record the voltage displayed DRB II at 20 inches. • Subtract the voltage recorded at 20 inches from the voltage recorded at 5 inches **Example** Voltage at 5 in. 3.8 Voltage at 20 in. −1.1 Difference 2.7	• The DRB II is showing an uninterrupted change of voltage between 5 and 20 inches of vacuum. • The voltage difference is between 2.3 and 2.9 volts • The DRB II is showing an interrupted change of voltage between 5 and 20 inches of vacuum. • The voltage difference is not between 2.3 and 2.9 volts.	• Repair vacuum line to the M.A.P. sensor for a restriction. • Replace the M.A.P. sensor

---

TEST DR-15 | STEP G | CHECKING SENSOR CALIBRATION (THROTTLE BODY TEMPERATURE SENSOR)

COMPLETE TEST DR-15E BEFORE PROCEEDING

PROCEDURE		TEST INDICATION	ACTION REQUIRED
• DRB II connected. • Engine cold. • Start the engine • Put the system in **Engine Running Test 63.**		• Display on the DRB II is reading between 3 and 5 volts. • Display on the DRB II is not reading between 3 and 5 volts.	• **Perform TEST DR-16.** • Replace the throttle body temperature sensor

---

TEST DR-15 | STEP D | CHECKING SENSOR CALIBRATION (THROTTLE POSITION SENSOR)

COMPLETE TEST DR-15C BEFORE PROCEEDING

PROCEDURE		TEST INDICATION	ACTION REQUIRED
• DRB II connected. • Engine running at idle. • Put the system into **Engine Running Test 69.**		• Display on the readout box is between 0 and .1 (one tenth) volt. • Display on the readout box is reading more than .1 (one tenth) volt.	• **Perform STEP E.** • Replace the throttle position sensor.

TEST DR-15 | STEP E | CHECKING SENSOR CALIBRATION (M.A.P. SENSOR)

COMPLETE TEST DR-15D BEFORE PROCEEDING

PROCEDURE		TEST INDICATION	ACTION REQUIRED
• DRB II connected. • Tee a vacuum gauge into the vacuum line at the M.A.P. sensor. • Start the engine. • Put the system into **Engine Running Test 68.**	VACUUM GAUGE	• Vacuum displayed on the DRB II is within 1 inch of vacuum shown on the vacuum gauge. • Vacuum displayed on the DRB II is not within 1 inch of vacuum shown on the vacuum gauge.	• **Perform STEP G.** • **Perform STEP F.**

TEST DR-16 | STEP A | CHECKING FOR FUEL FOULED SPARK PLUGS

COMPLETE TEST DR-15G BEFORE PROCEEDING

PROCEDURE		TEST INDICATION	ACTION REQUIRED
• Remove the spark plugs.	LOOK FOR WET FUEL	• Spark plugs are dry. NOTE: It is normal for spark plugs to be black after an engine has been started cold • Spark plugs are wet with fuel.	• Spark plugs OK. **Perform STEP B.** • Clean and reinstall. Do not install new spark plugs. • Check for gasoline in the crankcase. Change oil and filter if required.

TEST DR-16 | STEP B | CHECKING HEATED AIR INTAKE SYSTEM

COMPLETE TEST DR-16A BEFORE PROCEEDING

PROCEDURE		TEST INDICATION	ACTION REQUIRED
• Engine cold. • Disconnect the air duct from the air cleaner snorkel. • Disconnect the vacuum supply hose to the heated air intake system air temperature sensor. • Connect an auxiliary vacuum supply to the air temperature sensor. • Apply at least 15 inches of vacuum.	DISCONNECT THIS HOSE AIR CLEANER BASE SENSOR	• Vacuum builds up, closes heated air door and then bleeds down opening the heated door. NOTE: With air temperature below 76°F. • Vacuum builds up but heated air door does not close. • Vacuum does not build up or does not bleed down. • Vacuum builds up, bleeds down, but heated air door does not open.	• **Perform tests as follows:** Federal **TEST DR-18.** California **TEST DR-19.** • Repair or replace door as required. • Replace air temperature sensor. • Repair or replace door as required.

1987–88 2.5L DIAGNOSTIC CHART—DRIVEABILITY TEST

THE FOLLOWING TEST MUST BEGIN WITH A WARM ENGINE

TEST DR-17	STEP A	CHECKING SENSOR CALIBRATION (ENGINE COOLANT TEMPERATURE SENSOR)	
COMPLETE TEST DR-1N OR DR-1A BEFORE PROCEEDING			
PROCEDURE		TEST INDICATION	ACTION REQUIRED
• DRB II connected. • Start the engine • Put the system in **Engine Running Test 64**.		• Display on the DRB II is reading between 180° and 250°	• **Perform STEP B**.
		• Display on the DRB II is not reading between 180° and 250°	• Replace the coolant sensor

TEST DR-17	STEP C	CHECKING SENSOR CALIBRATION (THROTTLE POSITION SENSOR)	
COMPLETE TEST DR-17B BEFORE PROCEEDING			
PROCEDURE		TEST INDICATION	ACTION REQUIRED
• DRB II connected • Put the system into **Engine Running Test 65**. • Slowly increase engine speed to 2,000 rpm		• As engine speed increases the voltage displayed on the DRB II also increases	• **Perform STEP D**
		• As engine speed increases the voltage displayed on the DRB II is not increasing	• Replace the throttle position sensor

TEST DR-17	STEP B	CHECKING SENSOR CALIBRATIONS (THROTTLE POSITION SENSOR)	
COMPLETE TEST DR 17-A BEFORE PROCEEDING			
PROCEDURE		TEST INDICATION	ACTION REQUIRED
• DRB II connected. • Engine warm. • Put the system in **Sensor Test 05**.		• Display on the DRB II should read as follows: **Throttle Fully Closed** 1 volt ± ½ volt NOTE: Make sure the cables attached to the throttle body are not misadjusted holding the throttle open. **In Between Closed and Open** You should see an uninterrupted change of voltage between closed and open throttle **Throttle Wide Open** at least 3½ volts	• If the voltage readings are within specifications, **perform STEP C**. • If the voltage readings are not within specifications, replace the throttle position sensor

TEST DR-17	STEP D	CHECKING SENSOR CALIBRATION (THROTTLE POSITION SENSOR)	
COMPLETE TEST DR-17C BEFORE PROCEEDING			
PROCEDURE		TEST INDICATION	ACTION REQUIRED
• DRB II connected • Engine running at idle • Put the system into **Engine Running Test 69**.		• Display on the DRB II is reading between 0 and 1 (one tenth) volt	• **Perform STEP E**
		• Display on the DRB II is reading more than 1 (one tenth) volt	• Replace the throttle position sensor

TEST DR-17	STEP E	CHECKING SENSOR CALIBRATION (M.A.P. SENSOR)	
COMPLETE TEST DR-17D BEFORE PROCEEDING			
PROCEDURE		TEST INDICATION	ACTION REQUIRED
• DRB II connected • Tee a vacuum gauge into the vacuum line at the M.A.P. sensor • Start the engine • Put the system into **Engine Running Test 66**.		• Vacuum displayed on the DRB II is within 1 inch of vacuum shown on the vacuum gauge	• **Perform STEP G**.
	VACUUM GAUGE	• Vacuum displayed on the DRB II is not within 1 inch of vacuum shown on the vacuum gauge	• **Perform STEP F**.

TEST DR-17	STEP G	CHECKING SENSOR CALIBRATION (THROTTLE BODY TEMPERATURE SENSOR)	
COMPLETE TEST DR-17E BEFORE PROCEEDING			
PROCEDURE		TEST INDICATION	ACTION REQUIRED
• DRB II connected • Start the engine • Put the system in **Engine Running Test 63**.		• Display on the DRB II is reading between 1 and 4 volts.	• **Perform STEP H**.
		• Display on the DRB II is not reading between 1 and 4 volts.	• Replace the throttle body temperature sensor.

TEST DR-17	STEP F	CHECKING SENSOR CALIBRATION (M.A.P. SENSOR)	
COMPLETE TEST DR-17E BEFORE PROCEEDING			
PROCEDURE		TEST INDICATION	ACTION REQUIRED
• DRB II connected • Engine warm. • Put the system in **Sensor Test 08**. • Disconnect the vacuum hose from the M.A.P. sensor • Connect an auxiliary vacuum supply to the M.A.P. sensor • Apply 5 inches of vacuum and record the voltage displayed on the DRB II • Slowly apply vacuum to 20 inches and watch display on DRB II		• Record the voltage displayed on the DRB II at 20 inches. • Subtract the voltage recorded at 20 inches from the voltage recorded at 5 inches. • The voltage difference is between 2.3 and 2.9 volts. **Example** Voltage at 5 in. 3.8 Voltage at 20 in. −1.1 Difference 2.7 • The DRB II is showing an uninterrupted change of voltage between 5 and 20 inches of vacuum.	• Repair vacuum line to the M.A.P. sensor for a restriction.
		• The DRB II is showing an interrupted change of voltage between 5 and 20 inches of vacuum. • The voltage difference is not between 2.3 and 2.9 volts	• Replace the M.A.P. sensor.

TEST DR-17	STEP H	CHECKING HEATED AIR INTAKE SYSTEM	
COMPLETE TEST DR-17G BEFORE PROCEEDING			
PROCEDURE		TEST INDICATION	ACTION REQUIRED
• Engine warm. • Disconnect the air duct from the air cleaner snorkel. • Disconnect the vacuum supply hose to the heated air intake system air temperature sensor. • Connect an auxiliary vacuum supply to the air temperature sensor. • Try to apply vacuum.		• Vacuum does not hold and heated air door is open.	• Perform Tests as follows: Federal TEST DR-18. California TEST DR-19.
		• Vacuum holds.	• Replace air temperature sensor.
	DISCONNECT THIS HOSE / AIR CLEANER BASE / SENSOR	• Heated air door not open.	• Repair or replace as required.

1987–88 2.5L DIAGNOSTIC CHART—DRIVEABILITY TEST

TEST DR-18	STEP A	CHECKING THE EGR SYSTEM – VACUUM SUPPLY FROM THE THROTTLE BODY TO THE EGR BACKPRESSURE VALVE

COMPLETE TEST DR-16A OR DR-17G BEFORE PROCEEDING

PROCEDURE		TEST INDICATION	ACTION REQUIRED
• Disconnect the vacuum line at the EGR back pressure valve that comes from the throttle body • Connect a vacuum gauge to this line • Start the engine • Disconnect idle speed motor • Raise engine speed to 2,500 rpm		• Vacuum gauge is reading at least 5 inches	• Remember what it is and **Perform STEP B**
		• No vacuum or vacuum below 5 inches	• Repair vacuum supply or vacuum from throttle body or solenoid

TEST DR-18	STEP C	CHECKING THE EGR VALVE OPERATION

COMPLETE TEST DR-18B BEFORE PROCEEDING

PROCEDURE		TEST INDICATION	ACTION REQUIRED
• Vacuum line disconnected from the EGR valve • Engine running • Idle speed motor disconnected • Connect an auxiliary vacuum supply to the EGR valve • With engine running at idle speed slowly apply vacuum		• Engine speed begins to drop when applied vacuum reaches 2½ to 3½ inches	• Perform STEP D.
		• Engine speed does not drop	• Replace EGR/back-pressure valve assembly

TEST DR-18	STEP B	CHECKING THE VALVE SUPPLY FROM THE BACKPRESSURE VALVE TO THE EGR VALVE

COMPLETE TEST DR-18A BEFORE PROCEEDING

PROCEDURE		TEST INDICATION	ACTION REQUIRED
• Engine running • Idle speed motor disconnected • Disconnect the vacuum gauge from the vacuum line and reconnect the vacuum line to the back pressure valve • Disconnect the vacuum line from the EGR valve and connect a vacuum gauge to it • Raise the engine speed to 2,500 rpm.		• Vacuum gauge is reading the same or near the same as seen in **STEP A.**	• Perform STEP C.
		• Vacuum gauge is not reading the same or near the same as seen in **STEP A.**	• Replace EGR/back pressure valve assembly

TEST DR-18	STEP D	CHECKING THE EGR VALVE VACUUM CHAMBER FOR LEAKS

COMPLETE TEST DR-18C BEFORE PROCEEDING

PROCEDURE		TEST INDICATION	ACTION REQUIRED
• Vacuum line disconnected from the EGR valve • Auxiliary vacuum supply connected to the EGR valve • Apply 10 inches of vacuum to EGR valve		• Vacuum should hold without bleeding for at least 10 seconds	• EGR diaphragm is OK **Perform TEST DR-19.**
		• Vacuum does not hold or bleeds down before 10 seconds	• Replace EGR/back-pressure valve assembly

TEST DR-19	STEP A	CHECKING SECONDARY IGNITION SYSTEM

COMPLETE TEST DR-18D BEFORE PROCEEDING

PROCEDURE		TEST INDICATION	ACTION REQUIRED
• Connect suitable engine analyzer to engine • Start engine and let engine speed stabilize for **two minutes.**		• Follow equipment manufacturer's procedure for secondary ignition testing and pattern analysis. **CAUTION: Make sure ignition coil output is checked in this testing. Open circuit secondary voltage should be at least 25,000 volts.** • Secondary ignition system okay	• Secondary pattern OK **Perform TEST DR-20.**
		• Secondary ignition not to specs	• Repair as required

TEST DR-20	STEP B	CHECKING SPARK ADVANCE

COMPLETE TEST DR-20A BEFORE PROCEEDING

PROCEDURE		TEST INDICATION	ACTION REQUIRED
• Tachometer connected to engine • Timing light connected to engine • Air cleaner removed (if necessary) • Engine at operating temperature • Reconnect the coolant sensor connector. **NOTE: The check engine lamp will not turn off until engine is restarted.** • Raise engine speed to 2,000 rpm.		• Timing is between 25° and 35° before top dead center	• Perform TEST DR-21.
		• Spark advance not within minimum specification.	• Defective logic board. Replace the SMEC.

TEST DR-20	STEP A	CHECKING BASIC IGNITION TIMING

COMPLETE TEST DR-19A BEFORE PROCEEDING

PROCEDURE		TEST INDICATION	ACTION REQUIRED
• Connect a tachometer to engine. • Connect a power timing light to engine. • Remove air cleaner (if necessary). • Start and run engine until operating temperature is reached. • Disconnect the engine coolant sensor connector and **do not reconnect it** **NOTE: The check engine lamp on the instrument panel must come on.**		• Basic timing is within 2° of specification as shown on the emission label.	• **Perform STEP B.**
		• Basic timing is not within 2° of specification as shown on the emission label.	• Adjust following basic ignition timing procedure.

TEST DR-21	STEP A	CHECKING FUEL SUPPLY AND RETURN SYSTEM

COMPLETE TEST DR-20B BEFORE PROCEEDING

PROCEDURE		TEST INDICATION	ACTION REQUIRED
• DRB II connected. • Install pressure gauge (Tool C3292) with (C4799 adapter) in fuel supply hose at throttle body. **CAUTION: Fuel is under high pressure. Refer to service manual for pressure release procedure.** • Put the system into the **Diagnostic Test Mode.** • Press and hold the ATM key on the DRB II.		• Fuel pressure is 14½ psi ± 1.	• Perform TEST DR-22.
		• Fuel pressure below 13½, record what it is.	• Perform STEP B.
		• Fuel pressure above 15½	• Perform STEP D.

1987–88 2.5L DIAGNOSTIC CHART—DRIVEABILITY TEST

TEST DR-21	STEP B	CHECKING FOR LOW FUEL PRESSURE

COMPLETE TEST DR-21A BEFORE PROCEEDING

PROCEDURE	TEST INDICATION	ACTION REQUIRED
• Turn ignition switch off. • DRB II connected. • Release fuel pressure. • Remove pressure gauge. • Reinstall hose to throttle body. • Install pressure gauge between filter and intank pump. • Turn ignition switch to the run position. • Press and hold the ATM key on the DRB II.	• Fuel pressure is 5 psi higher than previously recorded pressure.	• Replace filter.
	• Fuel pressure still below 13½ psi.	• **Perform STEP C.**

INSTALL PRESSURE GAUGE

FUEL FILTER

TEST DR-21	STEP D	CHECKING FOR HIGH FUEL PRESSURE

COMPLETE TEST DR-21A BEFORE PROCEEDING

PROCEDURE	TEST INDICATION	ACTION REQUIRED
• DRB II connected. • Turn the ignition switch off. • Pressure gauge connected. • Remove fuel return hose (small one) from throttle body. • Connect a suitable length of fuel hose to throttle body and put open end into an approved gasoline container (2-gallon size). • Turn the ignition switch to the run position. • Press and hold the ATM key on the DRB II.	• Fuel pressure is 14½ psi ± ½.	• Check fuel return lines for kinks or restrictions including return line check valve inside fuel tank.
	• Fuel pressure is above 15½ psi.	• Replace pressure regulator valve.

REMOVE HOSE

RETURN HOSE

FUEL PRESSURE RETURN HOSE

TEST DR-21	STEP C	CHECKING FOR LOW FUEL PRESSURE

COMPLETE TEST DR-21B BEFORE PROCEEDING

PROCEDURE	TEST INDICATION	ACTION REQUIRED
• Turn ignition switch off. • DRB II connected. • Release fuel pressure. • Remove pressure gauge from before filter and reinstall between filter and throttle body. • Turn ignition switch to the run position. • Press and hold the ATM key on the DRB II. **CAUTION: Fuel pressure must not exceed 25 psi or damage to the fuel pressure regulator will result.** • **Very gently, squeeze fuel return line at throttle body and immediately let go.**	• Fuel pressure increases above operating pressure.	• Replace pressure regulator valve.
	• Fuel pressure does not increase.	• Replace intank fuel pump. **NOTE:** Before replacing pump, look for contamination in the fuel tank that may be plugging pump filter. Also make sure electrical connections are not corroded.

PRESSURE GAUGE

SUPPLY HOSE

FUEL PRESSURE SUPPLY HOSE

TEST DR-22	STEP A	CHECKING THE OXYGEN SENSOR OPERATION

COMPLETE TEST DR-21A BEFORE PROCEEDING

PROCEDURE	TEST INDICATION	ACTION REQUIRED
• Connect the DRB II to the engine harness connector. • Put the system in **Engine Running Mode**. • Start the engine and wait 2 minutes. • Press the read/hold key until **Hold** is displayed to increase engine rpm.	• Display on the DRB II is switching between 0 to 1.	• **Perform TEST DR-23.**
	• Display on the DRB II is 0.	• Check for an engine vacuum leak. • Check for a grounded oxygen sensor wire. • Check for a plugged fuel injector.
	• Display on the DRB II is 1.	• Perform STEP B.

DRB II

TEST DR-22	STEP B	CHECKING FOR A RICH ENGINE OPERATING CONDITION

COMPLETE TEST DR-22A BEFORE PROCEEDING

PROCEDURE	TEST INDICATION	ACTION REQUIRED
• DRB II connected. • Turn the engine off. • Disconnect the distributor pickup connector. • Make sure the system is still in the engine running mode. • Crank the engine at wide open throttle for 10 seconds while looking at the display on the DRB II. • Crank engine again for 10 seconds at wide open throttle while looking at the display on the DRB II.	• Display on the DRB II changes to 0.	• Replace the fuel injector. **NOTE:** Before replacing the fuel injector make sure the lower O ring is not split or rolled over.
	• Display on the DRB II does not change to 0.	• Perform TEST NO. 24.

TEST DR-23	STEP A	CHECKING THROTTLE BODY MINIMUM AIR FLOW

COMPLETE TEST DR-22A BEFORE PROCEEDING

PROCEDURE	TEST INDICATION	ACTION REQUIRED
• DRB II connected. • Disconnect and plug the vacuum supply hose to the heated air temperature door. • Remove the air cleaner assembly. • Connect a tachometer to the engine. • Disconnect the tee connector in the PCV valve vacuum supply hose. • Install Tool C-5004 (.125″ orifice) into the PCV vacuum supply hose. • Start the engine and let it idle for one minute. • Put the system into **Engine Running Test 70.**	• Tachometer is reading as follows Low Mileage (below 1,000 miles) 2.2L 700 – 1300 rpm 2.5L 650 – 1250 rpm Broken-in (above 1,000 miles) 2.2L 1100 – 1300 rpm 2.5L 1050 – 1250 rpm	• Perform TEST DR-24.
	• Tachometer is not reading within above specifications	• Replace the throttle body casting assembly

DISCONNECT

INSTALL C-5004 IN HOSE

TEST NO. DR-24

COMPLETE TEST DR-22B OR 23A BEFORE PROCEEDING

AT THIS POINT IN THE DRIVEABILITY TEST PROCEDURE YOU HAVE DETERMINED ALL OF THE ENGINE CONTROL SYSTEMS ARE OPERATING AS THEY WERE DESIGNED THEREFORE, THEY ARE NOT THE CAUSE OF THE DRIVEABILITY PROBLEM.

THE FOLLOWING ADDITIONAL ITEMS SHOULD BE CHECKED AS POSSIBLE CAUSES.

1. **ENGINE VACUUM** – MUST BE AT LEAST 13 INCHES IN NEUTRAL
2. **ENGINE VALVE TIMING** – TO SPECIFICATIONS
3. **ENGINE COMPRESSION** – TO SPECIFICATIONS
4. **ENGINE EXHAUST SYSTEM** – MUST BE FREE OF ANY RESTRICTIONS
5. **ENGINE PCV SYSTEM** – MUST FLOW FREELY
6. **ENGINE DRIVE SPROCKETS** – CAM, CRANK AND INTERMEDIATE SHAFTS
7. **TORQUE CONVERTOR STALL SPEED** – TO SPECIFICATIONS
8. **POWER BRAKE BOOSTER** – NO INTERNAL VACUUM LEAKS
9. **FUEL CONTAMINATION** – HIGH ALCOHOL AND WATER CONTENT

ANY ONE OR MORE OF THESE ITEMS CAN CREATE A DRIVEABILITY RELATED PROBLEM THEY CANNOT BE OVERLOOKED AS POSSIBLE CAUSES

1987–88 2.5L DIAGNOSTIC CHART — CHARGING SYSTEM TEST

TEST CH-1	STEP A	CHECKING CHARGING SYSTEM FOR FAULT CODES	
PROCEDURE	**TEST INDICATION**	**CIRCUIT**	**ACTION REQUIRED**
• Connect DRB II to the engine harness connector.	88-12-55	No fault codes	**Perform TEST CH-2.**
	88-11-12-16-55	Battery voltage sense	**Perform TEST CH-3.**
• Put the system in Diagnostic Test Mode.	88-12-41-46-55 88-12-46-55	Alternator field (charging system output to high)	**Perform TEST CH-4.**
• RECORD ALL CODES.	88-12-41-55 88-12-41-47-55 88-12-47-55	Alternator field (charging system output to low)	**Perform TEST CH-5.**
• Erase fault codes.			

• Start engine.

• Let engine run for 7 minutes at idle rpm.

• Raise engine speed above 1,500 rpm for 30 seconds.

• Turn engine off.

• Put the system in Diagnostic Test Mode.

• RECORD ALL CODES

If the same code appears before and after the engine is started, the problem still exists. Proceed to test indications.

If a code does not reappear after the engine is started, the problem no longer exists. Perform STEP B.

TEST CH-1	STEP B	CHECKING CHARGING SYSTEM FOR INTERMITTENT FAILURES
COMPLETE TEST CH-1A BEFORE PROCEEDING		

The majority of intermittent failures are caused by wiring and connections. One way to find them is to duplicate the problem. Since the SMEC can remember where they are, the ATM and Sensor Tests can be used in an attempt to locate them.

• If the following fault code does not reappear, use the **ATM Test** as indicated.

Fault Code	**ATM Test**
41*	09

* Connect a voltmeter to the field control wire terminal of the alternator and watch pulsations of meter.

Once in the correct test, wiggle all the connectors and wires in the circuit. When the bad connection or wire is located the ATM test will be interrupted.

• If the following fault code does not reappear, use the **Sensor Test** as indicated.

Fault Code	**Sensor Test**
16	07

Once in the correct test mode, wiggle all the connectors and wires in the circuit. When the bad connection or wire is located the display on the DRB II will change.

TEST CH-2	STEP A	CHECKING SENSOR CALIBRATION (BATTERY TEMPERATURE SENSOR)	
COMPLETE TEST CH-1A BEFORE PROCEEDING			
PROCEDURE		**TEST INDICATION**	**ACTION REQUIRED**
• DRB II connected • Put the system in Engine Running Test 61.		• Display on the DRB II is reading between 2 (two tenths) and 3 volts	• Perform STEP B.
		• Display on the DRB II is not reading between 2 (two tenths) and 3 volts	• Defective logic board. Replace the SMEC.

TEST CH-3	STEP A	CHECKING FOR FAULT CODE 16 – BATTERY VOLTAGE SENSING CIRCUIT	
COMPLETE TEST CH-1A BEFORE PROCEEDING			
PROCEDURE	VIEW FROM TERMINAL END	**TEST INDICATION**	**ACTION REQUIRED**
• Turn the ignition switch off. • Disconnect the 60-way connector • Connect a voltmeter between the J1 (RD) wire in cavity No. 41 of the 60-way connector and ground		• Voltmeter reads battery voltage.	• Defective logic board. Replace the SMEC. **CAUTION:** Before replacing the SMEC, make sure the J1 terminal in cavity No. 41 of the 60-way connector is not damaged causing a poor connection.
		• Voltmeter reads 0.	• Repair the J1 (RD) wire of cavity No. 41 for an open circuit to the wiring harness splice.

TEST CH-2	STEP B	CHECKING CHARGING SYSTEM OPERATING VOLTAGE	
COMPLETE TEST CH-2A BEFORE PROCEEDING			
PROCEDURE		**TEST INDICATION**	**ACTION REQUIRED**
• DRB II connected • Put the system in Engine Running Test 67.		• Display on the DRB II is reading between 13 and 15 volts.	• Check battery per service manual procedure • Check for a battery drain condition.
		• Display on the DRB II is not reading between 13 and 15 volts.	• Check alternator per service manual procedure.

TEST CH-4	STEP A	CHECKING FOR FAULT CODE 46 OR 41-46 – ALTERNATOR FIELD CIRCUIT (CHARGING SYSTEM OUTPUT TOO HIGH)	
COMPLETE TEST CH-1A BEFORE PROCEEDING			
PROCEDURE		**TEST INDICATION**	**ACTION REQUIRED**
• DRB II connected. • Turn the ignition switch off. • Disconnect the 14-way connector from the SMEC. • Separate the 14-way connector. • Reconnect the half of the connector that contains cavities No. 1 thru 7 to the SMEC. • Connect the positive lead of an analog voltmeter to the R3 (DG) wire in cavity No. 14 in the half of the 14-way connector that is not connected to the SMEC.	• Connect the negative lead of the voltmeter to R31 (DG/OR) wire in cavity No. 11 of the same connector. • Put the system in ATM Test 09.	• Voltmeter is pulsating between 0 and 12 volts.	• Defective power board. Replace the SMEC. **CAUTION:** Before replacing the SMEC, make sure the R3 terminal in cavity No. 14 and the R31 terminal in cavity No. 11 of the 14-way connector are not spread apart causing a poor connection.
		• Voltmeter reads 0 volts.	• Perform STEP B.

ANALOG VOLTMETER

14-WAY CONNECTOR

1987–88 2.5L DIAGNOSTIC CHART—CHARGING SYSTEM TEST

TEST CH-4	STEP B	CHECKING ALTERNATOR FIELD CONTROL WIRE FOR A SHORT TO GROUND (R3 CIRCUIT)
COMPLETE TEST CH-4A BEFORE PROCEEDING		

PROCEDURE		TEST INDICATION	ACTION REQUIRED
• Half of 14 way connector with cavities No 8-14 disconnected from the SMEC. • Ignition switch in the run position • Positive lead of the voltmeter connected to the R3 (DG) wire in cavity No 14 of the 14 way connector.		• Voltmeter reads battery voltage	• Perform STEP C.
• Move the negative lead of the voltmeter from cavity No. 11 of the 14 way connector to ground		• Voltmeter reads 0-1 volts	• Repair alternator field circuit for a short to ground

TEST CH-4	STEP C	CHECKING THE CHARGING SYSTEM CONTROL OF THE SMEC FOR A SHORT CIRCUIT (R3 CIRCUIT)
COMPLETE TEST CH-4B BEFORE PROCEEDING		

PROCEDURE		TEST INDICATION	ACTION REQUIRED
• Half of 14 way connector with cavities No 8-14 disconnected. • Turn the ignition switch off. • Disconnect the 60-way connector from the SMEC. • Connect an ohmmeter between the R3 (DG) wire in cavity No. 14 of the 60-way connector and ground	VIEW FROM TERMINAL END	• Ohmmeter shows open.	• Defective logic board. Replace the SMEC.
		• Ohmmeter shows continuity.	• Repair the R3 (DG) wire of the 60-way connector for a short to ground

TEST CH-5	STEP A	CHECKING FOR FAULT CODE 41 OR 41-47 OR 47 – ALTERNATOR FIELD (CHARGING SYSTEM OUTPUT TOO LOW)
COMPLETE TEST CH-1A BEFORE PROCEEDING		

PROCEDURE		TEST INDICATION	ACTION REQUIRED
• DRB II connected • Connect the negative lead of a voltmeter to the battery negative post • Put the system in ATM Test 09		• Voltmeter reads 0 volts at both alternator field terminals	• Repair the J2 wire to the alternator field for an open circuit to the wiring harness splice
• Touch the positive lead of the voltmeter to each of the alternator field terminals		• Voltmeter reads battery voltage at one alternator field terminal and is pulsating between 0 and battery voltage at the other terminal	• Check for a loose alternator drive belt, check the battery or alternator following the service manual procedure
		• Voltmeter reads battery voltage at both alternator field terminals	• Perform STEP B.

TEST CH-5	STEP B	CHECKING THE ALTERNATOR FIELD CONTROL WIRE (R3 CIRCUIT) FOR AN OPEN CIRCUIT TO THE SMEC
COMPLETE TEST CH-5A BEFORE PROCEEDING		

PROCEDURE		TEST INDICATION	ACTION REQUIRED
• DRB II connected • Turn the ignition switch off • Disconnect the 14-way connector from the S.MEC. • Connect a voltmeter to the R3 (DG) wire in cavity No. 14 of the 14 way connector and ground • Turn the ignition switch to the run position		• Voltmeter reads battery voltage	• Perform STEP C.
		• Voltmeter reads 0 volts	• Repair the R3 (DG) wire of cavity No. 14 of the 14 way connector for an open circuit to the alternator

TEST CH-5	STEP C	CHECKING THE CHARGING SYSTEM CONTROL CIRCUIT TO THE SMEC (R31 CIRCUIT)
COMPLETE TEST CH-5B BEFORE PROCEEDING		

PROCEDURE		TEST INDICATION	ACTION REQUIRED
• DRB II connected • SMEC 14-way connector disconnected. • Turn the ignition switch off. • Separate the SMEC 14-way connector • Reconnect the half of the connector that contains cavities No. 1 thru 7 to the SMEC. • Connect the positive lead of the analog voltmeter to the R3 (DG) wire in cavity No. 14 in the half of the 14 way connector that is not connected to the SMEC.	• Connect the negative lead of the voltmeter to the R31 (DG/OR) wire in cavity No. 11 of the same connector. • Put the system in ATM Test 09	• Voltmeter is pulsating between 0 and 12 volts	• Defective power board. Replace the SMEC. CAUTION: Before replacing the SMEC, check the R3 and R31 terminals in cavities No. 11 and 14 to make sure they are not spread apart causing a poor connection.
		• Voltmeter reads 0 volts	• Perform STEP D.

TEST CH-5	STEP D	CHECKING THE CHARGING SYSTEM CONTROL WIRE FOR AN OPEN CIRCUIT TO THE SMEC (R31 CIRCUIT)
COMPLETE TEST CH-5C BEFORE PROCEEDING		

PROCEDURE		TEST INDICATION	ACTION REQUIRED
• SMEC 14-way connector disconnected. • Turn the ignition switch off. • Disconnect the 60-way connector. • Connect an ohmmeter between the R31 (DG/OR) wire in cavity No. 11 of the 14-way connector and the R31 (DG/OR) wire in cavity No. 14 of the 60-way connector.	VIEW FROM TERMINAL END	• Ohmmeter shows continuity.	• Defective logic board. Replace the SMEC. CAUTION: Before replacing the SMEC, check the R31 terminal in cavity No. 14 of the 60-way connector to make sure it is not damaged causing a poor connection.
		• Ohmmeter shows open.	• Repair the R31 (DG/OR) wire of the 60-way connector for an open circuit to the 14-way connector.

1987–88 2.5L DIAGNOSTIC CHART SPEED CONTROL SYSTEM TEST

TEST SC-1	STEP A	CHECKING SPEED CONTROL SYSTEM FOR FAULT CODES

PROCEDURE	TEST INDICATION	CIRCUIT	ACTION REQUIRED
• Connect DRB II to the engine harness connector	88-55 88-12-55	No fault codes	Perform STEP B.
• Put the system into the Diagnostic Test Mode	88-34-55 88-12-34-55	Speed control servo	Perform TEST SC-2A.
• RECORD ALL CODES	88-15-55 88-12-15-55	Speed sensor	Perform Driveability TEST DR-3.

TEST SC-1	STEP B	CHECKING SPEED CONTROL SWITCH INPUTS TO THE SMEC
COMPLETE TEST SC-1A BEFORE PROCEEDING		

PROCEDURE	TEST INDICATION			ACTION REQUIRED
• DRB II connected. • Put the system into Sensor Test 09	On 00	Set 10	Resume 01	• Perform TEST SC-3A.
NOTE: Make sure speed control switch is in the off position.	On Blank	Set Blank	Resume Blank	• Perform TEST SC-4A.
• While looking at the DRB II display; a) move on/off switch to the on position. b) press the set button c) press the resume button • Record display readings.	On Blank	Set 10	Resume 10	• Perform TEST SC-5A.
	On 00	Set 00	Resume 00	• Perform TEST SC-6A.

1987–88 2.5L DIAGNOSTIC CHART—SPEED CONTROL SYSTEM TEST

TEST SC-2	STEP A	CHECKING FOR FAULT CODE 34, SPEED CONTROL SERVO (VACUUM SOLENOID)
COMPLETE TEST SC-1A BEFORE PROCEEDING		

PROCEDURE	TEST INDICATION	ACTION REQUIRED
• DRB II connected • Connect a voltmeter to the X36 (TN/RD) wire of the speed control servo harness connector and ground. • Put the system into ATM Test 08 • Turn the speed control switch to the on position	• Voltmeter is pulsating between 0 and 12 volts	• Perform STEP B.
	• Voltmeter is reading battery voltage	• Perform STEP E.
	• Voltmeter is reading between 0 and 1 volt.	• Perform STEP F.

TEST SC-2	STEP B	CHECKING FOR FAULT CODE 34 – SPEED CONTROL (VENT SOLENOID)
COMPLETE TEST SC-2A BEFORE PROCEEDING		

PROCEDURE	TEST INDICATION	ACTION REQUIRED
• Turn ignition switch off • Connect a voltmeter to the X35 (LG/RD) wire at the speed control servo harness connector and ground. • Turn the ignition switch to the run position • Turn the speed control switch on	• Voltmeter is reading battery voltage	• Perform STEP C.
	• Voltmeter is reading between 0 and 1 volt.	• Perform STEP D.

TEST SC-2	STEP E	CHECKING THE VACUUM SOLENOID CONTROL WIRE FOR AN OPEN CIRCUIT TO THE SMEC (X36 CIRCUIT)
COMPLETE TEST SC-2A BEFORE PROCEEDING		

PROCEDURE	TEST INDICATION	ACTION REQUIRED
• Turn the ignition switch off. • Disconnect the 60-way connector. • Connect a voltmeter to the X36 (TN/RD) wire in cavity No. 53 of the 60-way connector and ground. • Turn the ignition switch to the run position.	• Voltmeter is reading battery voltage	• Defective logic board Replace the SMEC. CAUTION: Before replacing the SMEC, check the X36 terminal in cavity No. 53 of the 60-way connector to make sure it is not damaged causing a poor connection.
VIEW FROM TERMINAL END	• Voltmeter reads 0 volts.	• Repair X36 (TN/RD) wire of cavity No. 53 for an open circuit to the speed control servo connector.

TEST SC-2	STEP F	CHECKING THE VACUUM SOLENOID CIRCUIT FOR A SHORT TO THE SMEC (X36 CIRCUIT)
COMPLETE TEST CS-2A BEFORE PROCEEDING		

PROCEDURE	TEST INDICATION	ACTION REQUIRED
• Voltmeter connected to the X36 (TN/RD) wire of the speed control servo harness and ground. • Disconnect the 60-way connector. • Turn the ignition to the run position.	• Voltmeter reads battery voltage.	• Defective logic board. Replace the SMEC.
	• Voltmeter is reading between 0 and 1 volt.	• Perform STEP G.

TEST SC-2	STEP C	CHECKING THE VENT SOLENOID WIRE FOR AN OPEN CIRCUIT TO THE SMEC (X35 CIRCUIT)
COMPLETE TEST SC-2B BEFORE PROCEEDING		

PROCEDURE	TEST INDICATION	ACTION REQUIRED
• Turn the ignition switch off. • Disconnect the 60 way connector • Connect a voltmeter to the X35 (LG/RD) wire in cavity No. 60 of the 60-way connector and ground • Turn the ignition switch to the run position	• Voltmeter is reading within one volt of battery voltage	• Defective logic board Replace the SMEC. CAUTION: Before replacing the SMEC, check the X35 terminal in cavity No. 60 of the 60-way connector to make sure it is not damaged causing a poor connection.
VIEW FROM TERMINAL END	• Voltmeter is reading between 0 and 1 volt.	• Repair X35 wire of cavity No. 60 for an open circuit to the speed control servo connector.

TEST SC-2	STEP D	CHECKING THE VENT SOLENOID CIRCUIT FOR A SHORT IN THE SMEC (X35 CIRCUIT)
COMPLETE TEST SC-2B BEFORE PROCEEDING		

PROCEDURE	TEST INDICATION	ACTION REQUIRED
• Voltmeter connected to the X35 (LG/RD) wire of the speed control servo harness and ground. • Disconnect the 60-way connector from the SMEC. • Turn the ignition to the run position.	• Voltmeter is reading battery voltage.	• Defective logic board Replace the SMEC.
	• Voltmeter is reading between 0 and 1 volt.	• Repair X35 (LG/RD) wire of cavity No. 60 for a short to ground from the SMEC to the speed control servo connector

TEST SC-2	STEP G	CHECKING THE POWER SUPPLY TO THE SPEED CONTROL SERVO (X30 CIRCUIT)
COMPLETE TEST CS-2F BEFORE PROCEEDING		

PROCEDURE	TEST INDICATION	ACTION REQUIRED
• Speed control switch in the on position. • Turn the ignition off. • Connect a voltmeter to the X30 (DB/RD) wire of the speed control servo harness connector and ground. • Turn the ignition switch to the run position.	• Voltmeter is reading battery voltage.	• Replace the speed control servo.
	• Voltmeter is still reading between 0 and 1 volt.	• Perform STEP H.

TEST SC-2	STEP H	CHECKING SPEED CONTROL POWER SUPPLY THROUGH THE BRAKE SWITCH (X30 CIRCUIT)
COMPLETE TEST SC-2G BEFORE PROCEEDING		

PROCEDURE	TEST INDICATION	ACTION REQUIRED
• Speed control switch in the on position. • Ignition switch in the run position. • Connect a voltmeter to the X30 (DB/RD) wire of the brake switch harness connector and ground.	• Voltmeter is reading battery voltage.	• Repair the X30 (DB/RD) wire for an open circuit to the speed control servo.
	• Voltmeter is still reading between 0 and 1 volt.	• Perform STEP I.

1987–88 2.5L DIAGNOSTIC CHART—SPEED CONTROL SYSTEM TEST

TEST SC-2	STEP I	CHECKING SPEED CONTROL POWER SUPPLY TO THE BRAKE SWITCH (X32 CIRCUIT)

COMPLETE TEST SC-2H BEFORE PROCEEDING

PROCEDURE		TEST INDICATION	ACTION REQUIRED
• Speed control switch in the on position. • Ignition switch in the run position. • Connect a voltmeter between the X32 (YL/RD) wire of the brake switch harness connector and ground.		• Voltmeter reads battery voltage.	• Check brake switch adjustment if okay, replace the brake switch
		• Voltmeter reads 0.	• Repair the X32 (YL/RD) wire for an open circuit to the wiring harness splice. **NOTE:** Make sure fuse for X32 circuit is not blown.

TEST SC-3	STEP A	CHECKING THE SPEED CONTROL SERVO GROUND CIRCUIT (X9 CIRCUIT)

COMPLETE TEST SC-1B BEFORE PROCEEDING

PROCEDURE		TEST INDICATION	ACTION REQUIRED
• Turn the ignition switch off. • Disconnect the speed control servo connector. • Connect an ohmmeter between the X9 (BK) wire of the speed control servo harness connector and ground.		• Ohmmeter is showing continuity.	• Perform STEP B.
		• Ohmmeter is showing open.	• Repair the X9 (BK) wire for an open circuit to the wiring harness splice.

TEST SC-3	STEP D	CHECKING PARK/NEUTRAL SWITCH INPUT TO THE SMEC

COMPLETE TEST SC-3B BEFORE PROCEEDING

PROCEDURE		TEST INDICATION	ACTION REQUIRED
• DRB II connected • System in the Switch Test Mode • Put gear selector in park, reverse, neutral, and drive and observe display on DRB II		• Display on the DRB II changes as the gear selector is moved from park to reverse, from reverse to neutral, from neutral to drive, and back to park. **NOTE:** It is not important what display changes to just make sure it changes	• Perform STEP F.
		• Display on the DRB II does not change when gear selector is moved	• Perform STEP E.

TEST SC-3	STEP E	CHECKING PARK/NEUTRAL SWITCH INPUT CIRCUIT TO THE SMEC (S4 CIRCUIT)

COMPLETE TEST SC-3D BEFORE PROCEEDING

PROCEDURE		TEST INDICATION	ACTION REQUIRED
• Turn ignition switch off • Disconnect the 60-way connector • Connect an ohmmeter to the S4 (BN/YL) wire in cavity No. 30 of the 60 way connector and ground. • Disconnect the battery quick disconnect. • Turn the ignition switch to the run position • Put gear selector in park, reverse, neutral, and drive and observe position	VIEW FROM TERMINAL END	• Ohmmeter shows continuity in all positions of the gear selector.	• Check S4 (BN/YL) wire of cavity No 30 for a short to ground • Check for a bad safety neutral switch
		• Ohmmeter shows no continuity in all positions of the gear selector.	• Repair S4 (BN/YL) wire of cavity No 30 for an open circuit to the safety neutral switch.
		• Ohmmeter reads as follows: **Park** - continuity **Reverse** - open **Neutral** - continuity **Drive** - open **NOTE:** Disregard any resistance readings Just make sure there is continuity	• Defective logic board. Replace the SMEC. **NOTE:** Before replacing the SMEC, check the S4 terminal in cavity No 30 of the 60 way connector to make sure it is not damaged causing a poor connection.

TEST SC-3	STEP B	CHECKING BRAKE SWITCH INPUT TO THE SMEC

COMPLETE TEST SC-3A BEFORE PROCEEDING

PROCEDURE		TEST INDICATION	ACTION REQUIRED
• DRB II connected. • Put the system into the **Switch Test Mode** • Press down on brake pedal.		• Display on the DRB II changes as brake pedal is depressed. **NOTE:** It is not important what display changes to just make sure it changes	• Perform STEP D.
		• Display on the readout box does not change when brake pedal is depressed.	• Perform STEP C.

TEST SC-3	STEP C	CHECKING BRAKE SWITCH INPUT CIRCUIT TO THE SMEC (D40 CIRCUIT)

COMPLETE TEST SC-3B BEFORE PROCEEDING

PROCEDURE		TEST INDICATION	ACTION REQUIRED
• Turn the ignition switch off. • Disconnect the 60-way connector. • Connect an ohmmeter between the D40 (WT/PK) wire in cavity No. 29 of the 60-way connector and ground. • Press down on brake pedal and then release.	VIEW FROM TERMINAL END	• Ohmmeter shows open when brake pedal is pressed down and continuity when released.	• Defective logic board. Replace the SMEC. **CAUTION:** Before replacing the SMEC, check the D40 terminal in cavity No. 29 of the 60-way connector to make sure it is not damaged causing a poor connection.
		• Ohmmeter does not read as above.	• Refer to the wiring diagram and check the D40 (WT/PK) wire of cavity No. 29 of the 60 way connector for an open circuit through the stop lamp bulb circuit to ground

TEST SC-3	STEP F	CHECKING THE SPEED CONTROL SERVO OPERATION

COMPLETE TEST SC-3D BEFORE PROCEEDING

PROCEDURE		TEST INDICATION	ACTION REQUIRED
• Connect the speed control servo connector • DRB II connected. • Disconnect the speed control servo vacuum supply hose from the power brake booster and connect an auxiliary vacuum supply to it. • Put the system into ATM **Test 06** • Continuously apply vacuum to servo.	DISCONNECT & CONNECT AN AUXILIARY VACUUM SUPPLY	• As the system turns on and off while vacuum is being applied, the throttle is opening and closing.	• Check vacuum supply to the speed control servo • Check speed sensor operation using **Engine Running Test 71.** Miles per hour shown on the readout box must be stable at all times. If not, replace the speed sensor.
		• As the system turns on and off while vacuum is being applied the throttle is not opening and closing.	• Replace the speed control servo. **NOTE:** Before replacing the servo, make sure there are no leaks or restrictions in the vacuum supply hose.

TEST SC-4	STEP A	CHECKING SPEED CONTROL SYSTEM POWER SUPPLY CIRCUIT (X30 AND X32 CIRCUITS)

COMPLETE TEST SC-1B BEFORE PROCEEDING

PROCEDURE		TEST INDICATION	ACTION REQUIRED
• DRB II connected. • System in Sensor Test **06** • Speed control switch in the on position. • Connect a jumper wire between the X30 (DB/RD) wire and the X32 (YL/RD) wire of the speed control switch harness connector located under the instrument panel. **NOTE:** Do not disconnect the speed control switch connector.		• 00 is displayed on the DRB II	• Replace the speed control switch.
		• Display on the DRB II is blank.	• Perform STEP B.

1987–88 2.5L DIAGNOSTIC CHART—SPEED CONTROL SYSTEM TEST

TEST SC-4	STEP B	CHECKING THE SPEED CONTROL SYSTEM POWER SUPPLY CIRCUIT (X30 CIRCUIT)

COMPLETE TEST SC-4A BEFORE PROCEEDING

PROCEDURE		TEST INDICATION	ACTION REQUIRED
• Turn the ignition switch off. • Connect a voltmeter between ground and the X30 (DB/RD) wire of the speed control switch harness connector. NOTE: Do not disconnect the speed control switch connector • Turn the ignition switch on		• Voltmeter reading is within one volt of battery voltage.	• Perform STEP C.
		• Voltmeter reading is 0	• Repair the X30 (DB/RD) wire for an open circuit to the fuse box.

VOLTMETER X30 DB/RD

TEST SC-4	STEP C	CIRCUIT THE SPEED CONTROL SYSTEM POWER SUPPLY CIRCUIT (X32 CIRCUIT)

COMPLETE TEST SC-4B BEFORE PROCEEDING

PROCEDURE		TEST INDICATION	ACTION REQUIRED
• Turn the ignition switch off • Disconnect the 60 way connector • Connect a voltmeter between ground and the X32 (YL/RD) wire in cavity No. 8 of the 60-way connector NOTE: Do not disconnect the speed control switch connector • Turn the ignition switch on	VIEW FROM TERMINAL END	• Voltmeter is reading battery voltage.	• Defective logic board. Replace the SMEC. NOTE: Before replacing the SMEC, check the X32 terminal in cavity No. 8 of the 60 way connector to make sure it is not damaged causing a poor connection.
		• Voltmeter reading is 0	• Repair the X32 (YL/RD) cavity No. 8 of the 60 way connector for an open circuit to the speed control switch

VOLTMETER

TEST SC-6	STEP A	CHECKING THE SPEED CONTROL SYSTEM RESUME CIRCUIT (D4 AND X30 CIRCUITS)

COMPLETE TEST SC-1B BEFORE PROCEEDING

PROCEDURE		TEST INDICATION	ACTION REQUIRED
• DRB II connected. • System in Sensor Test 09 • Speed control switch in the on position. • Connect a jumper wire between the D4 (WT) wire and the X30 (DB/RD) wire of the speed control switch harness connector. NOTE: Do not disconnect the speed control switch connector		• 01 is displayed on the DRB II	• Replace the speed control switch
		• 00 is displayed on the DRB II.	• Perform STEP B.

D4 WT JUMPER X30 DR/RD

TEST SC-5	STEP A	CHECKING SPEED CONTROL SYSTEM SET CIRCUIT

COMPLETE TEST SC-1B BEFORE PROCEEDING

PROCEDURE		TEST INDICATION	ACTION REQUIRED
• DRB II connected. • System in Sensor Test 09. • Speed control switch in the on position. • Connect a jumper wire between the X30 (DB/RD) wire and the X31 (BN/RD) wires of the speed control switch harness connector. NOTE: Do not disconnect the speed control switch connector.		• 00 is displayed on the DRB II.	• Replace the speed control switch.
		• 10 is displayed on the DRB II.	• Perform STEP B.

X30 DB/RD JUMPER X31 BR/RD

TEST SC-5	STEP B	CHECKING SPEED CONTROL SYSTEM SET CIRCUIT (X31 CIRCUIT)

COMPLETE TEST SC-5A BEFORE PROCEEDING

PROCEDURE		TEST INDICATION	ACTION REQUIRED
• Turn the ignition switch off • Disconnect the 60-way connector. • Connect a voltmeter between ground and to the X31 (BN/RD) wire in cavity No. 9 of the 60-way connector. NOTE: Do not disconnect the speed control switch connector. • Turn the ignition switch on.	VIEW FROM TERMINAL END	• Voltmeter is reading battery voltage.	• Defective logic board. Replace the SMEC. NOTE: Before replacing the SMEC, check the X31 terminal in cavity No. 9 of the 60-way connector for an open circuit to the speed control switch.
		• Voltmeter reading is 0.	• Repair the X31 (BN/RD) wire of cavity No. 9 of the 60 way connector for an open circuit to the speed control switch.

VOLTMETER

TEST SC-6	STEP B	CHECKING THE SPEED CONTROL SYSTEM RESUME CIRCUIT (X33 CIRCUIT)

COMPLETE TEST SC-6A BEFORE PROCEEDING

PROCEDURE		TEST INDICATION	ACTION REQUIRED
• Turn the ignition switch off • Disconnect the 60-way connector • Connect a voltmeter between ground and the X33 (WT/LG) wire in cavity No. 7 of the 60-way connector. NOTE: Do not disconnect the speed control switch connector. • Turn the ignition switch on • Press resume switch.	VIEW FROM TERMINAL END	• Voltmeter is reading battery voltage.	• Defective logic board. Replace the SMEC. NOTE: Before replacing the SMEC, check the X33 terminal in cavity No. 7 of the 60-way connector for an open circuit to the speed control switch.
		• Voltmeter reading is 0.	• Repair the X33 (WT/LG) wire of cavity No. 7 of the 60-way connector for an open circuit to the speed control switch.

VOLTMETER

1989–91 2.5L DIAGNOSTIC CHART—NO START TEST

1989–91 2.5L DIAGNOSTIC CHART—NO START TEST

TEST NS-3 | CHECKING THE SMEC, WET PLUGS & ENGINE TIMING
Perform TEST NS-2 Before Proceeding

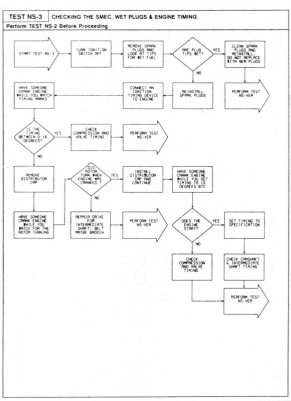

TEST NS-4 | CHECKING IGNITION COIL DRIVER, OPEN CIRCUITS, & DEFECTIVE SMEC
Perform TEST NS-1 Before Proceeding

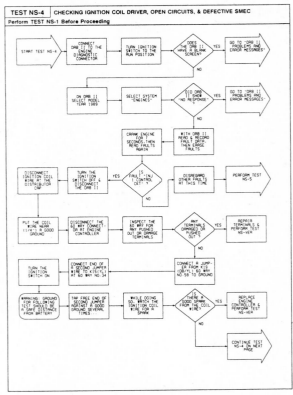

TEST NS-4 | CONTINUED - CHECKING IGNITION COIL DRIVER, OPEN CIRCUITS, & DEFECTVE SMEC

TEST NS-5 | CHECKING FOR POWER FEED TO COIL PRIMARY, PRIMARY CONTROL CIRCUITS, & COIL
Perform TEST NS-4 Before Proceeding

1989–91 2.5L DIAGNOSTIC CHART—NO START TEST

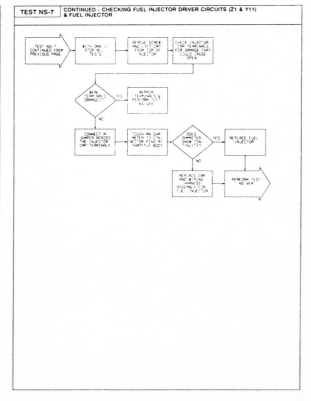

1989–91 2.5L DIAGNOSTIC CHART—NO START TEST

5 FUEL SYSTEM

1989–91 2.5L DIAGNOSTIC CHART — NO START TEST

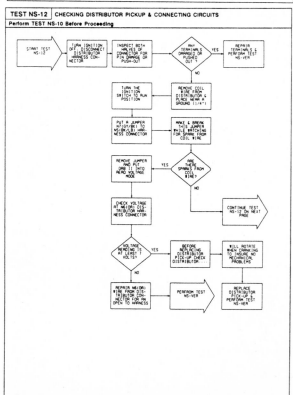

1989–91 2.5L DIAGNOSTIC CHART—NO START TEST

TEST NS-12 | CONTINUED - CHECKING DISTRIBUTOR PICKUP & CONNECTING CIRCUITS

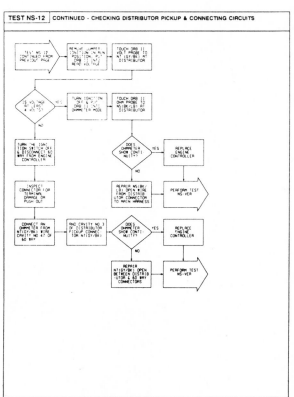

TEST NS-13 | CHECKING AUTO SHUTDOWN RELAY FAULT & PULL IN COIL CIRCUITS (K14 & K19)
Perform TEST NS-10 Before Proceeding

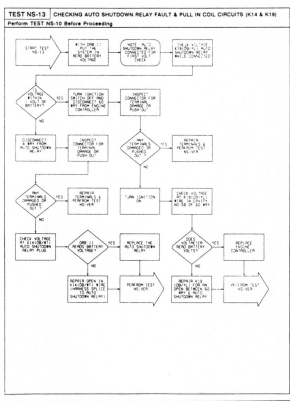

TEST NS-14 | CHECKING POWER CIRCUIT (K14) TO PULL IN COIL AND AUTO SHUTDOWN RELAY
Perform TEST NS-10 Before Proceeding

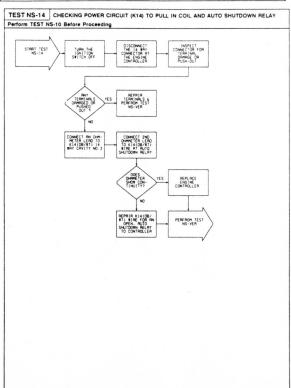

TEST NS-15 | CHECKING POWER FEED CIRCUITS (J2 & Z1) TO AUTO SHUTDOWN RELAY, AND DEFECTIVE AUTO SHUTDOWN RELAY
Perform TEST NS-10 Before Proceeding

1989–91 2.5L DIAGNOSTIC CHART—NO START TEST

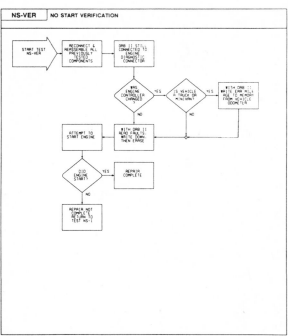

1989–91 2.5L DIAGNOSTIC CHART—DRIVEABILITY TEST

1989–91 2.5L DIAGNOSTIC CHART—DRIVEABILITY TEST

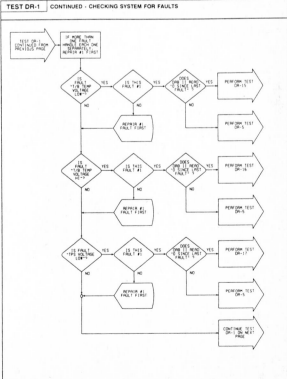

1989–91 2.5L DIAGNOSTIC CHART—DRIVEABILITY TEST

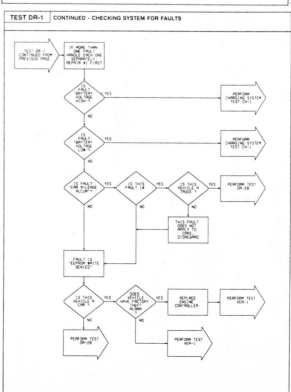

1989–91 2.5L DIAGNOSTIC CHART—DRIVEABILITY TEST

TEST DR-2 | CHECKING OUTPUT CIRCUITS OF SMEC
Perform TEST DR-1 Before Proceeding

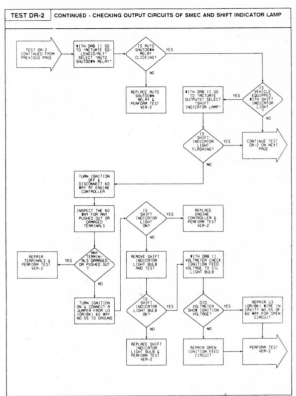

TEST DR-2 | CONTINUED - CHECKING OUTPUT CIRCUITS OF SMEC AND SHIFT INDICATOR LAMP

TEST DR-2 | CONTINUED - CHECKING BRAKE SWITCH INPUT CIRCUIT TO SMEC

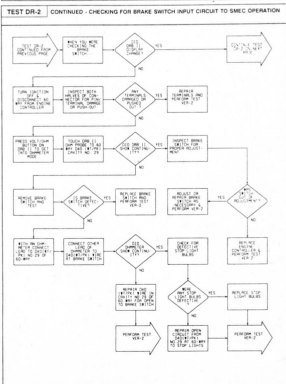

TEST DR-2 | CONTINUED - CHECKING FOR BRAKE SWITCH INPUT CIRCUIT TO SMEC OPERATION

1989–91 2.5L DIAGNOSTIC CHART — DRIVEABILITY TEST

TEST DR-2 | CONTINUED - CHECKING SWITCH INPUTS TO THE SMEC

TEST DR-2 | CONTINUED - CHECKING THE A/C PUSH BUTTON SWITCH INPUT

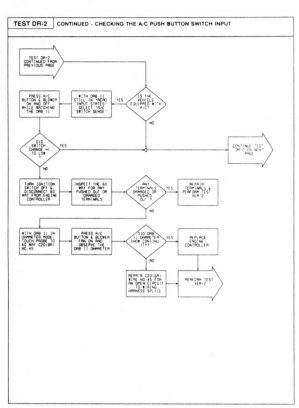

TEST DR-2 | CONTINUED - CHECKING THE EMISSION MAINTENANCE REMINDER LAMP

TEST DR-2 | CONTINUED - CHECKING THE AUTOMATIC IDLE SPEED MOTOR OPERATION

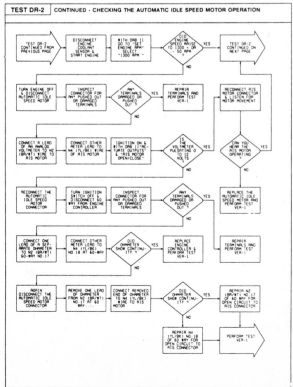

1989–91 2.5L DIAGNOSTIC CHART—DRIVEABILITY TEST

TEST DR-2 CONTINUED - CHECKING THE AUTOMATIC IDLE SPEED MOTOR OPERATION

TEST DR-2 CONTINUED - CHECKING THE SMEC GROUND CIRCUITS

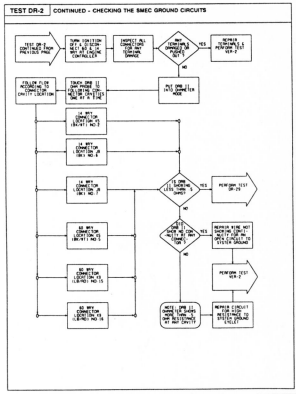

TEST DR-3 INTERMITTENT TEST FOR SOLENOIDS AND RELAYS
Perform TEST DR-1 Before Proceeding

TEST DR-4 INTERMITTENT TEST FOR MAP SENSOR SIGNAL
Perform TEST DR-1 Before Proceeding

1989–91 2.5L DIAGNOSTIC CHART—DRIVEABILITY TEST

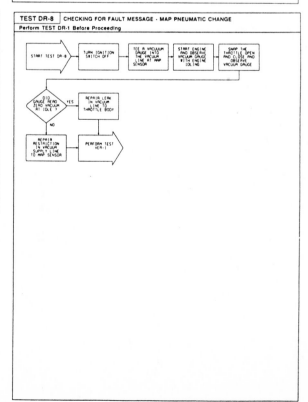

1989–91 2.5L DIAGNOSTIC CHART—DRIVEABILITY TEST

TEST DR-9 CHECKING FOR FAULT MESSAGE · MAP VOLTAGE LOW
Perform TEST DR-1 Before Proceeding

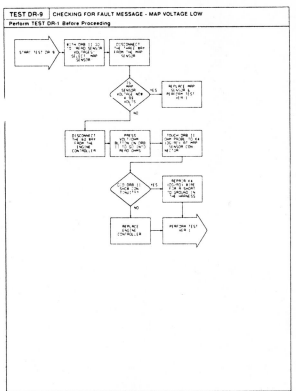

TEST DR-10 CHECKING FOR FAULT MESSAGE · MAP VOLTAGE TOO HIGH
Perform TEST DR-1 Before Proceeding

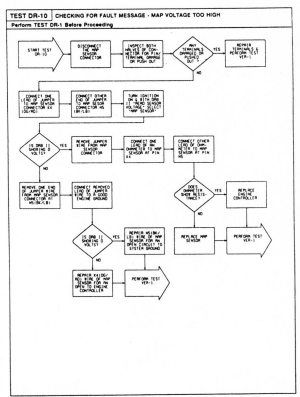

TEST DR-11 CHECKING FOR FAULT MESSAGE · VEHICLE SPEED SIGNAL
Perform TEST DR-1 Before Proceeding

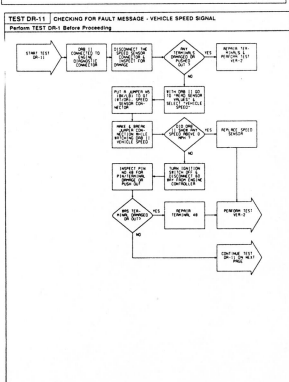

TEST DR-11 CONTINUED · CHECKING FOR FAULT MESSAGE · VEHICLE SPEED SIGNAL

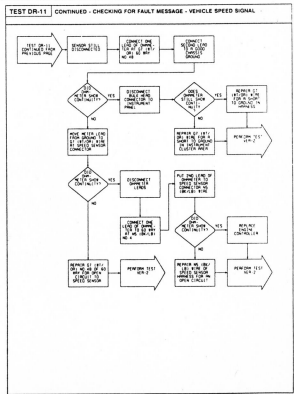

5 FUEL SYSTEM

1989–91 2.5L DIAGNOSTIC CHART—DRIVEABILITY TEST

TEST DR-12 CHECKING FOR FAULT MESSAGE - OXYGEN SENSOR SIGNAL
Perform TEST DR-1 Before Proceeding

TEST DR-13 CHECKING FOR FAULT MESSAGE - COOLANT VOLTAGE LOW
Perform TEST DR-1 Before Proceeding

TEST DR-14 CHECKING FOR FAULT MESSAGE - COOLANT VOLTAGE HIGH
Perform TEST DR-1 Before Proceeding

TEST DR-15 CHECKING FOR FAULT MESSAGE - T/B TEMP VOLTAGE LOW
Perform TEST DR-1 Before Proceeding

1989–91 2.5L DIAGNOSTIC CHART–DRIVEABILITY TEST

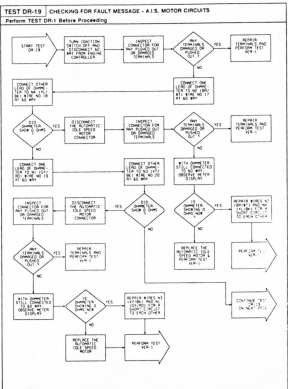

5 FUEL SYSTEM

1989–91 2.5L DIAGNOSTIC CHART — DRIVEABILITY TEST

TEST DR-19 CONTINUED - CHECKING FOR FAULT MESSAGE - A.I.S. MOTOR CIRCUITS

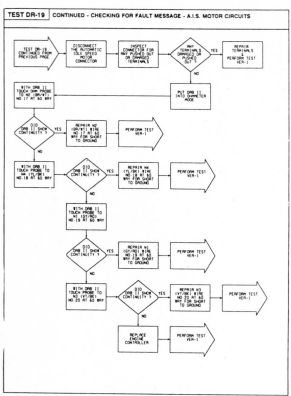

TEST DR-20 CHECKING FOR FAULT MESSAGE - PURGE SOLENOID CKT
Perform TEST DR-1 Before Proceeding

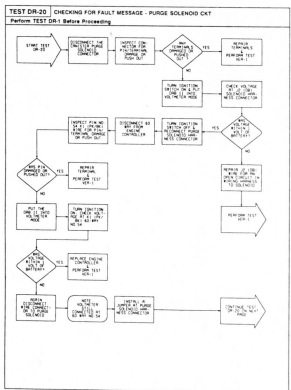

TEST DR-20 CONTINUED - CHECKING FOR FAULT MESSAGE - PURGE SOLENOID CKT

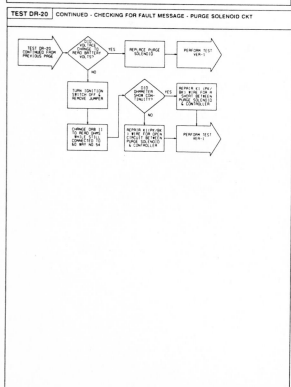

TEST DR-21 CHECKING FOR FAULT MESSAGE - EGR SOLENOID CIRCUIT
Perform TEST DR-1 Before Proceeding

1989–91 2.5L DIAGNOSTIC CHART — DRIVEABILITY TEST

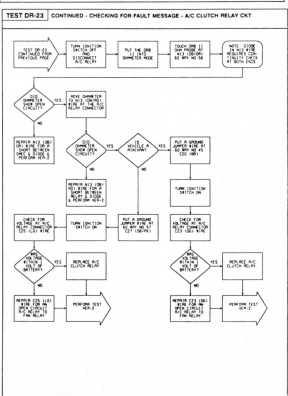

5 FUEL SYSTEM

1989–91 2.5L DIAGNOSTIC CHART—DRIVEABILITY TEST

TEST DR-24 | CHECKING RADIATOR & A/C FAN RELAYS
Perform **TEST DR-23** Before Proceeding

TEST DR-25 | CHECKING FOR FAULT MESSAGE - RADIATOR FAN RELAY
Perform **TEST DR-1** Before Proceeding

TEST DR-26 | CHECKING FOR FAULT MESSAGE - PTU SOLENOID CIRCUIT
Perform **TEST DR-1** Before Proceeding

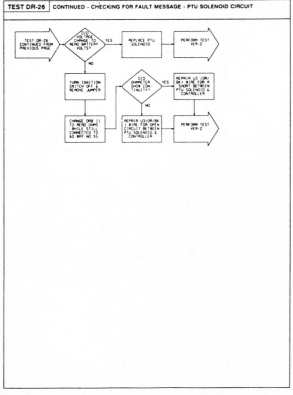

TEST DR-26 | CONTINUED - CHECKING FOR FAULT MESSAGE - PTU SOLENOID CIRCUIT

1989–91 2.5L DIAGNOSTIC CHART—DRIVEABILITY TEST

1989–91 2.5L DIAGNOSTIC CHART–DRIVEABILITY TEST

1989–91 2.5L DIAGNOSTIC CHART – DRIVEABILITY TEST

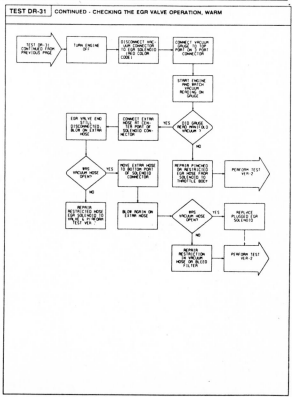

5 FUEL SYSTEM

1989–91 2.5L DIAGNOSTIC CHART—DRIVEABILITY TEST

1989–91 2.5L DIAGNOSTIC CHART—DRIVEABILITY TEST

TEST DR-34 | CHECKING THE OXYGEN SENSOR OPERATION
Perform TEST DR-33 Before Proceeding

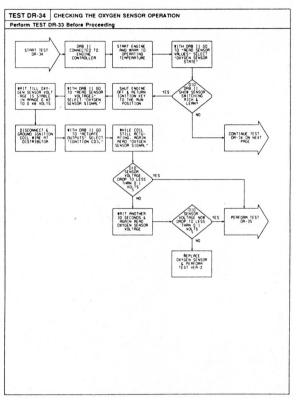

TEST DR-34 | CONTINUED - CHECKING THE OXYGEN SENSOR OPERATION

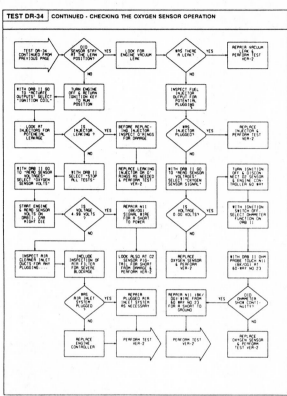

TEST DR-35 | CHECKING THROTTLE BODY MINIMUM AIR FLOW
Perform TEST DR-34 Before Proceeding

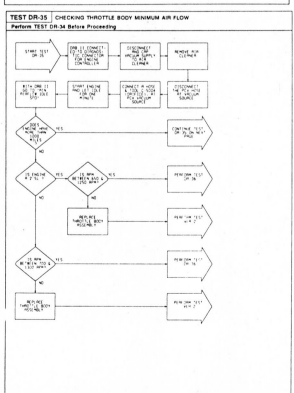

TEST DR-35 | CONTINUED - CHECKING THROTTLE BODY MINIMUM AIR FLOW

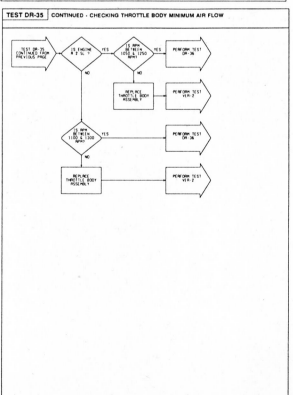

1989–91 2.5L DIAGNOSTIC CHART—DRIVEABILITY TEST

TEST DR-36	OTHER POSSIBLE CAUSES OF DRIVEABILITY RELATED PROBLEMS
Perform TEST DR-35 Before Proceeding	

AT THIS POINT IN THE DRIVEABILITY TEST PROCEDURE YOU HAVE DETERMINED THAT ALL OF THE ENGINE CONTROL SYSTEMS ARE OPERATING AS THEY WERE DESIGNED. THEREFORE, THEY ARE **NOT THE CAUSE OF THE DRIVEABILITY PROBLEM.**

THE FOLLOWING ADDITIONAL ITEMS SHOULD BE CHECKED AS POSSIBLE CAUSES:

1. **ENGINE VACUUM** - MUST BE AT LEAST 13 INCHES IN NEUTRAL.
2. **ENGINE VALVE TIMING** - TO SPECIFICATIONS.
3. **ENGINE COMPRESSION** - TO SPECIFICATIONS.
4. **ENGINE EXHAUST SYSTEM** - MUST BE FREE OF ANY RESTRICTIONS.
5. **ENGINE PCV SYSTEM** - MUST FLOW FREELY.
6. **ENGINE DRIVE SPROCKETS** - CAM, CRANK AND INTERMEDIATE SHAFTS.
7. **TORQUE CONVERTOR STALL SPEED** - TO SPECIFICATIONS.
8. **POWER BRAKE BOOSTER** - NO INTERNAL VACUUM LEAKS.
9. **FUEL CONTAMINATION** - HIGH ALCOHOL AND WATER CONTENT.

ANY ONE OR MORE OF THESE ITEMS CAN CREATE A DRIVEABILITY RELATED PROBLEM. THEY CAN NOT BE OVERLOOKED AS POSSIBLE CAUSES.

1989-91 2.5L DIAGNOSTIC CHART—SPEED CONTROL SYSTEM TEST

1989–91 2.5L DIAGNOSTIC CHART—SPEED CONTROL SYSTEM TEST

1989–91 2.5L DIAGNOSTIC CHART—SPEED CONTROL SYSTEM TEST

5 FUEL SYSTEM

1989–91 2.5L DIAGNOSTIC CHART—CHARGING SYSTEM DIAGNOSIS

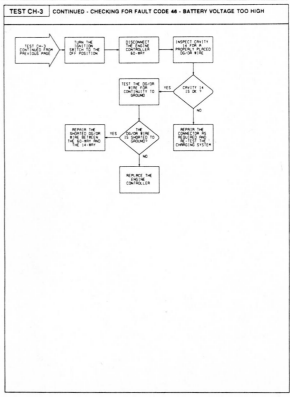

1989–91 2.5L DIAGNOSTIC CHART — CHARGING SYSTEM DIAGNOSIS

TEST CH-4 | CHECKING FOR FAULT CODE 47 - BATTERY VOLTAGE TOO LOW
Perform TEST CH-1 Before Proceeding

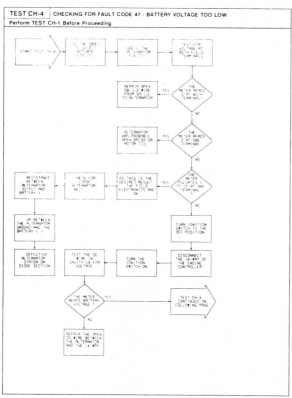

TEST CH-4 | CONTINUED - CHECKING FOR FAULT CODE 47 - BATTERY VOLTAGE TOO LOW

TEST CH-5 | CHECKING FOR INTERMITTENT FAULT CODES
Perform TEST CH-1 Before Proceeding

TEST CH-6 | CHECKING THE CHARGING SYSTEM WITH NO CODES
Perform TEST CH-1 Before Proceeding

DRBII PROBLEMS AND ERROR MESSAGES

COMPONENT TEST PROCEDURE

Fuel System Pressure Test

—————————— CAUTION ——————————
Fuel system pressure must be released as previously described each time a fuel hose is to be disconnected. Take precautions to avoid the risk of fire.

1. Remove fuel intake hose from throttle body and connect fuel system pressure testers C–3292, and C–4749, or equivalent, between fuel filter hose and throttle body.
2. Start engine and read gauge. Pressure should be 14.5 psi (100 kPa).

NOTE: ATM tester C–4805 or equivalent can be used. With ignition in RUN, depress ATM button. This activate the fuel pump and pressure system

3. If fuel pressure is below specifications:
   a. Install tester between fuel filter hose and fuel line.
   b. Start engine. If pressure is now correct, replace fuel filter. If no change is observed, gently squeeze return hose. If pressure increases, replace pressure regulator. If no change is observed, problem is either a plugged pump filter sock or defective fuel pump.
4. If pressure is above specifications:
   a. Remove fuel return hose from throttle body. Connect a substitute hose and place other end of hose in clean container.
   b. Start engine. If pressure is now correct, check for restricted fuel return line. If no change is observed, replace fuel regulator.

Component Replacement

—————————— CAUTION ——————————
The fuel injection system is under a constant pressure of approximately 14.5 psi (100 kPa). Before servicing any part of the fuel injection system, the system pressure must be released. Use a clean shop towel to catch any fuel spray and take precautions to avoid the risk of fire.

Fuel System Pressure Release

1. Loosen gas cap to release tank pressure.
2. Remove wiring harness connector from injector.
3. Ground 1 terminal of injector.
4. Connect jumper wire to second terminal and touch battery positive post for no longer than 10 seconds. This releases system pressure.
5. Remove jumper wire and continue fuel system service.

THROTTLE BODY

Removal and Installation

1. Remove air cleaner.
2. Perform fuel system pressure release.
3. Disconnect negative battery cable.
4. Disconnect vacuum hoses and electrical connectors.
5. Remove throttle cable and, if so equipped, speed control and transaxle (or transmission) kickdown cables.
6. Remove return spring.
7. Remove fuel intake and return hoses.
8. Remove throttle body mounting screws and lift throttle body from vehicle.

9. When installing throttle body, use a new gasket. Install throttle body and torque mounting screws to 175 inch lbs. (20 Nm).

10. Install fuel intake and return hoses using new original equipment type clamps.

11. Install return spring.

12. Install throttle cable and, if so equipped, install kickdown and speed control cables.

13. Install wiring connectors and vacuum hoses.

14. Install air cleaner.

15. Reconnect negative battery cable.

FUEL FITTINGS

Removal and Installation

1. Remove air cleaner assembly.

2. Perform fuel system pressure release.

3. Disconnect negative battery cable.

4. Loosen fuel intake and return hose clamps. Wrap a shop towel around each hose, twist and pull off each hose.

5. Remove each fitting and note inlet diameter. Remove copper washers.

6. To install, replace copper washers with new washers.

7. Install fuel fittings in proper ports and torque to 175 inch lbs. (20 Nm).

8. Using new original equipment type hose clamps, install fuel return and supply hoses.

9. Reconnect negative battery cable.

10. Test for leaks using ATM tester C–4805 or equivalent. With ignition in the **RUN** position depress ATM button. This will activate pump and pressurize the system. Check for leaks.

11. Reinstall air cleaner assembly.

FUEL PRESSURE REGULATOR

Removal and Installation

1. Remove air cleaner assembly.

2. Perform fuel system pressure release.

3. Disconnect negative battery cable.

4. Remove 3 screws attaching pressure regulator to throttle body. Place a shop towel around inlet chamber to contain any fuel remaining in the system.

5. Pull pressure regulator from throttle body.

6. Carefully remove O-ring from pressure regulator and remove gasket.

7. To install, place new gasket on pressure regulator and carefully install new O-ring.

8. Position pressure regulator on throttle body press into place.

9. Install 3 screws and torque to 40 inch lbs. (5 Nm).

10. Connect negative battery cable.

11. Test for leaks using ATM tester C–4805 or equivalent. With ignition in the **RUN** position depress ATM button. This will activate pump and pressurize the system. Check for leaks.

12. Reinstall air cleaner assembly.

FUEL INJECTOR

Removal and Installation

1. Remove air cleaner assembly.

2. Perform fuel system pressure release.

3. Disconnect negative battery cable.

4. Remove fuel pressure regulator.

5. Remove Torx® screw holding down injector cap.

6. With 2 small prying tools, lift cap off injector using slots provided.

7. Using a small prying tool placed in hole in front of electrical connector, gently pry injector from pod.

Throttle body mounting — 4 cylinder engines

Fuel fitting service — Single Point fuel injection

Fuel pressure regulator servicing — Single Point fuel injection

8. Make sure injector lower O-ring has been removed from pod.

9. To install, place a new lower O-ring on injector and a new O-ring on injector cap. The injector will have upper O-ring already installed.

10. Put injector cap on injector. (Injector and cap are keyed). Cap should sit on injector without interference. Apply a light coating of castor oil or petroleum jelly on O-rings. Place assembly in pod.

11. Rotate cap and injector to line up attachment hole.

12. Push down on cap until it contacts injector pod.

13. Install Torx® screw and torque to 35–45 inch lbs. (4–5 Nm).

14. Install fuel pressure regulator.

15. Connect negative battery cable.

16. Test for leaks using ATM tester C–4805 or equivalent. With ignition in the **RUN** position depress ATM button. This will activate pump and pressurize the system. Check for leaks.

17. Reinstall air cleaner assembly.

Injector cap removal — Single Point fuel injection

Fuel injector removal — Single Point fuel injection

Fuel injector servicing — Single Point fuel injection

Fuel injector terminal identification — Single Point fuel injection

Fuel injector installation — Single Point fuel injection

Throttle position sensor servicing — Single Point fuel injection

THROTTLE POSITION SENSOR

Removal and Installation

1. Disconnect negative battery cable.
2. Remove air cleaner.
3. Disconnect 3 way connector at throttle position sensor.
4. Remove 2 screws mounting throttle position sensor to throttle body.

5. Lift throttle position sensor off throttle shaft.
6. To install, install throttle position sensor to throttle body, position connector toward rear of vehicle.
7. Connect 3 way connector at throttle position sensor.
8. Install air cleaner.
9. Connect negative battery cable.

THROTTLE BODY TEMPERATURE SENSOR

Removal and Installation

1. Remove air cleaner.
2. Disconnect throttle cables from throttle body linkage.
3. Remove 2 screws from throttle cable bracket and lay bracket aside.
4. Disconnect wiring connector.
5. Unscrew sensor.
6. To install, apply heat transfer compound to tip portion of new sensor.
7. Install and torque to 100 inch lbs. (11 Nm).
8. Connect wiring connector.
9. Install throttle cable bracket with 2 screws.
10. Connect throttle cables to throttle body linkage and install clips.
11. Install air cleaner.

AUTOMATIC IDLE SPEED (AIS) MOTOR ASSEMBLY

Removal and Installation

1. Remove air cleaner.
2. Disconnect negative battery cable.
3. Disconnect 4 pin connector on AIS.
4. Remove temperature sensor from throttle body housing.
5. Remove 2 Torx® head screws.
6. Remove AIS from throttle body housing, making sure that O-ring is with AIS.
7. To install, be sure that pintle is in the retracted position. If pintle measures more than 1 in. (25mm), it must be retracted by using ATM test code No. 03. (Battery must be connected for this operation.)
8. Install new O-ring on AIS.
9. Install AIS into housing making sure O-ring is in place.
10. Install 2 Torx® head screws.
11. Connect 4 pin connector to AIS.
12. Install temperature sending unit into throttle body housing.
13. Connect negative battery cable.

Throttle body temperature sensor servicing — Single Point fuel injection

MINIMUM IDLE SPEED

Adjustment

1. Before adjusting the idle on fuel injected vehicles, the following items must be checked:
    a. AIS motor has been checked for operation.
    b. Engine has been checked for vacuum or EGR leaks.
    c. Engine timing has been checked and set to specifications.
    d. Coolant temperature sensor has been checked for operation.
2. Connect a tachometer and timing light to engine.
3. Close AIS by using ATM tester C–4805 or equivalent, ATM test code No. 03.
4. Connect a jumper to radiator fan so that it will run continuously.
5. Start and run the engine for 3 minutes to allow the idle speed to stabilize.
6. Check engine rpm and compare the result with the specifications listed on the under hood emission control sticker.
7. If idle rpm is not within specifications, use tool C–4804 or equivalent to turn the idle speed adjusting screw to obtain 800 ± 10 rpm. If the under hood emission sticker specifications are different, use those values for adjustment.

NOTE: If idle will not adjust down, check for binding linkage, speed control servo cable adjustment or throttle shaft binding.

8. Turn off the engine, disconnect tachometer, reinstall AIS wire and remove jumper wire from fan motor.

FUEL TANK

REMOVAL AND INSTALLATION

NOTE:—All Wheel Drive vehicles, have a fuel tank that is made of plastic. Care should be taken to avoid damaging this tank. The fuel tank in AWD vehicles is mounted at the side of the vehicle instead of the rear.

1. Release the fuel system pressure. Refer to fuel system pressure release procedure in this section.

——————— **CAUTION** ———————
Never smoke when working around gasoline! Avoid all sources of sparks or ignition. Gasoline vapors are EXTREMELY volatile!

2. Disconnect battery negative cable.
3. Raise the vehicle and support properly.
4. Remove drain tube rubber cap on left rail and connect a siphon hose to drain tube. Drain fuel into a safe gasoline container.
5. Remove screws supporting filler tube to inner and outer quarter panel.
6. Disconnect wiring and lines from the tank.
7. Position a transmission jack to support the fuel tank and remove the bolts from fuel tank straps.
8. Lower tank slightly, and carefully work filler tube from tank.

9. Lower tank, disconnect vapor separator rollover valve hose and remove the fuel tank and insulator pad from vehicle.

To install:
10. Support the fuel tank with a transmission jack. Connect the vapor separator rollover valve hose and position insulator pad on fuel tank.

NOTE: Be certain vapor vent hose is clipped to the tank and not pinch between tank and floor pan during

TORQUE SPECIFICATIONS

Component	English	Metric
AIS Motor		
Multi-Point Fuel Injection:	17 inch lbs.	2 Nm
Carburetor air horn retaining screws:	30 inch lbs.	3 Nm
Carburetor mounting nuts		
2.2L engine:	17 ft. lbs.	23 Nm
2.6L engine:	13 ft. lbs.	17 Nm
EGR tube flange-to-intake plenum		
3.0L engine:	200 inch lbs.	22 Nm
Fuel injector rail assembly		
2.5L turbo engines:	21 ft. lbs.	28 Nm
3.0L engines:	10 ft. lbs.	13 Nm
Fuel injector Torx® screw		
Single point injection:	35–45 inch lbs.	4–5 Nm
Fuel pressure damper		
Multi-point injection systems:	30 ft. lbs.	41 Nm
Fuel pressure regulator attaching screws		
Single point injection:	40 inch lbs.	5 Nm
3.0L engines:	77 inch lbs.	9 Nm
3.3L engines:	65 inch lbs.	7 Nm
Fuel supply and return tube hold-down bolt		
3.0L engine:	95 inch lbs.	10 Nm
Fuel tank strap bolts:	40 ft. lbs.	54.2 Nm
Heated oxygen sensor:	20 ft. lbs.	27 Nm
Mechanical Fuel Pump-to-engine block:	21 ft. lbs.	28 Nm
Throttle body fuel fittings		
Single point injection:	15 ft. lbs.	20 Nm
Throttle body mounting screws		
Single point injection:	175 inch lbs.	20 Nm
Throttle position sensor		
Multi-Point Fuel Injection:	17 inch lbs.	2 Nm
Throttle body temperature sensor		
Single point injection:	100 inch lbs.	11 Nm
Vacuum crossover tube hold-down bolt		
3.0L engine:	95 inch lbs.	10 Nm

6 Chassis Electrical

QUICK REFERENCE INDEX

GENERAL INDEX

HEATING AND AIR CONDITIONING

Service such as blower motor and heater core replacement on 1984–87 models, requires the removal of the Heater/Evaporator unit from the vehicle. Two persons will be required for the operation.

NOTE: Properly discharge the refrigerant system before any work requiring the disconnecting of the refrigerant lines. Refer to Section 1 for the proper discharging, evacuating and recharging procedures.

Heater/Evaporator Unit

REMOVAL AND INSTALLATION

1984-87 Models

CAUTION

The air conditioning system contains refrigerant under high pressure. Severe personal injury may result from improper service procedures. If the knowledge and necessary equipment are not on hand, have the system serviced by qualified service the refrigerant system completely.

---

1. Discharge the air conditioning system. See the CAUTION notice above.
2. Block the vehicle wheels and apply the parking brake.
3. Disconnect the negative battery cable. Drain the cooling system.

CAUTION

When draining the coolant, keep in mind that cats and dogs are attracted by the ethylene glycol antifreeze, and are quite likely to drink any that is left in an uncovered container or in puddles on the ground. This will prove fatal in sufficient quantity. Always drain the coolant into a sealable container. Coolant should be reused unless it is contaminated or several years old.

---

4. Remove the passenger side lower instrument panel.
5. Remove the steering column lower cover.
6. Remove the right side cowl and sill trim.
7. Remove the mounting bolt from the right side instrument panel to the right cowl.
8. Loosen the (2) brackets supporting the lower edge to air conditioning and heater unit housing.
9. Remove the mid-reinforcement instrument panel trim molding.
10. Remove the attaching screws from the right side to center of the steering column.
11. From the engine compartment; disconnect the vacuum line at brake booster and water valve.
12. Remove the hoses from the heater core. Plug the heater tubes.
13. Disconnect the air conditioning plumbing at the H-valve.
14. Remove the (4) nuts from engine compartment package mounting studs.
15. From the passenger compartment, pull the right side of lower instrument panel rearward until it reaches the passenger seat. Disconnect the electrical connectors and temperature control cable.
16. Remove the hangar strap from the unit assembly and bend rearward.
17. Carefully remove the unit assembly from the vehicle.
18. Place the heater/evaporator unit assembly on a work bench.
19. Remove the vacuum harness attaching screw and remove the harness through the access hole in the cover.
20. Remove the (13) attaching screws from the cover and remove the cover. The temperature control door will come out with the cover.

21. Remove the retaining bracket screws and the remove heater core assembly.
22. Remove the evaporator core assembly.
23. Disconnect the actuator linkage from the recirculation door and remove the vacuum line. Remove the actuator retaining screws and remove the actuator.
24. Remove the (4) attaching screws from the recirculation door cover to evaporator/heater assembly. Lift the cover from the unit and remove the recirculation door from its housing.
25. Remove the (5) attaching screws from the blower assembly sound helmet.
26. Remove the retaining clamp from the blower wheel hub and slide the blower wheel from the blower motor shaft.
27. Remove the blower motor (3) mounting screws from the helmet and remove the blower motor assembly.
To install:
28. Install the blower wheel to the blower motor shaft and secure it with the retaining clamp.
29. Feed the blower motor electrical wires through the access hole in the sound helmet and lower the blower motor into helmet.
30. Secure the blower motor with the (3) mounting screws.
31. Install the blower assembly and helmet into the fan scroll and secure it with (5) retaining screws.
32. Install the recirculation door into its housing. Place the recirculation door cover onto the unit and secure with the (4) retaining screws.
33. Install the actuator shaft onto the recirculation door and slide the actuator into its bracket. Secure the actuator assembly with (2) nuts.
34. Install the evaporator core into the unit.
35. Install the heater core into the unit and secure the core tube retaining bracket with attaching screws.
36. Install the unit cover and secure with (13) attaching screws.
37. Install the vacuum harness through the access hole in the cover and secure the vacuum harness.
38. Place the heater/evaporator assembly into the vehicle and position it against the dash panel.
39. Install the hangar strap.
40. Connect the temperature control cable, vacuum and electrical connectors.
41. Install the (4) retaining nuts to the unit mounting studs from the engine compartment.
42. Connect the air conditioning plumbing to the H-valve.
43. Connect the vacuum line at the brake booster and water valve.
44. Install the attaching screws from the right side to the center of the steering column.
45. Install the mid-reinforcement instrument panel trim molding.
46. Tighten the (2) brackets supporting the lower edge to the heater/evaporator unit housing.

Evaporator/Heater assembly

Removing and installing the heater core assembly

Blower motor removal and installation — 1984-90 models

Heater/evaporator assembly components

Removing and installing actuator and linkage on the blower housing

Removing or installing the evaporator

47. Install the mounting bolt from the right side of the instrument panel to the right cowl.
48. Install the right side cowl and sill trim.
49. Install the steering column lower cover.
50. Install the passenger side lower instrument panel.
51. Connect the heater hoses to heater core in the engine compartment.
52. Connect the negative battery cable.
53. Fill the cooling system.
54. Evacuate, charge and leak test the air conditioning system.

Blower Motor

REMOVAL AND INSTALLATION

1. Disconnect the negative battery cable.
2. Remove the air intake duct and top half of the fan shroud.
3. Disconnect the blower connector.

Air conditioning and heating system — vacuum circuits

Actuator assemblies

Instrument panel ventilation ducts and hoses

4. Remove the blower motor cooling tube.

5. Remove the retaining nuts and washers from the studs holding the blower.

6. Pull the air conditioning lines inboard and upward while removing the blower assembly from the vehicle. Remove the spring clip fastening the blower wheel to the blower shaft and pull off the wheel.

To install:

7. Install the blower wheel to the shaft and install the spring clip. Inspect the blower mounting plate seal and repair, as necessary. Apply rubber adhesive to the seal to aid in assembly.

8. Install the blower into the housing and install the washers and nuts.

9. Install the cooling tube.

10. Connect the connector.

11. Install the fan shroud and air intake duct.

12. Connect the negative battery cable and check the blower motor for proper operation.

Blower Motor Resistor

REMOVAL AND INSTALLATION

The resistor block is located at the left rear corner of the engine compartment on Caravan, Voyager and Town & Country.

1. Disconnect the negative battery cable.

2. Remove the glovebox, if necessary. Locate the resistor block and disconnect the wire harness.

3. Remove the attaching screws and remove the resistor from the housing.

4. Make sure there is no contact between any of the coils before installing.

5. The installation is the reverse of the removal procedure. Make sure the foam seal is in good condition.

6. Connect the negative battery cable and check the blower system for proper operation.

Resistor block removal or installation

Heater Core and Evaporator

REMOVAL AND INSTALLATION

1984–90

1. Disconnect the negative battery cable. Properly discharge the air conditioning system, if equipped. Drain the cooling system.

2. Remove the lower steering column cover.

3. Remove the lower reinforcement under the steering column, right side cowl and sill trim. Remove the bolt holding the right side instrument panel to the right cowl.

4. Loosen the 2 brackets supporting the lower edge of the heater housing. Remove the instrument panel trim covering and reinforcement. Remove the retaining screws from the right side of the steering column.

5. Disconnect the vacuum lines at the brake booster and water valve.

6. Clamp off the heater hoses at the heater core and remove

* = HOSE CLAMP

WATER VALVE

HEATER HOSES

Heater hose routing — V6 engines

them from the heater core tubes. Plug the ends to prevent leakage.

7. Disconnect the H-valve at the water valve and remove it. Remove the retaining nuts at the package tray mounting studs. Remove the drain tube.

8. Disconnect the blower motor wiring and temperature control cable. Disconnect the vacuum harness at the top of the heater unit.

9. Remove the retaining nuts from the package mounting studs at the firewall. Disconnect the hanger strap from the package and rotate it aside.

10. Pull the right side of the instrument panel out as far as possible. Fold the carpeting and insulation back to provide a little more working room and to prevent spillage from staining the carpeting.

11. Remove the entire housing assembly from the dash panel and remove it from the vehicle.

12. To disassemble the housing assembly, remove the vacuum diaphragm and retaining screws from the cover and remove the cover.

13. Remove the retaining screw from the heater core and/or evaporator and remove from the housing assembly.

To install:

14. Remove the temperature control door from the unit and clean the unit out with solvent. Lubricate the lower pivot rod and its well and install. Wrap the heater core and/or evaporator with foam tape and place in position. Secure with the screws.

15. Assemble the unit, making sure all vacuum tubes are properly routed.

16. Install the assembly to the vehicle and connect the vacuum harness. Install the nuts to the firewall and install the condensation tube. Fold the carpeting back into position.

17. Connect the hanger strap from the package and rotate it aside. Install the 2 brackets supporting the lower edge of the heater housing. Connect the blower motor wiring, resistor wiring and the temperature control cable.

18. Install the retaining screws from the right side to the steering column. Install the instrument panel trim covering and reinforcement.

19. Install the bolt holding the right side instrument panel to the right cowl. Install the lower reinforcement under the steering column, right side cowl and sill trim.

20. Connect the vacuum lines at the brake booster and water valve.

21. Connect the heater hoses to the core tubes.

22. Using new gaskets, install the H-valve and connect the refrigerant lines. Install the condensation tube.

23. Evacuate and recharge the air conditioning system, if equipped. Add 2 oz. of refrigerant oil during the recharge. Fill the cooling system.

24. Connect the negative battery cable and check the entire climate control system for proper operation and leaks.

25. Connect the negative battery cable and check the entire climate control system for proper operation and leakage.

1991

1. Disconnect the negative battery cable. Properly discharge the air conditioning system, if equipped. Drain the cooling system.

2. Remove the steering column cover and left and right side under panel silencers.

3. Remove the center bezel by unclipping it from the instrument panel.

4. Remove the accessory switch carrier and the heater/air conditioning control head.

5. Remove storage bin and lower right instrument panel.

6. Disconnect the blower motor lead under the right side of the instrument panel.

7. Remove the right side 40-way connector wiring bracket.

8. Remove the lower right reinforcement, body computer bracket and mid-to-lower reinforcement as an assembly.

9. Disconnect the vacuum lines at the brake booster and water valve.

10. Clamp off the heater hoses near the heater core and remove the hoses from the core tubes. Plug the hose ends and the core tubes to prevent spillage of coolant.

11. If equipped with air conditioning, remove the H-valve and condensation tube.

12. Disconnect the temperature control cable and vacuum harness at the connection at the top of the unit.

13. Remove the retaining nuts from the package mounting studs at the firewall. Disconnect the hanger strap from the package and rotate it aside.

To install:

14. Remove the temperature control door from the unit and clean the unit out with solvent. Lubricate the lower pivot rod and its well and install. Wrap the heater core and/or evaporator with foam tape and place in position. Secure with the screws.

15. Assemble the unit, making sure all vacuum tubes are properly routed.

16. Install the assembly to the vehicle and connect the vacuum harness. Install the nuts to the firewall and install the condensation tube. Fold the carpeting back into position.

17. Connect the hanger strap from the package and rotate it aside. Install the 2 brackets supporting the lower edge of the heater housing. Connect the blower motor wiring, resistor wiring and the temperature control cable.

18. Install the retaining screws from the right side to the steering column. Install the instrument panel trim covering and reinforcement.

19. Assemble the unit, making sure all vacuum tubes are properly routed.

20. Install the assembly to the vehicle and connect the vacuum harness. Install the nuts to the firewall and install the condensation tube. Fold the carpeting back into position.

21. Connect the hanger strap from the package and rotate it aside. Connect the blower motor wiring and temperature control cable.

23. Install the lower right reinforcement, body computer bracket and mid-to-lower reinforcement as an assembly.

24. Install the right side 40-way connector wiring bracket.

25. Install the lower right instrument panel and storage bin.

26. Install the heater/air conditioning control head and accessory switch carrier.

27. Install the center bezel to the instrument panel.

28. Install the under panel silencers and steering column cover.

29. Install the vacuum lines at the brake booster and water valve.

30. Connect the heater hoses to the core tubes.

31. Using new gaskets, install the H-valve and connect the re-

A/C CONTROL TEMPERATURE CABLE

LAMP

VACUUM CONNECTOR

A/C-HEATER CONTROL

Air conditioning and heater control head removal

frigerant lines. Install the condensation tube.

32. Evacuate and recharge the air conditioning system, if equipped. Add 2 oz. of refrigerant oil during the recharge. Fill the cooling system.

33. Connect the negative battery cable and check the entire climate control system for proper operation and leaks.

34. Connect the negative battery cable and check the entire climate control system for proper operation and leakage.

Climate Control Head

REMOVAL AND INSTALLATION

1. Disconnect the negative battery cable.
2. Remove the necessary bezel(s) in order to gain access to the control head.
3. Remove the screws that fasten the control head to the instrument panel.
4. Pull the unit out and unplug the electrical and vacuum connectors. Disconnect the temperature control cable by pushing the flag in and pulling the end from its seat.
5. Remove the control head from the instrument panel.
6. The installation is the reverse of the removal proceed that fasten the control head to the instrument panel.

Heater/Air Conditioning Control Cables

REMOVAL AND INSTALLATION

1. Disconnect the negative battery cable.

2. Remove the necessary bezel(s) in order to gain access to the control head.
3. Remove the screws that fasten the control head to the instrument panel.
4. Pull the unit out and disconnect the temperature control cable by pushing the flag in and pulling the end from its seat.
5. The temperature control cable end is located at the bottom of the heater/air conditioning housing. Disconnect the cable end by pushing the flag in and pulling the end from its seat.
6. Disconnect the self-adjusting clip from the blend air or mode door crank.
7. Take note of the cable's routing and remove the from the vehicle.
To install:
8. Install the cable by routing it in exactly the same position as it was prior to removal.
9. Connect the self-adjusting clip to the door crank and click the flag into the seat.
10. Connect the upper end of the cable to the control head.
11. Place the temperature lever on the coolest side of its travel. Allowing the self-adjusting clip to slide on the cable, rotate the blend air door counterclockwise by hand until it stops.
12. Cycle the lever back and forth a few times to make sure the cable moves freely.
13. Connect the negative battery cable and check the entire climate control system for proper operation.

Receiver/Drier

REMOVAL AND INSTALLATION

1. Disconnect the negative battery cable.
2. Properly discharge the air conditioning system.
3. Remove the nuts that fasten the refrigerant lines to sides of the receiver/drier assembly.
4. Remove the refrigerant lines from the receiver/drier and discard the gaskets. Cover the exposed ends of the lines to minimize contamination.
5. Remove the mounting strap bolts and remove the receiver/drier from the engine compartment.
To install:
6. Transfer the mounting strap to the new receiver/drier.
7. Coat the new gaskets with wax-free refrigerant oil and install. Connect the refrigerant lines to the receiver/drier and tighten the nuts.
8. Evacuate and recharge the air conditioning system. Add 1 oz. of refrigerant oil during the recharge. Check for leaks.

Expansion Valve (H-Valve)

TESTING

1. Connect a manifold gauge set or charging station to the air conditioning system. Verify adequate refrigerant level.
2. Disconnect and plug the vacuum hose at the water control valve.
3. Disconnect the low pressure or differential pressure cut off switch connector and jump the wires inside the boot.
4. Close all doors, windows and vents to the passenger compartment.
5. Set controls to **MAX A/C**, full heat and high blower speed.
6. Start the engine and hold the idle speed at 1000 rpm. After the engine has reached normal operating temperature, allow the passenger compartment to heat up to create the need for maximum refrigerant flow into the evaporator.
7. The discharge (high pressure) gauge should read 140–240 psi and suction (low pressure) gauge should read 20–30 psi, providing the refrigerant charge is sufficient.
8. If the suction side is within specifications, freeze the ex-

pansion valve control head using a very cold substance (liquid CO2 or dry ice) for 30 seconds:

    a. If equipped with a silver H-valve used with fixed displacement compressor, the suction side pressure should drop to 15 in. Hg vacuum. If not, the expansion valve is stuck open and should be replaced.

    b. If equipped with a black H-valve used with variable displacement compressor, the discharge pressure should drop about 15 percent. If not, the expansion valve is stuck open and should be replaced.

9. Allow the expansion valve to thaw. As it thaws, the pressures should stabilize to the values in Step 7. If not, replace the expansion valve.

10. Once the test is complete, put the vacuum line and connector back in the original locations, and perform the overall performance test.

REMOVAL AND INSTALLATION

1. Disconnect the negative battery cable.
2. Properly discharge the air conditioning system.
3. Disconnect the low or differential pressure cut off switch.

4. Remove the attaching bolt at the center of the refrigerant plumbing sealing plate.
5. Pull the refrigerant lines assembly away from the expansion valve. Cover the exposed ends of the lines to minimize contamination.
6. Remove the 2 Torx® screws that mount the expansion valve to the evaporator sealing plate.
7. Remove the valve and discard the gaskets.

To install:

8. Transfer the low pressure cutoff switch to the new valve, if necessary.
9. Coat the new "figure-8" gasket with wax-free refrigerant oil and install to the evaporator sealing plate.
10. Install the expansion valve and torque the Torx® screws to 100 inch lbs.
11. Lubricate the remaining gasket and install with the blower motor lead under the right side of the instrument panel.
12. Connect the refrigerant lines and sealing plate, tighten to 200 inch lbs. (23 Nm).
13. Connect the electrical leads and connect the negative battery cable.
14. Evacuate and properly recharge the air conditioning system.

AUXILIARY HEATER/AIR CONDITIONER

Expansion Valve

REMOVAL AND INSTALLATION

1. Disconnect the negative battery cable.
2. Properly discharge the air conditioning system.
3. Remove the bolt that secures the refrigerant lines to the evaporator sealing plate and separate the parts. Discard the gasket. Cover the exposed ends of the lines to minimize contamination.
4. Remove the middle bench, if equipped. Remove the interior left lower quarter trim panel.
5. Remove the 7 screws that attach the air distribution duct to the floor and unit. Pull the distribution duct straight up to remove.
6. Remove the 6 screws from the top surface of the unit and remove the unit cover.
7. Pull the evaporator and expansion valve straight up in order to clear the extension tube pilots and remove from the vehicle. Cover the exposed ends of the lines to minimize contamination.
8. Remove the Torx® screws and remove the expansion valve from the evaporator. Discard the gasket.

To install:

9. Lubricate the gasket with wax-free refrigerant oil and assemble the expansion valve and evaporator.
10. Lubricate the gasket with wax-free refrigerant oil and install the evaporator and expansion valve assembly to the refrigerant lines and install the bolt.

Rear air conditioning/heater assembly components

11. Install the unit cover and air distribution duct.
12. Install the interior trim cover and middle bench.
13. Evacuate and recharge the air conditioning system.
14. Connect the negative battery cable and check the entire climate control system for proper operation and leaks.

Blower Motor

REMOVAL AND INSTALLATION

1. Disconnect the negative battery cable.
2. Remove the middle bench, if equipped. Remove the left lower quarter trim panel.
3. Remove 1 blower scroll cover to floor screw and 7 scroll to unit screws.
4. Remove the blower relay.
5. Rotate the blower scroll cover from under the unit.
6. Remove the fan from the blower motor, remove the 3 motor attaching screws and remove the motor from the unit.
7. The installation is the reverse of the removal procedure.
8. Connect the negative battery cable and check the blower motor for proper operation.

Blower Motor Resistor

REMOVAL AND INSTALLATION

1. Disconnect the negative battery cable.
2. Remove the middle bench, if equipped. Remove the left lower quarter trim panel.
3. Disconnect the wiring harness from the resistor.
4. Remove the screws that attach the resistor to the rear unit and remove the resistor.
5. The installation is the reverse of the removal procedure.
6. Connect the negative battery cable and check for proper operation.

Heater Core

REMOVAL AND INSTALLATION

1. Disconnect the negative battery cable. Pinch off the hoses to the rear heater core.
2. Raise the vehicle and support safely. Disconnect the underbody heater hoses from the rear heater core tubes.
3. Remove the middle bench, if equipped. Remove the interior left lower quarter trim panel.
4. Remove the 7 screws that attach the air distribution duct to the floor and unit. Pull the distribution duct straight up to remove.
5. Remove the 6 screws from the top surface of the unit and remove the unit cover.
6. Pull the heater core straight up and out of the unit.
7. The installation is the reverse of the removal procedure.
8. Connect the negative battery cable and check for leaks.

Evaporator

REMOVAL AND INSTALLATION

1. Disconnect the negative battery cable.
2. Properly discharge the air conditioning system.
3. Remove the unit cover and duct.
4. Remove the middle bench, if equipped. Remove the interior left lower quarter trim panel.
5. Remove the 7 screws that attach the air distribution duct to the floor and unit. Pull the distribution duct straight up to remove.

6. Remove the 6 screws from the top surface of the unit and remove the unit cover.
7. Pull the evaporator and expansion valve straight up in order to clear the extension tube pilots and remove from the vehicle. Cover the exposed ends of the lines to minimize contamination.
8. Remove the Torx® screws and remove the expansion valve from the evaporator. Discard the gasket.

To install:
9. Lubricate the gasket with wax-free refrigerant oil and assemble the expansion valve and evaporator.
10. Lubricate the gasket with wax-free refrigerant oil and install the evaporator and expansion valve assembly to the refrigerant lines and install the bolt.
11. Install the unit cover and air distribution duct.
12. Install the interior trim cover and middle bench.
13. Evacuate and recharge the air conditioning system. If the evaporator was replaced, measure the amount of oil that was in the original evaporator and add that amount during the recharge.
14. Connect the negative battery cable and check the entire climate control system for proper operation and leaks.

Rear heater assembly — underbody hose routing

Rear air conditioning assembly — underbody line routing

Blower motor noise/vibration diagnosis

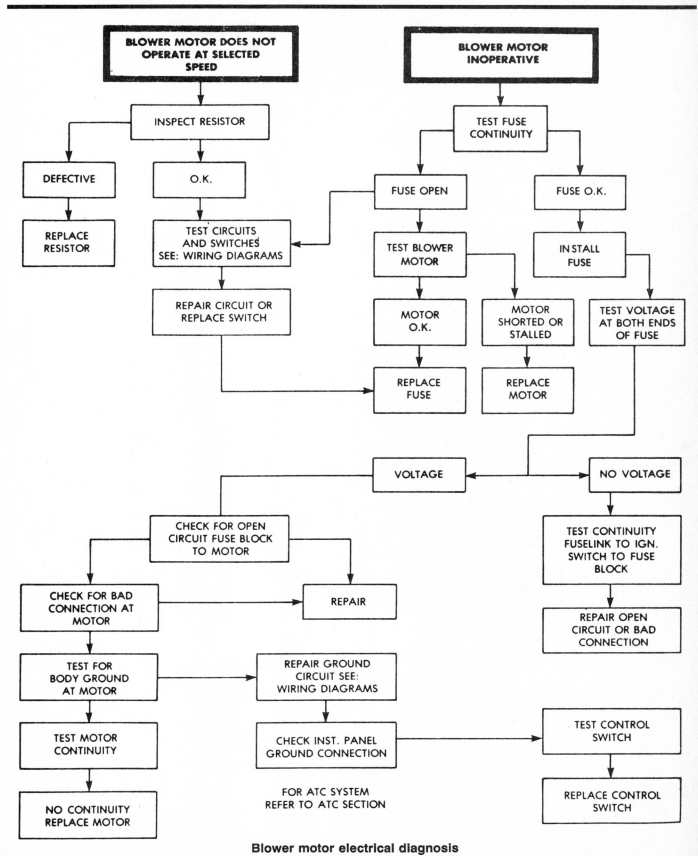

Blower motor electrical diagnosis

Refrigerant Lines

REMOVAL AND INSTALLATION

1. Disconnect the negative battery cable.
2. Properly discharge the air conditioning system.
3. Raise the vehicle and support safely.
4. Remove the nuts or bolts that attach the refrigerant line sealing plates to the adjoining components. If the lines are connected with flare nuts, use a back-up wrench when disassembling. Cover the exposed ends of the lines to minimize contamination.

5. Remove the support mount.
6. Remove the lines and discard the gaskets or O-rings.

To install:

7. Coat the new gaskets or O-rings with wax-free refrigerant oil and install. Connect the refrigerant lines to the adjoining components and tighten the nuts or bolts.
8. Install the support mount.
9. Evacuate and recharge the air conditioning system.
10. Connect the negative battery cable and check the entire climate control system for proper operation and leaks.

RADIO

REMOVAL AND INSTALLATION

1. Disconnect the negative battery cable. Remove the control knobs by pulling them from the mounting stalks. Remove the three (3) screws from the top of the radio trim bezel.
2. Remove the ash tray to gain access to the trim bezel lower screws.
3. Remove the two (2) screws from the lower portion of the trim bezel.
4. Pull outward on the left side of bezel to unsnap the mounting clips. Remove the bezel.
5. Remove the radio to instrument panel retaining screws.
6. Pull the radio through the front of the instrument panel and unplug the wiring harness, ground strap and antenna plug.
7. Connect the radio wiring harness, ground strap and antenna lead.
8. Position the radio into the instrument panel and install the retaining screws.
9. Install the trim bezel and secure it with the lower and upper retaining screws. Install the ash tray.

Radio assembly removal

Antenna

REMOVAL AND INSTALLATION

1. Remove the radio.
2. Disconnect the antenna cable from the radio.
3. Remove the antenna cable from the harness retaining clips.
4. Unscrew the antenna mast from the upper adapter.
5. Remove the cap mounting nut.
6. Remove the adapter and mounting gasket.
7. From beneath the fender remove the antenna lead and body assembly.
8. Install the new antenna body and cable assembly from under fender.
9. Install the adapter gasket, adapter and cap nut.
10. Install the antenna cable through harness mounting clips and install the cable into radio receiver.
11. Install the radio into the instrument panel.

Antenna removal

WINDSHIELD WIPERS

Wiper Blade

Refer to "General Information and Maintenance" for removal and installation procedure.

Wiper Arm (Windshield)

REMOVAL AND INSTALLATION

1. Remove the head cover from the wiper arm base.
2. Remove the arm to pivot attaching nut.
3. Remove the wiper arm from pivot using a rocking motion.
4. With the wiper motor in Park position, position the arm on the pivot shaft. Choose a point where the tip of the left wiper arm is approximately 2 to 3 inches above the windshield cowl top, and the right arm 1 to 1.5 inches above the windshield cowl top.
5. Install the attaching nut and torque to 120 in. lbs.
6. Install the pivot head cover on the wiper arm.

Wiper arm servicing

Wiper Arm (Liftgate)

REMOVAL AND INSTALLATION

1. Insert Tool C-3982 or the equivalent between the wiper arm and wiper motor output shaft.

Windshield wiper motor and linkage assemblies

NOTE: The use of screwdrivers or other prying tool may damaged the spring clip in the base of the arm, while trying to release the arm. Damage of the spring clip will result in the arm coming off the shaft regardless of how carefully it is installed.

2. Lift the arm and remove it from motor output shaft.

3. With motor in the Park position, position the arm on the motor output shaft. Choose a point where the tip of blade is about 38mm parallel with the bottom lower edge of liftgate glass. Push the wiper arm onto the motor shaft.

Windshield Wiper Motor

REMOVAL AND INSTALLATION

1. The motor and wiper linkage are serviced as a unit. Disconnect the negative battery cable. Remove the wiper arm and blade assemblies. Refer to the windshield wiper arm removal and installation procedure in this section.

2. Open the hood and remove the cowl plenum grille and plastic screen.

3. Remove the hoses from the turret connector. Remove the pivot mounting screws.

4. Disconnect the motor wiring connector from the motor.

5. Remove the retaining nut from the wiper motor shaft to linkage drive crank, and remove the drive crank from the wiper motor shaft.

6. Remove the wiper motor assembly mounting screws and nuts, and remove the wiper motor.

To install:

7. Position the wiper motor against it's mounting surface and secure in position with the mounting screws and nuts Connect the wiring harness.

8. Install the linkage drive crank onto the wiper motor shaft and secure it with the retaining nut. Torque the nut to 95 in. lbs.

9. Install cowl plenum grille plastic screen.

10. Connect hoses to turret connector.

11. Install the cowl plenum grille. Connect the negative battery cable. Close the hood.

12. Install the windshield wiper arm and blade assemblies.

Liftgate Wiper Motor

REMOVAL AND INSTALLATION

1. Disconnect the negative battery cable. Remove the wiper arm and blade assembly.

Liftgate wiper arm installation

2. Open the liftgate and remove the trim panel.

3. Remove the four (4) mounting screws from liftgate wiper motor and bracket assembly.

4. Disconnect the electrical harness connector and remove the liftgate motor.

To install:

5. Install the liftgate wiper motor and bracket assembly. Secure it with the mounting screws.

6. Connect the wiring harness to the wiper motor.

7. Install the liftgate trim panel and secure it with the mounting screws.

8. Install the liftgate wiper arm and blade assembly.

Windshield Wiper Linkage

Refer to the Wiper Motor procedures in this section.

INSTRUMENTS AND SWITCHES

Instrument Cluster Assembly

WARNING: Before servicing the instrument cluster or components, disconnect the negative battery.

REMOVAL AND INSTALLATION

1. Disconnect the negative battery cable. Remove the cluster assembly bezel mounting (7) screws and remove the cluster bezel.

2. On vehicles equipped with an automatic transaxle, remove the steering column lower cover. Disconnect the shift indicator wire.

3. Remove the cluster assembly retaining screws.

4. Carefully pull the cluster assembly from the panel and disconnect the speedometer cable.

5. Remove the cluster assembly wiring harness.

6. Remove the cluster assembly past the right side of the steering column.

To install:

7. Position the cluster assembly to the dash from the right side of the steering column.

8. Connect the cluster wiring.

9. Connect the speedometer cable.

10. Install the cluster assembly and retaining screws.

11. On models equipped with an automatic transaxle, place the selector lever in (D) Drive position.

12. Connect the shift indicator wire to the steering column shift housing. Route the wire on the outside of slotted flange.

13. Place the shift lever in (P) Park position to make the indicator self-adjust.

14. Connect the shift indicator wire.

15. Install the steering column lower cover.

16. Install the cluster assembly bezel. Secure the bezel with the retaining screws.

NOTE: The following instruments can be serviced after removing the instrument cluster mask/lens. Do not completely remove the cluster assembly if only instrument service or cluster bulb replacement is necessary.

Instrument cluster mask/lens — 1984-90 models

Fuel Gauge

REMOVAL AND INSTALLATION

1. Disconnect the negative battery cable. Remove the cluster bezel retaining screws and remove the cluster bezel.

2. Remove the cluster mask/lens.

3. Remove the fuel gauge attaching screws to cluster assembly and remove the fuel gauge.

4. Position the replacement gauge to the cluster assembly and secure it with attaching screws.

5. Install the cluster mask/lens, bezel and bezel retaining screws.

Upper instrument panel and cluster mounting — 1984-90 models, 1991 models similar

Voltmeter

REMOVAL AND INSTALLATION

1. Disconnect the negative battery cable. Remove the cluster bezel retaining screws and remove the cluster bezel.
2. Remove the cluster mask/lens.
3. Remove the voltmeter attaching screws to cluster assembly and remove the voltmeter.
4. Position the replacement voltmeter to cluster assembly and secure with the attaching screws.
5. Install the cluster mask/lens, bezel and bezel retaining screws.

Temperature Gauge

REMOVAL AND INSTALLATION

1. Disconnect the negative battery cable. Remove the cluster bezel retaining screws and remove the cluster bezel.
2. Remove the cluster mask/lens.
3. Remove the temperature/oil pressure gauge attaching screws to cluster assembly and remove the temperature gauge.
4. Position the replacement temperature/oil pressure gauge to cluster assembly and secure with the attaching screws.
5. Install the cluster mask/lens, bezel and bezel retaining screws.

Oil Pressure Gauge

REMOVAL AND INSTALLATION

1. Disconnect the negative battery cable. Remove the cluster bezel retaining screws and remove the cluster bezel.

Printed circuit board mounting screw location

Shift indicator and message center mounting on the instrument cluster

2. Remove the cluster mask/lens.
3. Remove the oil pressure/temperature gauge attaching screws to cluster assembly and remove the temperature gauge.
4. Position the replacement oil pressure/temperature gauge to cluster assembly and secure with the attaching screws.
5. Install the cluster mask/lens, bezel and bezel retaining screws.

Printed Circuit Board

REMOVAL AND INSTALLATION

1. Disconnect the negative battery cable.
2. Remove the instrument cluster from the instrument panel.
3. Remove the circuit board retaining screws.
4. Remove the lamp sockets, by twisting them out.
5. Carefully remove the circuit board.
6. Install the new circuit board in position and install the lamp sockets.
7. Connect the negative battery cable.

Cluster Lamp Bulbs

REMOVAL AND INSTALLATION

1. Disconnect the negative battery cable. Remove the cluster bezel retaining screws and remove the cluster bezel.
2. Remove the cluster mask/lens.
3. Remove the gauge assembly in front of blown bulbs and replace the bulbs.
4. Install the gauge to the cluster assembly.
5. Install the cluster mask/lens, bezel and bezel retaining screws.

Cluster Lamp Sockets

REMOVAL AND INSTALLATION

All cluster lamp sockets are twist out sockets and are removed from the rear of the instrument cluster. Refer to Instrument Cluster Removal and Installation procedure in this section.

Instrument Panel (Lower)

REMOVAL AND INSTALLATION

——————— CAUTION ———————
Before servicing the lower instrument panel, chock the wheels. Servicing the steering column may cause an automatic transaxle to come out of the (P) Park position.

Always release the parking brake before the release cable is disconnected. Disconnecting the parking brake cable without releasing the parking brake may cause personal injury.

1. Block the vehicle wheels and release the parking brake. Disconnect the negative battery cable.
2. Remove the steering column lower left cover.
3. Remove the side cowl and the sill molding.
4. Remove the instrument panel silencer and reinforcement.
5. Loosen the bolt in the side cowl, but do not remove the bolt.
6. Place the gear selector into the (N) Neutral position and disconnect the shift indicator cable.
7. Remove the steering wheel.
8. Remove the (5) nuts securing the steering column to the support bracket.
9. Lower the steering column. Use a cover to protect the steering column and the front seat.

SPEAKER GRILLE

DEFROSTER GRILLE

MOULDING

REINFORCEMENT

SILENCER

STEERING COLUMN COVER

INSTRUMENT PANEL UPPER

INSTRUMENT PANEL LOWER

Instrument panel assembly — 1984-90 models

10. Remove the right side instrument panel trim molding.

11. Remove the (9) screws securing the lower panel to the upper panel and mid-reinforcement.

12. Lower the instrument panel approximately six inches.

13. Disconnect the park brake release cable, heater attachment or air conditioning control cables, antenna and wiring connectors from the radio and fresh air ducts.

14. Disconnect the electrical connections and label them with tape for identification.

15. Pry the A-pillar garnish off the door opening weatherstrip at the panel bolt.

16. Pull the weatherstrip from the body and remove the lower panel from the vehicle.

To install:

17. Position the lower panel into the vehicle.

18. Install the weatherstrip and garnish molding.

19. Connect the park brake release cable, heater attachment or air conditioning control cables, antenna and wiring connectors to the radio and fresh air ducts.

20. Connect all electrical connections.

21. Secure the lower instrument panel to upper panel and mid-reinforcement with (9) retaining screws.

22. Install the right side instrument panel trim molding.

23. Raise the steering column and install the (5) nuts securing steering column to the support bracket.

24. Install the steering wheel.

25. Connect the shift indicator cable.

26. Install the lower reinforcement, silencer and the lower left steering column cover. Connect the negative battery cable.

Instrument Panel (Upper)

REMOVAL AND INSTALLATION

1. Disconnect the negative battery cable. Separate the lower instrument panel from the upper half (see Steps 1 through 12 of the Lower Instrument Panel procedure).

2. Disconnect the speedometer cable from the engine compartment.

3. Remove (2) nuts at the steering column floating bracket.

4. Disconnect the gear shift selector indicator wire.

5. Disconnect the electrical connector at the radio speakers.

6. Remove the radio speaker and defroster grilles.

7. Remove the (2) mounting screws from each side cowl bracket.

8. Remove the (4) upper panel attaching screws from the defroster duct slots and the (2) screws next to the radio speakers.

9. Pull the panel and disconnect the speedometer cable from the speedometer.

10. Remove upper instrument panel from vehicle.

To install:

11. Position the upper instrument panel into the vehicle.

12. Connect the speedometer cable.

13. Install the (6) upper panel attaching screws.

14. Install the cowl bracket retaining screws.

15. Install the radio speaker and defroster grilles.

16. Connect the radio speaker wiring.

17. Connect the gear shift selector indicator wire.

18. Install the retaining nuts at the steering column floating bracket.

19. Connect the speedometer cable in the engine compartment.

20. Install the lower panel to the upper.

Forward Console

REMOVAL AND INSTALLATION

1. Disconnect the negative battery cable. Remove the cigar lighter and ash receiver.

Forward console mounting

2. Remove the retaining screws securing the forward console to the upper mounting bracket.

3. Remove the retaining screws securing the forward console to the lower bracket.

4. Pull the console rearward and disconnect the cigar lighter and illumination electrical wiring connectors.

5. Remove the forward console from vehicle.

6. Position the forward console into the vehicle.

7. Connect the cigar lighter and illumination wiring connectors.

8. Install the console lower bracket retaining screws.

9. Install the console upper bracket retaining screws.

10. Install the cigar lighter and ash receiver.

Windshield Wiper Switch

The windshield wiper switch on all 1984-90 models is an stalk mounted control. On 1991 models, the wiper switch is mounted on the instrument cluster pod.

REMOVAL AND INSTALLATION

1984-90 Models With Standard Steering Column

1. Disconnect negative battery cable.

2. Remove the steering wheel horn pad assembly.

3. Remove the lower steering column cover, silencer and reinforcement.

4. Remove the wiper switch wiring harness from the steering column retainer.

5. Remove the wash/wipe switch cover. Rotate the cover upward.

6. Disconnect the wipe/wash seven terminal electrical connector. Disconnect intermittent the wipe switch electrical connector or speed control electrical connector, if equipped.

7. Unlock the steering column and turn the wheel so that the access hole provided in the wheel base is in the 9 o'clock position.

8. Reach through the access hole using a small screwdriver and loosen the turn signal lever mounting screw.

9. Remove the wipe/wash switch assembly the from steering column.

10. Slide the circular hider up the control stalk and remove the (2) screws that attach the control stalk sleeve to wipe/wash switch.

11. Remove the wipe/wash switch control knob from the multifunction control stalk. Rotate the control stalk to full clockwise position and pull the shaft from the switch.

To install:

12. Install the stalk shaft into the wash/wipe switch and rotate full counterclockwise.

13. Install the wash/wipe switch control knob onto the end of the multifunction control stalk.

14. Install (2) retaining screws that secure the wipe/wash switch to the control stalk sleeve.

15. Install the wipe/wash switch assembly to the steering column.

16. Install and tighten the turn signal lever screw (through the access hole).

17. Connect the wipe/wash seven terminal electrical connector. Connect the intermittent wipe switch electrical connector or speed control electrical connector, if equipped.

18. Install the wash/wipe switch cover.

19. Secure the wiring harness into the steering column retainer.

20. Install the reinforcement, silencer and lower steering column cover.

21. Install the steering wheel horn pad assembly.

21. Connect the negative batter cable.

1984-90 Models With Tilt Steering Column

1. Disconnect the negative battery cable.

Removing the wiper switch — standard steering column

2. Remove the horn cover pad from the steering wheel. Remove steering column cover. Remove the steering wheel nut.

3. Remove the steering wheel using puller C-3428B or equivalent.

4. Carefully remove the plastic cover from the locking plate. Install locking plate depressing tool C-4156 or equivalent onto the steering shaft. Depress the locking plate and remove the retaining ring from the mounting groove using a small screwdriver. To avoid difficulty when removing the retaining ring, the full load of the upper bearing spring should not be relieved. Remove the locking plate, canceling cam, and upper bearing spring.

5. Remove the switch stalk actuator screw and arm.

6. Remove the hazard warning knob.

7. Disconnect the wipe/wash seven terminal electrical connector. Disconnect the intermittent wipe switch electrical connector or speed control electrical connector, if equipped.

8. Remove the turn signal switch (3) retaining screws.

9. Tape the connectors at end of the wiring to prevent snagging when removing. Place the shift bowl in low (1st) position. Remove the switch and wiring.

10. Remove the ignition key lamp located next to the hazard warning knob.

11. Insert a thin screwdriver into the lock release slot next to the lock cylinder mounting and depress the spring latch at the bottom of the slot. Remove the lock cylinder.

12. Insert a straightened paper clip or similar piece of wire with a hook bent on one end into the exposed loop of the wedge spring of key buzzer switch. Pull on the clip to remove both spring and switch.

NOTE: If the wedge spring is dropped, it could fall into steering column, requiring complete disassembly of the column.

13. Remove the column housing cover (3) screws and remove the housing cover.

14. Use a punch, and tap the wiper switch pivot pin from the lock housing. Use tape to hold the dimmer switch rod in place.

15. Remove the wipe/wash switch assembly.

16. Slide the circular hider up the control stalk and remove the (2) screws that attach the control stalk sleeve to the wipe/wash switch.

17. Remove the wipe/wash switch control knob from the multifunction control stalk. Rotate the control stalk to full clockwise position and pull the shaft from the switch.

To install:

18. Install the stalk shaft into the wash/wipe switch and rotate full counterclockwise.

19. Install the wash/wipe switch control knob on the end of the multifunction control stalk.

20. Install the (2) retaining screws that secure the wipe/wash switch to the control stalk sleeve.

21. Install the wipe/wash switch assembly to the steering column.

22. Install the wiper switch pivot pin.

23. Install the housing cover and secure with retaining screws.

24. Install the lock cylinder.

25. Assemble the wedge spring to key buzzer and install the key buzzer switch.

26. Install the ignition key lamp.

27. With the shift bowl in low (1st) position, install the turn signal switch and secure with retaining screws.

28. Connect the wipe/wash seven terminal electrical connector. Connect the intermittent wipe switch electrical connector or speed control electrical connector, if equipped.

29. Secure the wiring harness in retainer.

30. Install the hazard warning knob.

31. Install the switch stalk actuator screw and arm.

32. Install the locking plate, canceling cam, and upper bearing spring. Install the locking plate. Depress the locking plate with tool C-4156 or equivalent and install the retaining ring in

groove of steering shaft. Install the plastic cover on locking plate.

33. Install the reinforcement, silencer and lower steering column cover.

34. Install the steering wheel and steering shaft nut.

35. Install the horn contact, horn pad and install the horn pad retaining screws.

36. Connect the negative battery cable.

1991 Models—Pod Mounted

1. Disconnect the negative battery cable.

2. Remove the cluster bezel retaining screws.

3. Tilt the steering column down, if equipped.

4. Pull the cluster bezel out enough to gain access to the switch retaining tabs.

5. Release the tabs and pull the switch from the cluster.

6. Install the switch in position and seat it firmly. Install the cluster bezel retaining screws.

7. Connect the negative battery cable.

Headlamp and Accessory Switches

On the 1991 models, the headlight switch is removed in the same manner as the windshield wiper switch. Refer to the windshield wiper switch removal procedure on these models.

REMOVAL AND INSTALLATION

1. Disconnect the negative battery cable. Remove the headlamp switch plate bezel.

2. Remove the switch plate (4) retaining screws and pull the switch plate rearward.

3. Disconnect the electrical connectors. Remove the headlamp switch knob and shaft by depressing button on the switch body. Pull the knob and shaft out of the switch.

4. Remove the (2) screws retaining the headlamp switch to switch plate assembly.

5. Remove the headlamp switch retainer.

To install:

6. Install the replacement switch into the headlamp switch plate with retainer.

7. Install the headlamp switch retaining screws to the switch plate assembly.

8. Install the headlamp switch knob and shaft.

9. Connect the electrical connectors.

10. Secure the headlamp switch plate with (4) attaching screws.

11. Install the headlamp switch plate bezel.

Steering column wiring connector identification

Headlight and accessory switches — 1984-90 models

Headlamp Dimmer Switch

REMOVAL AND INSTALLATION

1. Remove the lower left steering column cover.
2. Tape the actuator control rod to prevent the rod from falling out.
3. Remove the dimmer switch retaining screws.
4. Disconnect the switch electrical connector and remove the switch.
5. Install a new switch and connect the electrical connector.
6. Position the actuator control rod into the dimmer switch and secure the switch onto the steering column.
7. Remove the tape from the actuator control rod.
8. Install the lower left steering column cover.

ADJUSTMENT

1. Loosen the dimmer switch retaining screws.
2. Insert a 24mm drill bit or pin in the adjusting pin hole. Push the switch lightly against the control rod to remove free play. Tighten the switch retaining screws while maintaining light pressure on the dimmer switch.
3. Remove the drill bit or pin.

Ignition Lock/Switch

REMOVAL AND INSTALLATION

Except Tilt Column

1. Disconnect the negative battery cable.
2. Remove the horn pad mounting screws from behind the steering wheel and remove the horn pad.
3. Remove the steering wheel nut, matchmark the steering wheel to the shaft and remove the steering wheel with a suitable puller.
4. Remove the hazard switch knob. Remove the slotted hexhead screw that attaches the wiper switch to the turn signal switch.
5. Remove the 3 screws and pull the turn signal switch out of the column as far as it will go. Unplug it below if necessary.
6. Remove the ignition switch key lamp.
7. Place the key in the **LOCK** position and remove the key.
8. Insert 2 suitable small diameter tools into both release holes and push inward to release the spring loaded lock retainers while simultaneously pulling the key lock cylinder out of its bore.
To install:
9. Install the key cylinder.

Removing the key lock cylinder — except on tilt wheel

Removing the key lock cylinder — tilt wheel

10. Install the ignition switch key lamp.
11. Install the turn signal switch and hazard switch knob. Connect the wires if they were disconnected.
12. Install the steering wheel torque the nut to 45 ft. lbs. (61 Nm).
13. Install the horn pad.
14. Connect the negative battery cable and check the lock cylinder for proper operation.
15. Install the lower column cover, if equipped.

Tilt Column

1. Disconnect the negative battery cable.
2. Remove the horn pad mounting screws from behind the steering wheel and remove the horn pad.
3. Remove the steering wheel nut, matchmark the steering wheel to the shaft and remove the steering wheel with a suitable puller.
4. Depress the lock plate with the proper depressing tool, remove the retaining ring from its groove and remove the tool, ring, lock plate, canceling cam and spring.
5. Remove the stalk actuator screw and arm.
6. Remove the hazard switch knob.
7. Remove the 3 screws and pull the turn signal switch out of the column as far as it will go. Unplug it below if necessary.

8. Remove the ignition key lamp.

9. Place the key in the **LOCK** position and remove the key. Insert a thin tool into the slot next to the switch mounting screw boss, depress the spring latch at the bottom of the slot releasing the lock and remove the lock cylinder.

To install:

10. Install the lock cylinder.

11. Install the ignition key lamp.

12. Install the turn signal switch, switch stalk actuator arm and hazard switch knob.

13. Install the spring, canceling cam and lock cylinder.

14. Install the steering wheel torque the nut to 45 ft. lbs. (61 Nm).

15. Install the horn pad.

16. Connect the negative battery cable and check the lock cylinder for proper operation.

17. Install the lower column cover, if equipped.

Brake Light Switch

REMOVAL AND INSTALLATION

1. Disconnect the negative battery cable.

2. Remove the switch mounting bracket assembly from the brake pedal bracket.

3. Remove the switch from its bracket.

4. The installation is the reverse of the removal procedure.

5. Connect the negative battery cable and check the switch for proper operation.

Speedometer Cable

REMOVAL AND INSTALLATION

1. Disconnect the speedometer cable in the engine compartment.

2. Remove the instrument cluster and disconnect the speedometer cable from the speedometer.

3. Service the cable as necessary. Connect the cable to the speedometer.

4. Install the instrument cluster. Connect the speedometer cable in the engine compartment.

LIGHTING

Headlights

REMOVAL AND INSTALLATION

Sealed Beam

1. Remove the headlight bezel retaining screws and remove the bezel.

2. Remove the headlamp retaining ring screws and remove the retaining ring. Do not disturb the headlamp adjusting crews.

3. Pull the sealed beam forward and disconnect the electrical connector.

4. Install the replacement beam and connect the electrical connector.

5. Install the retaining ring.

6. Install the headlight bezel.

Sealed beam headlamp replacement

Aero headlamp replacement

Tail, stop, turn signal, back-up and side marker lamp replacement

License lamp assembly replacement

Aerodynamic Headlamp

1. From the engine compartment, remove the three wire connector behind the headlamp assembly.
2. Rotate the bulb retaining ring counterclockwise and remove the retaining ring and lamp bulb.
3. Install the replacement bulb and retaining ring assembly. Rotate the ring clockwise.
4. Connect the three wire connector.

Signal and Marker Lights
REMOVAL AND INSTALLATION

Front Park, Turn Signal and Side Marker

1. Remove the headlamp bezel retaining screws and remove the bezel.
2. Twist the bulb from the lamp socket.
3. Install the replacement bulb and twist into position.
4. Install the headlamp bezel and retaining screws.

Rear Tail, Stop, Turn Signal, Back Up, Side Marker and License Lamp

1. To replace the bulb, remove (4) attaching screws.
2. Pull out the lamp assembly. Twist the socket from the lamp and replace the bulb.
3. Install the replacement bulb and twist the socket into the lamp assembly.
4. Position the lamp assembly in place and secure with (4) attaching screws.

TRAILER WIRING

Wiring the truck for towing is fairly easy. There are a number of good wiring kits available and these should be used, rather than trying to design your own. All trailers will need brake lights and turn signals as well as tail lights and side marker lights. Most states require extra marker lights for overly wide trailers. Also, most states have recently required back-up lights for trailers, and most trailer manufacturers have been building trailers with back-up lights for several years.

Additionally, some Class I, most Class II and just about all Class III trailers will have electric brakes.

Add to this number an accessories wire, to operate trailer internal equipment or to charge the trailer's battery, and you can have as many as seven wires in the harness.

Determine the equipment on your trailer and buy the wiring kit necessary. The kit will contain all the wires needed, plus a plug adapter set which included the female plug, mounted on the bumper or hitch, and the male plug, wired into, or plugged into the trailer harness.

When installing the kit, follow the manufacturer's instructions. The color coding of the wires is standard throughout the industry.

One point to note, some domestic vehicles, and most imported vehicles, have separate turn signals. On most domestic vehicles, the brake lights and rear turn signals operate with the same bulb. For those vehicles with separate turn signals, you can purchase an isolation unit so that the brake lights won't blink whenever the turn signals are operated, or, you can go to your local electronics supply house and buy four diodes to wire in series with the brake and turn signal bulbs. Diodes will isolate the brake and turn signals. The choice is yours. The isolation units are simple and quick to install, but far more expensive than the diodes. The diodes, however, require more work to install properly, since they require the cutting of each bulb's wire and soldering in place of the diode.

One final point, the best kits are those with a spring loaded cover on the vehicle mounted socket. This cover prevents dirt and moisture from corroding the terminals. Never let the vehicle socket hang loosely. Always mount it securely to the bumper or hitch.

CIRCUIT PROTECTION

Fuse Block

The fuse block and relay bank is located on the driver's side under the lower instrument panel. The fuse block contains fuses for various circuits as well as circuit breakers, horn relay, ignition lamp thermal time delay, and the turn signal flasher. The hazard warning flasher is mounted into a bracket below the fuse block. The individual fuse and relay locations can be found in the wiring diagrams at the end of this section.

Fusible Links

The main wiring harnesses are equipped with fusible links to protect against harness damage should a short circuit develop.

Never replace a fusible link with standard wire. Only fusible link wire of the correct gauge with hypalon insulation should be used.

When a fusible link blows, it is very important to locate and repair the short. Do not just replace the link to correct the problem.

Always disconnect battery negative cable when servicing the electrical system.

REPLACEMENT

1. Disconnect the negative battery cable.
2. Cut off the remaining portion of the blown fusible link flush with the multiple connection insulator. Take care not to cut any of the other fusible links.

Fusible link repair

3. Carefully remove about one inch of insulation from the main harness wire at a point one inch away from the connection insulator.
4. Remove one inch of insulation from the replacement fusible link wire and wrap the exposed area around the main harness wire at the point where the insulation was removed.
5. Heat the splice with a high temperature soldering gun and apply resin type solder until it runs freely. Remove the soldering gun and confirm that a "bright" solder joint has been made. Resolder if "cold" (dull) joint.
6. Cut the other end of the fusible link off at a point just behind the small single wire insulator. Strip one inch of insulation from fusible link and connection wires. Wrap and solder.
7. After the connections have cooled, wrap the splices with at least three layers of electrical tape.

Troubleshooting Basic Turn Signal and Flasher Problems

Most problems in the turn signals or flasher system can be reduced to defective flashers or bulbs, which are easily replaced. Occasionally, problems in the turn signals are traced to the switch in the steering column, which will require professional service.

F = Front   R = Rear   ● = Lights off   ○ = Lights on

Problem		Solution
Turn signals light, but do not flash		· Replace the flasher
No turn signals light on either side		· Check the fuse. Replace if defective. · Check the flasher by substitution · Check for open circuit, short circuit or poor ground
Both turn signals on one side don't work		· Check for bad bulbs · Check for bad ground in both housings
One turn signal light on one side doesn't work		· Check and/or replace bulb · Check for corrosion in socket. Clean contacts. · Check for poor ground at socket
Turn signal flashes too fast or too slow		· Check any bulb on the side flashing too fast. A heavy-duty bulb is probably installed in place of a regular bulb. · Check the bulb flashing too slow. A standard bulb was probably installed in place of a heavy-duty bulb. · Check for loose connections or corrosion at the bulb socket
Indicator lights don't work in either direction		· Check if the turn signals are working · Check the dash indicator lights · Check the flasher by substitution

Troubleshooting Basic Turn Signal and Flasher Problems

Most problems in the turn signals or flasher system can be reduced to defective flashers or bulbs, which are easily replaced. Occasionally, problems in the turn signals are traced to the switch in the steering column, which will require professional service.

F = Front   R = Rear   ● = Lights off   o = Lights on

Problem		Solution
One indicator light doesn't light		· On systems with 1 dash indicator: See if the lights work on the same side. Often the filaments have been reversed in systems combining stoplights with taillights and turn signals. Check the flasher by substitution · On systems with 2 indicators: Check the bulbs on the same side Check the indicator light bulb Check the flasher by substitution

Troubleshooting Basic Lighting Problems

Problem	Cause	Solution
Lights		
One or more lights don't work, but others do	· Defective bulb(s) · Blown fuse(s) · Dirty fuse clips or light sockets · Poor ground circuit	· Replace bulb(s) · Replace fuse(s) · Clean connections · Run ground wire from light socket housing to car frame
Lights burn out quickly	· Incorrect voltage regulator setting or defective regulator · Poor battery/alternator connections	· Replace voltage regulator · Check battery/alternator connections
Lights go dim	· Low/discharged battery · Alternator not charging · Corroded sockets or connections · Low voltage output	· Check battery · Check drive belt tension; repair or replace alternator · Clean bulb and socket contacts and connections · Replace voltage regulator
Lights flicker	· Loose connection · Poor ground · Circuit breaker operating (short circuit)	· Tighten all connections · Run ground wire from light housing to car frame · Check connections and look for bare wires
Lights "flare"—Some flare is normal on acceleration—if excessive, see "Lights Burn Out Quickly"	· High voltage setting	· Replace voltage regulator

Troubleshooting Basic Lighting Problems

Problem	Cause	Solution
Lights glare—approaching drivers are blinded	• Lights adjusted too high • Rear springs or shocks sagging • Rear tires soft	• Have headlights aimed • Check rear springs/shocks • Check/correct rear tire pressure
Turn Signals		
Turn signals don't work in either direction	• Blown fuse • Defective flasher • Loose connection	• Replace fuse • Replace flasher • Check/tighten all connections
Right (or left) turn signal only won't work	• Bulb burned out • Right (or left) indicator bulb burned out • Short circuit	• Replace bulb • Check/replace indicator bulb • Check/repair wiring
Flasher rate too slow or too fast	• Incorrect wattage bulb • Incorrect flasher	• Flasher bulb • Replace flasher (use a variable load flasher if you pull a trailer)
Indicator lights do not flash (burn steadily)	• Burned out bulb • Defective flasher	• Replace bulb • Replace flasher
Indicator lights do not light at all	• Burned out indicator bulb • Defective flasher	• Replace indicator bulb • Replace flasher

Troubleshooting Basic Dash Gauge Problems

Problem	Cause	Solution
Coolant Temperature Gauge		
Gauge reads erratically or not at all	• Loose or dirty connections • Defective sending unit • Defective gauge	• Clean/tighten connections • Bi-metal gauge: remove the wire from the sending unit. Ground the wire for an instant. If the gauge registers, replace the sending unit. • Magnetic gauge: disconnect the wire at the sending unit. With ignition ON gauge should register COLD. Ground the wire; gauge should register HOT.
Ammeter Gauge—Turn Headlights ON (do not start engine). Note reaction		
Ammeter shows charge Ammeter shows discharge Ammeter does not move	• Connections reversed on gauge • Ammeter is OK • Loose connections or faulty wiring • Defective gauge	• Reinstall connections • Nothing • Check/correct wiring • Replace gauge

Troubleshooting Basic Dash Gauge Problems

Problem	Cause	Solution
Oil Pressure Gauge		
Gauge does not register or is inaccurate	• On mechanical gauge, Bourdon tube may be bent or kinked	• Check tube for kinks or bends preventing oil from reaching the gauge
	• Low oil pressure	• Remove sending unit. Idle the engine briefly. If no oil flows from sending unit hole, problem is in engine.
	• Defective gauge	• Remove the wire from the sending unit and ground it for an instant with the ignition ON. A good gauge will go to the top of the scale.
	• Defective wiring	• Check the wiring to the gauge. If it's OK and the gauge doesn't register when grounded, replace the gauge.
	• Defective sending unit	• If the wiring is OK and the gauge functions when grounded, replace the sending unit
All Gauges		
All gauges do not operate	• Blown fuse	• Replace fuse
	• Defective instrument regulator	• Replace instrument voltage regulator
All gauges read low or erratically	• Defective or dirty instrument voltage regulator	• Clean contacts or replace
All gauges pegged	• Loss of ground between instrument voltage regulator and car	• Check ground
	• Defective instrument regulator	• Replace regulator
Warning Lights		
Light(s) do not come on when ignition is ON, but engine is not started	• Defective bulb	• Replace bulb
	• Defective wire	• Check wire from light to sending unit
	• Defective sending unit	• Disconnect the wire from the sending unit and ground it. Replace the sending unit if the light comes on with the ignition ON.
Light comes on with engine running	• Problem in individual system	• Check system
	• Defective sending unit	• Check sending unit (see above)

Troubleshooting the Heater

Problem	Cause	Solution
Blower motor will not turn at any speed	• Blown fuse	• Replace fuse
	• Loose connection	• Inspect and tighten
	• Defective ground	• Clean and tighten
	• Faulty switch	• Replace switch
	• Faulty motor	• Replace motor
	• Faulty resistor	• Replace resistor

Troubleshooting the Heater

Problem	Cause	Solution
Blower motor turns at one speed only	• Faulty switch • Faulty resistor	• Replace switch • Replace resistor
Blower motor turns but does not circulate air	• Intake blocked • Fan not secured to the motor shaft	• Clean intake • Tighten security
Heater will not heat	• Coolant does not reach proper temperature • Heater core blocked internally • Heater core air-bound • Blend-air door not in proper position	• Check and replace thermostat if necessary • Flush or replace core if necessary • Purge air from core • Adjust cable
Heater will not defrost	• Control cable adjustment incorrect • Defroster hose damaged	• Adjust control cable • Replace defroster hose

Troubleshooting Basic Windshield Wiper Problems

Problem	Cause	Solution
Electric Wipers		
Wipers do not operate— Wiper motor heats up or hums	• Internal motor defect • Bent or damaged linkage • Arms improperly installed on linking pivots	• Replace motor • Repair or replace linkage • Position linkage in park and reinstall wiper arms
Electric Wipers		
Wipers do not operate— No current to motor	• Fuse or circuit breaker blown • Loose, open or broken wiring • Defective switch • Defective or corroded terminals • No ground circuit for motor or switch	• Replace fuse or circuit breaker • Repair wiring and connections • Replace switch • Replace or clean terminals • Repair ground circuits
Wipers do not operate— Motor runs	• Linkage disconnected or broken	• Connect wiper linkage or replace broken linkage
Vacuum Wipers		
Wipers do not operate	• Control switch or cable inoperative • Loss of engine vacuum to wiper motor (broken hoses, low engine vacuum, defective vacuum/fuel pump) • Linkage broken or disconnected • Defective wiper motor	• Repair or replace switch or cable • Check vacuum lines, engine vacuum and fuel pump • Repair linkage • Replace wiper motor
Wipers stop on engine acceleration	• Leaking vacuum hoses • Dry windshield • Oversize wiper blades • Defective vacuum/fuel pump	• Repair or replace hoses • Wet windshield with washers • Replace with proper size wiper blades • Replace pump

WIRING DIAGRAMS

1984-85 Caravan/Voyager

CHARGING SYSTEM (2.6 LITRE)

CHARGING SYSTEM (2.6 LITRE)

HK 5

HK 6

STARTER SYSTEM (2.2 LITRE)

STARTER SYSTEM (2.6 LITRE)

HK 7

HK 8

1984-85 Caravan/Voyager

ELECTRONIC SPARK ADVANCE SYSTEM (2.2 LITRE)   HK 9

ELECTRONIC SPARK ADVANCE SYSTEM (2.2 LITRE)   HK 10

HK 11   ELECTRONIC IGNITION SYSTEM (2.6 LITRE)

WINDSHIELD WIPER SYSTEM   HK 12

1984-85 Caravan/Voyager

HK 13   INTERMITTENT WIPER SYSTEM

INTERMITTENT WIPER SYSTEM   HK 14

HK 15   FRONT END LIGHTING

FRONT END LIGHTING   HK 16

1984-85 Caravan/Voyager

HK 17 — HORN SYSTEM

HK 18 — HEADLAMP SWITCH

HK 19 — IGNITION SWITCH

HK 20 — SPEED CONTROL SYSTEM

1984-85 Caravan/Voyager

| HK 21 | AIR CONDITIONING SYSTEM (2.2 LITRE) |

| AIR CONDITIONING SYSTEM (2.2 LITRE) | HK 22 |

| HK 23 | AIR CONDITIONING SYSTEM (2.6 LITRE) |

| AIR CONDITIONING SYSTEM (2.6 LITRE) | HK 24 |

1984-85 Caravan/Voyager

HK 25   AIR CONDITIONING SYSTEM

RADIATOR FAN MOTOR   HK 26

HK 27   HEATER SYSTEM

RADIATOR FAN MOTOR
(2.6 LITRE CALIFORNIA ONLY)   HK 28

1984-85 Caravan/Voyager

OIL PRESSURE AND
TEMPERATURE SYSTEM (2.6 LITRE)

HK 29

OIL PRESSURE AND
TEMPERATURE SYSTEM (2.6 LITRE)

HK 30

WARNING LAMP MODULE SYSTEM

HK 31

WARNING LAMP MODULE SYSTEM

HK 32

1984-85 Caravan/Voyager

HK 33 — SEAT BELT WARNING SYSTEM

DOME AND COURTESY LAMPS — HK 34

HK 35 — DOME AND BODY COURTESY LAMPS

DOME AND BODY COURTESY LAMPS — HK 36

1984-85 Caravan/Voyager

| HK 37 | STOP/TURN & HAZARD FLASHER SYSTEM |

| STOP/TURN & HAZARD FLASHER SYSTEM | HK 38 |

| HK 39 | PRINTED CIRCUIT BOARD |

| PRINTED CIRCUIT BOARD CONNECTORS | HK 40 |

1984-85 Caravan/Voyager

VISUAL MESSAGE CENTER
PRINTED CIRCUIT BOARD

HK 41	VISUAL MESSAGE CENTER PRINTED CIRCUIT BOARD CONNECTOR

H/LP SWITCH CONTROLLED INTERIOR LIGHTING	HK 42

HK 43	ELECTRONICALLY TUNED RADIOS

ELECTRONICALLY TUNED RADIOS	HK 44

1984-85 Caravan/Voyager

HK 45 — DOOR LOCK SYSTEM

DOOR LOCK SYSTEM — HK 46

LEFT DOOR			
B+ POLARITY	B- POLARITY	SWITCH SECTION	WINDOW MOVEMENT
LB	WT	1	LEFT FRONT UP
WT	LB	1	LEFT FRONT DOWN
PK/RD●	VT	2	RIGHT FRONT UP
VT	PK/RD●	2	RIGHT FRONT DOWN
TN	BK	SWITCH	FEED & GROUND

HK 47 — WINDOW LIFT SYSTEM

RIGHT DOOR		
B+ POLARITY	B- POLARITY	WINDOW MOVEMENT & SWITCH
WT	LB	DOWN-FROM DOOR SWITCH
LB	WT	UP-FROM DOOR SWITCH
VT	PK/RD●	DOWN-FROM MASTER SWITCH
PK/RD●	VT	UP-FROM MASTER SWITCH
TN	-	FEED

WINDOW LIFT SYSTEM — HK 48

1984-85 Caravan/Voyager

HK 49   POWER SEAT SYSTEM

POWER SEAT SYSTEM   HK 50

HK 51   LIFT GATE RELEASE

LIFT GATE RELEASE   HK 52

1984-85 Caravan/Voyager

LIFTGATE AJAR WARNING &
LIFTGATE WIPER AND WASHER SYSTEM

LIFTGATE WIPER AND WASHER SYSTEM HK 54

HK 55 ELECTRICALLY HEATED REAR WINDOW

ELECTRICALLY HEATED REAR WINDOW HK 56

1984-85 Caravan/Voyager

HK 57 — REAR LIGHTING

REAR LIGHTING — HK 58

Instrument Panel to Steering Column Wiring (HK 59)

CAV	CIRCUIT	DESCRIPTION
1	—	NOT USED
2	H4 18BK	HORN & KEY-IN LAMP GROUND (STANDARD COLUMN)
3	H3 20BK/RD*	GROUND FROM HORN SWITCH
4	D6 18LG	LEFT FRONT TURN SIGNAL
5	D5 18TN	RIGHT FRONT TURN SIGNAL
6	D32 18PK	HAZARD FLASHER FEED
7	D2 18RD/BK*	FEED FROM TURN SIGNAL FLASHER
8	D8 18DG/RD*	LEFT REAR TURN SIGNAL
9	D7 18BR/RD*	RIGHT REAR TURN SIGNAL
10	D4 18WT	FEED FROM BRAKE SWITCH
11	—	NOT USED
12	V3 18BR*	WINDSHIELD WIPER LOW SPEED
13	V4 18RD	WINDSHIELD WIPER HIGH SPEED
14	V5 18DG/YL*	WINDSHIELD WIPER MOTOR
15	V6 18DB	WINDSHIELD WIPER SWITCH FEED
16	V10 20BR	WINDSHIELD WASHER MOTOR
17	H4 18BK*	INTERMITTENT WIPE SWITCH GROUND
18	H40 18BK/LG*	INTERMITTENT WIPE MODULE GROUND
19	M26 20LB	KEY-IN BUZZER
20	M26 20LB	KEY-IN BUZZER
20	M16 20BK/LB*	LEFT FRONT DOOR JAMB SWITCH GROUND
21	—	NOT USED
22	—	NOT USED
23	—	NOT USED
24	J15 20YL/RD*	IGNITION KEY LAMP FEED
24	J15 20YL/RD*	IGNITION KEY LAMP FEED
25	H4 18BK	IGNITION KEY LAMP GROUND (TILT COLUMN)

VIEWED FROM WIRE SIDE OF 25 WAY CONNECTOR

(MOUNTED ON INSTR-PANEL LEFT OF STEERING COLUMN)

INSTRUMENT PANEL TO STEERING COLUMN WIRING

HK 59

Steering Column Switch to Panel Wiring (HK 60)

VIEWED FROM TERMINAL END OF CONNECTORS

CAV	CIRCUIT	DESCRIPTION
1	—	NOT USED
2	M4 18BK*	HORN&KEY-IN LAMP GROUND(STANDARD COLUMN)
3	H3 18BK/RD*	HORN SWITCH GROUND
4	D6 18LG	LEFT FRONT TURN SIGNAL
5	D5 18TN	RIGHT FRONT TURN SIGNAL
6	D32 18PK	HAZARD FLASHER FEED
7	D2 18RD	TURN SIGNAL FLASHER FEED
8	D8 18DG/RD*	LEFT REAR TURN SIGNAL
9	D7 18BR/RD*	RIGHT REAR TURN SIGNAL
10	D4 18WT	BRAKE SWITCH FEED
11	—	NOT USED
12	V3 18BR* / V3 18BR*	INTERMITTENT WIPE MODULE / WINDSHIELD WIPER LOW SPEED
13	V4 18RD	WINDSHIELD WIPER HIGH SPEED
14	V5 18DG / V5 18DG	INTERMITTENT WIPE MODULE / WINDSHIELD WIPER MOTOR
15	V6 18DB	WINDSHIELD WIPER SWITCH FEED
16	V10 18BR / V10 18BR	INTERMITTENT WIPE MODULE / WINDSHIELD WASHER MOTOR
17	H4 18BK	INTERMITTENT WIPE SWITCH GROUND
18	H40 18BK/LG*	INTERMITTENT WIPE MODULE GROUND
19	M26 20LB	KEY-IN BUZZER
20	M16 20BK/LB*	LEFT FRONT DOOR JAMB SWITCH GROUND
21		
22		
23		
24	J15 18YL*	IGNITION KEY LAMP FEED
25	H4 18BK	IGNITION KEY LAMP GROUND (TILT COLUMN)

TURN SIGNAL SWITCH CONNECTOR

WINDSHIELD WIPER SWITCH CONNECTOR

KEY-IN BUZZER SWITCH CONNECTOR

IGNITION KEY LAMP SWITCH CONNECTOR

(PLUGGED INTO STEERING COLUMN 25 WAY CONNECTOR)

STEERING COLUMN SWITCH TO PANEL WIRING

HK 60

1984-85 Caravan/Voyager

VIEWED FROM TERMINAL
END OF CONNECTORS

VIEWED FROM WIRE SIDE
OF 25 WAY CONNECTOR

CAV	CIRCUIT	DESCRIPTION
1	M2 18BK/YL●	DOOR SWITCH GROUND-DOME LAMP
1	M2 18YL	DOOR SWITCH GROUND-DOME LAMP
2	M1 18BK/PK●	DOME LAMP FEED
2	M1 18PK	DOME LAMP FEED
3	G4 18DB	FUEL GAUGE SENDING UNIT
4	B2 18VT	BACK-UP LAMPS
5	M16 18BK/LB●	LEFT FRONT DOOR JAMB SWITCH
6	M4 18TN/BK●	TAIL GATE OPEN SWITCH
7	G10 18LG	SEAT BELT WARNING SWITCH
8	L7 18BR	TAIL,LICENSE & SIDE MARKER LAMPS
9	D8 18DG	LEFT REAR TURN SIGNAL LAMP
10	D7 18BR	RIGHT REAR TURN SIGNAL LAMP
11	Y20 16BR/WT●	REAR WASHER
12	Y16 16DB/PK●	REAR WIPER-PARK
13	Y13 16BR/LG●	REAR WIPER-RUN
14	————	NOT USED
15	M3 18TN	DOOR AJAR
16	G40 18LB	LOW FUEL
17	X42 14BK/GY●	LIFTGATE RELEASE
18	————	NOT USED
19	M1 18PK	DOME LAMP FEED
20	M2 18YL	DOOR SWITCH GROUND-DOME LAMP
20	M2 18YL	DOOR SWITCH GROUND-DOME LAMP
21		NOT USED
22		NOT USED
23		NOT USED
24	C15 12BK	HEATED REAR WINDOW-EBL
25		NOT USED

(MOUNTED ON PARKING
BRAKE LEFT SIDE)

CAV	CIRCUIT	DESCRIPTION	
1	M2 20YL	DOOR SWITCH GROUND-DOME LAMP	
2	M1 18PK	DOME LAMP FEED	
3	G4 20DB/YL●	FUEL GAUGE SENDING UNIT	
4	B2 18VT/BK●	BACK-UP LAMPS	INSTR-PANEL
5	M16 20BK/LB●	KEY-IN SWITCH	WIRING CONNECTOR
5	M16 20BK/LB●	LEFT FRONT DOOR JAMB SWITCH GROUND	
6	M4 20TN/BK●	TAIL GATE OPEN SWITCH	
7	G10 20LG	SEAT BELT WARNING SWITCH	
8	L78 18BK/YL●	TAIL,LICENSE & SIDE MARKER LAMPS	
9	D8 18DG/RD●	LEFT REAR TURN SIGNAL LAMP	
10	D7 18BR/RD●	RIGHT REAR TURN SIGNAL LAMP	
11	V20 18BR/WT●	REAR WASHER	
12	Y16 16DB	REAR WIPER-PARK	
13	Y13 16BR	REAR WIPER-RUN	INSTR-PANEL
14		NOT USED	WIRING CONNECTOR
15	M3 20TN/RD●	DOOR AJAR	
16	G40 20LB/BK●	LOW FUEL	
17	X42 16BK	LIFT GATE RELEASE	
18		NOT USED	
19	M1 18PK	DOME LAMP FEED	
19	M1 18PK	DOME LAMP FEED	BODY WIRING
20	M2 18YL	DOOR SWITCH GROUND-DOME LAMP	CONNECTOR
20	M2 18YL	DOOR SWITCH GROUND-DOME LAMP	
21			
22			
23			
24	C15A 12BK/OR●	HEATED REAR WINDOW-EBL	INSTR-PANEL
25		NOT USED	WIRING CONNECTOR

(PLUG INTO BODY 25 WAY CONNECTOR)

| HK 61 | BODY TO INSTRUMENT PANEL WIRING |

| INSTRUMENT PANEL TO BODY WIRING | HK 62 |

	ENGINE COMPARTMENT CIRCUITS	CAVITY
X30 20DB/RD ●	SPEED CONTROL	1
X31 20BR/RD ●	SPEED CONTROL	2
X33 20WT/RD ●	SPEED CONTROL	3
J10 12PK ●	IGNITION SWITCH	4
-		5
-		6
P5 20BK	BRAKE WARNING LAMP SWITCH	7
H2 16DG/RD●	HORN	8
S2 18YL	STARTER RELAY-IGNITION	9
J2 14DB	IGNITION RUN CURCUIT	10
-		-
G2 20VT	ENGINE WARNING LAMP(TEMPERATURE)	11
G6 20GY	ENGINE WARNING LAMP(OIL PRESSURE)	12
-		-
D6 18LG	LEFT TURN SIGNAL LAMP	13
D5 18TN	RIGHT TURN SIGNAL LAMP	14
-		-
-		15
-		16
S40 18BR/YL●	LIFTGATE RELEASE	17
-		18
V10 20BR	WINDSHIELD WASHER MOTOR	19
V11 20BK/TN●	LOW WASHER FLUID INDICATOR LAMP	20
B1 18WT	BACK-UP LAMP SWITCH	21
B2 18VT/BK●	BACK-UP LAMP SWITCH	22
V3 18BR●	WINDSHIELD WIPER MOTOR	23
V4 18RD	WINDSHIELD WIPER MOTOR	24
L7 18BK/YL●	PARK,TURN SIGNAL & SIDE MARKER LAMPS	25
		26
V5 18DG	WINDSHIELD WIPER MOTOR	27
V6 18DB	WINDSHIELD WIPER MOTOR	28
L4 16VT●	HEADLAMP(LOW BEAM)	29
L3 16RD	HEADLAMP(HIGH BEAM)	30
R3 14PK	BATTERY-HAZARD FLASHER	31
C2 16DB/YL●	AIR CONDITIONING LOW PRESSURE SWITCH	32
-		33
-		34
R6 12BK	BATTERY FEED	35
C13 12BK/RD●	ELECTRICALLY HEATED REAR WINDOW	36
J1 12RD	IGNITION SWITCH	37
-		38
G60 20GY/YL●	OIL PRESSURE GAUGE	39
-		40

TERMINAL END OF DISCONNECT

SMALL INDEX

LARGE INDEX

| HK 63 | 40 WAY BULKHEAD DISCONNECT |

1984-85 Caravan/Voyager

40 way bulkhead connector 1984-85

WIRE COLOR CODES
BK BLACK · BR BROWN · DB DARK BLUE · DG DARK GREEN · GY GRAY · LB LIGHT BLUE · LG LIGHT GREEN · OR ORANGE · PK PINK · RD RED · TN TAN · VT VIOLET · WT WHITE · YL YELLOW · * WITH TRACER

CAV	COLOR	DESCRIPTION
1	DB/RD*	SPEED CONTROL (WITH OPTIONS HARNESS)
2	BK/RD*	SPEED CONTROL (WITH OPTIONS HARNESS)
3	WT/RD*	SPEED CONTROL (WITH OPTIONS HARNESS)
4	PK*	IGNITION SWITCH
5		
6		
7	GY*	BRAKE WARNING LAMP
8	DG/RD*	HORN
9	YL	IGNITION START
10	DB	IGNITION RUN
11	VT	TEMPERATURE
12	GY	OIL PRESSURE LAMP
13	LG	LEFT TURN SIGNAL
14	TN	RIGHT TURN SIGNAL
15		
16		
17	BR/BL*	LIFTGATE RELEASE (WITH OPTIONS HARNESS)
18	BR	WINDSHIELD WASHER
19	BK/TN*	WINDSHIELD WASHER FLUID LAMP (W/OPTS HARNESS)
20	WT	BACK-UP LAMP SWITCH FEED
21	LG	BACK-UP LAMP
22	VT/BK*	BACK-UP LAMP
23	BR*	WINDSHIELD WIPER LOW SPEED FEED
24	RD	WINDSHIELD WIPER HIGH SPEED FEED
25	BK/Y*	PARKING LAMPS
26		
27	DG/YL*	WINDSHIELD WIPER MOTOR PARK RETURN AND INTERMITTENT WIPE SIGNAL
28	DB	WINDSHIELD WIPER SWITCH FEED & PARK FEED
29	VT*	HEADLAMP LOW BEAM
30	RD	HEADLAMP HIGH BEAM
31	PK	HAZARD FLASHER
32	DBL/YL*	A/C CLUTCH
33		
34	BK	BATTERY FEED
35	BK/RD*	HEATED REAR WINDOW (WITH OPTIONS HARNESS)
36	RD	IGNITION SWITCH FEED
37		
38		
39	GY/YL*	OIL PRESSURE GAUGE
40		

40 Way Bulkhead Disconnect

40 way bulkhead connector 1984-85

25 way instrument panel-to-steering column connector 1984-85 Caravan/Voyager

WIRE COLOR CODES
BK BLACK · BR BROWN · DB DARK BLUE · DG DARK GREEN · GY GRAY · LB LIGHT BLUE · LG LIGHT GREEN · OR ORANGE · PK PINK · RD RED · TN TAN · VT VIOLET · WT WHITE · YL YELLOW · * WITH TRACER

CAV	COLOR	DESCRIPTION
2	BK	HORN & KEY-IN LAMP GROUND (STANDARD COLUMN)
3	BK/RD*	GROUND FROM HORN SWITCH
4	LG	LEFT FRONT TURN SIGNAL
5	TN	RIGHT FRONT TURN SIGNAL
6	PK	FEED FROM HAZARD FLASHER
7	RD*	FEED FROM TURN SIGNAL FLASHER
8	DG/RD*	LEFT REAR TURN SIGNAL
9	BR/RD*	RIGHT REAR TURN SIGNAL
10	WT	FEED FROM BRAKE SWITCH
11		
12	BR*	WINDSHIELD WIPER LOW SPEED
13	RD	WINDSHIELD WIPER HIGH SPEED
14	DG/YL*	WINDSHIELD WIPER MOTOR PARK RETURN & INTERMITTENT WIPE SIGNAL
15	DB	WINDSHIELD WIPER SWITCH FEED & MOTOR PARK FEED
16	BR	WINDSHIELD WASHER MOTOR
17	BK*	WINDSHIELD WIPER SWITCH GROUND
18	BK/LG*	INTERMITTENT WIPE MODULE GROUND
19	LB	KEY-IN BUZZER
20	BL/LB*	GROUND FROM LEFT FRONT DOOR JAMB SWITCH
21		
22		
23		
24	YU/RD*	KEY-IN LAMP FEED
25	BK	KEY-IN GROUND WIRE

25 Way Instrument Panel to Steering Column Connector

25 way instrument panel-to-steering column connector 1984-85 Caravan/Voyager

25 way instrument panel-to-body connector 1984-85 Caravan/Voyager

WIRE COLOR CODES
BK BLACK · BR BROWN · DB DARK BLUE · DG DARK GREEN · GY GRAY · LB LIGHT BLUE · LG LIGHT GREEN · OR ORANGE · PK PINK · RD RED · TN TAN · VT VIOLET · WT WHITE · YL YELLOW · * WITH TRACER

CAV	COLOR	DESCRIPTION
1	YL / YL/BK*	DOOR SWITCH GROUND TO I/P WIRING, DOME & REAR CARGO LAMP GROUND
2	PK / BK/PK*	COURTESY LAMP FEED I/P WIRING, DOME & CARGO LAMP FEED
3	DB	FUEL GAUGE
4	VT	BACK-UP LAMPS
5	BK/LB*	LEFT FRONT DOOR JAMB SWITCH
6	LG/TN*	LIFTGATE AJAR LAMP
7	LG	SEAT BELT WARNING
8	BK	TAIL-SIDE MARKER & LICENSE LAMPS
9	BK/DG*	LEFT REAR STOP & TURN SIGNAL LAMP
10	BR	RIGHT REAR STOP & TURN SIGNAL LAMP
11	BR/WT*	LIFTGATE WASHER MOTOR FEED
12	DB	LIFTGATE WIPER MOTOR
13	BR	LIFTGATE WIPER MOTOR
14		
15	TN	DOOR AJAR SWITCH
16	LB	LOW FUEL
17	BK/GY*	LIFTGATE POWER RELEASE
18		
19	PK	FRONT DOOR COURTESY LAMP
20	YL	DOOR SWITCH & COURT. LAMP GROUND
21		
22		
23		
24	BK	HEATED REAR WINDOW
25		

25 Way Instrument Panel to Body Connector

25 way instrument panel-to-body connector 1984-85 Caravan/Voyager

Fuse block and relay bank — 1984-85 Caravan/Voyager

FUSE COLOR CODE
LG LIGHT GREEN · NAT NATURAL · TN TAN · VT VIOLET · YL YELLOW

CAV	FUSE/COLOR	ITEMS
1	20 AMP YL	HAZARD FLASHER
2	20 AMP YL	BACK-UP LAMPS
3	30 AMP C/BRKR	POWER WINDOWS
4	30 AMP LG	A/C & HEATER BLOWER MOTOR
5	20 AMP YL	PARK, TAIL, SIDEMARKER & LICENSE LAMPS, CLOCK DISPLAY DIMMING
6	20 AMP YL	STOP DOME, CARGO, VANITY MIRROR IGNITION SWITCH & DOOR COURTESY LAMPS, IGNITION LAMP TIME DELAY RELAY
7	25 AMP NAT	HORNS, CIGAR LIGHTER, BUZZER OR CHIMES, DIGITAL CLOCK & RADIO MEMORY
8	30 AMP C/BRKR	POWER DOOR LOCKS & POWER SEATS
9	5 AMP YL	RADIO & CLOCK DISPLAY
10	20 AMP YL	TURN SIGNAL LAMPS, A/C CLUTCH, A/C FAN RELAY COIL & HEATED REAR WINDOW RELAY
11	20 AMP YL	WINDSHIELD WIPER & WASHER
12	3 AMP VT	CLUSTER, A/C & HEATER CONTROL SWITCH TITLE, RADIO & ASH RECEIVER LAMPS
13	5 AMP YL	FUEL, VOLTAGE, OIL & TEMP GAUGES, BRAKE WARNING, SEAT BELT, OIL & TEMPERATURE LAMPS, BUZZER OR CHIMES, WARNING LAMP MODULE & SPEED CONTROL
14	6 AMP C/BRKR	REAR WASH WIPE & LIFTGATE RELEASE
15		
16		

Fuse Block and Relay Bank

Fuse block and relay bank — 1984-85 Caravan/Voyager

HK 1   FUSE APPLICATION CHART

FUSE APPLICATION CHART   HK 2

HK 3   CHARGING SYSTEM (2.2 LITRE)

CHARGING SYSTEM (2.2 LITRE)   HK 4

1986 Caravan/Voyager

CHARGING SYSTEM (2.6 LITRE)

HK 5

CHARGING SYSTEM (2.6 LITRE)

HK 6

STARTER SYSTEM (2.2 LITRE)

HK 7

STARTER SYSTEM (2.6 LITRE)

HK 8

1986 Caravan/Voyager

HK 9 — ELECTRONIC SPARK ADVANCE SYSTEM (2.2 LITRE)

ELECTRONIC SPARK ADVANCE SYSTEM (2.2 LITRE) — HK 10

HK 11 — ELECTRONIC IGNITION SYSTEM (2.6 LITRE)

WINDSHIELD WIPER SYSTEM — HK 12

1986 Caravan/Voyager

HK 13   INTERMITTENT WIPER SYSTEM

INTERMITTENT WIPER SYSTEM   HK 14

HK 15   FRONT END LIGHTING

FRONT END LIGHTING   HK 16

1986 Caravan/Voyager

HK 17   HORN SYSTEM

HEADLAMP SWITCH   HK 18

HK 19   IGNITION SWITCH

ELECTRONIC SPEED CONTROL SYSTEM   HK 20

1986 Caravan/Voyager

FEDERAL/CANADA SEA LEVEL
AUTOMATIC AND MANUAL TRANSMISSIONS (WITHOUT AIR CONDITIONING)

FEDERAL, ALTITUDE, CALIFORNIA
AUTOMATIC AND MANUAL TRANSMISSION
(WITH AND WITHOUT AIR CONDITIONING)

| HK 21 | CARBURETOR WIRING 2.2 LITRE |

| UNDERHOOD LIGHT | HK 22 |

| HK 23 | AIR CONDITIONING SYSTEM (2.2 LITRE) |

| AIR CONDITIONING SYSTEM (2.2 LITRE) | HK 24 |

1986 Caravan/Voyager

| HK 25 | AIR CONDITIONING SYSTEM (2.6 LITRE) |

| AIR CONDITIONING SYSTEM (2.6 LITRE) | HK 26 |

| HK 27 | AIR CONDITIONING SYSTEM |

| RADIATOR FAN MOTOR | HK 28 |

1986 Caravan/Voyager

HEATER SYSTEM

RADIATOR FAN MOTOR
(2.6 LITRE CALIFORNIA ONLY)

HK 30

HK 31

OIL PRESSURE AND
TEMPERATURE SYSTEM (2.2 LITRE)

OIL PRESSURE AND
TEMPERATURE SYSTEM (2.6 LITRE)

HK 32

1986 Caravan/Voyager

| HK 33 | *WARNING LAMP MODULE SYSTEM* | | *WARNING LAMP MODULE SYSTEM* | HK 34 |

| HK 35 | *SEAT BELT WARNING SYSTEM* | | *DOME AND COURTESY LAMPS* | HK 36 |

1986 Caravan/Voyager

HK 37   DOME AND BODY COURTESY LAMPS

DOME AND BODY COURTESY LAMPS   HK 38

HK 39   STOP/TURN AND HAZARD FLASHER SYSTEM

STOP/TURN AND HAZARD FLASHER SYSTEM   HK 40

1986 Caravan/Voyager

HK 41 — PRINTED CIRCUIT BOARD

LEFT PRINTED CIRCUIT BOARD CONNECTOR

RIGHT PRINTED CIRCUIT BOARD CONNECTOR

PRINTED CIRCUIT BOARD CONNECTORS — HK 42

WARNING LIGHT MODULE
PRINTED CIRCUIT BOARD

HK 43 — WARNING LIGHT MODULE
PRINTED CIRCUIT BOARD CONNECTOR

HEADLAMP SWITCH
CONTROLLED INTERIOR LIGHTING — HK 44

1986 Caravan/Voyager

1986 Caravan/Voyager

WINDOW LIFT SYSTEM

LEFT DOOR			
B+ POLARITY	B- POLARITY	SWITCH SECTION	WINDOW AND MOVEMENT
LB	WT	1	LEFT FRONT UP
WT	LB	1	LEFT FRONT DOWN
PK/WT•	VT	2	RIGHT FRONT UP
VT	PK/RD•	2	RIGHT FRONT DOWN
TN	BK		SWITCH FEED AND GROUND

RIGHT DOOR		
B+ POLARITY	B- POLARITY	WINDOW MOVEMENT AND SWITCH
WT	LB	DOWN-FROM DOOR SWITCH
LB	WT	UP-FROM DOOR SWITCH
VT	PK/WT•	DOWN-FROM MASTER SWITCH
PK/WT•	VT	UP-FROM MASTER SWITCH
TN	-	FEED

HK 49   WINDOW LIFT SYSTEM

WINDOW LIFT SYSTEM   HK 50

MOTOR INSULATOR POLARITY		
+POLARITY	-POLARITY	SEAT MOVEMENT
YL/BL•	RD/BL•	FORWARD
RD/BL•	YL/BL•	REARWARD
YL/WT•	RD/WT•	REAR UP
RD/WT•	YL/WT•	REAR DOWN
YL/GN•	RD/GN•	FRONT UP
RD/GN•	YL/GN•	FRONT DOWN
BK/RD•	—	FEED
	BK	GROUND

HK 51   POWER SEAT SYSTEM

POWER SEAT SYSTEM   HK 52

1986 Caravan/Voyager

HK 53   LIFT GATE RELEASE

CONSOLE LIGHTING   HK 54

LIFTGATE AJAR WARNING AND
LIFTGATE WIPER AND WASHER SYSTEM
HK 55

LIFTGATE WIPER AND WASHER SYSTEM   HK 56

1986 Caravan/Voyager

| HK 57 | ELECTRICALLY HEATED REAR WINDOW | | ELECTRICALLY HEATED REAR WINDOW | HK 58 |

| HK 59 | REAR LIGHTING | | REAR LIGHTING | HK 60 |

1986 Caravan/Voyager

| HK | 61 | POWER REMOTE MIRRORS |

| POWER REMOTE MIRRORS | HK | 62 |

INSTRUMENT PANEL TO
STEERING COLUMN WIRING

| HK | 63 |

STEERING COLUMN SWITCH
TO PANEL WIRING

| HK | 64 |

1986 Caravan/Voyager

VIEWED FROM WIRE SIDE
OF 25 WAY CONNECTOR

CAV	CIRCUIT	DESCRIPTION
1	M2 18BK/YL●	DOOR SWITCH GROUND-DOME LAMP
2	M1 18BK/PK●	DOME LAMP FEED
2	M1 18PK	DOME LAMP FEED
3	G4 18DG	FUEL GAUGE SENDING UNIT
4	B2 18VT	BACK-UP LAMPS
5	M16 18BK/LB●	LEFT FRONT DOOR JAMB SWITCH
6	M4 18TN/BK	TAIL GATE OPEN SWITCH
7	G10 18LG	SEAT BELT WARNING SWITCH
8	L7 18BK	TAIL, LICENSE AND SIDE MARKER LAMPS
9	D8 18DG	LEFT REAR TURN SIGNAL LAMP
10	D7 18BR	RIGHT REAR TURN SIGNAL LAMP
11	V20 18BR/WT●	REAR WASHER
12	V16 18DG/PK●	REAR WIPER-PARK
13	V13 18BR/LG●	REAR WIPER-RUN
14	———	NOT USED
15	M3 18TN	DOOR AJAR
16	G40 18LB	LOW FUEL
17	X42 14BK/GY●	LIFTGATE RELEASE
18	———	NOT USED
19	M1 18PK	DOME LAMP FEED
20	M2 18YL	DOOR SWITCH GROUND-DOME LAMP
21	———	NOT USED
22	———	NOT USED
23	———	NOT USED
24	C15 12BK	HEATED REAR WINDOW-EBL
25	———	NOT USED

(MOUNTED ON PARKING
BRAKE LEFT SIDE)

HK 65	BODY TO INSTRUMENT PANEL WIRING

VIEWED FROM TERMINAL
END OF CONNECTORS

CAV	CIRCUIT	DESCRIPTION
1	M2 20YL	DOOR SWITCH GROUND-DOME LAMP
2	M1 18PK	DOME LAMP FEED
3	G4 20DB/YL●	FUEL GAUGE SENDING UNIT
4	B2 18VT/BK●	BACK-UP LAMPS
5	M16 20BK/LB●	KEY-IN SWITCH
5	M16 20BK/LB●	LEFT FRONT DOOR JAMB SWITCH GROUND
6	M4 20TN/BK●	TAIL GATE OPEN SWITCH
7	G10 20LG	SEAT BELT WARNING SWITCH
8	L7 18BK/YL●	TAIL, LICENSE AND SIDE MARKER LAMPS
9	D8 18DG/RD●	LEFT REAR TURN SIGNAL LAMP
10	D7 18BR/RD●	RIGHT REAR TURN SIGNAL LAMP
11	V20 18BR/WT●	REAR WASHER
12	V16 16DB/PK●	REAR WIPER-PARK
13	V13 18BR	REAR WIPER-RUN
14	———	NOT USED
15	M3 20TN/RD●	DOOR AJAR
16	G40 20LB/RD●	LOW FUEL
17	X42 16BK	LIFT GATE RELEASE
18	———	NOT USED
19	M1 18PK	DOME LAMP FEED
19	M1 18PK	DOME LAMP FEED
20	M2 18YL	DOOR SWITCH GROUND-DOME LAMP
20	M2 18YL	DOOR SWITCH GROUND-DOME LAMP
24	C15 12BK/OR●	HEATED REAR WINDOW-EBL
25	———	NOT USED

(PLUG INTO BODY 25 WAY CONNECTOR)

HK 66	INSTRUMENT PANEL TO BODY WIRING

TERMINAL END OF DISCONNECT

SMALL INDEX

LARGE INDEX

	ENGINE COMPARTMENT CIRCUITS	CAVITY
L1 12OR●	HEADLAMP SWITCH	1
-	-	2
B7 12RD/PK●	VAN CONVERSION	3
-	-	4
L4 18VT	HEADLAMP LOW BEAM	5
L3 14RD/OR●	HEADLAMP HIGH BEAM	6
X30 20DB/RD●	SPEED CONTROL	7
X31 20BR/RD●	SPEED CONTROL	8
X34 20WT/RD●	SPEED CONTROL	9
-	-	10
-	-	11
-	-	12
-	-	13
S4 18BR/YL●	LIFTGATE GROUND	14
-	-	15
-	-	16
G2 20VT	WATER TEMPERATURE SENDING UNIT	17
G6 20GY	OIL PRESSURE LAMP	18
G60 20GY/YL●	OIL PRESSURE SENDING UNIT	19
U3 20OR/LG●	SHIFT INDICATOR LAMP	20
D6 18LG	LEFT TURN SIGNAL LAMP	21
D5 18TN	RIGHT TURN SIGNAL LAMP	22
A3 14PK	BATTERY-HAZARD FLASHER	23
-	-	24
S40 18BR/LB●	LIFTGATE RELEASE	25
L7 18BK/YL●	SPLICE-SIDEMARKER AND PARK AND TURN SIGNAL LAMPS	26
B1 18WT	BACK-UP LAMP SWITCH	27
B2 18VT/BK●	BACK-UP LAMP SWITCH	28
V10 20BR	WINDSHIELD WASHER MOTOR	29
V11 20BK/TN●	LOW WASHER FLUID INDICATOR LEVEL SENSOR	30
S2 18YL	STARTER RELAY-IGNITION	31
H2 18DG/RD●	HORN	32
T21 20GY/LB●	TACHOMETER	33
P5 20GY/BK●	BRAKE WARNING LAMP SWITCH	34
V5 18DG	WINDSHIELD WIPER MOTOR	35
V6 18DB	WINDSHIELD WIPER MOTOR	36
C2 14DB/OR●	AIR CONDITIONING DAMPED PRESSURE SWITCH	37
-	-	38
-	-	39
-	-	40
-	-	41
G7 20WT/OR●	SPEED INDICATOR	42
-	-	43
-	-	44
V3 18BR	WINDSHIELD WIPER MOTOR	45
V4 12RD/YL●	WINDSHIELD WIPER MOTOR	46
J2 14DB	SPLICE-IGNITION RUN CIRCUIT	47
C13 12BK/RD●	ELECTRICALLY HEATED REAR WINDOW	48
J1 12RD	IGNITION SWITCH	49
J10 12PK	IGNITION SWITCH	50

HK 67	50 WAY BULKHEAD DISCONNECT

TERMINAL END OF DISCONNECT

SMALL INDEX

LARGE INDEX

CAVITY		INSTRUMENT PANEL CIRCUITS
1	B1A 12RD/WT●	IGNITION SWITCH FEED (BATTERY FEED)
2	-	-
3	B7 14RD/PK●	VAN CONVERSION (BATTERY SUPPLY)
4	-	-
5	L4 14VT●	HEADLAMP LOW BEAM
6	L3 14RD/OR● L3 16RD/OR●	HEADLAMP HIGH BEAM
7	X30 20DB/RD●	SPEED CONTROL
8	X31 20BR/RD●	SPEED CONTROL
9	X34 20WT/RD●	SPEED CONTROL
10	-	-
11	-	-
12	-	-
13	-	-
14	S40 20BR/LB●	LIFTGATE GROUND
15	-	-
16	-	-
17	G20 20VT/YL●	TEMPERATURE SEND
18	G6 20GY	OIL PRESSURE LAMP
19	G60 20GY/YL●	OIL PRESSURE SEND
20	U3 20 OR/LG●	UP-SHIFT LAMP
21	D6 20LG D6 18LG	LEFT TURN SIGNAL LAMP LEFT TURN SIGNAL SWITCH
22	D5 20TN D5 18TN	RIGHT TURN SIGNAL LAMP RIGHT TURN SIGNAL SWITCH
23	A3 14PK	HAZARD FLASHER
24	-	-
25	S4 20BR/YL●	LIFTGATE RELEASE (A/TRANSMISSION)
26	L7 18BK/YL●	PARKING LAMPS
27	B1 18WT	BACK-UP LAMP SWITCH FEED
28	B2 18VT/BK●	BACK-UP LAMP
29	V10 20BR	WINDSHIELD WASHER MOTOR
30	V11 20BK/TN●	LOW WASHER FLUID
31	S2 14YL	IGNITION START
32	H2 18DG/RD●	HORNS
33	-	-
34	P5 20GY/BK●	BREAK WARNING LAMP
35	V5 18DG	WINDSHIELD WIPER SWITCH
36	V6 18DB	WINDSHIELD WIPER SWITCH
37	C2 16DB/OR●	AIR CONDITIONER LOW PRESSURE SWITCH
38	-	-
39	-	-
40	-	-
41	-	-
42	G7 20 WT/OR●	SPEED SENSOR
43	-	-
44	-	-
45	V3 18BR/WT●	WINDSHIELD WIPER LOW SPEED FEED
46	V4 18RD/YL●	WINDSHIELD WIPER HIGH SPEED FEED
47	J2 14DB	IGNITION RUN/START
48	C13 12BK/RD●	HEATED REAR WINDOW
49	J1 12RD	IGNITION SWITCH FEED
50	J10 12PK/BK●	IGNITION SWITCH FEED

HK 68	50 WAY BULKHEAD DISCONNECT

1986 Caravan/Voyager

HK 69   FUSEBLOCK MODULE AND RELAY BANK

VAN CONVERSION WIRING   HK 70

1986 Caravan/Voyager

HK 1   FUSE APPLICATION CHART

FUSE APPLICATION CHART   HK 2

1987 Caravan/Voyager

CHARGING SYSTEM (2.2 LITRE)

HK 3

CHARGING SYSTEM (2.2 LITRE)

HK 4

CHARGING SYSTEM (2.6 LITRE)

HK 5

CHARGING SYSTEM (2.6 LITRE)

HK 6

1987 Caravan/Voyager

| HK 7 | STARTER SYSTEM (2.2 LITRE) |

| STARTER SYSTEM (2.6 LITRE) | HK 8 |

| HK 9 | ELECTRONIC SPARK ADVANCE SYSTEM (2.2 LITRE) |

| ELECTRONIC SPARK ADVANCE SYSTEM (2.2 LITRE) | HK 10 |

1987 Caravan/Voyager

HK 11 | ELECTRONIC IGNITION SYSTEM (2.6 LITRE)

CARBURETOR WIRING (2.2 LITRE) | HK 12

HK 13 | INTERMITTENT WIPER SYSTEM

INTERMITTENT WIPER SYSTEM | HK 14

1987 Caravan/Voyager

HK 15   FRONT END LIGHTING

FRONT END LIGHTING   HK 16

HK 17   HORN SYSTEM

HEADLAMP SWITCH   HK 18

1987 Caravan/Voyager

| HK | 19 | IGNITION SWITCH |

(CARBURETOR ENGINES)
ELECTRONIC SPEED CONTROL SYSTEM | HK | 20 |

| HK | 21 | UNDERHOOD LIGHT |

REAR HEATER | HK | 22 |

1987 Caravan/Voyager

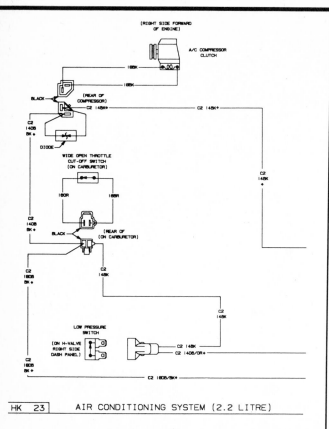

HK 23 AIR CONDITIONING SYSTEM (2.2 LITRE)

AIR CONDITIONING SYSTEM (2.2 LITRE) HK 24

AIR CONDITIONING SYSTEM
(2.6 LITRE CALIFORNIA)

HK 25

AIR CONDITIONING SYSTEM
(2.6 LITRE CALIFORNIA)

HK 26

1987 Caravan/Voyager

AIR CONDITIONING SYSTEM
(2.6 LITRE) FEDERAL/CANADA

HK 27

AIR CONDITIONING SYSTEM
(2.6 LITRE) FEDERAL/CANADA

HK 28

HK 29   AIR CONDITIONING SYSTEM

(2.2 LITRE)

RADIATOR FAN MOTOR   HK 30

1987 Caravan/Voyager

HK 31	HEATER SYSTEM

RADIATOR FAN MOTOR (2.6 LITRE CALIFORNIA ONLY)	HK 32

HK 33	OIL PRESSURE AND TEMPERATURE SYSTEM (2.2 LITRE)

OIL PRESSURE AND TEMPERATURE SYSTEM (2.6 LITRE)	HK 34

1987 Caravan/Voyager

| HK | 35 | WARNING LAMP MODULE SYSTEM | | HK | 36 |

| HK | 36 |

WARNING LAMP MODULE SYSTEM

| HK | 37 | SEAT BELT WARNING SYSTEM | | DOME AND COURTESY LAMPS | HK | 38 |

1987 Caravan/Voyager

HK 39 — DOME AND BODY COURTESY LAMPS

DOME AND BODY COURTESY LAMPS — HK 40

HK 41 — STOP/TURN AND HAZARD FLASHER SYSTEM

STOP/TURN AND HAZARD FLASHER SYSTEM — HK 42

1987 Caravan/Voyager

OIL PRESSURE GAUGE
GAUGE ALERT MODULE
LEFT TURN SIGNAL LAMP
OIL PRESSURE LAMP
TEMPERATURE GAUGE
TEMPERATURE LAMP
ILLUMINATION LAMPS
ILLUMINATION LAMPS
2-WAY GRAY CONNECTOR (SEE PG 35)
HIGH BEAM LAMP
EMR MODULE CONNECTOR (SEE PG 35)
FUEL GAUGE
GATE AJAR WARNING LAMP
BRAKE LAMP
POWER LOSS LAMP
ILLUMINATION LAMPS
HIGH TEMPERATURE LAMP
ILLUMINATION LAMP
SEAT BELT LAMP
RIGHT TURN SIGNAL LAMP
CHECK EGR LAMP
LOW VOLTS LAMP
LOW OIL LAMP
VOLT METER

| HK 43 | PRINTED CIRCUIT BOARD |

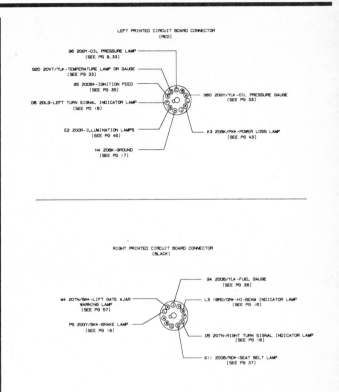

LEFT PRINTED CIRCUIT BOARD CONNECTOR (RED)

B6 20GY-OIL PRESSURE LAMP (SEE PG 9,33)
G20 20VT/YL*-TEMPERATURE LAMP OR GAUGE (SEE PG 33)
B5 20DB*-IGNITION FEED (SEE PG 35)
D6 20LG-LEFT TURN SIGNAL INDICATOR LAMP (SEE PG 16)
E2 20OR-ILLUMINATION LAMPS (SEE PG 46)
H4 20BK-GROUND (SEE PG 17)
G60 20GY/YL*-OIL PRESSURE GAUGE (SEE PG 33)
K3 20BK/PK*-POWER LOSS LAMP (SEE PG 43)

RIGHT PRINTED CIRCUIT BOARD CONNECTOR (BLACK)

B4 20DB/YL*-FUEL GAUGE (SEE PG 38)
M4 20TN/BK*-LIFT GATE AJAR WARNING LAMP (SEE PG 57)
P5 20GY/BK*-BRAKE LAMP (SEE PG 19)
L3 18RD/OR*-HI-BEAM INDICATOR LAMP (SEE PG 16)
D5 20TN-RIGHT TURN SIGNAL INDICATOR LAMP (SEE PG 16)
G11 20DB/RD*-SEAT BELT LAMP (SEE PG 37)

| PRINTED CIRCUIT BOARD CONNECTORS | HK 44 |

LOW FUEL
DOOR AJAR
LOW FUEL RELAY
WASHER FLUID
NOT USED
6 5 4 3 2 1

WARNING LIGHT MODULE
PRINTED CIRCUIT BOARD

M3 20TN/RD* DOOR AJAR LAMP (SEE PG 35)
B5 20DB/WT* IGNITION 12 VOLT (SEE PG 35)
H4 20BK GROUND (SEE PG 35)
B40 20LB/BK* LOW FUEL SIGNAL LAMP (SEE PG 35)
V11 20BK/TN* LOW WASHER FLUID LAMP (SEE PAGE 35)

| HK 45 | WARNING LIGHT MODULE PRINTED CIRCUIT BOARD CONNECTOR |

TO HEADLAMP SWITCH (SEE PG 18)
FUSE#12 (4 AMP)
E1 20TN
TO HEATED REAR WINDOW SWITCH (SEE PG 59)
E2 200R
TO REAR HEATER CONTROL LAMP (SEE PG 22)
E2 200R
CLUSTER CONNECTORS (UNDER CLUSTER LEFT SIDE)
E2 200R
E2 200R
TO PRINTED CIRCUIT BOARD CLUSTER LAMPS (SEE PG 44)
RED
GRAY
E2 200R
TO CONSOLE LIGHTING (SEE PG 56)
E2 200R
TO OVERHEAD CONSOLE (SEE PG 73,74)
E2 200R
E2 200R
H4 20BK
E2 200R
BLACK
H4 20BK
E2 200R
TO RADIO (SEE PG 47)
LIFT GATE RELEASE SWITCH ILLUMINATION (SEE PG 95)
H4 20BK
E2 200R
REAR WIPER SWITCH ILLUMINATION (SEE PG 57)
200R
20BK
H4 20BK
TO A/C AND HEATER CONTROL LAMP
TO GROUND SPLICE (SEE PG 17)
TO GROUND SPLICE (SEE PG 17)

| HK 46 | HEADLAMP SWITCH CONTROLLED INTERIOR LIGHTING |

1987 Caravan/Voyager

ELECTRONICALLY TUNED RADIOS

HK 47

ELECTRONICALLY TUNED RADIOS

HK 48

HK 49

DOOR LOCK SYSTEM

DOOR LOCK SYSTEM

HK 50

1987 Caravan/Voyager

HK 51 | WINDOW LIFT SYSTEM

WINDOW LIFT SYSTEM | HK 52

HK 53 | POWER SEAT SYSTEM

POWER SEAT SYSTEM | HK 54

1987 Caravan/Voyager

LIFTGATE RELEASE

CONSOLE LIGHTING

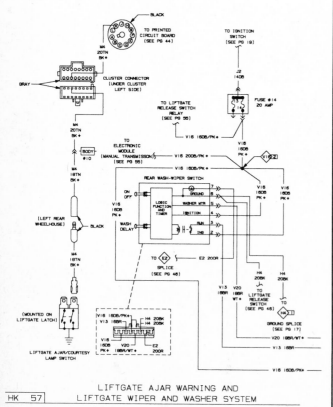

LIFTGATE AJAR WARNING AND
LIFTGATE WIPER AND WASHER SYSTEM

LIFTGATE WIPER AND WASHER SYSTEM

1987 Caravan/Voyager

| HK 59 | ELECTRICALLY HEATED REAR WINDOW | | ELECTRICALLY HEATED REAR WINDOW | HK 60 |

| HK 61 | REAR LIGHTING | | REAR LIGHTING | HK 62 |

1987 Caravan/Voyager

POWER REMOTE MIRRORS

| HK | 63 |

LEVER POSITION	CIRCUIT	MIRROR DIRECTION
A	P-B,S-K,T-L	UP
B	N-B,R-C,V-F	RIGHT
C	P-H,S-D,T-E	DOWN
D	N-A,R-J,V-M	LEFT

POWER MIRROR SWITCH FUNCTION

POWER MIRROR SWITCH

POWER REMOTE MIRRORS

| HK | 64 |

| HK | 65 | OVERHEAD CONSOLE (LIGHTING) |

OVERHEAD CONSOLE (ELECTRONICS)

| HK | 66 |

1987 Caravan/Voyager

B7 12RD/TN ◆ — TO FUSIBLE LINK (SEE PG 4,6)

TO TURN SIGNAL FLASHER (SEE PG 41)

D1 18BK

G2 14BK

FUSE #10 (20 AMP)

TO IGNITION SWITCH (SEE PG 19)

D1 20BK ◆

#3

B7 14RD PK ◆

D1 20BK ◆   J6 14TN

H4 20BK   B7 14RD/PK ◆

B7 14RD/PK ◆

B7 14RD/PK ◆

IGNITION RELAY (TAPE TO HARNESS LEFT SIDE)

BATT FEED

IGN ACC RUN

J6 14TN

YELLOW MOLD

RED MOLD

H4 20BK

TO LOWER CONSOLE (SEE PG 17)

LOCATED LEFT SIDE NEAR BULKHEAD CONNECTOR

| HK | 67 | | VAN CONVERSION WIRING |

V6 18DB-WINDSHIELD WIPER MOTOR
V1 18DB-WINDSHIELD WIPER SWITCH FEED

V16 16DB/PK ◆ -ELECTRONIC MODULE
RR WASH-WIPE SYSTEM
V16 16DB/PK ◆ -LIFTGATE RELEASE RELAY
G5 20DB/WT ◆ -GAUGES, CHIMES,
SPEED CONTROL AND
FUEL PACER LAMP

INSTRUMENT PANEL LAMPS — E2 20 OR
E1 20 TN

TURN SIGNAL FLASHER — D1 18BK
D2 18RD/BK ◆

J2 14DB-IGNITION RUN FEED
J2 14DB-IGNITION RUN FEED
D1 20BK/WT ◆ -VAN CONVERSION RELAY
X12 20RD/WT ◆ -RADIO

IGNITION TIME DELAY RELAY — J15 20YL/RD ◆
W2 20YL
W11 18PK/LB ◆

Q2 14BK IGNITION ACC FEED

M1 18PK - STOP AND DOME LAMPS

POWER DOOR LOCKS AND SEAT-W5 12RD

L8 18PK/RD ◆ -TAIL LAMPS
L1 12RD/WT ◆ -BATTERY FEED

HORN RELAY — H1 14VT
H3 20BK/RD ◆
H2 18DG/RD ◆

A3 14PK
D31 18BK/WT ◆ — HAZARD FLASHER

HEATER OR A/C FEED-C1 12BR

Q20 12BK/RD ◆ -IGNITION RUN FEED

B1 18WT-REAR HEATER SWITCH
B1 18WT-BACK-UP LAMPS

POWER WINDOWS-W1 12TN

H1 14VT — HORNS AND CIGAR LIGHTER FEED
X1 14RD

FRONT OF FUSEBLOCK

FUSE #	AMPS	COLOR
1	20	YELLOW
2	20	YELLOW
3	30	CIRCUIT BREAKER(POWER WINDOW)OPTION
4	30	LIGHT GREEN
5	20	YELLOW
6	20	YELLOW
7	25	NATURAL
8	30	CIRCUIT BREAKER (POWER DOOR LOCKS OR SEAT) OPTION
9	10	RED
10	20	YELLOW
11	20	YELLOW
12	4	PINK
13	5	TAN
14	20	YELLOW
15	BLANK	
16	BLANK	

| | FUSEBLOCK MODULE AND RELAY BANK | HK | 68 |

TERMINAL END OF DISCONNECT

SMALL INDEX

LARGE INDEX

	ENGINE COMPARTMENT CIRCUITS	CAVITY
L1 12RD ◆	HEADLAMP SWITCH	1
V3 18BR ◆	WINDSHIELD WIPER MOTOR	2
B7 12RD/TN ◆	VAN CONVERSION	3
V4 18RD/YL ◆	WINDSHIELD WIPER MOTOR	4
L4 16YT ◆	HEADLAMP LOW BEAM	5
L3 14RD	HEADLAMP HIGH BEAM	6
X30 20BR/RD ◆	SPEED CONTROL	7
X31 20BR/RD ◆	SPEED CONTROL	8
X34 20WT/RD ◆	SPEED CONTROL	9
-		10
-		11
-		12
-		13
54B 18BR/YL ◆	LIFTGATE GROUND	14
-		15
-		16
G2 20VT	WATER TEMPERATURE SENDING UNIT	17
G6 20GY	OIL PRESSURE SWITCH	18
G60/20GY/YL ◆	OIL PRESSURE SENDING UNIT	19
U3 200R/LG ◆	SHIFT INDICATOR LAMP	20
D6 18LG	LEFT TURN SIGNAL LAMP	21
D5 18TN	RIGHT TURN SIGNAL LAMP	22
A3 14PK	BATTERY-HAZARD FLASHER	23
-		24
	LIFTGATE RELEASE	25
L7 18BK/YL ◆	SPLICE-SIDEMARKER AND PARK AND TURN SIGNAL LAMPS	26
B1 18WT	BACK-UP LAMP SWITCH	27
B2 18WT/BK ◆	BACK-UP LAMP SWITCH	28
V10 20BR	WINDSHIELD WASHER MOTOR	29
V11 20BK/TN ◆	LOW WASHER FLUID INDICATOR LEVEL SENSOR	30
S2 18YL	STARTER RELAY-IGNITION	31
H2 18DG/RD ◆	HORN	32
-		33
P5 20BK	BRAKE WARNING LAMP SWITCH	34
V5 18DG	WINDSHIELD WIPER MOTOR	35
V6 18DB	WINDSHIELD WIPER MOTOR	36
C2 14DB/OR ◆	AIR CONDITIONING DAMPED PRESSURE SWITCH	37
-		38
G31 20VT/LG ◆	AMBIENT TEMPERATURE SENSOR	39
G32 20BK/LB ◆	AMBIENT TEMPERATURE SENSOR	40
-		41
G7 20WT/OR ◆	SPEED INDICATOR	42
-		43
-		44
-		45
-		46
J2 14DB	SPLICE-IGNITION RUN CIRCUIT	47
C13 12BK/RD ◆	ELECTRICALLY HEATED REAR WINDOW	48
J1 12RD	IGNITION SWITCH	49
J10 12PK ◆	IGNITION SWITCH	50

| HK | 69 | | 50 WAY BULKHEAD DISCONNECT |

TERMINAL END OF DISCONNECT

SMALL INDEX

LARGE INDEX

CAVITY		INSTRUMENT PANEL CIRCUITS
1	L1 12RD/WT ◆	IGNITION SWITCH FEED (BATTERY FEED)
2	V3 18BR/WT ◆	WINDSHIELD WIPER LOW SPEED FEED
3	B7 14RD/PK ◆	VAN CONVERSION (BATTERY SUPPLY)
4	V4 18RD/YL ◆	WINDSHIELD WIPER HIGH SPEED FEED
5	L4 14VT ◆	HEADLAMP LOW BEAM
6	L3 14RD/OR ◆	HEADLAMP HIGH BEAM
	L3 16RD/OR ◆	
7	X30 20BR/RD ◆	SPEED CONTROL
8	X31 20BR/RD ◆	SPEED CONTROL
9	X33 20WT/RD ◆	SPEED CONTROL
10	-	-
11	-	-
12	-	-
13	-	-
14	S40 20BR/LB ◆	LIFTGATE GROUND
15	-	-
16	-	-
17	G20 20VT/YL ◆	TEMPERATURE SEND
18	G6 20GY	OIL PRESSURE LAMP
19	G60 20GY/YL ◆	OIL PRESSURE SEND
20	U3 20 OR/LG ◆	UP-SHIFT LAMP
21	D6 20LG	LEFT TURN SIGNAL LAMP
	D6 18LG	LEFT TURN SIGNAL SWITCH
22	D5 20TN	RIGHT TURN SIGNAL LAMP
	D5 18TN	RIGHT TURN SIGNAL SWITCH
23	A3 14PK	HAZARD FLASHER
24	-	-
25	S4 18BR/YL ◆	LIFTGATE RELEASE (A/TRANSMISSION)
	S4 20BR/YL ◆	
26	L7 18BK/YL ◆	PARKING LAMPS
27	B1 18WT	BACK-UP LAMP SWITCH FEED
28	B2 18WT/BK ◆	BACK-UP LAMP SWITCH
29	V10 20BR	WINDSHIELD WASHER MOTOR
30	V11 20BK/TN ◆	LOW WASHER FLUID
31	S2 14YL	IGNITION START
32	H2 18DG/RD ◆	HORNS
33	-	-
34	P5 20GY/BK ◆	BRAKE WARNING LAMP
35	V5 18DG	WINDSHIELD WIPER SWITCH
36	V6 18DB	WINDSHIELD WIPER SWITCH
37	C2 18DB/OR ◆	AIR CONDITIONER LOW PRESSURE SWITCH
38	-	-
39	G31 20VT/LG ◆	AMBIENT TEMPERATURE (OVERHEAD CONSOLE)
40	G32 20BK/LB ◆	AMBIENT TEMPERATURE (OVERHEAD CONSOLE)
41	-	-
42	G7 20 WT/OR ◆	SPEED SENSOR
	G7 20 WT/OR ◆	SPEED SENSOR
43	-	-
44	-	-
45	-	-
46	-	-
47	J2 14DB	IGNITION RUN/START
48	C13 12BK/RD ◆	HEATED REAR WINDOW
49	J1 12RD	IGNITION SWITCH FEED
50	J10 12PK/BK ◆	IGNITION SWITCH FEED

| | 50 WAY BULKHEAD DISCONNECT | HK | 70 |

1987 Caravan/Voyager

VIEWED FROM WIRE SIDE OF 25 WAY CONNECTOR

CAV	CIRCUIT	DESCRIPTION
1	L7 18BK	TAIL, LICENSE AND SIDE MARKER LAMPS
2	D8 18DG	LEFT REAR TURN SIGNAL LAMP
3	M16 18BK/LB*	LEFT FRONT DOOR JAMB SWITCH
4	91Q 18LG	SEAT BELT WARNING SWITCH
5	D7 18BR	RIGHT REAR TURN SIGNAL LAMP
6	52 18VT	BACK-UP LAMPS
7	G4 18DB	FUEL GAUGE SENDING UNIT
8	M1 18BK/PK*	MAP LAMP FEED
9	M2 18BK/YL*	DOOR SWITCH GROUND-DOME LAMP
10	M4 18TN/BK*	TAIL GATE OPEN SWITCH
11	X42 14BK/GY*	LIFTGATE RELEASE
12	—	NOT USED
13	M3 18TN	DOOR AJAR
14	G40 18LB	LOW FUEL
15	M11 18PK/LB*	DOME LAMP DEFEAT
16	V20 18BR/WT*	REAR WASHER
17	V16 18DB/PK*	REAR WIPER-PARK
18	V13 18BR/LG*	REAR WIPER-RUN
19	M11 18PK/LB*	DOME LAMP DEFEAT
20	M2 18YL	DOOR SWITCH GROUND-DOME LAMP
21	—	NOT USED
22	—	NOT USED
23	—	NOT USED
24	C15 12BK	HEATED REAR WINDOW-EBL
25	Z1 14DG/BK*	FUEL PUMP FEED

(MOUNTED ON PARKING BRAKE LEFT SIDE)

| HK 71 | BODY TO INSTRUMENT PANEL WIRING |

VIEWED FROM TERMINAL END OF CONNECTORS

CAV	CIRCUIT	DESCRIPTION
1	L7 18BK/YL*	TAIL, LICENSE AND SIDE MARKER LAMPS
2	D8 18DG/RD*	LEFT REAR TURN SIGNAL LAMP
3	M16 20BK/LB*	LEFT FRONT DOOR JAMB SWITCH GROUND
3	M16 20BK/LB*	LEFT FRONT DOOR JAMB SWITCH GROUND
4	91Q 20LG	SEAT BELT WARNING SWITCH
5	D7 18BR/RD*	RIGHT REAR TURN SIGNAL LAMP
6	52 18VT/BK*	BACK-UP LAMPS
7	G4 20DB/YL*	FUEL GAUGE SENDING UNIT
8	M1 18PK	DOME LAMP FEED
9	M2 20YL	DOOR SWITCH GROUND-DOME LAMP
10	M4 20TN/BK*	TAIL GATE OPEN SWITCH

INSTRUMENT-PANEL WIRING CONNECTOR

CAV	CIRCUIT	DESCRIPTION
11	X42 18BK	LIFT GATE RELEASE
12	—	NOT USED
13	M3 20TN/RD*	DOOR AJAR
14	G40 20LB/RD*	LOW FUEL
15	M11 18PK/LB*	DOME LAMP DEFEAT
16	V20 18BR/WT*	REAR WASHER
17	V16 18DB/PK*	REAR WIPER-PARK
18	V13 18BR	REAR WIPER-RUN

INSTR-PANEL WIRING CONNECTOR

CAV	CIRCUIT	DESCRIPTION
19	M1 18PK / M1 18PK	DOME LAMP FEED / DOME LAMP FEED
20	M2 18YL / M2 18YL	DOOR SWITCH GROUND-DOME LAMP / DOOR SWITCH GROUND-DOME LAMP

BODY WIRING CONNECTOR

CAV	CIRCUIT	DESCRIPTION
24	C15 12BK/OR*	HEATED REAR WINDOW-EBL
25	—	NOT USED

INSTRUMENT-PANEL WIRING CONNECTOR

[PLUG INTO BODY 25 WAY CONNECTOR]

| INSTRUMENT PANEL TO BODY WIRING | HK 72 |

VIEWED FROM WIRE SIDE OF 25 WAY CONNECTOR

CAV	CIRCUIT	DESCRIPTION
1	—	NOT USED
2	H4 18BK	HORN GROUND
3	H3 20BK/RD*	GROUND FROM HORN SWITCH
4	D6 18LG	LEFT FRONT TURN SIGNAL
5	D5 18TN	RIGHT FRONT TURN SIGNAL
6	D32 18PK*	HAZARD FLASHER FEED
7	D2 18RD/BK*	FEED FROM TURN SIGNAL FLASHER
8	D8 18DG/RD*	LEFT REAR TURN SIGNAL
9	D7 18BR/RD*	RIGHT REAR TURN SIGNAL
10	D4 18VT	FEED FROM BRAKE SWITCH
11	—	NOT USED
12	V3 18BR*	WINDSHIELD WIPER LOW SPEED
13	V4 18RD/YL*	WINDSHIELD WIPER HIGH SPEED
14	V5 18DG	WINDSHIELD WIPER MOTOR
15	V1 18DB	WINDSHIELD WIPER SWITCH FEED
16	V10 20BR	WINDSHIELD WASHER MOTOR
17	H4 18BK	INTERMITTENT WIPE SWITCH GROUND
18	H40 18BK/LG* / H40 18BK/LG*	INTERMITTENT WIPE MODULE GROUND / TO CHIME GROUND
19	M26 20LB / M26 20LB	KEY-IN BUZZER / KEY-IN BUZZER
20	M16 20BK/LB*	LEFT FRONT DOOR JAMB SWITCH GROUND
21	—	NOT USED
22	—	NOT USED
23	—	NOT USED
24	J15 20YL/RD* / J15 20YL/RD*	IGNITION KEY LAMP FEED / IGNITION KEY LAMP FEED
25	H4 18BK	IGNITION KEY LAMP GROUND

(MOUNTED ON INSTR-PANEL LEFT OF STEERING COLUMN)

| HK 73 | INSTRUMENT PANEL TO STEERING COLUMN WIRING |

VIEWED FROM TERMINAL END OF CONNECTORS

CAV	CIRCUIT	DESCRIPTION
1	—	NOT USED
2	H4 18BK	HORN GROUND
3	H3 18BK/RD*	HORN SWITCH GROUND
4	D6 18LG	LEFT FRONT TURN SIGNAL
5	D5 18TN	RIGHT FRONT TURN SIGNAL
6	D32 18PK	HAZARD FLASHER FEED
7	D2 18RD	TURN SIGNAL FLASHER FEED
8	D8 18DG/RD*	LEFT REAR TURN SIGNAL
9	D7 18BR/RD*	RIGHT REAR TURN SIGNAL
10	D4 18VT	BRAKE SWITCH FEED

TURN SIGNAL SWITCH CONNECTOR

CAV	CIRCUIT	DESCRIPTION
11	—	NOT USED
12	V3 18BR* / V3 18BR*	INTERMITTENT WIPE MODULE / WINDSHIELD WIPER LOW SPEED
13	V4 18RD	WINDSHIELD WIPER HIGH SPEED
14	V5 18DG / V5 18DG	INTERMITTENT WIPE MODULE / WINDSHIELD WIPER MOTOR
15	V1 18DB	WINDSHIELD WIPER SWITCH FEED
16	V10 18BR / V10 18BR	INTERMITTENT WIPE MODULE / WINDSHIELD WASHER MOTOR
17	H4 18BK	INTERMITTENT WIPE SWITCH GROUND
18	H40 18BK/LG*	INTERMITTENT WIPE MODULE GROUND

WINDSHIELD WIPER SWITCH CONNECTOR

CAV	CIRCUIT	DESCRIPTION
19	M26 20LB	KEY-IN BUZZER
20	M16 20BK/LB*	LEFT FRONT DOOR JAMB SWITCH GROUND

KEY-IN BUZZER SWITCH CONNECTOR

CAV	CIRCUIT	DESCRIPTION
21	—	NOT USED
22	—	NOT USED
23	—	NOT USED

CAV	CIRCUIT	DESCRIPTION
24	J15 18YL	IGNITION KEY LAMP FEED
25	H4 18BK	IGNITION KEY LAMP GROUND

IGNITION KEY LAMP SWITCH CONNECTOR

(PLUGGED INTO STEERING COLUMN 25 WAY CONNECTOR)

| STEERING COLUMN SWITCH TO PANEL WIRING | HK 74 |

1987 Caravan/Voyager

Fuse block and relay bank — 1987 Caravan/Voyager

AMPS	FUSE COLOR CODE
3	VT VIOLET
4	PK PINK
5	TN TAN
10	RD RED
20	YL YELLOW
25	NAT NATURAL
30	LG LIGHT GREEN

CAVITY	FUSE/COLOR	ITEMS FUSED
13	5 AMP TN	FUEL VOLTAGE, OIL AND TEMPERATURE GAUGES, BRAKE WARNING, LIFTGATE OPEN, SEAT BELT WARNING MODULE, UPSHIFT, AND POWER LOSS LAMPS, CHIMES AND SPEED CONTROL
14	20 AMP YL	REAR WASH WIPE AND LIFTGATE RELEASE ELECTRONIC MODULE (MANUAL TRANSMISSION)
15	20 AMP YL	SPOTLIGHT
16	20 AMP YL	SPOTLIGHT

CAVITY	FUSE/COLOR	ITEMS FUSED
1	20 AMP YL	HAZARD FLASHER
2	20 AMP YL	BACK-UP LAMPS, A/D FAN AND CLUTCH RELAY, HEATED REAR WINDOW SWITCH, REAR SEAT HEATER AND OVERHEAD CONSOLE
3	30 AMP C/BRKR SILVER CAN	POWER WINDOW MOTORS
4	30 AMP LG	A/C, OR HEATER BLOWER MOTOR
5	20 AMP YL	PARK, TAIL, SIDE MARKER AND LICENSE LAMPS, CLOCK, RADIO AND OVERHEAD CONSOLE DISPLAY INTENSITY
6	20 AMP YL	STOP, DOME, CARGO, VANITY MIRROR, IGNITION SWITCH, DOOR COURTESY, READING, AND UNDERSEAT STORAGE LAMPS, IGNITION SWITCH LAMP TIME DELAY RELAY
7	25 AMP NAT	CONSOLE AND EMISSION MAINTENANCE REMINDER LAMPS, HORNS, CIGAR LIGHTER, CLOCK AND RADIO MEMORY, CHIMES AND PREMIUM SPEAKER POWER AMPLIFIER FEED
8	30 AMP C/BRKR SILVER CAN	POWER DOOR LOCKS, SEATS AND MIRRORS
9	10 AMP RD	RADIO
10	20 AMP YL	TURN SIGNAL LAMPS AND VAN CONVERSION
11	20 AMP YL	WINDSHIELD WIPER AND WASHERS
12	4 AMP PK	CLUSTER, A/C AND HEATER CONTROL, SWITCH TITLE, ASH RECEIVER, RADIO CIGAR LIGHTER, OVERHEAD CONSOLE AND REAR SEAT HEATER LAMPS

Fig. 8—Fuse Block and Relay Bank S/H-K

Fuse block and relay bank — 1987 Caravan/Voyager

50 way bulkhead connector — 1987 Caravan/Voyager

WIRE COLOR CODES	
BK BLACK	LB LIGHT BLUE
BR BROWN	LG LIGHT GREEN
DB DARK BLUE	OR ORANGE
DG DARK GREEN	PK PINK
GY GRAY	RD RED
	TN TAN
	VT VIOLET
	WT WHITE
	YL YELLOW
	* WITH TRACER

CAV	WIRE COLOR	DESCRIPTION
36	DB	WINDSHIELD WIPER SWITCH & PARK FEED
37	DB/OR*	LOW PRESSURE SWITCH AND A/C CLUTCH
38	BK/PK*	LIMITED POWER WARNING LAMP
39	VT/LG*	AMBIENT AIR
40	BK/LB	AMBIENT AIR
41	WT/PK*	BRAKE SENSE (EFI)
42	WT/OR	SPEED SENSOR (2 WIRES 1 WIRE EFI)
43		
44		
45		
46		
47	DB	IGNITION RUN/START
48	BR/RD*	HEATED REAR WINDOW
49	RD	IGNITION SWITCH FEED
50	PK*	IGNITION SWITCH FEED

CAV	WIRE COLOR	DESCRIPTION
1	RD*	BATTERY FEED
2	BR*	WINDSHIELD WIPER LOW SPEED
3	RD/PK*	BATTERY FEED (VAN CONVERSION)
4	RD/YL*	WINDSHIELD WIPER HIGH SPEED
5	VT*	HEADLAMP LOW BEAM
6	RD/OR*	HEADLAMP HIGH BEAM
7	DB/RD*	SPEED CONTROL
8	BR/RD*	SPEED CONTROL
9	WT/RD*	SPEED CONTROL
10	YL/RD*	SPEED CONTROL (EFI ONLY)
11		
13		
14	BK/LB*	LIFTGATE RELEASE
15		
17	VT/YL*	TEMPERATURE SENDING UNIT
18	GY	OIL PRESSURE LAMP
19	GY/YL*	OIL PRESSURE SENDING UNIT
20	OR/LG*	UPSHIFT LAMP (MANUAL TRANSMISSION)
21	TN	LEFT TURN SIGNAL
22	TN	RIGHT TURN SIGNAL
23	PK	HAZARD FLASHER
24	DG/BK*	FUEL PUMP FEED (EFI)
25	BK/YL*	LIFTGATE RELEASE
26	BK/YL*	PARKING LAMPS
27	WT	BACK-UP LAMPS
28	VT/BR	BACK-UP LAMPS
29	BR	WINDSHIELD WASHER
30	BK/TN*	LOW WINDSHIELD WASHER FLUID
31	YL	IGNITION START
32	DG/RD*	HORN
33	BK	
34	GY/BR*	BRAKE WARNING LAMP
35	DG	WINDSHIELD WIPER MOTOR PARK RETURN & INTERMITTENT WIPE SIGNAL

Fig. 9—50 Way Bulkhead Disconnect

50 way bulkhead connector — 1987 Caravan/Voyager

25 way Instrument panel to steering column connector — 1987 Caravan/Voyager

WIRE COLOR CODES	
BK BLACK	OR ORANGE
BR BROWN	PK PINK
DB DARK BLUE	RD RED
DG DARK GREEN	TN TAN
GY GRAY	VT VIOLET
LB LIGHT BLUE	WT WHITE
LG LIGHT GREEN	YL YELLOW
	* WITH TRACER

CAV	WIRE COLOR	DESCRIPTION
20	BU/LB*	GROUND FROM LEFT FRONT DOOR JAMB SWITCH
21		
22		
23		
24	YL/RD*	KEY-IN LAMP FEED
25	BK	KEY-IN GROUND WIRE

CAV	WIRE COLOR	DESCRIPTION
1	BK	HORN & KEY-IN LAMP GROUND (STANDARD COLUMN)
2	DG	GROUND FROM HORN SWITCH
3	BK/LB*	GROUND FROM HORN SWITCH
4	LG	LEFT FRONT TURN SIGNAL
5	TN	RIGHT FRONT TURN SIGNAL
6	VT	FEED FROM HAZARD FLASHER
7	PK*	FEED FROM TURN SIGNAL FLASHER
8	DG/RD*	LEFT REAR TURN SIGNAL
9	BR/RD*	RIGHT REAR TURN SIGNAL
10	WT	FEED FROM BRAKE SWITCH
11		
12	BR*	WINDSHIELD WIPER LOW SPEED
13	RD/YL*	WINDSHIELD WIPER HIGH SPEED
14	DG	WINDSHIELD WIPER MOTOR PARK
15	DB	WINDSHIELD WIPER RETURN & INTERMITTENT WIPE SWITCH FEED & MOTOR PARK FEED
16	BR	WINDSHIELD WASHER MOTOR
17	BK	INTERMITTENT WIPE SWITCH GROUND
18	BK/LG*	INTERMITTENT WIPE MODULE GROUND
19	LB	KEY-IN BUZZER

Fig. 10—25 Way Instrument Panel to Steering Column Connector

25 way Instrument panel to steering column connector — 1987 Caravan/Voyager

25 way Instrument panel to body connector — 1987 Caravan/Voyager

WIRE COLOR CODES	
BK BLACK	OR ORANGE
BR BROWN	PK PINK
DB DARK BLUE	RD RED
DG DARK GREEN	TN TAN
GY GRAY	VT VIOLET
LB LIGHT BLUE	WT WHITE
LG LIGHT GREEN	YL YELLOW
	* WITH TRACER

CAV	WIRE COLOR	DESCRIPTION
20	YL	DOOR SWITCH GROUND FRONT DOOR COURTESY LAMP FEED
21		
22		
23		
24	BK	HEATED LIFTGATE WINDOW
25	DG/BK*	FUEL PUMP FEED

CAV	WIRE COLOR	DESCRIPTION
1	BK	TAIL, SIDE MARKER & LICENSE LAMPS
2	YL	LEFT REAR STOP & TURN SIGNAL LAMP
3	BK/LB*	LEFT FRONT DOOR JAMB SWITCH
4	LG	SEAT BELT WARNING SWITCH
5	BR	RIGHT REAR STOP & TURN SIGNAL LAMP
6	VT	BACK-UP LAMPS
7	DB	FUEL GAUGE SENDING UNIT
8	BK/PK*	DOME & CARGO LAMP FEED
9	BK/YL*	DOOR SWITCH GROUND DOME LAMP
10	BK/YL*	LIFTGATE AJAR LAMP
11	BK/GY*	LIFTGATE POWER RELEASE
12		
13	TN	DOOR AJAR SWITCHES
14	LB	LOW FUEL
15	PK/LB*	DOME LAMP FEED
16	BR/WT*	LIFTGATE WASHER MOTOR FEED
17	BK/GY*	LIFTGATE WIPER MOTOR
18	DB/RD*	LIFTGATE WIPER MOTOR RUN
19	PK/LB*	FRONT DOOR COURTESY LAMP

Fig. 11—25 Way Instrument Panel to Body Connector

25 way Instrument panel to body connector — 1987 Caravan/Voyager

S-HK 1 — FUSE APPLICATION CHART

FUSE APPLICATION CHART — S-HK 2

S-HK 3 — CHARGING SYSTEM

CHARGING SYSTEM — S-HK 4

1988 Caravan/Voyager

S-HK 5 STARTER SYSTEM 2.5L ENGINE

STARTER SYSTEM 3.0L ENGINE S-HK 6

S-HK 7 IGNITION SWITCH

STOP LAMP AND SPEED CONTROL SWITCH S-HK 8

1988 Caravan/Voyager

ELECTRONIC FUEL INJECTION
IGNITION SYSTEM 2.5L ENGINE

S-HK 9

ELECTRONIC FUEL INJECTION
IGNITION SYSTEM 2.5L ENGINE

S-HK 10

ELECTRONIC FUEL INJECTION
IGNITION SYSTEM 2.5L ENGINE

S-HK 11

ELECTRONIC FUEL INJECTION
IGNITION SYSTEM 2.5L ENGINE

S-HK 12

1988 Caravan/Voyager

ELECTRONIC FUEL INJECTION
IGNITION SYSTEM 2.5L ENGINE

S-HK 13

ELECTRONIC FUEL INJECTION
IGNITION SYSTEM 3.0L ENGINE

S-HK 14

ELECTRONIC FUEL INJECTION
IGNITION SYSTEM 3.0L ENGINE

S-HK 15

ELECTRONIC FUEL INJECTION
IGNITION SYSTEM 3.0L ENGINE

S-HK 16

1988 Caravan/Voyager

ELECTRONIC FUEL INJECTION
IGNITION SYSTEM 3.0 L ENGINE

S-HK 17

ELECTRONIC FUEL INJECTION
IGNITION SYSTEM 3.0 L ENGINE

S-HK 18

OIL PRESSURE AND
S-HK 19 | TEMPERATURE SYSTEM (2.5 & 3.0 LITRE)

UNDERHOOD LAMP

S-HK 20

1988 Caravan/Voyager

S-HK 21 · FRONT END LIGHTING

FRONT END LIGHTING · S-HK 22

S-HK 23 · HORN SYSTEM

HEADLAMP SWITCH · S-HK 24

1988 Caravan/Voyager

S-HK	25	HEADLAMP SWITCH CONTROLLED INTERIOR LAMPS

	CONSOLE LAMPS	S-HK	26

S-HK	27	OVERHEAD CONSOLE LAMPS

	OVERHEAD CONSOLE LAMPS	S-HK	28

1988 Caravan/Voyager

S-HK | 29 | DOME AND BODY COURTESY LAMPS

DOME AND BODY COURTESY LAMPS | S-HK | 30

S-HK | 31 | SEAT BELT WARNING SYSTEM

DOME AND COURTESY LAMPS | S-HK | 32

1988 Caravan/Voyager

S-HK 33 — WARNING LAMP MODULE SYSTEM

WARNING LAMP MODULE SYSTEM — S-HK 34

S-HK 35 — LIFTGATE AJAR WARNING AND LIFTGATE WIPER AND WASHER SYSTEM

LIFTGATE WIPER AND WASHER SYSTEM — S-HK 36

1988 Caravan/Voyager

S-HK 37 | INTERMITTENT WIPER SYSTEM

INTERMITTENT WIPER SYSTEM | S-HK 38

S-HK 39 STOP/TURN AND HAZARD FLASHER SYSTEM

STOP/TURN AND HAZARD FLASHER SYSTEM | S-HK 40

1988 Caravan/Voyager

LEFT PRINTED CIRCUIT BOARD CONNECTOR
(RED)

G28 22WT/BR* EMR LAMP
(SEE SH 33)

G6 22GY-OIL PRESSURE LAMP*
(SEE SH 18)

G20 22VT/YL*-TEMPERATURE LAMP OR GAUGE
(SEE SH 18)

D6 18LG-LEFT TURN SIGNAL INDICATOR LAMP
(SEE SH 22, 40)

E2 22OR-ILLUMINATION LAMPS
(SEE SH 25)

H4 18BK-GROUND
(SEE SH 23, 33)

M4 22TN/BK*-LIFTGATE AJAR
(SEE SH 35)

G5 22DB*- IGNITION FEED
(SEE SH 8, 33)

G60 22GY/YL*-OIL PRESSURE GAUGE
(SEE SH 18)

K3 22BK/PK*-CHECK GAUGES
(SEE SH 11, 15, 33)

RIGHT PRINTED CIRCUIT BOARD CONNECTOR
(BLACK)

G11 22DB/RD*-SEAT BELT LAMP
(SEE SH 31)

P5 22GY/BK*-BRAKE LAMP
(SEE SH 7)

D5 20TN-RIGHT TURN SIGNAL
INDICATOR LAMP
(SEE SH 22, 40)

L3 18RD/OR*-HI-BEAM INDICATOR LAMP
(SEE SH 22)

G5 22DB*-IGNITION FEED
(SEE SH 8)

G4 20DB/YL*-FUEL GUAGE
(SEE SH 34)

T21 22GY/LB*-TACHOMETER
(SEE SH 12, 17, 34)

S-HK	41	PRINTED CIRCUIT BOARD CONNECTORS

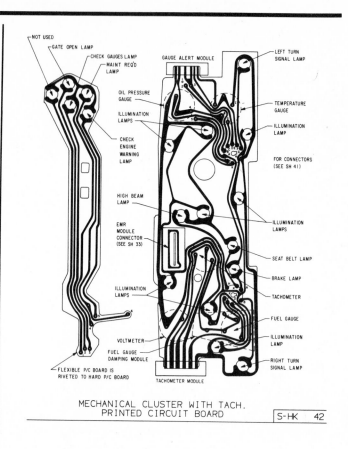

NOT USED

GATE OPEN LAMP

CHECK GAUGES LAMP

MAINT REQ'D LAMP

GAUGE ALERT MODULE

OIL PRESSURE GAUGE

ILLUMINATION LAMPS

CHECK ENGINE WARNING LAMP

HIGH BEAM LAMP

EMR MODULE CONNECTOR
(SEE SH 33)

ILLUMINATION LAMPS

VOLTMETER

FUEL GAUGE DAMPING MODULE

FLEXIBLE P/C BOARD IS RIVETED TO HARD P/C BOARD

LEFT TURN SIGNAL LAMP

TEMPERATURE GAUGE

ILLUMINATION LAMP

FOR CONNECTORS
(SEE SH 41)

ILLUMINATION LAMPS

SEAT BELT LAMP

BRAKE LAMP

TACHOMETER

FUEL GAUGE

ILLUMINATION LAMP

RIGHT TURN SIGNAL LAMP

TACHOMETER MODULE

MECHANICAL CLUSTER WITH TACH.
PRINTED CIRCUIT BOARD

		S-HK	42

MAINT REQ'D LAMP

OIL PRESSURE LAMP

ILLUMINATION LAMPS

CHECK GAUGES LAMP

HIGH BEAM LAMP

EMR MODULE CONNECTOR
(SEE SH 33)

FUEL GAUGE DAMPING MODULE

ILLUMINATION LAMPS

VOLTMETER

FLEXIBLE P/C BOARD IS RIVETED
TO HARD P/C BOARD

LEFT TURN SIGNAL LAMP

TEMPERATURE LAMP

ILLUMINATION LAMPS

FUEL GAUGE

GATE OPEN LAMP

BRAKE LAMP

FOR CONNECTORS
(SEE SH 41)

ILLUMINATION LAMP

SEAT BELT LAMP

RIGHT TURN SIGNAL LAMP

MECHANICAL CLUSTER W/O TACH
PRINTED CIRCUIT BOARD

S-HK	43	

LOW FUEL LAMP

LOW FUEL RELAY

LOW FUEL LAMP

IGNITION

LOW FUEL SIGNAL

NOT USED

DOOR AJAR LAMP

LOW WASHER FLUID LAMP

WARNING LIGHT MODULE
PRINTED CIRCUIT BOARD

H4 18BK *
GROUND
(SEE SH 33)

G40 22LB/BK *
LOW FUEL SIGNAL LAMP
(SEE SH 33,34)

G5 22DB/WT *
IGNITION 12 VOLT
(SEE SH 33)

M3 22TN/RD *
DOOR AJAR LAMP
(SEE SH 33)

V11 22BK/TN *
LOW WASHER FLUID LAMP
(SEE SH 37)

WARNING LIGHT MODULE
PRINTED CIRCUIT BOARD CONNECTOR

		S-HK	44

1988 Caravan/Voyager

S-HK 45 | ELECTRONICALLY TUNED RADIOS

ELECTRONICALLY TUNED RADIOS | S-HK 46

S-HK 47 | HEATER SYSTEM 2.5L AND 3.0L ENGINE

AIR CONDITIONING SYSTEM CONTROL
2.5L AND 3.0L ENGINE | S-HK 48

1988 Caravan/Voyager

S-HK 49 AIR CONDITIONING SYSTEM 2.5L ENGINE

AIR CONDITIONING SYSTEM 2.5L ENGINE S-HK 50

S-HK 51 AIR CONDITIONING SYSTEM 3.0L ENGINE

AIR CONDITIONING SYSTEM 3.0L ENGINE S-HK 52

1988 Caravan/Voyager

S-HK 53   REAR HEATER AND A/C SYSTEM

REAR HEATER AND A/C SYSTEM   S-HK 54

S-HK 55   REAR HEATER-ONLY

REAR WINDOW DEFOGGER   S-HK 56

1988 Caravan/Voyager

S-HK 57 WINDOW LIFT SYSTEM

WINDOW LIFT SYSTEM S-HK 58

LEFT DOOR			
B+ POLARITY	B− POLARITY	SWITCH SECTION	WINDOW AND MOVEMENT
LB	WT	1	LEFT FRONT UP
WT	LB	1	LEFT FRONT DOWN
PK/WT*	YT	2	RIGHT FRONT UP
YT	PK/RD*	2	RIGHT FRONT DOWN
TN	BK	SWITCH	FEED AND GROUND

RIGHT DOOR		
B+ POLARITY	B− POLARITY	WINDOW AND MOVEMENT
WT	LB	DOWN-FROM DOOR SWITCH
LB	WT	UP-FROM DOOR SWITCH
YT	PK/WT*	DOWN-FROM MASTER SWITCH
PK/WT*	YT	UP-FROM MASTER SWITCH
TN		FEED

S-HK 59 POWER SEAT SYSTEM

POWER SEAT SYSTEM S-HK 60

MOTOR INSULATOR POLARITY		
+POLARITY	−POLARITY	SEAT MOVEMENT
YL/BL*	RD/BL*	FORWARD
RD/BL*	YL/BL*	REARWARD
YL/WT*	RD/WT*	REAR UP
RD/WT*	YL/WT*	REAR DOWN
YL/GN*	RD/GN*	FRONT UP
RD/GN*	YL/GN*	FRONT DOWN
BK/RD*		FEED
	BK	GROUND

1988 Caravan/Voyager

S-HK 61   DOOR LOCK SYSTEM

DOOR LOCK SYSTEM   S-HK 62

POWER MIRROR SWITCH FUNCTION		
LEVER POSITION	CIRCUIT	MIRROR DIRECTION
A	SK, TL, PB	UP
B	NG, VF, RC	RIGHT
C	SD, TE, PH	DOWN
D	NA, VM, RJ	LEFT

VIEW OF SWITCH INDEXING FROM FRONT OF SWITCH

S-HK 63   POWER REMOTE MIRRORS

POWER REMOTE MIRRORS   S-HK 64

1988 Caravan/Voyager

S-HK 65   LIFTGATE RELEASE

VAN CONVERSION WIRING   S-HK 66

S-HK 67   REAR LIGHTING & TRAILER TOW

REAR LIGHTING & TRAILER TOW   S-HK 68

1988 Caravan/Voyager

CAV	IGNITION SYSTEM CIRCUITS		SHEET NO.
1	K4 18DG/RD*	MAP SENSOR	10
2	—	—	
3	K10 20TN/WT*	COOLANT SENSOR	12
4	N5 18BK/LB*	SENSOR RETURN	12
5	K5 16BK*	SIGNAL GROUND	9
6	—	—	
7	X33 20WT	S/C RESUME	13
8	X32 20YL/RD*	S/C ON/OFF	13
9	X31 20BR/RD*	S/C SET	13
10	Z1 16DG/BK*	Z1 INPUTOR	13
11	—	—	
12	K14 18DB*	FJ2	11
13	K8 18VT*	5 VOLT SUPPLY	10
14	R31 20DG/OR*	ALT FIELD CONTROL	10
15	K9 18LB/RD*	POWER GROUND	11
16	K9 18LB/RD*	POWER GROUND	11
17	N2 18BR*	AUTOMATIC IDLE SPEED MOTOR	8
18	N4 18YL/BK*	AUTOMATIC IDLE SPEED MOTOR	8
19	N1 18GY/RD*	AUTOMATIC IDLE SPEED MOTOR	8
20	N3 18VT/BK*	AUTOMATIC IDLE SPEED MOTOR	8
21	K13 20BK/RD*	T/B TEMP SENSOR	9
22	K7 18OR/DB*	THROTTLE POSITION SENSOR	9
23	N11 18BK/DG*	OXYGEN SENSOR	9
24	—	—	
25	—	—	
26	—	—	
27	—	—	
28	—	—	
29	D40 18WT/PK*	BRAKE SWITCH	13
30	S4 20BR/YL*	PARK/NEUTRAL SWITCH	9
31	DK20 20LG	SCI RECEIVE	11
32	—	—	
33	K16 20VT/YL*	INJECTOR CONTROL 1	10
34	K15 20YL	DWELL CONTROL	10
35	—	—	
36	Z6 20LB/BK*	NOT USED	13
37	—	—	
38	—	—	
39	—	—	
40	S6 20GY/YL*	EGR SOLENOID	12
41	J1 16RD	DIRECT BATTERY	11
42	—	—	
43	—	—	
44	—	—	
45	C20 18BR	A/C CLUTCH INPUT	11
46	—	—	
47	N7 18GY*	REFERENCE PICKUP	12
48	G7 20WT/OR*	VEH SPEED PICKUP	12
49	—	—	
50	T21 20GY/LB*	TACH SIGNAL	12
51	DK21 20PK	SCI TRANSMIT	11
52	N6 18OR	8 VOLT INPUT	12
53	X36 20TN/RD*	SPEED CONTROL VAC	13
54	K1 20PK*	PURGE SOLENOID	10
55	U31 18OR/BK*	SIL	13
56	N13 20DB/OR*	A/C HOT C/O	11
57	C27 20DB/PK*	RAD FAN RELAY	11
58	K19 20DB/YL*	ASD RELAYR	11
59	K3 20BK/PK*	POWER LOSS LAMP	11
60	X35 20LG/RD*	SPEED CONTROL VENT	13

SHORT TAB

LONG TAB

CONNECTOR #1
VIEWED FROM WIRE
END OF CONNECTOR

(2.5 LITRE) SINGLE MODULE
ENGINE CONTROLLER-60 WAY

S-HK 69

CONNECTOR #2

CAV	IGNITION SYSTEM CIRCUITS		SHEET NO.
1	N6 18OR	8 VOLT OUTPUT	12
2	K5 16BK/ *	SIGNAL GROUND	9
3	K14 18DB/ *	FJ2 OUTPUT	11
4	J2 14DB	J2 INPUT	13
5	—	—	
6	J9 16BK	POWER GROUND	11
7	J9 16BK	POWER GROUND	11
8	K16 20VT/YL*	INJECTOR CONTROL 1	10
9	Y11 18WT	INJECTOR DRIVER 1	13
10	—	—	
11	R31 20DG/OR*	ALT FIELD CONTROL	10
12	J5 18BK/YL*	IGNITION COIL DRIVER	11
13	K15 20YL	DWELL CONTROL	10
14	R3 18DG	ALT FIELD DRIVER	13

(2.5 LITRE) SINGLE MODULE
ENGINE CONTROLLER-14 WAY

S-HK 70

CAV	IGNITION SYSTEM CIRCUITS		SHEET NO.
1	K4 18DG/RD*	MAP SENSOR	16
2	—	—	
3	K10 20TN/WT*	COOLANT SENSOR	17
4	N5 18BK/LB*	SENSOR RETURN	17
5	K5 16BK*	SIGNAL GROUND	14
6	—	—	
7	X33 20WT	S/C RESUME	18
8	X32 20YL/RD*	S/C ON/OFF	18
9	X31 20BR/RD*	S/C SET	18
10	Z1 16DG/BK*	Z1 INPUT	18
11	Y11	—	
12	K14 18DB*	FJ2	15
13	K8 18VT/YL*	5 VOLT SUPPLY	16
14	R31 20DG/OR*	ALT FIELD CONTROL	16
15	K9 18LB/RD*	POWER GROUND	15
16	K9 18LB/RD*	POWER GROUND	15
17	N2 18BR*	AUTOMATIC IDLE SPEED MOTOR	16
18	N4 18YL/BK*	AUTOMATIC IDLE SPEED MOTOR	16
19	N1 18GY/RD*	AUTOMATIC IDLE SPEED MOTOR	16
20	N3 18VT/BK*	AUTOMATIC IDLE SPEED MOTOR	16
21	K13 20BK/RD*	CHARGE TEMP SENSOR	17
22	K7 18OR/DB*	THROTTLE POSITION SENSOR	16
23	N11 18BK/DG*	OXYGEN SENSOR	14
24	—	—	
25	—	—	
26	—	—	
27	—	—	
28	—	—	
29	D40 18WT/PK*	BRAKE SWITCH	18
30	S4 20BR/YL*	PARK/NEUTRAL SWITCH	16
31	DK20 20LG	SCI RECEIVE	15
32	—	—	
33	K16 20VT/YL*	INJECTOR CONTROL 1	16
34	K15 20YL	DWELL CONTROL	16
35	—	—	
36	Z6 20LB/BK*	FUEL MONITOR	14
37	—	—	
38	—	—	
39	—	—	
40	S6 20GY/YL*	EGR SOLENOID	14
41	J1 16RD	DIRECT BATTERY	15
42	—	—	
43	—	—	
44	—	—	
45	C20 18BR	A/C CLUTCH INPUT	15
46	—	—	
47	N7 18GY*	REFERENCE PICKUP	17
48	G7 20WT/OR*	VEH SPEED PICKUP	17
49	Y7 18TN/RD*	HIGH DATA RATE PICKUP	17
50	T21 20GY/LB*	TACH SIGNAL	17
51	DK21 20PK	SCI TRANSMIT	15
52	N6 18OR	8 VOLT INPUT	17
53	X36 20TN/RD*	SPEED CONTROL VAC	18
54	K1 20PK*	PURGE SOLENOID	14
55	U31 18OR/BK*	LOCK-UP T/C	18
56	N13 20DB/OR*	A/C HOT C/O	15
57	C27 20DB/PK*	RAD FAN RELAY	15
58	K19 20DB/YL*	ASD RELAY	15
59	K3 20BK/PK*	POWER LOSS LAMP	15
60	X35 20LG/RD*	SPEED CONTROL VENT	18

SHORT TAB

LONG TAB

CONNECTOR #1
VIEWED FROM WIRE
END OF CONNECTOR

(3.0 LITRE) SINGLE MODULE ENGINE
CONTROLLER-60 WAY

S-HK 71

CONNECTOR #2

CAV	IGNITION SYSTEM CIRCUITS		SHEET NO.
1	N6 18OR	8 VOLT OUTPUT	17
2	K5 16BK*	SIGNAL GROUND	14
3	K14 18DB*	FJ2 OUTPUT	15
4	J2 14DB	J2 INPUT	14
5	Y13 18YL/WT*	INJECTOR DRIVER 3	18
6	J9 16BK	POWER GROUND	15
7	J9 16BK	POWER GROUND	15
8	K16 20VT/YL*	INJECTOR CONTROL 1	16
9	Y11 18WT	INJECTOR DRIVER 1	18
10	Y12 18TN	INJECTOR DRIVER 2	18
11	R31 20DG/OR*	ALT FIELD CONTROL	16
12	J5 18BK/YL*	IGNITION COIL DRIVER	15
13	K15 20YL	DWELL CONTROL	16
14	R3 18DG	ALT FIELD DRIVER	18

(3.0 LITRE) SINGLE MODULE ENGINE
CONTROLLER-14 WAY

S-HK 72

ENGINE COMPARTMENT CIRCUITS		CAVITY
L1 12RD*	HEADLAMP SWITCH	1
V3 18BR*	WINDSHIELD WIPER MOTOR	2
B7 12RD/TN*	VAN CONVERSION	3
V4 18RD/YL*	WINDSHIELD WIPER MOTOR	4
L4 16VT*	HEADLAMP LOW BEAM	5
L3 16RD	RIGHT HEADLAMP	6
L3 16RD	LEFT HEADLAMP	
X30 20DB/RD*	SPEED CONTROL	7
X31 22BR/WT*	SPEED CONTROL	8
X33 20WT*	SPEED CONTROL	9
X32 20YL/RD*	60-WAY	10
	———	11
	———	12
	———	13
S4 18BR/YL*	LIFTGATE GROUND	14
	———	15
	———	16
G2 20VT	WATER TEMPERATURE SENDING UNIT	17
G6 20GY	OIL PRESSURE SWITCH	18
G60 20GY/YL*	OIL PRESSURE SENDING UNIT	19
G31 18OR/BK*	SHIFT INDICATOR LAMP	20
D6 18LG	LEFT TURN SIGNAL LAMP	21
D5 18TN	RIGHT TURN SIGNAL LAMP	22
A3 14PK	BATTERY-HAZARD FLASHER	23
Z1 14DG/BK*	FUEL PUMP FEED	24
S40 18BR/LB*	LIFTGATE RELEASE	25
L7 18BK/YL*	SPLICE-SIDEMARKER AND PARK	26
L7 18BK/YL*	AND TURN SIGNAL LAMPS	
B1 18WT	BACK-UP LAMP SWITCH	27
B2 18VT/BK*	BACK-UP LAMP SWITCH	28
V10 20BR	WINDSHIELD WASHER MOTOR	29
V11 20BK/TN*	LOW WASHER FLUID INDICATOR LEVEL SENSOR	30
S2 18YL	STARTER RELAY-IGNITION	31
H2 18DG/RD*	HORN	32
T21 20GY/LB*	TACHOMETER	33
P5 20BK	BRAKE WARNING LAMP SWITCH	34
V5 18DG	WINDSHIELD WIPER MOTOR	35
V6 18DB	WINDSHIELD WIPER MOTOR	36
C20 18DB/OR*	AIR CONDITIONING DAMPED PRESSURE SWITCH	37
K3 20BK/PK*	POWER LOSS	38
G31 20VT/LG*	AMBIENT TEMPERATURE SENSOR	39
G32 20BK/LB*	AMBIENT TEMPERATURE SENSOR	40
D40 18WT/PK*	60-WAY	41
G7 20WT/OR*	SPEED INDICATOR	42
	———	43
Z6 20LB/BK*	NOT USED	44
	———	45
	———	46
J2 14DB		47
J2 14DB	SPLICE-IGNITION RUN CIRCUIT	
C13 12BK/RD*	ELECTRICALLY HEATED REAR WINDOW	48
J1 12RD	IGNITION SWITCH	49
J10 12PK*	IGNITION SWITCH	50

■ (CAVITY 20 CIRCUIT FOR 2.5L ONLY)

S-HK 73   50 WAY BULKHEAD DISCONNECT

CAVITY		INSTRUMENT PANEL CIRCUITS	SHEET
1	L1 12RD/WT*	IGNITION SWITCH FEED (BATTERY FEED)	4, 24
2	V3 18BR/WT*	WINDSHIELD WIPER LOW SPEED FEED	38
3	B7 14RD/PK*	VAN CONVERSION (BATTERY SUPPLY)	3, 66
4	V4 18BR/WT*	WINDSHIELD WIPER HIGH SPEED FEED	38
5	L4 14VT*	HEADLAMP LOW BEAM	21, 24
6	L3 14RD/OR*	HEADLAMP HIGH BEAM	21, 24
	L3 16RD/OR*		
7	X30 20DB/RD*	SPEED CONTROL	8
8	X31 22BR/WT*	SPEED CONTROL	8, 13, 18
9	X33 22WT/RD*	SPEED CONTROL	8, 13, 18
10	X32 22YL/RD*	SPEED CONTROL	8, 13, 18
11		———	
12		———	
13		———	
14	S40 22BR/LB*	LIFTGATE GROUND	65
15		———	
16		———	
17	G20 22VT/YL*	TEMPERATURE SEND	19
18	G6 22GY	OIL PRESSURE LAMP	19
19	G60 22GY/YL*	OIL PRESSURE SEND	19
20	U3 22OR/LG*	UP-SHIFT LAMP	13, 33
21	D6 18LG	LEFT TURN SIGNAL LAMP	22, 40
	D6 18LG	LEFT TURN SIGNAL SWITCH	
22	D5 18TN	RIGHT TURN SIGNAL LAMP	21, 40
	D5 18TN	RIGHT TURN SIGNAL SWITCH	
23	A3 16PK/WT*	HAZARD FLASHER	3, 39
24	Z1 14DG/BK*	FUEL PUMP FEED	13, 18
25	S4 18BR/YL*	LIFTGATE RELEASE (A/TRANSMISSION)	5, 6, 25, 65
	S4 20BR/YL*		
26	L7 18BK/WT*	PARKING LAMPS	22, 24
27	B1 18WT	BACK-UP LAMP SWITCH FEED	6, 50, 51
28	B2 18VT/BK*	BACK-UP LAMP	5, 6, 33
29	V10 18BR	WINDSHIELD WASHER MOTOR	33, 37
30	V11 22BK/TN*	LOW WASHER FLUID	33, 37
31	S2 14YL	IGNITION START	6, 7
32	H2 18DG/RD*	HORNS	23
33	T21 22GY/LB*	TACHOMETER	12, 17, 33
34	P5 22GY/BK*	BRAKE WARNING LAMP	7
35	V5 18DG	WINDSHIELD WIPER SWITCH	38
36	V6 18DB	WINDSHIELD WIPER SWITCH	38
37	C20 22DB/OR*	AIR CONDITIONER LOW PRESSURE SWITCH	48, 49, 51
38	K3 22BK/PK*	POWER LOSS	11, 15, 33
39	G31 22VT/LG*	AMBIENT TEMPERATURE (OVERHEAD CONSOLE)	28
40	G32 22BK/LB*	AMBIENT TEMPERATURE (OVERHEAD CONSOLE)	28
41	D40 18WT/PK*	BRAKE SENSE	8, 13, 18
42	G7 22WT/OR*	SPEED SENSOR	12, 17, 65
43		———	
44		NOT USED	
45		———	
46		———	
47	J2 14DB	IGNITION RUN/START	3, 7, 10, 14
48	C13 12BK/RD*	HEATED REAR WINDOW	3, 56
49	J1 12RD	IGNITION SWITCH FEED	4, 7
50	J10 12PK/BK*	IGNITION SWITCH FEED	4, 7

50 WAY BULKHEAD DISCONNECT   S-HK 74

CAV	CIRCUIT	DESCRIPTION	
1	———	NOT USED	
2	H4 18BK	HORN GROUND	
3	H3 20BK/RD*	GROUND FROM HORN SWITCH	
4	D6 18LG	LEFT FRONT TURN SIGNAL	
5	D5 18TN	RIGHT FRONT TURN SIGNAL	
6	D32 18PK*	HAZARD FLASHER FEED	
7	D2 18RD/BK*	FEED FROM TURN SIGNAL FLASHER	
8	D8 18DG/RD*	LEFT REAR TURN SIGNAL	
9	D7 18BR/RD*	RIGHT REAR TURN SIGNAL	
10	D4 18WT	FEED FROM BRAKE SWITCH	
11	———	NOT USED	
12	V3 18BBR*	WINDSHIELD WIPER LOW SPEED	
13	V4 18RD/BK*	WINDSHIELD WIPER HIGH SPEED	
14	V5 18DG	WINDSHIELD WIPER MOTOR	
15	V1 18DB	WINDSHIELD WIPER SWITCH FEED	
16	V10 20BR	WINDSHIELD WASHER MOTOR	
17	H4 18BK	INTERMITTENT WIPE SWITCH GROUND	
18	H40 18BK/LG*	INTERMITTENT WIPE MODULE GROUND	
	H40 18BK/LG*	TO CHIME GROUND	
19	M26 20LB	KEY-IN BUZZER	
	M26 20LB	KEY-IN BUZZER	
20	M16 20BK/LB*	LEFT FRONT DOOR JAMB SWITCH GROUND	
21	———	NOT USED	
22	———	NOT USED	
23	———	NOT USED	
24	J15 20YL/RD*	IGNITION KEY LAMP FEED	
	J15 20YL/RD*	IGNITION KEY LAMP FEED	
25	H4 18BK	IGNITION KEY LAMP GROUND	

VIEWED FROM WIRE SIDE OF 25 WAY CONNECTOR

(MOUNTED ON INSTRU-PANEL LEFT OF STEERING COLUMN)

INSTRUMENT PANEL TO STEERING COLUMN WIRING

S-HK 75

VIEWED FROM TERMINAL END OF CONNECTORS   STRG COLUMN

CAV	CIRCUIT	DESCRIPTION	SHEET
1		NOT USED	—
2	H4 18BK	HORN GROUND	23
3	H3 18BK/RD*	HORN SWITCH GROUND	23
4	D6 18LG	LEFT FRONT TURN SIGNAL	40
5	D5 18TN	RIGHT FRONT TURN SIGNAL	40
6	D32 18PK	HAZARD FLASHER FEED	39
7	D2 18RD	TURN SIGNAL FLASHER FEED	39
8	D8 18DG/RD*	LEFT REAR TURN SIGNAL	40
9	D7 18BR/RD*	RIGHT REAR TURN SIGNAL	40
10	D4 16WT	BRAKE SWITCH FEED	8, 39

TURN SIGNAL SWITCH CONNECTOR

11	———	NOT USED	—
12	V3 18BR*	INTERMITTENT WIPE MODULE	37
	V3 18BR*	WINDSHIELD WIPER LOW SPEED	37
13	V4 18RD	WINDSHIELD WIPER HIGH SPEED	37
14	V5 18DG	INTERMITTENT WIPE MODULE	37
	V5 18DG	WINDSHIELD WIPER MOTOR	
15	V1 18DB	WINDSHIELD WIPER SWITCH FEED	37
16	V10 18BR	INTERMITTENT WIPE MODULE	33, 37
	V10 18BR	WINDSHIELD WASHER MOTOR	
17	H4 18BK	INTERMITTENT WIPE SWITCH GROUND	37
18	H40 18BK/LG*	INTERMITTENT WIPE MODULE GROUND	38

WINDSHIELD WIPER SWITCH CONNECTOR

19	M26 20LB	KEY-IN BUZZER	32
20	M16 20BK/LB*	LEFT FRONT DOOR JAMB SWITCH GROUND	32

KEY-IN BUZZER SWITCH CONNECTOR

21	———	NOT USED	—
22	———	NOT USED	—
23	———	NOT USED	—

24	J15 18YL	IGNITION KEY LAMP FEED	32
25	H4 18BK	IGNITION KEY LAMP GROUND	32

IGNITION KEY LAMP SWITCH CONNECTOR

(PLUGGED INTO STEERING COLUMN 25 WAY CONNECTOR)

STEERING COLUMN SWITCH TO PANEL WIRING

S-HK 76

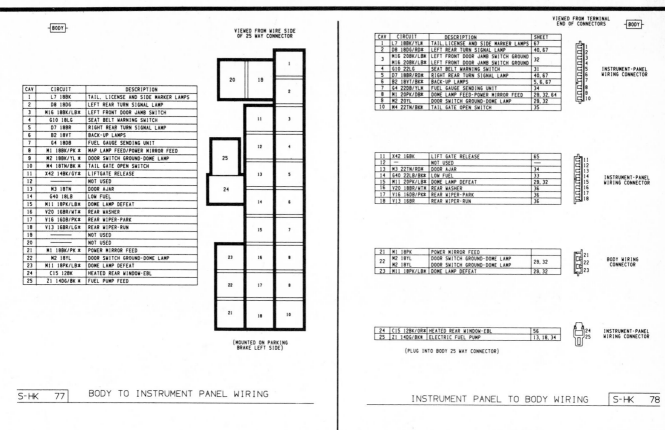

-[BODY]-

VIEWED FROM WIRE SIDE
OF 25 WAY CONNECTOR

CAV	CIRCUIT	DESCRIPTION
1	L7 18BK	TAIL, LICENSE AND SIDE MARKER LAMPS
2	D8 18DG	LEFT REAR TURN SIGNAL LAMP
3	M16 18BK/LB*	LEFT FRONT DOOR JAMB SWITCH
4	G10 18LG	SEAT BELT WARNING SWITCH
5	D7 18BR	RIGHT REAR TURN SIGNAL LAMP
6	B2 18VT	BACK-UP LAMPS
7	G4 18DB	FUEL GAUGE SENDING UNIT
8	M1 18BK/PK *	MAP LAMP FEED/POWER MIRROR FEED
9	M2 18BK/YL*	DOOR SWITCH GROUND-DOME LAMP
10	M4 18TN/BK *	TAIL GATE OPEN SWITCH
11	X42 14BK/GY*	LIFTGATE RELEASE
12	———	NOT USED
13	M3 18TN	DOOR AJAR
14	G40 18LB	LOW FUEL
15	M11 18PK/LB*	DOME LAMP DEFEAT
16	V20 16BR/WT*	REAR WASHER
17	V16 16DB/PK*	REAR WIPER-PARK
18	V13 16BR/LG*	REAR WIPER-RUN
19	———	NOT USED
20	———	NOT USED
21	M1 18BK/PK *	POWER MIRROR FEED
22	M2 18YL	DOOR SWITCH GROUND-DOME LAMP
23	M11 18PK/LB*	DOME LAMP DEFEAT
24	C15 12BK	HEATED REAR WINDOW-EBL
25	Z1 14DG/BK*	FUEL PUMP FEED

(MOUNTED ON PARKING
BRAKE LEFT SIDE)

VIEWED FROM TERMINAL
END OF CONNECTORS   -[BODY]-

CAV	CIRCUIT	DESCRIPTION	SHEET
1	L7 18BK/YL*	TAIL,LICENSE AND SIDE MARKER LAMPS	67
2	D8 18DG/RD*	LEFT REAR TURN SIGNAL LAMP	40,67
3	M16 20BK/LB*	LEFT FRONT DOOR JAMB SWITCH GROUND	32
	M16 20BK/LB*	LEFT FRONT DOOR JAMB SWITCH GROUND	32
4	G10 22LG	SEAT BELT WARNING SWITCH	31
5	D7 18BR/RD*	RIGHT REAR TURN SIGNAL LAMP	40,67
6	B2 18VT/BK*	BACK-UP LAMPS	5,6,67
7	G4 22DB/YL*	FUEL GAUGE SENDING UNIT	34
8	M1 20PK/DB*	DOME LAMP FEED-POWER MIRROR FEED	28,32,64
9	M2 20YL	DOOR SWITCH GROUND-DOME LAMP	28,32
10	M4 22TN/BK*	TAIL GATE OPEN SWITCH	35

INSTRUMENT-PANEL
WIRING CONNECTOR

11	X42 16BK	LIFT GATE RELEASE	65
12	———	NOT USED	—
13	M3 22TN/RD*	DOOR AJAR	34
14	G40 22LB/BK*	LOW FUEL	33
15	M11 20PK/LB*	DOME LAMP DEFEAT	28,32
16	V20 18BR/WT*	REAR WASHER	36
17	V16 16DB/PK*	REAR WIPER-PARK	36
18	V13 16BR	REAR WIPER-RUN	36

INSTRUMENT-PANEL
WIRING CONNECTOR

21	M1 18PK	POWER MIRROR FEED	
22	M2 18YL	DOOR SWITCH GROUND-DOME LAMP	28,32
	M2 18YL	DOOR SWITCH GROUND-DOME LAMP	
23	M11 18PK/LB*	DOME LAMP DEFEAT	28,32

BODY WIRING
CONNECTOR

24	C15 12BK/OR*	HEATED REAR WINDOW-EBL	56
25	Z1 14DG/BK*	ELECTRIC FUEL PUMP	13,18,34

INSTRUMENT-PANEL
WIRING CONNECTOR

(PLUG INTO BODY 25 WAY CONNECTOR)

S-HK 77	BODY TO INSTRUMENT PANEL WIRING

INSTRUMENT PANEL TO BODY WIRING | S-HK 78 |

DOME LAMPS-M1 20PK/DB* ———
BATTERY FEED-C13 12BK/RD* ———
REAR A/C SWITCH LAMP — E2 22OR ——
INSTRUMENT PANEL LAMPS — E2 20OR
                          E1 18TN

TURN SIGNAL   D1 18BK ——
FLASHER   D2 18RD/BK* ——

                  J15 20YL/RD* ——
IGNITION TIME   M2 20YL ——
DELAY RELAY   M11 20PK/LB* ——

POWER DOOR LOCKS AND
SEAT-W5 12RD
                  X1 16RD ——
HORN RELAY   H3 18BK/RD* ——
                  H2 18DG/RD* ——

HEATER OR A/C FEED-C1 12BR ——
POWER WINDOWS-W1 12TN ——
                  X1 16RD ——
                  X1 16RD ——

V6 18DB-WINDSHIELD WIPER MOTOR
V1 18DB-WINDSHIELD WIPER SWITCH FEED
V16 16DB/PK*-ELECTRONIC MODULE
         RR WASH-WIPE SYSTEM
V16 16DB/PK*-LIFTGATE RELEASE RELAY
G5 20DB/WT*-GAUGES,CHIMES

J2 14DB-IGNITION RUN FEED
J2 14DB-IGNITION RUN FEED

D1 20BK/WT*-VAN CONVERSION RELAY
D1 18BK-TURN SIGNALS
X12 20RD/WT*-RADIO
Q2 14BK-IGNITION AACC FEED
D3 18PK-STOP LAMPS
D3 18PK-CHIME
L8 18PK/RD*-TAIL LAMPS
L1 12RD/WT*-BATTERY FEED
A3 16PK/WT* ——
D31 18BK/WT*——HAZARD FLASHER

O20 12BK/RD*- IGNITION RUN TO FEED
B1 16WT-REAR HEATER SWITCH

X1 16RD——HORNS AND CIGAR LIGHTER FEED

FRONT OF FUSEBLOCK

FUSE #	AMPS	COLOR	SHEET #
1	20	YELLOW	1,38
2	20	YELLOW	2,7,28,50,51,53,56
3	30	CIRCUIT BREAKER (POWER WINDOW) OPTION	2,7,57,59
4	30	LIGHT GREEN	2,7,47-48
5	20	YELLOW	1,24
6	20	YELLOW	1,8,31,40
7	25	NATURAL	1,24,31,45
8	30	CIRCUIT BREAKER (POWER DOOR LOCKS OR SEAT) OPTION	1,57,59,61
9	10	RED	2,7,45
10	20	YELLOW	2,39,66
11	20	YELLOW	2,7,38
12	4	PINK	1,25,28,35,45,53,55,56
13	5	TAN	2,3,8,10
14	20	YELLOW	2,3,8,35,65
15	10	RED	2,3,26,32-45,56,64
16	BLANK		

S-HK 79	FUSEBLOCK MODULE AND RELAY BANK

1988 Caravan/Voyager

S-HK 1 — FUSE APPLICATION CHART

FUSE APPLICATION CHART — S-HK 2

S-HK 3 — CHARGING SYSTEM

CHARGING SYSTEM — S-HK 4

1989 Caravan/Voyager

S-HK 5 — STARTER SYSTEM 2.5L ENGINE

STARTER SYSTEM 3.0L ENGINE — S-HK 6

S-HK 7 — STARTER SYSTEM 3.0L ENGINE WITH ELECTRONIC TRANSAXLE

IGNITION SWITCH — S-HK 8

1989 Caravan/Voyager

ELECTRONIC FUEL INJECTION
IGNITION SYSTEM (2.5L ENGINE)

S-HK 9

ELECTRONIC FUEL INJECTION
IGNITION SYSTEM (2.5L ENGINE)

S-HK 10

ELECTRONIC FUEL INJECTION
IGNITION SYSTEM (2.5L ENGINE)

S-HK 11

ELECTRONIC FUEL INJECTION
IGNITION SYSTEM (2.5L ENGINE)

S-HK 12

1989 Caravan/Voyager

ELECTRONIC FUEL INJECTION
IGNITION SYSTEM (2.5L ENGINE)

S-HK 13

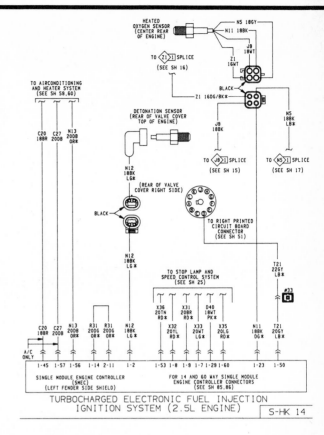

TURBOCHARGED ELECTRONIC FUEL INJECTION
IGNITION SYSTEM (2.5L ENGINE)

S-HK 14

TURBOCHARGED ELECTRONIC FUEL INJECTION
IGNITION SYSTEM (2.5L ENGINE)

S-HK 15

TURBOCHARGED ELECTRONIC FUEL INJECTION
IGNITION SYSTEM(2.5L ENGINE)

S-HK 16

1989 Caravan/Voyager

SINGLE MODULE ENGINE CONTROLLER
(SMEC)
(LEFT FENDER SIDE SHIELD)

FOR 14 AND 60 WAY SINGLE MODULE
ENGINE CONTROLLER CONNECTORS
(SEE SH 85,86)

TURBOCHARGED ELECTRONIC FUEL INJECTION
IGNITION SYSTEM (2.5L ENGINE)

S-HK 17

SINGLE MODULE ENGINE CONTROLLER
(SMEC)
(LEFT FENDER SIDE SHIELD)

FOR 14 AND 60 WAY SINGLE MODULE
ENGINE CONTROLLER CONNECTORS
(SEE SH 85,86)

TURBOCHARGED ELECTRONIC FUEL INJECTION
IGNITION SYSTEM (2.5L ENGINE)

S-HK 18

SINGLE MODULE ENGINE CONTROLLER
(SMEC)
(LEFT FENDER SIDE SHIELD)

FOR SINGLE MODULE ENGINE CONTROLLER
CONNECTORS
(SEE PG 87,88)

ELECTRONIC FUEL INJECTION
IGNITION SYSTEM 3.0L ENGINE

S-HK 19

SINGLE MODULE ENGINE CONTROLLER
(SMEC)
(LEFT FENDER SIDE SHIELD)

FOR SINGLE MODULE ENGINE CONTROLLER
CONNECTORS
(SEE PG 87,88)

ELECTRONIC FUEL INJECTION
IGNITION SYSTEM 3.0L ENGINE

S-HK 20

1989 Caravan/Voyager

| S-HK 21 | ELECTRONIC FUEL INJECTION IGNITION SYSTEM 3.0L ENGINE | |

| | ELECTRONIC FUEL INJECTION IGNITION SYSTEM 3.0 L ENGINE | S-HK 22 |

| S-HK 23 | ELECTRONIC FUEL INJECTION IGNITION SYSTEM 3.0 L ENGINE | |

| | OIL PRESSURE AND TEMPERATURE SYSTEM (2.5 & 3.0 LITRE) | S-HK 24 |

1989 Caravan/Voyager

S-HK 25 | SPEED CONTROL AND STOP LAMP SWITCH

UNDERHOOD LAMP | S-HK 26

S-HK 27 | FRONT END LIGHTING

FRONT END LIGHTING | S-HK 28

1989 Caravan/Voyager

S-HK 29 | HORN SYSTEM

HEADLAMP SWITCH | S-HK 30

S-HK 31 | HEADLAMP SWITCH CONTROLLED INTERIOR LAMPS

CONSOLE LAMPS | S-HK 32

1989 Caravan/Voyager

S-HK 33 | OVERHEAD CONSOLE LAMPS

OVERHEAD CONSOLE LAMPS | S-HK 34

S-HK 35 | DOME AND BODY COURTESY LAMPS

DOME AND BODY COURTESY LAMPS | S-HK 36

1989 Caravan/Voyager

S-HK 37 | SEAT BELT WARNING SYSTEM

DOME AND COURTESY LAMPS | S-HK 38

S-HK 39 | WARNING LAMP MODULE SYSTEM

WARNING LAMP MODULE SYSTEM | S-HK 40

1989 Caravan/Voyager

S-HK 41 | STOP/TURN AND HAZARD FLASHER SYSTEM

STOP/TURN AND HAZARD FLASHER SYSTEM | S-HK 42

S-HK 43 | INTERMITTENT WIPER SYSTEM

INTERMITTENT WIPER SYSTEM | S-HK 44

1989 Caravan/Voyager

| S-HK 45 | LIFTGATE AJAR WARNING AND LIFTGATE WIPER AND WASHER SYSTEM |

| LIFTGATE WIPER AND WASHER SYSTEM | S-HK 46 |

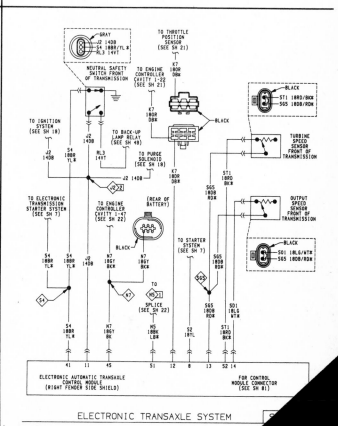

| S-HK 47 | ELECTRONIC TRANSAXLE SYSTEM |

| ELECTRONIC TRANSAXLE SYSTEM |

1989 Caravan/Voyager

ELECTRONIC VEHICLE INFORMATION CENTER
ENGINE COMPARTMENT SENSORS

S-HK 49

WARNING LIGHT MODULE
PRINTED CIRCUIT BOARD

WARNING LIGHT MODULE
PRINTED CIRCUIT BOARD CONNECTOR

S-HK 50

IT BOARD CONNECTORS

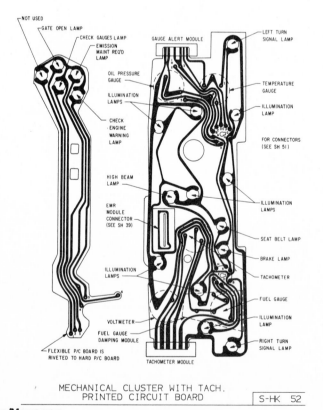

MECHANICAL CLUSTER WITH TACH.
PRINTED CIRCUIT BOARD

S-HK 52

1989 Caravan/Voyager

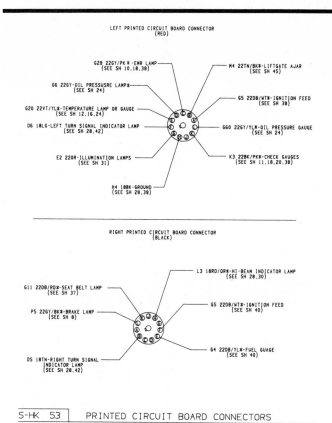

LEFT PRINTED CIRCUIT BOARD CONNECTOR (RED)

G28 22GY/PK✳-EMR LAMP (SEE SH 10,18,39)
M4 22TN/BK✳-LIFTGATE AJAR (SEE SH 45)
G6 22GY-OIL PRESSURE LAMP✳ (SEE SH 24)
G5 22DB/WT✳-IGNITION FEED (SEE SH 39)
G20 22VT/YL✳-TEMPERATURE LAMP OR GAUGE (SEE SH 12,16,24)
G60 22GY/YL✳-OIL PRESSURE GAUGE (SEE SH 24)
D6 18LG-LEFT TURN SIGNAL INDICATOR LAMP (SEE SH 28,42)
E2 220R-ILLUMINATION LAMPS (SEE SH 31)
K3 22BK/PK✳-CHECK GAUGES (SEE SH 11,18,20,39)
H4 18BK-GROUND (SEE SH 28,39)

RIGHT PRINTED CIRCUIT BOARD CONNECTOR (BLACK)

G11 22DB/RD✳-SEAT BELT LAMP (SEE SH 37)
L3 18RD/OR✳-HI-BEAM INDICATOR LAMP (SEE SH 28,30)
P5 22GY/BK✳-BRAKE LAMP (SEE SH 8)
G5 22DB/WT✳-IGNITION FEED (SEE SH 40)
G4 22DB/YL✳-FUEL GUAGE (SEE SH 40)
D5 18TN-RIGHT TURN SIGNAL INDICATOR LAMP (SEE SH 28,42)

| S-HK 53 | PRINTED CIRCUIT BOARD CONNECTORS |

EMISSION MAINT REQ'D LAMP
LEFT TURN SIGNAL LAMP
OIL PRESSURE LAMP
TEMPERATURE LAMP
ILLUMINATION LAMPS
CHECK GAUGES LAMP
ILLUMINATION LAMPS
FUEL GAUGE
HIGH BEAM LAMP
GATE OPEN LAMP
EMR MODULE CONNECTOR (SEE SH 39)
BRAKE LAMP
FUEL GAUGE DAMPING MODULE
ILLUMINATION LAMPS
ILLUMINATION LAMP
VOLTMETER
SEAT BELT LAMP
RIGHT TURN SIGNAL LAMP
FLEXIBLE P/C BOARD IS RIVETED TO HARD P/C BOARD

MECHANICAL CLUSTER W/O TACH.
PRINTED CIRCUIT BOARD

| S-HK 54 |

| S-HK 55 | ELECTRONICALLY TUNED RADIOS |

ELECTRONICALLY TUNED RADIOS

| S-HK 56 |

1989 Caravan/Voyager

S-HK 57 | HEATER SYSTEM 2.5L AND 3.0L ENGINE

RADIATOR FAN SYSTEM WITH HEATER
2.5L & 3.0L ENGINE | S-HK 58

S-HK 59 | AIR CONDITIONING SYSTEM 2.5L ENGINE

AIR CONDITIONING SYSTEM 2.5L ENGINE | S-HK 60

1989 Caravan/Voyager

S-HK 61 | AIR CONDITIONING SYSTEM 3.0L ENGINE

AIR CONDITIONING SYSTEM 3.0L ENGINE | S-HK 62

S-HK 63 | REAR HEATER AND A/C SYSTEM

REAR HEATER AND A/C SYSTEM | S-HK 64

1989 Caravan/Voyager

S-HK 65 — REAR HEATER-ONLY

REAR WINDOW DEFOGGER — S-HK 66

S-HK 67 — POWER WINDOW LIFT SYSTEM

LEFT DOOR			
B+ POLARITY	B- POLARITY	SWITCH SECTION	WINDOW AND MOVEMENT
LB	WT	1	LEFT FRONT UP
WT	LB	1	LEFT FRONT DOWN
PK/WT*	VT	2	RIGHT FRONT UP
VT	PK/RD*	2	RIGHT FRONT DOWN
TN	BK		SWITCH FEED AND GROUND

POWER WINDOW LIFT SYSTEM — S-HK 68

RIGHT DOOR			
B+ POLARITY	B- POLARITY	SWITCH SECTION	WINDOW AND MOVEMENT
WT	LB		DOWN-FROM DOOR SWITCH
LB	WT		UP-FROM DOOR SWITCH
VT	PK/WT*		DOWN-FROM MASTER SWITCH
PK/WT*	VT		UP-FROM MASTER SWITCH
TN	-		FEED

1989 Caravan/Voyager

S-HK 69   POWER REAR QUARTER WINDOW

POWER REAR QUARTER WINDOW
AND POWER SUN ROOF   S-HK 70

S-HK 71   POWER SEAT SYSTEM

MOTOR INSULATOR POLARITY		
+POLARITY	-POLARITY	SEAT MOVEMENT
YL/BL*	RD/BL*	FORWARD
RD/BL*	YL/BL*	REARWARD
YL/WT*	RD/WT*	REAR UP
RD/WT*	YL/WT*	REAR DOWN
YL/GN*	RD/GN*	FRONT UP
RD/GN*	YL/GN*	FRONT DOWN
BK/RD*	—	FEED
—	BK	GROUND

POWER SEAT SYSTEM   S-HK 72

1989 Caravan/Voyager

6–121

S-HK 73 — DOOR LOCK SYSTEM

DOOR LOCK SYSTEM — S-HK 74

S-HK 75 — POWER REMOTE MIRRORS

POWER REMOTE MIRRORS — S-HK 76

1989 Caravan/Voyager

| S-HK 77 | LIFTGATE RELEASE | | VAN CONVERSION WIRING | S-HK 78 |

| S-HK 79 | REAR LIGHTING & TRAILER TOW | | REAR LIGHTING & TRAILER TOW | S-HK 80 |

1989 Caravan/Voyager

SHORT TAB

LONG TAB

CONNECTOR #2
VIEWED FROM WIRE
END OF CONNECTOR

CAV	WIRE CODE	IGNITION SYSTEM CIRCUITS	SHEET
1	RL2 16LG*	PRINDIAL SWITCH	47
2	RL1 14TN/BK*	BACK UP LIGHT RELAY	49
3	RL3 14VT	BACK UP LIGHT RELAY	49
4	MX2 20WT/BK*	CCD BUS (—)	49
5	MX1 20BK/VT	CCD BUS (+)	49
6	—		—
7	—		—
8	S2 18YL	STARTER RELAY	48
9	GP3 18BK/LG*	TRANS. SOLENOIDS & PRESSURE SWITCH	47
10	—		—
11	J2 14DB	NEUTRAL SAFETY SWITCH	48
12	K7 18OR/DB*	(SMEC) SINGLE MODULE CONTROLLER	48
13	SG5 18DB/RD*	OUTPUT & TURBINE SPEED SENSOR	48
14	SO1 18LG/WT*	OUTPUT SPEED SENSOR	48
15	SA1 18LG	SAFETY SHUTDOWN RELAY	47
16	SF1 16RD	TRANS. SOLENOIDS & PRESSURE SWITCH	47
17	SF1 16RD	SAFETY SHUTDOWN RELAY	47
18	—		—
19	SC2 18WT/DB*	TRANS. SOLENOIDS & PRESSURE SWITCH	47
20	SC1 18LB	TRANS. SOLENOIDS & PRESSURE SWITCH	47
21	—		—
22	—		—
23	—		—
24	—		—
25	—		—
26	—		—
27	—		—
28	—		—
29	—		—
30	—		—
31	—		—
32	—		—
33	—		—
34	—		—
35	—		—
36	—		—
37	—		—
38	—		—
39	—		—
40	—		—
41	S4 18BR/YL*	NEUTRAL SAFETY SWITCH	48
42	NS2 18VT*	PRINDIAL SWITCH	47
43	MX1 20BK/VT*	CCD BUS (+)	49
44	MX2 20WT/BK*	CCD BUS (—)	49
45	N7 18GY/BK*	DISTRIBUTOR	48
46	—		—
47	GP2 18YL/BK*	TRANS. SOLENOIDS & PRESSURE SWITCH	47
48	—		—
49	—		—
50	GP1 18DG	TRANS. SOLENOIDS & PRESSURE SWITCH	47
51	N5 18BK/LB*	SIGNAL GROUND	48
52	ST1 18RD/BK*	TURBINE SPEED SENSOR	48
53	N51 18BK/YL*	SIGNAL GROUND	47
54	N51 18BK/YL*	SIGNAL GROUND	47
55	—		—
56	J11 16RD*	DIRECT BATTERY FEED	47
57	J81 18BK	SIGNAL GROUND	47
58	J81 18BK	SIGNAL GROUND	47
59	SC3 18BK/YL*	TRANS. SOLENOIDS & PRESSURE SWITCH	47
60	SC4 18BK	TRANS. SOLENOIDS & PRESSURE SWITCH	47

ELECTRONIC AUTOMATIC
S-HK 81 | TRANSAXLE CONTROL MODULE CONNECTOR

CAV	CIRCUIT	FUNCTION	SHEET
1	SC1 18LB	LOW REV SOLENOID	47
2	SC4 18BR	OVERDRIVE SOLENOID	47
3	SC2 18WT/DB*	LOW REV SOLENOID	47
4	SC3 18PK/YL*	LOW REV SOLENOID	47
5	GP2 18YL/BK*	PRESSURE SWITCH	47
6	SF1 16RD	SWITCHED BATTERY	47
7	GP1 18DG	PRESSURE SWITCH	47
8	GP3 18BK/LG*	PRESSURE SWITCH	47

TRANSAXLE SOLENOID CONNECTOR | S-HK 82

SHORT TAB

LONG TAB

CONNECTOR #1
VIEWED FROM WIRE
END OF CONNECTOR

CAV		IGNITION SYSTEM CIRCUITS	SHEET NO.
1	K4 20DG/RD*	MAP SENSOR	10
2	—		—
3	K10 20TN/WT*	COOLANT SENSOR	12
4	N5 18BK/LB*	SENSOR RETURN	12
5	K5 16BK/WT*	SIGNAL GROUND	9
6	MX1 20BK/VT*	CCD BUS (+)	49
7	X33 20WT/LG*	S/C RESUME	13,25
8	X32 20YL/RD*	S/C ON/OFF	13,25
9	X31 20BR/RD*	S/C SET	13,25
10	B1 18WT	B1 VOLTAGE SENSE	13
11	—		—
12	K14 18DB*	FJ2	11
13	K8 20VT/WT*	5 VOLT SUPPLY	10
14	R31 20DG/OR*	ALT FIELD CONTROL	10
15	K9 18LB/RD*	POWER GROUND	11
16	K9 18LB/RD*	POWER GROUND	11
17	N2 18BR/WT*	AUTOMATIC IDLE SPEED MOTOR	9
18	N4 18YL/BK*	AUTOMATIC IDLE SPEED MOTOR	9
19	N1 18GY/RD*	AUTOMATIC IDLE SPEED MOTOR	9
20	N3 18VT/BK*	AUTOMATIC IDLE SPEED MOTOR	9
21	K13 18BK/RD*	T/B TEMP SENSOR	9
22	K7 18OR/DB*	THROTTLE POSITION SENSOR	9
23	N11 18BK/DG*	OXYGEN SENSOR	9
24	—		—
25	—		—
26	—		—
27	—		—
28	—		—
29	D40 18WT/PK*	BRAKE SWITCH	13,25
30	S4 20BR/YL*	PARK/NEUTRAL SWITCH	12
31	DK20 20LG	SCI RECEIVE	11
32	—		—
33	K16 20VT/YL*	INJECTOR CONTROL 1	10
34	K15 20YL	DWELL CONTROL	10
35	—		—
36	—		—
37	G29 20GY/PK	EMISS MAINT REMAINDER LAMP	10
38	—		—
39	—		—
40	S6 20GY/YL*	EGR SOLENOID	10
41	J11 16RD	DIRECT BATTERY	11
42	—		—
43	—		—
44	—		—
45	C20 18BR	A/C CLUTCH INPUT	11
46	MX2 20WT/BK*	CCD BUS (—)	49
47	N7 18GY/BK*	REFERENCE PICKUP	12
48	G7 20WT/OR*	VEH SPEED PICKUP	12
49	—		—
50	T21 22GY/LB*	TACH SIGNAL	13
51	DK21 20PK	SCI TRANSMIT	11
52	N6 18OR	8 VOLT INPUT	12
53	X36 20TN/RD*	SPEED CONTROL VAC	13,25
54	K1 20PK/BK*	PURGE SOLENOID	10
55	U3 20OR/BK*	SIL	13
56	N13 20DB/PK*	A/C HOT C/O	11
57	C27 20DB/PK*	RAD FAN RELAY	11
58	DK19 20DB/YL*	ASD RELAY	11
59	K3 20BK/PK*	POWER LOSS LAMP	11
60	X35 20LG/RD*	SPEED CONTROL VENT	13,25

SINGLE MODULE ENGINE
S-HK 83 | CONTROLLER-60 WAY 2.5L EFI ENGINE

CONNECTOR #2

CAV		IGNITION SYSTEM CIRCUITS	SHEET NO.
1	N6 18OR	8 VOLT OUTPUT	12
2	K5 16BK*	SIGNAL GROUND	9
3	K14 18DB*	FJ2 OUTPUT	11
4	J2 14DB	J2 INPUT	10
5	—		—
6	J9 16BK	POWER GROUND	11
7	J9 16BK	POWER GROUND	11
8	K16 20VT/YL*	INJECTOR CONTROL 1	10
9	Y11 18WT/DB*	INJECTOR DRIVER 1	13
10	—		—
11	R31 20DG/OR*	ALT FIELD CONTROL	10
12	J5 18BK/GY*	IGNITION COIL DRIVER	11
13	K15 20YL	DWELL CONTROL	10
14	R3 18DG	ALT FIELD DRIVER	13

SINGLE MODULE ENGINE CONTROLLER-14 WAY
2.5L EFI ENGINE | S-HK 84

1989 Caravan/Voyager

CAV	IGNITION SYSTEM CIRCUITS		SHEET NO.
1	K4 18DG/RD*	MAP SENSOR	17
2	N12 18BK/LG	KNOCK SENSOR	14
3	K10 20TN/WT*	COOLANT SENSOR	16
4	N5 18BK/LB*	SENSOR RETURN	17
5	K5 16BK/WT*	SIGNAL GROUND	15
6	MX1 20BK/VT*	CCD BUS (+)	49
7	X33 20WT/LG*	S/C RESUME	14,25
8	X32 20YL/RD*	S/C ON/OFF	14,25
9	X31 20BR/RD*	S/C SET	14,25
10	B1 18WT	VOLTAGE SENSOR	16
11	—	—	—
12	K14 18DB/WT*	FJ2	16
13	K8 18VT/WT*	5 VOLT SUPPLY	18
14	R31 20DG/OR*	ALT FIELD CONTROL	14
15	K9 18LB/RD*	POWER GROUND	15
16	K9 18LB/RD*	POWER GROUND	15
17	N2 18BR/WT*	AUTOMATIC IDLE SPEED MOTOR	18
18	N4 18YL/BK*	AUTOMATIC IDLE SPEED MOTOR	18
19	N1 18GY/WT*	AUTOMATIC IDLE SPEED MOTOR	18
20	N3 18VT/BK*	AUTOMATIC IDLE SPEED MOTOR	18
21	—	—	—
22	K7 18OR/DB*	THROTTLE POSITION SENSOR	18
23	N11 18BK/DG*	OXYGEN SENSOR	14
24	—	—	—
25	—	—	—
26	Y7 18TN/YL*	FUEL SYNC PICK-UP	16
27	—	—	—
28	—	—	—
29	D40 18WT/PK*	BRAKE SWITCH	14,25
30	S4 20BR/YL*	PARK/NEUTRAL SWITCH	17
31	DK20 20LG	SCI RECEIVE	16
32	Y1 20GY/WT	INJECTOR CONTROL #2	18
33	K16 20VT/YL*	INJECTOR CONTROL #1	18
34	K15 20YL	DWELL CONTROL	18
35	—	—	—
36	—	—	—
37	G29 20GY/PK	EMISS MAINT REMINDER LAMP	18
38	Y4 20LB	BARO READ	15
39	Y6 20GY/BK*	WASTE GATE SOLENOID	15
40	—	—	—
41	J11 16RD	DIRECT BATTERY	15
42	—	—	—
43	—	—	—
44	—	—	—
45	C20 18BR	A/C CLUTCH INPUT	14
46	MX2 20WT/BK*	CCD BUS (—)	49
47	N7 18GY/BK*	REFERENCE PICKUP	16
48	G7 20WT/OR*	VEH SPEED PICKUP	17
49	—	—	—
50	T21 20GY/LB*	TACH SIGNAL	14
51	DK21 20PK	SCI TRANSMIT	16
52	N6 18OR	8 VOLT INPUT	16
53	X36 20TN/RD*	SPEED CONTROL VAC	14,25
54	K1 20PK/BK*	PURGE SOLENOID	15
55	U3 10OR/BK*	SHIFT INDICATOR LAMP	15
56	N13 20DB/OR*	A/C HOT C/O	14
57	C27 20DB	RAD FAN RELAY	14
58	DK19 20DB/YL*	ASD RELAY	16
59	K3 20BK/PK*	POWER LOSS LAMP	18
60	X35 20LG/RD*	SPEED CONTROL VENT	14,25

SINGLE MODULE ENGINE CONTROLLER-60 WAY 2.5L TURBO ENGINE | S-HK 85

CONNECTOR #2

CAV	IGNITION SYSTEM CIRCUITS		SHEET NO.
1	N6 18OR	8 VOLT OUTPUT	16
2	K5 16BK*	SIGNAL GROUND	15
3	K14 18DB*	FJ2 OUTPUT	16
4	J2 14DB	J2 INPUT	16
5	Y1 20GY/WT*	INJECTOR CONTROL 2	18
6	J9 16BK	POWER GROUND	15
7	J9 16BK	POWER GROUND	15
8	K16 20VT/YL*	INJECTOR CONTROL 1	18
9	Y11 18WT/DB*	INJECTOR DRIVER 1	16
10	Y12 18TN	INJECTOR DRIVER 2	16
11	R31 20DG/OR*	ALT FIELD CONTROL	14
12	J5 18BK/GY*	IGNITION COIL DRIVER	16
13	K15 20YL	DWELL CONTROL	16
14	R3 18DG	ALT FIELD DRIVER	16

SINGLE MODULE ENGINE CONTROLLER-14 WAY 2.5L TURBO ENGINE | S-HK 86

CAV	IGNITION SYSTEM CIRCUITS		SHEET NO.
1	K4 20DG/RD*	MAP SENSOR	21
2	—	—	—
3	K10 20TN/WT*	COOLANT SENSOR	22
4	N5 18BK/LB*	SENSOR RETURN	22
5	K5 16BK/WT*	SIGNAL GROUND	19
* 6	MX1 20BK/VT*	CCD BUS (+)	49
7	X33 20WT/LG*	S/C RESUME	23,25
8	X32 20YL/RD*	S/C ON/OFF	23,25
9	X31 20BR/RD*	S/C SET	23,25
10	Z1 16DG/BK*	SENSE	23
11	—	—	—
12	K14 18DB/WT*	FJ2	20
13	K8 20VT/WT*	5 VOLT SUPPLY	21
14	R31 20DG/OR*	ALT FIELD CONTROL	21
15	K9 18LB/RD*	POWER GROUND	20
16	K9 18LB/RD*	POWER GROUND	20
17	N2 18BR/WT*	AUTOMATIC IDLE SPEED MOTOR	21
18	N4 18YL/BK*	AUTOMATIC IDLE SPEED MOTOR	21
19	N1 18GY/WT*	AUTOMATIC IDLE SPEED MOTOR	21
20	N3 18VT/BK*	AUTOMATIC IDLE SPEED MOTOR	21
21	—	—	—
22	K7 18OR/DB*	THROTTLE POSITION SENSOR	21
23	N11 18BK/DG*	OXYGEN SENSOR	19
24	—	—	—
25	—	—	—
26	—	—	—
27	—	—	—
28	—	—	—
29	D40 18WT/PK*	BRAKE SWITCH	23,25
30	S4 20BR/YL*	PARK/NEUTRAL SWITCH	21
31	DK20 20LG	SCI RECEIVE	20
32	—	—	—
33	K16 20VT/YL*	INJECTOR CONTROL 1	21
34	K15 20YL	DWELL CONTROL	21
35	—	—	—
36	—	—	—
37	G28 20GY/PK*	EMISS MAINT REMINDER LAMP	—
38	—	—	—
39	—	—	—
40	S6 20GY/YL	EGR SOLENOID	19
41	J11 16RD	DIRECT BATTERY	20
42	—	—	—
43	—	—	—
44	—	—	—
45	C20 18BR	A/C CLUTCH INPUT	20
* 46	MX2 20WT/BK*	CCD BUS (—)	49
47	N7 18GY/BK*	REFERENCE PICKUP	22
48	G7 20WT/OR*	VEH SPEED PICKUP	22
49	Y7 18TN/YL*	HIGH DATA RATE PICKUP	22
50	T21 20GY/LB*	TACH SIGNAL	22
51	DK21 20PK	SCI TRANSMIT	20
52	N6 18OR	8 VOLT INPUT	22
53	X36 20TN/RD*	SPEED CONTROL VAC	23,25
54	K1 20PK/PK*	PURGE SOLENOID	19
** 55	U3 20OR/BK*	LOCK-UP T/C	23
56	N13 20DB/OR*	A/C HOT C/O	20
57	C27 20DB/PK*	RAD FAN RELAY	20
58	DK19 20DB/YL*	ASD RELAY	20
59	K3 20BK/PK*	POWER LOSS LAMP	20
60	X35 20LG/RD*	SPEED CONTROL VENT	23,25

*WITH ELECTRONIC TRANSMISSION
**WITHOUT ELECTRONIC TRANSMISSION

SINGLE MODULE ENGINE CONTROLLER-60 WAY 3.0L EFI ENGINE | S-HK 87

CONNECTOR #2

CAV	IGNITION SYSTEM CIRCUITS		SHEET NO.
1	N6 18OR	8 VOLT OUTPUT	22
2	K5 16BK/WT*	SIGNAL GROUND	19
3	K14 18DB/WT*	FJ2 OUTPUT	20
4	J2 14DB	J2 INPUT	19
5	Y13 18YL/WT*	INJECTOR DRIVER 3	23
6	J9 16BK	POWER GROUND	20
7	J9 16BK	POWER GROUND	20
8	K16 20VT/YL*	INJECTOR CONTROL 1	21
9	Y11 18WT/DB*	INJECTOR DRIVER 1	23
10	Y12 18TN	INJECTOR DRIVER 2	23
11	R31 20DG/OR*	ALT FIELD CONTROL	21
12	J5 18BK/GY*	IGNITION COIL DRIVER	20
13	K15 20YL	DWELL CONTROL	21
14	R3 18DG	ALT FIELD DRIVER	23

SINGLE MODULE ENGINE CONTROLLER-14 WAY 3.0L EFI ENGINE | S-HK 88

1989 Caravan/Voyager

ENGINE COMPARTMENT CIRCUITS		CAVITY
L1 12RD*	HEADLAMP SWITCH	1
V3 18BR*	WINDSHIELD WIPER MOTOR	2
B7 12RD/TN*	VAN CONVERSION	3
V4 18RD/YL*	WINDSHIELD WIPER MOTOR	4
L4 16VT*	HEADLAMP LOW BEAM	5
L3 16RD	RIGHT HEADLAMP	
L3 16RD	LEFT HEADLAMP	6
X30 20DB/RD*	SPEED CONTROL	7
X31 20BR/RD*	SPEED CONTROL	8
X33 20VT/LG*	SPEED CONTROL	9
X32 20YL/RD*	SPEED CONTROL	10
** MX2 20WT/BK*	CCD BUS (—)	11
** MX1 20BK	CCD BUS (+)	12
		13
S4 18BR/YL*	LIFTGATE GROUND	14
G29 20GY/PK*	EMISS MAINT REMINDER LAMP	15
		16
G2 20VT	WATER TEMPERATURE SENDING UNIT	17
G6 20GY	OIL PRESSURE SWITCH	18
G60 20GY/YL*	OIL PRESSURE SENDING UNIT	19
U3 20OR/BK*	SHIFT INDICATOR LAMP	20
D6 18LG	LEFT TURN SIGNAL LAMP	21
D5 18TN	RIGHT TURN SIGNAL LAMP	22
A3 14PK	BATTERY-HAZARD FLASHER	23
Z1 14DG/BK*	FUEL PUMP FEED	24
S40 18BR/LB*	LIFTGATE RELEASE	25
L7 18BK/YL*	SPLICE-SIDEMARKER AND PARK	
L7 18BK/YL*	AND TURN SIGNAL LAMPS	26
B1 18PK*	BACK-UP LAMP SWITCH	
** B1 18WT	BACK-UP LAMP SWITCH	27
B2 18VT/BK*	BACK-UP LAMP SWITCH	28
V10 20BR	WINDSHIELD WASHER MOTOR	29
V11 20BK/TN*	LOW WASHER FLUID INDICATOR LEVEL SENSOR	30
** S2 18YL	STARTER RELAY-IGNITION	31
H2 18DG/RD*	HORN	32
T21 20GY/LB*	TACHOMETER	33
P5 20BK	BRAKE WARNING LAMP SWITCH	34
V5 18DG	WINDSHIELD WIPER MOTOR	35
V8 18DB	WINDSHIELD WIPER MOTOR	36
C20 18DB/OR*	AIR CONDITIONING DAMPED PRESSURE SWITCH	37
K3 20BK/PK*	POWER LOSS	38
G31 20VT/LG*	AMBIENT TEMPERATURE SENSOR	39
G32 20BK/LB*	AMBIENT TEMPERATURE SENSOR	40
D40 18WT/PK*	60-WAY BRAKE SENSE	41
G7 20WT/OR*	SPEED INDICATOR	42
		43
		44
		45
		46
J2 14DB		
J2 14DB	SPLICE-IGNITION RUN CIRCUIT	47
C13 12BK/RD*	ELECTRICALLY HEATED REAR WINDOW	48
J1 12RD	IGNITION SWITCH	49
J10 12PK*	IGNITION SWITCH	50

■ (CAVITY 20 CIRCUIT FOR 2.5L ONLY)
* ALL ENGINES
** 3.0L ELECTRONIC AUTOMATIC TRANSAXLE

SMALL INDEX / LARGE INDEX
TERMINAL END OF DISCONNECT

S-HK 89 | 50 WAY BULKHEAD DISCONNECT

CAVITY		INSTRUMENT PANEL CIRCUITS	SHEET
1	L1 12RD/WT*	IGNITION SWITCH FEED (BATTERY FEED)	4,30
2	V3 18BR/WT*	WINDSHIELD WIPER LOW SPEED FEED	44
3	B7 14RD/PK*	VAN CONVERSION (BATTERY SUPPLY)	3,78
4	V4 18RD/YL*	WINDSHIELD WIPER HIGH SPEED FEED	44
5	L4 14VT*	HEADLAMP LOW BEAM	27,30
6	L3 14RD/OR*	HEADLAMP HIGH BEAM	27,30
	L3 16RD/OR*		
7	X30 22DB/RD*	SPEED CONTROL	25
8	X31 22BR/RD*	SPEED CONTROL	23,25
9	X33 22WT	SPEED CONTROL	23,25
10	X32 22YL/RD*	SPEED CONTROL	23,25
11	MX2 20WT/BK*	CCD BUS (—)	49
12	MX1 20BK	CCD BUS (+)	49
13			—
14	S40 22BR/LB*	LIFTGATE GROUND	5,6,77
15	G28 22GY/PK*	EMISS MAINT REMINDER LAMP	10,18
16			—
17	G20 22VT/YL*	TEMPERATURE SEND	12,16,24
18	G6 22GY	OIL PRESSURE LAMP	24
19	G60 22GY/YL*	OIL PRESSURE SEND	24
20	U3 22OR/LG*	UP-SHIFT LAMP	5,39
21	D6 18LG	LEFT TURN SIGNAL LAMP	
	D6 18LG	LEFT TURN SIGNAL SWITCH	28,42
22	D5 18TN	RIGHT TURN SIGNAL LAMP	
	D5 18TN	RIGHT TURN SIGNAL SWITCH	27,42
23	A3 18PK/WT*	HAZARD FLASHER	3,5,6,7,41
24	Z1 14DG/BK*	FUEL PUMP FEED	11,13,16,23
25	S4 18BR/YL*	LIFTGATE RELEASE (A/TRANSMISSION)	5,6,7,77
	S4 20BR/YL*		
26	L7 18BK/YL*	PARKING LAMPS	28,30
27	B1 18WT	BACK-UP LAMP SWITCH FEED	5,6,49,60
28	B2 18VT/BK*	BACK-UP LAMP	5,6,49
29	V10 18BR	WINDSHIELD WASHER MOTOR	43
30	V11 22BK/TN*	LOW WASHER FLUID	39,43
31	S2 14YL	IGNITION START	5,6,8
32	H2 18DG/RD*	HORNS	29
33	T21 22GY/LB*	TACHOMETER	13,14,22,39
34	P5 22GY/BK*	BRAKE WARNING LAMP	8
35	V5 18DG	WINDSHIELD WIPER SWITCH	44
36	V8 18DB	WINDSHIELD WIPER SWITCH	44
37	C2 20DB/OR*	AIR CONDITIONER LOW PRESSURE SWITCH	59,61
38	K3 22BK/PK*	POWER LOSS	11,18,20,39
39	G31 22VT/LG*	AMBIENT TEMPERATURE (OVERHEAD CONSOLE)	34
40	G32 22BK/LB*	AMBIENT TEMPERATURE (OVERHEAD CONSOLE)	34
41	D40 18WT/PK*	BRAKE SENSE	23,25
42	G7 22WT/OR*	SPEED SENSOR	12,17,22,27
43			—
44		NOT USED	—
45			—
46			—
47	J2 14DB	IGNITION RUN/START	3,8,10,16,19
48	C13 12BK/RD*	HEATED REAR WINDOW	3,66
49	J1 12RD	IGNITION SWITCH FEED	4,8
50	J10 12PK/BK*	IGNITION SWITCH FEED	4,8

TERMINAL END OF DISCONNECT
SMALL INDEX / LARGE INDEX

S-HK 90 | 50 WAY BULKHEAD DISCONNECT

STRG COLUMN

CAV	CIRCUIT	DESCRIPTION
1		NOT USED
2	H4 18BK	HORN GROUND
3	H3 20BK/RD*	GROUND FROM HORN SWITCH
4	D6 18LG	LEFT FRONT TURN SIGNAL
5	D5 18TN	RIGHT FRONT TURN SIGNAL
6	D32 18PK/BK*	HAZARD FLASHER FEED
7	D2 18RD/BK*	FEED FROM TURN SIGNAL FLASHER
8	D8 18DG/RD*	LEFT REAR TURN SIGNAL
9	D7 18BR/RD*	RIGHT REAR TURN SIGNAL
10	D4 18WT	FEED FROM BRAKE SWITCH
11		NOT USED
12	V3 18BR/WT*	WINDSHIELD WIPER LOW SPEED
13	V4 18RD/YL*	WINDSHIELD WIPER HIGH SPEED
14	V5 18DG	WINDSHIELD WIPER MOTOR
15	V1 18DB	WINDSHIELD WIPER SWITCH FEED
16	V10 18BR	WINDSHIELD WASHER MOTOR
17	H4 18BK	INTERMITTENT WIPE SWITCH GROUND
18	H40 18BK/LG*	INTERMITTENT WIPE MODULE GROUND
	H40 18BK/LG*	TO CHIME GROUND
19	M26 22LB	KEY-IN BUZZER
	M26 22LB	KEY-IN BUZZER
20	M16 20BK/LB*	LEFT FRONT DOOR JAMB SWITCH GROUND
21		NOT USED
22		NOT USED
23		NOT USED
24	J15 20YL/RD*	IGNITION KEY LAMP FEED
	J15 20YL/RD*	IGNITION KEY LAMP FEED
25	H4 18BK	
	H4 20BK	

VIEWED FROM WIRE SIDE OF 25 WAY CONNECTOR

(MOUNTED ON INSTR-PANEL LEFT OF STEERING COLUMN)

S-HK 91 | INSTRUMENT PANEL TO STEERING COLUMN WIRING

VIEWED FROM TERMINAL END OF CONNECTORS STRG COLUMN

CAV	CIRCUIT	DESCRIPTION	SHEET
1		NOT USED	—
2	H4 18BK	HORN GROUND	29
3	H3 18BK/RD*	HORN SWITCH GROUND	29
4	D6 18LG	LEFT FRONT TURN SIGNAL	42
5	D5 18TN	RIGHT FRONT TURN SIGNAL	42
6	D32 18PK	HAZARD FLASHER FEED	41
7	D2 18RD	TURN SIGNAL FLASHER FEED	41
8	D8 18DG/RD*	LEFT REAR TURN SIGNAL	42
9	D7 18BR/RD*	RIGHT REAR TURN SIGNAL	42
10	D4 18WT	BRAKE SWITCH FEED	25,41

TURN SIGNAL SWITCH CONNECTOR

11		NOT USED	—
12	V3 18BR*	INTERMITTENT WIPE MODULE	43
	V3 18BR*	WINDSHIELD WIPER LOW SPEED	43
13	V4 18RD	WINDSHIELD WIPER HIGH SPEED	43
14	V5 18DG	INTERMITTENT WIPE MODULE	43
	V5 18DG	WINDSHIELD WIPER MOTOR	43
15	V1 18DB	WINDSHIELD WIPER SWITCH FEED	43
16	V10 18BR	INTERMITTENT WIPE MODULE	43
	V10 18BR	WINDSHIELD WASHER MOTOR	43
17	H4 18BK	INTERMITTENT WIPE SWITCH GROUND	43
18	H40 18BK/LG*	INTERMITTENT WIPE MODULE GROUND	43,48

WINDSHIELD WIPER SWITCH CONNECTOR

19	M26 20LB	KEY-IN BUZZER	38
20	M16 20BK/LB*	LEFT FRONT DOOR JAMB SWITCH GROUND	38

KEY-IN BUZZER SWITCH CONNECTOR

21		NOT USED	—
22		NOT USED	—
23		NOT USED	—

24	J15 18BK/YL*	IGNITION KEY LAMP FEED	38
25	H4 18BK	IGNITION KEY LAMP GROUND	38

IGNITION KEY LAMP SWITCH CONNECTOR

(PLUGGED INTO STEERING COLUMN 25 WAY CONNECTOR)

S-HK 92 | STEERING COLUMN SWITCH TO PANEL WIRING

1989 Caravan/Voyager

VIEWED FROM WIRE SIDE
OF 25 WAY CONNECTOR

—[BODY]—

CAV	CIRCUIT	DESCRIPTION
1	L7 18BK	TAIL, LICENSE AND SIDE MARKER LAMPS
2	D8 18DG	LEFT REAR TURN SIGNAL LAMP
3	M16 18BK/LB*	LEFT FRONT DOOR JAMB SWITCH
4	G10 18LG	SEAT BELT WARNING SWITCH
5	D7 18BR	RIGHT REAR TURN SIGNAL LAMP
6	B2 18VT	BACK-UP LAMPS
7	G4 18DB	FUEL GAUGE SENDING UNIT
8	M1 18BK/PK* (2)	MAP LAMP FEED/POWER MIRROR FEED
9	M2 18BK/YL*	DOOR SWITCH GROUND-DOME LAMP
10	M4 18TN/BK*	TAIL GATE OPEN SWITCH
11	X42 14BK/GY*	LIFTGATE RELEASE
12		NOT USED
13	M3 18TN	DOOR AJAR
14	G40 18LB	LOW FUEL
15	M11 18PK/LB*	DOME LAMP DEFEAT
16	V20 16BR/WT*	REAR WASHER
17	V16 16DB/PK*	REAR WIPER-PARK
18	V13 16BR/LG*	REAR WIPER-RUN
19		NOT USED
20		NOT USED
21	M1 18BK/PK*	POWER MIRROR FEED
22	M2 18YL	DOOR SWITCH GROUND-DOME LAMP
23	M11 18PK/LB*	DOME LAMP DEFEAT
24	C15 12BK	HEATED REAR WINDOW-EBL
25	Z1 14DG/BK *	FUEL PUMP FEED

(MOUNTED ON PARKING
BRAKE LEFT SIDE)

S-HK 93	BODY TO INSTRUMENT PANEL WIRING

VIEWED FROM TERMINAL
END OF CONNECTORS   —[BODY]—

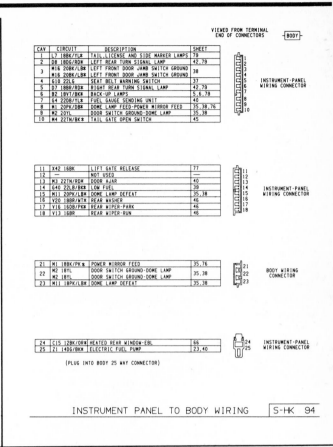

CAV	CIRCUIT	DESCRIPTION	SHEET
1	L7 18BK/YL*	TAIL, LICENSE AND SIDE MARKER LAMPS	79
2	D8 18DG/RD*	LEFT REAR TURN SIGNAL LAMP	42,79
3	M16 20BK/LB*	LEFT FRONT DOOR JAMB SWITCH GROUND	38
3	M16 20BK/LB*	LEFT FRONT DOOR JAMB SWITCH GROUND	
4	G10 22LG	SEAT BELT WARNING SWITCH	37
5	D7 18BR/RD*	RIGHT REAR TURN SIGNAL LAMP	42,79
6	B2 18VT/BK*	BACK-UP LAMPS	5,6,79
7	G4 22DB/YL*	FUEL GAUGE SENDING UNIT	40
8	M1 20PK/DB*	DOME LAMP FEED-POWER MIRROR FEED	35,38,76
9	M2 20YL	DOOR SWITCH GROUND-DOME LAMP	35,38
10	M4 22TN/BK*	TAIL GATE OPEN SWITCH	45

INSTRUMENT-PANEL
WIRING CONNECTOR

11	X42 16BK	LIFT GATE RELEASE	77
12	—	NOT USED	—
13	M3 22TN/RD*	DOOR AJAR	40
14	G40 22LB/BK*	LOW FUEL	39
15	M11 20PK/LB*	DOME LAMP DEFEAT	35,38
16	V20 18BR/WT*	REAR WASHER	46
17	V16 16DB/PK*	REAR WIPER-PARK	46
18	V13 16BR	REAR WIPER-RUN	46

INSTRUMENT-PANEL
WIRING CONNECTOR

21	M1 18BK/PK*	POWER MIRROR FEED	35,76
22	M2 18YL	DOOR SWITCH GROUND-DOME LAMP	35,38
22	M2 18YL	DOOR SWITCH GROUND-DOME LAMP	
23	M11 18PK/LB*	DOME LAMP DEFEAT	35,38

BODY WIRING
CONNECTOR

24	C15 12BK/OR*	HEATED REAR WINDOW-EBL	66
25	Z1 14DG/BK*	ELECTRIC FUEL PUMP	23,40

INSTRUMENT-PANEL
WIRING CONNECTOR

(PLUG INTO BODY 25 WAY CONNECTOR)

INSTRUMENT PANEL TO BODY WIRING	S-HK 94

DOME LAMPS-M1 20PK/DB*
BATTERY FEED-C13 12BK/RD*
REAR A/C SWITCH LAMP — E2 220R
INSTRUMENT PANEL LAMPS ⌐ E2 200R
└ E1 18TN
PWR VENT ⌐ Q20 12BK/OR*
WINDOW └ W41 16YL/RD*
TURN SIGNAL ⌐ D1 18BK
FLASHER └ D2 18RD/BK*
⌐ J15 20YL/RD*
IGNITION TIME │ M2 20YL
DELAY RELAY └ M11 20PK/LB*
POWER DOOR LOCKS AND
SEAT-W5 12RD
⌐ X1 16RD
HORN RELAY ┤ H3 18BK/RD*
└ H2 18DG/RD*
HEATER OR A/C FEED-C1 12BK
POWER WINDOWS-W1 12TN

V6 18DB-WINDSHIELD WIPER MOTOR
V1 18DB-WINDSHIELD WIPER SWITCH FEED
V16 16DB/PK*-ELECTRONIC MODULE
RR WASH-WIPE SYSTEM
V16 16DB/PK*-LIFTGATE RELEASE RELAY
G5 20DB/WT*-GAUGES,CHIMES
G5 22DB/WT*
J2 14DB-IGNITION RUN FEED
J2 14DB-IGNITION RUN FEED
D1 20BK/WT*-VAN CONVERSION RELAY
D1 18BK-TURN SIGNALS
X12 20RD/WT*-RADIO
Q2 14BK-IGNITION ACC FEED
D3 18PK-STOP LAMPS
D3 18PK-CHIME
L8 18PK/RD*-TAIL LAMPS
L1 12RD/WT*-BATTERY FEED
A3 16PK/WT*
D31 18BK/WT*⌐ HAZARD FLASHER
Q20 12BK/RD*- IGNITION RUN TO FEED
B1 16WT-REAR HEATER SWITCH
X1 16RD ⌐ HORNS AND CIGAR LIGHTER FEED
X1 16RD ┘

FRONT OF FUSEBLOCK

FUSE #	AMPS	COLOR	SHEET #
1	20	YELLOW	1,41
2	20	YELLOW	2,5,6,8,34,60,62,63,66,70
3	30	CIRCUIT BREAKER (POWER WINDOW) OPTION	2,8,67,71
4	30	LIGHT GREEN	2,8,57,59,61
5	20	YELLOW	1,30
6	20	YELLOW	1,25,37,42
7	25	NATURAL	1,30,37,49,55
8	30	CIRCUIT BREAKER (POWER DOOR LOCKS OR SEAT) OPTION	1,67,71,73
9	10	RED	2,8,55
10	20	YELLOW	2,41,78
11	20	YELLOW	2,8,44
12	4	PINK	1,31,34,45,55,63,65,66
13	5	TAN	2,3,8,10,16,25
14	20	YELLOW	2,3,8,10,16,25,43,77
15	10	RED	2,3,25,32,35,38,55,66,76
16	25	NATURAL	2,8,34,69,70

S-HK 95	FUSEBLOCK MODULE AND RELAY BANK

1989 Caravan/Voyager

AS-HK 1   FUSE APPLICATION CHART

FUSE APPLICATION CHART   AS-HK 2

AS-HK 3   CHARGING SYSTEM (2.5L TBI ENGINE)

CHARGING SYSTEM (2.5L TBI ENGINE)   AS-HK 4

1990 Caravan/Voyager

AS-HK 5   CHARGING SYSTEM (2.5L TURBO ENGINE)

CHARGING SYSTEM (2.5L TURBO ENGINE)   AS-HK 6

CHARGING SYSTEM
(3.0L & 3.3L ENGINE)

AS-HK 7

CHARGING SYSTEM
(3.0L & 3.3L ENGINE)   AS-HK 8

1990 Caravan/Voyager

AS-HK 9 — STARTER SYSTEM (2.5L TBI ENGINE)

STARTER SYSTEM (2.5L TURBO ENGINE) — AS-HK 10

AS-HK 11 — STARTER SYSTEM WITH ELECTRONIC TRANSAXLE (2.5L TURBO ENGINE)

STARTER SYSTEM (3.0L ENGINE) WITHOUT ELECTRONIC TRANSAXLE — AS-HK 12

1990 Caravan/Voyager

AS-HK 13 | STARTER SYSTEM WITH ELECTRONIC TRANSAXLE (3.0L & 3.3L ENGINE)

IGNITION SWITCH | AS-HK 14

ELECTRONIC FUEL INJECTION IGNITION SYSTEM (2.5L ENGINE) | AS-HK 15

AS-HK 16 | ELECTRONIC FUEL INJECTION IGNITION SYSTEM (2.5L ENGINE)

1990 Caravan/Voyager

ELECTRONIC FUEL INJECTION
IGNITION SYSTEM (2.5L ENGINE)

AS-HK 17

ELECTRONIC FUEL INJECTION
IGNITION SYSTEM (2.5L ENGINE)

AS-HK 18

ELECTRONIC FUEL INJECTION
IGNITION SYSTEM (2.5L ENGINE)

AS-HK 19

ELECTRONIC FUEL INJECTION
IGNITION SYSTEM (3.0 L ENGINE)

AS-HK 20

1990 Caravan/Voyager

ELECTRONIC FUEL INJECTION
IGNITION SYSTEM (3.0L ENGINE)

AS-HK 21

ELECTRONIC FUEL INJECTION
IGNITION SYSTEM (3.0L ENGINE)

AS-HK 22

ELECTRONIC FUEL INJECTION
IGNITION SYSTEM (3.0L ENGINE)

AS-HK 23

ELECTRONIC FUEL INJECTION
IGNITION SYSTEM (3.0 L ENGINE)

AS-HK 24

1990 Caravan/Voyager

ELECTRONIC FUEL INJECTION
IGNITION SYSTEM (3.3L ENGINE)

AS-HK 25

ELECTRONIC FUEL INJECTION
IGNITION SYSTEM (3.3L ENGINE)

AS-HK 26

AS-HK 27

ELECTRONIC FUEL INJECTION
IGNITION SYSTEM (3.3L ENGINE)

ELECTRONIC FUEL INJECTION
IGNITION SYSTEM (3.3 L ENGINE)

AS-HK 28

1990 Caravan/Voyager

ELECTRONIC FUEL INJECTION
IGNITION SYSTEM (3.3 L ENGINE)

AS-HK 29

OIL PRESSURE AND TEMPERATURE
SYSTEM (2.5, 3.0 & 3.3 LITRE)

AS-HK 30

TURBOCHARGED ELECTRONIC FUEL INJECTION
IGNITION SYSTEM (2.5L ENGINE)

AS-HK 31

TURBOCHARGED ELECTRONIC FUEL INJECTION
IGNITION SYSTEM (2.5L ENGINE)

AS-HK 32

1990 Caravan/Voyager

TURBOCHARGED ELECTRONIC FUEL INJECTION
IGNITION SYSTEM (2.5L ENGINE)

AS-HK 33

TURBOCHARGED ELECTRONIC FUEL INJECTION
IGNITION SYSTEM (2.5L ENGINE)

AS-HK 34

AS-HK 35 | SPEED CONTROL AND STOP LAMP SWITCH

UNDERHOOD LAMP

AS-HK 36

1990 Caravan/Voyager

AS-HK 37   FRONT END LIGHTING

FRONT END LIGHTING   AS-HK 38

AS-HK 39   FRONT END LIGHTING WITH DAYTIME RUNNING LIGHTS

FRONT END LIGHTING WITH DAYTIME RUNNING LIGHTS   AS-HK 40

1990 Caravan/Voyager

AS-HK 41 | DAYTIME RUNNING LIGHT MODULE WIRING

ELECTRONIC VEHICLE INFORMATION CENTER
ENGINE COMPARTMENT SENSORS | AS-HK 42

AS-HK 43 | HORN SYSTEM

HEADLAMP SWITCH | AS-HK 44

1990 Caravan/Voyager

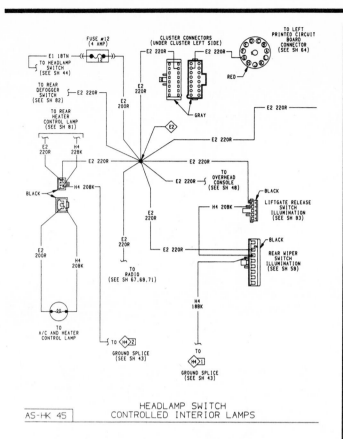

AS-HK 45 — HEADLAMP SWITCH CONTROLLED INTERIOR LAMPS

CONSOLE LAMPS — AS-HK 46

AS-HK 47 — OVERHEAD CONSOLE LAMPS

OVERHEAD CONSOLE LAMPS — AS-HK 48

1990 Caravan/Voyager

AS-HK 49 | DOME AND BODY COURTESY LAMPS

DOME AND BODY COURTESY LAMPS | AS-HK 50

AS-HK 51 | SEAT BELT WARNING SYSTEM

DOME AND COURTESY LAMPS | AS-HK 52

1990 Caravan/Voyager

AS-HK 53 | WARNING LAMP MODULE SYSTEM

WARNING LAMP MODULE SYSTEM | AS-HK 54

AS-HK 55 | STOP/TURN AND HAZARD FLASHER SYSTEM

STOP/TURN AND HAZARD FLASHER SYSTEM | AS-HK 56

1990 Caravan/Voyager

AS-HK 57 | INTERMITTENT WIPER SYSTEM

INTERMITTENT WIPER SYSTEM | AS-HK 58

AS-HK 59 | LIFTGATE AJAR WARNING AND
LIFTGATE WIPER AND WASHER SYSTEM

LIFTGATE WIPER AND WASHER SYSTEM | AS-HK 60

1990 Caravan/Voyager

ELECTRONIC TRANSAXLE SYSTEM

AS-HK 61

ELECTRONIC TRANSAXLE SYSTEM

AS-HK 62

WARNING LIGHT MODULE
PRINTED CIRCUIT BOARD

LEFT PRINTED CIRCUIT BOARD CONNECTOR
(RED)

G29 22GY/PK* -EMR LAMP
(SEE SH 17,22,26,34,53)

G6 22GY-OIL PRESSURE LAMP*
(SEE SH 30)

G20 22VT/YL*-TEMPERATURE LAMP OR GAUGE
(SEE SH 26,30)

D6 18LG-LEFT TURN SIGNAL INDICATOR LAMP
(SEE SH 38,40,56)

E2 22OR-ILLUMINATION LAMPS
(SEE SH 45)

H4 18BK-GROUND
(SEE SH 53)

H4 18BK-GROUND
(SEE SH 43,53)

M4 22TN/BK*-LIFTGATE AJAR
(SEE SH 59)

G5 22DB/WT*-IGNITION FEED
(SEE SH 53)

G60 22GY/YL*-OIL PRESSURE GAUGE
(SEE SH 30)

K3 22BK/PK*-CHECK GAUGES
(SEE SH 17,22,26,34,53)

WARNING LIGHT MODULE
PRINTED CIRCUIT BOARD CONNECTOR

AS-HK 63

H4 18BK
GROUND
(SEE SH 53)

GRAY

G40 22LB/BK*
LOW FUEL SIGNAL LAMP

G5 22DB/WT *
IGNITION 12 VOLT
(SEE SH 53)

M3 22TN/RD *
DOOR AJAR LAMP
(SEE SH 53)

V11 22BK/TN *
LOW WASHER FLUID LAMP
(SEE SH 53)

RIGHT PRINTED CIRCUIT BOARD CONNECTOR
(BLACK)

G11 22DB/RD*-SEAT BELT LAMP
(SEE SH 51)

P5 22GY/BK*-BRAKE LAMP
(SEE SH 14)

D5 18TN-RIGHT TURN SIGNAL
INDICATOR LAMP
(SEE SH 38,40,56,59)

L3 18RD/OR*-HI-BEAM INDICATOR LAMP
(SEE SH 38,40,41)

G5 22DB/WT*-IGNITION FEED
(SEE SH 54)

G4 22DB/YL*-FUEL GUAGE
(SEE SH 54)

T21 22GY/LB*-TACHOMETER
(SEE SH 19,24,25,34,54)

PRINTED CIRCUIT BOARD CONNECTORS

AS-HK 64

1990 Caravan/Voyager

MECHANICAL CLUSTER WITH TACH.
PRINTED CIRCUIT BOARD

AS-HK 65

MECHANICAL CLUSTER W/O TACH.
PRINTED CIRCUIT BOARD

AS-HK 66

ELECTRONICALLY TUNED RADIOS

AS-HK 67

ELECTRONICALLY TUNED RADIOS

AS-HK 68

1990 Caravan/Voyager

AS-HK 69 | 2 SPEAKER STEREO RADIOS

2 SPEAKER STEREO RADIOS | AS-HK 70

AS-HK 71 | 4 SPEAKER STEREO RADIOS

4 SPEAKER STEREO RADIOS | AS-HK 72

1990 Caravan/Voyager

RADIATOR FAN SYSTEM WITH HEATER
(2.5L, 3.0L & 3.3L ENGINE)

AS-HK 73

HEATER SYSTEM
(2.5L, 3.0L & 3.3L ENGINE)

AS-HK 74

AS-HK 75 | AIR CONDITIONING SYSTEM (2.5L ENGINE)

AIR CONDITIONING SYSTEM (2.5L ENGINE) | AS-HK 76

1990 Caravan/Voyager

AS-HK 77

AIR CONDITIONING SYSTEM
(3.0L & 3.3L ENGINE)

AIR CONDITIONING SYSTEM (3.0L & 3.3L ENGINE)

AS-HK 78

AS-HK 79

REAR HEATER AND A/C SYSTEM

REAR HEATER AND A/C SYSTEM

AS-HK 80

1990 Caravan/Voyager

6-147

1990 Caravan/Voyager

AS-HK 85   POWER REAR QUARTER WINDOW

POWER REAR QUARTER
WINDOW AND POWER SUN ROOF   AS-HK 86

AS-HK 87   POWER SEAT SYSTEM

POWER SEAT SYSTEM   AS-HK 88

1990 Caravan/Voyager

DOOR LOCK SYSTEM | AS-HK 89

DOOR LOCK SYSTEM | AS-HK 90

AS-HK 91 | POWER REMOTE MIRRORS

POWER REMOTE MIRRORS | AS-HK 92

1990 Caravan/Voyager

AS-HK 93 — LIFTGATE RELEASE

VAN CONVERSION WIRING — AS-HK 94

AS-HK 95 — REAR LIGHTING & TRAILER TOW

REAR LIGHTING & TRAILER TOW — AS-HK 96

1990 Caravan/Voyager

CAV	WIRE CODE	IGNITION SYSTEM CIRCUITS	SHEET
1	RL2 16LG*	PRINDIAL SWITCH	61
2	RL1 14TN/BK*	BACK UP LIGHT RELAY	42
3	RL3 14VT	BACK UP LIGHT RELAY	42
4	MX2 20WT/BK*	CCD BUS (—)	42
5	MX1 20BK/VT*	CCD BUS (+)	42
6	—	—	—
7	—	—	—
8	S2 14YL	STARTER RELAY	62
9	GP3 18BK/LG*	TRANS. SOLENOIDS & PRESSURE SWITCH	61
10	—	—	—
11	J2 14DB	NEUTRAL SAFETY SWITCH	62
12	K7 18OR/DB*	(SMEC) SINGLE MODULE CONTROLLER	62
13	SG5 18DB/RD*	OUTPUT & TURBINE SPEED SENSOR	62
14	SO1 18LG/WT*	OUTPUT SPEED SENSOR	62
15	SA1 18LG	SAFETY SHUTDOWN RELAY	61
16	SF1 16RD	TRANS. SOLENOIDS & PRESSURE SWITCH	61
17	SF1 16RD	SAFETY SHUTDOWN RELAY	61
18	—	—	—
19	SC2 18WT/DB*	TRANS. SOLENOIDS & PRESSURE SWITCH	61
20	SC1 18LB	TRANS. SOLENOIDS & PRESSURE SWITCH	61
21	—	—	—
22	—	—	—
23	—	—	—
24	—	—	—
25	—	—	—
26	—	—	—
27	—	—	—
28	—	—	—
29	—	—	—
30	—	—	—
31	—	—	—
32	—	—	—
33	—	—	—
34	—	—	—
35	—	—	—
36	—	—	—
37	—	—	—
38	—	—	—
39	—	—	—
40	—	—	—
41	S4 18BR/YL*	NEUTRAL SAFETY SWITCH	62
42	NS2 18VT*	PRINDIAL SWITCH	61
43	MX1 20BK/VT*	CCD BUS (+)	42
44	MX2 20WT/BK*	CCD BUS (—)	42
45	N7 18GY/BK*	DISTRIBUTOR	62
46	—	—	—
47	GP2 18YL/BK*	TRANS. SOLENOIDS & PRESSURE SWITCH	61
48	—	—	—
49	—	—	—
50	GP1 18DG	TRANS. SOLENOIDS & PRESSURE SWITCH	61
51	NS5 18BK/LB*	SIGNAL GROUND	62
52	ST1 18RD/BK*	TURBINE SPEED SENSOR	62
53	NS1 18BK/YL*	SIGNAL GROUND	61
54	NS1 18BK/YL*	SIGNAL GROUND	61
55	—	—	—
56	J11 16RD	DIRECT BATTERY FEED	61
57	J91 18BK/RD*	SIGNAL GROUND	61
58	J91 18BK/RD*	SIGNAL GROUND	61
59	SC3 18PK/YL*	TRANS. SOLENOIDS & PRESSURE SWITCH	61
60	SC4 18BR	TRANS. SOLENOIDS & PRESSURE SWITCH	61

SHORT TAB

LONG TAB

VIEWED FROM WIRE END OF CONNECTOR

AS-HK 97 ELECTRONIC AUTOMATIC TRANSAXLE CONTROL MODULE CONNECTOR

CAV	CIRCUIT	FUNCTION	SHEET
1	SC1 18LB	LOW REV SOLENOID	61
2	SC4 18BR	OVERDRIVE SOLENOID	61
3	SC2 18WT/DB*	LOW REV SOLENOID	61
4	SC3 18PK/YL*	LOW REV SOLENOID	61
5	GP2 18YL/BK*	PRESSURE SWITCH	61
6	SF1 16RD	SWITCHED BATTERY	61
7	GP1 18DG	PRESSURE SWITCH	61
8	GP3 18BK/LG*	PRESSURE SWITCH	61

TRANSAXLE SOLENOID CONNECTOR **AS-HK 98**

CAV	WIRE CODE	IGNITION SYSTEM CIRCUITS	SHEET NO.
1	K4 20DG/RD*	MAP SENSOR SIGNAL	16
2	K10 20TN/WT*	TEMPERATURE SENSOR SIGNAL	18
3	J11 16RD/WT*	DIRECT BATTERY FEED	17
4	N5 18BK/LB*	SIGNAL GROUND	18
5	K5 16BK*	SIGNAL GROUND	15
6	K8 20VT/WT*	MAP SENSOR SIGNAL	16
7	N6 180R	8 VOLT OUTPUT	18
8	B1 18WT	VOLTAGE SENSOR	19
9	J2 14DB	SOLENOID	16
10	—	—	—
11	K9 16LB/RD*	POWER GROUND	17
12	K9 16LB/RD*	POWER GROUND	17
13	—	—	—
14	—	—	—
15	—	—	—
16	Y11 18WT/DB*	INJECTOR	19
17	—	—	—
18	—	—	—
19	J5 18BK/GY*	IGNITION COIL	17
20	R3 18DG	ALTERNATOR	18
21	K13 18BK/RD*	CHARGE TEMP SENSOR	15
22	K7 18OR/DB*	THROTTLE POSITION SENSOR	15
23	—	—	—
24	N7 18GY/BK*	DISTRIBUTOR PICKUP SIGNAL	18
25	DK21 20PK	SCI (TRANSMIT)	17
26	MX1 20BK/VT*	CCD BUS (+)	42
27	C20 18BR	A/C CLUTCH INPUT	17
28	—	—	—
29	D40 18WT/PK*	BRAKE SWITCH SIGNAL	35
30	S4 20BR/YL*	PARK/NEUTRAL SWITCH SIGNAL	18
31	C27 200R/PK*	RADIATOR FAN RELAY	17
32	K3 20BK/PK*	CHECK ENGINE WARNING LAMP	17
33	X36 20TN/RD*	SPEED CONTROL (VACUUM)	35
34	N13 20DB/OR*	A/C CLUTCH RELAY SIGNAL	17
35	S6 20GY/YL*	EGR SOLENOID SIGNAL (CALIF)	16
36	—	—	—
37	—	—	—
38	—	—	—
39	N1 18GY/RD*	AUTO IDLE SPEED MOTOR(A15-3)	15
40	N2 18BR*	AUTO IDLE SPEED MOTOR(A15-1)	15
41	N11 18BK/DG*	OXYGEN SENSOR SIGNAL	15
42	—	—	—
43	T21 20GY/LB*	TACHOMETER SIGNAL	19
44	—	—	—
45	DK20 20LG	SCI (RECEIVE)	17
46	MX2 20WT/BK*	CCD BUS (—)	42
47	G7 20WT/OR*	DISTANCE SENSOR SIGNAL	18
48	X31 20BR/RD*	SPEED CONTROL SET	35
49	X32 20YL/RD*	SPEED CONTROL ON/OFF	35
50	X33 20WT/LG*	SPEED CONTROL RESUME	35
51	K18 20DG/YL*	AUTO SHUTDOWN SIGNAL	17
52	K1 20PK/BK*	PURGE SOLENOID SIGNAL	16
53	X35 20LG/RD*	SPEED CONTROL (VENT)	35
54	U3 200R/BK*	SHIFT INDICATOR LAMP	19
55	—	—	—
56	G29 20GY/PK*	EMISS MAINT REMINDER LAMP	16
57	—	—	—
58	—	—	—
59	N3 18VT/BK*	AUTO IDLE SPEED MOTOR(A15-4)	15
60	N4 18YL/BK*	AUTO IDLE SPEED MOTOR(A15-3)	15

SHORT TAB

LONG TAB

VIEWED FROM WIRE END OF CONNECTOR

AS-HK 99 SINGLE BOARD ENGINE CONTROLLER CONNECTOR (2.5L TBI)

CAV	WIRE CODE	IGNITION SYSTEM CIRCUITS	SHEET NO.
1	K4 20DG/RD*	MAP SENSOR SIGNAL	33
2	K10 20TN/WT*	TEMPERATURE SENSOR SIGNAL	32
3	J11 16RD/WT*	DIRECT BATTERY FEED	32
4	N5 18BK/LB*	SIGNAL GROUND	33
5	K5 16BK/WT*	SIGNAL GROUND	31
6	K8 20VT/WT*	MAP SENSOR SIGNAL	34
7	N6 180R	8 VOLT OUTPUT	32
8	Z1 16DG/BK*	INJECTOR	32
9	—	—	—
10	—	—	—
11	K8 16LB/RD*	POWER GROUND	31
12	K8 16LB/RD*	POWER GROUND	31
13	Y14 16LB/BR*	INJECTOR	32
14	Y13 18YL/WT*	INJECTOR	32
15	Y12 18TN	INJECTOR	31
16	Y11 18WT/DB*	INJECTOR	31
17	—	—	—
18	—	—	—
19	J5 18BK/GY*	IGNITION COIL	32
20	R3 18DG	ALTERNATOR	32
21	—	—	—
22	K7 18OR/DB*	THROTTLE POSITION SENSOR	34
23	—	—	—
24	N7 18GY/BK*	DISTRIBUTOR PICKUP SIGNAL	32
25	DK21 20PK	SCI (TRANSMIT)	32
26	MX1 20BK/VT*	CCD BUS (+)	42 *
27	C20 18BR	AC CLUTCH INPUT	33
28	—	—	—
29	D40 18WT/PK*	BRAKE SWITCH SIGNAL	35
30	S4 20BR/YL*	PARK/NEUTRAL SWITCH SIGNAL	34
31	C27 200R/PK*	RADIATOR FAN RELAY	33
32	K3 20BK/PK*	CHECK ENGINE WARNING LAMP	34
33	X36 20TN/RD*	SPEED CONTROL (VACUUM)	35
34	N13 20DB/OR*	AC CLUTCH RELAY SIGNAL	33
35	—	—	—
36	Y6 20LG/BK*	WASTEGATE SOLENOID	31
37	—	—	—
38	—	—	—
39	N1 18GY/RD*	AUTOMATIC IDLE SPEED MOTOR(A15-3)	34
40	N2 180R/WT*	AUTOMATIC IDLE SPEED MOTOR(A15-1)	34
41	N11 18BK/DG*	OXYGEN SENSOR SIGNAL	32
42	N12 18TN/RD*	DETONATION SENSOR SIGNAL	32
43	T21 20GY/LB*	TACHOMETER SIGNAL	34
44	T7 18TN/YL*	DISTRIBUTOR	32
45	DK20 20LG	SCI (RECEIVE)	32
46	MX2 20WT/BK*	CCD BUS (—)	42 *
47	G7 20WT/OR*	DISTANCE SENSOR SIGNAL	33
48	X31 20BR/RD*	SPEED CONTROL SET	35
49	X32 20YL/RD*	SPEED CONTROL ON/OFF	35
50	X33 20WT/LG*	SPEED CONTROL RESUME	35
51	K18 20DG/YL*	AUTO SHUTDOWN SIGNAL	32
52	K1 20PK/BK*	PURGE SOLENOID SIGNAL	31
53	X35 20LG/RD*	SPEED CONTROL (VENT)	35
54	U3 200R/BK*	SHIFT INDICATOR LAMP	
55	Y4 20LB	BARO PRESS READ SOLENOID	31
56	G29 20GY/PK*	EMISS MAINT REMINDER LAMP	34
57	—	—	—
58	—	—	—
59	N3 18VT/BK*	AUTOMATIC IDLE SPEED MOTOR(A15-4)	34
60	N4 18YL/BK*	AUTOMATIC IDLE SPEED MOTOR(A15-3)	34

SHORT TAB

LONG TAB

VIEWED FROM WIRE END OF CONNECTOR

*ELECTRONIC TRANSMISSION ONLY

AS-HK 100 SINGLE BOARD ENGINE CONTROLLER CONNECTOR (2.5L TURBO)

1990 Caravan/Voyager

CAV	WIRE CODE	IGNITION SYSTEM CIRCUITS	SHEET
1	K4 200G/RD*	MAP SENSOR SIGNAL	23
2	K10 20TN/WT*	TEMPERATURE SENSOR SIGNAL	24
3	J11 16RD/WT*	DIRECT BATTERY FEED	22
4	N5 18BK/LB*	SIGNAL GROUND	24
5	K5 18BK/WT*	SIGNAL GROUND	21
6	K8 20VT/WT*	MAP SENSOR SIGNAL	23
7	N6 180R	8 VOLT OUTPUT	24
8	Z1 16DG/BK*	INJECTOR	20
9	J2 14DB	SOLENOID	21
10	—	—	—
11	K9 16LB/RD*	POWER GROUND	22
12	K9 16LB/RD*	POWER GROUND	22
13	—	—	—
14	Y13 18YL/WT*	INJECTOR	20
15	Y12 18TN	INJECTOR	20
16	Y11 18WT/DB*	INJECTOR	20
17	—	—	—
18	—	—	—
19	J5 18BK/GY*	IGNITION COIL	22
20	R3 180G	ALTERNATOR	20
21	—	—	—
22	K7 18OR/DB*	THROTTLE POSITION SENSOR	23
23	—	—	—
24	N7 18GY/BK*	DISTRIBUTOR PICKUP SIGNAL	24
25	DK21 20PK	SCI (TRANSMIT)	22
* 26	MX1 20BK/VT*	CCD BUS (+)	42
27	C20 18BR	A/C CLUTCH INPUT	22
28	—	—	—
29	D40 18WT/PK*	BRAKE SWITCH SIGNAL	35
30	N4 20BR/YL*	PARK/NEUTRAL SWITCH SIGNAL	23
31	C27 200G/PK*	RADIATOR FAN RELAY	22
32	K3 20BK/PK*	CHECK ENGINE WARNING LAMP	22
33	X36 20TN/RD*	SPEED CONTROL (VACUUM)	35
34	N13 200B/OR*	A/C CLUTCH RELAY SIGNAL	22
35	S6 20GY/YL*	EGR SOLENOID SIGNAL (CALIF)	21
36	—	—	—
37	—	—	—
38	—	—	—
39	N1 18GY/RD*	AUTOMATIC IDLE SPEED MOTOR (AIS-3)	23
40	N2 18OR/WT*	AUTOMATIC IDLE SPEED MOTOR (AIS-1)	23
41	N11 18BK/DG*	OXYGEN SENSOR SIGNAL	21
42	—	—	—
43	T21 20GY/LB*	TACHOMETER SIGNAL	24
44	Y7 18TN/YL*	DISTRIBUTOR	24
45	DK20 20LG	SCI (RECEIVE)	22
* 46	MX2 20WT/BK*	CCD BUS (—)	42
47	G7 20VT/OR*	DISTANCE SENSOR SIGNAL	24
48	X31 20BR/RD*	SPEED CONTROL SET	35
49	X32 20YL/RD*	SPEED CONTROL ON/OFF	35
50	X33 20VT/LG*	SPEED CONTROL RESUME	35
51	K19 200G/YL*	AUTO SHUTDOWN	22
52	K1 20PK/BK*	PURGE SOLENOID SIGNAL	21
53	X35 20LG/RD*	SPEED CONTROL (VENT)	20,35
54	U3 200R/BK*	SHIFT INDICATOR LAMP	20
55	—	—	—
56	G29 20GY/PK*	EMISS MAINT REMINDER LAMP	21
57	—	—	—
58	—	—	—
59	N3 18VT/BK*	AUTOMATIC IDLE SPEED MOTOR (AIS-4)	23
60	N4 18YL/BK*	AUTOMATIC IDLE SPEED MOTOR (AIS-3)	23

SHORT TAB · LONG TAB · VIEWED FROM WIRE END OF CONNECTOR

*ELECTRONIC TRANSMISSION ONLY

AS-HK 101	SINGLE BOARD ENGINE CONTROLLER CONNECTOR (3.0L ENGINE)

CAV	WIRE CODE	IGNITION SYSTEM CIRCUITS	SHEET NO.
1	K4 200G/RD*	MAP SENSOR SIGNAL	27
2	K10 20TN/WT*	TEMPERATURE SENSOR SIGNAL	29
3	J11 16RD/WT*	DIRECT BATTERY FEED	26
4	N5 18BK/LB*	SIGNAL GROUND	29
5	K5 18BK/WT*	SIGNAL GROUND	25
6	K8 20VT/WT*	MAP SENSOR SIGNAL	27
7	N6 180R	8 VOLT OUTPUT	28
8	Z1 16DG/BK*	INJECTOR	28
9	J2 14DB	SOLENOID	25
10	—	—	—
11	K9 16LB/RD*	POWER GROUND	26
12	K9 16LB/RD*	POWER GROUND	26
13	—	—	—
14	Y13 18YL/WT*	INJECTOR	29
15	Y12 18TN	INJECTOR	29
16	Y11 18WT/DB*	INJECTOR	29
17	J6 18DB/BK*	IGNITION COIL	29
18	J7 18DB/BK*	IGNITION COIL	29
19	J5 18DB/GY*	IGNITION COIL	29
20	R3 18DG	ALTERNATOR	28
21	K13 18BK/RD*	CHARGE TEMP SENSOR	27
22	K7 18OR/DB*	THROTTLE POSITION SENSOR	27
23	—	—	—
24	N7 18GY/BK*	DISTRIBUTOR PICKUP SIGNAL	28
25	DK21 20PK	SCI (TRANSMIT)	26
26	MX1 20BK/VT*	CCD BUS (+)	42
27	C20 18BR	A/C CLUTCH INPUT	26
28	—	—	—
29	D40 18WT/PK*	BRAKE SWITCH SIGNAL	35
30	N4 20BR/YL*	PARK/NEUTRAL SWITCH SIGNAL	27
31	C27 200R/PK*	RADIATOR FAN RELAY	26
32	K3 20BK/PK*	CHECK ENGINE WARNING LAMP	26
33	X36 20TN/RD*	SPEED CONTROL (VACUUM)	35
34	N13 200B/OR*	A/C CLUTCH RELAY SIGNAL	26
35	S6 20GY/YL*	EGR SOLENOID SIGNAL (CALIF)	25
36	—	—	—
37	—	—	—
38	—	—	—
39	N1 18GY/RD*	AUTOMATIC IDLE SPEED MOTOR (AIS-3)	27
40	N2 18OR/WT*	AUTOMATIC IDLE SPEED MOTOR (AIS-1)	27
41	N11 18BK/DG*	OXYGEN SENSOR SIGNAL	27
42	N12 18BK/LG*	DETONATION SENSOR SIGNAL	28
43	T21 20GY/LB*	TACHOMETER SIGNAL	25
44	Y7 18TN/YL*	DISTRIBUTOR	29
45	DK20 20LG	SCI (RECEIVE)	26
46	MX2 20WT/BK*	CCD BUS (—)	42
47	G7 20VT/OR*	DISTANCE SENSOR SIGNAL	28
48	X31 20BR/RD*	SPEED CONTROL SET	35
49	X32 20YL/RD*	SPEED CONTROL ON/OFF	35
50	X33 20WT/LG*	SPEED CONTROL RESUME	35
51	K19 200G/YL*	AUTO SHUTDOWN	26
52	K1 20PK/BK*	PURGE SOLENOID SIGNAL	25
53	X35 20LG/RD*	SPEED CONTROL (VENT)	35
54	—	—	—
55	—	—	—
56	G29 20GY/PK*	EMISS MAINT REMINDER LAMP	26
57	—	—	—
58	—	—	—
59	N3 18VT/BK*	AUTOMATIC IDLE SPEED MOTOR (AIS-4)	27
60	N4 18YL/BK*	AUTOMATIC IDLE SPEED MOTOR (AIS-3)	27

SHORT TAB · LONG TAB · VIEWED FROM WIRE END OF CONNECTOR

SINGLE BOARD ENGINE CONTROLLER CONNECTOR (3.3L ENGINE)	AS-HK 102

CAV	WIRE CODE	ENGINE COMPARTMENT CIRCUITS	SHEET
1	L1 12RD*	HEADLAMP SWITCH	4,44
2	V3 18BR*	WINDSHIELD WIPER MOTOR	58
3	B7 12RD/TN*	VAN CONVERSION	3,84
4	V4 18RD/YL*	WINDSHIELD WIPER MOTOR	58
5	L4 16VT*	HEADLAMP LOW BEAM	37,39,41,44
6	L3 16RD / L33 16RD/BK* / L3 16RD	RIGHT HEADLAMP / LEFT HEADLAMP / DRL ONLY	37,39,41,44
7	X30 200B/RD*	SPEED CONTROL	35
8	X31 20BR/RD*	SPEED CONTROL	35
9	X33 20WT/LG*	SPEED CONTROL	35
10	X32 20YL/RD*	SPEED CONTROL	35
11	MX2 20WT/BK*	CCD BUS (—)	42
12	MX1 20BK	CCD BUS (+)	42
13	—	—	—
14	S4 18BR/YL*	LIFTGATE GROUND	8,93
15	G29 20GY/PK*	EMISS MAINT REMINDER LAMP	16,53
16	L33 16RD/BK*	DRL	37,40,41
17	G2 20VT	WATER TEMPERATURE SENDING UNIT	30
18	G6 20GY	OIL PRESSURE SWITCH	30
19	G60 20GY/YL*	OIL PRESSURE SENDING UNIT	30
20	U3 200R/BK*	SHIFT INDICATOR LAMP	9,53
21	D6 18LG	LEFT TURN SIGNAL LAMP	38,40,56
22	D5 18TN	RIGHT TURN SIGNAL LAMP	37,39,56
23	A3 14PK	BATTERY-HAZARD FLASHER	3,8,55
24	Z1 14DG/BK*	FUEL PUMP FEED	19,54
25	S40 18BR/LB*	LIFTGATE RELEASE	8,62,93
26	L7 18BK/YL* / L7 18BK/YL*	SPLICE-SIDEMARKER AND PARK / AND TURN SIGNAL LAMPS	38,40,44
27	B1 18WT	BACK-UP LAMP SWITCH	9,42,76,82
28	B2 18YL/BK*	BACK-UP LAMP SWITCH	9,42,95
29	V10 20BR	WINDSHIELD WASHER MOTOR	57
30	V11 20BK/TN*	LOW WASHER FLUID INDICATOR LEVEL SENSOR	53,57
31	S2 18YL	STARTER RELAY-IGNITION	9,14
32	H2 18DG	HORN	43
33	T21 20GY/LB*	TACHOMETER	19,53
34	P5 20BK	BRAKE WARNING LAMP SWITCH	14
35	V5 180G	WINDSHIELD WIPER MOTOR	58
36	V6 18DB	WINDSHIELD WIPER MOTOR	58
37	C20 18DB/OR*	AIR CONDITIONING DAMPED PRESSURE SWITCH	75
38	K3 20BK/PK*	POWER LOSS	17,53
39	G31 20VT/LG*	AMBIENT TEMPERATURE SENSOR	48
40	G32 20DB/LB*	AMBIENT TEMPERATURE SENSOR	48
41	D40 18WT/PK*	60-WAY BRAKE SENSE	35
42	G7 20WT/OR*	SPEED INDICATOR	18,93
43	—	—	—
44	—	—	—
45	—	—	—
46	L20 14LG/BK*	DRL MODULE	41,44
47	J2 14DB / J2 14DB	SPLICE-IGNITION RUN CIRCUIT	3,14,16,35,73
48	C13 12BK/RD*	ELECTRICALLY HEATED REAR WINDOW	3,82
49	J1 12RD	IGNITION SWITCH	4,14
50	J10 12PK*	IGNITION SWITCH	4,14

SMALL INDEX · LARGE INDEX · TERMINAL END OF DISCONNECT

■ DAYTIME RUNNING LIGHTS ONLY

AS-HK 103	50 WAY BULKHEAD DISCONNECT (2.5L TBI)

CAV	WIRE CODE	ENGINE COMPARTMENT CIRCUITS	SHEET	
1	L1 12RD*	HEADLAMP SWITCH	6,44	
2	V3 18BR*	WINDSHIELD WIPER MOTOR	58	
3	B7 12RD/TN*	VAN CONVERSION	5,94	
4	V4 18RD/YL*	WINDSHIELD WIPER MOTOR	58	
5	L4 16VT*	HEADLAMP LOW BEAM	37,39,41,44	
6	L3 16RD / L33 16RD/BK* / L3 16RD	RIGHT HEADLAMP / LEFT HEADLAMP / DRL ONLY	37,39,41,44	
7	X30 200B/RD*	SPEED CONTROL	35	
8	X31 20BR/RD*	SPEED CONTROL	35	
9	X33 20WT/LG*	SPEED CONTROL	35	
10	X32 20YL/RD*	SPEED CONTROL	35	
11	MX2 20WT/BK*	CCD BUS (—)	42	**
12	MX1 20BK	CCD BUS (+)	42	**
13	—	—	—	
14	S4 18BR/YL*	LIFTGATE GROUND	10,93	
15	G29 20GY/PK*	EMISS MAINT REMINDER LAMP	34,53	
16	L33 16RD/BK*	DRL	37,40,41	
17	G2 20VT	WATER TEMPERATURE SENDING UNIT	30	
18	G6 20GY	OIL PRESSURE SWITCH	30	
19	G60 20GY/YL*	OIL PRESSURE SENDING UNIT	30	
20	U3 200R/BK*	SHIFT INDICATOR LAMP	34,53	
21	D6 18LG	LEFT TURN SIGNAL LAMP	38,40,56	
22	D5 18TN	RIGHT TURN SIGNAL LAMP	37,39,56	
23	A3 14PK	BATTERY-HAZARD FLASHER	5,10,11,55	
24	Z1 14DG/BK*	FUEL PUMP FEED	32,54	
25	S4 18DG/YL* / S4 18BR/YL*	LIFTGATE GROUND	10,11,62,93	**
26	L7 18BK/YL* / L7 18BK/YL*	SPLICE-SIDEMARKER AND PARK / AND TURN SIGNAL LAMPS	38,40,44	
27	B1 18WT / B1 18WT	BACK-UP LAMP SWITCH	10,76, 42,82	**
28	B2 18YL/BK*	BACK-UP LAMP SWITCH	10,42,95	
29	V10 20BR	WINDSHIELD WASHER MOTOR	57	
30	V11 20BK/TN*	LOW WASHER FLUID INDICATOR LEVEL SENSOR	53,57	
31	S2 18YL	STARTER RELAY-IGNITION	10,11,14	
32	H2 18DG/RD*	HORN	43	
33	T21 20GY/LB*	TACHOMETER	34,53	
34	P5 20BK	BRAKE WARNING LAMP SWITCH	14	
35	V5 180G	WINDSHIELD WIPER MOTOR	58	
36	V6 18DB	WINDSHIELD WIPER MOTOR	58	
37	C20 18DB/OR*	AIR CONDITIONING DAMPED PRESSURE SWITCH	75	
38	K3 20BK/PK*	CHECK ENGINE LAMP	34,53	
39	G31 20VT/LG*	AMBIENT TEMPERATURE SENSOR	48	
40	G32 20DB/LB*	AMBIENT TEMPERATURE SENSOR	48	
41	D40 18WT/PK*	60-WAY BRAKE SENSE	35	
42	G7 20WT/OR*	SPEED INDICATOR	33,93	
43	—	—	—	
44	—	—	—	
45	—	—	—	
46	L20 14LG/BK*	DRL MODULE	41,44	
47	J2 14DB / J2 14DB	SPLICE-IGNITION RUN CIRCUIT	5,14,32,35,73	
48	C13 12BK/RD*	ELECTRICALLY HEATED REAR WINDOW	5,82	
49	J1 12RD	IGNITION SWITCH	6,14	
50	J10 12PK*	IGNITION SWITCH	6,14	

SMALL INDEX · LARGE INDEX · TERMINAL END OF DISCONNECT

■ DAYTIME RUNNING LIGHTS ONLY
* MANUAL TRANSMISSION ONLY
** ELECTRONIC AUTOMATIC TRANSAXLE

50 WAY BULKHEAD DISCONNECT (2.5L TURBO)	AS-HK 104

1990 Caravan/Voyager

CAV	WIRE CODE	ENGINE COMPARTMENT CIRCUITS	SHEET
1	L1 12RD*	HEADLAMP SWITCH	8,44
2	V3 18BR*	WINDSHIELD WIPER MOTOR	58
3	B7 12RD/TN*	VAN CONVERSION	7,94
4	V4 18RD/YL*	WINDSHIELD WIPER MOTOR	58
5	L4 16VT*	HEADLAMP LOW BEAM	37,39,41,44
6	L3 16RD	RIGHT HEADLAMP	37,38,
	L33 16RD/BK*	LEFT HEADLAMP	41,44
	L3 16RD	DRL ONLY	
7	X30 20DB/RD*	SPEED CONTROL	35
8	X31 20BR/RD*	SPEED CONTROL	35
9	X33 20WT/LG*	SPEED CONTROL	35
10	X32 20YL/RD*	SPEED CONTROL	35
11	MX2 20WT/BK*	CCD BUS (−)	42
12	MX1 20BK/VT*	CCD BUS (+)	42
13	—	—	—
14	S4 18BR/YL*	LIFTGATE GROUND	12,93
15	G29 20GY/PK*	EMISS MAINT REMINDER LAMP	21,26,53
16	L33 16RD/BK*	DRL	37,40,41
17	G20 20VT	WATER TEMPERATURE SENDING UNIT	29,30
18	G6 20GY	OIL PRESSURE LAMP	30
19	G60 20GY/YL*	OIL PRESSURE SENDING UNIT	30
20	U3 20OR/BK*	SHIFT INDICATOR LAMP	12,53
21	D6 18LG	LEFT TURN SIGNAL LAMP	38,40,56
22	D5 18TN	RIGHT TURN SIGNAL LAMP	37,39,56
23	A3 14PK	BATTERY-HAZARD FLASHER	7,12,13,55
24	Z1 14DG/BK*	FUEL PUMP FEED	20,28,54
25	S4 18BR/YL*	LIFTGATE GROUND	13,62,93
	S4 18BR/YL*		
26	L7 18BK/YL*	SPLICE-SIDEMARKER AND PARK	38,40,44
	L7 18BK/YL*	AND TURN SIGNAL LAMPS	
27	B1 18WT	BACK-UP LAMP SWITCH	12,42, 77,82
28	B2 18VT/BK*	BACK-UP LAMP SWITCH	12,42,95
29	V10 20BR	WINDSHIELD WASHER MOTOR	57
30	V11 20BK/TN*	LOW WASHER FLUID INDICATOR LEVEL SENSOR	53,57
31	S2 18YL	STARTER RELAY-IGNITION	12,13,14
32	H2 18DG/RD*	HORN	43
33	T21 20GY/LB*	TACHOMETER	24,25,53
34	P5 20BK	BRAKE WARNING LAMP SWITCH	14
35	V5 18DG	WINDSHIELD WIPER MOTOR	58
36	V6 18DB	WINDSHIELD WIPER MOTOR	58
37	C20 18DB/OR*	AIR CONDITIONING DAMPED PRESSURE SWITCH	22,26,53
38	K3 20BK/PK*	CHECK ENGINE LAMP	77
39	G31 20VT/LG*	AMBIENT TEMPERATURE SENSOR	48
40	G32 20BK/LB*	AMBIENT TEMPERATURE SENSOR	48
41	D40 18WT/PK*	60-WAY BRAKE SENSE	35
42	G7 20WT/OR*	SPEED INDICATOR	24,28,93
43	—		—
44	—		—
45	—		—
46	L20 14LG/BK*	DRL MODULE	41,44
47	J2 14DB	SPLICE-IGNITION RUN CIRCUIT	7,14,21, 25,35,73
	J2 14DB		
48	C13 12BK/RD*	ELECTRICALLY HEATED REAR WINDOW	7,82
49	J1 12RD	IGNITION SWITCH	8,14
50	J10 12PK*	IGNITION SWITCH	8,14

■ DAYTIME RUNNING LIGHTS ONLY

SMALL INDEX — LARGE INDEX

TERMINAL END OF DISCONNECT

50 WAY BULKHEAD DISCONNECT (3.0L & 3.3L)

AS-HK 105

CAV	WIRE CODE	INSTRUMENT PANEL CIRCUITS	SHEET
1	L1 12RD/WT*	IGNITION SWITCH FEED (BATTERY FEED)	
2	V3 18BR/WT*	WINDSHIELD WIPER LOW SPEED FEED	
3	B7 14RD/PK*	VAN CONVERSION (BATTERY SUPPLY)	
4	V4 18RD/YL*	WINDSHIELD WIPER HIGH SPEED FEED	
5	L4 14VT*	HEADLAMP LOW BEAM	
6	L3 14RD/OR*	HEADLAMP HIGH BEAM	
7	X30 22DB/RD*	SPEED CONTROL	
8	X31 22BR/RD*	SPEED CONTROL	
9	X33 22WT	SPEED CONTROL	
10	X32 22YL/RD*	SPEED CONTROL	
11	MX2 20WT/BK*	CCD BUS (−)	
12	MX1 20BK	CCD BUS (+)	
13	—		
14	S40 22BR/LB*	LIFTGATE GROUND	
15	G29 22GY/PK*	EMISS MAINT REMINDER LAMP	
16	L33 16RD/BK*	REAR FOG LAMP FEED	
17	G20 22VT/YL*	TEMPERATURE SEND	
18	G6 22GY	OIL PRESSURE LAMP	
19	G60 22GY/YL*	OIL PRESSURE SEND	
20	U3 22OR/LG*	UP-SHIFT LAMP	
21	D6 18LG	LEFT TURN SIGNAL LAMP	
	D6 18LG	LEFT TURN SIGNAL SWITCH	
22	D5 18TN	RIGHT TURN SIGNAL LAMP	
	D5 18TN	RIGHT TURN SIGNAL SWITCH	
23	A3 16PK/WT*	HAZARD FLASHER	
24	Z1 14DG/BK*	FUEL PUMP FEED	
25	S4 18BR/YL*	LIFTGATE RELEASE (A/TRANSMISSION)	
	S4 20BR/YL*		
26	L7 18BK/YL*	PARKING LAMPS	
27	B1 18WT	BACK-UP LAMP SWITCH FEED	
28	B2 18VT/BK*	BACK-UP LAMP SWITCH	
29	V10 18BR	WINDSHIELD WASHER MOTOR	
30	V11 22BK/TN*	LOW WASHER FLUID	
31	S2 14YL	IGNITION START	
32	T21 22GY/LB*	TACHOMETER	
33	P5 22GY/BK*	BRAKE WARNING LAMP	
34	V5 18DG	WINDSHIELD WIPER SWITCH	
35	V6 18DB	WINDSHIELD WIPER SWITCH	
36	C2 20DB/OR*	AIR CONDITIONER LOW PRESSURE SWITCH	
37	K3 22BK/PK*	CHECK ENGINE LAMP	
38	G31 22VT/LG*	AMBIENT TEMPERATURE (OVERHEAD CONSOLE)	
39	G32 22BK/LB*	AMBIENT TEMPERATURE (OVERHEAD CONSOLE)	
40	D40 18WT/PK*	BRAKE SENSE	
41	G7 22WT/OR*	SPEED SENSOR	
42	—		
43	—		
44	—		
45	—		
46	L20 14LG/WT*	BATTERY FEED	
47	J2 14DB	IGNITION RUN/START	
48	C13 12BK/RD*	HEATED REAR WINDOW	
49	J1 12RD	IGNITION SWITCH FEED	
50	J10 12PK*	IGNITION SWITCH FEED	

TERMINAL END OF DISCONNECT

SMALL INDEX — LARGE INDEX

50 WAY BULKHEAD DISCONNECT

AS-HK 106

STRG COLUMN

CAV	CIRCUIT	DESCRIPTION
1	—	NOT USED
2	H4 18BK	HORN GROUND
3	H3 18BK/RD*	GROUND FROM HORN SWITCH
4	D6 18LG	LEFT FRONT TURN SIGNAL
5	D5 18TN	RIGHT FRONT TURN SIGNAL
6	D32 18PK/BK*	HAZARD FLASHER FEED
7	D2 18RD/BK*	FEED FROM TURN SIGNAL FLASHER
8	D8 18DG/RD*	LEFT REAR TURN SIGNAL
9	D7 18BR/RD*	RIGHT REAR TURN SIGNAL
10	D4 18WT	FEED FROM BRAKE SWITCH
11	V3 18BR/WT*	WINDSHIELD WIPER INTERMITTANT WIPE
12	V3 18BR/WT*	WINDSHIELD WIPER LOW SPEED
	V3 18BR/WT*	
13	V4 18RD/YL*	WINDSHIELD WIPER HIGH SPEED
14	V5 18DG	WINDSHIELD WIPER MOTOR
15	V6 18DB	WINDSHIELD WIPER SWITCH FEED
16	V10 18BR	WINDSHIELD WASHER MOTOR
17	—	NOT USED
18	H40 18BK/LG*	INTERMITTENT WIPER MODULE GROUND
	H40 18BK/LG*	TO CHIME GROUND
19	M26 22LB	KEY-IN BUZZER
	M26 22LB	KEY-IN BUZZER
20	M16 22BK/LB*	LEFT FRONT DOOR JAMB SWITCH GROUND
21	—	NOT USED
22	—	NOT USED
23	—	NOT USED
24	J15 20YL/RD*	IGNITION KEY LAMP FEED
	J15 20YL/RD*	IGNITION KEY LAMP FEED
25	H4 18BK	
	H4 20BK	

VIEWED FROM WIRE SIDE OF 25 WAY CONNECTOR

(MOUNTED ON INSTR-PANEL LEFT OF STEERING COLUMN)

INSTRUMENT PANEL TO STEERING COLUMN WIRING

AS-HK 107

VIEWED FROM TERMINAL END OF CONNECTORS — STRG COLUMN

CAV	CIRCUIT	DESCRIPTION	SHEET
1	—	NOT USED	—
2	H4 18BK	HORN GROUND	43
3	H3 18BK/RD*	HORN SWITCH GROUND	43
4	D6 18LG	LEFT FRONT TURN SIGNAL	56
5	D5 18TN	RIGHT FRONT TURN SIGNAL	56
6	D32 18PK	HAZARD FLASHER FEED	55
7	D2 18RD	TURN SIGNAL FLASHER FEED	55
8	D8 18DG/RD*	LEFT REAR TURN SIGNAL	56
9	D7 18BR/RD*	RIGHT REAR TURN SIGNAL	56
10	D4 18WT	BRAKE SWITCH FEED	35,55

TURN SIGNAL SWITCH CONNECTOR

11	V3 18BR*	INTERMITTENT WIPER MODULE	57
12	V3 18BR*	INTERMITTENT WIPER MODULE	57
	V3 18BR/WT*	WINDSHIELD WIPER LOW SPEED	
13	V4 18RD	WINDSHIELD WIPER HIGH SPEED	57
14	V5 18DG	INTERMITTENT WIPER MODULE	
	V5 18DG	WINDSHIELD WIPER MOTOR	57
15	V6 18DB	WINDSHIELD WIPER SWITCH FEED	57
16	V10 18BR	INTERMITTENT WIPER MODULE	
	V10 18BR	WINDSHIELD WASHER MOTOR	57
17	—	NOT USED	—
18	H40 18BK/LG*	INTERMITTENT WIPER MODULE GROUND	42,58

WINDSHIELD WIPER SWITCH CONNECTOR

19	M26 20LB	KEY-IN BUZZER	52
20	M16 20BK/LB*	LEFT FRONT DOOR JAMB SWITCH GROUND	52

KEY-IN BUZZER SWITCH CONNECTOR

21	—	NOT USED	—
22	—	NOT USED	—
23	—	NOT USED	—

24	J15 18BK/YL*	IGNITION KEY LAMP FEED	52
25	H4 18BK	IGNITION KEY LAMP GROUND	52

IGNITION KEY LAMP SWITCH CONNECTOR

(PLUGGED INTO STEERING COLUMN 25 WAY CONNECTOR)

STEERING COLUMN SWITCH TO PANEL WIRING

AS-HK 108

1990 Caravan/Voyager

VIEWED FROM WIRE SIDE
OF 25 WAY CONNECTOR

[BODY]

CAV	CIRCUIT	DESCRIPTION
1	L7 16BK	TAIL, LICENSE AND SIDE MARKER LAMPS
2	D8 18DG	LEFT REAR TURN SIGNAL LAMP
3	M16 18BK/LB*	LEFT FRONT DOOR JAMB SWITCH
4	G10 18LG	SEAT BELT WARNING SWITCH
5	D7 18BR	RIGHT REAR TURN SIGNAL LAMP
6	B2 18VT	BACK-UP LAMPS
7	G4 18DB	FUEL GAUGE SENDING UNIT
8	M1 18BK/PK* (2)	MAP LAMP FEED/POWER MIRROR FEED
9	M2 18BK/YL*&18YL	DOOR SWITCH GROUND-DOME LAMP
10	M4 18TN/BK *	TAIL GATE OPEN SWITCH
11	X42 14BK/GY*	LIFTGATE RELEASE
12	——	NOT USED
13	M3 18TN	DOOR AJAR
14	G40 18LB	LOW FUEL
15	M11 18PK/LB * (2)	DOME LAMP DEFEAT
16	V20 18BR/WT*	REAR WASHER
17	V16 16DB/PK*	REAR WIPER-PARK
18	V13 16BR/LG*	REAR WIPER-RUN
19	——	NOT USED
20	——	NOT USED
21	M1 18BK/PK *	POWER MIRROR FEED
22	M2 18YL (2)	DOOR SWITCH GROUND-DOME LAMP
23	M11 18PK/LB*	DOME LAMP DEFEAT
24	C15 12BK	HEATED REAR WINDOW-EBL
25	Z1 14DG/BK *	FUEL PUMP FEED

(MOUNTED ON PARKING
BRAKE LEFT SIDE)

AS-HK 109 | BODY TO INSTRUMENT PANEL WIRING

VIEWED FROM TERMINAL
END OF CONNECTORS

[BODY]

CAV	CIRCUIT	DESCRIPTION	SHEET
1	L7 18BK/YL*	TAIL,LICENSE AND SIDE MARKER LAMPS	95
2	D8 18DG/RD*	LEFT REAR TURN SIGNAL LAMP	56,95
3	M16 20BK/LB*	LEFT FRONT DOOR JAMB SWITCH GROUND	52
3	M16 20BK/LB*	LEFT FRONT DOOR JAMB SWITCH GROUND	
4	G10 22LG	SEAT BELT WARNING SWITCH	51
5	D7 18BR/RD*	RIGHT REAR TURN SIGNAL LAMP	56,95
6	B2 18VT/BK*	BACK-UP LAMPS	9,10,12,95
7	G4 22DB/YL*	FUEL GAUGE SENDING UNIT	54
8	M1 20PK/DB*	DOME LAMP FEED-POWER MIRROR FEED	49,52,92
9	M2 20YL	DOOR SWITCH GROUND-DOME LAMP	49,52
10	M4 22TN/BK*	TAIL GATE OPEN SWITCH	59

INSTRUMENT-PANEL
WIRING CONNECTOR

11	X42 16BK	LIFT GATE RELEASE	93
12	—	NOT USED	—
13	M3 22TN/RD*	DOOR AJAR	54
14	G40 22LB/BK*	LOW FUEL	53
15	M11 20PK/LB*	DOME LAMP DEFEAT	49,52
16	V20 18BR/WT*	REAR WASHER	60
17	V16 16DB/PK*	REAR WIPER-PARK	60
18	V13 16BR	REAR WIPER-RUN	60

INSTRUMENT-PANEL
WIRING CONNECTOR

21	M1 18BK/PK*	POWER MIRROR FEED	49,92
22	M2 18YL	DOOR SWITCH GROUND-DOME LAMP	49,52
22	M2 18YL	DOOR SWITCH GROUND-DOME LAMP	
23	M11 18PK/LB*	DOME LAMP DEFEAT	49,52

BODY WIRING
CONNECTOR

24	C15 12BK/OR*	HEATED REAR WINDOW-EBL	82
25	Z1 14DG/BK*	ELECTRIC FUEL PUMP	20,28,54

(PLUG INTO BODY 25 WAY CONNECTOR)

INSTRUMENT-PANEL
WIRING CONNECTOR

INSTRUMENT PANEL TO BODY WIRING | AS-HK 110

DOME LAMPS-M1 20PK/DB*
BATTERY FEED-C13 12BK/RD*
REAR A/C SWITCH LAMP — E2 220R
INSTRUMENT PANEL LAMPS — E2 200R, E1 18TN

V6 18DB-WINDSHIELD WIPER MOTOR
V1 18DB-WINDSHIELD WIPER SWITCH FEED
V16 16DB/PK*-ELECTRONIC MODULE
RR WASH-WIPE SYSTEM
V16 16DB/PK*-LIFTGATE RELEASE RELAY
G5 20DB/WT*-GAUGES
G5 22DB/WT*-CHIMES
J2 14DB-IGNITION RUN FEED
J2 14DB-IGNITION RUN FEED

TURN SIGNAL FLASHER — D2 18RD/BK*, D1 18BK/PK*
TIME DELAY RELAY — J15 20YL/RD*, M2 20YL, M11 20PK/LB*
POWER DOOR LOCKS AND SEAT-WS 12RD
HORN RELAY — X1 16RD, H3 18BK/RD*, H2 18DG/RD*

D1 18BK/PK*-VAN CONVERSION RELAY
D1 18BK/PK*-TURN SIGNALS
X12 20RD/WT*-RADIO
Q2 14BK-IGNITION ACC FEED
D3 18PK*-STOP LAMPS
D3 18PK-CHIME
L8 18PK/RD*-TAIL LAMPS
L1 12RD/WT*-BATTERY FEED
A3 16PK/WT*
D31 18BK/WT* — HAZARD FLASHER
Q20 12BK/OR*-IGNITION RUN TO FEED
B1 16WT-REAR HEATER SWITCH

HEATER OR A/C FEED-C1 12BR
POWER WINDOWS-W1 12TN
X1 16RD, X1 16RD — HORNS AND CIGAR LIGHTER FEED

FRONT OF FUSEBLOCK

FUSE #	AMPS	COLOR	SHEET #
1	20	YELLOW	1,55
2	20	YELLOW	2,9,10,12,14,48,76,78,79,82
3	30	CIRCUIT BREAKER (POWER WINDOW) OPTION	2,14,83,87
4	30	LIGHT GREEN	2,14,74,75,77
5	20	YELLOW	1,44
6	20	YELLOW	1,35,51,56
7	25	NATURAL	1,42,44,51,67,69,71
8	30	CIRCUIT BREAKER (POWER DOOR LOCKS OR SEAT) OPTION	1,83,87,89
9	10	RED	2,14,67,69,71
10	20	YELLOW	2,55,94
11	20	YELLOW	2,14,58
12	4	PINK	1,44,45,48,59,67,69,71,79,81,82
13	5	TAN	2,3,5,7,14,16,35
14	20	YELLOW	2,3,5,7,14,16,35,59,93
15	10	RED	2,3,5,7,46,49,52,67,69,71,82,92
16	—	NOT USED	

AS-HK 111 | FUSEBLOCK MODULE AND RELAY BANK

1990 Caravan/Voyager

FUSE APPLICATION CHART

AS-HK 1

FUSE APPLICATION CHART

AS-HK 2

FUSE APPLICATION CHART

AS-HK 3

CHARGING SYSTEM (2.5L ENGINE)

AS-HK 4

1991 Caravan/Voyager and Town & Country

CHARGING SYSTEM (2.5L ENGINE)

AS-HK 5

CHARGING SYSTEM
(3.0L & 3.3L ENGINE)

AS-HK 6

CHARGING SYSTEM
(3.0L & 3.3L ENGINE)

AS-HK 7

STARTER SYSTEM (2.5 ENGINE)

AS-HK 8

1991 Caravan/Voyager and Town & Country

STARTER SYSTEM (3.0L ENGINE)
WITH 3 SPEED AUTOMATIC

AS-HK 9

STARTER SYSTEM WITH ELECTRONIC
TRANSAXLE (3.0L & 3.3L ENGINE)

AS-HK 10

IGNITION SWITCH

AS-HK 11

ELECTRONIC FUEL INJECTION
IGNITION SYSTEM (2.5L ENGINE)

AS-HK 12

1991 Caravan/Voyager and Town & Country

ELECTRONIC FUEL INJECTION
IGNITION SYSTEM (2.5L ENGINE)

AS-HK 13

ELECTRONIC FUEL INJECTION
IGNITION SYSTEM (2.5L ENGINE)

AS-HK 14

ELECTRONIC FUEL INJECTION IGNITION
SYSTEM (2.5L ENGINE)

AS-HK 15

ELECTRONIC FUEL INJECTION
IGNITION SYSTEM (2.5L ENGINE)

AS-HK 16

1991 Caravan/Voyager and Town & Country

1991 Caravan/Voyager and Town & Country

ELECTRONIC FUEL INJECTION
IGNITION SYSTEM (3.0L ENGINE)

AS–HK 21

ELECTRONIC FUEL INJECTION
IGNITION SYSTEM (3.3L ENGINE)

AS–HK 22

ELECTRONIC FUEL INJECTION
IGNITION SYSTEM (3.3L ENGINE)

AS–HK 23

ELECTRONIC FUEL INJECTION IGNITION
SYSTEM (3.3L ENGINE)

AS–HK 24

1991 Caravan/Voyager and Town & Country

ELECTRONIC FUEL INJECTION IGNITION SYSTEM (3.3 L ENGINE)

AS-HK 25

ELECTRONIC FUEL INJECTION IGNITION SYSTEM (3.3L ENGINE)

AS-HK 26

AIR CONDITIONING SYSTEM (2.5L ENGINE)

AS-HK 27

AIR CONDITIONING SYSTEM (2.5L ENGINE)

AS-HK 28

1991 Caravan/Voyager and Town & Country

AS-HK 29

AS-HK 30

AS-HK 31

AS-HK 32

1991 Caravan/Voyager and Town & Country

1991 Caravan/Voyager and Town & Country

AS-HK 37

ANTI-LOCK BRAKE SYSTEM

OIL AND TEMPERATURE WARNING SYSTEM
2.5L ENGINE

AS-HK 38

AS-HK 39

OIL AND TEMPERATURE WARNING SYSTEM
3.0L ENGINE

OIL AND TEMPERATURE WARNING SYSTEM
3.3L ENGINE

AS-HK 40

1991 Caravan/Voyager and Town & Country

FRONT END LIGHTING

AS-HK 41

FRONT END LIGHTING

AS-HK 42

SPEED CONTROL AND STOP LAMP SWITCH

AS-HK 43

HORN SYSTEM

AS-HK 44

1991 Caravan/Voyager and Town & Country

AS–HK 45 | INTERMITTENT WIPER SYSTEM

INTERMITTENT WIPER SYSTEM | AS–HK 46

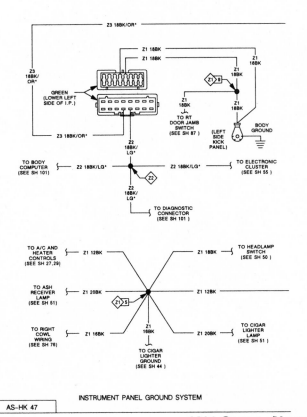

INSTRUMENT PANEL GROUND SYSTEM

AS–HK 47

INSTRUMENT PANEL GROUND SYSTEM

AS–HK 48

1991 Caravan/Voyager and Town & Country

AS–HK 49

AS–HK 50

AS–HK 51

AS–HK 52

1991 Caravan/Voyager and Town & Country

STOP/TURN AND HAZARD
FLASHER SYSTEM

AS-HK 53

STOP/TURN AND HAZARD
FLASHER SYSTEM

AS-HK 54

ELECTRONIC CLUSTER

AS-HK 55

ELECTRONIC CLUSTER

AS-HK 56

1991 Caravan/Voyager and Town & Country

HEATER SYSTEM
(2.5L, 3.0L, 3.3L ENGINE)

AS-HK 57

2 SPEAKER STEREO RADIOS

AS-HK 58

2 SPEAKER STEREO RADIOS

AS-HK 59

ELECTRONICALLY TUNED STEREO RADIO
WITH STANDARD SPEAKERS

AS-HK 60

1991 Caravan/Voyager and Town & Country

ELECTRONICALLY TUNED STEREO RADIO
WITH STANDARD SPEAKERS

AS-HK 61

ELECTRONICALLY TUNED STEREO RADIO
WITH NAME BRAND SPEAKERS

AS-HK 62

ELECTRONICALLY TUNED STEREO RADIO
NAME BRAND SPEAKERS

AS-HK 63

REAR HEATER AND A/C SYSTEM

AS-HK 64

1991 Caravan/Voyager and Town & Country

REAR HEATER AND A/C SYSTEM

AS-HK 65

LIFTGATE WIPER AND WASHER SYSTEM

AS-HK 66

LIFTGATE WIPER AND WASHER SYSTEM

AS-HK 67

FOG LAMPS

AS-HK 68

1991 Caravan/Voyager and Town & Country

AS-HK 69

FOG LAMPS

REAR WINDOW DEFOGGER

AS-HK 70

AS-HK 71

LIFTGATE RELEASE

WARNING LAMP CENTER

AS-HK 72

1991 Caravan/Voyager and Town & Country

DOOR AJAR SYSTEM

AS-HK 73

SEAT BELT WARNING SYSTEM

AS-HK 74

POWER MIRROR SYSTEM

AS-HK 75

POWER MIRROR SYSTEM

AS-HK 76

1991 Caravan/Voyager and Town & Country

DOOR LOCK SYSTEM

AS-HK 77

DOOR LOCK SYSTEM

AS-HK 78

LEFT DOOR CONNECTOR AND DOOR LOCK SWITCH FUNCTION		
B+ POLARITY	B- POLARITY	DOOR LOCK FUNCTION
OR/VT*	PK/VT*	LOCK
PK/VT*	OR/VT*	UNLOCK
PK	—	FEED

RIGHT DOOR CONNECTOR AND DOOR LOCK SWITCH FUNCTION		
B+ POLARITY	B- POLARITY	DOOR LOCK FUNCTION
OR/VT*	PK/VT*	LOCK
PK/VT*	OR/VT*	UNLOCK
PK	—	FEED

POWER WINDOW LIFT SYSTEM

AS-HK 79

MASTER SWITCH PWR WINDOWS		
B+	B-	WINDOW/ MOVEMENT
LB	WT	LEFT UP
WT	LB	LEFT DOWN
BR/WT*	VT/WT*	RIGHT UP
VT/WT*	BR/WT*	RIGHT DOWN
TN	—	FEED
—	BK	GROUND

POWER WINDOW LIFT SYSTEM

AS-HK 80

RIGHT DOOR		
B+ POLARITY	B- POLARITY	WINDOW AND MOVEMENT
VT	BR	DOWN-FROM DOOR SWITCH
BR	VT	UP-FROM DOOR SWITCH
VT/WT*	BR/WT*	DOWN-FROM MASTER SWITCH
BR/WT*	VT/WT*	UP-FROM MASTER SWITCH
TN	—	FEED

1991 Caravan/Voyager and Town & Country

COURTESY LAMP SYSTEM

AS-HK 81

COURTESY LAMP SYSTEM

AS-HK 82

ILLUMINATED ENTRY SYSTEM

AS-HK 83

OVERHEAD CONSOLE LAMPS

AS-HK 84

1991 Caravan/Voyager and Town & Country

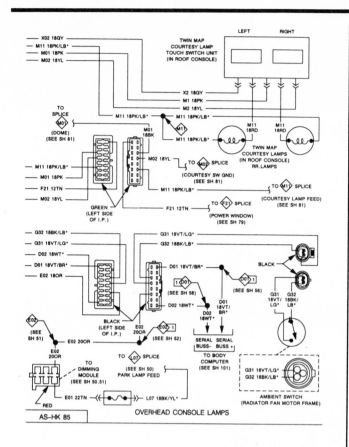

OVERHEAD CONSOLE LAMPS

AS-HK 85

POWER REAR QUARTER WINDOW

AS-HK 86

POWER SEAT SYSTEM

AS-HK 87

MOTOR INSULATOR POLARITY		
+POLARITY	−POLARITY	SEAT MOVEMENT
YL/LB*	RD/LB*	FORWARD
RD/LB*	YL/LB*	REARWARD
YL/WT*	RD/WT*	REAR UP
RD/WT*	YL/WT*	REAR DOWN
YL/LG*	RD/LG*	FRONT UP
RD/LG*	YL/LG*	FRONT DOWN
RD	—	FEED
—	BK	GROUND

ELECTRIC FUEL PUMP AND GAUGE SYSTEM

AS-HK 88

1991 Caravan/Voyager and Town & Country

REAR LIGHTING & TRAILER TOW

AS-HK 89

REAR LIGHTING & TRAILER TOW

AS-HK 90

VAN CONVERSION WIRING

AS-HK 91

FRONT END LIGHTING WITH
DAYTIME RUNNING LIGHTS

AS-HK 92

1991 Caravan/Voyager and Town & Country

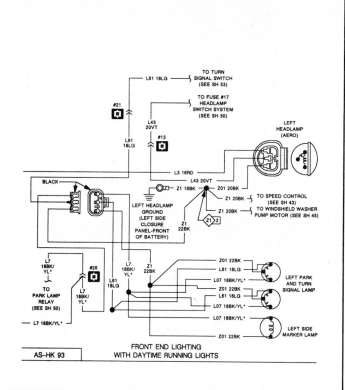

FRONT END LIGHTING
WITH DAYTIME RUNNING LIGHTS

AS-HK 93

DAYTIME RUNNING LIGHT MODULE WIRING

AS-HK 94

UNDERHOOD LAMP

AS-HK 95

RADIATOR FAN SYSTEM WITH HEATER
(2.5L ENGINE ONLY)

AS-HK 96

1991 Caravan/Voyager and Town & Country

RADIATOR FAN SYSTEM WITH HEATER
(3.0L & 3.3L ENGINE ONLY)

AS-HK 97

4 WHEEL DRIVE VACUUM SOLENOID SYSTEM

AS-HK 98

4 WHEEL DRIVE VACUUM SOLENOID SYSTEM

AS-HK 99

ELECTRIC FUEL PUMP AND GAUGE
SYSTEM (4 WHEEL DRIVE)

AS-HK 100

1991 Caravan/Voyager and Town & Country

AS-HK 101

BODY COMPUTER

AS-HK 102

BODY COMPUTER

AS-HK 103

BODY COMPUTER

AS-HK 104

BODY CONNECTOR

1991 Caravan/Voyager and Town & Country

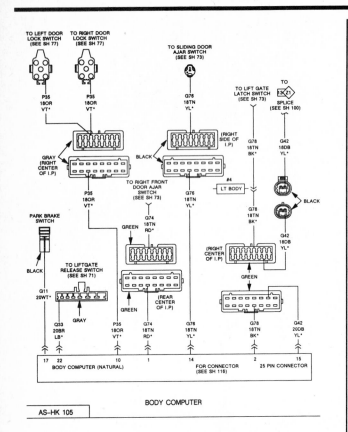

BODY COMPUTER

AS-HK 105

50 WAY BULKHEAD DISCONNECT — AS-HK 106

CAV	WIRE CODE	INSTRUMENT PANEL CIRCUITS	SHEET
1	A3 12RD/WT*	IGNITION SWITCH FEED (BATTERY FEED)	5,7
2	A6 12RD/BK*	BATTERY FEED - PARK LAMPS	5,7
3	A18 14RD/PK*	VAN CONVERSION (BATTERY SUPPLY)	91
4	G19 20LG/BK*	ABS WARNING LAMP	72
5	—	—	—
6	L3 14RD/OR*	HEADLAMP HIGH BEAM	41
7	V30 22BR/RD*	SPEED CONTROL	43
8	V31 20BR/RD*	SPEED CONTROL	43
9	V33 20WT/LG*	SPEED CONTROL	43
10	V32 20YL/RD*	SPEED CONTROL	43
11	D2 18WT/BK*	CCD BUS (-)	56
12	D1 18WT/BR*	CCD BUS (+)	56
13	L43 20VT	FUSE 10 LT HEADLAMP	42
14	L44 20VT/RD*	FUSE TO RT HEADLAMP	41
15	G24 22GY/PK*	EMISS MAINT REMINDER LAMP	72
16	G34 16RD/BK*	DAYTIME RUNNING LIGHT MODULE TO HI-BM IND	72
17	G20 22VT/YL*	TEMPERATURE SEND	38, 39,40
18	G6 22GY	OIL PRESSURE SEND	38, 39,40
19	G60 22GY/YL*	OIL PRESSURE SEND	38, 39,40
20	L39 18LB	FUSED FOG LAMP FEED	69
21	L61 18LG	LEFT TURN SIGNAL LAMP	54
22	L60 18TN	RIGHT TURN SIGNAL LAMP	54
23	A15 14PK	HAZARD FLASHER	54
24	V4 18RD/YL*	WIPER MOTOR HIGH SPEED	46
25	V3 18BR/WT*	WIPER MOTOR LOW SPEED	46
26	L7 18BK/YL*	PARKING LAMPS	42
27	F20 18WT	BACK-UP LAMP SWITCH FEED	89
28	L1 18VT/BK*	BACK-UP LAMP	89
29	V10 18BR	WINDSHIELD WASHER MOTOR	45
30	G29 22BK/TN*	LOW WASHER FLUID	46
31	A41 14YL	IGNITION START	11
32	X2 18DG/RD*	HORNS	44
33	C21 18DB/OR*	AIR CONDITIONING	27, 29
34	G4 20GY/BK*	BRAKE WARNING LAMP	104
35	V5 18DG	WINDSHIELD WIPER SWITCH	46
36	V6 18DB	WINDSHIELD WIPER MOTOR	46
	V6 18DB	WINDSHIELD WIPER MOTOR	46
37	B3 20LG/DB*	LEFT RR WHEEL SENSOR	34
38	B4 20LG	LEFT RR WHEEL SENSOR	34
39	B1 20YL/DB*	RIGHT RR WHEEL SENSOR	34
40	B2 20YL	RIGHT RR WHEEL SENSOR	34
41	K29 20WT/PK*	BRAKE SENSE	43
42	L50 18WT/OR*	SPEED SENSOR	89
43	D11 20WT/VT*	DIAG. ANTI-LOCK BRAKES	37
44	D12 20OR	DIAG. ANTI-LOCK BRAKES	37
45	A61 14DG/BK*	FUEL PUMP FEED	88, 100
46	L20 14LG/WT*	BATTERY FEED	50
47	A21 14DB	IGNITION RUN/START	4
48	A4 12BK/RD*	HEATED REAR WINDOW	4, 6
49	A1 12RD	IGNITION SWITCH FEED	7
50	A2 12PK/BK*	IGNITION SWITCH FEED	5,7

TERMINAL END OF DISCONNECT

SMALL INDEX

LARGE INDEX

50 WAY BULKHEAD DISCONNECT (2.5L ENGINE) — AS-HK 107

CAV	WIRE CODE	INSTRUMENT PANEL CIRCUITS	SHEET
1	A3 12RD*	IGNITION SWITCH FEED	5,7
2	A6 10RD	BATTERY FEED	5,7
3	A18 12RD/BK*	VAN CONVERSION	91
4	G19 20LG/OR*	ABS WARNING	72
5	—	—	—
6	L33 16RD	LEFT HEADLAMP	41
6	L3 16RD/OR*	DRL ONLY	41
7	V30 20DB/RD*	SPEED CONTROL	43
8	V31 20BR/RD*	SPEED CONTROL	43
9	V33 20WT/LG*	SPEED CONTROL	43
10	V32 20YL/RD*	SPEED CONTROL	43
11	D2 20WT/BK*	CCD BUS (-)	56
12	D1 20VT/BR*	CCD BUS (+)	56
13	L43 20VT	FUSE TO LT HEADLAMP	42
14	L44 20VT/RD*	FUSE TO RT HEADLAMP	41
15	G24 20GY/PK*	EMISS MAINT REMINDER LAMP	72
16	L33 16RD	DRL	72
17	G20 20VT/YL*	WATER TEMPERATURE SENDING UNIT	38,39,40
18	G6 20GY	OIL PRESSURE SWITCH	38,39,40
19	G60 20GY/YL*	OIL PRESSURE SENDING UNIT	38,39,40
20	L39 18LB	FUSED FOG LAMP FEED	69
21	L61 18LG	LEFT TURN SIGNAL LAMP	54
22	L60 18TN	RIGHT TURN SIGNAL LAMP	54
23	A15 14PK	BATTERY-HAZARD FLASHER	54
24	V4 18RD/YL*	WIPER MOTOR-HIGH SPEED	46
25	V3 18BR/WT	WIPER MOTOR-LOW SPEED	46
26	L7 18BK/YL*	SPLICE-SIDEMARKER AND PARK	42
	L7 18BK/YL*	AND TURN SIGNAL LAMPS	
27	F20 18W	BACK-UP LAMP SWITCH	89
28	L1 18VT/BK*	BACK-UP LAMP SWITCH	89
29	V10 20BR	WINDSHIELD WASHER MOTOR	45
30	G29 20BK/TN*	LOW WASHER FLUID INDICATOR LEVEL SENSOR	46
31	A41 18YL	STARTER RELAY-IGNITION	11
32	X2 18DG/RD*	HORN	44
33	C21 18DB/OR*	AIR CONDITIONING	27,29
34	G9 20GY/BK*	BRAKE WARNING LAMP SWITCH	104
35	V5 18DG	WINDSHIELD WIPER MOTOR	46
36	V6 18DB	WINDSHIELD WIPER MOTOR	46
37	—	—	—
38	—	—	—
39	—	—	—
40	—	—	—
41	K29 18WT/PK*	60-WAY BRAKE SENSE	43
42	—	—	—
43	—	—	—
44	—	—	—
45	A61 14DG/BK*	FUEL PUMP FEED	88
46	L20 14LG/WT*	BATTERY FEED	50
47	A21 14DB	SPLICE-IGNITION RUN CIRCUIT	4
48	A4 12BK/RD*	ELECTRICALLY HEATED REAR WINDOW	4,6
49	A1 12RD	IGNITION SWITCH	7
50	A2 12PK*	IGNITION SWITCH	5,7

SMALL INDEX — LARGE INDEX

TERMINAL END OF DISCONNECT

50 WAY BULKHEAD DISCONNECT (3.0L & 3.3L) — AS-HK 108

CAV	WIRE CODE	INSTRUMENT PANEL CIRCUITS	SHEET
1	A3 12RD*	IGNITION SWITCH FEED	5, 7
2	A6 10RD	BATTERY FEED	5, 7
3	A18 12RD/BK*	VAN CONVERSION	91
4	G19 20LG/OR*	ABS WARNING	72
5	—	—	—
6	L33 16RD	LEFT HEADLAMP	41
6	L3 16RD/OR*	DRL ONLY	41
7	V30 20DB/RD*	SPEED CONTROL	43
8	V31 20BR/RD*	SPEED CONTROL	43
9	V33 20WT/LG*	SPEED CONTROL	43
10	V32 20YL/RD*	SPEED CONTROL	43
11	D2 20WT/BK*	CCD BUS (-)	56
12	D1 20VT/BR*	CCD BUS (+)	56
13	L43 20VT/BR*	FUSE TO LT HEADLAMP	42
14	L44 20VT/RD*	FUSE TO RT HEADLAMP	41
15	G24 20GY/PK*	EMISS MAINT REMINDER LAMP	72
16	L33 16RD	DRL	72
17	G20 20VT/YL*	WATER TEMPERATURE SENDING UNIT	38,39,40
18	G6 20GY	OIL PRESSURE SWITCH	38,39,40
19	G60 20GY/YL*	OIL PRESSURE SENDING UNIT	38,39,40
20	L39 18LB	FUSED FOG LAMP FEED	69
21	L61 18LG	LEFT TURN SIGNAL LAMP	54
22	L60 18TN	RIGHT TURN SIGNAL LAMP	54
23	A15 14PK	BATTERY-HAZARD FLASHER	54
24	V4 18RD/YL*	WIPER MOTOR-HIGH SPEED	46
25	V3 18BR/WT	WIPER MOTOR-LOW SPEED	46
26	L7 18BK/YL*	SPLICE-SIDEMARKER AND PARK	42
	L7 18BK/YL*	AND TURN SIGNAL LAMPS	42
27	F20 18WT	BACK-UP LAMP SWITCH	89
	F20 18WT		89
28	L1 18VT/BK*	BACK-UP LAMP SWITCH	89
29	V10 20BR	WINDSHIELD WASHER MOTOR	45
30	G29 20BK/TN*	LOW WASHER FLUID INDICATOR LEVEL SENSOR	46
31	A41 18YL	STARTER RELAY-IGNITION	11
	A41 18YL	STARTER RELAY-IGNITION	11
32	X2 18DG/RD*	HORN	44
33	C21 18DB/OR*	AIR CONDITIONING	27,29
34	G9 20GY/BK*	BRAKE WARNING LAMP SWITCH	104
35	V5 18DG	WINDSHIELD WIPER MOTOR	46
36	V6 18DB	WINDSHIELD WIPER MOTOR	46
37	B3 20LG/DB*	LEFT RR WHEEL SENSOR	34
38	B4 20LG*	LEFT RR WHEEL SENSOR	34
39	B1 20YL/DB*	RIGHT RR WHEEL SENSOR	34
40	B2 20YL*	RIGHT RR WHEEL SENSOR	34
41	K29 18WT/PK*	60-WAY BRAKE SENSE	43
42	L50 18WT/TN*	SPEED INDICATOR	89
43	D11 20WT/VT*	DIAG. ANTI-LOCK BRAKES	37
44	D12 20OR	DIAG. ANTI-LOCK BRAKES	37
45	A61 14DG/BK*	FUEL PUMP FEED	88,100
46	L20 14LG/WT*	BATTERY FEED	50
47	A21 14DB	SPLICE-IGNITION RUN CIRCUIT	4
48	A4 12BK/RD*	ELECTRICALLY HEATED REAR WINDOW	4,6
49	A1 12RD	IGNITION SWITCH	7
50	A2 12PK*	IGNITION SWITCH	5,7

SMALL INDEX — LARGE INDEX

TERMINAL END OF DISCONNECT

1991 Caravan/Voyager and Town & Country

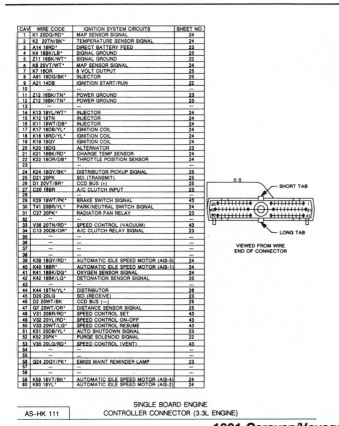

CAV	WIRE CODE	IGNITION SYSTEM CIRCUITS	SHEET NO.
1	K1 20DG/RD*	MAP SENSOR SIGNAL	13
2	K2 20TN/BK*	TEMPERATURE SENSOR SIGNAL	15
3	A14 18RD/WT*	DIRECT BATTERY FEED	14
4	K4 18BK/LB*	SIGNAL GROUND	15
5	Z11 16BK/WT*	SIGNAL GROUND	15
6	K6 20VT/WT*	MAP SENSOR SIGNAL	13
7	K7 18OR	8 VOLT OUTPUT	15
8	E20 16WT	IGNITION FEED	16
9	A2 14DB	IGNITION START/RUN	13
10	—	—	—
11	Z12 16BK/TN*	POWER GROUND	14
12	Z12 16BK/TN*	POWER GROUND	14
13	—	—	—
14	—	—	—
15	—	—	—
16	K11 18WT/DB*	INJECTOR	15
17	—	—	—
18	—	—	—
19	K19 18GY	IGNITION COIL	14
20	K20 18DG	ALTERNATOR	15
21	—	—	—
22	K22 18OR/DB*	THROTTLE POSITION SENSOR	12
23	—	—	—
24	K24 18GY/BK*	DISTRIBUTOR PICKUP SIGNAL	15
25	D21 20PK	SCI (TRANSMIT)	14
26	D1 20VT/BR*	CCD BUS (+)	12
27	C20 18BR	A/C CLUTCH INPUT	14
28	—	—	—
29	K29 18WT/PK*	BRAKE SWITCH SIGNAL	43
30	T41 20BR/YL*	PARK/NEUTRAL SWITCH SIGNAL	15
31	C27 20PK	RADIATOR FAN RELAY	14
32	—	—	—
33	Y36 20TN/RD*	SPEED CONTROL (VACUUM)	43
34	C13 20DB/OR*	A/C CLUTCH RELAY SIGNAL	14
35	K35 20GY/YL*	EGR SOLENOID SIGNAL (CALIF)	13
36	—	—	—
37	—	—	—
38	—	—	—
39	K39 18GY/RD*	AUTOMATIC IDLE SPEED MOTOR (AIS-3)	12
40	K40 18BR/WT*	AUTOMATIC IDLE SPEED MOTOR (AIS-1)	12
41	K41 18BK/DG*	OXYGEN SENSOR SIGNAL	12
42	—	—	—
43	—	—	—
44	—	—	—
45	D20 20LG	SCI (RECEIVE)	14
46	D2 20WT/BK*	CCD BUS (-)	12
47	G7 20WT/OR*	DISTANCE SENSOR SIGNAL	15
48	V31 20BR/RD*	SPEED CONTROL SET	43
49	V32 20YL/RD*	SPEED CONTROL ON/OFF	43
50	V33 20WT/LG*	SPEED CONTROL RESUME	43
51	K51 20DB/YL*	AUTO SHUTDOWN SIGNAL	14
52	K52 20PK/BK*	PURGE SOLENOID SIGNAL	13
53	V35 20LG/RD*	SPEED CONTROL (VENT)	43
54	K54 20OR/BK*	PACK THROTTLE UNLOCK SOLENOID	16
55	—	—	—
56	G24 20GY/PK*	EMISS MAINT REMINDER LAMP	13
57	—	—	—
58	—	—	—
59	K54 18VT/BK*	AUTOMATIC IDLE SPEED MOTOR (AIS-4)	12
60	K60 18YL/BK*	AUTOMATIC IDLE SPEED MOTOR (AIS-3)	12

SHORT TAB / LONG TAB

VIEWED FROM WIRE END OF CONNECTOR

SINGLE BOARD ENGINE CONTROLLER CONNECTOR (2.5L ENGINE)

AS-HK 109

CAV	WIRE CODE	IGNITION SYSTEM CIRCUITS	SHEET NO.
1	K1 20DG/RD*	MAP SENSOR SIGNAL	18
2	K2 20TN/BK*	TEMPERATURE SENSOR SIGNAL	20
3	A14 18RD*	DIRECT BATTERY FEED	19
4	K4 18BK/LB*	SIGNAL GROUND	20
5	Z11 16BK/WT*	SIGNAL GROUND	18
6	K6 20VT/WT*	MAP SENSOR SIGNAL	20
7	K7 18OR	8 VOLT OUTPUT	20
8	A61 16DG/BK*	INJECTOR	17
9	A21 14DB	IGNITION START/RUN	18
10	—	—	—
11	Z12 16BK/TN*	POWER GROUND	19
12	Z12 16BK/TN*	POWER GROUND	19
13	—	—	—
14	K13 18YL/WT*	INJECTOR	17
15	K12 18TN	INJECTOR	17
16	K11 18WT/DB*	INJECTOR	17
17	—	—	—
18	—	—	—
19	K19 18GY	IGNITION COIL	19
20	K20 18DG	ALTERNATOR	17
21	—	—	—
22	K22 18OR/DB*	THROTTLE POSITION SENSOR	20
23	—	—	—
24	K24 18GY/BK*	DISTRIBUTOR PICKUP SIGNAL	20
25	D21 20PK	SCI (TRANSMIT)	19
26	D1 20VT/BR*	CCD BUS (+)	17
27	C20 18BR	A/C CLUTCH INPUT	19
28	—	—	—
29	K29 18WT/PK*	BRAKE SWITCH SIGNAL	43
30	T41 20BR/YL*	PARK/NEUTRAL SWITCH SIGNAL	20
31	C27 20PK	RADIATOR FAN RELAY	19
32	—	—	—
33	V36 20TN/RD*	SPEED CONTROL (VACUUM)	43
34	C13 20DB/OR*	A/C CLUTCH RELAY SIGNAL	19
35	—	—	—
36	—	—	—
37	—	—	—
38	—	—	—
39	K39 18GY/RD*	AUTOMATIC IDLE SPEED MOTOR (AIS-3)	20
40	K40 18BR*	AUTOMATIC IDLE SPEED MOTOR (AIS-1)	20
41	K41 18BK/DG*	OXYGEN SENSOR SIGNAL	18
42	—	—	—
43	—	—	—
44	K44 18TN/YL*	DISTRIBUTOR	20
45	D20 20LG	SCI (RECEIVE)	19
46	D2 20WT/BK	CCD BUS (—)	17
47	G7 20WT/OR*	DISTANCE SENSOR SIGNAL	20
48	V31 20BR/RD*	SPEED CONTROL SET	43
49	V32 20YL/RD*	SPEED CONTROL ON/OFF	43
50	V33 20WT/LG*	SPEED CONTROL RESUME	43
51	K51 20DB/YL*	AUTO SHUTDOWN SIGNAL	19
52	K52 20PK*	PURGE SOLENOID SIGNAL	18
53	V35 20LG/RD*	SPEED CONTROL (VENT)	43
54	—	—	—
55	—	—	—
56	G24 20GY/PK*	EMISS MAINT REMINDER LAMP	18
57	—	—	—
58	—	—	—
59	K59 18VT/BK*	AUTOMATIC IDLE SPEED MOTOR (AIS-4)	20
60	K60 18YL*	AUTOMATIC IDLE SPEED MOTOR (AIS-2)	20

SHORT TAB / LONG TAB

VIEWED FROM WIRE END OF CONNECTOR

SINGLE BOARD ENGINE CONTROLLER CONNECTOR (3.0L ENGINE)

AS-HK 110

CAV	WIRE CODE	IGNITION SYSTEM CIRCUITS	SHEET NO.
1	K1 20DG/RD*	MAP SENSOR SIGNAL	24
2	K2 20TN/BK*	TEMPERATURE SENSOR SIGNAL	24
3	A14 18RD*	DIRECT BATTERY FEED	23
4	K4 18BK/LB*	SIGNAL GROUND	25
5	Z11 16BK/WT*	SIGNAL GROUND	22
6	K6 20VT/WT*	MAP SENSOR SIGNAL	24
7	K7 18OR	8 VOLT OUTPUT	25
8	A61 16DG/BK*	INJECTOR	25
9	A21 14DB	IGNITION START/RUN	22
10	—	—	—
11	Z12 16BK/TN*	POWER GROUND	23
12	Z12 16BK/TN*	POWER GROUND	23
13	—	—	—
14	K13 18YL/WT*	INJECTOR	24
15	K12 18TN	INJECTOR	24
16	K11 18WT/DB*	INJECTOR	24
17	K17 18DB/YL*	IGNITION COIL	24
18	K18 18RD/YL*	IGNITION COIL	24
19	K19 18GY	IGNITION COIL	24
20	K20 18DG	ALTERNATOR	23
21	K21 18BK/RD*	CHARGE TEMP SENSOR	24
22	K22 18OR/DB*	THROTTLE POSITION SENSOR	24
23	—	—	—
24	K24 18GY/BK*	DISTRIBUTOR PICKUP SIGNAL	25
25	D21 20PK	SCI (TRANSMIT)	25
26	D1 20VT/BR*	CCD BUS (+)	25
27	C20 18BR	A/C CLUTCH INPUT	23
28	—	—	—
29	K29 18WT/PK*	BRAKE SWITCH SIGNAL	43
30	T41 20BR/YL*	PARK/NEUTRAL SWITCH SIGNAL	24
31	C27 20PK	RADIATOR FAN RELAY	23
32	—	—	—
33	V36 20TN/RD*	SPEED CONTROL (VACUUM)	43
34	C13 20DB/OR*	A/C CLUTCH RELAY SIGNAL	23
35	—	—	—
36	—	—	—
37	—	—	—
38	—	—	—
39	K39 18GY/RD*	AUTOMATIC IDLE SPEED MOTOR (AIS-3)	24
40	K40 18BR*	AUTOMATIC IDLE SPEED MOTOR (AIS-1)	24
41	K41 18BK/DG*	OXYGEN SENSOR SIGNAL	24
42	K42 18BK/LG*	DETONATION SENSOR SIGNAL	25
43	—	—	—
44	K44 18TN/YL*	DISTRIBUTOR	26
45	D20 20LG	SCI (RECEIVE)	23
46	D2 20WT/BK	CCD BUS (—)	25
47	G7 20WT/OR*	DISTANCE SENSOR SIGNAL	25
48	V31 20BR/RD*	SPEED CONTROL SET	43
49	V32 20YL/RD*	SPEED CONTROL ON/OFF	43
50	V33 20WT/LG*	SPEED CONTROL RESUME	43
51	K51 20DB/YL*	AUTO SHUTDOWN SIGNAL	23
52	K52 20PK*	PURGE SOLENOID SIGNAL	22
53	V35 20LG/RD*	SPEED CONTROL (VENT)	43
54	—	—	—
55	—	—	—
56	G24 20GY/PK*	EMISS MAINT REMINDER LAMP	23
57	—	—	—
58	—	—	—
59	K59 18VT/BK*	AUTOMATIC IDLE SPEED MOTOR (AIS-4)	24
60	K60 18YL*	AUTOMATIC IDLE SPEED MOTOR (AIS-2)	24

SHORT TAB / LONG TAB

VIEWED FROM WIRE END OF CONNECTOR

SINGLE BOARD ENGINE CONTROLLER CONNECTOR (3.3L ENGINE)

AS-HK 111

IGNITION START/RUN A21 14DB
DIMMED ILLUMINATION FEED E1 22TN
LAMP FEED L7 18BK/YL*
RADIO FEED X12 20RD/WT*
TURN SIGNAL FEED L5 18BK*
WIPER MOTOR V8 18DB
IGNITION ACCESSORY FEED A31 14BK*
HAZARD FEED L9 18BK*
BATTERY FEED A15 14PK

HEATED MIRROR FEED C16 20LB/YL*
EBL SWITCH C15 12BK*
BODY LAMPS A4 12BK/RD* M1 18PK

HEADLAMP A3 12RD*
BLOWER MOTOR C1 12DG
POWER WINDOWS F21 12TN
IGNITION ACCESSORY/RUN A22 12BK/OR*
POWER SEATS, LOCK & HORN F35 12RD
HEADLAMP (LO) L4 14VT/WT*
LEFT HEADLAMP L43 20VT
RIGHT HEADLAMP L44 20VT/RD*
PARK LAMPS A6 12RD/BK*

SEE OWNERS MANUAL 527075
IGNITION START/RUN G5 20DB*
SPEED CONTROL V34 20WT/RD*
REAR WIPER V23 18BR/PK*

FOG LAMPS F61 18WT/OR*
PARK LAMPS F63 18PK/RD*
FEED F62 16RD
LAMPS/WIPER F20 16WT
IGN ACCESSORY/RUN A22 12BK/OR*
STOP LAMP F32 18PK/DB*
A/C F36 16WT*
BATT FEED A3 12RD*

FUSE #	AMPS	COLOR	SHEET #
1	20	YELLOW	53
2	10	RED	70, 76
3	20	YELLOW	76, 81
4	—	NOT USED	—
5	20	YELLOW	46
6	20	YELLOW	53
7	10	RED	58, 60, 62
8	—	NOT USED	—
9	7.5	BROWN	50
10	—	NOT USED	—
11	—	NOT USED	—
12	—	NOT USED	—
13	20	YELLOW	66
14	2	GRAY	43
15	10	RED	72
16	—	NOT USED	—
17	10	RED	50
18	10	RED	41
19	20	YELLOW	43
20	20	YELLOW	64
21	20	YELLOW	69
22	20	YELLOW	50
23	20	YELLOW	44
24	20	YELLOW	89
25	30	CIRCUIT BREAKER	79
26	30	LT GREEN	27, 29, 57
27	30	CIRCUIT BREAKER	44
28	—	NOT USED	—

FUSE BLOCK

AS-HK 112

1991 Caravan/Voyager and Town & Country

CAV	WIRE CODE	IGNITION SYSTEM CIRCUITS
1	—	NOT USED
2	—	NOT USED
3	—	NOT USED
4	—	NOT USED
5	—	NOT USED
6	—	NOT USED
7	—	NOT USED
8	—	NOT USED
9	—	NOT USED
10	—	NOT USED
11	L60 18TN	RT FT TURN SIGNAL
12	L62 18BR/RD*	RT RR STOP & TURN SIG LP
13	L59 18TN/LG*	FLASHER FEED
14	L63 18DG/RD*	LT RR STOP & TURN SIG LP
15	L61 18LG	LT FT TURN SIGNAL
16	L53 18BR	STOP LAMP FEED
17	Z1 18BK	GROUND
18	L4 14VT/WT	HEADLAMP (LO-BEAM)
19	L2 14LG	HEADLAMP DIMMER SWITCH
20	L3 14RD/OR*	HEADLAMP (HI-BEAM)
21	L20 14LG/WT*	OPTICAL HORN
22	—	NOT USED
23	—	NOT USED
24	—	NOT USED

MULTI-FUNCTION SWITCH CONNECTOR

AS-HK 113

RELAY BLOCK

AS-HK 114

CAV	CIRCUIT	DESCRIPTION
1	E2 18OR	DIMMABLE LAMP FEED
2	D1 18VT/BR*	SERIAL BUSS B+
3	D2 18WT*	SERIAL BUSS B-
4	G32 18BK/LB*	EXT TEMP SENSOR RETURN
5	G31 18VT/LG*	EXT TEMP SENSOR SIGNAL
6	M2 18YL	DOOR JAMB SWITCHES
7	Q41 18WT	IGNITION FEED
8	—	NOT USED
9	Z1 18BK	GROUND
10	—	NOT USED
11	Z1 18BK	GROUND
12	M11 18PK/LB*	SWITCHED COURTESY LAMP FEED
13	M1 18PK	READING AND VISOR LAMP FEED

AS-HK 115   OVERHEAD CONSOLE CONNECTOR

WHITE

CAV	CIRCUIT	DESCRIPTION	SHEET
1	G74 18TN/RD*	DOOR AJAR SWITCH RT FRONT DOOR	105
2	G78 18TN/BK*	LIFTGATE/DECK LID AJAR SWITCH	105
3	—	NOT USED	—
4	G9 20GY/BK*	BRAKE WARNING	104
5	—	NOT USED	—
6	—	NOT USED	—
7	L60 18TN	RT FRONT TURN SIGNAL	104
8	—	NOT USED	—
9	D14 18LB	DECODE - HIGH INST CLUSTER	104
10	P35 18 OR/VT*	POWER DOOR LOCK B+ LOCK	105
11	G60 22GY/YL*	OIL PRESSURE SENDING UNIT	104
12	D13 18OR/DB*	DECODE - LOW INST CLUSTER	104
13	—	NOT USED	—
14	G76 18TN/YL*	DOOR AJAR SWITCH REAR DOOR	105
15	G42 20DB/YL*	SIGNAL GROUND	105
16	—	NOT USED	—
17	G11 20WT/BK*	PARK BRAKE SWITCH	105
18	—	NOT USED	—
19	L81 18LG	LT FRONT TURN SIGNAL	104
20	L94 20OR/WT*	LO BEAM RELAY COIL	104
21	L2 16LG	HEADLAMP DIMMER SWITCH FEED	104
22	Q33 20BR/LB*	SP - SENSE - GND FROM LIFT GATE	105
23	G8 20GY	LOW OIL PRESSURE WARNING	104
24	—	NOT USED	—
25	G20 22VT/YL*	WATER TEMP SENDING UNIT	104

BODY COMPUTER CONNECTOR   AS-HK 116

1991 Caravan/Voyager and Town & Country

BLUE

CAV	CIRCUIT	DESCRIPTION	SHEET
1	G75 18TN	DOOR AJAR SWITCH LEFT FRONT DOOR	102
2	G26 20LB	KEY-IN BUZZER CHIME	103
3	E17 20YL/BK*	ELEC DISPLAY	103
4	E92 20OR/BK*	SW POD TO ILLUM MOD DIMMING CONTROL	103
5	G4 20DB	FUEL TANK SENDING UNIT	102
6	G5 20DB/WT*	IGN RUN/START FEED	102
7	D1 18VT/BR*	SERIAL BUSS B+	101
8	M1 18PK	COURTESY, DOME, VISOR LAMPS	102
9	—	NOT USED	—
10	V5 18DG	WIPER MOTOR FEED	101
11	V6 18DB	WIPER MOTOR	101
12	V7 18DG/WT*	PULSE WIPE PARK (B-) DWELL	103
13	G16 20BK/LB*	CHIME GROUND	102
14	G10 20LG/RD*	SEAT BELT WARNING	102
15	G29 22BK/TN*	LOW WASH FLUID INDICATOR	101
16	M22 18WT	ILLUMINATED ENTRY RELAY GROUND	103
17	V9 18DG/YL*	PULSE WIPE INTERMITTENT	103
18	V10 18BR	WASH PUMP MOTOR	101
19	Z2 18BK/LG*	GROUND	101
20	D2 18WT/BK*	SERIAL BUSS B-	101
21	P38 20OR/WT*	AUTO DOOR LOCK RELAY COIL B+	103
22	M51 18YL/RD*	KEY IN LIGHT GROUND	103
23	G13 18DB/RD*	SEAT BELT LAMP	102
24	—	NOT USED	—
25	M2 18YL	GROUND FOR COURTESY LAMPS	102

AS-HK 117   BODY COMPUTER CONNECTOR

GRAY

CAV	CIRCUIT	DESCRIPTION
1	—	NOT USED
2	M1 18PK	ILLUMINATION
3	D13 18OR/DB*	DECODE-LOW INST CLUST TO BCOMP
4	—	NOT USED
5	D14 18LB	DECODE-HIGH INST CLUST TO BCOMP
6	E2 20OR	I/P DIMMABLE ILLUMINATION
7	Z2 18BK/LG*	GROUND
8	G6 20GY	LOW OIL PRESSURE
9	D2 18WT/BK*	SERIAL BUSS B+
10	D1 18VT/BR*	SERIAL BUSS B+
11	G5 20DB/WT*	IGN RUN/START
12	—	NOT USED
13	—	NOT USED
14	Z3 20BK/OR*	GROUND

ELECTRONIC CLUSTER CONNECTOR

AS-HK 118

SHORT TAB

LONG TAB

VIEWED FROM WIRE
END OF CONNECTOR

CAV	WIRE CODE	IGNITION SYSTEM CIRCUITS	SHEET
1	T1 16LG*	PRNDL SWITCH	32
2	T2 14TN/BK*	BACK UP LIGHT RELAY	33
3	T3 14VT	BACK UP LIGHT RELAY	33
4	D2 20WT/BK*	CCD BUS(-)	33
5	D1 20BK/VT	CCD BUS(+)	33
6	—	—	—
7	—	—	—
8	A41 YL	STARTER RELAY	31
9	T9 18OR/BK*	OVERDRIVE PRESSURE SWITCH	32
10	—	—	—
11	A21 14DB	NEUTRAL SAFETY SWITCH	31
12	K22 18OR/DB*	(SMEC) SINGLE MODULE CONTROLLER	31
13	T13 10DB/BK*	SPEED SENSOR GROUND	31
14	T14 18LG/WT*	OUTPUT SPEED SENSOR	31
15	T15 18LG	SAFETY SHUTDOWN RELAY	32
16	T16 16RD	TRANS. SOLENOIDS & PRESSURE SWITCH	32
17	T16 16RD	SAFETY SHUTDOWN RELAY	32
18	—	—	—
19	T19 18WT	TRANS. SOLENOIDS & PRESSURE SWITCH	32
20	T20 18LB	TRANS. SOLENOIDS & PRESSURE SWITCH	32
21	—	—	—
22	—	—	—
23	—	—	—
24	—	—	—
25	—	—	—
26	—	—	—
27	—	—	—
28	—	—	—
29	—	—	—
30	—	—	—
31	—	—	—
32	—	—	—
33	—	—	—
34	—	—	—
35	—	—	—
36	—	—	—
37	—	—	—
38	—	—	—
39	—	—	—
40	—	—	—
41	T41 18BR/YL*	NEUTRAL SAFETY SWITCH	31
42	T42 18VT*	PRNDL SWITCH	32
43	D1 20VT/BR*	CCD BUS (+)	33
44	D2 20WT/BK*	CCD BUS (-)	33
45	K24 18GY/BK*	DISTRIBUTOR	31
46	—	—	—
47	T47 18YL/BK*	TRANS. SOLENOIDS & PRESSURE SWITCH	32
48	—	—	—
49	—	—	—
50	T50 18DG	TRANS. SOLENOIDS & PRESSURE SWITCH	32
51	K4 18BK/LB*	SIGNAL GROUND	31
52	T52 18RD/BK*	TURBINE SPEED SENSOR	31
53	Z14 18BK/YL*	SIGNAL GROUND	32
54	Z14 18BK/YL*	SIGNAL GROUND	32
55	—	—	—
56	A14 16RD*	DIRECT BATTERY GROUND	32
57	Z13 18BK/RD*	SIGNAL GROUND	32
58	Z13 18BK/RD*	SIGNAL GROUND	32
59	T59 18BK	TRANS. SOLENOIDS & PRESSURE SWITCH	32
60	T60 18BR	TRANS. SOLENOIDS & PRESSURE SWITCH	32

AS-HK 119   ELECTRONIC AUTOMATIC
TRANSAXLE CONTROL MODULE CONNECTOR

BLUE

CAV	CIRCUIT	DESCRIPTION
1	—	NOT USED
2	—	NOT USED
3	L60 18 TN	RT FT TURN SIGNAL
4	—	NOT USED
5	L61 18 LG	LT FT TURN SIGNAL
6	G19 20 LG*	ANTI-LOCK BRAKE WARNING
7	G5 20 DB*	IGN RUN/START FEED
8	G13 18DB/RD*	SEAT BELT LAMP
9	G34 16RD/BK*	HI BEAM INDICATOR
10	G24 22GY/PK*	EMISSION MAINTENANCE LAMP
11	Z3 20BK/OR*	GROUND
12	—	NOT USED
13	—	NOT USED
14	G9 20GY*	BRAKE WARNING LAMP

WARNING LAMP CENTER CONNECTOR

AS-HK 120

1991 Caravan/Voyager and Town & Country

GREEN

CAV	CIRCUIT	DESCRIPTION	SHEET NO.
1	—	NOT USED	—
2	L50 18WT/TN*	STOP LAMP SWITCH	89
3	G75 18TN	LEFT FRONT DOOR AJAR SWITCH	73
4	M11 18PK/LB*	SWITCHED COURTESY LAMP FEED	81
5	G78 18TN/BK*	LIFTGATE AJAR SWITCH	73
6	M2 18YL	GROUND FOR COURTESY LAMPS	81
7	G4 20DB	FUEL TANK SENDING UNIT	88, 100
8	—	NOT USED	—
9	L1 18VT/BK*	BACK UP LAMP FEED	89
10	L1 18VT/BK*	BACK UP LAMP FEED	89
	L1 18VT/BK*	BACK UP LAMP FEED	89
11	L62 18BR/RD*	RT RR TURN AND STOP LAMP	89
12	G10 20LG/RD*	SEAT BELT WARNING SWITCH	74
13	G16 20BK/LB*	CHIME GROUND	102
14	L63 18DG/RD*	LT RR TURN AND STOP LAMP	89
15	G42 20DB/YL*	SIGNAL GROUND	100
16	—	NOT USED	

LEFT BODY CONNECTOR

AS-HK 121

CAV	CIRCUIT	DESCRIPTION	SHEET NO.
1	Z1 18BK	GROUND	49
	Z1 18BK	GROUND	49
2	E2 20OR	I/P ILLUMINATION	49
3	L59 18TN/LG*	FLASHER FEED	49
4	L53 18BK	STOP LAMP FEED	49
5	L50 18WT/TN*	STOP LAMP SW	49
6	L55 18PK/BK*	SW FEED FROM HAZARD UNIT	49
7	L9 18BK/WT*	FUSED HAZARD FLASHER FEED	49
8	L5 18BK/PK*	TURN SIGNAL FLASHER UNIT	49

LEFT POD CONNECTOR

CAV	CIRCUIT	DESCRIPTION	SHEET NO.
1	V22 18BR/YL*	WASH DELAY - RR WIPER	45
2	V21 18DB/RD*	ON/OFF SW - RR WIPER	45
3	V6 18DB	WINDSHIELD WIPER MOTOR	45
	V6 18DB	WINDSHIELD WIPER MOTOR	45
4	V10 18BR	WASH PUMP MOTOR	45
5	Z3 20BK/OR*	GROUND	45
6	E2 20OR	I/P ILLUMINATION	45
7	—	NOT USED	—
8	—	NOT USED	—

RIGHT POD CONNECTOR

STEERING COLUMN SWITCH
TO PANEL WIRING

AS-HK 122

LT BODY

CAV	CIRCUIT	DESCRIPTION	SHEET
1	L7 18BK/YL*	LICENSE LAMP FEED	90
2	Z1 12BK	GROUND	90
3	C15 12BK*	EBL	70
4	G78 18TN/BK*	DECK LID AJAR SWITCH	73
5	—	NOT USED	—
6	M11 18PK/LB*	SWITCHED COURTESY LAMP FEED	82
7	V20 16BK/WT*	WASH PUMP GROUND	67
8	Q2 14LG/BK*	LIFTGATE RELEASE	71
9	—	NOT USED	—
10	L50 18WT/TN*	CHMSL FEED	90
11	M2 18YL	LIFTGATE JAMB SWITCH	82
12	—	NOT USED	—
13	—	NOT USED	—

RT BODY

CAV	CIRCUIT	DESCRIPTION	SHEET
1	V21 18DB/RD*	RR WIPER ON/OFF SIGNAL	66
2	—	NOT USED	—
3	—	NOT USED	—
4	X57 18BR/LB*	LEFT REAR SPEAKER B-	61, 63
5	—	NOT USED	—
6	X58 18DB/OR*	RIGHT REAR SPEAKER B-	61, 63
7	V22 18BR/YL*	RR WIPER DELAY	66
8	F20 18WT	REAR WIPER PARK	66
9	X51 18BR/YL	LEFT REAR SPEAKER B+	61, 63
10	—	NOT USED	—
11	X52 18DB/WT*	RIGHT REAR SPEAKER B+	61, 63
12	—	NOT USED	—
13	—	NOT USED	—

BODY CONNECTORS

AS-HK 123

CAV	WIRE CODE	IGNITION SYSTEM CIRCUITS	SHEET
1	B1 20YL/DB*	RIGHT REAR WHEEL SENSOR(-)	34
2	B2 20YL	RIGHT REAR WHEEL SENSOR(+)	34
3	B3 20LG/DB*	LEFT REAR WHEEL SENSOR(-)	34
4	B4 20LG	LEFT REAR WHEEL SENSOR(+)	34
5	Z1 16BK	GROUND	35
6	B6 20WT/DB*	RIGHT FRONT WHEEL SENSOR(-)	34
7	B7 20WT	RIGHT FRONT WHEEL SENSOR(+)	34
8	B8 20RD/DB*	LEFT FRONT WHEEL SENSOR(-)	34
9	B9 20RD	LEFT FRONT WHEEL SENSOR(+)	34
10	B210 20RD/BK*	ABS TRANSDUCER RETURN(-)	35
11	D11 20WT/VT*	DIAGNOSTICS	37
12	D12 20OR	DIAGNOSTICS	37
13	L50 18WT/TN*	STOP LAMP SWITCH	36
14	G9 20GY/BK*	BRAKE WARNING LAMP SWITCH	36
15	G19 29 LG/OR*	ABS WARNING LAMP	37
16	—	NOT USED	—
17	B217 14RD	LOW ACCUMULATOR	35
18	B218 20WT/OR*	PRIMARY PRESSURE /DPA	35
19	B219 20DB	(ABS)	35
20	T40 14BR	STARTER RELAY CONTACT TO SOLENOID	35
21	—	NOT USED	—
22	—	NOT USED	—
23	—	NOT USED	—
24	—	NOT USED	—
25	—	NOT USED	—
26	—	NOT USED	—
27	—	NOT USED	—
28	—	NOT USED	—
29	—	NOT USED	—
30	—	NOT USED	—
31	—	NOT USED	—
32	—	NOT USED	—
33	—	NOT USED	—
34	—	NOT USED	—
35	—	NOT USED	—
36	—	NOT USED	—
37	—	NOT USED	—
38	—	NOT USED	—
39	—	NOT USED	—
40	—	NOT USED	—
41	—	NOT USED	—
42	B242 20BR*	LEFT FRONT BUILD VALVE	36
43	B243 20DG/BK*	LEFT FRONT DELAY VALVE	36
44	—	NOT USED	—
45	B245 20WT/LG*	LEFT FRONT ISOLATE VALVE	36
46	B246 20BR/RD*	RIGHT FRONT BUILD VALVE	36
47	B47 16RD/LB*	MODULE FEED	37
48	B248 20DG*	RIGHT FRONT DELAY VALVE	36
49	B249 20WT/TN*	RIGHT FRONT ISOLATE VALVE	36
50	B47 16RD/LB*	MODULE FEED	37
51	B251 20WT*	LEFT REAR ISOLATE VALVE	36
52	B252 20BR/TN*	RIGHT AND NLEFT REAR BUILD VALVE	36
53	—	NOT USED	—
54	B254 20DG/OR*	RIGHT AND LEFT REAR DELAY VALVE	36
55	B255 20WT/PK*	RIGHT AND LEFT REAR ISOLATOR VALVE	36
56	—	NOT USED	—
57	B57 20BR/BK*	ABS SYSTEM RELAY COIL FEED	36
58	B258 20GY/LB*	TRANSDUCER FEED(+)	35
59	—	NOT USED	—
60	A21 14DB	IGNITION START RUN	37

SHORT TAB

LONG TAB

VIEWED FROM WIRE
END OF CONNECTOR

ANTI-LOCK BRAKE
SYSTEM CONTROLLER CONNECTOR

AS-HK 124

1991 Caravan/Voyager and Town & Country

CAV	CIRCUIT	DESCRIPTION	SHEET
1	B82 12BR*	ABS PUMP MOTOR FEED	35
2	Z1 14BK	GROUND	35

CAV	CIRCUIT	DESCRIPTION	SHEET
1	Z1 16BK	GROUND	35
2	B210 20RD/BK*	TRANSDUCER RETURN (–)	35
3	—	NOT USED	—
4	G9 20GY*	BRAKE WARNING LAMP	35
5	B21 14GY	ABS PUMP MOTOR CONTROL	35
6	T40 14BR	STARTER RELAY CONTACT	35
7	B258 20GY/LB*	TRANSDUCER FEED (+)	35
8	B219 20DB	(ABS)	35
9	B218 20WT/OR*	PRIMARY PRESSURE/DPA	35
10	B217 14RD	LOW ACCUMULATOR	35

CAV	CIRCUIT	DESCRIPTION
1	T47 18YL*	KICK-DOWN PRESSURE SWITCH
2	T50 18DG	LOW REV PRESSURE SWITCH
3	T9 18OR*	OVERDRIVE PRESSURE SWITCH
4	T16 16RD	SWITCHED BATTERY FEED
5	T59 18PK	UD SOLENOID
6	T60 18BR	OD SOLENOID
7	T20 18LB	LR/LU SOLENOID
8	T19 18WT	KICK DOWN/LOW AND REVERSE

CAV	CIRCUIT	DESCRIPTION	SHEET
1	B245 20WT/LG*	LEFT FRONT ISOLATE VALVE	36
2	B243 20DG/BK*	LEFT FRONT DECAY VALVE	36
3	B242 20BR*	LEFT FRONT BUILD VALVE	36
4	B254 20DG/OR*	RIGHT AND LEFT REAR DECAY VALVE	36
5	B255 20WT/PK*	RIGHT AND LEFT REAR ISOLATOR VALVE	36
6	B249 20WT/TN*	RIGHT FRONT ISOLATE VALVE	36
7	B248 20DG/WT*	RIGHT FRONT DECAY VALVE	36
8	B246 20BR/RD*	RIGHT FRONT BUILD VALVE	36
9	B252 20BR/TN*	RIGHT AND LEFT REAR BUILD VALVE	36
10	B251 20WT*	LEFT REAR ISOLATE VALVE	36

DK GRAY

AS–HK 125	ABS PUMP MOTOR CONNECTORS

TRANSAXLE SOLENOID CONNECTOR	AS–HK 126

1991 Caravan/Voyager and Town & Country

TORQUE SPECIFICATIONS

Component	English	Metric
Expansion valve Torx® screws:	100 inch lbs.	11 Nm
Linkage drive crank-to-wiper motor shaft:	95 inch lbs.	11 Nm
Refrigerant lines and sealing plate:	17 ft. lbs. 23 Nm	
Steering wheel nut:	45 ft. lbs.	61 Nm
Wiper arm attaching nut:	10 ft. lbs.	14 Nm

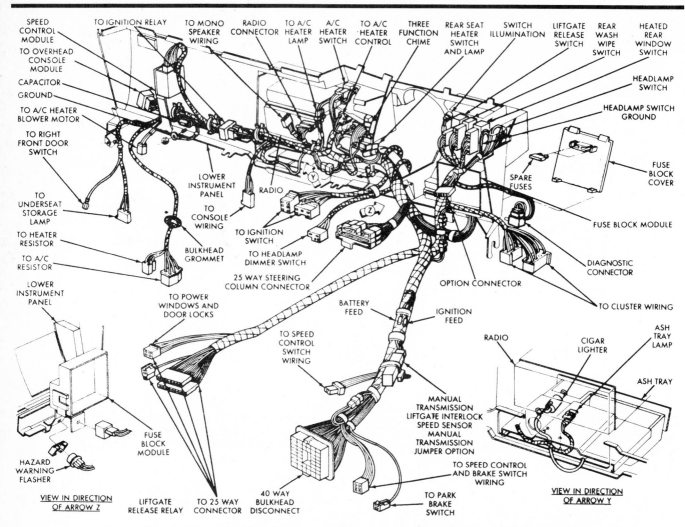

SPEED CONTROL MODULE
TO OVERHEAD CONSOLE MODULE
CAPACITOR
GROUND
TO A/C HEATER BLOWER MOTOR
TO RIGHT FRONT DOOR SWITCH
TO UNDERSEAT STORAGE LAMP
TO HEATER RESISTOR
TO A/C RESISTOR
LOWER INSTRUMENT PANEL

TO IGNITION RELAY
TO MONO SPEAKER WIRING
RADIO CONNECTOR
TO A/C HEATER LAMP
A/C HEATER SWITCH
TO A/C HEATER CONTROL
THREE FUNCTION CHIME
REAR SEAT HEATER SWITCH AND LAMP
SWITCH ILLUMINATION
LIFTGATE RELEASE SWITCH
REAR WASH WIPE SWITCH
HEATED REAR WINDOW SWITCH

HEADLAMP SWITCH
HEADLAMP SWITCH GROUND
FUSE BLOCK COVER
SPARE FUSES
FUSE BLOCK MODULE
DIAGNOSTIC CONNECTOR
TO CLUSTER WIRING

LOWER INSTRUMENT PANEL
TO CONSOLE WIRING
RADIO
TO IGNITION SWITCH
TO HEADLAMP DIMMER SWITCH
25 WAY STEERING COLUMN CONNECTOR
BULKHEAD GROMMET
OPTION CONNECTOR

TO POWER WINDOWS AND DOOR LOCKS
TO SPEED CONTROL SWITCH WIRING
BATTERY FEED
IGNITION FEED

HAZARD WARNING FLASHER
FUSE BLOCK MODULE
LIFTGATE RELEASE RELAY
TO 25 WAY CONNECTOR
40 WAY BULKHEAD DISCONNECT
MANUAL TRANSMISSION LIFTGATE INTERLOCK SPEED SENSOR MANUAL TRANSMISSION JUMPER OPTION
TO PARK BRAKE SWITCH
TO SPEED CONTROL AND BRAKE SWITCH WIRING

RADIO
CIGAR LIGHTER
ASH TRAY LAMP
ASH TRAY

VIEW IN DIRECTION OF ARROW Z
VIEW IN DIRECTION OF ARROW Y

Instrument panel wiring harness and component location — 1990–91 Models

Drive Train

7

QUICK REFERENCE INDEX

GENERAL INDEX

UNDERSTANDING THE MANUAL TRANSMISSION

Because of the way an internal combustion engine breathes, it can produce torque, or twisting force, only within a narrow speed range. Most modern, overhead valve engines must turn at about 2,500 rpm to produce their peak torque. By 4,500 rpm they are producing so little torque that continued increases in engine speed produce no power increases.

The torque peak on overhead camshaft engines is, generally, much higher, but much narrower.

The manual transmission and clutch are employed to vary the relationship between engine speed and the speed of the wheels so that adequate engine power can be produced under all circumstances. The clutch allows engine torque to be applied to the transmission input shaft gradually, due to mechanical slippage. The car can, consequently, be started smoothly from a full stop.

The transmission changes the ratio between the rotating speeds of the engine and the wheels by the use of gears. 4-speed or 5-speed transmissions are most common. The lower gears allow full engine power to be applied to the wheels during acceleration at low speeds.

The clutch drive plate is a thin disc, the center of which is splined to the transmission input shaft. Both sides of the disc are covered with a layer of material which is similar to brake lining and which is capable of allowing slippage without roughness or excessive noise.

The clutch cover is bolted to the engine flywheel and incorporates a diaphragm spring which provides the pressure to engage the clutch. The cover also houses the pressure plate. The driven disc is sandwiched between the pressure plate and the smooth surface of the flywheel when the clutch pedal is released, thus forcing it to turn at the same speed as the engine crankshaft.

The transmission contains a mainshaft which passes all the way through the transmission, from the clutch to the halfshafts. This shaft is separated at one point, so that front and rear portions can turn at different speeds.

Power is transmitted by a countershaft in the lower gears and reverse. The gears of the countershaft mesh with gears on the mainshaft, allowing power to be carried from one to the other. All the countershaft gears are integral with that shaft, while several of the mainshaft gears can either rotate independently of the shaft or be locked to it. Shifting from one gear to the next causes one of the gears to be freed from rotating with the shaft and locks another to it. Gears are locked and unlocked by internal dog clutches which slide between the center of the gear and the shaft. The forward gears usually employ synchronizers; friction members which smoothly bring gear and shaft to the same speed before the toothed dog clutches are engaged.

The clutch is operating properly if:

1. It will stall the engine when released with the vehicle held stationary.

2. The shift lever can be moved freely between 1st and reverse gears when the vehicle is stationary and the clutch disengaged.

A clutch pedal free-play adjustment is incorporated in the linkage. If there is about 1–2 in. (25–50mm) of motion before the pedal begins to release the clutch, it is adjusted properly. Inadequate free-play wears all parts of the clutch releasing mechanisms and may cause slippage. Excessive free-play may cause inadequate release and hard shifting of gears.

Some clutches use a hydraulic system in place of mechanical linkage. If the clutch fails to release, fill the clutch master cylinder with fluid to the proper level and pump the clutch pedal to fill the system with fluid. Bleed the system in the same way as a brake system. If leaks are located, tighten loose connections or overhaul the master or slave cylinder as necessary.

Front wheel drive cars do not have conventional rear axles or drive shafts. Instead, power is transmitted from the engine to a transaxle, or a combination of transmission and drive axle, in one unit. Both the transmission and drive axle accomplish the same function as their counterparts in a front engine/rear drive axle design. The difference is in the location of the components.

In place of a conventional driveshaft, a front wheel drive design uses two driveshafts, sometimes called halfshafts, which couple the drive axle portion of the transaxle to the wheels. Universal joints or constant velocity joints are used just as they would in a rear wheel drive design.

Manual Transaxle

Identification

Seven manual transaxles, built by Chrysler, are used; a 4-speed, A-460 and six 5-speeds; A-465, A-520, A-523, A-525, A-555 and A-568. All of these transaxles are based on the same design and components, therefore servicing each is almost identical. The transmission and differential are contained together in a single die-cast aluminum case. All of the transmissions are fully synchronized in all gears. Dexron®II automatic transmission type fluid (models through 1986) or 5W-30 motor oil (1987 and later models) is used for lubrication. The transaxle model, build date and final drive ratio are stamped on a tag that is attached to the top of the transaxle. Always give the tag information when ordering parts for the unit.

Adjustments

SHIFT LINKAGE

NOTE: If a hard shifting situation is experienced, determine if the cables are binding and need replacement, or if a linkage adjustment is necessary. Disconnect both cables at the transaxle and move the selector through the various positions. If the selector moves freely an adjustment may be all that is necessary; if not, cable replacement might be indicated.

1. Working over the left front fender, unscrew the lock pin, from the transaxle selector shaft housing.

Transaxle pinned in the neutral position to adjust gearshift linkage

Cable operated gearshift linkage

Remove the pull up ring and boot

2. Reverse the lock pin so that the long end faces down and insert into the same threaded hole it was removed from. Push the selector shaft into the selector housing while inserting the pin. A hole in the selector shaft will align with the lock pin, allowing the pin to be threaded into the housing. This will lock the selector shaft into the neutral position.

3. From inside the vehicle, remove the gearshift knob by pulling straight up. Remove the reverse pull up ring by first removing the retaining nut and then pull the ring up and off of the lever.

4. Remove the shift lever boot. Remove the console.

5. For models built through 1987: Fabricate two adjusting lock pins out of $3/16$ in. rod. Total length of the pins should be 5 inches with a hook shaped on one end.

6. Loosen the selector and cross-over cable end adjusting/retainer bolts. Be sure the transaxle end of the cables are connected.

7. Install one adjusting lock pin on the side of the lever bracket in hole provided while moving lever slightly to help alignment. Install the other lock pin at the rear of the lever bracket (cross-over cable). Be sure that both cable end pieces are free to move.

8. After pins are inserted, the cable ends will be positioned to the correct adjustment point. Tighten the adjustment/retainer bolts to 55 inch lbs.

9. On model built in late 1986 and later: Loosen the selector and crossover cable adjusting screws. Remove the adjusting screw tool and attached spacer block from the shifter support.

10. Install the adjusting screw tool through the attached spacer, and screw the tool into the base of the shifter tower base.

11. Tighten the adjusting screw tool to 20 in. lbs.

12. Tighten the selector/crossover cable retaining screws to 70 in. lbs. Proper torque on the selector/crossover cable bracket is very important for proper operation.

13. Remove the adjusting screw tool and attach it to the bracket.

14. Check the gearshift cables for proper connection to the transaxle.

15. Install console and remainder of the removed parts.

16. Remove the selector housing lock pin at the transaxle and install it in the reversed position (see Step 1). Tighten the lock pin to 105 inch lbs. check gear shift operation.

Back-up Light Switch

The back-up light switch is located at the upper left side of the transaxle case. The switch is screwed into the transaxle and serviced by replacement. No adjustment is possible.

Remove the center console

Install the adjusting screw tool as shown

Adjusting the crossover cable

Adjusting the selector cable

Gearshift cable connections at the transaxle

MANUAL TRANSAXLE

REMOVAL AND INSTALLATION

NOTE: Transaxle removal does not require engine removal.

1. Disconnect the negative battery cable from the battery.
2. Install a sling or lifting bracket to the No. 4 cylinder exhaust manifold mounting bolt (through 1987), or the battery ground strap bolt (1988 and later). Place an engine support device across the engine compartment and connect to the sling. Tighten until slight upward pressure is applied to the engine.
3. Disconnect the gearshift operating control from the transaxle selector lever.
4. Loosen the wheel lug nuts slightly. Raise and support the front of the vehicle.
5. Remove both front wheel and tire assemblies. Remove the

5-speed manual transaxle — component identification

Engine support fixture installed

Remove the clutch housing bolts

4- and 5-speed transaxle components — left side

4- and 5-speed transaxle components — right side

left front engine splash shield. Drain the fluid from the transaxle.

6. Remove the left front mount from the transaxle. Remove the speedometer cable adapter and pinion from the transaxle.

7. Disconnect the front sway bar. Disconnect the anti-rotational link (anti-hop damper) from the cross member bracket, do not remove the bracket from the transaxle. Remove both lower ball joint-to-steering knuckle mounting bolts. Pry the ball joint from the steering knuckle. Remove the halfshaft from the drive wheel hub.

8. Remove the halfshafts from the differential.

9. Remove the back-up light switch connector.

10. Remove the engine mount bracket from the front crossover.

11. Remove the front mount insulator through bolt. Place a suitable floor jack or transmission jack under the transaxle and raise to gently support.

12. Remove the top bell housing bolts.

13. Remove the left engine mount at rear cover plate. Remove the starter motor.

14. Secure the transaxle to the jack and remove the lower bell housing bolts. Check that all transaxle support mounts or through bolts are removed. Slide the jack and transaxle away from the engine and lower assembly.

To install:

15. To install the transaxle; make two locating pins for extra same thread bolts that are slightly longer than the mounting

bolts. Cut the heads off with a hacksaw, remove any burrs or sharp edges with a file. Install the bolts into the rear of the engine and guide the transaxle over them. After the transaxle is in position, remove the guide bolts and install mounting bolts.

16. Raise the transaxle into position and slide it over the locating pins. Install the top bell housing bolts.

17. Install the front mount insulator through bolt. Install the left engine mount and the starter motor.

18. Install the halfshafts.

19. Connect the sway bar and anti-hop/rotation link. Install the front wheels and lower the vehicle.

20. Install the speedometer drive and cable. Connect the throttle and shift linkage. Remove the engine support and connect the negative battery cable. Fill the transaxle with the correct lubrication fluid.

4-Speed Manual Transaxle Overhaul

TRANSAXLE CASE DISASSEMBLY

1. Remove the transaxle from the vehicle and position on suitable holding fixture.

4- and 5-speed transaxle components — front

4- and 5-speed transaxle components — top

4- and 5-speed transaxle components — rear

2. Remove the differential cover bolts and the stud nuts, then remove the cover.

3. Remove the differential bearing retainer bolts.

4. Using tool No. L-4435 or equivalent spanner, rotate the differential bearing retainer to remove it.

5. Remove the extension housing bolts, differential assembly and extension housing.

6. Unbolt and remove the selector shaft housing.

7. Remove the stud nuts and the bolts from the rear end cover then pry off the rear end cover.

8. Remove the large snapring from the intermediate shaft rear ball bearing.

9. Remove the bearing retainer plate by tapping it with a plastic hammer.

10. Remove the 3rd/4th shift fork rail.

11. Remove the reverse idler gear shaft and gear.

12. Remove the input shaft gear assembly and the intermediate shaft gear assembly.

13. To remove the clutch release bearing, remove the E-clips from the clutch release shaft, then disassemble the clutch shaft components.

14. Remove the input shaft seal retainer bolts, the seal, the retainer assembly and the select shim.

15. Remove the reverse shift lever E-clip and flat washer and disassemble the reverse shift lever components.

16. Press the input shaft front bearing cup from the transaxle case.

17. Unbolt and remove the intermediate shaft front bearing retaining strap.

18. Remove the intermediate shaft front bearing and oil feeder using a bearing puller.

19. Press the intermediate shaft front bearing with the oil feeder into the transaxle case. The bearing identification letters must be facing upward during installation.

20. Install the intermediate shaft front bearing retaining strap.

21. Press the input shaft front bearing cup into the transaxle case.

INTERMEDIATE SHAFT

NOTE: The 1st/2nd, the 3rd/4th shift forks are interchangeable, however, the synchronizer stop rings are not. The 1st and 2nd synchronizer stop rings have a larger diameter than the other stop rings.

1. Remove the intermediate shaft rear bearing snapring.

2. Remove the intermediate shaft rear bearing with a bearing puller.

3. Remove the 3rd/4th synchronizer hub snapring.

4. Matchmark then remove the 3rd/4th synchronizer hub and the 3rd speed gear using a puller.

5. Install the 1st speed gear thrust washer, 1st speed gear, stop ring and 1–2 synchronizer assembly

6. Install the 1–2 synchronizer snapring.

7. Install the 2nd speed gear and stop ring.

8. Install the retaining ring and split thrust washer. Install the 3rd speed gear and the 3–4 synchronizer. Install the hub snapring.

9. Install the intermediate shaft rear bearing and retaining snapring.

10. Install the intermediate shaft front bearing.

NOTE: Pay attention to the following when servicing the intermediate shaft: When assembling the intermediate shaft, make sure the speed gears turn freely and have a minimum of 0.076mm endplay. When installing the 1st speed gear thrust washer make sure the chamfered edge is facing the pinion gear. When installing the 1st/2nd synchronizer make sure the relief faces the 2nd speed gear. Use an arbor press to install the intermedi-

4-speed manual transaxle — component identification

ate shaft rear bearing, the 3rd/4th synchronizer hub and the 3rd speed gear. When installing the 3-4 synchronizer hub and 3rd speed gear, index the snapring 90° to the split washer. During the installation of synchronizer ring assemblies, make sure that all the matchmarks are aligned.

SELECTOR SHAFT HOUSING

1. Remove the snapring from the selector shaft boot and remove the boot.
2. Pry the shaft oil seal from the selector shaft housing.
3. With a small prybar positioned against the gearshift selector, compress the crossover and push the E-clip from the selector shaft. Remove the E-clip to release the selector shaft.
4. Withdraw the selector shaft from the selector housing.
5. Remove the plate stop retaining bolts and remove the stop.
6. Disassemble the selector shaft housing components.
7. Assemble the selector shaft housing components in the reverse order of removal. Use a new back-up lamp switch gasket if needed. Install the plate stop with the retaining bolts.
8. Install the plate stop with the retaining bolts.
9. Insert the selector shaft into the housing.
10. Compress the gearshift selector and install the E-clip.
11. Clean the bore and drive a new oil seal into the housing using the proper tool.
12. Place the boot onto the shaft and retain with the snapring.

DIFFERENTIAL BEARING RETAINER

1. Pry the oil seal from the retainer.
2. Remove the retainer cup with a puller. Be careful not to damage the oil baffle and the select shim .
3. Remove the oil baffle and the select shim from the retainer cup.
4. Drive the oil baffle and select shim into the retainer cup using the proper tool.
5. Drive the retainer cup into the retainer using the proper tool.
6. Drive in a new retainer oil seal.

EXTENSION HOUSING

1. Pry the oil seal from the extension housing.
2. Pull the extension cup from the extension housing using the proper tool.
3. Remove the O-ring and oil baffle from the housing.
4. Install a new O-ring into the groove on the outside of the housing.
5. Press the oil baffle in the housing using the proper tool.
6. Press the bearing cup into the extension housing using the proper tool.
7. Install a new housing oil seal.

INPUT SHAFT

1. Remove the input shaft rear and front bearing cones using a suitable puller.
2. Mount the bearing retainer plate on wood blocks and press the input shaft rear bearing cup from the plate.
3. Before pressing in the bearing cup, bolt the support plate onto the retainer plate.
4. With the support plate in place, press the bearing cup into the retainer plate.
5. Press the front and rear bearing cones onto the input shaft using the proper tool.

Bearing Endplay Adjustment

Shim thickness calculation and endplay adjustment need only

be done if any of the following parts are replaced: transaxle case, input shaft seal retainer, bearing retainer plate, rear end cover, input shaft or input shaft bearings.

If any of the above components were replaced, use the following procedure to adjust the bearing preload and proper bearing turning torque.

1. Select a gauging shim which will give 0.025–0.250mm of endplay.

NOTE: Measure the original shim from the input shaft seal retainer and select a shim 0.25mm thinner than the original for the gauging shim.

2. Install the gauging shim on the bearing cup and the input shaft seal retainer.
3. Alternately tighten the input shaft seal retainer bolts until the retainer is bottomed against the case. Torque the bolts to 21 ft. lbs.

NOTE: The input shaft seal retainer is used to draw the input shaft front bearing cup the proper distance into the case bore.

4. Oil the input shaft bearings with A.T.F. (1984–87) or SAE 5W-30 engine oil (1988) and install the input shaft in the case. Install the bearing retainer plate with the input shaft rear bearing cup pressed in and the end cover installed. Torque all bolts and nuts to 21 ft. lbs.
5. Position the dial indicator to check the input shaft endplay. Apply moderate load, by hand, to the input shaft splines. Push toward the rear while rotating the input shaft back and forth a number of times and to settle out the bearings. Zero the dial indicator. Pull the input shaft toward the front while rotating the input shaft back and forth a number of times to settle out the bearings. Record the endplay.
6. The shim required for proper bearing preload is the total of the gauging shim thickness, plus endplay, plus (constant) preload of 0.050–0.076mm. Combine shims, if necessary, to obtain a shim within 0.04mm of the required shim.
7. Remove the input shaft seal retainer and gauging shim. Install the shim(s) selected in Step 6 and install the input shaft seal retainer with a ⅛ in. bead of RTV sealant.

NOTE: Keep RTV sealant out of the oil slot.

8. Tighten the input shaft seal retainer bolts to 21 ft. lbs.

NOTE: The input shaft seal retainer is used to draw the input shaft front bearing cup the proper distance into the case bore.

9. Using special tool L-4508 and an inch lb. torque wrench, check the input shaft turning torque. The turning torque should be 1–5 inch lbs. for new bearings or a minimum of 1 inch lb. for used bearings. If the turning torque is too high, install a 0.04mm thinner shim. If the turning torque is too low, install a 0.04mm thicker shim.
10. Check the input shaft turning torque. Repeat Step 9 until the proper bearing turning torque is obtained.

DIFFERENTIAL

1. Remove the bearing cone from the differential case.
2. Remove the ring gear bolts and separate the gear from the differential case. The ring gear bolts are epoxy patch type bolts and not to be reused.
3. Using a steel punch and hammer, knock the pinion shaft split pin from the ring gear and differential case.
4. Withdraw the pinion shaft(s) from the differential case.
5. Rotate the side gears to align them with the case opening and remove the thrust washers, side gears and pinion gears.

NOTE: Shim thickness calculation and bearing preload adjustment need only be done if any of the follow-

1. Snap ring
2. 5th speed synchronizer retainer
3. Spring
4. 5th speed synchronizer
5. not used
6. Stop ring
7. 5th speed gear
8. Snap ring
9. Intermediate shaft bearing
10. 4th speed gear
11. Synchronizer stop ring
12. Snap ring
13. Synchronizer stop ring
14. Synchronizer spring
15. 3rd speed gear
16. Snap ring
17. Thrust washer
18. 2nd speed gear
19. Synchronizer stop ring
20. 1st and 2nd gear synchronizer
21. Snap ring
22. Synchronizer spring
23. 1st speed gear
24. Thrust washer
25. Intermediate shaft
26. Pin
27. Not used
28. Roller bearing
29. Oil feeder
30. Snap ring
31. 5th speed gear
32. Bearing cup
33. Bearing cone
34. Input shaft
35. Bearing cone
36. Bearing cup

4-speed transaxle gear train

ing parts are replaced: transaxle case, input shaft seal retainer, bearing retainer plate, rear end cover, input shaft or input shaft bearings. If any of the those components were replaced, refer to the appropriate section to adjust the bearing preload, proper bearing turning torque or side gear endplay.

1. In their original order, install the side gears, pinion gears and pinion gear washers.
2. Insert the pinion shaft(s) into the differential case making sure that the hole in the shaft is aligned with the roll pin opening in the case.

3. Insert the pinion shaft roll pin(s) into the notched opening(s) on the side of the differential case and drive them into place.
4. Connect the ring gear to the differential case using new bolts. Torque the bolts in a criss-cross pattern to the proper specification.
5. Attach special tool L-4410 to a suitable extension handle and press the bearing cone onto the differential case.
6. Refer to the appropriate section to check and adjust the bearing preload, if necessary.

Bearing Preload Adjustment Procedure

1. Remove the bearing cup and existing shim from the differential bearing retainer.

1. Bearing cone
2. Roll pin
3. Differential shaft
4. Washer package
5. Side gear
6. Pinion washer
7. Pinion
8. Final drive gear
9. Differential case
10. Mounting bolt

4-speed transaxle — differential assembly

2. Select a gauging shim which will give 0.025–0.250mm endplay.

NOTE: Measure the original shim from the differential bearing retainer and select a shim 0.38mm thinner than the original for the gauging shim.

3. Install the gauging shim in the differential bearing retainer and press in the bearing cup. Installation of the oil baffle is not necessary when checking differential assembly endplay.

4. Lubricate the differential bearings with A.T.F. (1984–87) or SAE 5W-30 engine oil (1988–89) and install the differential assembly in the transaxle case.

5. Inspect the extension housing for damage and replace it as necessary. Apply a 1/8 in. bead of RTV sealant to the extension flange. Install the extension housing and differential bearing retainer. Tighten the bolts to 21 ft. lbs.

6. Position the transaxle with the bell housing facing down on the workbench and secure with C-clamps. Position the dial indicator.

7. Apply a medium load to the ring gear, by hand, in the downward direction while rolling the differential assembly back and forth a number of times to settle the bearings. Zero the dial indicator. To obtain endplay readings, apply a medium load upward by hand while rolling the differential assembly back and forth a number of times to settle out the bearings. Record the endplay.

8. The shim required for proper bearing preload is the total of the gauging shim thickness, plus endplay, plus (constant) preload of 0.25mm. Combine shims if necessary, to obtain a shim within 0.05mm of the shim(s).

9. Remove the differential bearing retainer. Remove the bearing cup and gauging shim. Properly install the oil baffle. Be sure the oil baffle is not damaged. Install the shim(s) selected in Step 8 and press the bearing cup into the differential bearing retainer.

10. Using a 1/8 in. bead of RTV sealant for gaskets, install the differential bearing retainer and extension housing. Tighten the bolts to 21 ft. lbs.

11. Using an appropriate tool and an inch lb. torque wrench, check the turning torque of the differential assembly. The turning torque should be 9–14 inch lbs. for new bearings or a minimum of 6 inch lbs. for used bearings. If the turning torque is too low, install a 0.05mm thicker shim.

12. Check the turning torque. Repeat Step 11 until the proper turning torque is obtained.

1. Extension seal
2. Extension with bushing
3. Extension O-ring seal
4. Retainer
5. Bearing cup
6. Magnet
7. Differential cover
8. Transaxle case
9. Bearing cup
10. Final drive spacer
11. Oil feed baffle
12. Bearing retainer
13. Seal
14. Oil scoop
15. Retainer plate
16. Vent
17. Bearing plate
18. Oil feed cover
19. not used
20. Drain plug
21. not used
22. Lock clip
23. Wave washer
24. Pivot washer
25. Reverse lever
26. Reverse idler spacer
27. Reverse idler gear
28. Reverse idler gear shaft
29. Spring pin
30. Clevis pin
31. Input shaft spacer
32. Input shaft seal
33. Retainer
34. Retainer bolt

4-speed transaxle — case components

TRANSAXLE CASE ASSEMBLY

1. Assemble the reverse shift lever components to the transaxle case and lock it in place with the E-clip.

2. Clean the input shaft bore and press in a new oil seal with special tool C-4674 or equivalent. Place the select shim into the retainer race and bolt the input shaft seal retainer onto the transaxle case. The drain hole on the retainer sleeve must be facing downward.

3. Assemble the clutch release shaft components in the reverse order of disassembly and secure the release lever with the E-clip. Insert the release shaft spline end through the bushing and engage it with the release shaft fork. Install the E-clip on the shaft groove to secure the shaft.

4. Install the shift fork and shift fork pads onto the intermediate shaft gear set. Install the intermediate and input shaft gear sets.

5. Install the reverse idler gear (with plastic stop) so that the roll pin on the end of the gear shaft aligns with the roll pin notch in the transaxle case. Lock the gear and engage the reverse shift lever. Make sure the plastic stop is firmly seated on the gear.

6. Install the 3-4 shift fork rail into the locating hole above the intermediate shaft assembly.

7. Remove all the excess sealant from the bearing retainer plate and run an ⅛ in. bead of RTV around the plate's seating surface. Keep the RTV away from the bolt holes. Align the locating dowel on the plate with the dowel on the transaxle case and install by tapping the plate with a rubber mallet. Install the intermediate shaft rear bearing snapring once the plate is in place.

8. Clean the excess sealant from the end cover and make sure the oil feeder hole is clear. Run a bead of RTV around the cover's seating surface and place the cover on the bearing retainer plate. Install the end cover bolts and torque to specification.

9. Clean the excess sealant from the selector shaft housing. If

the back-up light switch was removed, install the switch with a new gasket. Run a ⅛ in. bead of RTV sealant around the cover's seating surface and install the housing with the housing bolts. Torque the bolts to specification.

10. Connect the differential to the extension housing. Use a new extension housing O-ring seal. Attach the housing with the housing bolts and torque the bolts to specification.

11. Seal the differential bearing retainer with RTV and tighten the retainer with special tool L-4435 or equivalent spanner wrench.

12. Install the differential bearing retainer bolts and torque them to specification.

13. If the magnet was removed from the differential cover, install it at this time. Clean the excess sealant from the differential cover and run a ⅛ in. bead of RTV around the cover's seating surface. Install the differential cover with the cover bolts. Torque the bolts to specification.

14. Remove the transaxle from the holding fixture and install it in the vehicle.

5-Speed Manual Transaxle Overhaul

TRANSAXLE CASE DISASSEMBLY

1. Remove the transaxle from the vehicle and position on suitable holding fixture.

2. Remove the extension outer bolts.

3. Remove the differential retainer outer bolts.

4. Remove the differential cover bolts and gently pry the cover from the extension.

5. Remove the extension housing bolts then separate the differential assembly and extension housing. Remove the O-ring seal and clean the RTV from extension housing. Discard the O-ring seal.

6. Unbolt and remove the differential retainer.

7. Remove the selector shaft housing assembly bolts and remove the selector shaft housing.

8. Unbolt and remove the rear end cover.

9. Remove the snapring from the 5th speed synchronizer strut retainer plate.

10. Unscrew the 5th speed shift fork set screw. Lift the 5th speed synchronizer sleeve and shift fork off the synchronizer hub. Retrieve the (3) winged struts and top synchronizer spring.

11. Use a puller to remove the 5th speed synchronizer hub. Retrieve the remaining synchronizer spring.

12. Slide the 5th speed gear off the intermediate shaft.

Removing and installing differential retainer outer bolts

Removing and installing differential cover bolts

Removing and installing extension housing outer bolts

Removing and installing differential cover

APPLY LOCTITE GASKET MAKER AS SHOWN · DIFFERENTIAL COVER · DIFFERENTIAL ASSEMBLY · DOWEL

Differential cover removed — component identification

DIFFERENTIAL BEARING RETAINER · BOOT · BOLTS · SOCKET · SEAL

Removing and installing differential bearing retainer bolts

EXTENSION · BOLTS · SOCKET · SEAL

Removing and installing extension housing inner bolts

DIFFERENTIAL ASSEMBLY · DIFFERENTIAL BEARING RETAINER · APPLY R.T.V. SEALANT AS SHOWN · MAGNET

Removing and installing differential bearing retainer

DIFFERENTIAL ASSEMBLY · APPLY R.T.V. SEALANT AS SHOWN · EXTENSION · O-RING

Removing and installing extension housing

BEARING CONE (2) · DIFFERENTIAL ASSEMBLY

Removing and installing differential assembly

Removing and installing selector shaft housing

Fifth speed synchronizer plate snapring removal

Selector shaft housing removed — component identification

Removing and installing 5th gear fork set screw

Removing and installing rear end cover

Removing and installing 5th speed synchronizer sleeve and fork

13. Using holding tool 6252 or equivalent, remove the input shaft 5th speed gear nut. This nut is not to be reused.

14. Remove the remaining bearing support plate bolts. Gently pry off the bearing support plate.

15. Remove the large snapring from the intermediate shaft rear ball bearing. Then, gently tap the lower surface of the bearing retainer plate with a plastic hammer to free it and lift it off the transaxle case. Clean the RTV sealer from both surfaces.

16. Unscrew the 5th speed shifter guide pin. Do the same with the 1st/2nd shift fork setscrew. Withdraw the 1st/2nd, 3rd/4th shift fork rail.

17. Slide out the reverse idler gear shaft, gear, and plastic stop.

18. Rotate the 3rd/4th shift fork to the left, and the 5th gear shifter to the right. Pull out the 5th speed shift rail. Pull out the input shaft and intermediate shaft assemblies.

19. Remove the 1st/2nd, 3rd/4th, and 5th speed shift forks.

20. To remove the clutch release bearing, remove the E-clips from the clutch release shaft, then disassemble the clutch shaft components.

21. Remove the input shaft seal retainer bolts, the seal, the retainer assembly and the select shim.

22. Remove the reverse shift lever E-clip and flat washer and disassemble the reverse shift lever components.

23. Press the input shaft front bearing cup from the transaxle case.

24. Unbolt and remove the intermediate shaft front bearing retaining strap.

25. Remove the intermediate shaft front bearing and oil feeder using a bearing puller.

26. Press the intermediate shaft front bearing with the oil feeder into the transaxle case. The bearing identification letters must be facing upward during installation.

27. Install the intermediate shaft front bearing retaining strap.

28. Press the input shaft front bearing cup into the transaxle case.

INTERMEDIATE SHAFT

NOTE: The 1st/2nd, the 3rd/4th shift forks are interchangeable, however, the synchronizer stop rings are not. The 1st and 2nd synchronizer stop rings have a larger diameter than the other stop rings.

1. Remove the intermediate shaft rear bearing snapring.

Fifth speed synchronizer removal

Removing and installing intermediate shaft 5th speed gear

Installing 5th speed synchronizer

Removing and installing input shaft 5th gear snapring

Removing and installing input shaft 5th speed gear

Removing and installing bearing retainer plate

Removing and installing bearing support plate bolts

Removing and installing 5th speed shifter guide pin

Removing and installing intermediate shaft rear bearing snapring

Removing and installing 1st/2nd shift fork set screw

Removing and installing shift fork rail

Removing and installing gear set from case

Removing and installing reverse idler gear shaft and gear

Gear set removed from case

Reverse idler gear and plastic stop

Shift forks and rails

Removing and installing clutch release shaft

Input shaft seal retainer components

Clutch release shaft components

Installing new input shaft seal

Removing and installing input shaft seal retainer

Reverse lever components

Removing and installing bearing retaining strap

2. Remove the intermediate shaft rear bearing with a bearing puller.

3. Remove the 3rd/4th synchronizer hub snapring.

4. Matchmark then remove the 3rd/4th synchronizer hub and the 3rd speed gear using a puller.

5. Remove the 2nd speed gear from the intermediate shaft and remove the 1–2 synchronizer hub snapring.

6. Pull the 1st speed gear and 1–2 synchronizer assembly from the intermediate shaft.

NOTE: The 1–2 synchronizer assembly components are not interchangeable with other synchronizers.

7. Install the 1st speed gear thrust washer, 1st speed gear, stop ring and 1–2 synchronizer assembly

8. Install the 1–2 synchronizer snapring.

9. Install the 2nd speed gear and stop ring.

10. Install the retaining ring and split thrust washer. Install the 3rd speed gear and the 3–4 synchronizer. Install the hub snapring.

11. Install the intermediate shaft rear bearing and retaining snapring.

12. Install the intermediate shaft front bearing.

Removing and installing intermediate shaft front bearing

Removing and installing intermediate shaft bearing snapring

Front bearing and oil feeder assembly

Intermediate shaft rear bearing removal

Installing intermediate shaft rear bearing

Installing 3rd/4th synchronizer hub and gear

Removing and installing 3rd/4th synchronizer hub snapring

Snapring and split thrust washer removal

3rd/4th synchronizer hub and 3rd speed gear removal

Split thrust washer installation position

Removing and installing 2nd speed gear and stop ring

Removing and installing 1st/2nd synchronizer hub snapring

NOTE: Pay attention to the following when servicing the intermediate shaft: When assembling the intermediate shaft, make sure the speed gears turn freely and have a minimum of 0.076mm endplay. When installing the 1st speed gear thrust washer make sure the chamfered edge is facing the pinion gear. When installing the 1st/2nd synchronizer make sure the relief faces the 2nd speed gear. Use an arbor press to install the intermediate shaft rear bearing, the 3rd/4th synchronizer hub and the 3rd speed gear. When installing the 3–4 synchronizer hub and 3rd speed gear, index the snapring 90° to the split washer. During the installation of synchronizer ring assemblies, make sure that all he matchmarks are aligned.

Removing and installing 1st speed gear and 1st/2nd synchronizer

Removing and installing 1st/2nd synchronizer assembly

Removing and installing 1st speed gear thrust washer

SNAP RING

LARGE SNAP RING

REAR BEARING

4TH SPEED GEAR

STOP RING (SMALL DIAMETER)

SNAP RING

3-4 SYNCHRONIZER ASSEMBLY

STOP RING (SMALL DIAMETER)

3RD SPEED GEAR

SNAP RING

SPLIT THRUST WASHER

2ND SPEED GEAR

STOP RING (LARGE DIAMETER)

SNAP RING

1-2 SYNCHRONIZER ASSEMBLY

STOP RING (LARGE DIAMETER)

1ST SPEED GEAR

THRUST WASHER (CHAMFERED EDGE MUST FACE TOWARD PINION GEAR)

INTERMEDIATE SHAFT

PINION GEAR

ANTI-SPIN PIN

Intermediate shaft assembly — exploded view

WINGED STRUT (3)

3-4 SYNCHRONIZER HUB

WINGED STRUT (3)

1-2 SYNCHRONIZER HUB

SYNCHRONIZER SPRING

3-4 SYNCHRONIZER SLEEVE

SYNCHRONIZER SPRINGS (2)

1-2 SYNCHRONIZER SLEEVE

SYNCHRONIZER SPRING

Exploded view — 1st/2nd and 3rd/4th synchronizers

SNAP RING

SYNCHRONIZER SPRING

WINGED STRUT

SYNCHRONIZER SLEEVE

MISSING TEETH

INTERMEDIATE SHAFT 5TH SPEED GEAR

5TH SPEED SYNCHRONIZER STRUT RETAINER

SYNCHRONIZER HUB

WINGED STRUT

SYNCHRONIZER SPRING

STOP RING (SMALL DIAMETER)

SNAP RING

INPUT SHAFT 5TH SPEED GEAR

Exploded view — 5th speed synchronizer assembly

MISSING TEETH

1-2 SYNCHRONIZER SLEEVE

1-2 HUB

MISSING TEETH

SYNCHRONIZER SPRING (2)

WINGED STRUT (3)

3-4 HUB

SYNCHRONIZER SPRING (2)

WINGED STRUT (3)

3-4 SYNCHRONIZER SLEEVE

Synchronizer sleeves — Identification

Removing and installing selector shaft snapring and boot

Removing and installing selector shaft seal

SELECTOR SHAFT HOUSING

1. Remove the snapring from the selector shaft boot and remove the boot.
2. Pry the shaft oil seal from the selector shaft housing.
3. With a small prybar positioned against the gearshift selector, compress the crossover and 5th speed load spring and push the E-clip from the selector shaft. Remove the E-clip to release the selector shaft.
4. Withdraw the selector shaft from the selector housing.
5. Remove the plate stop retaining bolts and remove the stop.

6. Disassemble the selector shaft housing components.
7. Assemble the selector shaft housing components in the reverse order of removal. Use a new back-up lamp switch gasket if needed.
8. Install the plate stop with the retaining bolts.
9. Insert the selector shaft into the housing.
10. Compress the gearshift selector and install the E-clip.
11. Clean the bore and drive a new oil seal into the housing using the proper tool.
12. Place the boot onto the shaft and retain with the snapring.

Removing and installing selector shaft E-clip

SELECTOR SHAFT

GEARSHIFT SELECTOR

CROSSOVER SPRING
UNLOAD PLATE

REVERSE OPERATING
LEVER

E-CLIP

GEARSHIFT BLOCKER
AND DETENT ASSEMBLY

5th SPEED LOAD SPRING
AND PIN

CROSSOVER
SPRING

STOP PIN

SELECTOR SHAFT HOUSING

BACK-UP LAMP
SWITCH GASKET

STOP PLATE

BACK-UP LAMP SWITCH

LOCK PIN

SCREWS

Selector shaft housing components

SELECTOR HOUSING

CROSSOVER
SPRING
UNLOAD
PLATE

SELECTOR
SHAFT

STOP PLATE

Removing and installing selector shaft

DIFFERENTIAL BEARING RETAINER

1. Pry the oil seal from the retainer.
2. Remove the retainer cup with a puller. Be careful not to damage the oil baffle and the select shim .

DO NOT
DAMAGE
OIL BAFFLE

DIFFERENTIAL
BEARING CUP

SCREWDRIVER

HAMMER

OIL SEAL

DIFFERENTIAL
BEARING
RETAINER

Differential bearing retainer seal removal

3. Remove the oil baffle and the select shim from the retainer cup.
4. Drive the oil baffle and select shim into the retainer cup using the proper tool.

Installing differential bearing retainer seal

Inserting shim and differential bearing cup

Removing and installing differential bearing retainer cup

5. Drive the retainer cup into the retainer using the proper tool.
6. Drive in a new retainer oil seal.

EXTENSION HOUSING

1. Pry the oil seal from the extension housing.
2. Pull the extension cup from the extension housing using the proper tool.
3. Remove the O-ring and oil baffle from the housing.
4. Install a new O-ring into the groove on the outside of the housing.
5. Press the oil baffle in the housing using the proper tool.
6. Press the bearing cup into the extension housing using the proper tool.
7. Install a new housing oil seal.

INPUT SHAFT

1. Remove the input shaft rear and front bearing cones using a suitable puller.
2. Mount the bearing retainer plate on wood blocks and press the input shaft rear bearing cup from the plate.

Differential bearing retainer assembly

Extension housing seal removal

Installing extension housing seal

Extension housing bearing cap removal

Extension housing components

Installing extension housing bearing cup

3. Before pressing in the bearing cup, bolt the support plate onto the retainer plate.

4. With the support plate in place, press the bearing cup into the retainer plate.

5. Press the front and rear bearing cones onto the input shaft using the proper tool.

Bearing Endplay Adjustment

Shim thickness calculation and endplay adjustment need only be done if any of the following parts are replaced: transaxle case, input shaft seal retainer, bearing retainer plate, rear end cover, input shaft or input shaft bearings.

If any of the above components were replaced, use the following procedure to adjust the bearing preload and proper bearing turning torque.

1. Select a gauging shim which will give 0.025–0.250mm of endplay.

NOTE: Measure the original shim from the input shaft seal retainer and select a shim 0.25mm thinner than the original for the gauging shim.

2. Install the gauging shim on the bearing cup and the input shaft seal retainer.

3. Alternately tighten the input shaft seal retainer bolts until the retainer is bottomed against the case. Torque the bolts to 21 ft. lbs.

Input shaft rear bearing cone removal

Input shaft rear bearing cone installation

Input shaft rear bearing cup removal

Input shaft front bearing cone removal

Input shaft rear bearing cup installation

Installing input shaft front bearing cone

NOTE: **The input shaft seal retainer is used to draw the input shaft front bearing cup the proper distance into the case bore.**

4. Oil the input shaft bearings with A.T.F. (1984–87) or SAE 5W-30 engine oil (1988–91) and install the input shaft in the case. Install the bearing retainer plate with the input shaft rear bearing cup pressed in and the support plate installed. Torque all bolts and nuts to 21 ft. lbs.

5. Position the dial indicator to check the input shaft endplay. Apply moderate load, by hand, to the input shaft splines. Push toward the rear while rotating the input shaft back and forth a number of times and to settle out the bearings. Zero the dial indicator. Pull the input shaft toward the front while rotating the input shaft back and forth a number of times to settle out the bearings. Record the endplay.

6. The shim required for proper bearing preload is the total of the gauging shim thickness, plus endplay, plus (constant) pre-load of 0.050–0.076mm. Combine shims, if necessary, to obtain a shim within 0.04mm of the required shim.

Checking input shaft bearing endplay to determine shim thickness

Checking input shaft bearing turning torque

mm	mm	inch
.62		.024
.66		.026
.70		.028
.74		.029
.78		.031
.82		.032
.86		.034
.90		.035
.94		.037
.98		.039
1.02		.040
1.06		.042
1.10		.043
1.14		.045
1.18		.046
1.22		.048
1.26		.050
1.30		.051
1.34		.053
1.36	(.66 + .70)	.054
1.40	(.66 + .74)	.055
1.44	(.70 + .74)	.057
1.48	(.70 + .78)	.059
1.52	(.74 + .78)	.060
1.56	(.74 + .82)	.061
1.60	(.78 + .82)	.063
1.64	(.78 + .86)	.065
1.68	(.82 + .86)	.066
1.72	(.82 + .90)	.068
1.76	(.86 + .90)	.069

Input shaft shim selection chart

7. Remove the input shaft seal retainer and gauging shim. Install the shim(s) selected in Step 6 and install the input shaft seal retainer with a ⅛ in. bead of RTV sealant.

NOTE: Keep RTV sealant out of the oil slot.

8. Tighten the input shaft seal retainer bolts to 21 ft. lbs.

NOTE: The input shaft seal retainer is used to draw the input shaft front bearing cup the proper distance into the case bore.

9. Using special tool L-4508 and an inch lb. torque wrench, check the input shaft turning torque. The turning torque should be 1–5 inch lbs. for new bearings or a minimum of 1 inch lb. for used bearings. If the turning torque is too high, install a 0.04mm thinner shim. If the turning torque is too low, install a 0.04mm thicker shim.

10. Check the input shaft turning torque. Repeat Step 9 until the proper bearing turning torque is obtained.

DIFFERENTIAL

1. Remove the bearing cone from the differential case.
2. Remove the ring gear bolts and separate the gear from the differential case. The ring gear bolts are epoxy patch type bolts and not to be reused.

3. Using a steel punch and hammer, knock the pinion shaft split pin from the ring gear and differential case.

4. Withdraw the pinion shaft(s) from the differential case.

5. Rotate the side gears to align them with the case opening and remove the thrust washers, side gears and pinion gears.

NOTE: Shim thickness calculation and bearing preload adjustment need only be done if any of the following parts are replaced: transaxle case, input shaft seal retainer, bearing retainer plate, rear end cover, input shaft or input shaft bearings. If any of the those components were replaced, refer to the appropriate section to adjust the bearing preload, proper bearing turning torque or side gear endplay.

6. In their original order, install the side gears, pinion gears and pinion gear washers. Leave the thrust washer out until after the side gear endplay is adjusted.

7. Insert the pinion shaft(s) into the differential case making sure that the hole in the shaft is aligned with the roll pin opening in the case.

8. Insert the pinion shaft roll pin(s) into the notched opening(s) on the side of the differential case and drive them into place.

9. Connect the ring gear to the differential case using new bolts. Torque the bolts in a criss-cross pattern to the proper specification.

To install:

10. Attach special tool L-4410 to a suitable extension handle and press the bearing cone onto the diffential case.

11. Refer to the appropriate section to check and adjust the

SPECIAL TOOL C-293

SPECIAL TOOL C-4996 (NOTE POSITION)

SPECIAL TOOL ADAPTER C-293-45 (USE 4 PIECES)

DIFFERENTIAL ASSEMBLY

DIFFERENTIAL BEARING CONE

Differential bearing cone removal

HAMMER

STEEL PUNCH

ROLL PIN HOLE

DIFFERENTIAL CASE

Removing and installing pinion shaft roll pin

ARBOR PRESS RAM

SPECIAL TOOL HANDLE C-4171

SPECIAL TOOL L-4410

DIFFERENTIAL ASSEMBLY

BEARING CONE

Differential bearing cone installation

PINION SHAFT

ROLE PIN HOLE

DIFFERENTIAL CASE

Removing and installing pinion shaft

DIFFERENTIAL CASE

RING GEAR

BOLTS MUST BE PROPERLY TORQUED

Removing and installing differential ring gear bolts and ring gear

DIFFERENTIAL CASE

PINION GEAR THRUST WASHER (2)

SIDE GEAR (2)

PINION GEAR (2)

Removing and installing pinion gears, side gears and thrust washers by rotating pinion gears to opening in differential case

Differential gear components

Checking side gear endplay

bearing preload, if necessary. Check the side gear endplay and select the proper dimension thrust washer.

Side Gear Endplay Adjustment

1. Once assembled, rotate the gears 2 complete revolutions in both a clockwise and counterclockwise direction.
2. Install special tool C-4996 on the bearing cone and mount a dial indicator so that the stylus of the dial rests on the surface of the tool.
3. Move one of the side gears up and down by hand and record the endplay.
4. Zero the dial and rotate the side gear in 90° increments an repeat Step 3.
5. Use the smallest endplay reading recorded and shim the side gear to within 0.025–0.330mm. For shimming, 4 select thrust washer sizes are available: 0.8mm, 0.9mm, 1.0mm, and 1.2mm.
6. Repeat Steps 1–4 for the other side gear.

Bearing Preload Adjustment Procedure

1. Remove the bearing cup and existing shim from the differential bearing retainer.
2. Select a gauging shim which will give 0.025–0.250mm endplay.

NOTE: Measure the original shim from the differential bearing retainer and select a shim 0.38mm thinner than the original for the gauging shim.

3. Install the gauging shim in the differential bearing retainer and press in the bearing cup. Installation of the oil baffle is not necessary when checking differential assembly endplay.
4. Lubricate the differential bearings with A.T.F. (1984–87) or SAE 5W-30 engine oil (1988–89) and install the differential assembly in the transaxle case.
5. Inspect the extension housing for damage and replace it as necessary. Apply a ⅛ in. bead of RTV sealant to the extension flange. Install the extension housing and differential bearing retainer. Tighten the bolts to 21 ft. lbs.
6. Position the transaxle with the bell housing facing down on the workbench and secure with C-clamps. Position the dial indicator.
7. Apply a medium load to the ring gear, by hand, in the downward direction while rolling the differential assembly back and forth a number of times to settle the bearings. Zero the dial indicator. To obtain endplay readings, apply a medium load up-

Checking differential bearing endplay to determine shim thickness

Checking differential bearing turning torque

Required Shim Combination		Total Thickness		Required Shim Combination		Total Thickness		Required Shim Combination		Total Thickness	
mm		mm	Inch	mm		mm	Inch	mm		mm	Inch
.50		.50	.020	.50 +	.70	1.20	.047	1.00 +	.70	1.70	.067
.75		.75	.030	.50 +	.75	1.25	.049	1.00 +	.75	1.75	.069
.80		.80	.032	.50 +	.80	1.30	.051	1.00 +	.80	1.80	.071
.85		.85	.034	.50 +	.85	1.35	.053	1.00 +	.85	1.85	.073
.90		.90	.035	.50 +	.90	1.40	.055	1.00 +	.90	1.90	.075
.95		.95	.037	.50 +	.95	1.45	.057	1.00 +	.95	1.95	.077
1.00		1.00	.039	.50 +	1.00	1.50	.059	1.00 +	1.00	2.00	.079
1.05		1.05	.041	.50 +	1.05	1.55	.061	1.00 +	1.05	2.05	.081
.50 +	.60	1.10	.043	1.00 +	.60	1.60	.063	1.05 +	1.05	2.10	.083
.50 +	.65	1.15	.045	1.00 +	.65	1.65	.065				

Differential bearing shim selection chart

ward by hand while rolling the differential assembly back and forth a number of times to settle out the bearings. Record the endplay.

8. The shim required for proper bearing preload is the total of the gauging shim thickness, plus endplay, plus (constant) preload of 0.25mm. Combine shims if necessary, to obtain a shim within 0.05mm of the shim(s).

9. Remove the differential bearing retainer. Remove the bearing cup and gauging shim. Properly install the oil baffle. Be sure the oil baffle is not damaged. Install the shim(s) selected in Step 8 and press the bearing cup into the differential bearing retainer.

10. Using a ⅛ in. bead of R.T.V. sealant for gaskets, install the differential bearing retainer and extension housing. Tighten the bolts to 21 ft. lbs.

11. Using an appropriate tool and an inch lb. torque wrench, check the turning torque of the differential assembly. The turning torque should be 9–14 inch lbs. for new bearings or a minimum of 6 inch lbs. for used bearings. If the turning torque is too low, install a 0.05mm thicker shim.

12. Check the turning torque. Repeat Step 11 until the proper turning torque is obtained.

TRANSAXLE CASE ASSEMBLY

1. Assemble the reverse shift lever components to the transaxle case and lock it in place with the E-clip.

2. Clean the input shaft bore and press in a new oil seal with special tool C-4674 or equivalent. Place the select shim into the retainer race and bolt the input shaft seal retainer onto the transaxle case. The drain hole on the retainer sleeve must be facing downward.

3. Assemble the clutch release shaft components in the reverse order of disassembly and secure the release lever with the E-clip. Insert the release shaft spline end through the bushing and engage it with the release shaft fork. Install the E-clip on the shaft groove to secure the shaft.

4. Install the shift forks and shift rails onto the intermediate gear shaft assembly.

5. Install the intermediate and input shaft gear sets into the transaxle case and make sure that the gears are in proper mesh. Once the gear sets are in place, rotate the 5th speed shifter to the right and the 1–2 and 3–4 shift forks to the left.

6. Install the reverse idler gear (with plastic stop) so that the roll pin on the end of the gear shaft aligns with the roll pin notch in the transaxle case. Lock the gear and engage the reverse shift lever. Make sure the plastic stop is firmly seated on the gear.

7. Install the 1–2, 3–4 and 5th speed shift fork rails into their respective locating holes.

8. Install and tighten the 1–2 shift fork set screw and 5th speed selector guide pin.

9. Remove all the excess sealant from the bearing retainer plate and run an ⅛ in. bead of RTV around the plate's seating surface. Keep the RTV away from the bolt holes. Align the plate with the transaxle case and install it. The plate will align with the oil trough and the 5th speed shift rail. Install the intermediate shaft rear bearing snapring once the plate is in place and seated.

10. Install the bearing support plate with the retaining bolts. Torque the bolts to specification.

11. Install the 5th speed gear onto the input shaft. Install a new gear nut with special holding tool 6252. The holding tool must be used to install the gear nut and the old nut must not be reused. Torque the nut to 190 ft. lbs. and remove the holding tool.

12. Install the intermediate shaft 5th speed gear, synchronizer hub and struts using special tool C-4888 or equivalent gear installer.

13. Position the 5th speed synchronizer sleeve and shift fork over the 5th speed shift rail and install it using the alignment marks for reference. Lock the fork to the rail with the set screw.

14. Install the 5th speed synchronizer strut retainer plate with the snapring.

15. Clean the excess sealant from the end cover and make sure the oil fill plug hole is clear. Run a bead of RTV around the cover's seating surface and place the cover on the bearing retainer plate. Install the end cover bolts and torque to specification.

16. Clean the excess sealant from the selector shaft housing. If the back-up light switch was removed, install the switch with a new gasket. Run a ⅛ in. bead of RTV sealant around the cover's seating surface and install the housing with the housing bolts. Torque the bolts to specification.

17. Apply RTV sealant to the portion of the differential bearing retainer that bolts to the ring gear to form a gasket.

18. Position the differential in the support saddles.

19. Connect the bearing retainer to the differential with the inner bolts and torque the bolts to specification.

20. Remove the O-ring seal from the extension housing and replace it with a new one. Remove the old sealant from the base of the extension and run a bead of new sealant.

21. Connect the extension to the other side of the differential with the outer bolts. Torque the bolts to specification.

22. Clean the excess sealant from the differential cover and run a ⅛ in. bead of RTV around the cover's seating surface. Install the differential cover with the cover bolts. Torque the bolts to specification.

23. Install the remaining extension and differential bearing retainer (outer) bolts and torque them to specification.

24. Remove the transaxle from the holding fixture and install it in the vehicle.

Halfshafts

The halfshafts used on your vehicle are of three piece con-

Halfshaft type and identification

Separating ball joint from the knuckle

Removing the driveshaft assembly

struction, and are unequal in length and material composition. A short solid interconnecting shaft is used on the left side and a longer tubular interconnecting shaft is installed on the right side.

The halfshaft assemblies are three piece units. Each shaft has a Tripod joint on the transaxle side, an interconnecting shaft and a Rzeppa joint on the wheel side. The Rzeppa joint mounts a splined stub shaft that connects with the wheel hub. The inner Tripod joint mounts a spring that maintains constant spline engagement with the transaxle. The design enables the halfshaft to be removed without dismantling the transaxle.

Models equipped with a turbo charged engine incorporate an equal length halfshaft system. This system includes and extra, intermediate shaft installed on the right side. This helps to pre-

Speedometer pinion removal and installation

Installing the inner shaft into the transaxle

Seal and wear sleeve lubrication points

vent torque steer induced by the power of the engine. The halfshaft removal procedure for all vehicles is the same.

REMOVAL AND INSTALLATION

1. Remove the cotter pin, lock and spring washer from the front axle ends.
2. Have a helper apply the service brakes and loosen the front axle hub retaining nut.
3. Raise and support the front of the vehicle on jackstands.
4. Remove the hub nut, washer and wheel assembly. Drain transaxle fluid.

NOTE: The speedometer drive pinion must be removed from the transaxle housing before the right side drive axle can be removed. Remove the retaining bolts and lift the pinion with cable connected from the housing.

5. Remove the clamp bolt that secures the ball joint stud with the steering knuckle.
6. Separate the ball joint from the knuckle by prying downward against the knuckle connecting point and the control arm. Take care not to damage the rubber boot.
7. Separate the outer CV (constant velocity) joint splines from the steering knuckle hub by holding the CV housing and pushing the knuckle out and away. If resistance is encountered, use a brass drift and hammer to gently tap the outer hub end of the axle. Do not pry on the outer wear sleeve of the CV joint.
8. After the outboard end of the drive axle has been removed from the steering knuckle, support the assembly and pull outward on the inner CV joint housing to remove the assembly from the transaxle.

WARNING: Do not pull on the shaft or the assembly will disconnect. Pull only on the inner CV joint housing.

9. Remove the halfshaft from under the vehicle and service as necessary.
To install:
10. To install the halfshaft; Hold the inner joint assembly by its housing, align and guide the shaft into the transaxle or intermediate shaft assembly.

11. Lubricate the outer wear sleeve and seal with multi-purpose grease. Push the steering knuckle outward and install the splined outer shaft into the drive hub. Install the steering knuckle assembly. Torque the ball joint clamp bolt to 70 ft. lbs. Hub nut (splined shaft nut) torque to 180 ft. lbs. Refill the transaxle with the proper lubrication fluid.

NOTE: If after installing the axle assembly, the inboard boot appears collapsed, vent the boot by inserting a thin round rod between the boot and the shaft. Massage the boot until is expands. Install a new clamp to prevent dirt from entering the boot.

CV-JOINT OVERHAUL

Inner Joint

1. With the halfshaft assembly removed from the vehicle, remove the clamps and boot.
2. Depending on the unit (GKN or Citroen) separate the tripod assembly from the housing as follows: Citroen type: Since

Installing the outer shaft into the hub

the trunion ball rollers are not retained on bearing studs a retaining ring is used to prevent accidental tripod/housing separation, which would allow roller and needle bearings to fall away.

In the case of the spring loaded inner CV-joints, if it weren't for the retaining ring, the spring would automatically force the tripod out of the housing whenever the shaft was not installed in the vehicle.

Separate the tripod from the housing by slightly deforming the retaining ring in 3 places, with a suitable tool.

WARNING: Secure the rollers to the studs during separation. With the tripod out of the housing secure the assembly with tape.

3. GKN type: Spring loaded GKN inboard CV-joints have tabs on the can cover that prevent the spring from forcing the tripod out of the housing. These tabs must be bent back with a pair of pliers before the tripod can be removed. Under normal conditions it is not necessary to secure the GKN rollers to their studs during separation due to the presence of a retainer ring on the end of each stud. This retention force can easily be overcome if the rollers are pulled or impacted. It is also possible to pull the rollers off by removing or installing the tripod with the connecting shaft at too high an angle, relative to the housing.

4. Remove the snapring from the shaft end groove, then remove the tripod with a brass punch.

To install:

5. Remove as much grease as possible from the assembly. Look at the ball housing races, and the components for excessive wear.

NOTE: DO NOT CLEAN THE INNER HOUSING WITH MINERAL SPIRITS OR SOLVENT. Solvents will destroy the rubber seals that are hidden in the housing and permit grease leakage. If wear is excessive, replace as necessary.

6. Fasten the new boot onto the interconnecting shaft. Install the tripod on the shaft as follows: G.K.N. type: Slide the tripod onto the shaft with the non-chamfered end facing the tripod retaining ring groove. Citroen type: Slide the tripod onto the shaft (both sides are the same).

Halfshaft assembly — exploded view

Separating the tripod from the housing

Rotate the cage and cross to remove the balls

Spring and cup installation

Removing the balls from the joint

7. Install the retainer snapring into the groove on the interconnecting shaft locking the tripod in position.

8. On G.K.N. type: Put two of the three packets of grease into the boot and the remaining pack into the housing. On Citroen type: Put two thirds of the packet of grease into the boot and the remaining grease into the housing.

9. Position the spring into the housing spring pocket with the cup attached to the exposed end of the spring. Place a small amount of grease in the spring cup.

10. On G.K.N type: Slip the tripod into the housing and bend down the retaining tabs. Make sure the tabs are holding the housing firmly. On Citroen type: Remove the tape holding the rollers and needle bearings in place. Hold the rollers and needles in place and install the housing. Install the retaining ring into the machined groove in the housing with a punch and plastic hammer. Hold the retaining collar in position with two C-clamps while installing the retainer ring.

WARNING: When installing the tripod, the spring must be centered in the housing to insure proper positioning.

11. Position the boot over the retaining groove in the housing and clamp in position.

Outer Joint

1. Remove the boot clamps and discard them.
2. Wipe away the grease to expose the joint.
3. Support the shaft in a vise (Cushion the vise jaws to prevent shaft damage). Hold the outer joint, and using a plastic hammer, give a sharp tap to the top of the joint body to dislodge it from the internal circlip.

4. If the shaft is bent carefully pry the wear sleeve from the CV-joint machined ledge.

5. Remove the circlip from the shaft and discard it.

NOTE: Replacement boot kits will contain this circlip.

6. Unless the shaft is damaged do not remove the heavy spacer ring from the shaft.

NOTE: If the shaft must be replaced, care must be taken that the new shaft is of the proper construction, depending on whether the inner joint is spring loaded or not. If the CV-joint was operating satisfactorily, and the grease down not appear contaminated, just replace the boot. If the outer joint is noisy or badly worn, replace the entire unit. The repair kit will include boot, clamps, retaining ring (circlip) and lubricant.

CAGE—ROTATE 90°, POSITION LONG OPENINGS BETWEEN BALL RACES—LIFT OUT

BALL RACE

CAGE WINDOW

Removing the cage and cross assembly form the housing

7. Wipe off the grease and mark the position of the inner cross, cage and housing with a dab of paint.

8. Hold the joint vertically in a vise. Do not crush the splines on the shaft.

9. Press down on one side of the inner race to tilt the cage and remove the balls from the opposite side.

10. If the joint is tight, use a hammer and brass drift pin to tap the inner race. Repeat this step until all balls have been removed. DO NOT hit the cage.

11. Tilt the cage and inner race assembly vertically and position the two opposing, elongated cage windows in the area between the ball grooves. Pull the cage out of the housing.

12. Turn the inner cross 90° and align the race lands with an elongated hole in the cage. Remove the inner race.

To install:

13. Position a new wear sleeve on the joint housing and install it using a suitable driver. Lubricate all of the components before assembly.

14. Align the parts according to paint markings.

15. Install one of the inner race lands into the cage window and feed the race into the cage.

16. Turn the cross 90° and align the opposing cage windows with the land, pivot another 90° and complete land installation.

17. When properly installed, the cross counter bore should be facing outward from the joint on G.K.N. type. The cross and cage chamfers will be facing out on Citroen type.

18. Apply the grease to the ball races. Install the balls into the raceway by tilting the cage and inner race assembly.

19. Fasten the boot to the shaft. Install the new retainer circlip provided. Position the outer joint on the splined end of the stub shaft, engage the splines and tap sharply to engage the circlip. Attempt to pull the shafts apart to see if the circlip is properly seated.

20. Position the large end of the boot and secure with a clamp. Install the halfshaft.

CLUTCH

Troubleshooting Basic Clutch Problems

Problem	Cause
Excessive clutch noise	Throwout bearing noises are more audible at the lower end of pedal travel. The usual causes are: • Riding the clutch • Too little pedal free-play • Lack of bearing lubrication A bad clutch shaft pilot bearing will make a high pitched squeal, when the clutch is disengaged and the transmission is in gear or within the first 2″ of pedal travel. The bearing must be replaced. Noise from the clutch linkage is a clicking or snapping that can be heard or felt as the pedal is moved completely up or down. This usually requires lubrication. Transmitted engine noises are amplified by the clutch housing and heard in the passenger compartment. They are usually the result of insufficient pedal free-play and can be changed by manipulating the clutch pedal.

Troubleshooting Basic Clutch Problems

Problem	Cause
Clutch slips (the car does not move as it should when the clutch is engaged)	This is usually most noticeable when pulling away from a standing start. A severe test is to start the engine, apply the brakes, shift into high gear and SLOWLY release the clutch pedal. A healthy clutch will stall the engine. If it slips it may be due to: • A worn pressure plate or clutch plate • Oil soaked clutch plate • Insufficient pedal free-play
Clutch drags or fails to release	The clutch disc and some transmission gears spin briefly after clutch disengagement. Under normal conditions in average temperatures, 3 seconds is maximum spin-time. Failure to release properly can be caused by: • Too light transmission lubricant or low lubricant level • Improperly adjusted clutch linkage
Low clutch life	Low clutch life is usually a result of poor driving habits or heavy duty use. Riding the clutch, pulling heavy loads, holding the car on a grade with the clutch instead of the brakes and rapid clutch engagement all contribute to low clutch life.

Understanding the Clutch

The purpose of the clutch is to disconnect and connect engine power from the transmission. A car at rest requires a lot of engine torque to get all that weight moving. An internal combustion engine does not develop a high starting torque, so it must be allowed to operate without any load until it builds up enough torque to move the car. Torque increases with engine rpm. The clutch allows the engine to build up torque by physically disconnecting the engine from the transmission, relieving the engine of any load or resistance. The transfer of engine power to the transmission (the load) must be smooth and gradual; if it weren't, drive line components would wear out or break quickly. This gradual power transfer is made possible by gradually releasing the clutch pedal. The clutch disc and pressure plate are the connecting link between the engine and transmission. When the clutch pedal is released, the disc and plate contact each other (clutch engagement), physically joining the engine and transmission. When the pedal is pushed in, the disc and plate separate (the clutch is disengaged), disconnecting the engine from the transmission.

The clutch assembly consists of the flywheel, the clutch disc, the clutch pressure plate, the throw out bearing and fork, the actuating linkage and the pedal. The flywheel and clutch pressure plate (driving members) are connected to the engine crankshaft and rotate with it. The clutch disc is located between the flywheel and pressure plate, and splined to the transmission shaft. A driving member is one that is attached to the engine and transfers engine power to a driven member (clutch disc) on the transmission shaft. A driving member (pressure plate) rotates (drives) a driven member (clutch disc) on contact and, in so doing, turns the transmission shaft. There is a circular diaphragm spring within the pressure plate cover (transmission side). In a relaxed state (when the clutch pedal is fully released), this spring is convex; that is, it is dished outward toward the transmission. Pushing in the clutch pedal actuates an attached linkage rod. Connected to the other end of this rod is the throw out bearing fork. The throw out bearing is attached to the fork. When the clutch pedal is depressed, the clutch linkage pushes the fork and bearing forward to contact the diaphragm spring of the pressure plate. The outer edges of the spring are secured to the pressure plate and are pivoted on rings so that when the center of the spring is compressed by the throw out bearing, the outer edges bow outward and, by so doing, pull the pressure plate in the same direction — away from the clutch disc. This action separates the disc from the plate, disengaging the clutch and allowing the transmission to be shifted into another gear. A coil type clutch return spring attached to the clutch pedal arm permits full release of the pedal. Releasing the pedal pulls the throw out bearing away from the diaphragm spring resulting in a reversal of spring position. As bearing pressure is gradually released from the spring center, the outer edges of the spring bow outward, pushing the pressure plate into closer contact with the clutch disc. As the disc and plate move closer together, friction between the two increases and slippage is reduced until, when full spring pressure is applied (by fully releasing the pedal), The speed of the disc and plate are the same. This stops all slipping, creating a direct connection between the plate and disc which results in the transfer of power from the engine to the transmission. The clutch disc is now rotating with the pressure plate at engine speed and, because it is splined to the transmission shaft, the shaft now turns at the same engine speed. Understanding clutch operation can be rather difficult at first; if you're still confused after reading this, consider the following analogy. The action of the diaphragm spring can be compared to that of an oil can bottom. The bottom of an oil can is shaped very much like the clutch diaphragm spring and pushing in on the can bottom and then releasing it produces a similar effect. As mentioned earlier, the clutch pedal return spring permits full release of the pedal and reduces linkage slack due to wear. As the linkage wears, clutch free-pedal travel will increase and free-travel will decrease as the clutch wears. Free-travel is actually throw out bearing lash.

The diaphragm spring type clutches used are available in two different designs: flat diaphragm springs or bent spring. The bent fingers are bent back to create a centrifugal boost ensuring quick re-engagement at higher engine speeds. This design enables pressure plate load to increase as the clutch disc wears and makes low pedal effort possible even with a heavy-duty clutch. The throw out bearing used with the bent finger design is 1¼ in.

long and is shorter than the bearing used with the flat finger design. These bearings are not interchangeable. If the longer bearing is used with the bent finger clutch, free-pedal travel will not exist. This results in clutch slippage and rapid wear.

The transmission varies the gear ratio between the engine and drive wheels. It can be shifted to change engine speed as driving conditions and loads change. The transmission allows disengaging and reversing power from the engine to the wheels.

CAUTION

The clutch driven disc contains asbestos, which has been determined to be a cancer causing agent. Never clean clutch surfaces with compressed air! Avoid inhaling any dust from any clutch surface! When cleaning clutch surfaces, use a commercially available brake cleaning fluid.

Adjustments

All models are equipped with a self-adjusting clutch. No free-play adjustment is possible.

Driven Disc and Pressure Plate

NOTE: Chrysler recommends the use of special tool #C4676 for disc alignment.

REMOVAL AND INSTALLATION

1. Remove the transaxle.
2. Matchmark the clutch cover and flywheel for easy reinstallation.
3. Insert special tool C4676 or its equivalent to hold the clutch disc in place.
4. Loosen the cover attaching bolts. Do this procedure in a diagonal manner, a few turns at a time to prevent warping the cover.

5. Remove the cover assembly and disc from the flywheel.
6. Remove the clutch release shaft and slide the release bearing off the input shaft seal retainer.
7. Remove the fork from the release bearing thrust plate.
8. Inspect the components. Replace as necessary.

To install:

9. Install the throw out bearing, fork and component parts.
10. Mount the clutch assembly on the flywheel (Mate the matchmarks if old unit is used). Install the clutch disc alignment tool. Hold the alignment tool in position and loosely install the pressure plate retaining bolts.
11. Tighten the bolts a few turns at a time in rotation. Tighten to 250 in. lbs.

RELEASE CABLE ADJUSTMENT

The clutch release cable cannot be adjusted. When the cable is properly installed, a spring in the clutch pedal adjusts the cable to the proper position, regardless of clutch disc wear.

Clutch Pedal

REMOVAL AND INSTALLATION

1. Disconnect the negative battery cable.
2. Under the drivers side of the instrument panel, remove the clutch pedal return spring from the pedal and bracket.
3. Remove the retainer bolt from the clutch cable, at the top of the pedal arm. Release the cable from the pedal bracket.
4. Remove the lockring washers and bushing from the pedal pivot. Carefully slide the pedal assembly off of the pivot.
5. Install the pedal in position on the pivot and install the lockring. Reconnect the clutch release cable.
6. Check the operation of the pedal and make sure the clutch release is working.
7. Connect the negative battery cable.

Clutch components

TORQUE		
LET.	N•m	IN. LBS.
Ⓐ	28	250

SPRING

RETAINER

CABLE ASSEMBLY

NUT AND WASHER Ⓐ

CLIP

BUMPER

CLUTCH PEDAL ASSEMBLY

CABLE ADJUSTER CLIP

VIEW IN DIRECTION OF ARROW Y

ADJUSTER PIVOT

GROMMET

BUSHING (2)

CLUTCH RELEASE LEVER

WASHER

LOCK RING

GROMMET

RETAINER

FORWARD

GROMMET

SPACER

PIVOT SHAFT

BRAKE PEDAL ASSEMBLY

BUSHING (2) (LUBRICATE)

POSITIONER ADJUSTER (LUBRICATE)

VIEW IN DIRECTION OF ARROW Z

SPRING

CLUTCH PEDAL ASSEMBLY

PAD

Clutch pedal mechanism and components

AUTOMATIC TRANSAXLE

Understanding Automatic Transaxles

The automatic transaxle allows engine torque and power to be transmitted to the drive wheels within a narrow range of engine operating speeds. The transaxle will allow the engine to turn fast enough to produce plenty of power and torque at very low speeds, while keeping it at a sensible rpm at high vehicle speeds. The transaxle performs this job entirely without driver assistance. The transaxle uses a light fluid as the medium for the transaxle of power. This fluid also works in the operation of various hydraulic control circuits and as a lubricant. Because the transaxle fluid performs all of these three functions, trouble within the unit can easily travel from one part to another. For this reason, and because of the complexity and unusual operating principles of the transaxle, a very sound understanding of the basic principles of operation will simplify troubleshooting.

THE TORQUE CONVERTER

The torque converter replaces the conventional clutch. It has three functions:

1. It allows the engine to idle with the vehicle at a standstill, even with the transaxle in gear.

2. It allows the transaxle to shift from range to range smoothly, without requiring that the driver close the throttle during the shift.

3. It multiplies engine torque to an increasing extent as vehicle speed drops and throttle opening is increased. This has the effect of making the transaxle more responsive and reduces the amount of shifting required.

The torque converter is a metal case which is shaped like a sphere that has been flattened on opposite sides. It is bolted to the rear end of the engine's crankshaft. Generally, the entire metal case rotates at engine speed and serves as the engine's flywheel.

The case contains three sets of blades. One set is attached directly to the case. This set forms the torus or pump. Another set is directly connected to the output shaft, and forms the turbine. The third set is mounted on a hub which, in turn, is mounted on a stationary shaft through a one-way clutch. This third set is known as the stator.

A pump, which is driven by the converter hub at engine speed, keeps the torque converter full of transaxle fluid at all times. Fluid flows continuously through the unit to provide cooling.

Under low speed acceleration, the torque converter functions as follows:

The torus is turning faster than the turbine. It picks up fluid at the center of the converter and, through centrifugal force, slings it outward. Since the outer edge of the converter moves faster than the portions at the center, the fluid picks up speed.

The fluid then enters the outer edge of the turbine blades. It then travels back toward the center of the converter case along the turbine blades. In impinging upon the turbine blades, the fluid loses the energy picked up in the torus.

If the fluid were now to immediately be returned directly into the torus, both halves of the converter would have to turn at approximately the same speed at all times, and torque input and output would both be the same.

In flowing through the torus and turbine, the fluid picks up two types of flow, or flow in two separate directions. It flows through the turbine blades, and it spins with the engine. The stator, whose blades are stationary when the vehicle is being accelerated at low speeds, converts one type of flow into another. Instead of allowing the fluid to flow straight back into the torus, the stator's curved blades turn the fluid almost 90° toward the direction of rotation of the engine. Thus the fluid does not flow as fast toward the torus, but is already spinning when the torus picks it up. This has the effect of allowing the torus to turn much faster than the turbine. This difference in speed may be compared to the difference in speed between the smaller and larger gears in any gear train. The result is that engine power output is higher, and engine torque is multiplied.

As the speed of the turbine increases, the fluid spins faster and faster in the direction of engine rotation. As a result, the ability of the stator to redirect the fluid flow is reduced. Under cruising conditions, the stator is eventually forced to rotate on its one-way clutch in the direction of engine rotation. Under these conditions, the torque converter begins to behave almost like a solid shaft, with the torus and turbine speeds being almost equal.

THE PLANETARY GEARBOX

The ability of the torque converter to multiply engine torque is limited. Also, the unit tends to be more efficient when the turbine is rotating at relatively high speeds. Therefore, a planetary gearbox is used to carry the power output of the turbine to the halfshafts.

Planetary gears function very similarly to conventional transaxle gears. However, their construction is different in that three elements make up one gear system, and, in that all three elements are different from one another. The three elements are: an outer gear that is shaped like a hoop, with teeth cut into the inner surface; a sun gear, mounted on a shaft and located at the very center of the outer gear; and a set of three planet gears, held by pins in a ring-like planet carrier, meshing with both the sun gear and the outer gear. Either the outer gear or the sun gear may be held stationary, providing more than one possible torque multiplication factor for each set of gears. Also, if all three gears are forced to rotate at the same speed, the gear set forms, in effect, a solid shaft.

Most modern automatics use the planetary gears to provide either a single reduction ratio of about 1.8:1, or two reduction gears: a low of about 2.5:1, and an intermediate of about 1.5:1.

Bands and clutches are used to hold various portions of the gear sets to the transaxle case or to the shaft on which they are mounted. Shifting is accomplished, then, by changing the portion of each planetary gear set which is held to the transaxle case or to the shaft.

THE SERVOS AND ACCUMULATORS

The servos are hydraulic pistons and cylinders. They resemble the hydraulic actuators used on many familiar machines, such as bulldozers. Hydraulic fluid enters the cylinder, under pressure, and forces the piston to move to engage the band or clutches.

The accumulators are used to cushion the engagement of the servos. The transaxle fluid must pass through the accumulator on the way to the servo. The accumulator housing contains a thin piston which is sprung away from the discharge passage of the accumulator. When fluid passes through the accumulator on the way to the servo, it must move the piston against spring pressure, and this action smooths out the action of the servo.

THE HYDRAULIC CONTROL SYSTEM

The hydraulic pressure used to operate the servos comes from the main transaxle oil pump. This fluid is channeled to the various servos through the shift valves. There is generally a manual shift valve which is operated by the transaxle selector lever and an automatic shift valve for each automatic upshift the transaxle provides: i.e., 2-speed automatics have a low/high shift valve, while 3-speeds have a 1–2 valve, and a 2–3 valve.

There are two pressures which effect the operation of these valves. One is the governor pressure which is affected by vehicle speed. The other is the modulator pressure which is affected by intake manifold vacuum or throttle position. Governor pressure rises with an increase in vehicle speed, and modulator pressure rises as the throttle is opened wider. By responding to these two pressures, the shift valves cause the upshift points to be delayed with increased throttle opening to make the best use of the engine's power output.

Most transaxles also make use of an auxiliary circuit for down shifting. This circuit may be actuated by the throttle linkage or the vacuum line which actuates the modulator, or by a cable or solenoid. It applies pressure to a special down shift surface on the shift valve or valves.

The transaxle modulator also governs the line pressure, used to actuate the servos. In this way, the clutches and bands will be actuated with a force matching the torque output of the engine.

The three speed automatic transaxle and differential are combined in a single housing and share the same Dexron®II type lubricant. Filter, fluid changes, and band adjustments are not require for average vehicle use. However, if the vehicle is used for constant heavy duty hauling, commercial use or more than 50% operation in heavy traffic, the fluid and filter should be changed every 15,000 miles.

Fluid Pan and Filter

REMOVAL AND INSTALLATION

1. Raise and support the front of the vehicle on jackstands.
2. Remove the splash shield if it will interfere with the fluid pan removal.
3. Place a suitable container that will hold at least four quarts of fluid under the oil pan. Loosen all of the pan bolts slightly until the fluid stats to drain. Loosen the bolts around the point where the fluid is draining to increase the flow.
4. When the bulk of the fluid has drained, remove the oil pan. Clean the dirt from the pan and magnet. Remove RTV sealant or gasket material from the pan and case mounting surfaces.
5. Remove the filter from the bottom of the valve body.

To install:

6. Install a new filter and gasket. Tighten the mounting screw to 40 inch lbs.

7. Apply a unbroken bead of RTV sealant to the oil pan and install on case. Tighten the mounting bolts to 165 inch lbs.

8. Remove the differential cover. Use a clean cloth and wipe the cover and magnet to remove dirt. Clean the mounting surfaces of the cover and case.

9. Apply an unbroken bead of RTV sealant to the differential cover and reinstall. Tighten the mounting bolts to 165 inch lbs. Install the splash shield, etc. and lower the vehicle.

10. Pour four quarts of Dexron II type fluid through the dipstick fill tube. Start the engine, with the parking and service brakes applied, move the gear selector through the various positions ending up in Park.

11. Add sufficient fluid, if necessary, to bring the level to ⅛ in. below the Add mark.

12. Check the fluid level after engine and transaxle have reached the normal operating temperature. The level should be within the Hot range on the dipstick.

NOTE: Always make sure that the dipstick is fully seated in its tube to prevent dirt from entering the transaxle.

Adjustments

KICKDOWN CABLE

1. Run the engine until the normal operating temperature is reached. Be sure the choke is fully opened.

Transaxle pan removal — out of vehicle view

2. Loosen the adjustment bracket lock bolt mounted on transaxle to engine flange.

3. Be sure that the adjustment bracket can slide freely. Clean as necessary.

4. Slide the bracket toward the engine as far as possible. Release the bracket and move the throttle lever to the right as far as it will go. tighten the adjustment lock bolt to 105 inch lbs.

Transaxle adjustment and maintenance points

LET.	TORQUE	
	N•m	IN. LBS.
Ⓐ	28	250
Ⓑ	12	105

GROMMET ON CABLE MUST BE
FIRMLY SEATED INTO DASH PANEL HOLE

Gearshift linkage routing and mounting

Removing the transaxle oil filter

KICKDOWN BAND (FRONT)

The kickdown band adjusting screw is located on left top front side of the transaxle case.

1. Clean the locknut, adjusting screw and area around with safe solvent and brush. Loosen the locknut and back it off about five turns.

2. Tighten the band adjusting screw to 72 inch lbs. Back the adjustment screw off 2½ turns. Hold the adjustment screw in position and tighten the locknut to 35 ft. lbs.

LOW/REVERSE BAND (REAR)

1. Drain the fluid and remove the oil pan from the transaxle.
2. Loosen and back off the locknut about five turns.
3. Tighten the band adjusting screw to 41 inch lbs.
4. Back off the adjusting screw 3½ turns and tighten the locknut to 10 ft. lbs. while holding the adjusting screw in position.
5. Install the oil pan and fill with Dexron II type fluid.

A-604 UPSHIFT AND KICKDOWN LEARNING PROCEDURE

A–604 Ultradrive Transaxle

In 1989, the A–604 4 speed, electronic transaxle was introduced; it is the first to use fully adaptive controls. The controls perform their functions based on real time feedback sensor information. Although, the transaxle is conventional in design, its functions are controlled by the ECM.

Since the A–604 is equipped with a learning function, each time the battery cable is disconnected, the ECM memory is lost. In operation, the transaxle must be shifted many times for the learned memory to be reinputed in the ECM; during this period, the vehicle will experience rough operation. The transaxle must be at normal operating temperature when learning occurs.

1. Maintain constant throttle opening during shifts. Do not move the accelerator pedal during upshifts.

2. Accelerate the vehicle with the throttle ⅛–½ open.

3. Make 15 to 20 1/2, 2/3 and 3/4 upshifts. Accelerating from a full stop to 50 mph each time at the aforementioned throttle opening is sufficient.

4. With the vehicle speed below 25 mph, make 5 to 8 wide open throttle kick downs to 1st gear from either 2nd or 3rd gear. Allow at least 5 seconds of operation in 2nd or 3rd gear prior to each kickdown.

5. With the vehicle speed greater than 25 mph, make 5 to part throttle to wide open throttle kick downs to either 3rd or 2nd gear from 4th gear. Allow at least 5 seconds of operation in 4th gear, preferably at road load throttle prior to performing the kickdown.

THROTTLE PRESSURE CABLE ADJUSTMENT

1. Run the engine until it reaches normal operating temperature.
2. Loosen the cable mounting bracket lock screw.
3. Position the bracket so that both alignment tabs are touching the transaxle case surface and tighten the lock screws.
4. Release the cross lock on the cable assembly by pulling the cross lock up.
5. To ensure proper adjustment, the cable must be free to slide all the way toward the engine against its stop after the cross lock is released.
6. Move the transaxle throttle control lever fully clockwise and press the cross lock down until it snaps into position.
7. Road test the vehicle and check the shift points.

THROTTLE PRESSURE ROD ADJUSTMENT

1. Run the engine until it reaches normal operating temperature.
2. Loosen the adjustment swivel lock screw.
3. To ensure proper adjustment, the swivel must be free to slide along the flat end of the throttle rod. Disassembly, clean and lubricate as required.
4. Hold the transaxle throttle control lever firmly toward the engine and tighten the swivel screw.
5. Road test the vehicle and check the shift points.

Neutral Starting/Back-up Light Switch

The neutral starting/back-up light switch is screwed into the side of the automatic transaxle. If the vehicle fails to start in either the Park or Neutral positions, or starts in any of the drive gears a problem with the switch is indicated.

TESTING

1. The Neutral/Park sensing part of the switch is the center terminal, while the back-up lights are controlled by the outer two terminals.
2. Remove the wiring connector from the switch. Use an ohmmeter or continuity tester and connect the leads between the center switch terminal and the transaxle case to test the Neutral/Park circuit. Continuity should exist only when the

THROTTLE CONTROL CABLE

LOCK SCREW

CROSS-LOCK

BRACKET

THROTTLE PRESSURE CABLE

THROTTLE CONTROL LEVER

SELECTOR LEVER

Throttle pressure cable mounting

LOCK-UP SOLENOID ELECTRICAL CONNECTOR

NEUTRAL/PARK SAFETY SWITCH

DIPSTICK HOLE

Lock-up solenoid and neutral safety switch location

gearshift is either in the Park or Neutral positions. Check the gearshift cable adjustment first before replacing the switch.
3. Connect an ohmmeter or continuity tester connected between the outer two terminals of the switch to check the back-up light. Continuity should be present when the gearshift selector is in the Reverse position.

REMOVAL AND INSTALLATION

1. Remove the wiring connector. Place a container under the switch to catch transaxle fluid and unscrew the switch.
2. Move the gearshift selector to the Park and Neutral positions and check to see that the switch operating fingers center in the case opening.
3. Screw the new switch and new mounting seal into the transaxle case. Tighten to 24 ft. lbs. Retest switch operation. Add transaxle fluid if needed.

Automatic Transaxle

REMOVAL AND INSTALLATION

NOTE: If the vehicle is going to be rolled while the transaxle is out of the vehicle, obtain 2 outer CV joints to install to the hubs. If the vehicle is rolled without the proper torque applied to the front wheel bearings, the bearings will be destroyed.

1. Disconnect the negative battery cable. If equipped with 3.0L or 3.3L engine, drain the coolant. Remove the dipstick.
2. Remove the air cleaner assembly if it is preventing access to the upper bell housing bolts. Remove the upper bell housing bolts and water tube, where applicable. Unplug all electrical connectors from the transaxle.
3. If equipped with a 2.2L or 2.5L engine, remove the starter attaching nut and bolt at the top of the bell housing.
4. Raise the vehicle and support safely. Remove the tire and wheel assemblies. Remove the axle end cotter pins, nut locks, spring washers and axle nuts.
5. Remove the ball joint retaining bolts and pry the control arm from the steering knuckle. Position a drain pan under the transaxle where the axles enter the differential or extension housing. Remove the axles from the transaxle or center bearing. Unbolt the center bearing and remove the intermediate axle from the transaxle, if equipped.
6. Drain the transaxle. Disconnect and plug the fluid cooler hoses. Disconnect the shifter and kickdown linkage from the transaxle, if equipped.
7. Remove the speedometer cable adaptor bolt and remove the adaptor from the transaxle.
8. Remove the starter. Remove the torque converter inspec-

tion cover, matchmark the torque converter to the flex plate and remove the torque converter bolts.

9. Using the proper equipment, support the weight of the engine.

10. Remove the front motor mount and bracket.

11. Position a suitable jack under the transaxle.

12. Remove the lower bell housing bolts.

13. Remove the left side splash shield. Remove the transaxle mount bolts.

14. Carefully pry the engine from the transaxle.

15. Slide the transaxle rearward until the locating dowels disengage from the mating holes in the transaxle.

16. Pull the transaxle completely away from the engine and remove it from the vehicle.

17. To prepare the vehicle for rolling, support the engine with a suitable support or reinstall the front motor mount to the engine. Then reinstall the ball joints to the steering knuckle and install the retaining bolt. Install the obtained outer CV joints to the hubs, install the washers and torque the axle nuts to 180 ft. lbs. (244 Nm). The vehicle may now be safely rolled.

To install:

18. Install the transmission securely on the transmission jack. Rotate the converter so it will align with the positioning of the flex plate.

19. Apply a coating of high temperature grease to the torque converter pilot hub.

20. Raise the transaxle into place and push it forward until the dowels engage and the bell housing is flush with the block.

21. Install the transaxle to bell housing bolts.

22. Jack the transaxle up and install the left side mount bolts. Install the torque converter bolts and torque to 55 ft. lbs. (74 Nm).

23. Install the front motor mount and bracket. Remove the engine and transaxle support fixtures.

24. Install the starter to the transaxle. Install the bolt finger tight if equipped with a 2.2L or 2.5L engine.

25. Install a new O-ring to the speedometer cable adaptor and install to the extension housing; make sure it snaps in place. Install the retaining bolt.

26. Connect the shifter and kickdown linkage to the transaxle, if equipped.

27. Install the axles and center bearing, if equipped. Install the ball joints to the steering knuckles. Torque the axle nuts to 180 ft. lbs. (244 Nm) and install new cotter pins. Install the splash shield and install the wheels. Lower the vehicle. Install the dipstick.

28. Install the upper bell housing bolts and water pipe, if removed.

29. If equipped with 2.2L or 2.5L engine, install the starter attaching nut and bolt at the top of the bell housing. Raise the vehicle again and tighten the starter bolt from underneath the vehicle. Lower the vehicle.

30. Connect all electrical wiring to the transaxle.

31. Install the air cleaner assembly, if it was removed. Fill the transaxle with the proper amount of Dexron®II.

32. Connect the negative battery cable and check the transaxle for proper operation. On the A-604 transaxle perform the upshift and kickdown learn procedure found earlier in this section.

POWER TRANSFER UNIT

Identification

For 1991 Chrysler introduced an All Wheel Drive (AWD) version of the Caravan/Voyager. The AWD equipped vehicles use the same basic drivetrain layout as the front wheel drive versions, with the exception of the rear driveline module. To transfer the power from the engine and transaxle, to the rear driveline module, these vehicles use an Power Transfer Unit (PTU).

The PTU is connected to the transaxle where the right halfshaft extension housing would be.

The PTU is a separate unit from the transaxle. It uses a standard hypoid type ring and pinion. The PTU is sealed from the transaxle and has its own oil sump. The unit uses SAE 85W-90 gear lube and holds 1.22 qts.

The PTU is not a repairable unit and can only be replaced. If you suspect the PTU has failed, take the vehicle to an authorized service center.

REAR DRIVE LINE MODULE

Identification

As an option in 1991, Chrysler offered All Wheel Drive (AWD) on Caravan/Voyager models. These models are basically the same as the front wheel drive versions, with the exception of the components needed for driving the rear wheels as well.

The power is transferred to the rear wheels through the Power Transfer Unit (PTU) attached to the transaxle. The power travels through the PTU to a torque tube that contains the cen-

Rear driveline module assembly — exploded view

Torque tube and overrunning clutch assemblies — exploded view

ter driveshaft. The power then enters an overrunning clutch assembly, attached to the front of the rear differential carrier.

The overrunning clutch assembly is separate from the rear carrier. The overrunning clutch assembly has an vacuum operated dog clutch, it is lubricated with Mopar ATF type 7176. The rear carrier is lubricated with SAE 85W-90 gear lube.

Rear Drive Line Assembly Module

REMOVAL AND INSTALLATION

1. Raise and safely support the rear of the vehicle.
2. Remove the right and left inner halfshaft joint mounting bolts.
3. Support the inner side of the halfshafft, by hanging it from the frame using a piece of wire. Do not allow the shafts to hang freely or the joints will be damaged.
4. Remove the mounting bolts from the rear side of the propeller shaft at, the rear carrier.
5. Support the propeller shaft.
6. Remove the viscous coupling retaining nut and slide the viscous coupling off the rear driveline assembly.
7. Disconnect the vacuum line at the driveline module. Also disconnect the electrical lead from the assembly.
8. Support the rear of the driveline module with a jack.
9. Remove the rear driveline module front mounting bolts. Partially lower the unit from the vehicle.
10. Remove the rear driveline module from the vehicle.
To install:
11. Position the driveline module in the vehicle. Install the front mounting bolts and tighten to 40 ft. lbs. (54 Nm).
12. Reconnect the vacuum line and electrical lead. Install the viscous coupling and nut. Tighten the nut to 120 ft. lbs. (162 Nm).

13. Connect the propeller shaft to the driveline module, tighten to 250 inch lbs. (28 Nm).
14. Connect the rear halshafts to the rear driveline module. Tighten the bolt to 45 ft. lbs. (61 Nm).
15. Lower the vehicle. Check the operation of the drive train.

Rear Halfshaft

REMOVAL AND INSTALLATION

1. Raise and safely support the rear of the vehicle.
2. Remove the rear wheel.
3. Remove the cotter pin, nut, lock and spring washer from the rear hub.
4. Remove the inner halfshaft retaining bolts.
5. The halshaft is spring loaded, push it in slightly and then tilt it down to remove it. Pull it out from under the vehicle.
To install:
6. Insert the end of the halshaft into the rear hub assembly.
7. Position it on the rear carrier unit and install the retaining bolts.
8. Tighten the retaining bolts to 45 ft. lbs. (61 Nm).
9. Install the hub nut, spring and lock washers, and cotter pin.
10. Install the wheel and tire assembly.

Drive Pinion

REMOVAL AND INSTALLATION

1. Raise and safely support the vehicle.
2. Remove the rear driveline module from the vehicle.
3. Remove the overrunning clutch case-to-rear carrier bolts. Separate the overrunning clutch case from the rear carrier.

Rear driveline module — seal locations

REAR
CARRIER HOUSING

OVERRUNNING
CLUTCH CASE

Overrunning clutch case to rear carrier bolts

REAR CARRIER
CASE

OVERRUNNING
CLUTCH CASE

Separating the housings

4. Remove the overrunning clutch outer race snapring and slide the clutch race off of the shaft.

5. Using a spline socket and a wrench, remove the pinion nut.

6. Remove the front carrier cover retaining bolts and remove the carrier cover.

7. Place a block of wood under the end of the pinion shaft. Tap the end of the pinion against the wood to remove the spacer from the shaft.

To install:

8. Install the front carrier onto the case and tighten the retaining nuts to 105 inch lbs. (12 Nm).

9. Clean and inspect the seal area, apply a light coat of oil to the drive pinion seal. Install the seal using a seal installer. The

OVERRUNNING
CLUTCH CASE

OVERRUNNING
CLUTCH INNER
RACE

SNAP
RING

Inner snapring removal — overrunning clutch case

OVERRUNNING
CLUTCH INNER
RACE

OVERRUNNING
CLUTCH CASE

Removing overrunning clutch inner race

PINION

OVERRUNNING CLUTCH
OUTER RACE

Overrunning clutch — outer race removal

seal must be installed with the spring towards the rear of the case.

10. Apply a light coat of oil onto the drive pinion spacer and slide it onto the pinion shaft with the tapered side facing out.

Removing the pinion nut

Removing the front carrier cover retaining bolts

Removing the front carrier cover and pinion

Removing the output flange, using 2 pry bars

Bolt tightening sequence — differential side gear

11. Apply a light coat of oil to the overrunning clutch seal and install with a seal installer, the seal must be installed with the spring facing outward.

12. Install the pinion nut and tighten to 150 ft. lbs. (203 Nm).

13. Install the overrunning clutch outer race and snapring. Apply Loctite® sealer to the overrunning clutch sealing surface and install the clutch case to the rear carrier. Tighten to 250 inch lbs. (28 Nm).

14. Install the rear driveline module into the vehicle. Check and fill the fluid as required.

Vacuum actuation schematic — solenoids de- energized

Vacuum actuation schematic — solenoids energized

Differential Side Gears

REMOVAL AND INSTALLATION

1. Raise and safely support the rear of the vehicle.
2. Disconnect both rear halshafts from the axle carrier assembly.
3. Using 2 prybars, remove the output shaft.
4. Remove the end cover retaining bolts and remove the end cover.
5. Remove the differential assembly from the rear driveline case.
6. Remove the ring gear bolts and separate the differential case from the differential body.

7. Using a punch and hammer, remove the differential pinion shaft pin.
8. Slide the differential pinion shaft out of the differential case.

To install:

9. Replace the pinion gears, shaft or washers as required.
10. Reverse steps 8 through 5 to assemble the differential. Torque the ring gear bolts to 70 ft. lbs. (95 Nm).
11. Install the differential into the module case. Clean and inspect sealer surfaces.
12. Apply Loctite® gasket eliminator or equivalent, and install the end cover. Tighten, in the sequence shown, to 250 inch lbs. (28 Nm).
13. Install the rear halfshafts and lower the vehicle.

Torque Tube

REMOVAL AND INSTALLATION

1. Raise and safely support the vehicle.
2. Remove the rear driveline module assembly from the vehicle.
3. Remove the viscous coupling, snapring and torque tube bearing shield.
4. Remove torque tube to overrunning clutch case bolts.
5. Slide the torque tube off of the torque shaft.
6. Install the torque tube onto the torque shaft. Install the Torque tube to overrunning clutch case bolts, tightening to 250 inch lbs. (28 Nm).
7. Install the bearing shield and snapring. Install the viscous coupling.
8. Install the driveline module into the vehicle. Lower The vehicle.

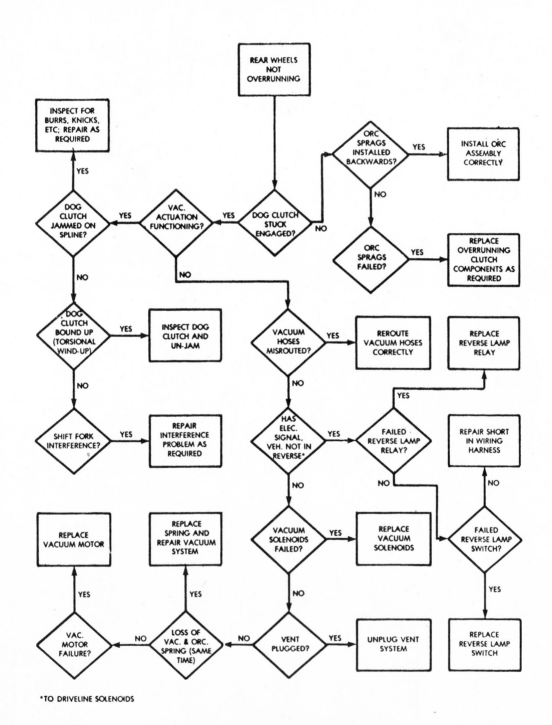

*TO DRIVELINE SOLENOIDS

Rear driveline vacuum shift motor diagnosis

TORQUE SPECIFICATIONS

Component	English	Metric
MANUAL TRANSAXLE		
Differential assembly turning torque		
New bearings:	9–14 inch lbs.	1–2 Nm
Used bearings:	6 inch lbs. (minimum)	0.7 Nm (minimum)
Differential bearing retainer:	21 ft. lbs.	29 Nm
Extension housing:	21 ft. lbs.	29 Nm
Input shaft bearings bearing retainer plate:	21 ft. lbs.	29 Nm
Input shaft seal retainer bolts:	21 ft. lbs.	29 Nm
Input shaft turning torque		
New bearings:	1–5 inch lbs.	0.1–0.6 Nm
Used bearings:	1 inch lb. (minimum)	0.1 Nm (minimum)
Selector/crossover cable retaining screws:	70 inch lbs.	8 Nm
Selector housing lock pin:	105 inch lbs.	12 Nm
Shift linkage adjustment/retainer bolts:	55 inch lbs.	6Nm
5th speed gear nut:	190 ft. lbs.	258 Nm
HALFSHAFTS		
Ball joint clamp bolt:	70 ft. lbs.	95 Nm
Hub nut:	180 ft. lbs.	245 Nm
CLUTCH		
Pressure plate bolts:	21 ft. lbs.	29 Nm
AUTOMATIC TRANSAXLE		
Differential cover bolts:	165 inch lbs.	18 Nm
Filter mounting screw:	40 inch lbs.	4 Nm
Kickdown cable adjustment lock bolt:	105 inch lbs.	12 Nm
Kickdown (front) band locknut:	35 ft. lbs.	48 Nm
Low/reverse (rear) band locknut:	10 ft. lbs.	(14 Nm
Neutral Start/Back-up Light Switch:	24 ft. lbs.	33 Nm
Oil pan mounting bolts:	165 inch lbs.	18 Nm
Torque converter bolts:	55 ft. lbs.	74 Nm
DRIVELINE		
Driveshaft-to-driveline module:	21 ft. lbs.	28 Nm
Rear drive line assembly module front mounting bolts:	40 ft. lbs.	54 Nm
Rear halshafts-to-rear driveline module:	45 ft. lbs.	61 Nm
Viscous coupling nut:	120 ft. lbs.	162 Nm

TORQUE SPECIFICATIONS

REAR DIFFERENTIAL

Differential end cover:	21 ft. lbs.	28 Nm
Differential ring gear bolts:	70 ft. lbs.	95 Nm
Front carrier-to-case nuts:	105 inch lbs.	12 Nm
Overrunning clutch case-to-rear carrier:	21 ft. lbs.	28 Nm
Pinion nut:	150 ft. lbs.	203 Nm
Torque tube-to-overrunning clutch case bolts:	21 ft. lbs.	28 Nm

Suspension and Steering

8

GENERAL INDEX

Alignment, wheel 8-10
Ball joints... 8-5
Front suspension
   Ball joints.. 8-5
   Hub and bearing............................. 8-8
   Knuckle and spindle 8-6
   Lower control arm 8-6
   MacPherson struts 8-4
   Springs 8-4
   Sway bar 8-6
   Troubleshooting.............................. 8-2
   Wheel alignment............................ 8-10
Front wheel bearings........................... 8-8
Ignition lock cylinder 8-20
Knuckles 8-6
Lower ball joint.................................... 8-5
Lower control arm................................ 8-6

MacPherson struts 8-4
Power steering pump
   Removal and installation 8-27
   Troubleshooting.............................. 8-27
Rear suspension
   Rear axle alignment........................ 8-15
   Shock absorbers 8-13
   Springs 8-12
   Sway bar 8-13
   Wheel bearings............................... 8-14
Shock absorbers 8-13
Specifications Charts
   Torque 8-29
   Wheel alignment............................ 8-10
Springs
   Front 8-4

Rear.. 8-12
Steering column
   Removal and installation 8-21
   Troubleshooting.............................. 8-15
Steering gear 8-25
Steering linkage 8-25
Steering wheel 8-19
Sway bar 8-6,13
Tie rod ends 8-25
Troubleshooting Charts
   Front suspension 8-2
   Ignition switch 8-17
   Power steering pump 8-27
   Steering column 8-15
   Turn signal switch 8-17
Turn signal switch 8-20
Wheel alignment.................................. 8-10

WHEELS

Front and Rear Wheel Assemblies

REMOVAL AND INSTALLATION

1. Place the vehicle transmission in PARK.
2. Block the wheel diagonally from the wheel being removed.
3. Remove the hub cap and loosen the lug nuts.
4. Raise the vehicle and place a jackstand underneath it on the side being raised.
5. Remove the lug nuts and the tire and wheel assembly.
6. Install the wheel on the vehicle and install the lug nuts.

The lug nuts should be tightened as much as possible, using a crossing or "X" pattern.

7. Lower the vehicle and final torque the wheel nuts to 95 ft. lbs. (129 Nm).

INSPECTION

With the wheel and tire assembly removed from the vehicle, check the tire and rim for visible signs of damage. Check the rim for bends in its outer edge, or cracks and chunks missing on alloy type wheels. Check the tire for uneven wear or other signs of possible damage. Replace any damaged rim or excessively worn tire.

FRONT SUSPENSION

Troubleshooting Basic Steering and Suspension Problems

Problem	Cause	Solution
Hard steering (steering wheel is hard to turn)	· Low or uneven tire pressure · Loose power steering pump drive belt · Low or incorrect power steering fluid · Incorrect front end alignment · Defective power steering pump · Bent or poorly lubricated front end parts	· Inflate tires to correct pressure · Adjust belt · Add fluid as necessary · Have front end alignment checked/adjusted · Check pump · Lubricate and/or replace defective parts
Loose steering (too much play in the steering wheel)	· Loose wheel bearings · Loose or worn steering linkage · Faulty shocks · Worn ball joints	· Adjust wheel bearings · Replace worn parts · Replace shocks · Replace ball joints
Car veers or wanders (car pulls to one side with hands off the steering wheel)	· Incorrect tire pressure · Improper front end alignment · Loose wheel bearings · Loose or bent front end components · Faulty shocks	· Inflate tires to correct pressure · Have front end alignment checked/adjusted · Adjust wheel bearings · Replace worn components · Replace shocks

Troubleshooting Basic Steering and Suspension Problems

Problem	Cause	Solution
Wheel oscillation or vibration trans-mitted through steering wheel	• Improper tire pressures • Tires out of balance • Loose wheel bearings • Improper front end alignment • Worn or bent front end compo-nents	• Inflate tires to correct pressure • Have tires balanced • Adjust wheel bearings • Have front end alignment checked/adjusted • Replace worn parts
Uneven tire wear	• Incorrect tire pressure • Front end out of alignment • Tires out of balance	• Inflate tires to correct pressure • Have front end alignment checked/adjusted • Have tires balanced

Front suspension components — exploded view

MacPherson Struts

A MacPherson Type front suspension, with vertical shock absorbers attached to the upper fender reinforcement and the steering knuckle, is used. Lower control arms, attached inboard to a crossmember and outboard to the steering knuckle through a ball joint, provide lower steering knuckle position. During steering maneuvers, the upper strut and steering knuckle turn as an assembly.

REMOVAL AND INSTALLATION

1. Loosen the front wheel lug nuts slightly. Raise and support the front of the vehicle on jackstands.
2. Remove the wheel and tire assemblies.

NOTE: If the original strut assemblies are to be installed, mark the camber eccentric bolt and strut for installment in same position.

3. Remove the lower camber bolt and nut(at the steering knuckle), and the knuckle bolt and nut. Remove the brake hose to strut bracket mounting bolt.
4. Remove the upper mounting nuts and washers on the fender shield in the engine compartment. Remove the strut assembly from the vehicle.
To install:
5. Inspect the strut assembly for signs of leakage. A slight amount of seepage is normal, fluid streaking down the side of the strut is not. Replacer the strut if leakage is evident. Service the strut and spring assembly as required.
6. Position the strut assembly under the fender well and loosely install the upper washers and nuts. Position the lower mount over the steering knuckle and loosely install the mounting and camber bolts and nuts. Attach the brake hose retaining bracket and tighten the mounting bolts to 10 ft. lbs.
7. Tighten the upper mount nuts to 20 ft. lbs. Index the camber bolt to reference mark and snug the nut. Install the nut on the mounting bolt and tighten slightly.
8. Mount a 4 in. (102mm) C-clamp over the inner edge of the strut and outer edge of the steering knuckle. Tighten the clamp just enough to eliminate any looseness between the knuckle and the strut. check the alignment of the camber bolt and strut reference marks. Tighten the mounting and camber nuts to 75 ft. lbs. plug ¼ turn more. Remove the C-clamp.
9. Install the wheel and tire assembly and lower the vehicle.

Clamp positioning for strut installation

Strut Spring

REMOVAL AND INSTALLATION

NOTE: A coil spring compressor Chrysler Tool C-4838 or equivalent is required.

1. Remove the strut and spring assembly from the vehicle.
2. Compress the coil spring with Chrysler Tool C-4838 or equivalent. Make sure the compressor is mounted correctly and tighten jaws evenly. If the spring slips from the compressor, bodily injury could occur.
3. Hold the strut center rod from turning and remove the assembly nut.

NOTE: The coil springs on each are rated differently. Be sure to mark the spring for side identification.

4. Remove the mount assembly and the coil spring. Inspect the assembly for rubber isolator deterioration, distortion, cracks and bonding failure. Replace as necessary. Check the mount bearings for binding and the retainers for bends and cracks. Replace as necessary.
To install:
5. Install the spring on the strut in compressed mode. Install the upper mount assembly. The spring seat tab and the end of the coil spring must be aligned. install assembly nut and tighten while holding the center strut rod in position. Tighten the nut to 60 ft. lbs.
6. Release the coil spring compressor.
7. Install the strut assembly on the vehicle.
8. Misalignment of the upper coil spring seat can cause interference between the coil spring and the inside of the mounting tower. A scraping noise on turns will be an indication if the problem. To correct, raise and support the vehicle to take the weight off of the front wheels. Use two wrenches, one on the top

TORQUE 27 N•m (20 FT. LBS.)

TORQUE 13 N•m (10 FT. LBS.)

TORQUE NUTS TO
100 N•m (75 FT. LBS.)
PLUS ¼ TURN

KNUCKLE BOLT

CAM BOLT

ADJUST CAMBER AND TOE WHEN REPLACING SHOCK ABSORBER

WASHER PLATE

MARK CAM LOCATION BEFORE REMOVING BOLTS

Strut removal

PARALLEL

BRACKET

SEAT RECESS

UPPER RETAINER TAB

Spring compressor installed position

of the center strut rod and one on the assembly nut. Turn both the strut rod and nut in the same direction. The spring will wind up and snap into position. Check the torque on the assembly nut (60 ft. lbs.).

Lower Ball Joint

The lower front suspension ball joints operate with no free play. The ball joint housing is pressed into the lower control arm with the joint stud retained in the steering knuckle with a (clamp) bolt.

On models from 1990, the lower ball joint is welded to the lower control arm. This requires the replacement of the complete lower control arm in the case of ball joint failure,

INSPECTION

With the weight of the vehicle resting on the ground, grasp the ball joint grease fitting, and attempt to move it. If the ball joint is worn the grease fitting will move easily. If movement is noted, replacement of the ball joint is recommended.

REMOVAL AND INSTALLATION

1984–89 Models

NOTE: Special Chrysler Tools C-4699-1 and C-4699-2 or equivalents are required to remove and install the ball joint form the lower control arm. If the tools are not on hand, remove the control arm and have an automotive machine shop press the ball joint out and in. Refer to the Lower Control Arm Section.

1. Remove the lower control arm. Pry off the seal from the ball joint.
2. Position a receiving cup, special tool C-4699-2 or its equivalent to support the lower control arm.
3. Install a 1⅛ in. deep socket over the stud and against the joint upper housing.
4. Press the joint assembly from the arm.

To install:

5. To install, position the ball joint housing into the control arm cavity.

Lower control arm assembly removal and installation

Installing the ball joint — models through 1989

LOWER CONTROL ARM

PRESS AND SUPPORT

RECEIVER CUP — C-4699-2

BALL JOINT

INSTALLER — C-4699-1

6. Position the assembly in a press with special tool C-4699-1 or its equivalent, supporting the control arm.

7. Align the ball joint assembly, then press it until the housing ledge stops against the control arm cavity down flange.

8. To install a new seal, support the ball joint housing with tool #C-4699-2 and place a new seal over the stud, against the housing.

9. With a 1½ in. socket, press the seal onto the joint housing with the seat against the control arm. Install control arm.

1990–91 Models

Refer to the lower control arm removal procedure for ball joint replacement on these models.

Lower Control Arm

REMOVAL AND INSTALLATION

1. Jack up the vehicle and support it with jackstands.
2. Remove the front inner pivot through bolt, the rear stub strut nut, retainer and bushing, and the ball joint-to-steering knuckle clamp bolts.
3. Separate the ball joint stud from the steering knuckle by prying between the ball stud retainer on the knuckle and the lower control arm.

WARNING: Pulling the steering knuckle out from the vehicle after releasing it from the ball joint can separate the inner CV joint.

4. Remove the sway bar-to-control arm nut and reinforcement and rotate the control arm over the sway bar. Remove the rear stub strut bushing, sleeve and retainer. Remove the control arm.

To install:

NOTE: The substitution of fasteners other than those of the grade originally used is not recommended.

5. Install the retainer, bushing and sleeve on the stub strut.

6. Position the control arm over the sway bar and install the rear stub strut and front pivot into the crossmember.

7. Install the front pivot bolt and loosely install the nut.

8. Install the stub strut bushing and retainer and loosely assembly the nut.

9. Position the sway bar bracket and stud through the control arm and install the retainer nut. Tighten the nuts to 25 ft. lbs. on 1984–1989 models and 50 ft. lbs. On 1990–91 models.

10. Install the ball joint stud into the steering knuckle and install the clamp bolt. Torque the clamp bolt to 70 ft. lbs. on 1984–89 models and 105 ft. lbs. on 1990–91 models.

11. Lower the vehicle, weight on wheels, and tighten the front pivot bolt to 105 ft. lbs. on 1984—89 models and 125 ft. lbs. on 1990–91 models. Tighten the rear stub strut nut to 70 ft. lbs.

Pivot Bushing

The front pivot bushing of the lower control arm can be replaced. Remove the control arm and have an automotive machine shop press the bushing out and in.

Sway Bar

The sway bar connects the control arms together and attaches to the front crossmember of the vehicle, Bumps, jounce and rebound affecting one wheel are partially transmitted to the other wheel to help stabilize body roll. The sway bar is attached to the control arms and crossmember by rubber-isolated bushings. All part are serviceable.

REMOVAL AND INSTALLATION

1. Raise and support the front of the vehicle on jackstands.
2. Remove the nuts, bolts and retainer connecting the sway bar to the control arms.
3. Remove the bolt that mount the sway bar to the crossmember. Remove the sway bar and crossmember mounting clamps from the vehicle.
4. Inspect the bushings for wear. Replace as necessary. End bushings are replaced by cutting or driving them from the retainer. Center bushings are split and are removed by opening the split and sliding from the sway bar.
5. Force the new end bushings into the retainers, allow about ½ in. (13mm) to protrude. Install the sway bar. Tighten the center bracket bolts to 25 ft. lbs. on 1984–89 models and 50 ft. lbs. on 1990–91 models. Place a jack under the control arm and raise the arm to normal design height. Tighten the outer bracket bolts to 25 ft. lbs. on 1984–89 models and 50 ft. lbs. on 1990–91 models. Lower the vehicle.

Steering Knuckle

The front suspension steering knuckle provides for steering, braking, front end alignment and supports the front driving hub and axle assembly.

REMOVAL AND INSTALLATION

NOTE: A tie rod end puller (Chrysler Tool C-3894A or equivalent) is necessary.

1. Remove the wheel cover, center hub cover, cotter pin, nut lock and spring washer from the front wheel.
2. Loosen the front hub nut and wheel lug nuts. Raise the front of the vehicle and support on jackstands.
3. Remove the wheel and tire assembly. Remove the center hub nut.
4. Disconnect the tie rod end from the steering knuckle arm with Tool C-3894A or equivalent. Disconnect the front brake hose bracket from the strut.

TORQUE 34 N•m (25 FT. LBS.)

SWAY BAR

TORQUE

RUBBER ISOLATOR

STRAP

Sway bar assembly mounting

5. Remove the caliper assembly and support it with a piece of wire. Do not permit the caliper to hang from the brake hose. Remove the disc brake rotor, inner pad and caliper mounting adapter.

6. Remove the clamp bolt that secures the ball joint and steering knuckle together.

7. Insure that the splined halfshaft is loose in the hub by tapping lightly with a brass drift and hammer. Separate the ball joint and steering knuckle. Pull the knuckle assembly out and away from the halfshaft. Remove the steering knuckle from the strut assembly.

To install:

8. Service hub, bearing, seal and steering knuckle as necessary.

9. Install the steering knuckle to the strut assembly. Install the halfshaft through the hub and steering knuckle. Connect

CAM BOLT NUT

ADAPTOR SCREW AND WASHER
216 N•m (160 FT. LBS.)

BRAKE CALIPER

WASHER
PLATE

SCREW
27 N•m (20 FT. LBS.)

HUB

RETAINER

BEARING

WASHER

COTTER
PIN

GASKET

KNUCKLE

NUT LOCK

WHEEL BOLT

HUB NUT
245 N•m (180 FT. LBS.)

STRUT DAMPER
(REFERENCE)

WEAR SLEEVE

SEAL

DRIVE SHAFT

STEERING LINKAGE
47 N•m (35 FT. LBS.)

CLAMP BOLT

LOWER CONTROL ARM
(REFERENCE)

Steering knuckle installation

the ball joint to the knuckle and tighten the clamp bolt to 70 ft. lbs. on 1984–89 models and 105 ft. lbs (145 Nm) on 1990–91 models.

10. Install the tie rod end and tighten the retaining nut to 35 ft. lbs. Install and bend the cotter pin.

11. Install the brake adapter, pads, rotor and caliper. Connect the brake hose bracket to the strut.

12. Install the center hub washer and retaining nut. Apply the brakes and tighten the nut to 180 ft. lbs. Install the spring washer, nut and new cotter pin. Install the wheel and tire assembly. Tighten the lug nuts to 95 ft. lbs. Lower the vehicle.

Front Hub and Bearing

REMOVAL AND INSTALLATION

Press In Type

NOTE: A special set of tools, C-4811 or the equivalent, is required to remove and install the hub and bearing. If the special tool is not on hand, remove the steering knuckle and take it to an automotive machine shop for bearing replacement.

1. Remove the cotter pin, nut lock and spring from the front halfshaft hub nut. Loosen the hub nut. Loosen the wheel lug nuts slightly.

2. Raise and safely support the vehicle on jackstands.

3. Remove the wheel assembly. Remove the center hub nut.

4. Disconnect the tie rod end from the steering arm. Disconnect the brake hose from the strut retainer. Remove the ball joint clamp nut.

5. Remove the brake caliper, suspend it with wire so that no strain is put on the brake hose. Remove the disc rotor.

6. Separate the knuckle from the control arm ball joint.

7. Pull the knuckle from the halfshaft. Tap the halfshaft with a brass hammer to loosen it if necessary. Use care so that the inner CV joint does not separate. Support the halfshaft.

8. Using tool C-4811, or equivalent. Back out one of the bearing and install the tool adapter bolt into the retainer threads.

9. Position the tool at the back of the knuckle and install two mounting bolts in the brake caliper mounting holes. Center the tool and tighten the caliper adapter mounting bolts and the retainer bolt.

10. Tighten the center threaded driver on the tool and push the hub from the knuckle.

11. Remove the tool from the front side of the knuckle. Carefully pry the grease seal from the knuckle. Press the bearing from the knuckle using tool C-4811.

To install:

12. Install a new bearing by using the puller adapter of tool C-4811. Install a new seal and lubricate. Install the bearing retainer and bolts, torque the bolts to 20 ft. lbs.

13. Press the hub into the bearing. Install a new wear/wipe seal. Install the halfshaft. Attach the ball joint and tie rod end. Install the brake rotor and caliper. Secure the brake hose. Tighten the clamp bolt to 70 ft. lbs. Tighten the tie rod end nut to 35 ft. lbs.

14. Install the washer and hub nut. Tighten the nut firmly. Install the wheel assemblies and tighten the lug nuts firmly.

15. Lower the vehicle. Tighten the center hub nut to 180 ft. lbs. Tighten the wheel lugs to 95 ft. lbs.

Removing the hub from the knuckle

Separating the ball joint stud from the knuckle assembly

Removing the outer bearing race

Removing the bearing from the knuckle

Installing the bearing in the knuckle

Installing the hub assembly

Bolt-In Type

Starting with 1989 eight-passenger model vehicles, a bolt in knuckle bearing is used. The bearing unit is serviced as a complete assembly. and is attached to the steering knuckle by four mounting bolts that are removed through a provided access hole in the hub flange.

1. Loosen the center splined retaining hub nut while the vehicle is on the ground. Loosen the wheel lug nuts slightly.

2. Raise and safely support the vehicle on jackstands.

3. Remove the wheel assembly. Remove the hub nut and washer.

4. Disconnect the tie rod end from the steering arm and the clamp bolt that retains the ball joint to the knuckle.

5. Remove the disc brake caliper and suspend it with wire so that there is no strain on the brake hose. Remove the rotor.

6. Separate the knuckle from the ball joint. Pull the knuckle assembly away from the halfshaft. Take care not separate the halfshaft inner CV joint. Support the halfshaft.

7. Remove the four hub and bearing retaining bolts. Remove the assembly.

To install:

8. Install the new bearing assembly and tighten the mounting bolts in a criss-cross manner to 45 ft. lbs.

9. Install a new wear sleeve seal. Lubricate the sealing surfaces with multi-purpose grease. Install the halfshaft through the hub.

10. Install the steering knuckle onto the lower control arm. Torque the clamp bolt to 70 ft. lbs. on 1984–89 models and 105 ft. lbs. on 1990–91 models.

11. Install the tie rod end. Tighten the nut to 35 ft. lbs. Install the brake disc rotor and caliper assembly.

12. Install and tighten the hub nut reasonably tight. Install the wheel assembly, tighten the lug nuts fairly tight. Lower the vehicle and tighten the hub nut to 180 ft. lbs. and the wheel lugs to 85 ft. lbs.

Removing the hub and bearing assembly from the knuckle — bolt on type

FRONT END ALIGNMENT

Front wheel alignment is the proper adjustment of all the interrelated suspension angles affecting the running and steering of the front wheels.

There are six basic factors which are the foundation of front wheel alignment, height, caster, camber, toe-in, steering axis inclination, and toe-out turns. of these basic factors, only camber and toe are mechanically adjustable. Any checks and required adjustments should be made to the camber first, then to the toe.

CAMBER

Camber is the number of degrees or inches the top of the wheel is tilted inward or outward from true vertical. Outward tilt is positive camber, inward-negative camber. Excessive camber (inward or outward) can cause poor handling, pulling and excessive tire wear.

TOE

Toe is measured in degrees or inches and is the distance that the front edges of the tires are closer or further apart then the rear edges. Front wheel drive vehicles usually have toe out which means that the outer edges are further apart than the inner. Incorrect toe adjustment will also cause poor handling and excessive tire wear.

WHEEL ALIGNMENT SPECIFICATIONS

Years	Model		Caster (Deg.) Range	Caster (Deg.) Preferred Setting	Camber (Deg.) Range	Camber (Deg.) Preferred Setting	Toe-In (in.)
1984	Caravan/Voyager	Front	①	②	0.25N–0.75P	0.30P	0.06
		Rear	—	—	1.00N–0.050P	0.25N	0
1985	Caravan/Voyager	Front	①	②	0.25N–0.75P	0.30P	0.06
		Rear	—	—	1.00N–0.050P	0.25N	0
1986	Caravan/Voyager	Front	①	②	0.25N–0.75P	0.30P	0.06
		Rear	—	—	1.00N–0.050P	0.25N	0
1987	Caravan/Voyager	Front	①	②	0.25N–0.75P	0.30P	0.06
		Rear	—	—	1.00N–0.050P	0.25N	0
1988	Caravan/Voyager	Front	①	②	0.25N–0.75P	0.30P	0.06
		Rear	—	—	1.00N–0.050P	0.25N	0
1989	Caravan/Voyager	Front	①	②	0.25N–0.75P	0.30P	0.06
		Rear	—	—	1.00N–0.050P	0.25N	0
1990	Caravan/Voyager	Front	①	②	0.25N–0.75P	0.30P	0.06
		Rear	—	—	1.00N–0.050P	0.25N	0
1991	Caravan/Voyager, Town & Country	Front	①	②	0.25N–0.75P	0.30P	0.06
		Rear	—	—	1.00N–0.050P	0.25N	0

N-Negative
P-Positive

① Not adjustable; maximum variation between sides should not exceed 1.5 degrees

② Van: 0.040P
Wagon: 0.70P

REAR SUSPENSION

The rear suspension consists of a tube and casting axle, shock absorbers and leaf springs. Stub axles are mounted to the axle and spring by U-bolts. It is possible to align both the camber and toe of the rear wheels.

The rear leaf springs are mounted by shackles and a fixed end bushing. the shackle angles have been selected to provide increasing suspension rates as the vehicle is loaded. These angles provide a comfortable unloaded ride and ample suspension trav-

LET	TORQUE	
A	35 FT. LBS.	47 N•m
B	70 IN. LBS.	7 N•m
C	95 FT. LBS.	129 N•m
D	80 FT. LBS.	108 N•m
E	60 FT. LBS.	81 N•m
F	45 FT. LBS.	61 N•m
G	50 FT. LBS.	68 N•m

Rear suspension components — 1984–88 models

LET	TORQUE	
A	35 FT. LBS.	47 N•m
B	105 FT. LBS.	142 N•m
C	80 FT. LBS.	108 N•m
D	65 FT. LBS.	88 N•m
E	45 FT. LBS.	61 N•m
F	85 FT. LBS.	115 N•m

Rear suspension components — 1989–91 models

Rear suspension components — 1991 All Wheel Drive models

el when the vehicle is loaded.

The rear shock absorbers are mounted at an angle, forward at the top and parallel to the springs. Greater stability and ride control are provided by this design.

WARNING: Do not install after market load leveling devices, air shocks or helper springs on your vehicle. These devices will cause the rear brake height sensing valve to adjust for a lighter lead than actually is contained.

Rear Springs

REMOVAL AND INSTALLATION

Front Wheel Drive Models

1. Raise and support the rear of the vehicle on jackstands. Locate the jackstands under the frame contact points just ahead of the rear spring fixed ends.
2. Raise the rear axle just enough to relieve the weight on the springs and support on jackstands.
3. Disconnect the rear brake proportioning valve spring. Disconnect the lower ends of the shock absorbers at the rear axle bracket.
4. Loosen and remove the nuts from the U-bolts. Remove the washer and U-bolts.
5. Lower the rear axle assembly to permit the rear springs to hang free. Support the spring and remove the four bolts that mount the fixed end spring bracket. Remove the rear spring shackle nuts and plate. Remove the shackle from the spring.
6. Remove the spring. Remove the fixed end mounting bolts from the bracket and remove the bracket. Remove the front pivot bolt from the front spring hanger.

To install:

7. Install the spring on the rear shackle and hanger. Start the shackle nuts but do not tighten completely.
8. Assembly the front spring hanger on the spring. Raise the front of the spring and install the four mounting bolts. Tighten the mounting bolts to 45 ft. lbs.
9. Raise the axle assembly and align the spring center bolts in correct position. Install the mounting U-bolts. Tighten the nuts to 60 ft. lbs.
10. Install the rear shock absorber to the lower brackets.
11. Lower the vehicle to the ground so that the full weight is on the springs. Tighten the mounting components as follows: Front fixed end bolt; 95 ft. lbs. Shackle nuts; 35 ft. lbs. Shock absorber bolts; 50 ft. lbs.
12. Raise and support the vehicle. Connect the brake valve spring and adjust the valve.

All Wheel Drive Models

1. Raise and support the rear of the vehicle on jackstands. Locate the jackstands under the chassis, ahead of the springs.
2. Raise the rear axle just enough to relieve the weight on the springs and support on jackstands.
3. Disconnect the rear brake proportioning valve spring. Disconnect the lower ends of the shock absorbers at the rear axle bracket.
4. Loosen and remove the nuts from the U-bolts. Remove the washer and U-bolts.
5. Lower the rear axle assembly to permit the rear springs to hang free. Support the spring and remove the four bolts that mount the fixed end spring bracket. Remove the rear spring shackle nuts and plate. Remove the shackle from the spring.
6. Remove the spring. Remove the fixed end mounting bolts from the bracket and remove the bracket. Remove the front pivot bolt from the front spring hanger.

7. Separate the rear shackle plate from the shackle and pin assembly. Remove the shackle and pin assembly from the spring.

To install:

8. Assemble the shackle and pin assembly, bushing and shackle plate on rear of spring and spring hanger. Start the shackle and pin assembly through bolts, do not tighten.

9. Assemble the front spring hanger to the front of the spring eye and install pivot bolt and nut. Do not tighten.

NOTE: Pivot bolt must inboard to prevent structural damage during spring installation.

10. Raise the front of the spring into position and install the 4 hanger bolts, tighten them to 45 ft. lbs. (61 Nm). Connect the actuator assembly for the proportioning valve.

11. Raise the axle assembly into position, centered under the spring center bolt.

12. Install the U-bolts, nuts and washers. Tighten the U-bolt nuts to 65 ft. lbs. (88 Nm).

13. Install the shock absorbers and start the bolts.

14. Lower the vehicle to the ground, with the full weight of the vehicle on the wheels. Tighten all of the fasteners in the following sequence and to the listed torques:

   a. Front pivot bolts – 105 ft. lbs. (142 Nm)

   b. Shackle and pin assembly through bolt nuts – 35 ft. lbs. (47 Nm).

   c. Shackle and pin assembly retaining bolts – 35 ft. lbs. (47 Nm)

   d. Shock absorber upper bolts – 85 ft. lbs. (115 Nm).

   e. Shock absorber lower bolts – 80 ft. lbs. (108 Nm).

15. Raise the vehicle and connect the proportioning valve.

Shock Absorbers

TESTING

Shock absorbers require replacement if the car fails to recover quickly after hitting a large bump or if it sways excessively following a directional change.

A good way to test the shock absorbers is to intermittently apply downward pressure to the side of the vehicle until it is moving up and down for almost its full suspension travel. Release it and observe its recovery. If the vehicle bounces once or twice after having been released and then comes to a rest, the shocks are alright. If the vehicle continues to bounce, the shock will probably require replacement.

REMOVAL AND INSTALLATION

1. Raise the vehicle and support it with jackstands.

2. Support the rear axle with a floor jack.

3. Remove the top and bottom shock absorber bolts.

4. Remove the shock absorbers.

5. Place the new shock in position and install the mounting bolts. Tighten to 80 ft. lbs. for the lower bolts and 85 ft. lbs for the upper bolts.

Sway Bar

REMOVAL AND INSTALLATION

All Wheel Drive Models

The sway bar interconnects both sides of the rear axle and attaches to the rear frame rails using 2 rubber isolated link arms. It is attached to the rear axle through rubber isolated bushings.

1. Raise and support the vehicle.

2. Remove the 2 lower bolts which hold the sway bar to the link arm on each side of the vehicle.

3. Loosen the bolts that attach the sway bar bushings to the rear axle housing.

4. While holding the sway bar in place, remove the 4 bushing retaining bolts and remove the sway bar from the axle.

To install:

5. Inspect the bushings and replace any that appear damaged.

6. Install the sway bar to the rear axle. The slits in the bushing should face up in the installed position. Do not tighten the bolts.

7. Install the 2 lower link bolts, do not tighten these.

8. Lower the vehicle so that all the weight is on the wheels. Tighten all of the bolts to the following torques:

Rear sway bar mounting — All Wheel Drive models

FRAME RAIL

LINK ARM

BOLT

FRAME RAIL BRACKET

SWAY BAR BUSHING

SWAY BAR

NUT

BOLT

BRAKE DRUM

REAR AXLE

REAR SPRING

FWD

SWAY BAR BUSHING RETAINER

Rear sway bar removal and installation — All Wheel Drive models

a. Bushing-to-axle bracket — 45 ft. lbs. (61 Nm)
b. Link arm-to-frame rail — 45 ft. lbs. (61 Nm)
c. Sway bar-to-link arm — 45 ft. lbs. (61 Nm)
d. Link arm bracket-to-frame rail 290 inch lbs. (33 Nm)

Rear Wheel Bearings

SERVICING

Front Wheel Drive Models

NOTE: Sodium-based grease is not compatible with lithium-based grease. Read the package labels and be careful not to mix the two types. If there is any doubt as to the type of grease used, completely clean the old grease from the bearing and hub before replacing.

Before handling the bearings, there are a few things that you should remember to do and not to do.
Remember to DO the following:
• Remove all outside dirt from the housing before exposing the bearing.
• Treat a used bearing as gently as you would a new one.
• Work with clean tools in clean surroundings.
• Use clean, dry canvas gloves, or at least clean, dry hands.
• Clean solvents and flushing fluids are a must.
• Use clean paper when laying out the bearings to dry.
• Protect disassembled bearings from rust and dirt. Cover them up.
• Use clean rags to wipe bearings.
• Keep the bearings in oil-proof paper when they are to be stored or are not in use.
• Clean the inside of the housing before replacing the bearing.

Do NOT do the following:
• Don't work in dirty surroundings.
• Don't use dirty, chipped or damaged tools.

• Try not to work on wooden work benches or use wooden mallets.
• Don't handle bearings with dirty or moist hands.
• Do not use gasoline for cleaning; use a safe solvent.
• Do not spin-dry bearings with compressed air. They will be damaged.
• Do not spin dirty bearings.
• Avoid using cotton waste or dirty cloths to wipe bearings.
• Try not to scratch or nick bearing surfaces.
• Do not allow the bearing to come in contact with dirt or rust at any time.

The rear wheel bearings should be inspected and relubricated whenever the rear brakes are serviced or at least every 30,000 miles. Repack the bearings with high temperature multi-purpose grease.

Check the lubricant to see if it is contaminated. If it contains dirt or has a milky appearance indicating the presence of water, the bearings should be cleaned and repacked.

Clean the bearings in kerosene, mineral spirits or other suitable cleaning fluid. Do not dry them by spinning the bearings. Allow them to air dry.

1. Raise and support the vehicle with the rear wheels off the floor.
2. Remove the wheel grease cap, cotter pin, nut-lock and bearing adjusting nut.
3. Remove the thrust washer and bearing.
4. Remove the drum from the spindle.
5. Thoroughly clean the old lubricant from the bearings and hub cavity. Inspect the bearing rollers for pitting or other signs of wear. Light discoloration is normal.
To install:
6. Repack the bearings with high temperature multi-purpose EP grease and add a small amount of new grease to the hub cavity. Be sure to force the lubricant between all rollers in the bearing.
7. Install the drum on the spindle after coating the polished spindle surfaces with wheel bearing lubricant.
8. Install the outer bearing cone, thrust washer and adjusting nut.
9. Tighten the adjusting nut to 20-25 ft. lbs. while rotating the wheel.
10. Back off the adjusting nut to completely release the preload from the bearing.
11. Tighten the adjusting nut finger-tight.
12. Position the nut-lock with one pair of slots in line with the cotter pin hole. Install the cotter pin.
13. Clean and install the grease cap and wheel.
14. Lower the vehicle.

All Wheel Drive Vehicles

The rear wheel bearings used on these models is a bolt in type unit, this is the same unit that is used on the front knuckle assembly.
1. Raise and support the vehicle.
2. Remove the wheel and tire assembly.
3. Remove the halfshaft flange retaining bolts and remove the halfshaft assembly.
4. Remove the wheel bearing mounting bolts and remove the wheel bearing and hub assembly.
To install:
5. Install the hub and bearing assembly, tighten the bolts to 96 ft. lbs (130 Nm) in a criss-cross pattern.

NOTE: Thoroughly clean the seal and wear sleeve, lubricate both before installation.

6. Install the halfshaft.
7. Install the washer and hub nut, with the brakes applied tighten the nut to 180 ft. lbs. (244 Nm).
8. Install the spring washer, nut lock and new cotter pin.
9. Install the wheel and tire assembly.

Rear Axle Alignment

Camber and Toe adjustment are possible through the use of shims. Shims are added or subtracted between the spindle mounting surface and the axle mounting plate. Each shim equals a wheel angle change of 0.3 degrees.

Troubleshooting the Steering Column

Problem	Cause	Solution
Will not lock	• Lockbolt spring broken or defective	• Replace lock bolt spring
High effort (required to turn ignition key and lock cylinder)	• Lock cylinder defective • Ignition switch defective • Rack preload spring broken or deformed • Burr on lock sector, lock rack, housing, support or remote rod coupling • Bent sector shaft • Defective lock rack • Remote rod bent, deformed • Ignition switch mounting bracket bent • Distorted coupling slot in lock rack (tilt column)	• Replace lock cylinder • Replace ignition switch • Replace preload spring • Remove burr • Replace shaft • Replace lock rack • Replace rod • Straighten or replace • Replace lock rack
Will stick in "start"	• Remote rod deformed • Ignition switch mounting bracket bent	• Straighten or replace • Straighten or replace
Key cannot be removed in "off-lock"	• Ignition switch is not adjusted correctly • Defective lock cylinder	• Adjust switch • Replace lock cylinder
Lock cylinder can be removed without depressing retainer	• Lock cylinder with defective retainer • Burr over retainer slot in housing cover or on cylinder retainer	• Replace lock cylinder • Remove burr
High effort on lock cylinder between "off" and "off-lock"	• Distorted lock rack • Burr on tang of shift gate (automatic column) • Gearshift linkage not adjusted	• Replace lock rack • Remove burr • Adjust linkage
Noise in column	• One click when in "off-lock" position and the steering wheel is moved (all except automatic column) • Coupling bolts not tightened • Lack of grease on bearings or bearing surfaces • Upper shaft bearing worn or broken • Lower shaft bearing worn or broken • Column not correctly aligned • Coupling pulled apart • Broken coupling lower joint • Steering shaft snap ring not seated	• Normal—lock bolt is seating • Tighten pinch bolts • Lubricate with chassis grease • Replace bearing assembly • Replace bearing. Check shaft and replace if scored. • Align column • Replace coupling • Repair or replace joint and align column • Replace ring. Check for proper seating in groove.

Troubleshooting the Steering Column (cont.)

Problem	Cause	Solution
Noise in column	• Shroud loose on shift bowl. Housing loose on jacket—will be noticed with ignition in "off-lock" and when torque is applied to steering wheel.	• Position shroud over lugs on shift bowl. Tighten mounting screws.
High steering shaft effort	• Column misaligned • Defective upper or lower bearing • Tight steering shaft universal joint • Flash on I.D. of shift tube at plastic joint (tilt column only) • Upper or lower bearing seized	• Align column • Replace as required • Repair or replace • Replace shift tube • Replace bearings
Lash in mounted column assembly	• Column mounting bracket bolts loose • Broken weld nuts on column jacket • Column capsule bracket sheared	• Tighten bolts • Replace column jacket • Replace bracket assembly
Lash in mounted column assembly (cont.)	• Column bracket to column jacket mounting bolts loose • Loose lock shoes in housing (tilt column only) • Loose pivot pins (tilt column only) • Loose lock shoe pin (tilt column only) • Loose support screws (tilt column only)	• Tighten to specified torque • Replace shoes • Replace pivot pins and support • Replace pin and housing • Tighten screws
Housing loose (tilt column only)	• Excessive clearance between holes in support or housing and pivot pin diameters • Housing support-screws loose	• Replace pivot pins and support • Tighten screws
Steering wheel loose—every other tilt position (tilt column only)	• Loose fit between lock shoe and lock shoe pivot pin	• Replace lock shoes and pivot pin
Steering column not locking in any tilt position (tilt column only)	• Lock shoe seized on pivot pin • Lock shoe grooves have burrs or are filled with foreign material • Lock shoe springs weak or broken	• Replace lock shoes and pin • Clean or replace lock shoes • Replace springs
Noise when tilting column (tilt column only)	• Upper tilt bumpers worn • Tilt spring rubbing in housing	• Replace tilt bumper • Lubricate with chassis grease
One click when in "off-lock" position and the steering wheel is moved	• Seating of lock bolt	• None. Click is normal characteristic sound produced by lock bolt as it seats.
High shift effort (automatic and tilt column only)	• Column not correctly aligned • Lower bearing not aligned correctly • Lack of grease on seal or lower bearing areas	• Align column • Assemble correctly • Lubricate with chassis grease
Improper transmission shifting—automatic and tilt column only	• Sheared shift tube joint • Improper transmission gearshift linkage adjustment • Loose lower shift lever	• Replace shift tube • Adjust linkage • Replace shift tube

Troubleshooting the Ignition Switch

Problem	Cause	Solution
Ignition switch electrically inoperative	• Loose or defective switch connector • Feed wire open (fusible link) • Defective ignition switch	• Tighten or replace connector • Repair or replace • Replace ignition switch
Engine will not crank	• Ignition switch not adjusted properly	• Adjust switch
Ignition switch wil not actuate mechanically	• Defective ignition switch • Defective lock sector • Defective remote rod	• Replace switch • Replace lock sector • Replace remote rod
Ignition switch cannot be adjusted correctly	• Remote rod deformed	• Repair, straighten or replace

Troubleshooting the Turn Signal Switch

Problem	Cause	Solution
Turn signal will not cancel	• Loose switch mounting screws • Switch or anchor bosses broken • Broken, missing or out of position detent, or cancelling spring	• Tighten screws • Replace switch • Reposition springs or replace switch as required
Turn signal difficult to operate	• Turn signal lever loose • Switch yoke broken or distorted • Loose or misplaced springs • Foreign parts and/or materials in switch • Switch mounted loosely	• Tighten mounting screws • Replace switch • Reposition springs or replace switch • Remove foreign parts and/or material • Tighten mounting screws
Turn signal will not indicate lane change	• Broken lane change pressure pad or spring hanger • Broken, missing or misplaced lane change spring • Jammed wires	• Replace switch • Replace or reposition as required • Loosen mounting screws, reposition wires and retighten screws
Turn signal will not stay in turn position	• Foreign material or loose parts impeding movement of switch yoke • Defective switch	• Remove material and/or parts • Replace switch
Hazard switch cannot be pulled out	• Foreign material between hazard support cancelling leg and yoke	• Remove foreign material. No foreign material impeding function of hazard switch—replace turn signal switch.

Troubleshooting the Turn Signal Switch (cont.)

Problem	Cause	Solution
No turn signal lights	• Inoperative turn signal flasher • Defective or blown fuse • Loose chassis to column harness connector • Disconnect column to chassis connector. Connect new switch to chassis and operate switch by hand. If vehicle lights now operate normally, signal switch is inoperative • If vehicle lights do not operate, check chassis wiring for opens, grounds, etc.	• Replace turn signal flasher • Replace fuse • Connect securely • Replace signal switch • Repair chassis wiring as required
Instrument panel turn indicator lights on but not flashing	• Burned out or damaged front or rear turn signal bulb • If vehicle lights do not operate, check light sockets for high resistance connections, the chassis wiring for opens, grounds, etc. • Inoperative flasher • Loose chassis to column harness connection • Inoperative turn signal switch • To determine if turn signal switch is defective, substitute new switch into circuit and operate switch by hand. If the vehicle's lights operate normally, signal switch is inoperative.	• Replace bulb • Repair chassis wiring as required • Replace flasher • Connect securely • Replace turn signal switch • Replace turn signal switch
Stop light not on when turn indicated	• Loose column to chassis connection • Disconnect column to chassis connector. Connect new switch into system without removing old.	• Connect securely • Replace signal switch
Stop light not on when turn indicated (cont.)	Operate switch by hand. If brake lights work with switch in the turn position, signal switch is defective. • If brake lights do not work, check connector to stop light sockets for grounds, opens, etc.	 • Repair connector to stop light circuits using service manual as guide
Turn indicator panel lights not flashing	• Burned out bulbs • High resistance to ground at bulb socket • Opens, ground in wiring harness from front turn signal bulb socket to indicator lights	• Replace bulbs • Replace socket • Locate and repair as required

Troubleshooting the Turn Signal Switch (cont.)

Problem	Cause	Solution
Turn signal lights flash very slowly	• High resistance ground at light sockets	• Repair high resistance grounds at light sockets
	• Incorrect capacity turn signal flasher or bulb	• Replace turn signal flasher or bulb
	• If flashing rate is still extremely slow, check chassis wiring harness from the connector to light sockets for high resistance	• Locate and repair as required
	• Loose chassis to column harness connection	• Connect securely
	• Disconnect column to chassis connector. Connect new switch into system without removing old. Operate switch by hand. If flashing occurs at normal rate, the signal switch is defective.	• Replace turn signal switch
Hazard signal lights will not flash— turn signal functions normally	• Blow fuse	• Replace fuse
	• Inoperative hazard warning flasher	• Replace hazard warning flasher in fuse panel
	• Loose chassis-to-column harness connection	• Conect securely
	• Disconnect column to chassis connector. Connect new switch into system without removing old. Depress the hazard warning lights. If they now work normally, turn signal switch is defective.	• Replace turn signal switch
	• If lights do not flash, check wiring harness "K" lead for open between hazard flasher and connector. If open, fuse block is defective	• Repair or replace brown wire or connector as required

STEERING

Steering Wheel

REMOVAL AND INSTALLATION

NOTE: A steering wheel puller (Chrysler tool C3428B or the equivalent) is required.

1. Disconnect the negative battery cable at the battery.

2. Remove the center horn pad assembly. On standard steering wheels the horn pad is retained by two screws which are removed from underneath the wheel. Premium steering wheels require that the horn pad be pried from internal retainers. Pry the horn pad up from the bottom edges of the steering wheel.

3. Disconnect the horn wires from the center pad. Remove the pad.

4. Mark the column shaft and wheel for reinstallation refer-

Steering wheel horn pad and wiring

Depressing the lock plate

Turn signal switch removal

ence and remove the steering wheel retaining nut.

5. Remove the steering wheel using a steering wheel puller (Chrysler Tool C3428B or the equivalent).

To install:

6. Line up the reference marks on the steering wheel and column shaft. Push wheel on to the shaft and draw into position with the mounting nut. Tighten the nut to 45 ft. lbs. Install the center horn pad after connecting the horn connectors. Connect the negative battery cable.

Turn Signal Switch

REMOVAL AND INSTALLATION

1. Disconnect the negative battery cable at the battery.
2. Remove the steering wheel. Remove the lower steering column cover, silencer panel and reinforcement.
3. The wiring harness is contained by a trough that is mounted on the side of the steering column. Remove the trough by prying the connectors from the column. New connectors may be required for installation.
4. Disconnect the turn signal wiring harness connector at the bottom of the steering column.
5. Disassemble the steering column for switch removal as follows:
6. On standard columns; remove the screw holding the wiper-washer switch to the turn signal switch. Allow the control stalk and switch to remain in position. Remove the three screws that attach the bearing retainer and turn signal switch to the upper bearing housing. Remove the turn signal and hazard warning switch assembly by gently pulling the switch up from the column while straightening the wires and guiding them up through the column opening. Be sure to disconnect the ground connector.
7. On models with tilt wheel; remove the plastic cover (if equipped) from the lock plate. Depress the lock plate and pry the retaining ring form mounting groove. (Chrysler Tool C4156 or equivalent is used to compress the lock plate). Remove the lock plate, canceling cam and upper bearing spring. Place the turn signal switch in right turn position. Remove the screw that attaches the link between the turn signal and wiper-washer switches. Remove the screw that attaches the hazard warning switch knob. Remove the three screws attaching the turn signal switch to the steering column. Remove the turn signal and hazard warning switch assembly by gently pulling the switch up from the column while straightening and guiding the wires up through the column opening.

To install:

8. On models with the standard column; lubricate the turn signal switch pivot hole with a white lube (such as Lubriplate). Thread the connector and wires through the column hole carefully. Position the turn signal switch and bearing retainer in place on the upper bearing housing and install the three mounting screws. Position the turn signal lever to turn signal pivot and secure with the mounting screws. Be sure the dimmer switch rod is in mounting pocket.

9. On models with tilt wheel; thread connector and wire harness through column hole. Position the turn signal switch in the upper column housing. Place the switch in the right turn position. Install the three mounting screws. Install the link between the turn signal switch and the wiper-washer switch pivot and secure mounting screw. Install the lock plate bearing spring, canceling cam and new retainer clip using Tool C4156 or equivalent. Install the hazard warning knob, screw.

10. Connect the wiring harness plug. Install the cover through wiring cover to the steering column.

11. Install the steering wheel and retaining nut. Connect battery cable and test the switch for operation.

Ignition Lock

REMOVAL AND INSTALLATION

For removal of the ignition switch refer to Section 6 of this manual.

1. Follow the turn signal switch removal procedure previously described.

2. Unclip the horn and key light ground wires.

3. Remove the retaining screw and move the ignition key lamp assembly out of the way.

4. Remove the four screws that hold the bearing housing to the lock housing.

5. Remove the snap ring from the upper end of the steering shaft.

6. Remove the bearing housing from the shaft.

7. Remove the lock plate spring and lock plate from the steering shaft.

8. Remove the ignition key, then remove the screw and lift out the buzzer/chime switch.

9. Remove the two screws attaching the ignition switch to the column jacket.

10. Remove the ignition switch by rotating the switch 90 degrees on the rod then sliding off the rod.

11. Remove the two mounting screws from the dimmer switch and disengage the switch from the actuator rod.

12. Remove the two screws that mount the bellcrank and slide the bellcrank up in the lock housing until it can be disconnect from the ignition switch actuator rod.

13. To remove the lock cylinder and lock levers place the cylinder in the lock position and remove the key.

14. Insert a small diameter screwdriver or similar tool into the lock cylinder release holes and push into the release spring loaded lock retainers. At the same time pull the lock cylinder out of the housing bore.

15. Grasp the lock lever and spring assembly and pull straight out of the housing.

16. If necessary the lock housing may be removed from the column jacket by removing the hex head retaining screws.

17. Installation is the reverse of removal. If the lock housing was removed tighten the lock housing screws to 90 inch pounds.

18. To install the dimmer switch, firmly seat the push rod into the switch. Compress the switch until two ⅛ in. (3mm) drill shanks can be inserted into the alignment holes. Reposition the upper end of the push rod in the pocket of the wash/wipe switch. With a light rearward pressure on the switch, install the two screws.

19. Grease and assemble the two lock levers, lock lever spring and pin.

20. Install the lock lever assembly in the lock housing. Seat the pin firmly into the bottom of the slots and make sure the lock lever spring leg is firmly in place in the lock casting notch.

21. Install the ignition switch actuator rod from the bottom

Ignition lock mounting

CAUTION: DO NOT REMOVE IGNITION LOCKING LINK

CAUTION: NEVER REMOVE SHAFT LOCK PLATE

Removing upper and lower column covers

DIMMER SWITCH

DIMMER SWITCH ROD

CONTROL STALK

SCREWDRIVER

SCREW (5)

LOWER COVER

Hazard warning switch removal

BEARING RETAINER AND GROUND PLATE

IGNITION LAMP GROUND

TURN SIGNAL GROUND

HAZARD WARNING SWITCH

through the oblong hole in the lock housing and attach it to the bellcrank onto its mounting surface. The gearshift lever should be in the park position.

22. Place the ignition switch on the ignition switch actuator rod and rotate it 90 degrees to lock the rod into position.

23. To install the ignition lock, turn the key to the lock position and remove the key. Insert the cylinder far enough into the housing to contact the switch actuator. Insert the key and press inward and rotate the cylinder.

Steering Column

REMOVAL AND INSTALLATION

1984–88 Models

1. Disconnect the negative battery cable from the battery. If the vehicle is equipped with a column mounted shift, pry the shift cable rod from the lever grommet at the bottom of the steering column. Remove the cable clip and cable from lower bracket.

2. Disconnect the wiring harness connector at the bottom of the steering column.

3. Remove the instrument panel lower steering column cover

LET	TORQUE N·m	TORQUE IN. LBS.
Ⓐ	10	90
Ⓑ	4	35
Ⓒ	3	24
Ⓓ	2	16

LOCK PLATE

LOCK PLATE SPRING

STEERING SHAFT

VIEW IN CIRCLE Z

JACKET ASSEMBLY

HOUSING

LOCK HOUSING

SPRING IN ASSEMBLED POSITION

LEVER ASSEMBLY

SPRING

LEVER

BELLCRANK ASSEMBLY

SCREW (4) Ⓑ

IGNITION SWITCH ROD

SCREW (4) Ⓐ

PLATE

BEARING HOUSING

KEY LAMP

PLUNGER

SPRING

SCREW Ⓒ

LOCK HOUSING LEVER

LOCK HOUSING COVER

SCREW (2) Ⓒ

VIEW IN DIRECTION OF ARROW Y

GEARSHIFT LEVER GATE

SCREW (4) Ⓑ

IGNITION SWITCH ROD

LAMP SCREW Ⓓ

SCREW (4) Ⓒ

BEARING

TURN SIGNAL AND FLASHER SWITCH ASSEMBLY

SCREW (3) Ⓒ

Upper steering column components — except Acustar column

TORQUE		
LET	POUNDS	NEWTON METERS
Ⓐ	45 FT.	61
Ⓑ	105 IN.	12
Ⓒ	20 IN.	2

Standard steering column components — except Acustar column

Acustar steering column components

Steering column coupler removal

Multi-function switch wiring

NOTE: Do not remove the roll pin from the steering column assembly connector.

6. Pull the steering column rearward, disconnecting the lower stub shaft from the steering gear connector. If the vehicle is equipped with speed control and a manual transmission, take care not to damage the control switch mounted on the clutch pedal.

To install:

7. Install the anti-rattle coupling spring into the lower coupling tube. Be sure that the spring snaps into the slot in the coupling.

8. Align the column lower shaft stub with coupling and insert. Raise the column and place bracket into position on the mounting studs. Loosely install the mounting nuts. Pull the column rearward and tighten the nuts to 105 inch lbs. Tighten stub shaft connector.

9. Connect and adjust the linkage. Connect all harnesses. Connect the shift indicator and adjust as required. Connect the gear shift indicator operating cable into the slot on the shift housing. Slowly move the gearshift from 1 to P. The pointer will now be properly adjusted. Install the instrument steering column cover.

1989–91 Models with Acustar Steering Column

1. Make sure the wheels are in the straight ahead position.
2. Disconnect the negative battery cable.
3. Pry the shift link rod out of the grommet on the bottom of the column, if equipped with an automatic transaxle.
4. Remove the steering wheel pad and disconnect the electrical leads.
5. Remove the steering wheel. Remove the upper coupling bolt retaining pin.
6. Remove the nut and bolt from the upper coupling and remove the upper coupling from the lower coupling.
7. For vehicles equipped with an automatic transaxle, disconnect the PRNDL cable from the PRNDL driver arm.
8. If equipped with a tilt column, remove the tilt lever. Remove the upper and lower ignition shroud trim.
9. Remove the turn signal/multifunction switch. Disconnect the electrical connectors at the bottom of the column.
10. Remove the upper and lower fixed shrouds, loosen the upper support bracket bolts.
11. Remove the lower dash panel and column support standoff bracket bolts.
12. Remove the column out through the passenger compartment.

PRNDL cable removal

and disconnect the bezel. On models with floor shift, unsnap and remove shroud cover extensions.

4. If automatic, remove the selector indicator set screw and pointer from the shift housing.

5. Remove the nuts that attach the steering column mounting bracket to the instrument panel support and lower the bracket.

To install:

13. Install a replacement grommet on the shift rod arm and lubricate it.

14. Install the column in the vehicle, position it on the attaching studs and loosely assemble the upper bracket nuts.

15. Make sure the wheels are still in a straight ahead position and align the upper and lower coupling. Install the coupling nut and tighten to 250 inch lbs. (28 Nm). Install the retaining pin.

16. Install the multifunction switch and connect the column wiring.

17. Install the upper fixed shroud.

18. Make sure the 2 plastic retainer are fully seated on the column bracket and tighten the bracket bolts to 105 inch lbs. (12 Nm).

19. Install the lower shroud. Position the shift lever, if equipped with an automatic transaxle, in the farthest down position and install the PRNDL cable.

20. Install the tilt lever and the lower dash panel cover. Install the steering wheel. Connect the shift link rod.

21. Check the transaxle linkage adjustment through all of the gear positions.

22. Connect the negative battery cable.

Steering Linkage

REMOVAL AND INSTALLATION

Tie Rod Ends

1. Jack up the front of the vehicle and support on jackstands.

2. Loosen the jam nut which connects the tie rod end to the rack.

3. Mark the tie rod position on the threads.

4. Remove the tie rod cotter pin and nut.

5. Using a puller, remove the tie rod from the steering knuckle.

NOTE: Count the number of turns when removing tie rod end. Install the new end the same amount of turns.

6. Unscrew the tie rod end from the rack.

To install:

7. Install a new tie rod end, screw in the same number of turns as removal. Tighten the jam nut to 55 ft. lbs..

8. Check the wheel alignment.

Steering Gear

The steering system (either manual or power) used on these vehicles is of the rack and pinion design.

The manual steering gear assembly consists of a tube which contains a toothed rack and a housing containing a straddle mounted, helical-cut pinion gear. Tie rods are connected to each end of the rack and an adjustable end (on each side) connects to the steering knuckles. A double universal joint attaches the pinion to the steering column shaft. Steering wheel movement is transmitted by the column shaft and the rack and pinion converts the rotational movement of the pinion to transverse movement of the rack. The manual steering gear is permanently lubricated at the factory and periodic lubrication is not necessary. The manual steering gear cannot be adjusted or serviced. If a malfunction occurs, the entire assembly must be replaced.

The power steering gear is similar to appearance, except for a rotary valve assembly and two fluid hose assemblies. The rotary valve assembly directs fluid from the power steering pump, through hoses, to either side of an internal rack piston. As steering wheel effort is applied, an internal torsion bar twists causing the rotary valve to direct the fluid behind an internal rack piston, which in turn builds up hydraulic pressure and assists in the turning effort.

Rubber boots seal the tie rods and rack assembly. Inspect the boots periodically for cuts, tears or leakage. Replace the boots as necessary.

REMOVAL AND INSTALLATION

Front Wheel Drive Models

1. Loosen the wheel lugs slightly. Raise and support the front of the vehicle at the frame point below the front doors, not on the front crossmember. Use jackstands for supporting.

2. Remove the front wheels and tire assemblies.

3. Remove the tie rod ends from the steering knuckles.

4. Lower and disconnect the steering column from the steering gear pinion shaft.

5. If equipped, remove the anti-rotation link from the crossmember and the air diverter valve from the left side of the crossmember.

6. Place a transmission jack, or floor jack with a wide lifting flange, under the front suspension K-crossmember. Support the crossmember and remove the four crossmember to frame attaching bolts. Slowly lower the crossmember until enough room is gained to remove the steering gear assembly. Place stands under the crossmember, if available.

7. Remove the splash and boot shields. If equipped with power steering, disconnect the power steering hoses.

8. Remove the bolts that attach the steering gear assembly to the crossmember. Remove the assembly from the left side of the vehicle.

To install:

9. Line up the gear pinion with the column. Installation is in the reverse order of removal. On models with manual steering, be sure the master serration of the steering gear aligns with the steering column connector. the right rear crossmember bolt is the alignment pilot for reinstallation. Install first and tighten.

10. Attach the gear to the K-frame and secure the K-frame. Secure the anti-rotation link. Secure the K-frame. Torque all crossmember attaching bolts to 90 ft. lbs. Steering gear mounting bolts are tightened to 250 inch lbs.

11. Connect the tie rod ends. Fill power steering reservoir (if equipped), start engine, turn the steering wheel from lock to lock and check for fluid leaks.

12. Check toe adjustment.

All Wheel Drive (AWD) Models

Before removing the steering gear on AWD models, the steering column must be removed to provide clearance for steering rack removal.

1. Raise and support the vehicle. Remove the wheel and tire assemblies.

2. Remove the steering column assembly from the vehicle.

3. Remove the tie rod ends from the steering knuckle using a suitable puller.

4. Remove the 2 bolts and the 2 nuts that attach the bridge assembly to the crossmember. The bolts and nuts can be reached through the access holes in the top of the bridge assembly.

5. Remove the crossmember to frame rail attaching bolts. Use a jack to lower the crossmember so that it is suspended from the lower control arms. It is necessary to remove the crossmember completely from the vehicle.

6. Disconnect and plug the power steering lines from the steering gear. Remove the hose retaining bracket from the crossmember.

7. Remove the 4 bolts that retain the steering gear to the bridge assembly.

NOTE: Note the position of each bolt as it is removed, there are different bolts for the left and right sides.

8. Remove the lower steering column coupler from the steer-

ing gear. Drive the roll pin from the coupler using a punch. If this is not done, there will not be enough clearance for rack removal.

9. Remove the steering gear from the vehicle by pulling it out through the drivers side wheel well. Rotate the gear to clear the frame rail.

To install:

10. Install the steering gear into the vehicle. Work it in through the left wheel opening, rotating it as needed.

11. Install the steering column coupler, make sure to fully seat the roll pin.

12. Install the steering gear mounting bolts. Do not torque them at this time, be sure to install them in the proper locations.

13. Install the steering hose bracket in position, tighten to 70 inch lbs. (8 Nm). Install the hoses on the steering rack and tighten them to 275 inch lbs. (31 Nm).

14. Raise the crossmember into position and install the bolts to the following torques:

    a. Crossmember-to-frame rail screw and washer—90 ft. lbs. (122 Nm)

    b. Crossmember-to-frame rail stud nut—90 ft. lbs. (122 Nm)

15. Install the bridge assembly onto the crossmember and tighten the mounting nuts to 50 ft. lbs. (68 Nm).

16. Install the outer tie rod ends on the steering knuckle and tighten the nuts, tighten to 38 ft. lbs. (52 Nm). Be sure to install a new cotter pin.

17. Install the wheel and tire assemblies. Lower the vehicle.

18. Connect the negative battery cable. Start the vehicle and check the power steering lines for leaks. Check the fluid level.

Crossmember assembly mounting

Bridge assembly removal — All Wheel Drive vehicles

Steering gear removal and installation

Boot Seals

REMOVAL AND INSTALLATION

1. Raise and support the front of the vehicle on jackstands.

2. Disconnect the tie rod end from the steering knuckle. Loosen the jam nut and unscrew the end. Count the number of turns required when removing the end.

Crossmember assembly — lowered for gear removal

3. Cut the inner boot clamp, use pliers to expand the outer clamp and remove.
4. Locate and mark for reinstallation, the location of the breather tube.
5. Use a small tool to lift the boot from inner mounting groove and slide boot from the shaft.

6. Install the new boot and clamps. Locate breather tube to reference mark. Lubricate boot and mounting groove with silicone type lubricant. Install the tie rod end the same number of turns as counted when removing.

Power Steering Pump

REMOVAL AND INSTALLATION

1. Disconnect the negative battery cable from the battery. Disconnect the vapor hose (canister) from the carburetor. Disconnect the A/C compressor clutch wire harness connector at the compressor.
2. Remove the power steering pump adjustment bolt. Remove the power steering hose bracket from mounting.
3. Raise and support the front of the vehicle on jackstands.
4. Disconnect the return hose from the steering gear and drain the fluid into a container.
5. Remove the right side splash shield if it interferes with pump removal. After the fluid has drained from the pump, disconnect and plug the hoses from the pump.
6. Remove the lower pivot bolt and nut from the pump mounting.
7. Remove the drive belt. Move the pump to the rear and remove the adjusting bracket.
8. Rotate the pump clockwise so that the drive pulley faces the rear of the vehicle. Remove the power steering pump.
To install:
9. Place the pump in position and install it in reverse order of removal. Install new O-ring seal on the pump hoses before installation. Tighten the tube nuts to 25 ft. lbs. Refer to belt adjustments in "General Information and Maintenance".
10. Lower the vehicle and connect the vapor hose and A/C compressor clutch switch harness.
11. Fill the power steering pump reservoir with fluid. Start the engine and turn the steering wheel from stop to stop, several times, to bleed the system. check the fluid level.

Troubleshooting the Power Steering Pump

Problem	Cause	Solution
Chirp noise in steering pump	• Loose belt	• Adjust belt tension to specification
Belt squeal (particularly noticeable at full wheel travel and stand still parking)	• Loose belt	• Adjust belt tension to specification
Growl noise in steering pump	• Excessive back pressure in hoses or steering gear caused by restriction	• Locate restriction and correct. Replace part if necessary.
Growl noise in steering pump (particularly noticeable at stand still parking)	• Scored pressure plates, thrust plate or rotor • Extreme wear of cam ring	• Replace parts and flush system • Replace parts
Groan noise in steering pump	• Low oil level • Air in the oil. Poor pressure hose connection.	• Fill reservoir to proper level • Tighten connector to specified torque. Bleed system by operating steering from right to left—full turn.
Rattle noise in steering pump	• Vanes not installed properly • Vanes sticking in rotor slots	• Install properly • Free up by removing burrs, varnish, or dirt

Troubleshooting the Power Steering Pump (cont.)

Problem	Cause	Solution
Swish noise in steering pump	• Defective flow control valve	• Replace part
Whine noise in steering pump	• Pump shaft bearing scored	• Replace housing and shaft. Flush system.
Hard steering or lack of assist	• Loose pump belt • Low oil level in reservoir **NOTE:** Low oil level will also result in excessive pump noise • Steering gear to column misalignment • Lower coupling flange rubbing against steering gear adjuster plug • Tires not properly inflated	• Adjust belt tension to specification • Fill to proper level. If excessively low, check all lines and joints for evidence of external leakage. Tighten loose connectors. • Align steering column • Loosen pinch bolt and assemble properly • Inflate to recommended pressure
Foaming milky power steering fluid, low fluid level and possible low pressure	• Air in the fluid, and loss of fluid due to internal pump leakage causing overflow	• Check for leaks and correct. Bleed system. Extremely cold temperatures will cause system aeration should the oil level be low. If oil level is correct and pump still foams, remove pump from vehicle and separate reservoir from body. Check welsh plug and body for cracks. If plug is loose or body is cracked, replace body.
Low pump pressure	• Flow control valve stuck or inoperative • Pressure plate not flat against cam ring	• Remove burrs or dirt or replace. Flush system. • Correct
Momentary increase in effort when turning wheel fast to right or left	• Low oil level in pump • Pump belt slipping • High internal leakage	• Add power steering fluid as required • Tighten or replace belt • Check pump pressure. (See pressure test)
Steering wheel surges or jerks when turning with engine running especially during parking	• Low oil level • Loose pump belt • Steering linkage hitting engine oil pan at full turn • Insufficient pump pressure	• Fill as required • Adjust tension to specification • Correct clearance • Check pump pressure. (See pressure test). Replace flow control valve if defective.
Steering wheel surges or jerks when turning with engine running especially during parking (cont.)	• Sticking flow control valve	• Inspect for varnish or damage, replace if necessary
Excessive wheel kickback or loose steering	• Air in system	• Add oil to pump reservoir and bleed by operating steering. Check hose connectors for proper torque and adjust as required.

TORQUE SPECIFICATIONS

Component	English	Metric
WHEELS		
Wheel lug nuts:	95 ft. lbs.	129 Nm
FRONT SUSPENSION		
Ball joint-to-knuckle clamp bolt		
1984-89:	70 ft. lbs.	95 Nm
1990-91:	105 ft. lbs.	145 Nm
Ball joint stud-to-steering knuckle clamp bolt		
1984-89:	70 ft. lbs.	95 Nm
1990-91:	105 ft. lbs.	143 Nm
Brake hose retaining bracket:	10 ft. lbs.	14 Nm
Coil spring assembly nut:	60 ft. lbs.	82 Nm
Front Hub and Bearing		
Press-in type		
Bearing retainer bolts:	20 ft. lbs.	27 Nm
Bolt-In Type		
Bearing mounting bolts:	45 ft. lbs.	61 Nm
Hub retaining nut:	180 ft. lbs.	245 Nm
Lower control arm front pivot bolt		
1984-89:	105 ft. lbs.	143 Nm
1990-91:	125 ft. lbs.	170 Nm
MacPherson strut		
Upper mount nuts:	20 ft. lbs.	27 Nm
Lower mounting and camber nuts:	75 ft. lbs. + ¼ turn	102 Nm + ¼ turn
Rear stub strut nut:	70 ft. lbs.	95 Nm
Steering knuckle-to-lower control arm clamp bolt		
1984-89:	70 ft. lbs.	95 Nm
1990-91:	105 ft. lbs.	143 Nm
Sway bar bracket stud nuts		
1984-89:	25 ft. lbs.	34 Nm
1990=91:	50 ft. lbs.	68 Nm
Sway Bar center bracket bolts		
1984-89:	25 ft. lbs.	34 Nm
1990-91:	50 ft. lbs.	68 Nm
Sway bar outer bracket bolts		
1984-89:	25 ft. lbs.	34 Nm
1990-91:	50 ft. lbs.	68 Nm
Tie rod end nut:	35 ft. lbs.	48 Nm
REAR SUSPENSION		
Hub and bearing assembly bolts		
All wheel drive:	96 ft. lbs	130 Nm
Shock absorber bolts		
Front wheel drive:	50 ft. lbs.	68 Nm
All wheel drive		
Upper bolts:	85 ft. lbs.	115 Nm
Lower bolts:	80 ft. lbs.	108 Nm

TORQUE SPECIFICATIONS

Component	English	Metric
Spring		
Front wheel drive models		
Hanger bolts:	45 ft. lbs.	61 Nm
U-bolt nuts:	60 ft. lbs.	82 Nm
Front fixed end bolt:	95 ft. lbs.	129 Nm
Shackle nuts:	35 ft. lbs.	48 Nm
All wheel drive models		
Hanger bolts:	45 ft. lbs.	61 Nm
U-bolt nuts:	65 ft. lbs.	88 Nm
Front pivot bolts:	105 ft. lbs.	142 Nm
Shackle and pin assembly through-bolt nuts:	35 ft. lbs.	47 Nm
Shackle and pin assembly retaining bolts:	35 ft. lbs.	47 Nm
Sway Bar		
All Wheel Drive Models		
Bushing-to-axle bracket:	45 ft. lbs.	61 Nm
Link arm-to-frame rail:	45 ft. lbs.	61 Nm
Sway bar-to-link arm:	45 ft. lbs.	61 Nm
Link arm bracket-to-frame rail:	24 ft. lbs.	33 Nm
	STEERING	
Crossmember-to-frame rail screw:	90 ft. lbs.	122 Nm
Crossmember-to-frame rail stud nut:	90 ft. lbs.	122 Nm
K-frame-to-crossmember attaching bolts:	90 ft. lbs.	122 Nm
Outer tie rod ends-to-steering knuckle nuts:	38 ft. lbs.	52 Nm
Power steering bridge assembly-to-crossmember:	50 ft. lbs.	68 Nm
Power steering hose bracket:	70 inch lbs.	8 Nm
Power steering hoses-to-steering rack:	23 ft. lbs.	31 Nm
Power steering pump tube nuts:	25 ft. lbs.	34 Nm
Steering column bracket mounting stud nuts:	105 inch lbs.	12 Nm
Steering gear mounting bolts:	21 ft. lbs.	28 Nm
Steering wheel nut:	45 ft. lbs.	61 Nm
Tie rod end jam nut:	55 ft. lbs.	75 Nm
Upper and lower steering shaft coupling nut:	21 ft. lbs.	28 Nm

Brakes

Troubleshooting the Brake System

Problem	Cause	Solution
Low brake pedal (excessive pedal travel required for braking action.)	• Excessive clearance between rear linings and drums caused by inoperative automatic adjusters	• Make 10 to 15 alternate forward and reverse brake stops to adjust brakes. If brake pedal does not come up, repair or replace adjuster parts as necessary.
	• Worn rear brakelining	• Inspect and replace lining if worn beyond minimum thickness specification
	• Bent, distorted brakeshoes, front or rear	• Replace brakeshoes in axle sets
	• Air in hydraulic system	• Remove air from system. Refer to Brake Bleeding.
Low brake pedal (pedal may go to floor with steady pressure applied.)	• Fluid leak in hydraulic system	• Fill master cylinder to fill line; have helper apply brakes and check calipers, wheel cylinders, differential valve tubes, hoses and fittings for leaks. Repair or replace as necessary.
	• Air in hydraulic system	• Remove air from system. Refer to Brake Bleeding.
	• Incorrect or non-recommended brake fluid (fluid evaporates at below normal temp).	• Flush hydraulic system with clean brake fluid. Refill with correct-type fluid.
	• Master cylinder piston seals worn, or master cylinder bore is scored, worn or corroded	• Repair or replace master cylinder
Low brake pedal (pedal goes to floor on first application—o.k. on subsequent applications.)	• Disc brake pads sticking on abutment surfaces of anchor plate. Caused by a build-up of dirt, rust, or corrosion on abutment surfaces	• Clean abutment surfaces
Fading brake pedal (pedal height decreases with steady pressure applied.)	• Fluid leak in hydraulic system	• Fill master cylinder reservoirs to fill mark, have helper apply brakes, check calipers, wheel cylinders, differential valve, tubes, hoses, and fittings for fluid leaks. Repair or replace parts as necessary.
	• Master cylinder piston seals worn, or master cylinder bore is scored, worn or corroded	• Repair or replace master cylinder

Troubleshooting the Brake System (cont.)

Problem	Cause	Solution
Decreasing brake pedal travel (pedal travel required for braking action decreases and may be accompanied by a hard pedal.)	• Caliper or wheel cylinder pistons sticking or seized • Master cylinder compensator ports blocked (preventing fluid return to reservoirs) or pistons sticking or seized in master cylinder bore • Power brake unit binding internally	• Repair or replace the calipers, or wheel cylinders • Repair or replace the master cylinder • Test unit according to the following procedure: (a) Shift transmission into neutral and start engine (b) Increase engine speed to 1500 rpm, close throttle and fully depress brake pedal (c) Slow release brake pedal and stop engine (d) Have helper remove vacuum check valve and hose from power unit. Observe for backward movement of brake pedal. (e) If the pedal moves backward, the power unit has an internal bind—replace power unit
Grabbing brakes (severe reaction to brake pedal pressure.)	• Brakelining(s) contaminated by grease or brake fluid • Parking brake cables incorrectly adjusted or seized • Incorrect brakelining or lining loose on brakeshoes • Caliper anchor plate bolts loose • Rear brakeshoes binding on support plate ledges • Incorrect or missing power brake reaction disc • Rear brake support plates loose	• Determine and correct cause of contamination and replace brakeshoes in axle sets • Adjust cables. Replace seized cables. • Replace brakeshoes in axle sets • Tighten bolts • Clean and lubricate ledges. Replace support plate(s) if ledges are deeply grooved. Do not attempt to smooth ledges by grinding. • Install correct disc • Tighten mounting bolts
Spongy brake pedal (pedal has abnormally soft, springy, spongy feel when depressed.)	• Air in hydraulic system • Brakeshoes bent or distorted • Brakelining not yet seated with drums and rotors • Rear drum brakes not properly adjusted	• Remove air from system. Refer to Brake Bleeding. • Replace brakeshoes • Burnish brakes • Adjust brakes

Troubleshooting the Brake System (cont.)

Problem	Cause	Solution
Hard brake pedal (excessive pedal pressure required to stop vehicle. May be accompanied by brake fade.)	• Loose or leaking power brake unit vacuum hose • Incorrect or poor quality brake-lining • Bent, broken, distorted brakeshoes • Calipers binding or dragging on mounting pins. Rear brakeshoes dragging on support plate.	• Tighten connections or replace leaking hose • Replace with lining in axle sets • Replace brakeshoes • Replace mounting pins and bushings. Clean rust or burrs from rear brake support plate ledges and lubricate ledges with molydisulfide grease. **NOTE:** If ledges are deeply grooved or scored, do not attempt to sand or grind them smooth—replace support plate.
	• Caliper, wheel cylinder, or master cylinder pistons sticking or seized • Power brake unit vacuum check valve malfunction	• Repair or replace parts as necessary • Test valve according to the following procedure: (a) Start engine, increase engine speed to 1500 rpm, close throttle and immediately stop engine (b) Wait at least 90 seconds then depress brake pedal (c) If brakes are not vacuum assisted for 2 or more applications, check valve is faulty
	• Power brake unit has internal bind	• Test unit according to the following procedure: (a) With engine stopped, apply brakes several times to exhaust all vacuum in system (b) Shift transmission into neutral, depress brake pedal and start engine (c) If pedal height decreases with foot pressure and less pressure is required to hold pedal in applied position, power unit vacuum system is operating normally. Test power unit. If power unit exhibits a bind condition, replace the power unit.
	• Master cylinder compensator ports (at bottom of reservoirs) blocked by dirt, scale, rust, or have small burrs (blocked ports prevent fluid return to reservoirs). • Brake hoses, tubes, fittings clogged or restricted	• Repair or replace master cylinder **CAUTION:** Do not attempt to clean blocked ports with wire, pencils, or similar implements. Use compressed air only. • Use compressed air to check or unclog parts. Replace any damaged parts.

Troubleshooting the Brake System (cont.)

Problem	Cause	Solution
Hard brake pedal (excessive pedal pressure required to stop vehicle. May be accompanied by brake fade.)	• Brake fluid contaminated with improper fluids (motor oil, transmission fluid, causing rubber components to swell and stick in bores) • Low engine vacuum	• Replace all rubber components, combination valve and hoses. Flush entire brake system with DOT 3 brake fluid or equivalent. • Adjust or repair engine
Dragging brakes (slow or incomplete release of brakes)	• Brake pedal binding at pivot • Power brake unit has internal bind • Parking brake cables incorrrectly adjusted or seized • Rear brakeshoe return springs weak or broken • Automatic adjusters malfunctioning • Caliper, wheel cylinder or master cylinder pistons sticking or seized • Master cylinder compensating ports blocked (fluid does not return to reservoirs).	• Loosen and lubricate • Inspect for internal bind. Replace unit if internal bind exists. • Adjust cables. Replace seized cables. • Replace return springs. Replace brakeshoe if necessary in axle sets. • Repair or replace adjuster parts as required • Repair or replace parts as necessary • Use compressed air to clear ports. Do not use wire, pencils, or similar objects to open blocked ports.
Vehicle moves to one side when brakes are applied	• Incorrect front tire pressure • Worn or damaged wheel bearings • Brakelining on one side contaminated • Brakeshoes on one side bent, distorted, or lining loose on shoe • Support plate bent or loose on one side • Brakelining not yet seated with drums or rotors • Caliper anchor plate loose on one side • Caliper piston sticking or seized • Brakelinings water soaked • Loose suspension component attaching or mounting bolts • Brake combination valve failure	• Inflate to recommended cold (reduced load) inflation pressure • Replace worn or damaged bearings • Determine and correct cause of contamination and replace brakelining in axle sets • Replace brakeshoes in axle sets • Tighten or replace support plate • Burnish brakelining • Tighten anchor plate bolts • Repair or replace caliper • Drive vehicle with brakes lightly applied to dry linings • Tighten suspension bolts. Replace worn suspension components. • Replace combination valve
Chatter or shudder when brakes are applied (pedal pulsation and roughness may also occur.)	• Brakeshoes distorted, bent, contaminated, or worn • Caliper anchor plate or support plate loose • Excessive thickness variation of rotor(s)	• Replace brakeshoes in axle sets • Tighten mounting bolts • Refinish or replace rotors in axle sets

Troubleshooting the Brake System (cont.)

Problem	Cause	Solution
Noisy brakes (squealing, clicking, scraping sound when brakes are applied.)	• Bent, broken, distorted brakeshoes • Excessive rust on outer edge of rotor braking surface	• Replace brakeshoes in axle sets • Remove rust
Noisy brakes (squealing, clicking, scraping sound when brakes are applied.) (cont.)	• Brakelining worn out—shoes contacting drum of rotor • Broken or loose holddown or return springs • Rough or dry drum brake support plate ledges • Cracked, grooved, or scored rotor(s) or drum(s) • Incorrect brakelining and/or shoes (front or rear).	• Replace brakeshoes and lining in axle sets. Refinish or replace drums or rotors. • Replace parts as necessary • Lubricate support plate ledges • Replace rotor(s) or drum(s). Replace brakeshoes and lining in axle sets if necessary. • Install specified shoe and lining assemblies
Pulsating brake pedal	• Out of round drums or excessive lateral runout in disc brake rotor(s)	• Refinish or replace drums, re-index rotors or replace

STANDARD BRAKE SYSTEM

Basic Operating Principles

Hydraulic systems are used to actuate the brakes of all modern automobiles. The system transports the power required to force the frictional surfaces of the braking system together from the pedal to the individual brake units at each wheel. A hydraulic system is used for two reasons. First, fluid under pressure can be carried to all parts of an automobile by small hoses-some of which are flexible-without taking up a significant amount of room or posing routing problems. Second, a great mechanical advantage can be given to the brake pedal end of the system, and the foot pressure required to actuate the brakes can be reduced by making the surface area of the master cylinder pistons smaller than that of any of the pistons in the wheel cylinders or calipers.

The master cylinder consists of a fluid reservoir and either a single or double cylinder and piston assembly. Double type master cylinders are designed to separate the front and rear braking systems hydraulically in case of a leak.

Steel lines carry the brake fluid to a point on the vehicle's frame near each of the vehicle's wheels. The fluid is then carried to the wheel cylinders by flexible tubes in order to allow for suspension and steering movements.

Each wheel cylinder contains two pistons, one at either end, which push outward in opposite directions. In disc brake systems, the cylinders are part of the calipers. One or four cylinders are used to force the brake pads against the disc, but all cylinders contain one piston only. All pistons employ some type of seal, usually made of rubber, to minimize fluid leakage. A rubber dust boot seals the outer end of the cylinder against dust and dirt. The boot fits around the outer end of the piston on disc brake calipers, and around the brake actuating rod on wheel cylinders.

The hydraulic system operates as follows: When at rest, the entire system, from the piston(s) in the master cylinder to those in the wheel cylinders or calipers, is full of brake fluid. Upon application of the brake pedal, fluid trapped in front of the master cylinder piston(s) is forced through the lines to the wheel cylinders. Here, it forces the pistons outward, in the case of drum brakes, and inward toward the disc, in the case of disc brakes. The motion of the pistons is opposed by return springs mounted outside the cylinders in drum brakes, and by internal springs or spring seals, in disc brakes.

Upon release of the brake pedal, a spring located inside the master cylinder immediately returns the master cylinder pistons to the normal position. The pistons contain check valves and the master cylinder has compensating ports drilled in it.

These are uncovered as the pistons reach their normal position. The piston check valves allow fluid to flow toward the wheel cylinders or calipers as the pistons withdraw. Then, as the return springs force the brake pads or shoes into the released position, the excess fluid reservoir through the compensating ports. It is during the time the pedal is in the released position that any fluid that has leaked out of the system will be replaced through the compensating ports.

Dual circuit master cylinders employ two pistons, located one behind the other, in the same cylinder. The primary piston is actuated directly by mechanical linkage from the brake pedal. The secondary piston is actuated by fluid trapped between the two pistons. If a leak develops in front of the secondary piston, it moves forward until it bottoms against the front of the master cylinder, and the fluid trapped between the pistons will operate the rear brakes. If the rear brakes develop a leak, the primary piston will move forward until direct contact with the secondary piston takes place, and it will force the secondary piston to actuate the front brakes. In either case, the brake pedal moves farther when the brakes are applied, and less braking power is available.

All dual-circuit systems use a switch to warn the driver when only half of the brake system is operational. This switch is located in a valve body which is mounted on the firewall or the frame below the master cylinder. A hydraulic piston receives pressure from both circuits, each circuit's pressure being applied to one end of the piston. When the pressures are in balance, the piston remains stationary. When one circuit has a leak, however, the greater pressure in that circuit during application of the brakes will push the piston to one side, closing the switch and activating the brake warning light.

In disc brake systems, this valve body also contains a metering valve and, in some cases, a proportioning valve. The metering valve keeps pressure from traveling to the disc brakes on the front wheels until the brake shoes on the rear wheels have contacted the drums, ensuring that the front brakes will never be used alone. The proportioning valve controls the pressure to the rear brakes to avoid rear wheel lock-up during very hard braking.

Warning lights may be tested by depressing the brake pedal and holding it while opening one of the wheel cylinder bleeder screws. If this does not cause the light to go on, substitute a new lamp, make continuity checks, and, finally, replace the switch as necessary.

The hydraulic system may be checked for leaks by applying pressure to the pedal gradually and steadily. If the pedal sinks very slowly to the floor, the system has a leak. This is not to be confused with a springy or spongy feel due to the compression of air within the lines. If the system leaks, there will be a gradual change in the position of the pedal with a constant pressure.

Check for leaks along all lines and at wheel cylinders. If no external leaks are apparent, the problem is inside the master cylinder.

Disc Brakes

BASIC OPERATING PRINCIPLES

Instead of the traditional expanding brakes that press outward against a circular drum, disc brake systems utilize a disc (rotor) with brake pads positioned on either side of it. Braking effect is achieved in a manner similar to the way you would squeeze a spinning phonograph record between your fingers. The disc (rotor) is a casting with cooling fins between the two braking surfaces. This enables air to circulate between the braking surfaces making them less sensitive to heat buildup and more resistant to fade. Dirt and water do not affect braking action since contaminants are thrown off by the centrifugal action of the rotor or scraped off the by the pads. Also, the equal clamping action of the two brake pads tends to ensure uniform,

straight line stops. Disc brakes are inherently self-adjusting.
There are three general types of disc brake:
1. A fixed caliper.
2. A floating caliper.
3. A sliding caliper.
The fixed caliper design uses two pistons mounted on either side of the rotor (in each side of the caliper). The caliper is mounted rigidly and does not move.

The sliding and floating designs are quite similar. In fact, these two types are often lumped together. In both designs, the pad on the inside of the rotor is moved into contact with the rotor by hydraulic force. The caliper, which is not held in a fixed position, moves slightly, bringing the outside pad into contact with the rotor. There are various methods of attaching floating calipers. Some pivot at the bottom or top, and some slide on mounting bolts. In any event, the end result is the same.

Drum Brakes

BASIC OPERATING PRINCIPLES

Drum brakes employ two brake shoes mounted on a stationary backing plate. These shoes are positioned inside a circular drum which rotates with the wheel assembly. The shoes are held in place by springs; this allows them to slide toward the drums (when they are applied) while keeping the linings and drums in alignment. The shoes are actuated by a wheel cylinder which is mounted at the top of the backing plate. When the brakes are applied, hydraulic pressure forces the wheel cylinder's actuating links outward. Since these links bear directly against the top of the brake shoes, the tops of the shoes are then forced against the inner side of the drum. This action forces the bottoms of the two shoes to contact the brake drum by rotating the entire assembly slightly (known as servo action). When pressure within the wheel cylinder is relaxed, return springs pull the shoes back away from the drum.

Most modern drum brakes are designed to self-adjust themselves during application when the vehicle is moving in reverse. This motion causes both shoes to rotate very slightly with the drum, rocking an adjusting lever, thereby causing rotation of the adjusting screw.

Power Boosters

Power brakes operate just as standard brake systems except in the actuation of the master cylinder pistons. A vacuum diaphragm is located on the front of the master cylinder and assists the driver in applying the brakes, reducing both the effort and travel he must put into moving the brake pedal.

The vacuum diaphragm housing is connected to the intake manifold by a vacuum hose. A check valve is placed at the point where the hose enters the diaphragm housing, so that during periods of low manifold vacuum brake assist vacuum will not be lost.

Depressing the brake pedal closes off the vacuum source and allows atmospheric pressure to enter on one side of the diaphragm. This causes the master cylinder pistons to move and apply the brakes. When the brake pedal is released, vacuum is applied to both sides of the diaphragm, and return springs return the diaphragm and master cylinder pistons to the released position. If the vacuum fails, the brake pedal rod will butt against the end of the master cylinder actuating rod, and direct mechanical application will occur as the pedal is depressed.

The hydraulic and mechanical problems that apply to conventional brake systems also apply to power brakes, and should be checked for if the tests below do not reveal the problem.
Test for a system vacuum leak as described below:
1. Operate the engine at idle without touching the brake pedal for at least one minute.
2. Turn off the engine, and wait one minute.

3. Test for the presence of assist vacuum by depressing the brake pedal and releasing it several times. Light application will produce less and less pedal travel, if vacuum was present. If there is no vacuum, air is leaking into the system somewhere.

Test for system operation as follows:

1. Pump the brake pedal (with engine off) until the supply vacuum is entirely gone.

2. Put a light, steady pressure on the pedal.

3. Start the engine, and operate it at idle. If the system is operating, the brake pedal should fall toward the floor if constant pressure is maintained on the pedal.

Power brake systems may be tested for hydraulic leaks just as ordinary systems are tested.

Your vehicle is equipped with pin slider type caliper front disc brakes and automatic adjuster equipped rear drum brakes. The brake system is diagonally split, with the left front and right rear brakes on one hydraulic system and the right front and left rear on the other. Should one side of the split system fail, the other should provide enough braking power to bring the vehicle to a stop. Other components included in the brake system are: A brake warning switch, master cylinder, a lead sensing dual proportioning valve, a brake booster and the necessary hoses and lines.

Adjustments

Periodic brake adjustment is not necessary as the front calipers are inherently self-adjusting, and the rear brakes are equipped with self-adjusters. In the event of a brake reline or component service requiring brake shoe removal, initial manual adjustment of the rear brake shoes will speed up servicing time. Front brake pads adjust themselves as the brake pedal is applied. After installing new front brake pads pump the brake pedal several times until a firm feeling is obtained. The pads will be incorrect adjustment.

DRUM BRAKES

1. To make an initial rear brake shoe adjustment, raise and support the rear of the vehicle on jackstands, so that both wheels are off the ground and can turn freely.

2. Remove the adjusting hole cover at the back of the brake mounting plates.

3. Be sure the parking brake is fully released and that there is slack in the brake cables.

4. Insert a brake adjusting tool through the hole in the backing plate until the adjuster star wheel is engaged. move the adjusting tool upward to turn the star wheel. Continue until a slight drag is felt when the wheel is rotated.

5. Insert a thin screwdriver or piece of stiff rod through the backing plate slot and push the adjuster lock tab away from the star wheel. Move the adjusting tool down while holding the locking tab out of the way. Back off the star wheel until the wheel turns freely without any brake drag. Install the adjusting slot cover.

6. Repeat the procedure for the other rear wheel. Adjust the parking brake after initial rear brake adjustment is finished. Check parking brake adjustment after applying several times, insure freedom from brake drag.

Brake Light Switch

The brake light switch is a self adjusting unit installed on the brake pedal shaft pivot pin.

REMOVAL AND INSTALLATION

1. Remove the old switch from the retaining bracket.

2. Install the new brake light switch into the bracket and push the switch as far forward as it will go.

3. The brake pedal will move forward slightly when the switch is pushed forward.

4. Pull back on the brake pedal gently. As the brake pedal is pulled back, the switch striker will move toward the switch. When the brake pedal can not be pull back any further, the switch will ratchet to the correct position. Very little movement is required, and no further adjustment is required.

Master Cylinder

The master cylinder is of tandem design, having an anodized aluminum body and a glass reinforced nylon reservoir. If the cylinder bore is pitted or scratched, the body must be replaced as honing will remove the anodized surface. The reservoir is indexed to prevent incorrect installation and the cap diaphragms are slotted to allow internal pressure to equalize. A secondary outlet tube leading from the master cylinder is connected to the differential valve mounted underneath the master cylinder. The front part of the valve supplied the right rear and left front brakes. The rear portion supplied the right rear and left front. The rear portion of the valve is connect to the primary outlet tube of the master cylinder.

REMOVAL AND INSTALLATION

1. Disconnect the primary and secondary brake lines at the master cylinder. Tape or plug the ends of the lines.

2. Remove the nuts attaching the master cylinder to the power brake booster.

3. Wrap a rag around the brake line tilting holes, slide the master cylinder straight away from the booster and remove from the vehicle. Take care not to spill any brake fluid on the finish. Flush off with water if any fluid is spilled.

To install:

4. Bench bleed the master cylinder. (See the Bleeding section). Install the master cylinder over the mounting studs. After aligning the master cylinder pushrod and mounting studs, hold the cylinder in position and start the attaching nuts but do not tighten completely. Install the brake lines but do not tighten completely.

5. After the brake lines are installed, tighten the cylinder mounting nuts fully and then the brake lines.

6. Finish bleeding the brake system.

OVERHAUL

The aluminum master cylinder cannot be rebuilt; service is limited to replacement.

Master cylinder — cutaway view

Removing the reservoir

Removing reservoir mounting grommets

Bleeding the master cylinder

Fluid Reservoir

REMOVAL AND INSTALLATION

1. Remove the master cylinder from the vehicle. Clean the outside of the reservoir and cylinder.
2. Remove the reservoir caps and empty the brake fluid. Do not reuse the old fluid.

3. Position the master cylinder in a vise. Pad the vise jaws and do not over tighten.
4. Rock the reservoir from side to side to loosen and lift up to remove from the master cylinder. Do not pry the reservoir with an tools. Damage to the reservoir will result.
5. Remove the old housing to reservoir mounting grommets. Clean the cylinder and reservoir grommet mounting surfaces.
To install:
6. Install new mounting grommets in the master cylinder housing.
7. Lubricate the mounting surfaces of the grommets with brake fluid.
8. Place the reservoir in position over the grommets and seat it into the grommets using a rocking motion.
9. Be sure that the reservoir is fully seated on the master cylinder and the bottom of the reservoir touches the top of the grommets.
10. Fill the reservoir with fresh brake fluid and bench bleed the master cylinder.

Power Brake Booster

REMOVAL AND INSTALLATION

1. Remove the nuts that attach the master cylinder to the power brake booster. Slowly and carefully slide the master cylinder away from the booster, off the mounting studs. Allow the cylinder to rest against the fender shield.
2. Disconnect the vacuum hose from the brake booster.
3. From the inside of the vehicle under the instrument panel, locate the point where the booster linkage connects to the brake pedal. Use a small tool and position between the center tang of the booster linkage to brake pedal retaining clip. Rotate the tool and pull the retainer from the pin. disconnect the brake pedal.
4. Remove the brake booster mounting nuts and unfasten the brackets mounting the steel water line at the firewall and left frame rail. On models equipped with a manual transmission, unfasten the clutch cable bracket at the shock tower and move it to the side.
5. The booster mounting bracket holes are slotted, slide the booster up and to the left. Tilt the booster inboard and up to remove from the engine compartment.
6. Position the power booster over the firewall mounting studs. Install the mounting nuts and tighten to 200-300 inch lbs.
7. install the steel heater line bracket and clutch cable bracket, if equipped.
8. Carefully install the master cylinder and tighten the mounting bolts to 200-300 inch lbs.
9. Connect the vacuum line to the power brake booster.
10. Connect the pedal linkage to the booster push rod after lubricating the pivot point with white grease. Install a new retainer clip. Check brake and stoplight operation.

Pressure Differential Switch/Warning Light

As mentioned before, the hydraulic brake system on your vehicle is diagonally split; the left front and right rear are part of one system and the right front and left rear part of the other. Both systems are routed through a pressure differential switch (located under the master cylinder) which is designed to warn the driver should a failure occur. If hydraulic pressure is lost in one side of the split system the switch will activate a warning light on the instrument panel, indicating that the brake system should be checked and repaired, if necessary. After repairs to the system have been made, the switch will automatically recenter itself and the light will go out.

Power brake unit/vacuum hose connections — 2.2L and 2.5L engines

Power brake unit/vacuum hose connections — 3.3L engine

Power brake unit/vacuum hose connections — 3.0L engine

Brake warning switch location

TESTING

To test the warning switch system, raise the front or rear of the vehicle and safely support with jackstands. Open a caliper or wheel cylinder bleeder valve while a helper holds pressure on the brake pedal. As fluid is lost through the bleeder, the dash lamp should light. If the lamp fails to light, check for a burned out bulb, disconnected socket, or a broken or disconnected wire at the switch. Replace the warning switch if the rest of the circuit members check out. Be sure to fill the master cylinder and bleed the brakes after repairs have been completed.

Height Sensing Fuel Proportioning Valve

All vehicles are equipped with a height sensing dual proportioning valve. The valve is located under the rear floor pan just forward of the rear axle. The valve automatically provides the proper brake balance between the front and rear brakes regard-

Height sensing proportioning valve assembly — late model, non-ABS equipped vehicles

Height sensing dual proportioning valve and adjustment points — early models

less of the vehicle load condition. the valve modulates the rear brakes sensing the loading condition of the vehicle through relative height movement between the rear axle and load floor.

The valve is mounted on a crossmember and connected to an adjustable lever on the rear axle by a large spring. When the vehicle is unloaded or lightly leaded, the hydraulic line pressure is minimized. As the vehicle is more heavily loaded and the ride height lowers, the spring moves the valve control arm to allow higher rear brake pressure.

NOTE: Because ride height determines rear brake pressure, the use of after market load leveling or capacity increasing devices should be avoided.

The proportioning section of the valve transmits full input pressure up to a certain point, called the split point. Beyond the split point the valve reduces the amount of pressure increase to the rear brakes according to a certain ratio. This means that on light brake pedal application equal pressure will be transmitted to the front and rear brakes. On harder pedal application, pressure transmitted to the rear brakes will be lower to prevent rear wheel lock-up and skid.

TESTING

NOTE: Two pressure gauges and adapter fittings (tool set C4007A or equivalent) are required of the following test.

If premature rear wheel lock-up and skid is experienced frequently, it could be an indication that the fluid pressure to the rear brakes is excessive and that a malfunction has occurred in the proportioning valve or an adjustment is necessary.

1. If a pressure gauge and adapter fittings are on hand, proceed with the following test.
2. Disconnect the external spring at the valve lever.
3. Install one pressure gauge and T-fitting in line from either master cylinder port to the brake valve assembly.
4. Install the second gauge to either rear brake outlet port between the valve assembly and the rear brake line. Bleed the rear brakes.
5. Have a helper apply and hold pedal pressure to get a reading on the valve inlet gauge and outlet gauge. The inlet pressure should be 500 psi and the outlet pressure should be 100-200 psi. If the required pressures are not present, replace the valve. If the test pressures are all right, adjust the external spring and arm.

Ⓐ = 3/8-24 THREAD
Ⓑ = 7/16-24 THREAD

Proper nut thread size and tube routing — non-ABS models

VALVE REMOVAL, INSTALLATION AND ADJUSTMENT

1. Raise and support the rear of the vehicle. Position jackstands at the rear contact pads so that the rear axle will hang free with the tires off the ground.
2. Loosen the rear axle mounted adjustable lever assembly and remove the actuating spring. Remove the brake lines from the proportioning valve and remove the valve.
3. Install the brake lines loosely in the proportioning valve and mount valve in position.
4. Tighten the brake lines, fill the master cylinder to the correct fluid level and bleed the brakes.
5. Confirm that the axle is hanging free and at full rebound position with the wheels and tires mounted.
6. Confirm that the actuating spring is connected between the proportioning valve and axle adjusting lever. the axle adjusting lever mounting bolts should be loose so that the bracket can be moved.
7. Push the control lever on the proportioning valve towards the valve until it is against the body and hold it in that position.
8. Move the axle lever up and away to apply tension to the spring. When all free play is taken out of the spring, but the spring is not stretched, tighten the mounting bolt that goes through the slotted side of the adjustment bracket. Tighten the anchor bolt. Both mounting bolts should be tightened to 150 inch lbs.

Brake Hoses

REMOVAL AND INSTALLATION

1. Right and left brake hoses are not interchangeable. Remove the connecter at the caliper, then remove the mounting bracket from the strut support and finally, remove the from the upper body mount and disconnect the hose from the steel line.

2. Always use a flare wrench to prevent rounding of the line fittings.
3. Install the new hose to the caliper first. Always use a new copper washer after making sure the mounting surfaces are clean. Tighten the caliper hose fitting. Install the strut bracket next, then attach the steel line fitting. Position the upper keyed end of the hose to the body bracket and secure it.
4. Rear brake hoses should be attached first to the trailing arm bracket and the to the floor pan tubes.
5. Keep the hose as straight as possible, avoid twisting.
6. Bleed the brake system.

Bleeding the Brake System

The purpose of bleeding the brakes is to expel air trapped in the hydraulic system. The system must be bled whenever the pedal feels spongy, indicating that compressible air has entered the system. It must also be bled whenever the system has been opened or repaired. You will need a helper to help bleed the system. Always use fresh brake fluid.

BENCH BLEEDING

Always bench bleed the master cylinder before installing it on the vehicle.
1. Place the master cylinder in a vise.
2. Connect two lines to the fluid outlet orifices, bend the lines upwards and insert the opened ends into the reservoir.
3. Fill the reservoir with brake fluid.
4. Using a wooden dowel, depress the pushrod slowly, allowing the pistons to return. do this several times until the air bubbles are all expelled.
5. Remove the bleeding tubes from the master cylinder, plug the outlets and install the caps.

NOTE: It is not necessary to bleed the entire system after replacing the master cylinder, provided that mas-

LET	TIGHTENING TORQUE	
Ⓐ	30 IN. LBS.	3 N•m
Ⓑ	70 IN. LBS.	8 N•m
Ⓒ	95 IN. LBS.	11 N•m
Ⓓ	105 IN. LBS.	12 N•m
Ⓔ	145 IN. LBS.	16 N•m
Ⓕ	24 FT. LBS.	18 N•m

TUBE

LOCK

LOCK

LOCK

CLIP

CLIP

CLIP

HOSE

CLIP

MASTER CYLINDER

VALVE ASSEMBLY

HOSE

TO HEIGHT SENSING VALVE

LEFT FRONT TUBE

LOCK

VIEW IN DIRECTION OF ARROW Z

VIEW IN DIRECTION OF ARROW Y

Brake line routing

Proper method for bleeding the brake system

Open the bleeder screw at least one full turn

ter cylinder has been bled and filled upon installation. However, if a soft pedal is experienced, bleed the entire system.

SYSTEM BLEEDING

CAUTION

Do not allow brake fluid to spill on the vehicle's finish; it will remove the paint. In case of a spill, flush the area with water.

1. The sequence for bleeding is right rear, left front, left rear and right front. If the vehicle is equipped with power brakes, remove the vacuum by applying the brakes several times. Do not run the engine while bleeding the brakes.

2. Clean all the bleeder screws. You may want to give each one a shot of penetrating solvent to help loosen the fitting. Seizure is a common problem with bleeder screws, which then brake off, sometimes requiring replacement of the part to which they are attached.

3. Check the fluid level in the master cylinder and fill with DOT 3 brake fluid, if necessary.

NOTE: Brake fluid absorbs moisture from the air. Don't leave the master cylinder or the fluid container uncovered any longer than necessary. Be careful handling the brake fluid, it is a great paint remover. If any brake fluid spills on the vehicle's finish, flush off with water immediately. Check the level of the fluid often when bleeding, and refill the reservoirs as necessary. Don't let them run dry, or you will have to repeat the process.

4. Attach a length of clear vinyl tubing to the bleeder screw at the wheel cylinder or caliper. Insert the other end of the tube into a clear, clean jar half filled with brake fluid. Start at a rear cylinder first, then bleed the opposite side front cylinder.

5. Have your assistant slowly depress the brake pedal. As this is done, open the bleeder screw ⅓-½ of a turn on wheel cylinders and at least one turn on calipers, and allow the fluid to run through the tube. Then close the bleeder screw before the pedal reaches the end of its travel. Have your assistant slowly release the pedal after the bleeder screw is closed. Repeat this process until no air bubbles appear in the expelled fluid.

6. Repeat the procedure on the other calipers and cylinders, checking the level of fluid in the master cylinder reservoir often. After you're done, there should be no sponginess in the brake pedal feel. If there is, either there is still air in the line, in which case the process should be repeated, or there is a leak somewhere, which of course must be corrected before moving the vehicle.

BENDIX SYSTEM 10
ANTI-LOCK BRAKE SYSTEM

System Description

Found on 1991 Caravan/Voyager/Town and Country (AS body), the Bendix System 10 will prevent wheel locking under heavy braking. By preventing wheel lock-up, maximum braking

effort is maintained while preventing loss of directional control. Additionally, some steering capability is maintained during the stop. The ABS system will operate regardless of road surface conditions.

There are conditions for which the ABS system provides no benefit. Hydroplaning is possible when the tires ride on a film of water, losing contact with the paved surface. This renders the vehicle totally uncontrollable until road contact is regained. Extreme steering maneuvers at high speed or cornering beyond the limits of tire adhesion can result in skidding which is independent of vehicle braking. For this reason, the system is named anti–lock rather than anti–skid.

Under normal braking conditions, the ABS system functions in the same manner as a standard brake system. The primary difference is that power assist is gained from hydraulic pressure rather than a conventional vacuum booster.

The system is a combination of electrical and hydraulic components, working together to control the flow brake fluid to the wheels when necessary. The pump and motor assembly pressurizes brake fluid from the reservoir and stores it within an accumulator for use in both normal power-assisted and ABS braking. The Controller Anti-lock Brake (CAB) is the electronic brain of the system, receiving and interpreting speed signals from 4 sensors at the wheels. The CAB will enter anti-lock mode when it senses impending wheel lock at any wheel and immediately controls the line pressure(s) to the affected wheel(s). The hydraulic assembly serves as both an integral master cylinder and the hydraulic booster assembly for the brake system. It contains the wheel circuit valves used to control the brake fluid pressure to each wheel circuit.

During anti-lock braking, line pressures are controlled or modulated by the rapid cycling of electronic valves within the hydraulic assembly. These valves can allow pressures within the system to increase, remain constant or decrease depending on the needs of the moment as registered by the CAB. The front wheels are controlled individually while the rear wheels receive the same electrical signal, based on the wheel with the greatest locking tendency. Anti-lock function is available above 3–5 mph.

The operator may hear a popping or clicking sound as the pump and/or control valves cycle on and off during normal operation. The sounds are due to normal operation and are not indicative of a system problem; under most conditions, the sounds are only faintly audible. If ABS is engaged, the operator may notice some pulsation in the pedal. If additional force is applied to the pedal during an ABS-engaged stop, the operator will notice extremely hard pedal feel. This is due to isolation of the master cylinder during ABS operation. Some pulsing may also be felt in

the body of the vehicle due to suspension movement as brake pressures apply and release at the individual wheels.

Although the ABS system prevents wheel lock–up under hard braking, as brake pressure increases, wheel slip is allowed to reach as high as 30%. This means that the rolling velocity of a given wheel is 30% less than that of a free–rolling wheel at a given speed. This slip will result in some tire chirp during ABS operation. The sound should not be interpreted as lock–up but rather as an indication of the system holding the wheel(s) just outside the point of lock–up. Additionally, since the ABS system turns off below 4 mph, the final few feet of an ABS–engaged stop may be completed with the wheels locked.

The Bendix system is equipped with built-in diagnostic capability. At every start-up, the CAB illuminates the dashboard warning lights and turns them off after checking the circuitry. When the vehicle reaches 3–5 mph, the CAB conducts a system check, briefly activating all the control valves to confirm their operation. This system check may be noticed by the operator as a series of rapid clicks during initial drive-off; the sound is normal and not indicative of a problem. Some fault conditions will cause the CAB to set and retain a trouble code which may be retrieved for diagnostic purposes. Stored fault codes will remain stored until cleared by the DRB II.

The CAB will illuminate the appropriate dashboard warning lamp according to the fault detected. It is possible to have a fault affecting only the ABS function; in this case, the ABS system will be disabled but the vehicle will retain normal braking capability.

SYSTEM COMPONENTS

Wheel Speed Sensors

The speed of each wheel is monitored by a wheel speed sensor (WSS). A toothed tone wheel rotates in front of the sensor, generating a small AC voltage which is transmitted to the CAB. Each speed sensor is individually removable; the tone wheels are permanently mounted to either the front outer constant velocity joint assemblies or the rear wheel hub assembly. The air gap between the sensor and the tone wheel is set by the correct installation of the sensor; the air gap is not adjustable.

Bendix System 10 Anti-lock brake system — component layout

WHEEL SPEED SENSOR

TONE WHEEL

Front wheel speed sensor and tone wheel — ABS equipped models

Integrated pump and motor assembly — ABS equipped models

Controller Anti-Lock Brake (CAB)

The CAB is located in the engine compartment under the battery tray. This computer—operating separately from other on-board controllers—monitors wheel speed signals as well as several internal functions. The CAB controls the wheel circuit valves once a locking tendency is detected. This pressure modulation continues until the locking tendency is no longer detected.

The CAB receives inputs from the wheel speed sensors, the boost pressure transducer, the primary pressure transducer, the brake light switch, the brake fluid level sensor, the differential pressure switch, ignition switch, starter relay, system relay voltage and a ground signal. Outputs managed by the CAB include the 10 modulator valves (3 build, 3 decay and 4 isolation), both dashboard warning lamps, system relay actuation, low fluid/parking brake output, and diagnostic communication including transmitting fault codes.

NOTE: The CAB found on 2wd Caravan, Voyager, and Town and Country vehicles is different from that on the 4wd versions. The controllers must not be interchanged.

Pump and Motor Assembly

The integral motor and pump assembly is mounted on rubber isolators to a to a transaxle bracket below the hydraulic assembly. Fluid is taken from the master cylinder reservoir, pressurized and sent to storage in both the piston accumulator and the hydraulic bladder accumulator. The pump/motor assembly is serviceable only as a unit and should never be disassembled. Hoses running to and from the pump unit should never be repaired but replaced as an assembly.

Hydraulic Assembly

The integral hydraulic assembly is located on the firewall and provides the function of the power booster and master cylinder. Other components provide the brake pressure modulation and system monitoring required by the ABS system. The hydraulic assembly consists of several components with individual function as described below. Note that although the components and their function may be discussed and tested separately, most components are not serviced individually.

BOOSTER/MASTER CYLINDER

The master cylinder uses a diagonally split configuration in normal braking. The 2 circuits are isolated so that a leak in one will not affect the other. During brake pedal application, the pushrod applies force to the boost control valve, allowing pressurized fluid from the accumulator to flow into the master cylinder chamber. This pressure within the booster servo applies pressure to the primary and secondary master cylinder pistons. The pressures generated by the primary and secondary pistons are used to apply the brakes during normal braking.

The pressure within the hydraulic booster is directly proportional to the pressure applied to the brake pedal. As with vacuum operated boosters, brake efficiency depends on road surface and the force applied to the pedal.

HYDRAULIC ACCUMULATORS

The external or bladder accumulator stores brake fluid from the pump under very high pressure; the pressurized fluid is available for hydraulic assist (boost) and/or ABS braking. The accumulator uses a diaphragm and nitrogen pre-charge of about 1000 psi. Normally, the pump will charge the accumulator to a working pressure of 1600–2000 psi. For this reason, all safety precautions must be observed before working on the hydraulic system. The pressures within the accumulator are sufficient to cause serious personal injury or damage to the vehicle.

The piston accumulator is an integral part of the pump/motor assembly. It contains a pre-charge of approximately 460 psi nitrogen gas. This accumulator cannot be removed from the pump/motor assembly; component service is not possible.

DUAL FUNCTION PRESSURE SWITCh

This switch is located on the bottom of the hydraulic assembly and monitors the pressure within the accumulator. When accumulator pressure falls below 1600 psi, the dual function pressure switch causes the pump/motor to energize. When accumulator pressure reaches 2000 psi, the pump/motor is shut off.

The second purpose of this switch is to provide a signal to the CAB when accumulator pressure falls below the 1000 psi minimum. An internal warning pressure switch is normally closed at working pressures, grounding pin 17 at the controller. Should the accumulator pressure drop below minimum, the switch opens, a voltage signal is detected at the CAB and is read as low pressure. At this warning pressure, the CAB disables the ABS function and illuminates the dash warning lamps. After 2 minutes of continuous low pressure, a low accumulator fault code is stored in memory.

Hydraulic assembly component location — ABS equipped models

PRESSURE TRANSDUCERS

The boost pressure transducer is mounted on the bottom of the hydraulic assembly and monitors boost servo pressure. The primary pressure transducer is found on the left side of the hydraulic assembly and monitors the pressure within the primary master cylinder.

Both transducers generate a signal of 0.25–5.0 volts directly proportional to the fluid pressure. The CAB compares these signals and confirms proper operation. If either of the signals exceeds a pre-planned range, the CAB will disable the anti-lock system.

DIFFERENTIAL PRESSURE SWITCH

The differential pressure switch is used to detect a pressure differential between the primary and secondary master cylinder hydraulic circuits. When the pressure difference is 300 psi or more, this switch grounds the output of the primary pressure transducer. The CAB receives 0.0 volts from the transducer and reacts by shutting down the ABS function and illuminating the dash warning lights.

FLUID LEVEL SENSOR

A float and magnetic reed switch monitor the fluid level within the master cylinder hydraulic reservoir. Located in the reservoir cap, the sensor signal is used an input to the CAB. If low fluid level is detected, the BRAKE warning lamp on the dash is illuminated. If the vehicle is in motion above 3 mph, the ABS will be disabled and the anti-lock warning lamp will light. If the vehicle is not moving (or is below 3 mph) the anti-lock lamp will not come on.

Hydraulic bladder (external) accumulator — ABS equipped models

Dashboard Warning Lamps

BRAKE WARNING LAMP

The red BRAKE warning lamp will be illuminated to warn the operator of conditions which may result in reduced braking ability. These conditions include:
- Parking brake not fully released.
- Low brake fluid.
- Low accumulator pressure.
- Hydraulic assembly or CAB

The lamp will also illuminate whenever the ignition switch is put in the **START** position or the ignition switch is turned to **ON**. Under these bulb test conditions, the lamp should stay illuminated for about 2 seconds.

——————— **CAUTION** ———————

Illumination of the BRAKE lamp indicates a condition affecting the braking ability of the vehicle. The vehicle should not be driven until the seriousness of the problem is determined. In most cases, conditions illuminating the BRAKE lamp will also illuminate the ANTI-LOCK warning lamp, disabling that system as well.

ANTI-LOCK WARNING LAMP

The amber ANTI-LOCK warning lamp is controlled by the CAB. If the controller detects a condition resulting in the shutdown of the ABS function, the ANTI-LOCK lamp will be lit. The ANTI-LOCK lamp is normally lit until the CAB completes its self-tests; if no faults are found, the lamp is turned off.

Display of the ANTI-LOCK warning lamp by itself indicates only that the ABS function has been disabled. Power-assisted normal braking is still available and the car may be driven with reasonable care.

NOTE: When starting the vehicle, the ANTI-LOCK lamp may stay on 1–30 seconds depending on the residual press the left front headlight (AS body) The relay controls the operation of the pump/motor assembly and is energized by a signal from the dual function pressure switch. The relay may be serviced individually.

The system relay controls the modulator valves and the anti-lock warning lamp relay. The system relay, near the pump/motor relay, controls power to the CAB after the start-up cycle.

The anti-lock warning lamp relay controls the dashboard warning lamp. When the relay is energized by the CAB, the dash lamp is held **OFF**. Thus, the lamp will light when the CAB fails, is disconnected or causes the ABS function to be discontinued. The CAB has the capability to turn the light on by itself by providing a separate ground.

Proportioning Valves

In place of the usual differential pressure proportioning valve, this system incorporates individual valves in each rear brake line. Located in the brake outlet ports of the hydraulic assembly,

Relay locations — ABS equipped models

these screw-in valves limit rear brake pressure after a certain pressure is reached. This improves front-to-rear brake balance during normal braking. Each proportioning valve may be serviced individually.

Diagnostic Connector

The ABS diagnostic connector is located on the left side of the steering column under the dash. The blue 6-pin connector is used for connecting diagnostic tools such as the DRB II.

Diagnosis and Testing

SERVICE PRECAUTIONS

——————— **CAUTION** ———————

This brake system uses hydraulic accumulators which, when fully charged, contain brake fluid at very high pressure. Before disconnecting any hydraulic lines, hoses or fittings be certain that the accumulator pressure is completely relieved. Failure to depressurize the accumulators may result in personal injury and/or vehicle damage.

- Certain components within the ABS system are not intended to be serviced or repaired individually. Only those components with removal and installation procedures should be serviced.
- The accumulator contains high pressure nitrogen gas to assist in pressurizing the system. The gas pressure is maintained even after fluid pressure in the system is reduced. Never puncture or attempt to disassemble this component.
- Do not use rubber hoses or other parts not specifically specified for the ABS system. When using repair kits, replace all parts included in the kit. Partial or incorrect repair may lead to functional problems and require the replacement of components.
- Lubricate rubber parts with clean, fresh brake fluid to ease assembly. Do not use lubricated shop air to clean parts; damage to rubber components may result.
- Use only DOT 3 brake fluid from an unopened container.
- If any hydraulic component or line is removed or replaced, it may be necessary to bleed the entire system.
- A clean repair area is essential. Always clean the reservoir and cap thoroughly before removing the cap. The slightest amount of dirt in the fluid may plug an orifice and impair the system function. Perform repairs after components have been thoroughly cleaned; use only denatured alcohol to clean components. Do not allow ABS components to come into contact with any substance containing mineral oil; this includes used shop rags.
- The Controller Anti-lock Brakes (CAB) is a microprocessor similar to other computer units in the vehicle. Insure that the ignition switch is **OFF** before removing or installing controller harnesses. Avoid static electricity discharge at or near the controller.

1. Turn the ignition switch **OFF** and leave it **OFF** during repairs unless specifically directed otherwise. Alternately, the negative battery cable may be disconnected; it must remain disconnected throughout the repairs.

2. Firmly apply and release the brake pedal a minimum of 40 times, using at least 50 lbs. of pedal force.

3. The pedal feel will become noticeably harder when the accumulator is completely discharged. Once this is felt, apply the brake pedal forcefully a few additional times. This will remove all hydraulic pressure from the system.

4. Do not turn the ignition switch **ON** or reconnect the battery cable after depressurizing the system unless service procedures specifically require it or all service operations have been performed.

NOTE: After the reserve pressure is depleted, the fluid level in the reservoir may rise above the MAX fill

mark. This is normal; the reservoir will not overflow unless the system was over filled to begin with.

5. Always wear safety goggles when disconnecting lines and fittings.

DIAGNOSTIC PROCEDURE

Diagnosis of the ABS system consists of 3 general steps, performed in order. The visual or preliminary inspection is always required before any other steps are taken. A functional test drive is performed to confirm the existence of a problem. The functional test will indicate the need for specific diagnostic tests to be performed.

Some diagnostic tests will require the ignition being left **ON** for a period of time. This could lead to lowered battery voltage and erroneous voltage readings within the system. Unless the battery is known to be in sound condition, connect a slow-charger to the battery when performing extended testing.

Visual Inspection

Before diagnosing an apparent ABS problem, make absolutely certain that the normal braking system is in correct working order. Many common brake problems (dragging lining, seepage, etc.) will affect the ABS system. A visual check of specific system components may reveal problems creating an apparent ABS malfunction. Performing this inspection may reveal a simple failure, thus eliminating extended diagnostic time.

1. Depressurize the system.
2. Inspect the brake fluid level in the reservoir.
3. Inspect brake lines, hoses, master cylinder assembly, brake calipers and cylinders for leakage.
4. Visually check brake lines and hoses for excessive wear, heat damage, punctures, contact with other parts, missing clips or holders, blockage or crimping.
5. Check the calipers and wheel cylinders for rust or corrosion. Check for proper sliding action if applicable.
6. Check the caliper and wheel cylinder pistons for freedom of motion during application and release.
7. Inspect the wheel speed sensors for proper mounting and connections.
8. Inspect the tone wheels for broken teeth or poor mounting.
9. Inspect the wheels and tires on the vehicle. They must be of the same size and type to generate accurate speed signals. Check also for approximately equal tire pressures.
10. Confirm the fault occurrence with the operator. Certain driver induced faults, such as not releasing the parking brake fully, will set a fault code and trigger the dash warning light(s). Excessive wheel spin on low-traction surfaces, high speed acceleration or riding the brake pedal may also set fault codes and trigger a warning lamp. These induced faults are not system failures but examples of vehicle performance outside the parameters of the CAB.
11. The most common cause of intermittent faults is not a failed sensor but a loose, corroded or dirty connector. Incorrect installation of the wheel speed sensor will cause a loss of wheel speed signal. Check harness and component connectors carefully.

Functional Check

If the visual inspections do not lead to resolution of the problem, the test drive, or functional check must be preformed. Keep in mind that the vehicle driven, may have a problem affecting its braking ability; check the brakes at a very low speed in a safe location before beginning an extended drive. A recommended method of testing and test driving for an ABS fault is:

1. Turn the ignition **ON** without starting the engine. Wait until both the BRAKE and ANTI-LOCK warning lights turn off. This will allow the pump to charge the system; if either or both warning lamps do not go off, proceed to Step 3.

2. Turn the ignition switch **OFF** for 15 seconds.
3. Start the engine. Wait for displays to achieve normal operation.
4. Place the shift lever in **P**. Using a full pedal stroke, slowly depress the brake pedal and release it.
5. Drive the vehicle carefully for a short distance. Achieve a speed of at least 20 mph; bring the vehicle to a full stop then accelerate to at least 20 mph.
6. If either the BRAKE or ANTI-LOCK warning lamps comes on, a fault has been detected by the CAB and, in most cases, a fault code has been entered into the memory.

Intermittent Faults

Most intermittent faults are caused by loose or faulty connections or wiring. Always check suspect circuits for poor mating of connector halves, improperly formed or damaged terminals. Any sign of corrosion or entry of foreign matter within a connecter shell is cause for suspicion.

Most of the system faults will cause the ABS system to be disabled for the entire ignition on-off cycle. These are termed latching faults; in this case the warning lamp(s) will remain illuminated, even if the problem self-corrects during operation. There are some conditions which will allow the ABS function to be restored during a driving cycle; if one of these non–latching conditions exists and then ceases to exist, the warning lamp(s) will go off. When diagnosing a complaint of intermittent warning lamp illumination, investigate the following causes:

● Low system voltage. Once the CAB detects the correct voltage, the ABS function will be restored.
● Low brake fluid level. Once the fluid level sensor reads a normal level, system function is restored.
● Low accumulator pressure. May occur after long or hard stopping or as a result of riding the brake pedal. Once correct minimum pressure is achieved, the system is restored.
● Any interruption of power to either the CAB or the hydraulic assembly. Check the main power circuits, relays, fusible links and all related wiring.

Diagnostic Mode

NOTE:Connect the DRB II or equivalent tester, according to instructions furnished with the tool. The system will enter diagnostic mode and prompt the operator through the assorted system checks and tests.

Component Replacement

—————— CAUTION ——————
This brake system uses a hydraulic accumulator which, when fully charged, contains brake fluid at very high pressure. Before disconnecting any hydraulic lines, hoses or fittings be certain that the accumulator pressure is completely relieved. Failure to depressurize the accumulator may result in personal injury and/or vehicle damage.

FILLING THE SYSTEM

1. Turn the ignition **OFF** and leave it **OFF** during inspection.
2. Depressurize the system.
3. Thoroughly clean the reservoir cap and the surrounding area.
4. Carefully remove reservoir cap, keeping all dirt out of the reservoir. Inspect the fluid level; fill to the top of the white screen in the front strainer if required. Do not overfill. Use only fresh DOT 3 brake fluid from unopened containers. Do not use any fluid containing a petroleum base. Do not use any fluid which has been exposed to water or moisture. Failure to use the correct fluid will affect system function and component life.
5. Replace the reservoir cap.

DRB-II MESSAGE	WARNING LAMPS		POSSIBLE CAUSES	DETECTED	LATCHING
	BRAKE	ANTI-LOCK			
CAB FAULT	—	ON	—Internal CAB fault	Anytime key on	YES
MODULATOR FAULT	—	ON	—Shorted or open solenoid or solenoid driver —Loose connector pin —Internal CAB fault	After drive-off until next ignition reset	YES
RIGHT REAR LEFT REAR RIGHT FRONT } SENSOR LEFT FRONT	—	ON	—Missing sensor signal caused by defective wheel speed sensor —CAB fault	Vehicle speed above 15 mph	YES
RIGHT REAR LEFT REAR RIGHT FRONT } CONTINUITY LEFT FRONT	—	ON	—Open or short in sensor, wiring or CAB	After start-up check, vehicle not in motion	YES
SYSTEM RELAY FAULT	—	ON	—System relay stuck on	During start-up check	YES
SOLENOID UNDERVOLTAGE FAULT	—	ON	—Low battery, low vehicle voltage —Open circuit on system relay output —System relay malfunction	During drive-off check	NO
ANTILOCK LAMP RELAY	—	—	—Open or stuck relay —Open wiring	During start-up check	NO
ANTILOCK LAMP	*	—	—Failed bulb or open wiring *If this code is set and a 2nd fault is detected, the brake lamp will light	During start-up check	—
LOW FLUID/PARK BRAKE FAULT	ON	ON ABOVE 3 MPH	—Low brake fluid —Parking brake engaged —Short to ground on low fluid wire	Anytime key on	NO
PRIMARY PRESSURE/ DIFFERENTIAL PRESSURE FAULT	ON DURING BRAKING	ON DURING BRAKING	—Hydraulic leak —Air in circuits —Malfunctioning pressure transducers	Anytime with brakes applied	NO
BOOST PRESSURE FAULT	ON DURING BRAKING	ON DURING BRAKING	—Malfunction in hydraulic booster or pressure transducers	Anytime with brakes applied	NO
EXCESS DECAY FAULT	—	ON	—Modulator fault —Incorrect tone wheels —Sensor fault —Hydroplaning —Long stop on ice	During ABS operation, if any 2 decay valves operate for more than 2 seconds	NO
LOW ACCUMULATOR FAULT	ON	ON	Malfunction in pump/motor system: —Dual function pressure switch —Pump/motor relay —Pump/motor assembly —Wiring faults	Anytime. Warning lamps light immed. Fault code sets after 2 min. of continuous detection	NO
NO RESPONSE	—	—	—Open circuit in diagnostic or data wiring or loose connectors —Defective CAB —Ignition off	Not a fault code. DRB-II cannot communicate with CAB.	—

DRB-II Fault Messages — Bendix ABS System 10

Cavity	Circuit	Function	Cavity	Circuit	Function
1	PS5 20YL	Right Rear Wheel Sensor	41		Not Used
2	PS7 20YL	Right Rear Wheel Sensor	42	B42 20BR/WT*	Left Front Build Valve
3	PS6 20LG	Left Rear Wheel Sensor	43	B43 20DG/BK*	Left Front Decay Valve
4	PS8 20LG	Left Rear Wheel Sensor	44	—	Not Used
5	P9 16BK	Signal Ground	45	B45 20WT/LG*	Left Front Isolate Valve
6	PS1 20WT	Right Front Wheel Sensor	46	B46 20BR/RD*	Right Front Build Valve
7	PS3 20WT	Right Front Wheel Sensor	47	J3 16RD/LB*	Solenoid 12V
8	PS2 20RD	Left Front Wheel Sensor	48	B48 20DB/WT*	Right Front Decay Valve
9	PS4 20RD	Left Front Wheel Sensor	49	B49 20WT/TN*	Right Front Isolate Valve
10	B10 20RD/BK*	Transducer Ground	50	J3 16RD/LB*	Solenoid 12V
11	B11 20WT/VT*	Diagnostic Enable	51	B51 20WT/BK*	Left Rear Isolate Valve
12	B12 20OR	Data Out	52	B52 20BR/TN*	Rear Build Valve
13	D4 18WT/TN*	Stop Lamp Switch	53	—	Not Used
14	P5 20GY/BK*	Brake Lamp/Low Fluid/Park	54	B54 20DG/OR*	Rear Decay Valve
15	P7 20LG*	Antilock Warning Lamp	55	B55 20WT/PK*	Right Rear Isolate Valve
16	B16 20BK/LB*	Low Fluid Output	56	—	Not Used
17	B17 14RD	Warning Pressure	57	B57 20BR/BK*	System Relay
18	B18 20WT	Primary Pres./Diff. Pres.	58	B58 20GY/LB*	Transducer Actuation 5V
19	B19 20DB	Boost Pressure	59	—	Not Used
21	through	Not Used	60	J2 14DB	Ignition 12V

ABS controller 60 pin connector — pin identification

Isolation Valves—open, allowing fluid to flow from primary and secondary circuits to wheel brakes.

Decay and Build Valves—closed.

The brake pedal is in the released position, the booster servo circuit is closed to accumulator pressure. Booster servo circuit, primary and secondary circuits receive fluid from fluid reservoir. All brake circuits closed (check valves) to fluid from booster servo circuit.

System schematic: Normal driving, brakes off — ABS equipped models

Isolation Valves—open to primary and secondary master cylinder fluid supply.
Decay and Build Valves—closed.

The brake pedal is applied. The travel of the brake pedal closes primary, secondary and booster servo circuits from fluid supply at the fluid reservoir. Brake fluid from the primary and secondary circuits flows through the open isolation valves and applies the wheel brakes. Fluid from the booster servo circuit does not flow to the wheel brakes. The fluid flow is blocked by the closed build valves and check valves.

Power Assist—The boost control valve shuttles between its three positions to provide power assisted braking.

System schematic: Normal driving, Brakes applied — ABS equipped models

For explanation purposes, assume all speed sensors are sending the same wheel speed information, requiring the same modulation at the same rate.

Isolation Valves—closed, isolating the wheel brakes from master cylinder primary and secondary fluid supplies. Build and decay valves are closed preventing any fluid from reaching the open isolation valves.
Decay and Build Valves—closed.

System schematic: ABS braking, hold pressure — ABS equipped models

Isolation Valves—closed, isolating the wheel brakes from the master cylinder primary and secondary fluid supplies.

Decay Valves—open, allowing release of fluid through decay valve to the fluid reservoir.

Build Valves—closed, blocking booster servo circuit fluid to wheel brakes.

System schematic: ABS braking, Decay pressure — ABS equipped models

Isolation Valves—closed, isolating wheel brakes from master cylinder primary and secondary fluid supplies and open to booster servo circuit pressure through open build valves.

Decay Valves—closed.

Build Valves—open, allowing booster servo circuit pressure to flow to wheel brakes through the isolation valves.

Power Assist—The boost control valve shuttles between its three positions to provide power assisted braking.

System schematic: ABS braking, build pressure — ABS equipped models

ABS system wiring schematic

BLEEDING THE SYSTEM

The brake system must be bled any time air is permitted to enter the system, through loosened or disconnected lines. It is important to realize that air in the system, will cause a primary pressure fault to be set in the controller.

The system must be bled any time a hose or line is disconnected. Bleeding is also required after replacement of the hydraulic unit, caliper or wheel cylinder.

When bleeding any part of the system, the reservoir must remain close to FULL at all times. Check the level frequently and top off the fluid as needed. Do not allow the pump to run continuously for more than 60 seconds. If it becomes necessary to run the pump extensively, allow several minutes of cooling time between each 60 second operation period. Severe damage will oc-

The dummy cap must be installed, when using pressure bleeding equipment

cur to the pump if it is not allowe‚
pump with no fluid in the system

Pressure Bleeding the Brake Lines

Only diaphragm pressure bleeding equipment should be u‚
The diaphragm prevents the entry of dirt and moisture into the
fluid.

1. Depressurize the system. The ignition must remain **OFF** throughout the bleeding procedure.
2. Thoroughly clean the reservoir caps and the surrounding area.
3. Remove both reservoir caps. Install the pressure bleeder adapter on one port and the dummy cap on the other port.
4. Attach pressure bleeding equipment. Charge the pressure bleeder to approximately 20 psi.
5. Brakes should be bled in the following order: Left rear, right rear, left front and right front. Connect a transparent hose to the caliper bleed screw. Submerge the other end of the hose in clean brake fluid in a clear glass container.
6. Turn the pressure bleeder on; open the caliper bleed screw ½–¾ turn and allow fluid into the container. Leave the bleeder open until the fluid is free of air bubbles.

NOTE: If the reservoir was drained or the hydraulic assembly removed from the car before bleeding, pump the brake pedal slowly once or twice while the bleed screw is open and fluid is flowing. This will aid the escape of air from the hydraulic assembly.

7. Close the bleeder screw, tightening it to 7.5 ft. lbs. (10 Nm).
8. Repeat the bleeding procedure at the other calipers. When bleeding is complete, close the pressure bleeder valve and slowly unscrew the adapter from the fluid reservoir. Failure to release reservoir pressure slowly will result in brake fluid spraying both the vehicle and those around it.
9. Use a clean syringe or similar device to remove the excess fluid from the reservoir. The system must not be left over filled.
10. Install the reservoir caps. Turn the ignition switch **ON**; the pump should charge the system, stopping after approximately 30 seconds or less.

Proper nut thread size and tube routing — ABS equipped models

PRESSURE HOSE
DRAULIC FITTING

PUMP MOTOR CONNECTOR

BATTERY TRAY

HIGH PRESSURE HOSE TUBE NUT

HIGH PRESSURE HOSE CLIP

Hose and line routing in engine compartment — ABS equipped models

Manual Bleeding of the Brake Lines

The individual lines may be bled manually at each wheel using the traditional 2 person method.

1. Depressurize the system. The ignition must remain **OFF** throughout the bleeding procedure.

2. Calipers should be bled in the following order: Left rear, right rear, left front and right front. Connect a transparent hose to the caliper bleed screw. Submerge the other end of the hose in clean brake fluid in a clear glass container.

3. Slowly pump the brake pedal several times. Use full strokes of the pedal and allow 5 seconds between strokes. After 2 or 3 strokes, hold pressure on the pedal keeping it at the bottom of its travel.

4. With pressure held on the pedal, open the bleed screw ½–¾ turn. Leave the bleed screw open until fluid stops flowing from the hose. Tighten the bleed screw and release the pedal.

5. Repeat Steps 3 and 4 until air-free fluid flows from the hose. Tighten the caliper bleed screw to 7.5 ft. lbs. (10 Nm).

6. Repeat the sequence at each remaining caliper.

NOTE: Check the fluid level in the reservoir frequently and maintain it near the full level.

7. When the bleeding is complete, bring the fluid level in the reservoir to the correct level. Install the reservoir cap. Turn the ignition switch **ON** and allow the system to pressurize.

Pump/Motor Assembly

REMOVAL AND INSTALLATION

———————— CAUTION ————————

This brake system uses a hydraulic accumulator which, when fully charged, contains brake fluid at very high pressure. Before disconnecting any hydraulic lines, hoses or fittings be certain that the accumulator pressure is completely relieved. Failure to depressurize the accumulator may result in personal injury and/or vehicle damage.

1. Disconnect the negative battery cable.
2. Depressurize the brake system.
3. Remove the fresh air intake ducts from the engine.
4. On Van/wagon vehicles, loosen the low pressure hose

clamp at the hydraulic unit. Remove the clip holding the high pressure line to the battery tray.

5. Disconnect the electrical connectors running across the engine compartment in the vicinity of the pump/motor high and low pressure hoses. One of these connectors is the one for the pump/motor assembly.

6. Disconnect the high and low pressure hoses from the hydraulic assembly. Cap or plug the reservoir fitting.

7. Disconnect the pump/motor electrical connector from the engine mount.

8. Remove the heat shield bolt from the front of the pump bracket. Remove the heat shield.

9. Lift the pump/motor assembly from the bracket and out of the vehicle.

To install:

10. Fit the pump motor assembly onto the bracket; install the heat shield and its retaining bolt.

11. Install the pump/motor electrical connector to the engine mount.

12. Connect the high and low pressure hose to the hydraulic assembly. Tighten the high pressure line to 145 inch lbs. (16 Nm). Tighten the hose clamp on the low pressure hose to 10 inch lbs (1 Nm).

13. Connect the electrical connectors which were removed for access.

14. Install the high pressure line retaining clip to the battery tray if it was removed.

15. Install the fresh air intake ducts.

16. Bleed the brake system.

High Pressure and Return Hoses

REMOVAL AND INSTALLATION

1. Remove the pump/motor assembly.

2. Carefully cut the wire ties (Van/wagons, 4 ties; others, 2 ties)) holding the hoses and wiring harnesses.

3. Remove the banjo bolt from the pump/motor assembly and remove the hoses.

4. When installing, lubricate the rubber O-ring for the high and low pressure hoses with clean brake fluid before installation.

5. Place the hoses in position and install the banjo bolt.

6. Use care when routing the wiring along the hoses; install new wire ties in the proper locations. Noted that the wiring harness is not held within all the wire ties.

7. Install the pump/motor assembly.

Hydraulic Assembly

REMOVAL AND INSTALLATION

———————— CAUTION ————————

This brake system uses a hydraulic accumulator which, when fully charged, contains brake fluid at very high pressure. Before disconnecting any hydraulic lines, hoses or fittings be certain that the accumulator pressure is completely relieved. Failure to depressurize the accumulator may result in personal injury and/or vehicle damage.

1. Depressurize the brake system.

2. Remove the air cleaner. Additionally, remove the windshield washer fluid bottle.

3. Disconnect all electrical connectors at the hydraulic assembly.

4. Use a syringe to remove as much fluid as possible from the reservoir.

5. Disconnect and remove the banjo bolt holding the high pressure hose to the hydraulic assembly.

6. Remove the hose from the steel tube and cap the tube.

STRAP HIGH AND LOW PRESSURE
HOSES TOGETHER—NOT ELECTRICAL
HARNESS

LOW PRESSURE LINE

HIGH PRESSURE LINE

TIE STRAP HIGH PRESSURE LINE AND
ELECTRICAL HARNESS ONLY

BATTERY TRAY CLIP

WRAP ALL HOSES AND ELECTRICAL
HARNESS

Correct position of tie straps — ABS equipped models

HYDRAULIC ASSEMBLY

PUSH ROD

PUSH ROD MUST BE INSTALLED IN
POSITION SHOWN

GASKET

SPACER

PIVOT SHAFT

MOUNTING NUT

RETAINER CLIP

Hydraulic assembly mounting and under dash connections — ABS equipped models

7. Disconnect the brake lines from the hydraulic assembly.
8. Use a small flat tool to release the retainer clip on the brake pedal pin. The center tang on the clip must be moved back enough to allow the lock tab to clear the pin. Disconnect the pushrod from the pedal pin.
9. Under the dash at the firewall, remove the 4 bolts holding the hydraulic assembly.
10. Remove the hydraulic assembly from the engine compartment.
To install:
11. Position the hydraulic assembly and install the retaining nuts. Tighten the nuts to 21 ft. lbs. (28 Nm).
12. Coat the contact surface of the pedal pin with all-purpose grease. Connect the pushrod to the pedal pin and install a new retainer clip. Make certain the lock tab on the retainer is firmly engaged.

WARNING: The hydraulic assembly pushrod must be in the correct position before assembly.

13. Install the brake lines and tighten them to 12 ft. lbs. (16 Nm). If the proportioning valves were removed, reinstall and tighten them to 30 ft. lbs. (40 Nm).

NOTE: Be certain the brake tubes are connected to the proper location.

14. Install the return hose to the reservoir or the steel tube.

15. Before connecting the pressure hose to the hydraulic assembly, make certain the washers are in their correct positions. Install the hose and tighten the banjo bolt to 13. ft. lbs. (17 Nm).
16. Fill the reservoir to the top of the strainer screen.
17. Connect all the electrical connectors to the hydraulic assembly.
18. Bleed the entire brake system.
19. Install the air cleaner and washer bottle (Van/wagon) and the fresh air intake duct and clamps.

Hydraulic Reservoir

REMOVAL AND INSTALLATION

———————— **CAUTION** ————————
This brake system uses a hydraulic accumulator which, when fully charged, contains brake fluid at very high pressure. Before disconnecting any hydraulic lines, hoses or fittings be certain that the accumulator pressure is completely relieved. Failure to depressurize the accumulator may result in personal injury and/or vehicle damage.

1. Depressurize the brake system.
2. Using a syringe or similar tool, remove as much brake fluid as possible from the reservoir.
3. Disconnect the high pressure hose banjo fitting and re-

move the hydraulic bladder accumulator from the hydraulic assembly.

4. Remove the 3 retaining pins holding the reservoir to the hydraulic assembly.

5. Use a blunt prying tool carefully installed between the reservoir and hydraulic assembly body to lift the reservoir. Use a rocking motion to gently lift the reservoir free of the grommets.

NOTE: Be extremely careful to avoid damaging or puncturing the reservoir.

6. Remove the fluid level sensor switch from the reservoir.

7. Use fingers only to remove the grommets from the hydraulic assembly. Discard the grommets.

To install:

8. Lubricate new grommets with clean brake fluid and install them onto the hydraulic assembly. Always use new grommets.

9. Install the fluid level switch into the reservoir. Position the reservoir on the grommets and press it into place using hand pressure only. A rocking motion is helpful; make certain the reservoir is fully seated in all 3 grommets.

NOTE: Do not attempt to pound the reservoir into place with a hammer or other tools. Damage will result.

10. Install the 3 locking pins to hold the reservoir in place.

11. Reinstall the high pressure hose banjo fitting onto the hydraulic assembly and torque the fitting to 10 ft. lbs. (13 Nm).

12. Install the hydraulic bladder accumulator onto the hydraulic assembly and tighten the fitting to 30 ft. lbs. (40 Nm).

13. Fill the reservoir to the top of the strainer screen with fresh clean fluid.

14. Bleed the entire brake system including the booster.

Proportioning Valves
REMOVAL AND INSTALLATION

—————————— CAUTION ——————————
This brake system uses a hydraulic accumulator which, when fully charged, contains brake fluid at very high pressure. Before disconnecting any hydraulic lines, hoses or fittings be certain that the accumulator pressure is completely relieved. Failure to depressurize the accumulator may result in personal injury and/or vehicle damage.

1. Depressurize the brake system.

2. Remove the air cleaner and intake duct.

3. Disconnect the high pressure and return hoses from the hydraulic unit.

4. Remove the brake tube and fitting from the proportioning valve.

5. Remove the proportioning valve from the hydraulic assembly.

To install:

6. Install the valve to the hydraulic assembly and tighten it to 30 ft. lbs. (40 Nm).

7. Install the brake line and tighten to 12 ft. lbs. (16 Nm).

8. Install the high pressure and return hoses. Tighten the high pressure hose fitting to 145 inch lbs (16 Nm.).

9. Install the air cleaner and the ductwork.

10. Only the affected brake circuit needs bleeding.

Bladder Accumulator
REMOVAL AND INSTALLATION

—————————— CAUTION ——————————
This brake system uses a hydraulic accumulator which, when fully charged, contains brake fluid at very high pressure. Before disconnecting any hydraulic lines, hoses or fittings be certain that the accumulator pressure is completely relieved. Failure to depressurize the accumulator may result in personal injury and/or vehicle damage.

Controller Anti-lock Brake (CAB) mounting location

1. Depressurize the brake system.

2. Loosen the accumulator fitting at the hydraulic assembly and remove the accumulator assembly.

3. Reinstall the accumulator and tighten the to 30 ft. lbs. (40 Nm).

4. Turn the ignition switch **ON**. Allow the pump to pressurize the system. Inspect the accumulator area carefully for any sign of leakage.

5. If any seepage or leaking is noted, turn the ignition **OFF** and fully depressurize the system before beginning any repairs.

Controller Anti-Lock Brakes (CAB)

REMOVAL AND INSTALLATION

1. Turn the ignition switch to the **OFF** position or disconnect the negative battery cable.

2. Remove the speed control servo (cruise control).

3. Double check that the ignition switch is **OFF** or that the battery cable is disconnected.

4. Disconnect the 60-pin wiring connector at the CAB.

5. Remove the 3 CAB mounting bolts and remove the controller from the vehicle.

To install:

6. Install the CAB and tighten the mounting bolts.

7. After checking that the ignition is **OFF** or the battery disconnected, connect the 60-pin harness to the controller. Make certain that the connector is properly seated and locked in place. Do not force the connector into place.

8. Reinstall the speed control servo.

9. If the vehicle is elevated, lower it to the ground. Connect the negative battery cable if it was removed.

10. Drive the vehicle following the test drive procedures listed under Diagnosis and Testing. If a warning lamp is on and/or a fault code set (not previously present), closely inspect the 60-pin connector at the CAB for looseness or improper mating.

Wheel Speed Sensors

REMOVAL AND INSTALLATION

Front Wheel

1. Elevate and safely support the vehicle. Remove the wheel and tire.

2. Remove the screw from the sensor retaining clip.

Front wheel speed sensor cable routing — ABS equipped models

Rear wheel speed sensor cable routing — All Wheel Drive (AWD) ABS equipped models

3. Carefully remove the sensor wiring grommet from the fender shield.

4. Disconnect the sensor wiring from the ABS harness.

5. Remove the screws holding the sensor wiring tube to the fender well.

6. Remove the retainer grommets from the bracket on the strut.

7. Remove the fastener holding the sensor head.

8. Carefully remove the sensor head from the steering knuckle. Do not use pliers on the sensor head; if it is seized in place, use a hammer and small punch to tap the edge of the sensor ear. The tapping and side-to-side motion will free the unit.

To install:

9. Before installation, coat the sensor with high temperature multi-purpose grease.

Rear wheel speed sensor cable routing — Front Wheel Drive (FWD) ABS equipped models

10. Connect the speed sensor to the ABS harness.

11. Push the sensor assembly grommet into the hole in the fender shield. Install the retainer clip and screw.

12. Install the sensor grommets into the brackets on the fender shield and strut. Install the retainer clip at the strut.

13. On Van/wagons, install the sensor wiring tube and tighten the retaining bolts to 35 inch lbs. (4 Nm).

14. Install the sensor to the knuckle. Install the retaining screw and tighten it to 60 inch lbs. (7 Nm).

NOTE: Proper installation of the sensor and its wiring is critical to system function. Make certain that wiring is installed in all retainers and clips. Wiring must be protected from moving parts and not be stretched during suspension movements.

15. Install the tire and wheel. Lower the vehicle to the ground.

Rear Wheel

1. Elevate and safely support the vehicle. Remove the wheel and tire.

2. Remove the sensor assembly grommet from the underbody and pull the harness through the hole in the body.

3. Disconnect the sensor wiring from the ABS harness.

4. Remove the 4 clips holding the sensor wiring along the underside.

5. Remove the attaching bracket holding the wiring to the frame rail.

6. On FWD Van/wagons, remove the nuts from the rear axle U-bolts. Remove the sensor mounting bracket.

7. Remove the fastener holding the sensor head.

8. Carefully remove the sensor head from the adapter assembly. Do not use pliers on the sensor head; if it is seized in place, use a hammer and small punch to tap the edge of the sensor ear. The tapping and side-to-side motion will free the unit.

To install:

9. Position the sensor bracket under the brake tube and start the outer attaching bolt by hand.

10. Align the brake tube clip and the bracket; install the retaining bolt.

11. Tighten both retaining bolts to 145 inch lbs. (17 Nm).

12. Before installation coat the sensor with high temperature, multi-purpose grease.

13. Install the sensor head into the rear axle and install the bolt. Tighten the bolt to 60 inch lbs. (7 Nm).

14. Carefully bend the rubber hose section of the sensor assembly toward the rear of the vehicle. Position the anti-rotation tab correctly and install the frame rail bracket. Tighten the bolt to 50 inch lbs. (5 Nm).

15. Connect the sensor wiring to the rear harness. Push the sensor assembly wiring grommet back into the hole.

15. Install the rear sensor grommet retaining bracket and tighten the 2 retaining bolts to 50 inch lbs. (5 Nm). Make certain the bracket does not pinch the sensor wiring.

16. Route the sensor wiring along the vehicle frame rail and install the 4 retaining clips.

17. install the rear wheel and tire; lower the vehicle to the ground.

Tone Rings

REMOVAL AND INSTALLATION

The front toothed wheel or tone ring is an integral part of the outer Constant Velocity (CV) joint. Should the ring become unusable, the CV-joint must be replaced. Likewise, the rear tone ring is an integral part of the hub assembly and cannot be replaced individually.

The tone rings may be inspected in place on the vehicle. After gaining access, inspect for any evidence of contact between the speed sensor and the ring. If any contact occurred, the cause must be found and corrected before new parts are installed.

Teeth on the wheels should be unbroken and uncracked. The teeth and the valleys on the ring should be reasonably clean. Excessive run out of the tone ring can cause an erratic wheel speed signal. Replace the ring if run out exceeds 0.010 in. (0.25mm).

The air gap between the tone ring and the sensor is not adjustable. It is established by the correct installation of the wheel speed sensor.

FRONT DISC BRAKES

────── **CAUTION** ──────

Brake shoes contain asbestos, which has been determined to be a cancer causing agent. Never clean the brake surfaces with compressed air! Avoid inhaling any dust from any brake surface! When cleaning brake surfaces, use a commercially available brake cleaning fluid.

The front disc brakes are of the single position, floating caliper type. The caliper "floats" through a rubber bushing, inserted into the inboard portion of the caliper, via a guide pin that is threaded into the mounting adapter. the mounting adapter for the caliper if fitted with two machined abutments that position and align the caliper. The guide pin and bushing, on the Kelsey-Hayes type caliper, control the movement of the caliper when the brakes are applied, providing a clamping force. The A.T.E. type caliper, uses two steel guide pins and mounting bushings to control the movement of the caliper upon brake application.

Disc Brake Pads

INSPECTION

1. Loosen the front wheel lug nuts slightly. Raise and support the front of the vehicle safely on jackstands. Remove the front wheel.

2. When the front wheels are off, the cutout built into the caliper housing will be exposed. Look through the opening and

Kelsey Hayes single pin disc brake caliper — exploded view

check the lining thickness of the inner and outer pads.

3. If a visual inspection does not give a clear picture of lining wear, a physical check will be necessary.

4. Refer to the following section covering pad removal and installation for instructions.

REMOVAL AND INSTALLATION

Kelsey-Hayes Type

NOTE: Three anti-rattle clips are provided on each brake caliper, take note of locations for installation purposes.

1. The Kelsey Hayes caliper uses one mounting pin. Loosen the wheel lug nuts slightly. Raise and safely support the front of the vehicle on jackstands. Remove the front wheel and tire assemblies.

CAUTION

On models equipped with ABS, the system pressure must be released before disconnecting any of the hydraulic lines. Failure to do so, can cause personal injury.

---

2. Siphon about one quarter of the brake fluid from the master cylinder and replace the cover caps.

3. Use the proper size socket wrench and remove the threaded caliper guide pin.

4. Insert a small prybar between the front edge of the caliper and the adapter rail. Apply steady upward pressure to loosen the adhesive seals. Remove the caliper by slowly sliding it up and off the adapter and disc rotor.

Removing the caliper and brake shoes as an assembly

Prying the outboard shoe assembly from the caliper

5. Support the caliper by hanging it out of the way on wire. Do not allow the caliper to be supported by the brake hose.

6. Observe the location of the anti-rattle clips. One clip is on the top of the inboard (closes to axle) brake pad. Another clip is on the bottom of the outboard brake pad, and the third is installed on the top finger of the caliper.

7. Slide the outboard brake pad from the adapter. Remove the brake disc rotor and remove the inboard pad.

8. Measure the brake lining and pad thickness. If the combined thickness at the thinnest point of the is ⅛ in. (3mm) or less replace both front wheel brake pad assemblies.

To install:

9. Check around the caliper piston and boot for signs of brake fluid leakage. Inspect the dust boot around the caliper piston for cuts and breaks. If the boot is damaged or fluid leakage is visible, the caliper should be serviced. Check the adapter and caliper mounting surfaces for rust and dirt, clean them with a wire brush.

10. Remove the protective paper from the gaskets mounted on the metal part of the brake pads. Install the anti-rattle clips in position. Install inner brake pad on the adapter.

11. Install the brake disc rotor and outer brake pad.

12. Press the caliper back into the caliper until it bottoms. If may be necessary to place a small piece of wood on the piston and use a C-clamp to retract the piston. If so, tighten the clamp with slow steady pressure. Stop when resistance is felt.

13. Lower the caliper over the brake pads and disc rotor. Install the caliper guide pin and tighten to 25-35 ft. lbs. Take care not to cross thread the guide pin.

14. After both calipers have been installed, fill the master cylinder and bleed the brakes if the caliper were rebuilt. If the calipers were not serviced, pump the brakes until a firm brake pedal is obtained.

15. Install the front wheels and lower the vehicle. After the vehicle is lowered, check the lug nut torque and tighten to required specification to 95 ft. lbs. Road test the vehicle and make several firm but not hard stops to wear off any dirt from the pads or rotor.

A.T.E. Type

NOTE: The caliper is equipped with one holddown spring running across the outboard fingers of the caliper, and is also equipped with an inner shoe to piston mounting clip.

1. The A.T.E. caliper uses two mounting pins. Loosen the wheel lugs slightly. Raise and safely support the front of the vehicle.

2. Remove the wheel and tire assembly.

─────────── CAUTION ───────────

On models equipped with ABS, the system pressure must be released before disconnecting any of the hydraulic lines. Failure to do so, can cause personal injury.

3. Loosen, but do not remove the two steel caliper guide pins. Back the pins out until the caliper can be moved freely.

4. Pull the lower end of the caliper out from the steering knuckle support. Roll the caliper up and away from the disc rotor. The disc brake pads will remain located in their caliper positions.

5. Take care, while servicing the pads, that strain is not put on the brake hose.

6. Pry the outboard pad toward the bottom opened end of the caliper. The pad is retained by a captured clip. Remove the pad.

7. Remove the inboard pad by pulling it outward from the caliper piston. It is retained by a captive clip.

To install:

8. Inspect the caliper. Check for piston seal leaks and boot damage. Service the caliper as required.

9. Press the caliper piston slowly back into the caliper bore. Use a small block of wood and a C-clamp, if necessary. Tighten the clamp slowly, and make sure the piston is not cocked. Gently bottom the piston in the caliper.

10. The inboard pads are interchangeable, the outboard pads are marked with an **L** or **R** relating to the side of the vehicle they are to be used on.

11. Place the inboard pad clip into the caliper piston and push into position on the piston.

12. Place the outboard pad retainer clip over the ears of the caliper and slide the pad into position. If the replacement pads are equipped with a noise suppression gasket, remove the protective paper from the gasket before installation.

13. Lower the caliper over the disc rotor and align the holddown spring under the machined surface of the steering knuckle. Install the caliper mounting pins, take care not to cross thread and tighten the pins to 18-26 ft. lbs. Pump the brake pedal several times to move the pads against the rotor. If the caliper has been rebuilt, or other system service completed, bleed the brake system.

14. Install the wheel and tire assembly. Lower the vehicle. Do not move the vehicle until a firm brake pedal is verified.

Caliper

OVERHAUL

1. Remove the caliper as described in the previous section.

2. Place rags on the upper control arm and place the caliper on top of the rags. Take care not to put strain on the brake hose. Place a small block of wood between the caliper piston and outer fingers.

3. Have a helper slowly depress the brake pedal to push the piston from the caliper bore using hydraulic pressure. If both front caliper pistons are to be removed, disconnect the brake hose, to the first caliper, at the frame bracket; plug the brake tube and repeat Steps 2 and 3. Never use air pressure to blow the pistons from their bores. The pistons are made of a plastic composition and can damage easily, or can fly out and cause personal injury.

4. Disconnect the flexible brake line from the caliper and remove the caliper to work area.

5. Position the caliper between padded jaws of a bench vise. Do not overtighten since excessive pressure can distort the caliper bore. Remove the dust boot.

6. Use a plastic tool and work the piston seal from the mounting groove. Do not use a metal tool; damage can result to the bore or burrs can be created on the edges of the machined seal groove.

7. Remove the guide pin bushing from the caliper. A wooden dowel makes a good tool for this purpose.

To install:

8. Clean all parts using a safe solvent or alcohol and blow dry if compressed air is on hand.

9. Inspect the piston bore for pitting or scores. Light scratches or pitting can be cleaned with crocus cloth and brake fluid. Deep scratches or pitting require honing.

10. Caliper hones are available from an auto parts supplier. Do not remove more than 0.001 in. (0.025mm) of material from the bore. Deep scratches or pitting require caliper replacement.

11. After cleaning up the caliper bore with crocus cloth or hone, remove all the dirt and grit by flushing the caliper with brake fluid. After flushing, wipe dry with a lintless rag. Flush the caliper a second time and dry.

12. Carefully reclamp the caliper in the padded vise jaws. Dip the new piston seal in clean brake fluid and install in caliper bore mounting groove. Use your fingers to work the seal into the groove until properly seated.

13. Coat the caliper piston and piston boot with clean brake fluid. Install the boot on the caliper piston. Install the piston

Double pin (A.T.E. type) disc brake caliper — exploded view

Loosening the caliper assembly

Removing the caliper assembly

into the caliper bore. Push the piston past the seal until bottomed in the caliper bore. Use even pressure around the edges of the piston to avoid cocking when installing the piston.

14. Position the lip of the dust boot into the counter bore of the caliper. Use a seal driver or suitable tool to install the boot edge.

15. Compress the edges of the new guide pin bushing with your fingers and install into position on the caliper. Press in on the bushing while working it into the caliper until fully seated. Be sure the bushing flanges extend evenly over the caliper casting on both sides when installed.

16. Install the brake pads and the caliper. Bleed the brakes after caliper service.

Brake Disc (Rotor)

REMOVAL AND INSTALLATION

1. Loosen the wheel lugs slightly. Raise and support the front of the vehicle on jackstands. Remove the front wheel and tire assembly. Relieve the brake system pressure if equipped with ABS.

2. Remove the disc brake caliper and outer brake pad.

3. Remove the disc brake rotor.

4. Service as necessary. Place the rotor in position and install the caliper assembly. Refer to Brake Pad Removal and Installation for detailed procedures, if necessary.

Removing the caliper piston dust boot

Removing the caliper piston seal

INSPECTION

If excessive run out, wobble or thickness variation is present, feedback through the brake pedal will be felt when the brakes are applied. Pedal pulsation, chatter, surge and increased pedal travel can be caused when the disc rotor is worn unevenly or deeply scored. Remove the rotor and have an automotive machine shop measure the wear and check for run out. The machine shop can refinish the braking surfaces if replacement is not necessary.

REAR DRUM BRAKES

CAUTION

Brake shoes contain asbestos, which has been determined to be a cancer causing agent. Never clean the brake surfaces with compressed air! Avoid inhaling any dust from any brake surface! When cleaning brake surfaces, use a commercially available brake cleaning fluid.

Brake Drums

REMOVAL AND INSTALLATION

1. Raise and support the rear of the vehicle on jackstands. Remove the wheels and tire assemblies.
2. Remove the brake shoe adjusting slot cover from the rear of backing plate.
3. Insert a thin tool through the adjusting slot and hold the adjusting lever away from the star wheel. Insert an adjusting tool and back off the star wheel by prying downward with the tool.
4. Remove the center hub dust cover, nut, washer, brake drum, hub and wheel bearings.

To install:
5. Inspect the brake lining and drum for wear. Inspect the wheel cylinder for leakage. Service as required.
6. Remove, clean, inspect and repack the wheel bearings. Install the brake drum. Tighten the hub nut to 240-300 inch lbs. and back off the nut until bearing pressure is released. Retighten the nut finger tight, align the cotter pin hole and install the cotter pin.
7. Adjust the rear brakes as described in the beginning of this section.

Rear drum brake assembly components

INSPECTION

Check the brake drum for any cracks, scores, grooves, or an out-of-round condition. Slight scores can be removed with Emory cloth, while extensive scoring or grooves will require machining. Have an automotive machine shop measure the wear and check the drum for run out. The shop will be able to turn the drum on a lathe, if necessary. Never have a drum turned more than 0.060 in. (1.5mm). If the drum is cracked, or worn more than the limit, replace.

Brake Shoes

REMOVAL AND INSTALLATION

NOTE: A pair of brake springs pliers or spring removal/installation tool and a retainer cap spring tool are good tools to have on hand for this job.

1. Raise and support the rear of the vehicle on jackstands. Remove the rear wheels and brake drums.

NOTE: Remove and install the brake shoes on one side at a time. Use the assembled side for reference.

CAUTION

Brake shoes contain asbestos, which has been determined to be a cancer causing agent. Never clean the brake surfaces with compressed air! Avoid inhaling any dust from any brake surface! When cleaning brake surfaces, use a commercially available brake cleaning fluid.

2. Use a pair of brake spring pliers or appropriate tool and remove the shoe return springs from the top anchor. Take note that the secondary shoe spring is on top of the primary shoe spring. Install in the same position at installation time.
3. Slide the closed eye of the adjuster cable off of the anchor

stud. Unhook the spring end and remove the cable, overload spring, cable guide and anchor plate.

4. Remove the adjusting lever from the spring by sliding forward to clear the pivot. Work the lever out from under the spring. Remove the spring from the pivot.
5. Unhook the bottom shoe-to-shoe spring from the secondary (back) shoe and disengage from the primary (front) shoe.
6. Spread the bottom of the brake shoes apart and remove the star wheel adjuster. Remove the parking brake strut and spring assembly.
7. Locate the shoe retainer nail head at the rear of the brake backing plate. Support the nail head with a finger, press in and twist the spring retainer washer with the special retainer tool or a pair of pliers. If you are using pliers, take care not to slip and pinch your fingers.
8. Remove the retainer, spring, inner washer and nail from both shoes. Remove the parking brake lever from the secondary brake shoe. Remove the shoes from the backing plate. Disconnect the parking brake lever from the brake cable.

To install:

9. Clean the backing plate with a safe solvent. Inspect the raised show support pads for rough or rusted contact areas. Clean and smooth as necessary. Clean and inspect the adjuster star wheels, apply a thin film of lubricant to the threads, socket and washer. Replace the star wheel if rust or threads show damage.
10. Inspect the holddown springs, return springs and adjuster spring. If the springs have been subjected to overheating or if their strength is questionable, replace the spring.
11. Inspect the wheel cylinder. If signs of leakage are present (a small amount of fluid inside the end boot is normal) rebuild or replace the cylinder.
12. Lubricate the shoe contact area pads on the backing plate with high temperature resistant white lube.
13. Engage the parking brake lever with the cable and install the lever on the secondary brake shoe. Engage the end of the brake shoe with the wheel cylinder piston and the top anchor. Install the retainer nail, washer, spring and retainer.
14. Position the primary shoe in like manner and install holddown pin assembly. Install the top anchor plate.
15. Install the parking brake strut and spring in position, press the lower part of the brake.
16. Straighten the adjuster cable and install the eye end over the top anchor. Be sure the lower spring end hook is facing inward.
17. Install the primary (front) shoe return spring. Place the

Removing brake shoe return springs

PRIMARY SHOE AND LINING

SECONDARY SHOE AND LINING

SHOE RETAINERS, SPRING AND NAIL

SPECIAL TOOL

Removing the shoe retainers, springs and pins

SUPPORT PLATE

SHOE CONTACT AREA(6)

Shoe contact pads on support plate

cable guide in position on the secondary (rear) shoe (keep cable out of the way) and install the return spring. Check the cable guide and ensure proper mounting position. Squeeze the anchor ends of the return springs with pliers until they are parallel.

18. Carefully install the star wheel between the brake shoes. The wheel end goes closest the secondary (back) shoe. Wind out the star wheel until snug contact between the brake shoes will hold it in position.

19. Install the adjusting lever spring over the pivot pin on the lower shoe web of the secondary shoe. Install the adjuster lever under the spring and over the pivot pin. Slide the lever rearward until it locks in position.

20. Thread the adjuster cable over the guide and hook the end of the overload spring on the adjuster lever. Make sure the cable is float on the guide and the eye end is against the anchor.

21. Check the operation of the adjuster by pulling the cable rearward. The star wheel should rotate upward as the adjuster lever engages the teeth.

22. Back off the star wheel, if necessary, and install the hub and drum. Adjust the brakes.

23. Repeat the procedures on the other rear wheel.

Wheel Cylinders

REMOVAL AND INSTALLATION

1. Jack up the rear of the vehicle and support it with jackstands.

―――――――――――― CAUTION ――――――――――――
On models equipped with ABS, the system pressure must be released before disconnecting any of the hydraulic lines. Failure to do so, can cause personal injury.

2. Remove the brake drums as previously outlined.

3. Visually inspect the wheel cylinder boots for signs of excessive leakage. Replace any boots that are torn or broken.

NOTE: A slight amount of fluid on the boots may not be a leak but may be a preservative fluid used at the factory.

4. If a leak has been discovered, remove the brake shoes and check for contamination. Replace the linings if they are soaked with grease or brake fluid.

5. Disconnect the brake line from the wheel cylinder.

6. Remove the wheel cylinder attaching bolts, then pull the wheel cylinder out of its support.

7. Position the wheel cylinder onto the backing plate and loosely install the mounting bolts. Start the brake line into the cylinder. Tighten the mounting bolts and the brake line. Install the brake shoes and brake drum. Adjust the brake shoes.

8. Bleed the brake system.

OVERHAUL

1. Pry the boots away from the cylinder and remove the boots and pistons.

2. Disengage the boot from the piston.

BLEEDER SCREW

COAT MOUNTING SURFACE WITH RTV SEALANT

WHEEL CYLINDER

Removing the wheel cylinder from the backing plate

Wheel cylinder assembly — exploded view

3. Slide the piston into the cylinder bore and press inward to remove the other boot, piston and spring.

4. Wash all parts (except rubber parts) in clean brake fluid thoroughly. Do not use a rag; lint will adhere to the bore.

5. Inspect the cylinder bores. Light scoring can usually be cleaned up with crocus cloth. Heavier scores can be cleaned up with a cylinder hone. Black stains are caused by the piston cups and are no cause of concern. Bad scoring or pitting means that the wheel cylinder should be replaced.

6. Dip the pistons and new cups in clean brake fluid, or apply lubricant that is sometimes packaged in the rebuilding kit prior to assembly.

To install:

7. Coat the wheel cylinder bore with clean brake fluid.

8. Install the expansion spring with the cup expanders.

9. Install the cups in each end of the cylinder with the open ends facing each other.

10. Assemble new boots on the piston and slide them into the cylinder bore.

11. Press the boot over the wheel cylinder until seated.

Parking brake cable routing

12. Apply RTV on the mounting surface of the backing plate. Install the wheel cylinder, and connect brake lines.
13. Install brake shoes, and drum. Adjust and bleed brakes.

Parking Brake

ADJUSTMENT

1. Raise and support the rear of the vehicle on jackstands. Apply and release the parking brake several times.
2. Clean the parking park adjustment bolts with a wire brush and lubricate the threads. Back off the adjusting nut until there is slack in the cable.
3. Check the rear brake adjustment, adjust as necessary.
4. Tighten the parking brake cable adjuster until the slight drag is felt when turning the rear wheel.
5. Loosen the cable until no drag is felt on either rear wheel. Back off adjusting nut two full turns more.
6. Apply and release the parking brake several times to ensure there is not rear wheel drag. Lower the vehicle.

REMOVAL AND INSTALLATION

Front Cable

1. Raise and support the front of the vehicle on jackstands.
2. Back off the adjuster nut until the cable can be released from the connectors.
3. Lift the floor mat for access to the floor pan. Force the seal surrounding the cable from the floor.

4. Pull the cable forward and disconnect from lever clevis. Remove the front cable from support bracket and vehicle.
5. Feed the new cable through the floor pan hole. Attach the front end of the cable to the parking brake lever clevis and support.
6. Engage intermediate cable and adjust.

Intermediate Cable

1. Back off the parking brake adjuster. Disengage the front cable and rear cables from the intermediate cable connector.
2. Remove the intermediate cable. Install the new cable and adjust.

Rear Cables

1. Raise and support the rear of the vehicle on jackstands.
2. Back off the cable adjustment and disconnect the rear cable (that is to be replaced) from the intermediate cable. Remove the rear cable from the mounting clips.
3. Remove the rear wheel and the brake shoes from the side requiring replacement.
4. Disconnect the cable from the rear brake apply lever. Compress the cable lock with a mini-hose clamp and pull the cable from the backing plate.
5. Install the new cable through the brake backing plate. Engage the locks. Attach the cable to the apply lever. Install the brake shoes, drum and wheel assembly.
6. Adjust the service brakes and parking brake.

BRAKE SPECIFICATIONS

Years	Model	Master Cylinder Bore	Brake Disc		Brake Drum		Wheel Cylinder or Caliper Bore Dia.	
			Minimum Thickness	Maximum Runout	Inside Diameter	Maximum Machine O/S	Front	Rear
1984-89	Caravan	0.94	0.80	0.005	9.000	9.060	2.36	0.75
	Voyager	0.94	0.80	0.005	9.000	9.060	2.36	0.75
1990-91	Caravan	0.94	0.80	0.003	7.874 ①	7.934 ②	2.12	0.62
	Voyager	0.94	0.80	0.003	7.874 ①	7.934 ②	2.12	0.62
	Town & Country	0.94	0.80	0.003	7.874 ①	7.934 ②	2.12	0.62

① Heavy Duty: 8.661 in.
② Heavy Duty: 8.721

TORQUE SPECIFICATIONS

Component	English	Metric
Accumulator pump/motor assembly		
High pressure hose-to-hydraulic assembly:	12 ft. lbs.	16 Nm
Low pressure hose-to-hydraulic assembly:	10 inch lbs	1 Nm
Hydraulic assembly attaching nuts:	21 ft. lbs.	28 Nm
Brake line to hydraulic assembly:	12 ft. lbs.	16 Nm
Proportioning valve attaching nuts:	30 ft. lbs.	40 Nm
Pressure line banjo bolt:	13 ft. lbs.	17 Nm
Bleeder screws:	8 ft. lbs.	10 Nm
Height sensing dual proportioning valve mounting bolts:	13 ft. lbs.	18 Nm
Master cylinder mounting bolts:	17-25 ft. lbs.	23-34 Nm
Power booster-to-firewall mounting stud nuts:	17-25 ft. lbs.	23-34 Nm
Hydraulic reservoir high pressure hose banjo fitting:	10 ft. lbs.	13 Nm
Hydraulic bladder accumulator-to-hydraulic assembly:	30 ft. lbs.	40 Nm
Front wheel speed sensor wiring tube retaining bolts:	35 inch lbs.	4 Nm
Front wheel sensor-to-knuckle retaining screw:	60 inch lbs.	7 Nm
Rear wheel speed sensor retaining bolts:	12 ft. lbs.	17 Nm
Rear wheel speed sensor-to-rear axle:	60 inch lbs.	7 Nm
Rear wheel speed sensor frame rail bracket bolt:	50 inch lbs.	5 Nm
Caliper guide pins		
Kelsey-Hayes type:	25-35 ft. lbs.	34-48 Nm
ATE type:	18-26 ft. lbs.	25-35 Nm
Wheel lug nuts:	95 ft. lbs.	129 Nm

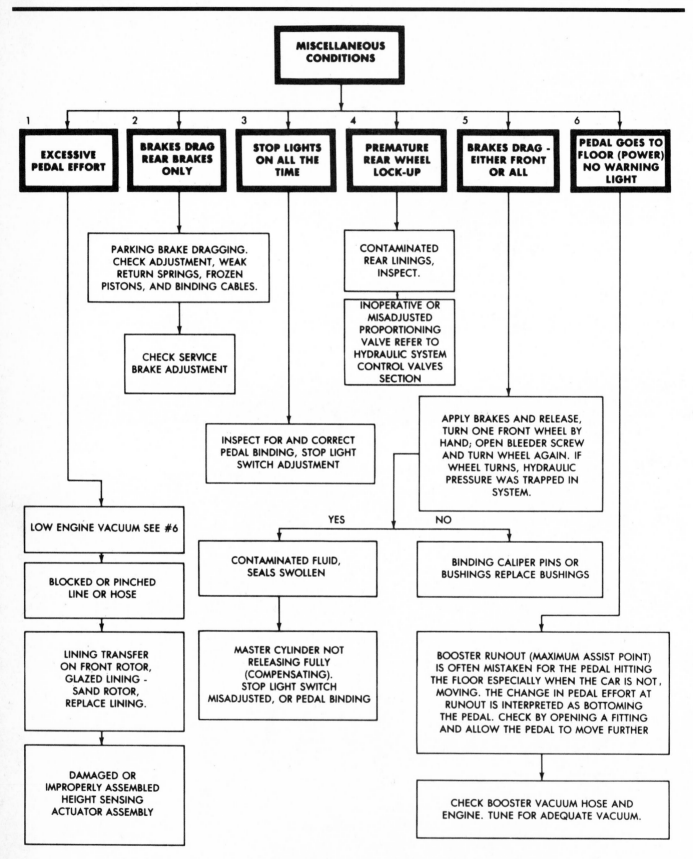

Basic brake condition diagnosis — Non-ABS equipped vehicles

10

Body

QUICK REFERENCE INDEX

GENERAL INDEX

Hood, Trunk Lid, Hatch Lid, Glass and Doors

Problem	Possible Cause	Correction
HOOD/TRUNK/HATCH LID		
Improper closure.	• Striker and latch not properly aligned.	• Adjust the alignment.
Difficulty locking and unlocking.	• Striker and latch not properly aligned.	• Adjust the alignment.
Uneven clearance with body panels.	• Incorrectly installed hood or trunk lid.	• Adjust the alignment.
WINDOW/WINDSHIELD GLASS		
Water leak through windshield	• Defective seal. • Defective body flange.	• Fill sealant • Correct.
Water leak through door window glass.	• Incorrect window glass installation. • Gap at upper window frame.	• Adjust position. • Adjust position.
Water leak through quarter window.	• Defective seal. • Defective body flange.	• Replace seal. • Correct.
Water leak through rear window.	• Defective seal. • Defective body flange.	• Replace seal. • Correct.
FRONT/REAR DOORS		
Door window malfunction.	• Incorrect window glass installation. • Damaged or faulty regulator.	• Adjust position. • Correct or replace.
Water leak through door edge.	• Cracked or faulty weatherstrip.	• Replace.
Water leak from door center.	• Drain hole clogged. • Inadequate waterproof skeet contact or damage.	• Remove foreign objects. • Correct or replace.
Door hard to open.	• Incorrect latch or striker adjustment.	• Adjust.
Door does not open or close completely.	• Incorrect door installation. • Defective door check strap. • Door check strap and hinge require grease.	• Adjust position. • Correct or replace. • Apply grease.
Uneven gap between door and body.	• Incorrect door installation.	• Adjust position.
Wind noise around door.	• Improperly installed weatherstrip. • Improper clearance between door glass and door weatherstrip. • Deformed door.	• Repair or replace. • Adjust. • Repair or replace.

EXTERIOR

Front Doors

REMOVAL AND INSTALLATION

Except 1991 Models

1. Open the front door and remove the inner door panel covering. Disconnect the interior light wiring harness and feed it through the access hole. Disconnect the door swing stop.
2. Open the door wide enough to gain access to the hinge bolts. Place a padded support under the door edge that will hold the door in a level position when the hinges have been unbolted from the frame.
3. Scribe around the door hinge on the door frame. Remove the hinge mounting bolts, lower hinge first, then the upper, from the door frame.
4. Remove the door.
5. Place the door on the padded support and install the hinge mounting bolts until they are snug enough to support the door, but not tight enough to prevent door adjustment. Adjust the door position until correctly aligned and tighten the hinge bolts. Adjust the striker as necessary. Connect the door stop and interior light harness. Install the inner trim panel.

1991 Models

1. Remove the door trim panel, silencer pad and water shield.
2. Disconnect all wire connectors and wire harness hold downs inside of the door, and push the harness through the access hole in the front of the door.
3. Open the door and support it with a jack, an assistant should also be used to hold the door.
4. Using a hammer and punch, drive the bottom hinge pin upward and remove the pin from the hinge.
5. Drive the upper hinge pin from the hinge and remove it. Separate the door from the vehicle.

To install:

6. Install the door assembly on the hinges.
7. Install the hinge pins, by tapping them into position.
8. The door should not require any re-alignment. Install the wiring harness into the door.
9. Install the trim panel.

ALIGNMENT

The front doors should be adjusted so that there is a ¼ in. (6mm) gap between the edge of the front fender and the edge of the door, and a ¼ in. (6mm) gap between the back edge of the door and the lock pillar. Adjust the door to position and raise or lower it so that the stamped edge line matches the body panel line. Secure the door in proper position after necessary adjustments.

Front Door Hinge

REMOVAL AND INSTALLATION

1991 Models

1. Raise the front of the vehicle slightly.
2. Remove the wheel and tire assembly.
3. Remove the inner fender, plastic splash shield retaining screws and remove the shield.
4. Support the door assembly. Remove the door retaining pin on the hinge to be replaced.
5. Remove the hinge plate retaining bolts from inside the fender well.
6. Remove the hinge assembly.

To install:

7. Install the hinge plate in position and install the retaining bolts. Do not tighten them completely.
8. Install the hinge pin and check the door alignment, there should be a ¼ in. (6mm) gap around the sides of the door.
9. Tighten the hinge mounting bolts.
10. Install the inner fender splash shield and install the wheel.
11. Lower the vehicle.

Sliding Door

REMOVAL AND INSTALLATION

NOTE: When removing the sliding door as an assembly, it is not necessary to remove or loosen bolts that would change the doors alignment.

Front door removal and installation

Sliding door trim mounting

* = CLEAN TRACK WITH
SUITABLE SOLVENT
AND LUBRICATE WITH
MULTI-PURPOSE GREASE

Sliding door center track cover and over travel stop mounting

1. Remove the sliding door upper track cover.
2. Remove the upper track over travel stop.
3. Remove the sill plate.
4. Remove the lower track over travel stop.
5. With the help of an assistant, roll the door back and out of its tracks.

To install:
6. Position the door carefully on its tracks and roll it into position.
7. Install the track over travel stops.
8. Install the sill plate.
9. Install the upper track cover.

ALIGNMENT

1. The gap between the back edge of the front door and the front edge of the sliding door should be $\frac{5}{16}$ in. (8mm). The gap between the sliding door edge and the quarter panel should be $\frac{1}{4}$ in. (6mm). The stamped edge line of the front door the sliding door and the quarter panel should be in line.

2. Remove the hinge trim panels and adjust the sliding door in the direction(s) required. Refer to the illustration provided for adjustment direction.

Liftgate

REMOVAL AND INSTALLATION

1. Support the liftgate in the full opened position.
2. Scribe a mark on the liftgate to mark the hinge positions.

Sliding door adjustments

3. Place masking tape on the roof edge and liftgate edge to protect the paint surfaces during removal and installation.
4. Remove the liftgate prop fasteners and remove the props.
5. Have a helper on hand to support the liftgate. Remove the hinge mounting bolts and remove the liftgate.
To install:
6. Raise the liftgate into position and install the hinge mounting bolts. Tighten the bolts until they are snug, but not tight enough to prevent liftgate adjustment.
7. Shift the liftgate until the hinge scribe marks are in position and tighten the hinge mounting bolts.
8. Attach and secure the liftgate props.

Liftgate assembly mounting

SLIDING DOOR

STABILIZER

STABILIZER SEAL

VIEW IN DIRECTION OF ARROW Y

SLIDING DOOR

RETAINER

LOCK CYLINDER

OUTSIDE HANDLE

OUTSIDE HANDLE PLATE

12 N•m (100 IN. LBS.)

VIEW IN DIRECTION OF ARROW W

LATCH REMOTE CONTROL

DOOR LATCH RELEASE LINK

DOOR LATCH LOCKING LINK

LATCH ASSEMBLY

ANTI RATTLE CLIP

KEY CYLINDER TO ACTUATOR LINK

STABILIZER ACTUATING LINK

ELECTRIC MOTOR TO LATCH LEVER LINK

ELECTRIC LOCKING MOTOR

STABILIZER ASSEMBLY

28 N•m (250 IN. LBS.)

VIEW IN DIRECTION OF ARROW X

4 N•m (35 IN. LBS.)

WEDGE

STABILIZER ASSEMBLY

28 N•m (250 IN. LBS.)

SLIDING DOOR

STABILIZER ACTUATING LINK

VIEW IN CIRCLE V

UPPER ROLLER

UPPER ROLLER BRACKET

12 N•m (105 IN. LBS.)

LATCH REMOTE LOCKING CONTROL ASSEMBLY

12 N•m (105 IN. LBS.)

REMOTE CONTROL BEZEL

4 N•m (35 IN. LBS.)

12 N•m (105 IN. LBS.)

LOWER ROLLER ASSEMBLY

LOWER ROLLER SUPPORT BRACKET

CENTER ROLLER ASSEMBLY

LATCH ASSEMBLY

95 N•m (70 FT. LBS.)

12 N•m (105 IN. LBS.)

Sliding door assembly — exploded view

Hood and hinge assembly

Hood latch components

Hood safety catch assembly

Hood release cable attachment

Hood

REMOVAL AND INSTALLATION

1. Raise the hood to its full open position.
2. Remove the cowl cover retaining screws, remove the wiper arms and remove the cowl cover.
3. Disconnect the under hood light connector.
4. Mark all bolt and hinge attachment points with a grease pencil or equivalent, to provide reference marks for installation.
5. Remove the top hood-to-hinge attaching bolts and loosen the bottom bolts until they can be removed by hand.
6. With the aid of a helper, support the hood and remove the hinge bolts.
7. Move the hood away from the vehicle and store it in a way to prevent it from being damaged.

To install:

8. With the aid of a helper, position the hood on the hinges and install the lower hinge bolt finger tight.
9. Install the remaining hinge bolts and align the hinge marks. Tighten the bolts.

NOTE: When the hood is properly aligned there should be a 4mm clearance at the fenders and the hood should be flush in height with the top of the fenders.

10. Connect the under hood light and install the cowl cover. Install the wiper arms.
11. Check the hood latch operation.

Exterior Moldings and Body Side Appliques

REMOVAL AND INSTALLATION

1991 Models

All of the 1991 models have various body moldings and applique panels, that are used to dress the appearance of the exterior of the vehicle. All of these trim pieces are either screwed or snapped in place.

1. Remove the screws that retain the trim piece being removed, these will be either under the edge of the trim or at the wheel openings. In some instances there will be clips holding the trim as well as screws. When removing front or rear bumper trim, be sure to remove all retaining bolts.
2. Once the screws are removed, lift the piece away from the vehicle, making sure no clips or screws are still in place.
3. When removing the side applique panels, they will need to be lifted slightly to release them from the tracks that retain them.

Exterior trim moldings

Body side applique panels

10 BODY

4. Install the replacement piece(s) in position and secure with screws or clips as needed. If replacing the trim piece, be sure to transfer any clips to the replacement. Install all front or rear bumper retaining bolts.

Bumpers

REMOVAL AND INSTALLATION

1. Remove the end cap to bumper mounting screw and the two end cap to fender nuts from both ends of the bumper. On 1991 models, remove the necessary trim pieces from the vehicle.

2. Remove the end cap to bumper nut and remove the end cap from both ends of the bumper.

3. Support the lower edge of the bumper on a padded jack.

4. Remove the bolts that mount the bumper to the body brackets and remove the bumper.

High line front bumper disassembly

Front bumper removal — low line front bumper

Rear bumper removal — 1991 models

Front bumper removal — high line bumper

High line rear bumper removal — 1991 models

54 N•m (40 FT. LBS.)

REAR BUMPER SUPPORT

28 N•m (250 IN. LBS.)

RUB STRIP

7 N•m (60 IN. LBS.)

REAR BUMPER

REAR BUMPER END CAP

3 N•m (24 IN. LBS.)

7 N•m (60 IN. LBS.)

Rear bumper removal — 1984-90 models

To install:

5. Place the bumper into the proper position, use a padded jack to support the bumper, and install the bracket to bumper mounting bolts. Tighten the bolts until they are snug. but not tight enough to prevent shifting of the bumper for proper centering.

6. Adjust bumper placement as required. Tighten the mounting bolts. Install the bumper end caps. On 1991 models install the trim pieces.

Grille

REMOVAL AND INSTALLATION

1984-1990 Models

1. Remove the screws from the headlamp bezels. Remove the screws from the sides of the grille.

2. Remove the screws from the grille to center support bracket.

3. Remove the grille.

4. Place the grille into position. Install the center support screws and the outer mounting screws. Center the grille and tighten the mounting screws.

5. Install the headlamp bezel screws.

1991 Models

There are 2 grille types used, one type incorporates the headlamp doors and the grille, the other is just the center grille assembly with separate headlamp doors.

1. Remove the bolt holding the grille to the radiator bracket, in front of the radiator.

RADIATOR CLOSURE PANEL BRACE

12 N•m (105 IN. LBS.)

GRILLE ADAPTER BRACKET

CLOSURE PANEL

12 N•m (105 IN. LBS.)

RADIATOR GRILL ASSEMBLY

FENDER

HEADLAMP BEZEL ADAPTOR

12 N•m (105 IN. LBS.)

1 N•m (12 IN. LBS.)

HEADLAMP BEZEL

Grille, headlamp bezel and adaptor removal — 1984-90 models

2. On the one piece models, remove the headlight and turn signal lenses.

Low line grille assembly removal — 1991 models

Side view mirror removal

High line grille assembly removal — 1991 models

3. Remove the screws that retain the grille to the front headlight assemblies.
4. Remove the grille from the vehicle.
5. Install the grille in position, make sure it is positioned correctly.

Outside Mirrors

REMOVAL AND INSTALLATION

1. Remove the door trim panel.
2. Remove the adjustment knob with an Allen wrench. Remove the screw cover plug and the mirror inner bezel mounting screws. Remove the bezel.
3. Remove the mirror mounting nuts and the mirror. If equipped with power mirrors, disconnect the electrical lead.
4. Place the mirror into position and install the mounting nuts. Connect the electrical lead, if equipped.

5. Place the bezel into position and install the mounting screws and cover plug.
6. Install the control knob and trim panel.

Antenna

Refer to Section 7 for antenna servicing under the Radio section.

Fenders and Splash Shields

REMOVAL AND INSTALLATION

1. Remove the splash shields from the inner fender wells.

NOTE: Raising the vehicle slightly and removing the wheel and tire, will make splash shield removal easier.

2. Remove the under vehicle splash shields where equipped, one will cover the transaxle and the other will be covering the accessory drive belts.
3. Remove the grille and headlamp assemblies.
4. Remove the bolts holding the vehicle jacking pad under the vehicle and remove the pad.
5. Remove the bolts holding the fender to the hinge pillar from inside the wheel opening.
6. Remove the bolts holding the fender to the rocker panel.
7. Remove the bolts holding the fender to the lower radiator panel.
8. Remove the remaining bolts along the top edge of the fender on the cowl side panel.
9. Remove the fender from the vehicle.
To install:
10. Install the fender in position on the vehicle.
11. Install the fender retaining bolts, but do not tighten.
12. Align the fender to ¼ in. (6mm) gap at the door and $^5/_{16}$ in. (8mm) at the edge of the hood.
13. Tighten all of the fender mounting bolts.
14. Install the splash shields, using new retainers.

Front fender removal and installation — 1984-90 models

Splash shield and cowl screen removal — 1984-90 models

Cowl cover and seal removal — 1991 models

Transaxle splash shield removal — 1991 models

Front splash shield removal — 1991 models

Front fender removal — 1991 models

INTERIOR

Door Panels

REMOVAL AND INSTALLATION

1. Lower the door glass until it is 3 in. (76mm) from the full down position.

2. Unlock the door and remove the remote door latch control handle bezel by prying the front of the bezel out and rearward.

3. Remove the arrest mounting screw, and on models with electric controls, pry out the power window switch bezel.

4. Remove the window crank handle on models with manual window regulators.

5. Remove the two edge inserts that cover the mounting

GLASS ANTI-RATTLE BUMPER

LATCH/LOCK REMOTE CONTROL

GLASS RUN

10 N•m (87 IN. LBS.)

FRONT DOOR LATCH

MOTOR/LATCH LINK

3 N•m (30 IN. LBS.)

LINK/MOTOR CLIP

ELECTRIC LOCKING MOTOR

SPACER

MANUAL WINDOW REGULATOR ASSEMBLY

HANDLE

3 N•m (30 IN. LBS.)

13 N•m (115 IN. LBS.)

Front door assembly — component view

screws for the door pull strap, and remove the mounting screws and strap.

6. Insert a wide flat tool between the panel and door frame and carefully twist the tool to unfasten the retainer clips from the door.

7. If the vehicle is equipped with power locks, slide the switch bezel through the trim panel.

8. Disconnect the courtesy lamp connector. Remove the door trim panel.

9. Remove the inner plastic cover and service the components as required.

To install:

10. Place sealer along the edges of the plastic liner and put the liner onto the door frame.

11. Potion the trim panel, slide the power lock bezel through the panel, connect the courtesy lamp.

12. Potion the panel clips over their mounting holes and push the panel against the door frame to lock the clips.

13. Install the pull strap, the arrest, widow handle/power switch, remote latch control/bezel.

FRONT DOOR

PLUG

FRONT DOOR TRIM

ARM REST

LATCH HANDLE BEZEL

CRANK

TRIM CLIP

MAP POCKET

PLUG

Front door trim panel removal

Interior Trim Panels

REMOVAL AND INSTALLATION

All of the trim panels on the interior of the vehicle can be removed easily, by removing their retaining screws and separating them from each other. Almost all of the trim pieces are fastened with screws, most of the screws are visible, however a few have removable caps.

The interior trim panels can be removed without removing any of the interior components of the vehicle, such as seats, etc. Remove the panels carefully to avoid damaging them. In some cases, the trim may be attached with a hidden retaining clip. If the panel is fixed with a clip, remove it by gently prying it away from the clip.

The following is a recommended sequence for removing the trim pieces. Since the trim pieces overlap, this method of removal will avoid any damage.

Left side garnish moldings and trim panel mounting — 1984-90 models

Right side garnish moldings and trim panel mounting — 1984-90 models

A-PILLAR/ROOF RAIL TRIM

UPPER TRACK COVER

WINDSHIELD SIDE GARNISH MOLDING

QUARTER TRIM INSERT

QUARTER TRIM PANEL

SCUFF PLATE

COWL TRIM SCUFF PLATE

B-PILLAR TRIM

Interior trim panel mounting — 1991 models

SHOULDER HARNESS ANCHORS

UPPER QUARTER TRIM PANEL

COAT HOOK

BRACKET

BRACKET

LOWER QUARTER TRIM PANEL

QUARTER TRIM INSERT

ASH TRAY

Interior quarter trim panel mounting — 1991 models

Interior trim panel mounting — 1991 models with rear air conditioning

1. Windshield surround trim and side garnish molding.
2. Front door scuff plate.
3. "B" pillar trim, seat belt cover and seat belt assembly.
4. Sliding door upper track cover.
5. Sliding door scuff plate.
6. Liftgate scuff plate.
7. Quarter panel trim. On 1991 Models, remove the upper quarter panel trim, then the lower. If equipped with rear air conditioning, remove the vents from the trim panels.

Install the trim panels by reversing the order in which they were removed. Be sure to position the panels correctly, this will help to avoid squeaks and possible warpage.

Door Locks/Latch

REMOVAL AND INSTALLATION

This procedure can be used for both the front and sliding doors.

1. Remove the door trim panel and inner cover.
2. Raise the window to the full up position.
3. Disconnect all the locking clips from the remote linkage at the latch.
4. Remove the retaining screws at the door edge and remove the latch assembly.
5. Position the latch to the door frame and secure it with the retaining screws.
6. Connect all of the remote linkage to the latch levers.
7. Check latch operation. Install the inner cover and door trim panel.

Door Glass Regulator

REMOVAL AND INSTALLATION

1. Remove the door trim panel and inner liner.
2. Remove the window glass from the regulator and the door.

Door latch assembly and striker — 1991 models

OUTSIDE HANDLE TO LATCH LINK
LOCK CYLINDER TO LATCH LINK
LATCH ASSEMBLY
ANTI-RATTLE CLIP
INSIDE LATCH RELEASE TO LATCH LINK
LOCK/LATCH REMOTE CONTROL
SPACER
LOCK PILLAR
STRIKER ASSEMBLY 95 N•m (70 FT. LBS.)
ELECTRIC LOCK MOTOR TO LATCH
INSIDE LOCK REMOTE CONTROL TO LATCH LINK

Door latch assembly, striker and linkage mounting — 1984-90 models

INSIDE LOCK BUTTON
BELL CRANK
FRONT LATCH
REAR LATCH
LATCH ROD
LOCK ROD
POWER LOCK ACTUATOR

Sliding door latch and linkage

STUD AND WASHER
GASKET
7 N•m (60 IN. LBS.)
FRONT WINDOW REGULATOR ASSEMBLY
GLASS
10 N•m (85 IN. LBS.)

Front door glass mounting

NOTE: The window glass is mounted to the regulator by two mounting studs and nuts. Raise the glass until the mounting nuts align with the large access hole. Remove the nuts. Raise the glass up through the door frame. Rotate the glass so that the mounting studs pass through the notch at the rear of the door and remove the glass from the door.

Electric Window Motor

REMOVAL AND INSTALLATION

1. Remove the window regulator. See procedure.
2. Remove the electric motor mounting screws and the motor.

3. If equipped with power windows, disconnect the wiring harness and remove the retainer clip.
4. Drill out the regulator mounting rivets. Their are five on vehicles equipped with electric windows, and six if equipped with manual windows.
5. Remove the regulator through the larger access hole. Rotate the regulator through the hole as required for removal.
To install:
6. Install the regulator to the mounting holes using ¼-20 × ½ in. screws and nuts. Tighten the screws to 90 inch lbs.
7. Install the window glass, connect the motor wiring harness, and install the inner liner and door trim panel.

Electric window regulator assembly — 1984-90 models

3. Place the window motor into the door and secure the mounting screws.
4. Install the window regulator.

Inside Rear View Mirror
REMOVAL AND INSTALLATION

1. Loosen the mounting set screw on the mounting arm.

Window regulator components — 1991 models

2. Slide the mirror off of the windshield mounting button.
3. Slide the mirror mounting arm over the mounting button and secure the set screw.

TIGHTENING SEQUENCE, POWER REGULATOR

Window regulator tightening sequence — 1984-90 models

Windshield molding and support spacer

Center the windshield and mark it at the support spacers

Correct positioning of the urethane compression spacers

6. Remove the windshield from the opening and place it on a suitable support, clean the inside of the glass. Apply clear glass primer in a 1 in. (25mm) path around the perimeter of the windshield and wipe with a clean cloth.

7. Apply a 15mm path of blackout primer around the top and sides of the windshield. Apply a 1 in. (25mm) path to the bottom of the windshield. Allow 3 minutes drying time.

8. Position the windshield bonding compression spacers around the opening for the windshield.

9. Apply a 10mm bead of urethane around the inside of the opening.

10. With the aid of a helper, install the windshield glass in position, aligning the reference marks made earlier. Push the windshield into position until it bottoms on the spacers and the top molding is flush with the roof line.

11. Clean excess urethane from the glass using a suitable solvent. Install the moldings.

12. Use pieces of masking tape around the windshield to hold the moulding until the urethane cures.

13. Install the cowl cover and the inside mirror.

14. When the urethane cures, remove the tape and water test the windshield for leaks.

Windshield Glass

REMOVAL AND INSTALLATION

NOTE: The removal and installation of the windshield must be done carefully, improper installation can cause the windshield to crack or shatter. An assistant must be used to insure that the windshield is positioned properly in the opening.

1. Remove the inside rearview mirror.

2. Remove the cowl cover and the windshield moldings. The moldings can be removed by pulling them upward.

3. Cut the urethane bonding from around the windshield using a sharp knife. Separate the windshield from the vehicle.
To install:

4. Clean the windshield area of old urethane bonding that may be loose. Clean the support spacers and reposition them on the studs.

5. With the aid of a helper, place the replacement windshield in the opening and position it in the center of the opening. Mark the glass at the supports, once it is centered, using a grease pencil or masking tape. This will help position it properly.

Stationary Glass

REMOVAL AND INSTALLATION

All of the fixed glass in the vehicle is removed and installed in the same manner as the windshield glass.

Front Seats

REMOVAL AND INSTALLATION

1. To remove the right front seat; raise and safely support the vehicle.

2. Remove the four nuts and washer that attach the seat to the floor pan.

3. Remove the seat.

4. Position the seat over and through the floor pan holes. Secure the seat with the nuts and washers.

5. To remove the left front seat: tilt the seat reward. Reach under the front of the seat and grab the cable near the clip that retains the cable to the lever. Pull the cable toward the driver's door until it is released from the lever assembly.

24 IN. LB. (3 N•m)

UPPER ADJUSTER COVER

LEFT FRONT SEAT

ELECTRIC SEAT ADJUSTER

24 IN. LB. (3 N•m)

LOWER ADJUSTER COVER

200 IN. LB. (23 N•m)

MANUAL SEAT ADJUSTER

24 IN. LB. (3 N•m)

200 IN. LB. (23 N•m)

RISER COVER

LATCH CONNECTOR WIRE

200 IN. LB. (23 N•m)

FLOOR PAN

SEAT RISER

70 FT. LB. (95 N•m)

Left front seat track and riser assembly

STOWAGE BOX CLOSURE PANEL

SPACER

24 IN. LB. (3•m)

TOOL RETAINER

WHEEL WRENCH

SEAT, RIGHT FRONT

24 IN. LB. (3 N•m)

STOWAGE BOX LATCH STRIKER

15 IN. LB. (2 N•m)

SOCKET

FRONT SEAT RISER

230 IN. LB. (26 N•m)

ROLLER ASSEMBLY

STOWAGE BOX DUST COVER

FLOOR PAN

350 IN. LB. (39 N•m)

STOWAGE BOX

LOCK CYLINDER

Right front seat track and riser assembly

(95 N•m) 70 FT. LBS.

Front seat and riser removal

6. Turn the cable ninety degrees and push it inward to separate the cable from the lever assembly.
7. Disconnect the electrical connectors. Remove the mounting nuts and washers and remove the seat.

8. Position the seat over the mounting holes and lower through the holes. Secure the seat with the nuts and washers. Connect the electrical wiring and cable.

Rear Seat Assembly

The rear seat assemblies can be removed without tools, they are of the quick release kind. To remove the assembly, pull the latch handle and tilt the seat assembly forward and lift it from its mounting. The seat can then be removed from the vehicle.

Seat Belt Systems
REMOVAL AND INSTALLATION

Front Seat Belts

OUTBOARD HARNESS AND LAP BELT

1. Remove the shoulder harness turning loop.
2. Remove the "B" pillar trim or quarter trim as needed, to gain access to the retractor assembly..
3. Remove the bolt holding the retractor assembly to the body and remove it from the vehicle.
4. Install the replacement belt in position and install any removed trim.

INBOARD BUCKLE

1. Lift the cover from over the mounting bolt.
2. Remove the bolt retaining the buckle to the seat riser.
3. Disconnect the seat belt sensor wire connector and remove the buckle from the vehicle.
4. Install the buckle in position and connect the electrical lead.

First rear seat riser assembly

Second rear seat riser and track assembly

Front seat belt mounting — 1984-90 models

Front seat belt mounting — 1991 models

Front inboard seat belt buckle

Rear Seat Belts

1984–90 MODELS

The rear seat belts in these vehicles are attached to the seat assembly mounting. The belt assemblies are retained by 1 bolt each. Remove the mounting bolt to remove the assembly. When installing replacement belts, tighten all mounting bolts to 350 inch lbs. (40 Nm).

1991 MODELS

The seat belt assemblies in these vehicles are 3 point types mounted to the body in the same manner as the front belts.

1. Remove the interior trim as needed to gain access to the retractor assembly.
2. Remove the bolt holding the lower lap belt anchor to the floor bracket.
3. Remove the bolt retaining the retractor assembly to the inner quarter panel.
4. Remove the belt assembly from the vehicle.
5. Install the replacement belt in position and install any trim that was removed.

Rear seat belt mounting — 1984-90 models

Rear seat belt mounting — 1991 models

Head lining assembly removal

Overhead console assembly mounting

Floor carpet and silencer assembly

Headliner

REMOVAL AND INSTALLATION

1. If equipped with an overhead console, disengage the sun visors from the console. Remove the screws retaining the console to the roof, disconnect the wiring and remove the console.
2. Remove the inboard sun visor clips, if not equipped with an overhead console. Remove the sun visors.
3. Remove the upper moldings as needed, to gain access to the headliner.
4. Remove the sliding door upper track cover.
5. Remove the right quarter trim panel.

6. Remove the dome lamp, if equipped.
7. Separate the lining from the vehicle and remove it from the vehicle.
To install:
8. Install the headliner in the vehicle, make sure it is positioned properly.
9. Install the dome lamp and install the right quarter trim panel.
10. Install the sliding door upper track cover.
11. Install any trim moulding that was removed.
12. Install the sun visor clips and the overhead console. Install he sun visors.
13. Install the dome light, if equipped.

Floor Carpeting and Silencers

REMOVAL AND INSTALLATION

1. Remove the front console, if equipped.
2. Remove all of the seat assemblies from the vehicle.
3. Remove the inboard seat belt buckle assemblies. Remove the door sill scuff plates.
4. Remove the rear seat anchor bezels.
5. Lift the carpeting and fold it toward the center of the vehicle, remove it through the sliding door.

Roof top luggage rack mounting

6. Lift the silencer pads from the floor and remove them from the vehicle.
To install:
7. Install the silencer pads in position first, make sure they are positioned correctly.

8. Place the carpeting in the vehicle through the sliding door. Unfold and position it.
9. Pull the carpet so that it is straight and even throughout the vehicle.
10. Install the rear seat anchor bezels. Install the rear seat assemblies.
11. Install the front seat assemblies. Install the inboard buckle assemblies.
12. Install the door sill scuff plates.
13. Install the center console assembly, if equipped.

Roof Top Luggage Rack

REMOVAL AND INSTALLATION

The center strips of the roof rack are stuck to the roof with an adhesive, they can be removed by heating them with a heat gun or lamp.
1. Slide the rail end covers from the side rails.
2. Remove the screws holding the rails to the roof.
3. Separate the luggage rack from the vehicle. Remove the center strips at this time, if they are to be removed.
To install:
4. Clean the area that the center strips mount to, if they were removed. All old adhesive must be removed.
5. Using new double sided trim tape, install the center strips.
6. Install the rack side rails to the roof. Make sure the gaskets are in position.
7. Install the rail end covers.

How to Remove Stains from Fabric Interior

For best results, spots and stains should be removed as soon as possible. Never use gasoline, lacquer thinner, acetone, nail polish remover or bleach. Use a 3′ x 3″ piece of cheesecloth. Squeeze most of the liquid from the fabric and wipe the stained fabric from the outside of the stain toward the center with a lifting motion. Turn the cheesecloth as soon as one side becomes soiled. When using water to remove a stain, be sure to wash the entire section after the spot has been removed to avoid water stains. Encrusted spots can be broken up with a dull knife and vacuumed before removing the stain.

Type of Stain	How to Remove It
Surface spots	Brush the spots out with a small hand brush or use a commercial preparation such as K2R to lift the stain.
Mildew	Clean around the mildew with warm suds. Rinse in cold water and soak the mildew area in a solution of 1 part table salt and 2 parts water. Wash with upholstery cleaner.
Water stains	Water stains in fabric materials can be removed with a solution made from 1 cup of table salt dissolved in 1 quart of water. Vigorously scrub the solution into the stain and rinse with clear water. Water stains in nylon or other synthetic fabrics should be removed with a commercial type spot remover.
Chewing gum, tar, crayons, shoe polish (greasy stains)	Do not use a cleaner that will soften gum or tar. Harden the deposit with an ice cube and scrape away as much as possible with a dull knife. Moisten the remainder with cleaning fluid and scrub clean.
Ice cream, candy	Most candy has a sugar base and can be removed with a cloth wrung out in warm water. Oily candy, after cleaning with warm water, should be cleaned with upholstery cleaner. Rinse with warm water and clean the remainder with cleaning fluid.

How to Remove Stains from Fabric Interior

For best results, spots and stains should be removed as soon as possible. Never use gasoline, lacquer thinner, acetone, nail polish remover or bleach. Use a 3' x 3" piece of cheesecloth. Squeeze most of the liquid from the fabric and wipe the stained fabric from the outside of the stain toward the center with a lifting motion. Turn the cheesecloth as soon as one side becomes soiled. When using water to remove a stain, be sure to wash the entire section after the spot has been removed to avoid water stains. Encrusted spots can be broken up with a dull knife and vacuumed before removing the stain.

Type of Stain	How to Remove It
Wine, alcohol, egg, milk, soft drink (non-greasy stains)	Do not use soap. Scrub the stain with a cloth wrung out in warm water. Remove the remainder with cleaning fluid.
Grease, oil, lipstick, butter and related stains	Use a spot remover to avoid leaving a ring. Work from the outisde of the stain to the center and dry with a clean cloth when the spot is gone.
Headliners (cloth)	Mix a solution of warm water and foam upholstery cleaner to give thick suds. Use only foam—liquid may streak or spot. Clean the entire headliner in one operation using a circular motion with a natural sponge.
Headliner (vinyl)	Use a vinyl cleaner with a sponge and wipe clean with a dry cloth.
Seats and door panels	Mix 1 pint upholstery cleaner in 1 gallon of water. Do not soak the fabric around the buttons.
Leather or vinyl fabric	Use a multi-purpose cleaner full strength and a stiff brush. Let stand 2 minutes and scrub thoroughly. Wipe with a clean, soft rag.
Nylon or synthetic fabrics	For normal stains, use the same procedures you would for washing cloth upholstery. If the fabric is extremely dirty, use a multi-purpose cleaner full strength with a stiff scrub brush. Scrub thoroughly in all directions and wipe with a cotton towel or soft rag.

Glossary

AIR/FUEL RATIO: The ratio of air to gasoline by weight in the fuel mixture drawn into the engine.

AIR INJECTION: One method of reducing harmful exhaust emissions by injecting air into each of the exhaust ports of an engine. The fresh air entering the hot exhaust manifold causes any remaining fuel to be burned before it can exit the tailpipe.

ALTERNATOR: A device used for converting mechanical energy into electrical energy.

AMMETER: An instrument, calibrated in amperes, used to measure the flow of an electrical current in a circuit. Ammeters are always connected in series with the circuit being tested.

AMPERE: The rate of flow of electrical current present when one volt of electrical pressure is applied against one ohm of electrical resistance.

ANALOG COMPUTER: Any microprocessor that uses similar (analogous) electrical signals to make its calculations.

ARMATURE: A laminated, soft iron core wrapped by a wire that converts electrical energy to mechanical energy as in a motor or relay. When rotated in a magnetic field, it changes mechanical energy into electrical energy as in a generator.

ATMOSPHERIC PRESSURE: The pressure on the Earth's surface caused by the weight of the air in the atmosphere. At sea level, this pressure is 14.7 psi at 32°F (101 kPa at 0°C).

ATOMIZATION: The breaking down of a liquid into a fine mist that can be suspended in air.

AXIAL PLAY: Movement parallel to a shaft or bearing bore.

BACKFIRE: The sudden combustion of gases in the intake or exhaust system that results in a loud explosion.

BACKLASH: The clearance or play between two parts, such as meshed gears.

BACKPRESSURE: Restrictions in the exhaust system that slow the exit of exhaust gases from the combustion chamber.

BAKELITE: A heat resistant, plastic insulator material commonly used in printed circuit boards and transistorized components.

BALL BEARING: A bearing made up of hardened inner and outer races between which hardened steel balls roll.

BALLAST RESISTOR: A resistor in the primary ignition circuit that lowers voltage after the engine is started to reduce wear on ignition components.

BEARING: A friction reducing, supportive device usually located between a stationary part and a moving part.

BIMETAL TEMPERATURE SENSOR: Any sensor or switch made of two dissimilar types of metal that bend when heated or cooled due to the different expansion rates of the alloys. These types of sensors usually function as an on/off switch.

BLOWBY: Combustion gases, composed of water vapor and unburned fuel, that leak past the piston rings into the crankcase during normal engine operation. These gases are removed by the PCV system to prevent the buildup of harmful acids in the crankcase.

BRAKE PAD: A brake shoe and lining assembly used with disc brakes.

BRAKE SHOE: The backing for the brake lining. The term is, however, usually applied to the assembly of the brake backing and lining.

BUSHING: A liner, usually removable, for a bearing; an anti-friction liner used in place of a bearing.

BYPASS: System used to bypass ballast resistor during engine cranking to increase voltage supplied to the coil.

CALIPER: A hydraulically activated device in a disc brake system, which is mounted straddling the brake rotor (disc). The caliper contains at least one piston and two brake pads. Hydraulic pressure on the piston(s) forces the pads against the rotor.

CAMSHAFT: A shaft in the engine on which are the lobes (cams) which operate the valves. The camshaft is driven by the crankshaft, via a belt, chain or gears, at one half the crankshaft speed.

CAPACITOR: A device which stores an electrical charge.

CARBON MONOXIDE (CO): A colorless, odorless gas given off as a normal byproduct of combustion. It is poisonous and extremely dangerous in confined areas, building up slowly to toxic levels without warning if adequate ventilation is not available.

CARBURETOR: A device, usually mounted on the intake manifold of an engine, which mixes the air and fuel in the proper proportion to allow even combustion.

CATALYTIC CONVERTER: A device installed in the exhaust system, like a muffler, that converts harmful byproducts of combustion into carbon dioxide and water vapor by means of a heat-producing chemical reaction.

CENTRIFUGAL ADVANCE: A mechanical method of advancing the spark timing by using flyweights in the distributor that react to centrifugal force generated by the distributor shaft rotation.

CHECK VALVE: Any one-way valve installed to permit the flow of air, fuel or vacuum in one direction only.

GLOSSARY

CHOKE: A device, usually a moveable valve, placed in the intake path of a carburetor to restrict the flow of air.

CIRCUIT: Any unbroken path through which an electrical current can flow. Also used to describe fuel flow in some instances.

CIRCUIT BREAKER: A switch which protects an electrical circuit from overload by opening the circuit when the current flow exceeds a predetermined level. Some circuit breakers must be reset manually, while most reset automatically

COIL (IGNITION): A transformer in the ignition circuit which steps up the voltage provided to the spark plugs.

COMBINATION MANIFOLD: An assembly which includes both the intake and exhaust manifolds in one casting.

COMBINATION VALVE: A device used in some fuel systems that routes fuel vapors to a charcoal storage canister instead of venting them into the atmosphere. The valve relieves fuel tank pressure and allows fresh air into the tank as the fuel level drops to prevent a vapor lock situation.

COMPRESSION RATIO: The comparison of the total volume of the cylinder and combustion chamber with the piston at BDC and the piston at TDC.

CONDENSER: 1. An electrical device which acts to store an electrical charge, preventing voltage surges.
2. A radiator-like device in the air conditioning system in which refrigerant gas condenses into a liquid, giving off heat.

CONDUCTOR: Any material through which an electrical current can be transmitted easily.

CONTINUITY: Continuous or complete circuit. Can be checked with an ohmmeter.

COUNTERSHAFT: An intermediate shaft which is rotated by a mainshaft and transmits, in turn, that rotation to a working part.

CRANKCASE: The lower part of an engine in which the crankshaft and related parts operate.

CRANKSHAFT: The main driving shaft of an engine which receives reciprocating motion from the pistons and converts it to rotary motion.

CYLINDER: In an engine, the round hole in the engine block in which the piston(s) ride.

CYLINDER BLOCK: The main structural member of an engine in which is found the cylinders, crankshaft and other principal parts.

CYLINDER HEAD: The detachable portion of the engine, fastened, usually, to the top of the cylinder block, containing all or most of the combustion chambers. On overhead valve engines, it contains the valves and their operating parts. On overhead cam engines, it contains the camshaft as well.

DEAD CENTER: The extreme top or bottom of the piston stroke.

DETONATION: An unwanted explosion of the air/fuel mixture in the combustion chamber caused by excess heat and compression, advanced timing, or an overly lean mixture. Also referred to as "ping".

DIAPHRAGM: A thin, flexible wall separating two cavities, such as in a vacuum advance unit.

DIESELING: A condition in which hot spots in the combustion chamber cause the engine to run on after the key is turned off.

DIFFERENTIAL: A geared assembly which allows the transmission of motion between drive axles, giving one axle the ability to turn faster than the other.

DIODE: An electrical device that will allow current to flow in one direction only.

DISC BRAKE: A hydraulic braking assembly consisting of a brake disc, or rotor, mounted on an axle, and a caliper assembly containing, usually two brake pads which are activated by hydraulic pressure. The pads are forced against the sides of the disc, creating friction which slows the vehicle.

DISTRIBUTOR: A mechanically driven device on an engine which is responsible for electrically firing the spark plug at a predetermined point of the piston stroke.

DOWEL PIN: A pin, inserted in mating holes in two different parts allowing those parts to maintain a fixed relationship.

DRUM BRAKE: A braking system which consists of two brake shoes and one or two wheel cylinders, mounted on a fixed backing plate, and a brake drum, mounted on an axle, which revolves around the assembly. Hydraulic action applied to the wheel cylinders forces the shoes outward against the drum, creating friction, slowing the vehicle.

DWELL: The rate, measured in degrees of shaft rotation, at which an electrical circuit cycles on and off.

ELECTRONIC CONTROL UNIT (ECU): Ignition module, module, amplifier or igniter. See Module for definition.

ELECTRONIC IGNITION: A system in which the timing and firing of the spark plugs is controlled by an electronic control unit, usually called a module. These systems have no points or condenser.

ENDPLAY: The measured amount of axial movement in a shaft.

ENGINE: A device that converts heat into mechanical energy.

EXHAUST MANIFOLD: A set of cast passages or pipes which conduct exhaust gases from the engine.

FEELER GAUGE: A blade, usually metal, of precisely predetermined thickness, used to measure the clearance between two parts. These blades usually are available in sets of assorted thicknesses.

F-Head: An engine configuration in which the intake valves are in the cylinder head, while the camshaft and exhaust valves are located in the cylinder block. The camshaft operates the intake valves via lifters and pushrods, while it operates the exhaust valves directly.

FIRING ORDER: The order in which combustion occurs in the cylinders of an engine. Also the order in which spark is distributed to the plugs by the distributor.

FLATHEAD: An engine configuration in which the camshaft and all the valves are located in the cylinder block.

FLOODING: The presence of too much fuel in the intake manifold and combustion chamber which prevents the air/fuel mixture from firing, thereby causing a no-start situation.

FLYWHEEL: A disc shaped part bolted to the rear end of the crankshaft. Around the outer perimeter is affixed the ring gear. The starter drive engages the ring gear, turning the flywheel, which rotates the crankshaft, imparting the initial starting motion to the engine.

FOOT POUND (ft.lb. or sometimes, ft. lbs.): The amount of energy or work needed to raise an item weighing one pound, a distance of one foot.

FUSE: A protective device in a circuit which prevents circuit overload by breaking the circuit when a specific amperage is present. The device is constructed around a strip or wire of a lower amperage rating than the circuit it is designed to protect. When an amperage higher than that stamped on the fuse is present in the circuit, the strip or wire melts, opening the circuit.

GEAR RATIO: The ratio between the number of teeth on meshing gears.

GENERATOR: A device which converts mechanical energy into electrical energy.

HEAT RANGE: The measure of a spark plug's ability to dissipate heat from its firing end. The higher the heat range, the hotter the plug fires.

HUB: The center part of a wheel or gear.

HYDROCARBON (HC): Any chemical compound made up of hydrogen and carbon. A major pollutant formed by the engine as a byproduct of combustion.

HYDROMETER: An instrument used to measure the specific gravity of a solution.

INCH POUND (in.lb. or sometimes, in. lbs.): One twelfth of a foot pound.

INDUCTION: A means of transferring electrical energy in the form of a magnetic field. Principle used in the ignition coil to increase voltage.

INJECTION PUMP: A device, usually mechanically operated, which meters and delivers fuel under pressure to the fuel injector.

INJECTOR: A device which receives metered fuel under relatively low pressure and is activated to inject the fuel into the engine under relatively high pressure at a predetermined time.

INPUT SHAFT: The shaft to which torque is applied, usually carrying the driving gear or gears.

INTAKE MANIFOLD: A casting of passages or pipes used to conduct air or a fuel/air mixture to the cylinders.

JOURNAL: The bearing surface within which a shaft operates.

KEY: A small block usually fitted in a notch between a shaft and a hub to prevent slippage of the two parts.

MANIFOLD: A casting of passages or set of pipes which connect the cylinders to an inlet or outlet source.

MANIFOLD VACUUM: Low pressure in an engine intake manifold formed just below the throttle plates. Manifold vacuum is highest at idle and drops under acceleration.

MASTER CYLINDER: The primary fluid pressurizing device in a hydraulic system. In automotive use, it is found in brake and hydraulic clutch systems and is pedal activated, either directly or, in a power brake system, through the power booster.

MODULE: Electronic control unit, amplifier or igniter of solid state or integrated design which controls the current flow in the ignition primary circuit based on input from the pick-up coil. When the module opens the primary circuit, the high secondary voltage is induced in the coil.

NEEDLE BEARING: A bearing which consists of a number (usually a large number) of long, thin rollers.

OHM: (Ω) The unit used to measure the resistance of conductor to electrical flow. One ohm is the amount of resistance that limits current flow to one ampere in a circuit with one volt of pressure.

OHMMETER: An instrument used for measuring the resistance, in ohms, in an electrical circuit.

OUTPUT SHAFT: The shaft which transmits torque from a device, such as a transmission.

OVERDRIVE: A gear assembly which produces more shaft revolutions than that transmitted to it.

OVERHEAD CAMSHAFT (OHC): An engine configuration in which the camshaft is mounted on top of the cylinder head and operates the valve either directly or by means of rocker arms.

OVERHEAD VALVE (OHV): An engine configuration in which all of the valves are located in the cylinder head and the camshaft is located in the cylinder block. The camshaft operates the valves via lifters and pushrods.

OXIDES OF NITROGEN (NOx): Chemical compounds of nitrogen produced as a byproduct of combustion. They combine with hydrocarbons to produce smog.

OXYGEN SENSOR: Used with the feedback system to sense the presence of oxygen in the exhaust gas and signal the computer which can reference the voltage signal to an air/fuel ratio.

PINION: The smaller of two meshing gears.

PISTON RING: An open ended ring which fits into a groove on the outer diameter of the piston. Its chief function is to form a seal between the piston and cylinder wall. Most automotive pistons have three rings: two for compression sealing; one for oil sealing.

PRELOAD: A predetermined load placed on a bearing during assembly or by adjustment.

PRIMARY CIRCUIT: Is the low voltage side of the ignition system which consists of the ignition switch, ballast resistor or resistance wire, bypass, coil, electronic control unit and pick-up coil as well as the connecting wires and harnesses.

PRESS FIT: The mating of two parts under pressure, due to the inner diameter of one being smaller than the outer diameter of the other, or vice versa; an interference fit.

GLOSSARY

RACE: The surface on the inner or outer ring of a bearing on which the balls, needles or rollers move.

REGULATOR: A device which maintains the amperage and/or voltage levels of a circuit at predetermined values.

RELAY: A switch which automatically opens and/or closes a circuit.

RESISTANCE: The opposition to the flow of current through a circuit or electrical device, and is measured in ohms. Resistance is equal to the voltage divided by the amperage.

RESISTOR: A device, usually made of wire, which offers a preset amount of resistance in an electrical circuit.

RING GEAR: The name given to a ring-shaped gear attached to a differential case, or affixed to a flywheel or as part a planetary gear set.

ROLLER BEARING: A bearing made up of hardened inner and outer races between which hardened steel rollers move.

ROTOR: 1. The disc-shaped part of a disc brake assembly, upon which the brake pads bear; also called, brake disc.
2. The device mounted atop the distributor shaft, which passes current to the distributor cap tower contacts.

SECONDARY CIRCUIT: The high voltage side of the ignition system, usually above 20,000 volts. The secondary includes the ignition coil, coil wire, distributor cap and rotor, spark plug wires and spark plugs.

SENDING UNIT: A mechanical, electrical, hydraulic or electromagnetic device which transmits information to a gauge.

SENSOR: Any device designed to measure engine operating conditions or ambient pressures and temperatures. Usually electronic in nature and designed to send a voltage signal to an on-board computer, some sensors may operate as a simple on/off switch or they may provide a variable voltage signal (like a potentiometer) as conditions or measured parameters change.

SHIM: Spacers of precise, predetermined thickness used between parts to establish a proper working relationship.

SLAVE CYLINDER: In automotive use, a device in the hydraulic clutch system which is activated by hydraulic force, disengaging the clutch.

SOLENOID: A coil used to produce a magnetic field, the effect of which is produce work.

SPARK PLUG: A device screwed into the combustion chamber of a spark ignition engine. The basic construction is a conductive core inside of a ceramic insulator, mounted in an outer conductive base. An electrical charge from the spark plug wire travels along the conductive core and jumps a preset air gap to a grounding point or points at the end of the conductive base. The resultant spark ignites the fuel/air mixture in the combustion chamber.

SPLINES: Ridges machined or cast onto the outer diameter of a shaft or inner diameter of a bore to enable parts to mate without rotation.

TACHOMETER: A device used to measure the rotary speed of an engine, shaft, gear, etc., usually in rotations per minute.

THERMOSTAT: A valve, located in the cooling system of an engine, which is closed when cold and opens gradually in response to engine heating, controlling the temperature of the coolant and rate of coolant flow.

TOP DEAD CENTER (TDC): The point at which the piston reaches the top of its travel on the compression stroke.

TORQUE: The twisting force applied to an object.

TORQUE CONVERTER: A turbine used to transmit power from a driving member to a driven member via hydraulic action, providing changes in drive ratio and torque. In automotive use, it links the driveplate at the rear of the engine to the automatic transmission.

TRANSDUCER: A device used to change a force into an electrical signal.

TRANSISTOR: A semi-conductor component which can be actuated by a small voltage to perform an electrical switching function.

TUNE-UP: A regular maintenance function, usually associated with the replacement and adjustment of parts and components in the electrical and fuel systems of a vehicle for the purpose of attaining optimum performance.

TURBOCHARGER: An exhaust driven pump which compresses intake air and forces it into the combustion chambers at higher than atmospheric pressures. The increased air pressure allows more fuel to be burned and results in increased horsepower being produced.

VACUUM ADVANCE: A device which advances the ignition timing in response to increased engine vacuum.

VACUUM GAUGE: An instrument used to measure the presence of vacuum in a chamber.

VALVE: A device which control the pressure, direction of flow or rate of flow of a liquid or gas.

VALVE CLEARANCE: The measured gap between the end of the valve stem and the rocker arm, cam lobe or follower that activates the valve.

VISCOSITY: The rating of a liquid's internal resistance to flow.

VOLTMETER: An instrument used for measuring electrical force in units called volts. Voltmeters are always connected parallel with the circuit being tested.

WHEEL CYLINDER: Found in the automotive drum brake assembly, it is a device, actuated by hydraulic pressure, which, through internal pistons, pushes the brake shoes outward against the drums.